WASHINGTONIANS

A Biographical Portrait of the State

Introduction by Roger Sale · Edited by David Brewster and David M. Buerge

SASQUATCH BOOKS

Sponsored by the 1989 Washington Centennial Commission

Printed in the United States of America
Typeset by the Typeworks

Library of Congress Cataloging-in-Publication Data
Washingtonians : a biographical portrait of the state

  Bibliography: p.
  Includes index.
  1. Washington (State)—Biography
2. Washington (State)—History.   I. Brewster, David,
1939-   .   II. Buerge, David M.   III. Washington Centennial Commission.
CT266.W37   1988   979.7'009'92   [B]   88-24008
ISBN 0-912365-16-1

Design by Ellen Ziegler, with Kris Morgan
Cover illustration by Larry Duke
Sponsored by the 1989 Washington Centennial Commission

Sasquatch Books
1931 Second Avenue
Seattle, Washington 98101
(206) 441-5555

Also by Sasquatch Books
  Northwest Best Places
  Seattle Best Places
  Seattle Cheap Eats
  Cooking with Eight Items or Less
  The Year in Bloom
  Three Years in Bloom
  The Fall of the House of WPPSS

PREFACE

Unquestionably, a landscape broods over this region, saturating our consciousness with its outsized presence. But history and a sense of the immediacy of the past do not haunt this land to the same degree. Indeed, as the state celebrates its centennial in 1989, we might even think our history is a scant one hundred years old, a mere three generations. But our soil lies much deeper than that. The geological and native histories of the land yield a sense of time and grandeur as powerful as the emotions one experiences on first entering an old-growth forest.

Excitingly, this region's sense of its history is still being thrashed out. This book is put together to give a sense of the contemporary debate about our traditions. What figures belong in the portrait gallery of greatness? What stories typify best the state's quest for its unique destiny? Which biographies distill the flaws and humor and distinctions of our people? Those questions are still being answered—still being posed—by writers only a few generations removed from the pioneers. We are at the exhilarating point of creating our sense of history.

For a dozen years as editor of *Seattle Weekly*, I have searched for essays that convey a sense of historical exploration, of forging a consciousness of our common past. I have long thought that many of the best of them, joined with other historians' similar excursions, would make a stimulating volume. A grant from the Centennial Commission has enabled us to pull together a rich feast of these essays by many hands, garnishing them with shorter portraits. As when our pioneer ancestors came into the country, so these writers are creating clearings in the dense forests, finding perches from which the whole vast landscape may be viewed.

The project of pulling all these varied perspectives together has required the help of many people. I would especially like to thank Keith Murray of the history department at Western Washington University for his careful review of the materials for historical accuracy; Deb Easter, our committed and meticulous copy editor; Lynn Getz, for her thorough research for supporting materials; Shiras Stamps-White, our enthusiastic and creative research assistant; and librarians Richard Caldwell of the Museum of History and Industry and Richard Engeman of the Special Collections Division of the University of Washington, for endless and timely assistance. For the Centennial Commission, Maura Craig provided encouragement and wonderfully prompt assistance. Stephanie Irving, our invaluable project coordinator, somehow kept us excited and organized through the entire complicated trek.

David Brewster

CONTENTS

VISIONARIES: Coming of Age, 1900–1945

CONTEMPORARIES: Modern Times, 1945–1989

INTRODUCTION

ROGER SALE

Many Americans can identify our fifty states if shown each in outline or as a piece in a jigsaw puzzle. Their shapes are so familiar that we seldom ask why many are oddly shaped: Texas has a chimney on its top, and, along with Florida, Oklahoma, and Idaho, has a panhandle; there are odd flanges in northwestern Pennsylvania, western Nebraska, and southwestern New Mexico. While rivers often dictated state boundaries, none does so consistently, and some do not do so at all. We know that forces, often mysterious and some quite arbitrary, were at work when a piece of land became a colony, a territory, or a state, and these created strange boundaries. We know also that the farther west we move from the original thirteen colonies the less likely we are to find that the boundaries were created to delineate some homogenous or unifying quality in the people living within those boundaries.

We seek kinship with the past more than with the future.

The northern border of Washington State was made by international treaty, the western by coastline, much of the southern by the Columbia River. In these instances rational decisions were made as to who would and would not be a Washingtonian. But rational decisions may not in real life make much sense, and what once made sense may not continue to do so. In the case of Washington, the crucial decision was made when Washington became a territory distinct from Oregon by the boundary of the Columbia. That effectively wedded two areas as Washington Territory—one cloudy, wet, forested; the other dry, open, river-dominated—and the marriage has, like many marriages, "worked," but without ever being entirely happy. The capital of the West is Seattle, of the East is Spokane, while the capital of the rationally made whole is neither. Western Washingtonians are citizens of what is sometimes called Ecotopia, which extends from the Alaska panhandle to northern California. Eastern Washingtonians are citizens of the Inland Empire, whose unmarked boundaries extend north into Canada, east into northern Idaho and Montana, and south into eastern Oregon.

How, then, make a history of Washington State?

In the writing of families, neighborhoods, churches, companies, cities, and perhaps countries, the model of a biography is often useful, because people and events can be

1

shaped into a story that creates what seems a living whole, and the metaphors of birth, growth, and decay seem valid and important. But it is more difficult to use such a model for Washington. The heart of its body is the capital in Olympia, and that heart is just too weak to make Washington seem like a body whose blood it pumps.

The essays in *Washingtonians* reflect this varied state. They were not first written to be part of "A Biographical Portrait." Nor, assembled here, the work of diverse hands and written over several decades, do they make a complete "biographical history" of the state, though they offer much material for which a history might be made. In this introductory essay, I wish to describe what sense of history seems to dominate here, and what implied sense of the job of the historian is offered. Then, with that in mind, I would like to suggest what a history of Washington, for all the sense that probably "it can't be done," needs most to bear in mind.

Part I, "Creators," embraces a sense that what we are looking for in our past is, if not heroes and heroines, dominant figures, the people who made a difference. Its view of history is "romantic," not in the sense that Vancouver, Stevens, Wilkes, and the others are romanticized, or made to look of epic stature, but in its belief that there *were* people who actually shaped events, and events to come. This is the way the history of exploring, pioneering, and settling has almost always been done, because these people were the first this, or the first that, and the importance of any one person is bound to be greater when the total number is small. Typically, these historians want to make their subject "more human" by darkening or mottling whatever simpler view they fear we might have inherited. Thus Archibald Menzies, who sailed with Vancouver, wrote: "What days those were.... Those books that Vancouver wrote—strange that he could put so much of himself into the printed page. He was a great captain." Without denying any of this, David Buerge shows how Vancouver had men flogged when they resisted being driven as hard as Vancouver drove himself and etches a little tragedy in showing how Vancouver struggled to escape the long shadow of Captain Cook, under whom Vancouver first explored, and whom he wished to emulate.

This historical method works excellently with "The Man We Call Seattle." Chief Seattle has suffered both from a sentimentalizing through Doc Smith's Victorian version of his "farewell" speech, and from a consequent deriding because he was sensitive to the wishes of white authorities and negotiated treaties rather than fight when reservations were made in Puget Sound. Here we already have the tragedy. Buerge's contribution is to show, in effect, how much of what later interpreters saw, Chief Seattle saw himself. The tragedy of his people was reaching its fifth act by the middle of the nineteenth century, and the old chief knew it. His was no failure of courage; he had been leading raids against various tribes for years. He had seen whites moving into the area for more than a generation, and he knew that the reds and whites would never truly live at peace with each other, because their ways

The importance of any one person is bound to be greater when the total number is small.

2

and means were too different. Since the whites were going to "win," he saw his job as that of getting as much for the native people as he could.

Though Buerge's knowledge of Puget Sound Indian languages is greater than Doc Smith's was, he wisely chooses to give us Smith's florid version of Seattle's speech to Stevens of January 10, 1854. It would be risky now to try to re-do the speech according to some notion of what Seattle is more likely to have said, just as it is risky now for whites to try to pronounce the man's name as he himself would have said it. Further, in showing us Smith's sense of Chief Seattle's tragedy and greatness, we have a mixing of white and red that gives us, in effect, the first important moment in the history of Washington State. At the heart of the speech, regardless of his actual words, is Seattle's mournful rebuke and warning to the conquerors. All histories of the state should properly begin with this announcement of what was ending as Washington was beginning.

The romantic impulse takes a different shape in the second section, "Visionaries." Those who came and made their fortunes, especially in the glory years of 1890–1910, became family dynasties, and so we have the Carkeeks leading to Guendolen Plestcheeff, the Stimsons to Dorothy Bullitt, the Blethens, a little later the Boeings, and, later still, the Clapps leading to Booth Gardner. Usually the money was made in not very interesting ways, often by someone realizing that Puget Sound soon would become urban, which meant that logging or mining was less profitable than real estate. The money-maker then gives way to a later family member who is more colorful, more interesting, or more interestingly deviant (the exception being the Boeings, where the fortune was made in exciting ways and the founder was the most interesting member).

In making these dynasties as important, as impressive, as full of anecdote as one can, many impulses are satisfied: the impulse to have important people, our equivalent of an aristocracy; the desire to have private life be more important than public life, especially if these private citizens can silently pull political strings; the need to think that the very rich are, and aren't, very different from you and me; the nostalgic hope that yesterday was a better time than today. It may reveal something that the only person in this section whose warts and real shortcomings are strongly noted is Woody Guthrie, a romantic and romanticized figure but from another tradition entirely than that of the family dynasties.

Finally, when we come to the last fifty years in the third section— "Contemporaries"— the wealthy families give way to the artists and writers. As important as Baker Ferguson, Tom Foley, and Archbishop Hunthausen may be, they remain square-jawed and decent, while the color, the mystery, the enduring legends and anecdotes now fall to Guy Anderson, Jacob Lawrence, Henry Gay, Bruce Lee, Tom Robbins—and the essays in this section barely begin to exhaust the list of others who might have been included here. In *Humboldt's Gift*, Saul Bellow writes about the role writers and artists in contemporary America can play, especially if they are mysterious, fail, are rebellious or eccentric,

Wealthy families give way to the artists and writers.

3

go mad, or die young. They confirm in an inverse way the American dream of success that is flattered in chronicling the dynasties of an earlier time. (Frank Chin may have managed to satisfy both impulses simultaneously, the one honoring success, the other failure and mystery, in his saga of Chinatown.) The frontier is closed, but not for these people. If many in an earlier time, like Bing Crosby and Ed Murrow, had to leave Washington to realize their talents, more frequently now such people can stay here and grow, or even move here in order to flourish.

So the essays here, not as part of their original intention but when assembled, begin to suggest, if not yet a history of Washington, a history of feelings about Washington as reflected in a contemporary mirror. How can we add to it? What can we add to this "romantic" view of our history?

White people, as we know, have seldom been content to live minimally.

Anyone who looks through the scholarly periodical literature about our state and region, or who pulls down books from the appropriate shelves of a library, knows that the trouble with most historical writing is that it is dull. Dull because it does not try to be interesting—much scholarly writing, alas, implies that to be interesting is to be unprofessional—and because it does not know how best to tell its story. Sensing this, most people prefer history that is biographical, anecdotal, colorful, personal, romantic. When my history of Seattle was published some years ago, the most frequent question asked me, even by people who had read the book, was "Who are your heroes?" There are people aplenty in the book, and many are admired, but there are no heroes, or villains either, because the *city* is the central figure, not the individuals. So a related question is: How to get at what's important in *Washington's* history, thereby avoiding dullness, without assuming that the basic unit of inquiry must be the individual Washingtonian?

Let us start with two facts about climate and topography: west of the Cascades evergreen forests dominate, while east of the mountains it is the Columbia River. In the centuries before whites moved into the territory, the forests and the Columbia were bounty to the people who lived here, all the bounty they needed, because the human population was small and the trees and fish numbered in the billions. (As for what the Columbia was to those people, Buerge has a fine essay here on the legends they told about it.) White people, as we know, have seldom been content to live minimally and to leave the land as they found it, and as soon as some whites moved into an area successfully, more have always followed, and, laterally, that has also been true for American blacks, Latinos, and Asian immigrants, our largest minority populations. So if the non-Indian people are going to do something to the land, what will it be?

They have done a great deal with the Columbia and its smaller companion, the Yakima, and what they have done is shape the history of Eastern Washington. One of the ironies of Woody Guthrie's "Roll On, Columbia" is that it was written for the Bonneville Power Administration precisely at the point when the BPA was working to make sure that the Columbia would never roll on again. The Columbia has become a series of lakes, the teacherous falls at the Cascades and The Dalles which scared the white settlers are no more, and the journeys made by salmon to spawn are the most arduous undergone by fish. The resultant irrigation and hydroelectric power have turned the dry volcanic soil into seedbed for wheat, fruit, and hops that has made it the most productive agricultural state in the northern United States. Also, the presence of the Columbia dictated where the huge Hanford nuclear power producing operation would be placed. The results cannot always be called pretty, and such powerful alterations of the environment are bound to seem at times frightening, but in such a vast dry world, nothing less than powerful alterations would have made a dent in it. You cannot have a little dam across the Columbia.

There seem to be two stumbling blocks to producing a full history of the relation of this great river to its people. The first is to recognize that it *is* a history, made up of events that did not have to happen and that altered both the land and the people: hydroelectric power, aluminum plants, orchards and vineyards, plutonium manufacture all are parts of the same story. That the view from Wenatchee is not the same as that from Yakima or Tri-Cities does not alter the fact that the river and the hot dry land have shaped the lives of all. The second stumbling block is more a matter of tone and perspective. In the wedding of East and West in Washington, the West has the people, and therefore the power and the influence. As a result, people close to the Columbia often feel, and often with reason, that people from the West are taking attitudes and making decisions that are unsympathetic and misunderstanding. One such attitude might be: the dams are all right, the irrigation is fine, but no Hanford. Or it might be: nothing larger than a case of wine is any good. In any event, the response of the Easterners is often nervous, defensive, aggressive, chauvinistic— all of which is too bad, and all of which gets in the way of the producing of clear-eyed, unapologetic history.

Something similar stands in the way of a fuller history when we come west of the mountains. Time was, and that time is not long past, when a shift in the value of logs and boards meant a shift in the entire economy of Washington and Oregon. To the extent that this had been true, it had never been importantly true, as became clear to everyone half a dozen years ago when major drops in the price of lumber wreaked havoc in logging towns but altered the urban economies hardly at all. What has been of prime importance in the wet Northwest has not been trees or fish but cities—in Washington, Seattle preeminently—and the significant history of the region is the history of Seattle. Once the trees were cut down, Seattle went about the business of becoming a major city, and never was a home for one of the biggest lumber firms or families. Likewise, while Seattle has always been home for many commercial fishers, its major relation to its water has always been the urban one of being a port, a hub for transportation around the Sound, north to Alaska, west to the Asiatic Pacific Rim.

You cannot have a little dam across the Columbia.

The first problem in understanding the history of Seattle has been the frequent inability, at times amounting almost to a refusal, to see the city as a city where a vast complex of powers are at work that are not easy to understand but which can be understood. Here the biographical model does hold, not in the sense that single individuals are major forces in Seattle's history, though of course some individuals cannot be ignored. The city's history is like that of a biography. Just as how a person works, acts with parents or children, plays tennis, thinks about money and death, are all related somehow even as they are also distinct and diverse, so too what happens at the Boeing Company, downtown, in commercial streets, at the University of Washington, etc., etc. are all diverse events that are creating and responding to forces which can be placed into a single focus. Unsurprisingly, it is always easier to see this, to look for the ways in which it is so, when some period in the past is in question. It is hard to write a history of now, and perhaps one can do no more than be alert for telltale signs.

Good times in Seattle have often produced a deadening sameness in whatever is built and thought.

Another obstacle to making good, full, urban history here is, like the defensive-aggressiveness one finds among people around the Columbia, a matter of attitude, in this case a complacent, uncritical acceptance of what has happened and is happening. Seattle is, unquestionably, a successful city, a place that has taken superb advantage of its great natural heritage of climate and topography, a place that has, from the 1873 announcement that the Northern Pacific Railroad would place its terminal in Tacoma to the layoff of fifty thousand workers at Boeing a century later, shown it can respond well to setbacks. But it has been much less successful in dealing with success. Good times in Seattle have often produced a deadening sameness in whatever is built and thought, an incuriosity about what created the success, an indiscriminateness about the quality and consequences of growth, and a dull sense that success once achieved must surely last forever.

So these are the problems—first, in seeing what units of study are most fruitful for the historian, second, in seeing what characteristic attitudes might get in the way—that show the limitations to the strictly biographical approach to history, which focuses primarily on individuals. Biographical historians tend to accept what happened without asking how it came about and, often, without any sense of how it might have been different, or better. They inform and entertain with good tales, but they have trouble getting readers to shift a perspective.

Interestingly, if we ask who might help these historians to gain focus and to overcome these attitudinal obstacles, the answer might well be people who are *near* the areas in question but are not *of* them. For instance, the historian of the Columbia River might well find—just to name people prominent in *Washingtonians* —that Baker Ferguson of Walla Walla or Tom Foley of Spokane could help precisely because they are interested but not involved. And the historian of Seattle might get similar help from Henry Gay of Shelton or, as I did once, from Murray Morgan of Tacoma. In writing the history of a place, where people are when they look can make a great difference. We instinctively feel that someone in, say, Minneapolis is not going to be the best historian of Seattle, and the chauvinist of the Columbia River rightly feels that someone in Seattle may not be able to see across the Cascades clearly. Which is why someone of the region but not of the actual place might be the perfect helper for the local historian.

If this is true, we must, for the time being at least, settle for two histories of our state, one East, one West. But our story, we must remember, has little more than begun, and it is unlikely that when Washington comes to celebrate its bicentennial that the histories which now seem possible, or impossible, will seem quite feasible then. A hundred years ago, someone assessing the future of the state-to-be might not have done better than to see Tacoma, rather than Seattle, as the hub of urban Puget Sound, and could have seen little along the Columbia River to locate the future of Eastern Washington there rather than in Walla Walla or Spokane.

If we project existing lines of force ahead a century, we might well feel that in 2089 the Columbia River basin could be best known for its wines, while Seattle could be little more than a regional headquarters for an economy whose central artery extends from Puyallup to Bellevue and north to Everett. It is hard, in 1989, to see how Puget Sound will cease to be the population center of the state, but, past that, little is sure. It took less than fifty years for Los Angeles to displace San Francisco as the leading city on the West Coast, and still less than that for Miami and Houston to supplant Atlanta and New Orleans as the premier cities of the South. We should not be surprised, thus, if in 2089 Kalama is the state's leading port.

If that thought boggles the mind, we can conveniently shift our gaze. As historians, we seek kinship with the past more than with the future, and so, as if to celebrate a sense that we now are not far removed from the outsized individuals of the frontier, we continue to find great appeal and truth in romantic history. So here is *Washingtonians*. ◂▪

CREATORS

BIRTH OF
A STATE:
BEGINNINGS
TO 1899

CREATORS

All peoples celebrate stories of their creation, and Washingtonians have one too, as complex as the Book of Genesis. It begins, as most do, with water. In the beginning there was a lot of water, but the discovery of the New World in the middle of it was looked upon as a colossal inconvenience by those who shared Columbus's dream of finding a short and direct ocean passage to Asia. A search for this passage along the convoluted east coast of the Americas was fruitless, so it was taken up along their west coast, particularly along the mysterious northern quadrant. A few explorers claimed actually to have found it, but their vague and fantastic accounts suggested to the wise that these were men more interested in the location of their next meal than in the fabled passage.

One whose account was given more credit than the rest was a Greek pilot whom the Spanish called Juan de Fuca. He claimed the discovery in 1592 of a great strait that after twenty days sailing led him from the Pacific Ocean to another sea. An Englishman, Michael Lok, got the story from the old man in Venice, and some two hundred years later, another Englishman, Captain James Cook, was sent to look for it along the northwest coast. He missed it but found instead the sea otter furs whose sale in China ignited the maritime fur trade. It remained for one of those traders, Charles Barkely, to find the great strait in 1787, very near where the old Greek said it would be found.

A creator without wisdom makes a mess of things.

Later the Spanish mapped the strait and much of the Olympic Peninsula besides, revealing for the first time something of the outline we recognize as Washington's. But the definitive line was drawn by George Vancouver during his exploration of the sounds and inlets branching from the strait's head. Because his maps filled in the last of the empty spaces, his was the last expedition sent to look for the northwest passage in the Pacific. For our purposes, the line he drew begins our story of creation. By separating the waters from the land, he brought forth our shores from the chaos of imagination for all the world to see.

Vancouver was also the first to see the value of what he discovered. In his enchanted eye, the lands at the head of the strait would give rise to thriving farms, bustling towns, and grand country estates. It would be a garden of England. But there came trouble to paradise. Even as Vancouver fancied English villages on the evergreen shores, an American fur trader out of Boston, Robert Gray, was claiming for his nation the great river he had just entered and named after his ship, the *Columbia Rediviva.*

In an odd sort of way, the United States took up the search for the northwest passage just as others were giving it up. Several geographers, including a talented amateur named Thomas Jefferson, suspected that Gray's River, the Columbia, might be the fabled River of the West, one of four great continental streams whose heads were believed to "interlock" somewhere in the unexplored interior. Whoever controlled the point of connection could command a freshwater route across the continent. Lewis and Clark's expedition established that the Columbia was indeed the River of the West, but they also showed that the Rocky Mountains eliminated in spectacular fashion the possibility of a water passage. Still, they had found a route west. If, as Vancouver surmised, the new land and its river were worth possessing, an overland connection to them was indispensable.

The contention between the United States and Great Britain over the Northwest took more than half a century to resolve, and during that period, several plans were put forward to carve up the territory. Here is where Lieutenant Charles Wilkes played his part. One of his officers performed admirable service to the American cause by losing his ship on the Columbia's treacherous bar. The loss convinced Wilkes that the river was a poor harbor and that if the United States claim to the Northwest was to have value, it must include Puget Sound. To bolster the claim he entered the Sound, with the aid of Vancouver's charts, and carried out the ancient conqueror's practice of broadcasting names to the four directions. Wilkes's report stressing the value of Puget Sound was delivered to the Senate at a crucial phase of negotiations about the Northwest, and it helped steel the Americans' resolve to have the national border follow the forty-ninth parallel to the sea rather than down the Columbia as the British wanted. Without that happening, there simply would not have been a Washington.

With these broad strokes the shape of the land was determined, but the shape of the commonwealth to inhabit it had yet to be established. American fur traders coming by sea or overland and a gaggle of contentious missionaries had poked about the Northwest with indifferent success. While the American government dawdled, the British had succeeded through their agent in the region, the Hudson's Bay Company, in creating a mercantile empire, skin for skin.

Wilkes himself thought the Company was doing a dandy job of running things in the area. They did it as it should be done, like the Navy, but most Americans would have none of it. It is ironic in this most unchurched corner of the country that Washington's beginnings should be so heavily influenced by the church, but missionaries provided the germ of the American community in the Northwest. When they failed to convert the native people in satisfying numbers, they sought to attract American settlers to fill the pews.

The missionaries led efforts to have the Northwest made part of the United States, but

If, as Vancouver surmised, the new land and its river were worth possessing, an overland connection to them was indispensable.

12

their petitions went unheeded in Congress. Then a band of desperate Cayuse, sick of encroaching settlers and of the diseases they brought, rose up and slaughtered Marcus and Narcissa Whitman and several others at the Waiilatpu mission on the Walla Walla River in 1847. The government was finally spurred into action. In the history of the West death had many shades. Among the hordes of single men who came out to seek their fortune, death was part of the gamble, and it could be absurdly comic, but the blood of women and of families was always dark. The blood shed at Waiilatpu and during the subsequent Cayuse War marked the birth of American government in the region, but it left an indelible stain on the christening garment.

It is fashionable now to condemn the missionaries, although it would be difficult to add condemnation to that which they heaped on one another at the time. They were not intentionally cruel or meanspirited. Their most striking failure would seem to have been their woeful lack of imagination in dealing with the native people who were generally predisposed to accommodate them. It would not be the last time relations between the two groups would fail.

Of all the victims of that tragedy, the figure of Narcissa Whitman excites the most attention. In the hands of church historians, she becomes a sainted martyr, but such hagiography fails to plumb the depths of her remarkable character. Part of the problem is Narcissa herself who, in her journal and letters, seeks often with iron command to discern the will of God and act upon it alone. We are luckier with Mary Richardson Walker, a figure no less complex than Narcissa Whitman but one who did not succeed in persuading herself to become a saint. Nancy Wilson Ross believes she suffered a martyrdom as complete as Narcissa's, and in her essay we are able to understand something of the travail of pioneer women.

The blood shed at Waiilatpu... marked the birth of American government in the region.

Women play a crucial role in Washington's creation, sometimes by dying horribly, but more importantly by living and striving. They are often described as standing beside their husbands, but it would be more accurate to say that they stood some distance apart. They were the ones who collected and pressed into books the flowers that disappeared after their husbands cut down the trees or sent the hogs to root in the meadows. They collected mineral specimens because they looked interesting rather than because they assayed well. The men appear generally to have seen the wilderness as an object to be won and whose value rested in what of it could be cut down, sawn up, dug out, or broken under the plow. Out of convention, women's perception of the wild was less aggressive, but it was often more subtle, and their recollections of the pioneering experience are generally less abstract, more immediate, and more interesting. The offspring of their creativity came not only from the children they bore but also in their constant efforts to tame the spirits of anarchy, to humanize a harsh frontier and make it habitable.

Among their homesteads and small towns, the pioneers created a robust, self-sufficient, and roughly egalitarian society whose brief existence many recalled wistfully as a time of innocence. By themselves, they got along tolerably well with the native people. Many pioneer men married native women and raised mixed-blood families, and in the towns especially there was plenty of opportunity for cooperation. Even when outrages led to interracial murder, frontier justice allowed for revenge only if it would settle the score.

If nothing else, the pioneers were practical. The emergence of Washington Territory in 1853 happened in part because citizens north of the Columbia resented the long trip south to Salem to attend sessions of government. These were the people who named their new creation Washington rather than Columbia because they feared people might confuse the latter choice with the District of Columbia.

Such innocence began to vanish with the advent of the new governor, Isaac Stevens. Stevens arrived on a euphoric tide of national expansion swollen by the conquest of Mexico and the first flexing of industrial muscle. He came with sweeping powers, and his own vast ambitions made him impatient of innocence or compromise. The region was soon plunged into a bloody race war whose dolorous effects divide us still. Events across the border in British Columbia suggest that violence was not the inevitable result of rapid settlement and development. Ironically, it was in the towns that settlers most opposed the policy of removing native peoples to isolated reservations, since it subtracted a valuable labor force from their economies. The war produced only bitterness and death, and the two races that might have cultivated the garden together ended up lacerated by the thorns of hostility.

The figures of Chief Seattle west of the Cascade Mountains and the prophet Smohalla east of them put us in touch with the anguish of a defeated people. Seattle sought always to cooperate with American authority, even when it was cruel. Smohalla attempted to isolate himself and his followers from it and resist it nonviolently when it imposed itself. Both succeeded to a degree: Seattle got and kept a reservation for his Suquamish, and Smohalla kept the flickering candle of an ancient heritage alive in a hurricane. But the land their people had held for millennia had been torn from their grasp in a single generation, and the people crushed so thoroughly that their dispossessors could safely ignore them.

With the land firmly in hand, change took place at a tremendous rate. Much of the process of development involved destruction on a massive scale: forests were scythed down, hills bored, rivers rerouted, whole ecosystems degraded or destroyed. Few lamented these changes—certainly the native people did, but they were only savages. Most saw them as signs of progress, but some were troubled by the enormity of it all.

As the harsher realities of frontier life gave way to less stringent conditions, and new issues absorbed people's attention, the older period—the age of creation—was viewed in softer light. The native fighter could be appreciated as a romantic, even heroic figure, although his children might languish in poverty. As newcomers poured in, what remained of native culture became a source of fascination. There had always been a few pioneers who

14

were genuinely interested in it, but more were surprised that outsiders should find it worthy of note. Gradually fragments were collected and preserved. The art was used to decorate, and myths and legends entertained. But of all the figures out of a romanticized past, few struck such a resonant chord among the newcomers as Coyote, the trickster-hero.

His actions in those earlier creation stories resembled what Washington's immigrant creators had experienced. Coyote had walked up the great river into the new land, still wet from birth, keen-eyed and oversexed, literally bursting with capacity. He had found the first people poor and benighted, and he had taught them new ways to live. He tamed the monsters bedeviling the earth, opened the wombs of fecundity, reshaped the land and made it habitable. These were the stories of an older creation, and they seemed prophetic. It was with them in mind that the native people had called the newcomers "Changers," after the mythical Changer—Coyote's counterpart west of the mountains—because of their fearful ability to transform the land. As was often the case with Coyote, the new creators' actions were accompanied by mayhem, violence, and pain, but it was always part of the older stories that Coyote should suffer for his foolishness in order to become wise.

A creator without wisdom makes a mess of things. Coyote learned that lesson, and it would be learned by those who followed in his footsteps. ◼

David M. Buerge

CAPTAINS COURAGEOUS

GEORGE VANCOUVER (1758–1798)

DAVID M. BUERGE

On March 19, 1778, the British ships *Resolution* and *Discovery,* under the command of Captain James Cook, dropped their anchors in the chill waters of Nootka Sound, on the west coast of British Columbia. Canoe-loads of native people eager to trade gathered about the ships and gave their crews an enthusiastic welcome. Among the items they offered were the thick, lustrous pelts of an animal the British had never seen before and which they nicknamed sea beaver. Threadbare after nearly two years at sea and knowing they were headed farther north, the sailors signaled their eagerness to obtain the furs and were surprised to find that the natives would part with them for scraps of metal, even the brass buttons from their coats. At that moment, the Northwest joined the world economy.

Captain Cook had left England on his third voyage of discovery in that momentous year of British-American relations, 1776. He made his way into the North Pacific via the Cape of Good Hope, New Zealand, and Tahiti. On his way he discovered the Hawaiian Islands, which he named the Sandwich Islands after his friend the Earl of Sandwich. On February 2, 1778, Cook's ships left Hawaiian waters and five weeks later raised the American coast. Storms prevented him from sighting the Columbia River or the Strait of Juan de Fuca, but a break in the weather enabled him to close with the land and bring his ships to Nootka.

With Cook's landing, the history of the Northwest Coast begins in earnest. The landing was all the more auspicious because Cook brought with him two men who were soon to have a tremendous impact on the region's history: John Ledyard, a marine corporal on board *Resolution,* and a young midshipman on the *Discovery* named George Vancouver. Neither man knew the other, and they played their later roles separately. Together they helped put into motion the currents that gave the Northwest much of the character it has today. And, as is often the case in history, the men were as much the victims of these currents as they were captains steering through them.

Compared to the South Sea Islands, Cook's Northwest landfall seemed wild and melancholy and its people appeared rougher and less attractive than the handsome Polynesians. To Ledyard, however, the dark spectacle of the North American coast, its

Vancouver brought to his new position a genuine passion for exploring, for what he termed "the science of discovery."

forested hills rising to a line of snowy peaks, was especially moving. Born in Groton, Connecticut, to a comfortable family, Ledyard soon found life in the narrow valleys and small towns of New England too confining. Work in an uncle's law firm bored him; so did student life at Dartmouth College. A short stint studying for the ministry convinced him he did not have a religious calling. And so in 1774, short of cash and unable to settle down, Ledyard went to sea—another life he promptly found unbearable. Jumping ship in England, he was arrested in Bristol and given the choice of sailing on a slaver to Guinea or joining the British army. He chose the latter, transferred to the marines, and in 1776 was assigned to serve on Captain Cook's *Resolution*. He was twenty-five years old. Two years later, Ledyard was standing on deck, transfixed by the wild scene before him.

Meanwhile, on board *Discovery,* George Vancouver was less impressed by the landscape than he was by Captain Cook, who had become his personal hero. On his father's side, Vancouver was descended from the old Dutch family of Van Couverden, whose castle in Drenth had been an important stronghold since the twelve hundreds. In 1699 an ancestor married an English girl at court and his children moved to England, anglicized their name, and attained positions in the King's service. Vancouver's father, John Jasper Vancouver, was deputy customs collector at Kings Lynn, a major port in Norfolk, and it was probably through these Tory connections that George, his youngest child, obtained a berth in 1772 on board the *Resolution* for Cook's second voyage. Vancouver was then fourteen years old.

John Elliott, a fellow midshipman on the voyage, remembered Vancouver as a "quiet, inoffensive young man." Beneath his deferential exterior, however, the boy was developing a passion for exploring that never left him. That voyage also kindled an admiration for Cook akin to worship, so in 1776 he joined Cook's third voyage as a midshipman on the *Discovery*.

Cook's instructions from the Admiralty directed him to search for the Northwest Passage, the fabled water link connecting the Pacific and Atlantic oceans that was believed to lie somehwere near sixty degrees north latitude. Cook would not find the passage, but the sea otter furs he obtained at Nootka and other places farther north would prove hardly less significant. When Cook's ships reached Canton in December 1778, Chinese merchants paid as much as 120 Spanish dollars for a prime pelt—the equivalent of several years of a sailor's pay. It was all Cook's officers could do to prevent mutiny as men tried to leave ship and head back to the Northwest Coast. In his journal, Cook commented on the profits that were likely to be made if a maritime fur trade could be established, but he would not live to play a part in it. On February 13, 1779, he was killed in the Hawaiian Islands during a confused fracas with the native people.

His death was counted a national tragedy, and the macabre details surrounding it were much on the public's mind when Cook's ships returned to England in October 1780.

Cook: a great captain

19

Of greater interest to London merchants were the stories about the fabulous profits made selling furs to the Chinese. The official version of Cook's journal for his third voyage would not be released until 1784, but enough information became available to permit London trader Richard Etches and several associates to form a company of their own and send two of Cook's veterans, Nathaniel Portlock and George Dixon, back to the Northwest Coast to gather furs. When they arrived they were surprised to find that English traders from China and India, who had also gotten wind of the fortunes made by Cook's sailors, had beaten them there.

As the British dreamed of fortunes in the fur trade, so did John Ledyard. In 1782 he was on board another ship, a sergeant of marines this time, bound for duty on the English blockade off Long Island. The American Revolution still had several months to run, but Ledyard was not about to take up arms against his countrymen. Jumping ship in Huntingdon Bay, he made his way to his uncle's house in Connecticut, where he hid until peace came in April.

He was nearly broke, but he possessed a copy of John Rickman's bootlegged journal of Cook's voyage, a lively and sometimes accurate account that came out fully three years before the official version. Using it as an outline and plagiarizing whole sections of it, Ledyard made up his own account and published it in 1783. He told how "skins which did not cost the purchaser sixpence sterling sold in China for 100 dollars." With the book as a kind of prospectus, Ledyard set to work convincing some merchant—any merchant—to finance his dream of leading a trading expedition to Nootka Sound. But American merchants were suffering from a postrevolutionary depression, so while some were tempted by Ledyard's scheme, none came forward with the money. Ledyard sailed off to France in 1785 in search of a patron.

In Paris he made contact with the American diplomatic community then made up of such figures as Benjamin Franklin, John Paul Jones, and the new ambassador, Thomas Jefferson. Ledyard became an intimate of Jefferson, who often invited him to the well-attended dinners at his townhouse, where Ledyard's accounts of his adventures and ideas about the maritime fur trade enlivened the conversation. Alarmed by the extent of Cook's explorations, France was planning a scientific expedition of her own, so she did not want a busy American adventurer complicating her schemes. A similar situation stymied him in Madrid. When Ledyard's luck seemed to have run out, Jefferson suggested an exploring expedition to the Northwest Coast. "I then proposed to him," Jefferson later wrote, "to go by land to Kamchatka, cross in some of the Russian vessels to Nootka Sound, fall down into the latitude of the Missouri, and penetrate to and through that to the United States."

Even Ledyard must have recognized Jefferson's ideas as fanciful, but by then his reputation as an adventurer and would-be explorer was the only collateral he could offer toward any plan to back his dream, so he agreed to try. In the summer of 1786 he found a patron in

Sir Joseph Banks, president of the London Royal Society, and began an astonishing trek to Russia, crossing from Hamburg into Sweden and then walking north beyond the Arctic Circle and around the Gulf of Bothnia to St. Petersburg. From there he headed east and managed to reach Yakutsk, less than five hundred miles from the Pacific, before he was arrested and sent back to Moscow. Like the other great powers, Russia wanted no foreigners interfering with her designs in the North Pacific, particularly in the fur trade.

Back in London by the summer of 1788 and once again short of cash, the indefatigable Ledyard hired himself out in support of one of Sir Joseph's own schemes, the exploration of Africa. An associate of Banks recalled being impressed by Ledyard's "manliness,... the breadth of his chest, the openness of his countenance, the inquietude of his eye." It was more than "inquietude." He had become a victim of his dreams, and in less than a year John Ledyard would be dead.

The tragic irony of Ledyard's life is that had he gone home to America in 1787, he might actually have realized his dream. One of those attending Jefferson's soirees in 1785, Charles Bullfinch (later the architect of the nation's capitol), had been deeply impressed by Ledyard. Returning to Boston in 1786, Bullfinch and his father met with the eminent trader Joseph Barrell and talked seriously about Ledyard's ideas. Boston ships had already commenced trading ginseng and liquor to Asian ports via the Cape of Good Hope, and it seemed a propitious time to enter this new venture. In the early months of 1787, Bullfinch, Barrell, and several other partners subscribed the enormous sum of fifty thousand dollars to outfit for a voyage to the North Pacific two vessels: the *Columbia Rediviva,* under the command of John Kendrick, and *Lady Washington,* under Robert Gray. Loaded with trade goods and high hopes, the ships left Boston Harbor on October 1, heading for Nootka Sound. On the same day, Ledyard was somewhere in Siberia, pacing through the forest in a line of Russian traders.

Nootka Sound was also much in the mind of Spanish officials who had read Cook's journals. Earlier, in 1774, they had sent an expedition into the North Pacific to see what the Russians were up to, and on August 8, its single ship *Santiago,* under the command of Juan Perez, anchored off the inlet. Native traders came on board and managed to steal two silver spoons belonging to the ship's second pilot, Esteban Martinez. Four years later, a lieutenant on board the *Discovery* traded a pewter basin for the same spoons and gave them to Cook, who wondered in his journal about their origin.

The Spanish recognized the reference and, in 1778, sent north another expedition under Martinez to look again at the Russians and to strengthen their claim to the coast. On Unalaska Island they met Russians who told them about the busy English fur trade emanating out of Nootka Sound. Hurrying south, Martinez reported this intelligence to his superiors. They ordered up another expedition, this time to extend the Spanish presence to Nootka.

The English had indeed been busy. From 1785 to 1789, as many as sixteen British ships visited the Northwest Coast. Besides making a fortune, their captains were adding to the knowledge of the coast itself. Between Cape Flattery and fifty-five degrees north latitude, Cook had carried out only the most cursory survey, and on his chart the coast was described by an uncomplicated line. The traders' discovery of several deep inlets, including the fabled Strait of Juan de Fuca, indicated the coast had a far more intricate configuration. In July 1788, Richard Etches wrote to Sir Joseph Banks suggesting the development of a prison colony on the Northwest Coast similar to one whose development Banks supported in Australia. As an added benefit, Etches proposed that the ship sent to guard the colony could be used to make a regular survey of the coast. This apparently was the germ from which the idea for an exploring expedition developed.

One of the most energetic English traders on the Northwest Coast at the time was Captain John Meares. Handsome, flamboyant, and something of a rogue, he came to the coast as an independent trader in 1786 and made Nootka his headquarters. In the summer of 1788 he claimed to have obtained a land grant from Maquinna, the paramount native leader in the area, and built a fort surrounded by a palisade. On a slipway of greased logs laid on the beach, he and a crew of Chinese shipwrights from Canton built the schooner *North West America*. Four days before it was launched, Robert Gray brought the *Lady Washington* into the harbor, followed a few days later by Kendrick.

That fall Meares returned to China and joined Etches' company. Meares' new partner, James Colnett, another Cook veteran, sailed back to Nootka in July of 1789 and was surprised to find a Spanish fort under construction at the site of the previous summer's activity. Nootka was getting dangerously international: a Spanish flotilla was anchored in the roadstead along with two American vessels.

The garrison at Fort San Miguel de Nutka was commanded by Martinez. On June 24, he had taken formal possession of the Sound in the name of the Spanish king and celebrated the event with the Americans as his invited guests. Next, he got down to the business of expelling the English traders from the coast. Since he had his hands full building the fort and presenting a bold front against the English, he allowed the Americans to stay since they posed no national threat and might even be useful. He even became friends with the affable Kendrick.

Such was the complicated situation when Colnett arrived in the *Argonaut*. Martinez at once demanded to know why he was trespassing on Spanish territory. Colnett informed him, with considerable spleen and no little pretense, that he came to take possession of the land for England. An argument ensued. Colnett called Martinez "a goddamned Spaniard" and Martinez had him seized along with his ship. The Americans disliked Colnett, a British rival, and participated in the affair to the extent of forging the manacles used to hold Colnett and training their loaded guns on the *Argonaut*. The next day, July 4, 1789,

Discovery on the rocks in Queen Charlotte Sound; from the 1789 edition of Vancouver's *Voyage*

Kendrick noisily celebrated Independence Day. A few days later the *North West America* and another ship, the *Princess Royal,* showed up. Martinez seized them as well and sent all three British vessels, their officers, and crews to Mexico under arrest.

This was the Nootka incident that pushed Spain and Great Britain to the brink of war. That took a while, since nearly six months passed before the government in London was aware of the particulars. In the meantime preparations were being made in London for an expedition to survey the Northwest Coast. On December 19, a 330-ton merchant vessel built in a yard on the Thames River was launched and christened *Discovery*. It was named after Cook's ship, and it was to be officered by many who had sailed with him. Henry Roberts, who had sailed with Cook on his second and third voyages, was captain, and one of the lieutenants was George Vancouver.

The ten years that intervened between the return of Cook's *Discovery* and the commissioning of its namesake had been important ones for Vancouver. Promoted to lieutenant immediately after his return, he had seen duty on the English Channel, the North Sea, and in the Caribbean where he had participated in a brief but noisy sea battle. It was during his long and hard years in the Caribbean that he established friendships with many of the men who would serve him later on and who left their names scattered along the circle of the globe. On board the *Europa* where Vancouver served four years, he came to know midshipmen Peter Puget and Joseph Baker as well as fellow lieutenants Zachary Mudge and Joseph Whidbey; another future eponym, James Vashon, was captain of the *Europa*. The man who became Vancouver's naval patron, Sir Alan Gardiner, shifted his

Alferez Manuel Quimper

Alferez Manuel Quimper was sent to the Northwest to strengthen Spanish claims to the area. With him were Commander Francisco de Eliza and Salvador Fidalgo. Quimper's party became the first to establish western presence in Washington when he settled near the Makah Indians on the outermost point of the Olympic Peninsula at Neah Bay. Quimper's stay in the area south of the Strait of Juan de Fuca lasted only a few years until the Nootka Convention when the Spanish agreed to vacate the area. Quimper documented his first encounter with the Makah Indians in a letter to the Viceroy.

From Spanish Explorations in the Strait of Juan de Fuca, *by Henry R. Wagner, Fine Arts Press, 1933.*

June 2, 1792

The day dawned clear and calm. At sunrise canoes full of Indians, men and women of all ages, began to come, asking for something with the word "pachito," and on not receiving anything called us "pizac," meaning "bad people," giving us to understand that the other vessels which had come to the port had given presents to everybody. I therefore found it necessary to have the calker cut up two large sheets of copper into small pieces to present to them. The men as well as the women wear a cloak of bark and wool hanging from the shoulders, the latter being distinguished by a breech clout which the men do not wear. They are of good figure, comely, of a clear brownish color and with regular features. In general all are of a good disposition. At 8 in the morning, the king, Huiquinanichi, sent out some canoes requesting me to come ashore. On my excusing myself he repeated his request by a brother, who with endearing demonstrations manifested to me that they were friends and that I could go ashore without any distrust. I therefore decided to do so together with the first pilot and an armed longboat, taking with me for my protection six of the soldiers. At 9 we landed and I was conducted by the brother of the king to his presence. In his house the chief of Fuca, named Macuina, had taken refuge. On asking him why he was not in his own country, he responded that it was because Martinez was in his port. Recognizing the first pilot, Don Gonzalo de Haro, he asked him if Martinez was in command of the sloop, seeing that she was in Nuca. To this answer was made that he need have no fear, as, although Martinez was in his port, he was not the chief in command of the frigate, but that another named Don Francisco de Eliza was, and that he should go to his port, as Eliza as well as Martinez desired to see him and entertain him. With these remarks he was content and satisfied, as well as the king, Huiquinanichi, to whom I gave three yards of scarlet cloth. Urging them to come to the sloop so I could entertain Macuina I went on board with all felicity. Huiquinanichi lives in a great house adorned with columns of huge figures which hold up three large pine timbers, as long as ninety feet and thick in proportion.

The entrance is a figure the mouth of which is a door. More than one hundred persons besides the king live in it. The other houses of his brothers and the chiefs are in proportion to the number they represent. All the Indians of both sexes and of all ages reach the number of one thousand or more. At 3:30 in the afternoon the king, Huiquinanichi, came out accompanied by Macuina, his father and his brothers. I received them with the greatest friendship, presenting a large copper sheet to Macuina and a half a one to the father of Huiquinanichi, declaring to Macuina that what had been told him on shore was true. At the same time the pilot presented to him two copper bracelets and some strings of beads for his wife and children. Still it was observed that this chief had no confidence in the friendship of Martinez nor in our words, because he asked the seamen if Martinez or Eliza was the captain of the frigate in Nuca. When they gave him the same answer as he had previously received he embraced us with much joy saying "Amigo amar a dios," words he had learned in Nuca. At sunset they returned to their settlement and I ordered a small gun fired for them all to go away. On shore they fired two musket shots. Night fell with the weather fine and calm and with nothing more to relate.

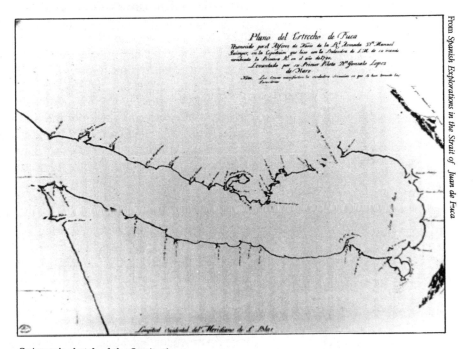

From *Spanish Explorations in the Strait of Juan de Fuca*

Quimper's sketch of the Strait of Juan de Fuca c. 1790s. Small bay at lower right is Discovery Bay

command of the West Indian Squadron to *Europa* in 1786. Like Cook, Gardiner was an energetic and progressive commander who kept his crews active and gave his officers ample opportunity to demonstrate their abilities.

After the American Revolution ended, there was a surplus of lieutenants in the British navy, and it was only by volunteering for extensive duty in places like the West Indies, where scurvy and yellow fever took a frightful toll even of officers, that one could hope for advancement. In the fall of 1787, Gardiner assigned Vancouver and Whidbey the task of surveying Port Royal and Kingston Harbor on the Island of Jamaica. It was a difficult job, given the size and complexity of the harbors, but the charts they produced were a source of pride to both men and caught the attention of their superiors. In early 1788, Vancouver was second in command of *Europa*. Even as John Ledyard lay dying in Cairo, retching out his life in a delirium of fever, Vancouver was being considered for an expedition to the far coast the American had despaired of reaching.

Before the *Discovery* and her consort, the brig *Chatham,* could sail, however, politics intervened. The ships had barely been commissioned when the Spanish ambassador in London delivered a protest, informing Westminster that an English ship violating Spanish waters in Nootka Sound had been seized. The prime minister, William Pitt, acted cautiously at first, but in April John Meares came booming into London, strenuously protesting the foul deeds done to him at Nootka Sound. Meares loudly informed the government that three ships rather than one had been seized. This news upped the diplomatic ante considerably, and Pitt issued the Spaniards stern demands and mobilized the fleet. Surprised by the British reaction at a time when she was unable to call on her allies quickly for support, Spain yielded on almost every point. In October of 1790, the two governments signed the Nootka Convention, under which Spain promised to allow British subjects to trade and settle on those parts of the coast it did not then occupy. Spain also promised to return the ships, buildings, and tracts of land it had seized at Nootka. To accomplish this, Britain agreed to send an emissary there to receive these spoils from the Spanish commandant.

The commander of the British surveying expedition bound for the Northwest Coast now being assembled in the Channel ports was the logical candidate for the emissary, so the government rushed to ready *Discovery* and *Chatham* for their new mission. In the meantime, however, Captain Roberts had been reassigned to lead another expedition to West Africa, and Vancouver was given his place, very likely at the suggestion of Sir Alan Gardiner, who had become a member of the Board of Admiralty.

Besides his demonstrated skills as navigator and surveyor, Vancouver also brought to his new position a genuine passion for exploring, for what he termed "the science of discovery." This expressed itself early in his naval career. In 1774, on Cook's second voyage, Vancouver had shinnied to the very end of *Resolution*'s bowsprit when Cook made his final tack southward into the ice-choked Antarctic. Walls of ice prevented him from going farther than seventy-two degrees ten minutes south, so as Cook prepared to come about and head back north, Vancouver, waving his hat and shouting, "Ne plus ultra!," became at that moment the man nearest the South Pole. When he finally made captain and was put in command of a major expedition, George Vancouver must have been acutely aware that as Cook's successor he would be judged against the man he most admired.

He set to work getting things under way. Many of the officers on board *Discovery* he selected from among his friends of the *Europa* days: Puget, Baker, Whidbey, and Mudge. Archibald Menzies, the lank Scot who was the expedition's botanist and became *Discovery*'s surgeon, had sailed to the Northwest Coast before and was a good friend of James Johnstone, master of the *Chatham* and one of the expedition's finest surveyors. Menzies owed his appointment to Sir Joseph Banks, with whom he had long corresponded on scientific matters. Banks went so far as to have the Admiralty give Vancouver special orders describing Menzies' role in the expedition, an intrusion upon Vancouver's prerogative that did not please him.

As spring approached, Vancouver saw to the provisioning of his ships which, prior to sailing, were "full so exactly like an Egg that there is no room to stow away one single box more in any part of the Ship." Among the supplies were eight thousand British-pounds' worth of trade goods for the natives they would meet, plus a good supply of fireworks— skyrockets, Roman candles, fountains, and pinwheels to overawe and delight them. There were also supplies of "antiscorbutics," sauerkraut, lemon and lime extracts, and other derivatives prescribed to allay the symptoms of scurvy. Their use had been pioneered by Cook, but it was not until after Vancouver's successful use of them during his voyage that the Admiralty ordered their use, particularly lime juice (hence the term "limey" to designate a British seaman), in the fleet. Finally, tucked away securely on each ship was a chronometer, still a revolutionary device the Board of Longitude had assigned to help compute their position.

On April 1, 1791, All Fools Day, the voyage began with the ships departing Falmouth on a gentle breeze. The men's minds, Vancouver wrote, were "not entirely free from serious and contemplative reflections. The remote and transitory places of abode were not likely to afford us any means of communicating with our native soil, our families, our friends or favorites, whom we were now leaving far behind."

Discovery proved a better sailer than *Chatham*. Not quite 100 feet long, *Discovery* carried a complement of 100 men besides being crammed with stores. On her best day she traveled 178 miles. Little more than 50 feet long on her keel, *Chatham* carried 45 men. Her instability required her to carry extra ballast, and this and other problems reduced her speed, much to Vancouver's annoyance and that of her own crew. Tortoiselike, the *Chatham* developed the curious habit of arriving at a destination before the *Discovery*. Vancouver hoped for a speedy passage to the Cape of Good Hope, but poor weather and the poorer performance of the *Chatham* added so many days to the journey that he felt required to break out the antiscorbutics and to fumigate the ships' holds with fires kindled in gunpowder mixed with vinegar. Only the cockroaches seemed not to mind the heat and stench the fires produced.

Twenty-three days out the Canary Islands rose on the horizon, and the ships put in at Santa Cruz. While *Chatham* took on more ballast and repairs were carried out on *Discovery*, whose head had been washed away by high seas, the men took their pleasure ashore. On the May 1 Sabbath a number of *Discovery*'s young gentlemen got into a fight with several from the *Chatham*. Spanish guards intervened and one who had his musket wrenched from him in the melee ran to get help. In the meantime, Vancouver chanced to arrive from a visit to a nearby town and tried to hurry the brawlers into boats and back to the ships. But the police came running at the head of an angry mob that threw the English, including Vancouver, into the bay. Angry and embarrassed, Vancouver avoided mentioning the incident in his regular report home, but word got out in crewmen's letters and it received notice in the London papers. Although a minor affair, it was the first of many that worked to cloud Vancouver's public image.

Adding to Vancouver's troubles was the onset of an illness that would kill him seven years later. Before he left England he suffered a bout that left him prostrate with exhaustion; shortly after leaving the Canaries, he endured another which nearly killed him before Menzies was able to nurse him back to a semblance of health with a special diet. The malady is likely to have been myxedema, a severe thyroid deficiency. At thirty-four, Vancouver was able to draw upon reserves of youthful energy. Like Ledyard, he too was a passionately driven man, but where Ledyard's object was the jagged edge of a native continent, Vancouver's was the image of Cook, the hero who masterfully strode the quarterdeck along that romantic shore.

From the Canaries the ships beat south to the Cape where for five weeks they waited repairs and resupply by dawdling provisioners. During their stay, a portentous transaction was being made at Nootka Sound. In July, the Bostonian John Kendrick had returned to the Sound and sailed past the guns of the Spanish fort, ignoring the call to leave and the summons to visit the new commandant, Lieutenant Don Francisco Eliza. Such was Kendrick's charm, though, that Eliza allowed him to stay. A few days later he pulled a fast one on the Spaniard by claiming a large part of the Sound for himself. The native Nootkans were also charmed by Kendrick, who on shore dressed in their clothes, ate their food, and spoke their language. In a gesture of friendship that may not have been spontaneous, Maquinna agreed to grant Kendrick more than three hundred square miles of territory in exchange for ten muskets—a grant that included the same lot he had traded to Meares. Out of sight of the Spanish authorities, Kendrick had Maquinna, several of his companions, and nine of the *Lady Washington*'s crew sign the deed. Celebrating the event in a manner similar to the Spanish marking of their earlier claim, Kendrick fired the ship's guns, unfurled a flag, and buried a bottle containing a copy of the document.

This was another fulfillment of John Ledyard's dream. Kendrick may have hoped to buy off the Spaniards, or he may have foreseen where the Anglo-Spanish dispute over the Sound would lead, but his act was one of vision and audacity almost twenty years before John Jacob Astor's claim at the mouth of the Columbia. Like Ledyard, Kendrick would never see anything come of his efforts, and the lack of national recognition of his claim prevented his kin from realizing any profit from it.

Kendrick was not the only heir to Ledyard's dream. A year earlier, Robert Gray returned to Boston in the *Columbia Rediviva* which Kendrick, who had stayed in the Pacific, had traded him for *Lady Washington*. Gray became the first American to sail around the world under his country's flag, and while his trip was not a commercial success, the fame it generated led his patrons to finance another voyage. The new nation was in the North Pacific to stay. On this second trip, Gray would establish a national claim to the Northwest that would never be given up.

The new nation was in the North Pacific to stay.

Just before Vancouver left the Cape in August, a Dutch East Indiaman ghosted in from Batavia with its crew stricken with dysentery. Many in the expedition became infected, and on the trip east the *Discovery*'s surgeon was felled by it, and Vancouver appointed Menzies to his place.

On the afternoon of September 26, the west coast of Australia rose above the horizon, a line of cliffs that resembled the coast of Cornwall. On the 28th the expedition discovered and entered King George Sound and took possession of the land, named New Cornwall, in the name of the king. Ashore to replenish water and wood for the galley stoves, Vancouver and his men surveyed the reaches of the Sound, but the wild land and the rude huts of its inhabitants, who apparently fled at their approach, did not impress them.

He followed Cook's route, coasting Australia and stopping briefly at Dusky Bay in New Zealand. Here the effects of the dysentery finally abated, and the men looked forward to their next landfall, Tahiti. Vancouver had visited the island four times before with Cook, and he decided to make an extended stopover, to treat his crews with fresh food, to resupply, and to make the repairs of which the wooden ships were constantly in need. The HMS *Bounty* under Captain William Bligh had called there only three years before, and the famous mutiny on the *Bounty* was still much on the public mind when Vancouver made his voyage. Mindful of this and the length of time—four weeks—he was to spend in this enchanted place, he restricted shore leave severely. The crew's disappointment was aggravated by the sweltering heat on board the ships and Vancouver's stubborn insistence on fumigating them with his stinking smudges.

Tensions rose. From the beginning of the voyage, Vancouver had been notably short-tempered, a condition due as much to his illness as to the heavy burden of command, but in

John Boit

The first solid American claim to the Northwest was made during Robert Gray's second voyage in 1792 when he named Columbia's River after his ship. John Boit, a crewman aboard the Columbia, logs the first crossing of this legendary river.

From Voyages of the "Columbia" to the Northwest Coast (1787-1790 and 1790-1793), *edited by Frederic W. Howay. Copyright © 1941 The Massachusetts Historical Society. Reprinted by permission.*

May 10, 1792

This day [12. N. Latt. 46° 7' W. Long. 122° 47'.] saw an appearance of a spacious harbour abrest the Ship, haul'd our wind for itt, observ'd two sand bars making off, with a passage between them to a fine river. Out pinnace and sent her in ahead and followed with the Ship under short sail, carried in from three to 7 f[atho]m, and when over the bar had 10 f[atho]m. Water quite fresh. the River extended to the NE as far as eye cou'd reach, and water fit to drink as far down as the *Bars,* at the entrance. we directed our course up this noble *river* in search of a Village. The beach was lin'd with Natives, who ran along shore following the Ship. Soon after above 20 Canoes came off, and brought a good lot of Furs and Salmon, which last they sold two for a board Nail. the furs we likewise bought cheap, for Copper and Cloth. they appear'd to view the Ship with the greatest astonishment and no doubt we was the first civilized people that they ever saw. We observ'd some of the same people we had before seen at Gray's harbour, and perhaps that was a branch of this same River. at length we arriv'd opposite to a large village, situate on the North side of the river about 5 leagues from the entrance, came too in 10 f[atho]m sand, about mile from shore. The river at this place was about 4 miles over. We purchas'd 4 Otter Skins for a Sheet of Copper, Beaver Skins, 2 Spikes each, and other land furs, 1 Spike each.

We lay in this place till the 20th May, during which time we put the Ship in good order and fill'd up all the *water* casks along side itt being very good. These Natives talk'd the same language as those farther South, but we cou'd not learn itt. Observ'd that the Canoes that came from down river brought no Otter Skins, and I believe the Otter constantly keeps in Salt water. they however always came well stocked with land furs and capitall Salmon. The tide sett down the whole time and was rapid. Whole trees sometimes come down with the *Stream.* The Indians inform'd us there was 50 Villages on the banks of this river. . . .

18. Shifted the Ship's berth to her Old Station abrest the Village *Chinoak,* command'd by a cheif name *Polack.* Vast many Canoes full of Indians from different parts of the river where constantly along side. Capt. Grays named this river *Colum-*

bia's, and the North entrance Cape Hancock, and the South Point *Adams.* This River in my opinion, wou'd be a fine place for to sett up a *Factory.* The Indians are very numerous, and appear'd very civill (not even offering to steal). during our short stay we collected 150 Otter, 300 Beaver, and twice the Number of other land furs. the river abounds with excellent *Salmon,* and most other River fish, and the Woods with plenty of Moose and Deer, the skins of which was brought us in great plenty, and the Banks produces a ground Nut, which is an excellent substitute for either bread or Potatoes, We found plenty of Oak, Ash, and Walnut trees, and clear ground in plenty, which with little labour might be made fit to raise such seeds as is nessescary for the sustenance of inhabitants, and in short a factory set up here and another at Hancock's River in the Queen Charlotte Isles, wou'd engross the whole trade of the NW coast (with the help [of] a few small coasting vessells).

20. This day left Columbia's River, and stood clear of the bars, and bore off to the Northward The Men at Columbia's River are strait limb'd, fine looking fellows, and the women are very pretty. they are all in a state of Nature, except the females, who wear a leaf Apron (perhaps *'twas* a fig leaf). But some of our gentlemen, that examin'd them pretty close, and *near,* both *within* and *without* reported that it was not a leaf but a nice wove mat in resemblance!! and so we go—thus, thus—and no Near!—!

John Boit

Tahiti his "violent passion" flared dramatically. For most of the stay, relations between him and the Tahitians were genial, but toward the end several incidents occurred that sparked his rage. An ax and a bag of linen were stolen, the latter a fairly serious loss, and Toweroo, a Hawaiian youth being returned to Molokai, had run off with his Tahitian lover. Vancouver threatened to burn the house of the suspected ax thief, and to lay waste to the entire district and destroy all its canoes unless it was returned. In a fit of temper he nearly strangled a man suspected as an accomplice in the theft of the linen. Terrified by his threats, the Tahitians fled, and it was only after earnest appeals were made by Tahitian chiefs and his own officers that Vancouver regained his composure. When Toweroo was hurriedly restored to him, Vancouver treated him without pity.

It was also Vancouver's misfortune to run afoul of a midshipman with a temperament more extreme than his own: Thomas Pitt, a close relative of the prime minister and the son of the first Baron Camelford. Pitt was a likable youth, but high-spirited to the point of instability and given to pranks that do not appear to have amused his captain. When he stole a barrel hoop to trade for the favors of a Tahitian girl, Vancouver had him flogged in the presence of the other midshipmen. He had him flogged again when he broke the binnacle glass while romping on the afterdeck with a shipmate, and once again after that. It was a punishment the proud youngster could not endure. He nursed the grudge and spent the next several years plotting to get even.

On January 24, 1792, Vancouver's ships left Tahiti and headed north. "It was not until the present moment," he later wrote, recalling a sense of elation and relief, "that our voyage could be considered as commenced; having now for the first time pointed our vessels' heads towards the grand object of the expedition."

The first destination was Hawaii, where he stopped for two weeks. Of all the places he visited, the Hawaiian Islands interested him the most, and he developed warm friendships with its prominent leaders, principally Kamehameha I, whom he would eventually persuade to submit to British dominion. If Vancouver had his faults he also had his virtues, and among these was a genuine respect for native societies and an ability to understand the distinctions governing relations among their leaders. Both were necessary to survival in Hawaii, which had entered upon a confused and violent stage in its political evolution. Vancouver refused to trade arms to Hawaiian leaders who desired them for their private armies to the point of seizing poorly guarded foreign vessels and killing their crews. This situation and his recollection of Cook's death may account for his panic when he mistook the normal burning of hillside fields for a signal to attack his ships. Menzies, who knew otherwise, tried to calm him, but the captain "behaved like a madman, raged and swore, which terrified the Indians." He demanded to be taken back to his ships in a native canoe, and when this upset in heavy surf, he thought it part of an attempt on his life and swam the rest of the way to a waiting longboat. He came to his senses and shortly afterward graciously entertained a visiting prince and his retinue with a display of fireworks. On March 17 they were off again, this time headed for the Northwest Coast.

Here is where Vancouver's story becomes especially significant for those who live in the Puget Sound region. He was the first to reveal its presence and importance to Western man, and his rapturous account of it attracted others and was the historic pretext for the rivalry between Great Britain and the United States over its possession.

He called the coast "New Albion," Sir Francis Drake's old name for it. Vancouver's instructions directed him to look for the Northwest Passage among the inlets Cook had missed. Vancouver's was the last expedition to do so, and the romance associated with that mythic strait appears to have heightened the sense of excitement and anticipation felt by all on board. Nearly four weeks out the appearance of a stupendous number of jellyfish heralded the approach of a continental grandeur. Trillions of these iridescent creatures covered the sea from horizon to horizon, and accompanied by great whales and lovely weather, the ships plowed through them for seven degrees of longitude. Thereafter there appeared driftwood, grass and seaweed, flocks of shags, ducks, and puffins. The weather turned. Finally, at about 4:00 a.m. on April 16, 1792, the tremendous coast materialized out of the fog and rain.

As they neared the entrance to the Strait of Juan de Fuca, they spied a sail approaching from the west.

Vancouver was near Point Cabrillo, about 115 miles north of San Francisco Bay. The boom of surf filled the air. In the days following, the ships nodded north past brave, wave-racked capes and big-shouldered hills, "beautifully green, with a luxurient herbages, interrupted with streaks of red earth." A gale carried them past Cape Mendocino, another past the present California-Oregon state line where they took pains to steer clear of the rocks, "so abundantly scattered along the coast."

Near the mouth of the Rogue River they met their first Indians, a people of "pleasing and courteous deportment," dressed in skins, who came out to trade, "with scrupulous honesty." On the 27th he was off the mouth of the Columbia blocked by its thundering bar, an opening he judged "not worthy of more attention." Historians have given Vancouver his lumps for these words, but he and several of his officers suspected a river entered the sea at that point. His early reputation as a perfectionist may have inspired the Admiralty's caution "not to pursue any inlet or river further than it shall appear to be navigable by vessels of such burthen as might safely navigate the Pacific Ocean." In light of these remarks, his seeming indifference appears more an expression of caution at the beginning of the survey than a failure of observation.

Passing and naming Point Grenville, he admired the "many detached rocks of various romantic forms" picketing the shore. As they neared the entrance to the Strait of Juan de Fuca, they spied a sail approaching from the west. This belonged to none other than the *Columbia Rediviva* under Robert Gray. Vancouver knew of Gray through John Meares's journal, which he was following at the time. In it, Meares accorded Gray the honor of first

The most lovely country that can be imagined.

circumnavigating what would become known as Vancouver Island. When the officers Vancouver sent over to visit Gray congratulated his achievement, he said with considerable astonishment that he had never done such a thing. In conversation as revealing of Gray's character as it was of Meares's, Gray told them that during an accidental meeting with Meares at Nootka Sound, he grew bored with his rival's boasts about the number of skins he had collected. Seeking to one-up him as much as throw him off Gray's own lucrative track, the American drolly informed him that he had discovered the Northwest Passage behind Nootka and even provided a fanciful map which, ironically, fairly approximated the actual passage separating Vancouver Island from the mainland. The gullible Meares recorded the story in his journal.

Gray apparently believed Vancouver was a rival trader. He mentioned his sighting of the river they had passed earlier, and from their comments about it and the fact that they had not entered it, Gray decided to head back south and try his luck. On May 11 he crossed the bar, named the river after his ship, and claimed it for the United States.

Rain obscured the opening mariners had thought might lead to an inland sea, a new Mediterranean. On April 30, however, a north wind unveiled a brilliant sky, and *Discovery* and *Chatham* passed between Tatoosh Island and Cape Flattery in the fabled Strait. To the north the shore was blue with mountains; to the south it rose up a great, crenelated wall capped with snow. Nothing they had seen before seemed quite so extraordinary. As they cleaved the glassy strait at a gentle three miles per hour, Midshipman Thomas Manby was moved to write: "Never was contrast greater, in this days sailing than with that we had long been accustomed too. It had more the aspect of enchantment than reality, with silent admiration each discerned the beauties of Nature, and nought was heard on board but expressions of delight murmered from every tongue." Even Vancouver, whose eighteenth-century prejudice for neat and ordered landscapes led him to dismiss the wild and untamed as "dreary" or "melancholy," was overwhelmed. "As we had no reason to imagine this country had ever been indebted for any of its decorations to the hand of man," he wrote in a famous passage, "I could not possibly believe that any uncultivated country had ever been discovered exhibiting so rich a picture."

He felt the tug of old England in the color and verdure of this new country, in its grand, parklike meadows, in much the same way that Ledyard felt the immediacy of his New England at Nootka. On May 2, in sight of the vast bulk of the peak he named Mount Baker, he anchored in Discovery Bay, near Port Townsend. On the 6th, a Sunday, he gave his men their first holiday since leaving the Cape of Good Hope. Joseph Whidbey spoke for many who would follow when he wrote a friend about the desirability of establishing a colony near the head of the Strait, "where there is a country equal to any in the world...the Farmer in this place would have nothing to do but put his plow in the ground... the Soil Capable in my opinion of producing anything offered to it."

On the 7th, Vancouver commenced surveying the southwest shore, entering and naming "Port Townshend" and "Hood's Channel." "As we advanced," he wrote, "the country seemed to improve in beauty." On the 8th he named "a remarkable high round mountain" Mount Rainier, after an old friend from his days patrolling the English Channel.

Many were curious about the signs of native life they observed on their way. They were fascinated by the sight of their first canoe burials, in which the dead were placed in lissome dugouts elevated on a wooden framework, but not enough to prevent one sailor from sawing one in half and using one end as a sentry box at camp. The tall poles the natives used to haul their duck-catching nets skyward mystified the English, who thought they might be gallows-poles. The people they met were cordial, even gracious, and seemed somehow to expect them. The women, unlike their Polynesian counterparts who offered themselves with frank abandon, were extremely modest and responded to the rough advances of the sailors, who believed all native women were alike, with shock. They fled in tears to their canoes, where they attempted to hide beneath blankets.

On the 15th, Vancouver returned to his ships and three days later raised sail to penetrate farther into the unknown sea. The *Chatham* headed up to the San Juans and the *Discovery* into the broad channel Vancouver named Admiralty Inlet. The weather held, and he continued to rhapsodize. "To describe the beauties of this region, will, on some future occasion, be a very grateful task to the pen of a skillful panegyrist. The serenity of the climate, the innumerable pleasing landscapes, and the abundant fertility that unassisted nature puts forth, require only to be enriched by the industry of man with villages, mansions, cottages, and other buildings, to render it the most lovely country that can be imagined." On the 19th he anchored off a low grassy point on Bainbridge Island that he named in honor of the Restoration of the Stuart Monarchy.

Here he took a walk through the lush meadow to an encampment whose temporary huts he mistook for a permanent village. Smeared with mud to prevent insect bites, the people there did not impress him as much as those who came from across the inlet—the Duwamish—to visit his ship with affecting ceremony. Among those at the camp, one wide-eyed child would preserve the memory of his visit. Later, he would take the name Seattle from an illustrious ancestor and give that name to an American city, but never be so impressed as he was at seeing the great Vancouver.

South of Restoration Point the waters were judged too hazardous to risk the larger ships. On the 20th, Lieutenants Puget and Whidbey were sent in small boats to survey the West Passage espied during a brief excursion into Port Orchard. When the *Chatham* returned from its cruise on the 25th, other boats were sent to explore the East Passage and Possession Sound. In this way the intricacies of Puget Sound and its adjacent waters were charted with such precision that, fifty years later, the American Wilkes Expedition could make only a few corrections.

Contacts with the native people remained cordial. At Commencement Bay, where Vancouver dined to a spectacular view of Mount Rainier, his men had to convince shocked Puyallups that the venison they offered them was not human flesh. Only once did the English meet with any hostility. This seems to have been provoked by the sailors fishing at the mouth of Minter Creek, near the head of Henderson Bay, but the menacing approach of armed men was halted by the discharge of a swivel gun above their heads. Bows that had been strung for a fight were quickly offered for trade.

At many spots on their survey the English saw the marks of smallpox on the faces of the people, and what looked like an abandoned village with skeletons scattered promiscuously along the beach suggested to them that the natives had recently endured the scourge of an epidemic. Vancouver surmised, accurately it seems, that the population had been decimated. Even the land seemed exhausted of its animal life. Native memories of the time likened his visit to a kind of epiphany, the fulfillment of a prophecy about the coming of strange beings during a time of cataclysm. While surveying Saratoga Passage (Wilkes's name), Whidbey was visited by a group of Skagits who were fascinated by the color of his skin. The prophecies told about the coming of white people. They thought his face might be painted white, but when he opened his waistcoat and showed them his skin, "their astonishment was inexpressible."

On June 3 and 4, Vancouver gave his exhausted men another well-deserved rest. On the shore of Port Gardiner Bay, at the site of the present Everett, he took possession of the land in the name of George III with cheers from his men and booming cannon. That done, *Discovery* and *Chatham* headed north, anchoring in Birch Bay on the 11th. The survey of the remarkable inland sea was complete, and Vancouver would never return.

After surveying the Georgia Strait, Vancouver headed to Nootka Sound where he met the *Daedalus*, the supply ship sent to replenish his depleted stores. He also met Don Juan Francisco de la Bodega y Quadra, the new commandant of Fort San Miguel and the commissioner appointed by the Spanish Crown to carry out the transfer at Nootka. Vancouver's diplomatic sense and Quadra's hospitality produced a warm friendship between the two men, and negotiations progressed in a pleasant round of dinners and celebrations. Yet, while Quadra was authorized to cede the occupancy of Nootka and restore property, he was not prepared to yield on the issue of sovereignty. This created an impasse, and the two men were forced to refer the matter to their respective governments. Eventually, Great Britain and Spain agreed to ignore the issue of sovereignty on unoccupied sections of the coast. To facilitate this, Nootka Sound, once the busiest port on the western shore, was abandoned by both countries. War was thereby avoided and the subsequent peace opened the door to British and American occupation of the coast.

After replenishing stores, Vancouver left Nootka in October. Quadra had informed him that Gray had entered a great river south on the coast and named it after his ship. On the 19th, Vancouver's ships hove to off the tempestuous bar, and he sent the smaller *Chatham* ahead into the surf. After a terrifying passage, its captain, William Broughton, brought his ship through and managed to survey one hundred miles of the river. In a prophetic insight, the *Chatham*'s clerk, Edward Bell, suggested the river might have connections deep in the continental interior and might be of interest to the Hudson's Bay Company. At Point Vancouver, near the present city of Vancouver, Broughton took possession of the river he named "Oragan" in the name of the king, but Ledyard's heirs would see to it that neither the name nor the claim stuck.

Although the survey of the Washington coast is enormously important to the history of the region, the few months Vancouver spent on it represented only a small fraction of his total survey. From the Columbia he sailed south to San Francisco Bay. His ships were the first foreign vessels to enter the port, and he spent considerable time exploring the Spanish settlements in California. In January of 1793 he returned to Hawaii where he remained until March, when he began his second season on the coast. He repeated the three-legged journey again, in 1793–94, carrying the survey up to Cook Inlet in what is now Alaska before he turned south for California, the west coast of South America and the Horn. On October 20, 1795, *Discovery* entered the Thames River where she was joined a month later by the *Chatham*.

The expedition was an enormous success; the survey was carried out to near perfection by the simple if exhausting process of tracing every foot of the shoreline. But unlike Cook's voyage, which men like Vancouver found inspiring, Vancouver's was not a happy one. In truth, he drove himself as hard as he drove his men, but the effort only made him irascible. He often exploded in wrath at his officers over unavoidable delays. When Menzies complained that his inattention to the greenhouse resulted in the destruction of much of its precious cargo, Vancouver had him arrested. As usual, the crew suffered most. When they grew weary and balked, he had them flogged; one man was flogged ten times, another who attempted to desert was given 144 lashes in two sessions. The bitterness that resulted followed the expedition home, where it continued to dog Vancouver.

On the other hand, he treated the native people with whom he came in contact with generosity, fairness, and respect. On only one occasion did he take life, when several canoe-loads of armed Tlingits bore down on one of his launches, and he ordered his men to fire into them. In his journal he expressed genuine grief over the incident, and it is interesting to compare his actions with the behavior of Gray and other traders, American and English, who believed that murdering a certain number of the people you traded with was simply part of business.

The *Discovery* crew was paid off on November 3, and Vancouver retired to the picturesque Thames village of Petersham on half-pay to work on his journal of the voyage. In spite of visits to the hot springs at Bristol, his health continued to decline. He was con-

The survey was carried out to near perfection by the simple if exhausting process of tracing every foot of the shoreline.

A boat encampment on Puget Sound, sketched by John Sykes

stantly short of money and hampered by disputes arising from the voyage. Spanish officials billed him for the expense of jailing his deserters, and there were hassles over expenses due him from the government. In spite of this, he wrote almost all of the five hundred thousand-word account of the voyage in language that was clear, direct, and elegant. The journals of other voyagers, like those of Cook, were ghostwritten, but for the sake of accuracy, Vancouver did it himself.

It was during this difficult time that Thomas Pitt, now the Baron Camelford, returned to England thirsting, he said, for Vancouver's blood. By this time Vancouver was suffering greatly from his disease. He had become bloated, his eyes protruded, and his hair had thinned to the point where he had to wear a wig for his portrait even though it was long out of style. Vancouver had sent Pitt home in disgrace on the *Daedalus,* and the new baron blamed him for the ruin of his naval career as well as the indignities he had suffered on the *Discovery*. He challenged Vancouver to a duel in an insulting letter that included money to pay Vancouver's traveling expenses to the selected site. Vancouver wrote in return that he did not feel called upon to "answer for his Public conduct in the exercise of his official duty," but that he was willing to submit to an examination of his conduct to any flag officer in the navy.

This enraged Camelford further, and he went to Petersham to confront Vancouver directly and demand satisfaction. Harried, Vancouver consulted friends and wrote Camelford another letter restating his position in the first. Camelford announced his intention of insulting Vancouver publicly in order to force him into a duel, and if he declined, he "would drive him from the Service, wou'd compel him to resign his Commission and would finally wherever he should meet him box it out and try which was the better Man." Vancouver's critics had charged him with arrogance, cruelty, and even embezzlement, so despite Camelford's obvious derangement, many took the baron's side. In September of 1796 Camelford met Vancouver and his brother John in London on Conduit Street near the latter's residence and proceeded to beat both of them with his cane. The affair was made the subject of a farcical caricature by James Gillray, "The Caneing in Conduit Street," that later appeared in print, to Vancouver's acute embarrassment.

The affair dragged on until Camelford left the country, making the last years of Vancouver's life miserable ones. Still, he continued writing and had almost finished the third and last volume of his journal when he died on May 12, 1798. He was not quite forty-one.

John Ledyard was thirty-eight when he died, burnt out by his unattainable dream. Even though Vancouver's accomplishments were immensely more substantial than Ledyard's, whose life was more a herald's than one who led the way, it is interesting to compare shipping statistics for the Northwest Coast in the years subsequent to both men's deaths. Between 1785 and 1794 about thirty five British ships traded there; in the next decade nine, and from 1805 to 1814, three. In 1788 two American ships visited the coast, in the next seven years fifteen, and between 1794 and 1805, about seventy. For a variety of historical reasons it would be the American captains, Ledyard's heirs, who dominated. The race was not always to the swift.

Exhausted by his labors, Vancouver died in circumstances almost as abject as Ledyard's. Although he never succeeded in escaping Cook's long shadow, his great work endured. Most of the landmarks he saw and mapped still bear the names he gave them, and two cities and a vast island are named after him. In the late evening of his life, Archibald Menzies recalled the man and the voyage: "What days those were—a fine group of officers—all gone now—a credit to the Captain—he chose them all, except me; Baker and Whidbey; yes, and Johnstone—they became Captains too—Mudge and Puget—Admirals both of them. Those books that Vancouver wrote—strange that he could put so much of himself into the printed page. He was a great Captain." ▄

LEGACY OF NAMES

CHARLES WILKES (1799–1877)

MURRAY MORGAN

Lieutenant Charles Wilkes—the man who named many things in Washington state—was the first official representative of the United States to visit Puget Sound. He came as commander of the United States Exploring Expedition of 1838–42, assigned to chart areas that might be of use to American commerce. His ships, *Vincennes* and *Porpoise*, reached the entrance to the Sound on May 2, 1841, exactly forty-nine years after George Vancouver got here for the British.

The difference in arrival dates was important. Under terms of the Convention of 1818, the United States and Great Britain shared equal rights in the territory lying between Spanish-America (forty-two degrees north latitude) and Russian-America (fifty-four degrees forty minutes). Political pressure was mounting to end the joint occupation. North of the Columbia River the British were well established; American presence was minimal.

As his men charted the waters discovered by Vancouver and familiar to the fur traders and farmers of the Hudson's Bay Company, Wilkes attached American names to every bay, harbor, inlet, point, or shoal Vancouver had neglected to christen. It was Wilkes who put in place most of the place names around the Sound.

Vancouver named the big things: Puget Sound, Admiralty Inlet, Hood Canal, Mount Rainier and Mount St. Helens, Whidbey and Vashon islands. Wilkes gave us Elliott Bay, Commencement Bay, Useless Bay, Quartermaster Harbor; such islands as Bainbridge, Blake, Fox, Hartstene, McNeil, Maury, and Waldron; nearly all of the inlets—Budd, Carr, Case, Dye, Eld, Hammersley, Henderson, Sinclair, and Totten; passages such as Agate, Colvos, Dana, Drayton, Peale, and Pickering; points innumerable (even the self-contradicting Point No Point), as well as assorted rocks.

There might have been more. Wilkes failed to win acceptance of "Naval Archipelago" for the San Juans, and was only partially successful in his attempt to call individual islands in that group after "distinguished officers late of the US Naval Service, viz. Rodgers, Chauncey, Hull, Shaw, Decatur, Jones, Blakely, Perry, Sinclair, Lawrence, Gordon, Percival, and others." Enough Hispanic names survive to reflect the fact that the Spanish were the first to reach the San Juans: Orcas, Sucia, Fidalgo.

It was Wilkes who put in place most of the place names around the Sound.

Argillite sea captain

From *Magnificent Voyagers*, Smithsonian Institution Press

In choosing historic naval figures to honor, Wilkes favored men who had fought the Barbary pirates, the British, or both. Captain William Bainbridge, who lost the frigate *Philadelphia* to the pirates in 1804 but captured the British *Java* in the War of 1812 (and earned the nickname "Old Ironsides" for his victorious ship the USS *Constitution*), has an island named for him. So does Bainbridge's friend, Stephen Decatur, who led a raid into Tripoli Harbor to burn the captured *Philadelphia*. Bainbridge served as Decatur's second when Decatur was killed in a duel with Captain James Barron. The evenhanded Wilkes named Barron Bay (now Yukon Harbor), west of Blake Island, for the better shot. The Blake of Blake Island was George Smith Blake, commander of the US Coast Survey.

Augustus C. Ludlow, killed at sea in the War of 1812, is honored by a port, as is Lieutenant Robert Gamble, who was only wounded. Allan Island is meant to honor a captain killed in battle, William Henry Allen, whose spelling of his patronym differed from Wilkes's. Sinclair Island in Skagit County is named for Arthur Sinclair Sr., who captained the thirty-two-gun *General Pike* against the British. Sinclair Inlet, however, bears the name of the sailing master of the *Porpoise,* who did most of the charting of the Sound north of the Tacoma Narrows.

After three years at sea, Wilkes had fallen from favor with all but a few of his officers. He did not let this greatly influence his name-giving. Lieutenant Henry Hartstene had been accused by Wilkes of cowardice during his rescue of sailors stranded on an Antarctic island, a feat Hartstene's fellow officers considered heroic. He quit the expedition and went home on the supply ship. Even so, Wilkes named one of the largest islands in the Sound for him. Another lieutenant, Augustus Case, had requested transfer to another ship while the expedition was in Australia. Wilkes assured him that there was not an officer in the flotilla he would not prefer to Case, but denied the request. Nevertheless, Case Inlet separates Hartstene Island from the Longbranch Peninsula.

The most peculiar of the names on Wilkes's chart is that of Vendovi Island, north of Bellingham Bay. Vendovi was a Fiji Island chieftain whom Wilkes had kidnapped to bring back to America to face charges that he had, a decade earlier, hosted a banquet at which ten crewmen from a New England whaler were the main course. Tall, lean, and stylish, Vendovi became such a favorite with the Yankees that he was permitted to don his royal feathers (and borrowed boots) to march in the Fourth of July parade the expedition staged near Nisqually. Vendovi never faced trial for alleged dietary indiscretions. The day after the *Vincennes* reached Brooklyn, ending its four-and-a-half-year voyage, he died. The expedition's scientists took a death mask, then detached his head. The skull became part of the Smithsonian Institution's inheritance of Wilkes Expedition artifacts. Alas, poor Vendovi.

The question lingers as to which of three men Elliott Bay is named for. Edmond Meany, in his study of Washington place names, decided on the expedition's chaplain as

The seizure by Captain Wilkes of the US warship *San Jacinto* of the British mail steamer *Trent*

the honoree. Further research has indicated that, however forgiving the standards applied by Wilkes in choosing Yankee names, Jared S. Elliott was unlikely to have been selected.

A stumpy, humorless prude who felt it his duty to shield the men of the expedition against all temptation, including the reading of novels, he incited mutinous, indeed sacrilegious, sentiments in Hawaii. Poor Jared attempted to persuade the resident missionaries to preserve the morals of the men of the expedition by sequestering the Christian Polynesian females while the fleet was in. The sailors counterattacked with complaints that the chaplain's relationship with the wife of one of the missionaries was a scandal to the arapane-birds.

Wilkes suspended the cleric from religious duties. Elliott resigned and demanded to be put ashore. Wilkes decided that to preserve the purity of the islands it would be necessary to keep the ex-chaplain aboard until they got to San Francisco. (Jared was left on the

William Fraser Tolmie

As superintendent of the Puget Sound Agricultural Company at Fort Nisqually, Dr. William Fraser Tolmie documented the trading, the travails, and the people of early Northwest life. Fort Nisqually was located just south of the mouth of the Nisqually River, where the delta enabled the settlers to grow crops.

From "Journal of Occurrences at Nisqually House," edited by Clarence B. Bagley, Washington Historical Quarterly, Vol. VI, No. 3, July 1915. Reprinted by permission of Pacific Northwest Quarterly.

December 1833

Wednesday 25th—This being Christmas day I gave the men a liberal Regale of eàtables and drinkables to make up in some measure for the bad living they have had all year here, and they enjoyed the feast as might be expected men would do who lived solely on soup since they came here. Weather still very cold—

Thursday 26th The men were allowed to rest from their labors, today as they are rather fagged after yesterday's indulgence—A hurricane or whirlwind passed and broke down the largest trees is its way like straws—

Friday 27th—Set all hands to work to square oak wood for making two Bastions of 12 sqr. each either for this place or Whidbey's Island, as they may be required—Rainy Weather.

December

Saturday 28th The men employed as yesterday Traded 6 beaver skins & three otters.—Weather Rainy—

Sunday 29th—Weather as yesterday—Held forth for about an hour, on religious subjects to the Indians who as usual collected for edification—

Monday 30th The men employed sawing and squaring oak wood for Bastions—The weather has again set in frosty—No trade

Tuesday 31st—The men employed as yesterday—Froze intensely during the last 24 hours—Many Indians have collected about the place who have a good many beaver, &c—They are very anxious to obtain supplies but are reluctant to give two beavers per blanket—To say the least of it, it was the most blind policy to begin the trade here in the spring at one beaver per blanket, when there were no opposition on the coast with the intention of afterwards raising the price to two.—Circumstanced as we have been here it has been no agreeable job to raise the price to two, as it exposed us to constant jarrings with the natives who are still in bad humour on that account. . . .

January 1834

Wednesday 1st Gave the men a blowout similar to that which they had on Christmas day, which afforded them ample enjoyment—The frosty weather continues—

June 1834

23rd Monday. Bourgeau with a couple of Indians have gone to gather more Cedar Bark. Pierre Charles has been busy at repairing the Boat. Plomondon, Brown and Louis working at the new Building. Ouvre doing sundry jobs besides attending to the Indians Mc Kee still very unwel with his left hand thumb, yet gets in water and brought up the Bark with his Oxen. The Indians are doing well and support us in meat. I have already one Cask Salted. Fair and very warm weather. . . .

26th Thursday. About a dozen of Cowlitz Indians arrived last evening with a few skins. They commenced to day to trade and of course very troublesome their Chiefs the greatest beggars I have known. In the evening Pierre Charles arrived with his party 500 pieces of Bark got by them which now makes 1100 pieces besides what was put on the store. Very warm weather.

27th Friday. The men kept at their employment About one P.M. Aniaveskum Mc Donald arrived from Vancouver with Letters. The Brigade from the Interior had arrived at that place on the 16th Inst. under Chief Factor Dease, accompanied by Messrs. Black and S. Mc Gillivery, all well in those quarters. The weather very warm.

28th Saturday. Trade continued with the Cowlitz Indians and I am happy to say that it was got over without much trouble at last, though yesterday I turned several out of the shop. Fair weather.

29 Sunday. Indians all away and the day was got over without seeing any. Cloudy weather.

30 Monday. Still employed at the new dwelling house. More Indians have come to trade, and everything got on in quietness. . . .

August 1834

23rd Sunday. I have this day got into my new dwelling house what is now done is well and I hope in a few days it will be completed. The mens house fairly covered and the Gable ends filled up. We have now about us three hundred Indians belonging to eight different tribes. A Chief by name Babillard got into a scrap with me, but the coward soon drew in his horns. This scamp has ever been troublesome as Ouvre says, and on that account I made him run from the Fort in a fright though provided all the time with a Brass bludgeon. The weather fine.

William Fraser Tolmie

24th Sunday. A great day for the Indians who assembled all here for a dance and to hear from me what was right to do. I made them a speech in the Flat Head language, which was understood by the Chief Frenchmen who was the linguist for the rest of the tribes present. Every one seemed to pay attention to what I said, and it is to be hoped that these Indians will become as good as those of the Interior. A Clallum chief arrived but could not see me owing to the number of Indians. There was about 250 men Women, Boys and Girls in the dance every one peaceable. The weather cloudy.

25th Monday. The men employed as usual. many of the Indians away to their homes. Pierre Charles has had another attack of the Ague but I am happy to remark it was a very slight one. Rained all day. . . .

28th Thursday. All the men employed indoors. Got the scythes put in order. Pierre Charles again sick of the ague. The weather fair.

29th Friday. Sent letters to Mr Yale by the Chief Nes Clam who proceeds to Langley. Some plastering done to the men's house, the flooring and division made for each family. Pierre Charles still sick. The natives keep going and coming with some skins and a little meat. The weather fair.

Augt. 30th 1834 Saturday. The plastering nearly completed. The Indians keep near us for the purpose of passing tomorrow with us. Fair weather.

31 Sunday. The men have kept at rest and the natives were also attentive to their devotions. The Returns of the month as follows,

193 Large Beaver	102 Rats
43 Small do.	53 Otters
3 lbs Cutting do.	7 Elk Skins
8 Black Bears	37 Deer
3 Fishers	9 Animals (the
24 Badgers	meat of)
42 Minks	13 Mats

Vincennes while Vendovi was invited to the Fourth of July festivities on Puget Sound.)

If not for the ex-chaplain, was Elliott Bay named for George Elliott? Again unlikely. George was a teenaged cabin boy who had received a cat-o'-nine for insubordination while on Puget Sound. That leaves Midshipman Samuel Elliott as the man aboard most likely to have his name bestowed upon a bay. His candidacy is bolstered by the fact that he was in the small boat party that surveyed the harbor. Not that Elliott Bay was considered important. Wilkes wrote that "the anchorage is of comparatively small extent, owing to the great depth of water as well as the extensive mud flats; these are exposed at low water. Three small streams enter the head of the bay, where good water may be obtained. I do not consider the bay a desirable anchorage: from the west it is exposed to the prevailing winds, and during their strength there is heavy sea."

In general, Wilkes observed the protocol of rank in bestowing names. Major waterways went to the officers. Thus we have inlets named for Lieutenants George M. Totten and Thomas A. Budd, his principal cartographers; for Lieutenant Case, whom Wilkes despised with reciprocity; and for Lieutenant Overton Carr, who rather liked his commander.

Lieutenant Cadwallader Ringgold, captain of the *Porpoise,* whose navigational ability led another officer to remark that "the mysterious properties of a right-angled triangle are utterly beyond his comprehension," was to have one of the major straits in the San Juans called for him; but later map makers decided on Rosario Strait, a shortening of the Spanish "Gran Canal de Nuestra Senora del Rosario la Marinera."

The midshipmen—officers-to-be—also had waterways named for them. Greek born George Musalas Colvocoresses, who was to write the most lively narrative of the expedition, left part of his patronym on the channel between Vashon Island and the Kitsap Peninsula, and on some rocks at the entrance to Port Ludlow. Wilkes, whose spelling was uncertain, did not even attempt Colvocoresses, calling both the passage and the rocks Colvos.

Midshipmen Henry Eld and George W. Hammersly had two of the southernmost inlets named for them, though Wilkes added an extra "e" to Hammersly's name. Midshipman William L. Maury, nephew of the hydrographer who had turned down command of the exploring expedition, is remembered by Maury Island—Wilkes choosing to ignore, for patriotic reasons, that Maury is really an extension of Vashon, which Vancouver had already christened.

George Sinclair, sailing master of the *Porpoise,* who supervised the actual charting cruise north of the Narrows (and whose journal is full of anti-Wilkes notations), was rewarded with an inlet between Bremerton and Port Orchard.

Notorious for his failure to praise his enlisted men personally, Wilkes was generous in putting their names on the map, so Puget Sound bristles with points named for the crew.

In general, Wilkes observed the protocol of rank in bestowing names.

Explorer Wilkes: flamboyant
obscurity

Point Whitehorn on the south side of Birch Bay is named after quarter-gunner Daniel Whitehorn, who left part of his hand at Nisqually when a howitzer exploded during the Independence Day celebration. Point Migley on Lummi Island, Point Fosdick on Fox, Green Point at the east entrance to Carr Inlet, and the Williamson Rocks off the western shore of Fidalgo Island bear the names of other gunners. Point White at the southwestern tip of Bainbridge is named for a captain of the forecastle; Hyde Point on McNeil for a carpenter's mate, Carter Point on Lummi for a petty officer, Gibson Point on Fox for a coxswain, and Point Wilson on Hartstene and Disney Point on Waldron for sailmakers.

The quartermasters, responsible for day-to-day navigation of the ship, were honored in general by Quartermaster Harbor, and individually by points Heyer, Piner, Pully (also known as Three Tree Point), Robinson, Southworth, and Williams. Quartermaster Dalco's name was shifted by usage to the passage between Tacoma and Vashon Island, Quartermaster Henderson's to an inlet.

A protuberance in Commencement Bay was named for crew member John Harmon, but the point disappeared in the reshaping of the waterfront. Sailor's mate Alvin Harris was to have had a point across the bay named for him but it is now called Browns Point for reasons unknown.

Islands were named for Lewis Herron, a barrel maker; J.L. Fox, assistant surgeon; Stephen E. Days, hospital steward; instrument maker John Brown; Frederick S. Stuart, captain's clerk; and William Speiden, purser. John Allshouse, a marine private later killed in an accident at San Francisco, had a small island in Carr Inlet named for him, but it is now known as Raft Island. A harbor off Hale Passage was named for Benjamin Vanderford, the pilot of the *Vincennes,* but the Indian name Wollachet (squirting clams) prevails.

The expedition's civilian scientists and their assistants, regarded by Wilkes much of the time as obligatory nuisances, were not neglected. Hale Passage between Fox Island and the mainland bears the name of the expedition's expert on languages. Horatio Hale compiled a dictionary of the Chinook Jargon and contributed to the studies of ethnography. (His mother, an editor of *Godey's Ladies Book,* wrote "Mary Had a Little Lamb.")

James Dwight Dana, who shipped as geologist but produced a celebrated study of coral zoophytes, had a passage named for him. So did the erudite Charles Pickering—zoologist, ichthyologist, herpetologist, and anthropologist—whose contribution to the expedition's publications, an anthropological study called *The Races of Man,* was to receive a memorably unkind review from Dr. Oliver Wendell Holmes: "The oddest collection of fragments that was ever seen...amorphous as a fog, unstratified as a dumpling, and heterogeneous as a low-priced sausage."

Drayton Passage between Anderson Island and the Longbranch Peninsula is named for the artist and map maker Joseph Drayton, who accompanied Wilkes on an overland

Charles Wilkes and his daughter

William Brackenridge

The "official" horticulturist on the Wilkes Expedition was part of the first American party to cross the Cascade Mountains. This account from William Brackenridge's diary kept during the trek along the Naches Trail in 1841 to Eastern Washington and Idaho offers a glimpse of the trek through a horticulturist's eye.

From "Our Official Horticulturist," edited by O.B. Sperlin, Washington Historical Quarterly, *Vol. XXI, No. 4, October 1930; Vol. XXII, No. 1, January 1931. Reprinted by permission of* Pacific Northwest Quarterly.

May 23rd, 1841

Oregon Country—Inland Expedition. Our route [a]cross the range lay somewhat to the north of Mt. R[ainier] where the finest timber exists that I ever beheld. For several days our route lay through dense forests of Spruce the stems so straight and clean that it was seldom you could find a branch closer than 150 feet to the ground. A prostrate trunk of a Spruce which we took with a tape line measured—length 265 ft. circumfe: (10 ft. from base) 35 ft. When this tree fell the top had broke[n] of[f], where it measured 18 inches in diameter, and allowing the top piece to be 20 ft. the whole height of Said tree when standing would be 285 ft. In deep moist valleys I have seen the Thuja, or Arbor Vita at least ⅓ more in circumference, but not so high by 100 ft. A Populus, or Cotton tree which we measured was upwards of 200 ft. high. Many of the Spruce stems which lay prostrate were so stout that when on horse back we could not see over them. On the decayed bark of such seedlings of the Spruce vegetated freely, forcing their roots through the bark, over the body of the trunk, till the[y] reached the ground so that when said trunk became entirely decayed, the roots of the young trees became robust [and] formed a sort of arch way, under which we occasionally rode.

[June] 12th, [1841]. At 10 A.M. made the Grand Coule[e]. The pass that led us into it was down a bank of loose rock about 500 feet high. Its breadth where we crossed it was about 5 miles. About the centre are several deep lakes bounded on the upper end be precipitous rocks. Here we found abundance of Ducks. I could observe no feature whatever that could lead one to suppose confidently that the valley had ever been the course of the Columbia, as it bears no traces of a sweeping current having passed through it at any time. On the contrary it presents in many places a rolling surface, with several rotund bluffs to the height of 700 feet. At the upper end of one of the lakes is a deep gap or hollow so that had water ever flowed through the Coule[e] this must have been the principal channel, and yet these rocks in place of being water worn or rounded of[f] are angular and show their natural disposition. The Coule[e] appeared to me to be like the seat of a former *Lake* or *Sea,* which by some convulsion or another had a gap formed in its banks by which its waters forced their way into the Columbia. There is a large tract of flat land in its bottom, but to[o] much impregnated with salt to raise crops or Grain on, but I should think admirably adapted for the raising of Sheep & Cattle, there being plenty of water and abundance of Good grass, both in the Coule[e] and within 20 miles of it on both sides. In the afternoon Mr. Maxwell came up with us—he loaned us several of the Companies Horses to help us along. The general course of the Coule[e] where we made it tends N & South. On leaving it we made a few miles on the opposite side & Camp'd on the prairie.

[July] 15th, [1841]. On the afternoon of this day the party reached Fort Nesqually, being absent exactly sixty days from the Ship. And casting a look back on that part of the Oregon that we had traversed it appears to me that we certainly must have viewed it in a very different light from the majority of writers that have come out so boldly in its favour. As an agricultural country to me it appears almost posetive that to take the upper lands (or those above Walla Walla) on an average, that Ten acres out of a Hundred would not pro-

duce Rye enough to cover expence of Seed and Labour. I have chosen Rye as being a grain that succeeds better on poor soil than any other that I know. And that not more than Two acres out of one Hundred would produce Wheat that would pay the farmer for his trouble. The valley extending from Colvile to Chimekane (Messrs Walker & Eel[l]s station), at Lapwia on the Kus-Kut-skii, (Mr. Spauldings station) and at Waiiletpu on the Walla Walla are the only three good tracts of land that we saw, or could learn anything of. Much has been said of the Willamette as a wheat Country but of that I can say nothing.—Nature seems to have designed the upper part of the Oregon more as a pastoral, or country for the raising of Cattle. That part of it pass'd over by us between Okanagan, by way of the Coule[e] to the River Spokane, & from that over to the Kus-Kutskii could not be surpassed as a sheep Country by any in the world, although I have not the least doubt but that the incursions of the Woolves and Indians on the herds might proove an obsticle to the Sheep farmer at the Commencement.

William Brackenridge

expedition from Nisqually to the Willamette Valley and later helped him prepare the final charts and supervised their engraving on copper: a useful man. Rich Passage bears the name of the useless William Rich, a weekend gardener who somehow won appointment as expedition botanist and botched the assignment. Not only was Rich cavalier about dissecting and identifying specimens, but a friend reported that he had done "nothing but smoke cigars and tell stories during the expedition."

Peale Passage between Hartstene and Squaxin islands was named for another of the expedition artists, Titian Ramsey Peale, the son of Charles Willson Peale who is remembered for several portraits of George Washington. Another professional painter, Alfred T. Agate, gave his name to the narrow pass at the northern tip of Bainbridge Island, to the continuing confusion of rock gatherers. (Similarly confusing is Point Partridge at the westernmost tip of Whidbey Island; it was named for an English family that Wilkes's brother married into.)

Dye Inlet (Dyes on Wilkes's chart) was named for the taxidermist John W. W. Dye, a dour chap who was the commander's superior when it came to misspelling: "The forrist trees of the largist size grow to the Very Warter's edge where you may cut a mast or stiack for a Line of Battle Ship. I never saw Sutch large forrist trees in any part of the world before...."

Some Wilkes place names reflect appearance or circumstance. The Narrows, Flattop Island, Yellow Island, and Point No Point are self-explanatory. Gig Harbor proved useful to the expedition's small boats. Useless Bay offered no shelter from storms. Commencement Bay was the starting point for the *Porpoise*'s survey north of the Narrows. Point Defiance "would bid defiance to any attack."

A few native names found their way onto Wilkes's charts, though he was profoundly unimpressed by the Indians. Scatchet Head on Whidbey Island is his version of Skagit. Several Indian names along Hood Canal—Tala Point, Toandos Peninsula, Suquamish Harbor, and Dabob Bay—seem to reflect the friendly relations between Lieutenant Case's surveying crew and the Twana tribesmen.

The British were not totally ignored. Anderson Island honors Alexander Canfield Anderson, the Hudson's Bay Company chief trader at Fort Nisqually, whose hospitality astonished Wilkes. Ketron Island was Wilkes's egregiously erratic spelling of the name of the superintendent of the Puget Sound Agricultural Company, William Kittson. McNeil Island was named for William Henry McNeill, the Yankee skipper of the HBC steamer *Beaver*.

The most mysterious names on the charts published after the return of the expedition are those of Gordon Island and Adolphus Island. No one knows who the islands, shown between Orcas and Sucia in the San Juans, were named for. It hardly matters; the islands don't exist. John Frazier Henry, the Seattle marine historian, has traced their existence to

"I never saw Sutch large forrist trees in any part of the world before...."

Midshipman William May, the son of George Washington's personal physician. May, who detested Wilkes and faced court-martial on two charges brought by him, seems to have inserted the fictitious Atlantises onto the charts as a way of embarrassing his commander.

Though one of the least modest men in naval history, Wilkes refrained from naming anything for himself. Perhaps he left that to posterity. Posterity proved unobliging. Around here the only thing bearing Wilkes name is a school on Bainbridge Island.

Wilkes's obscurity was flamboyantly earned. He was not the sort of man bureaucrats or politicians were inclined to honor. He was arrogant (he acknowledged that he was the only American capable of carrying out his assignment), secretive (on a voyage lasting four and half years he never confided to his subordinate officers where they were going next), suspicious (he suspected a cabal had formed to discredit him), brutal even by the disciplinary standards of the wooden ship navy (a court-martial found him guilty of exceeding the maximum number of lashes), impetuous (he needlessly risked his ships by entering the tricky harbor at Sydney, Australia, in the dark), and insubordinate (denied promotion to acting captain, he waited until well at sea, promoted himself, and raised the flag of a commodore). Even so, Wilkes could not understand his unpopularity.

After his official visit to the secretary of the Navy on his return to Washington, Wilkes boasted of telling that worthy, "I was entirely independent of him and well knew I had friends who would have justice done me." Asked by the secretary to explain an anonymous letter that charged members of the expedition with misbehavior, "I took the letter, threw it upon the floor, put my foot upon it, and gave it a kick....I felt he deserved this rebuke."

At a banquet celebrating the expedition's return he bawled out the audience, which included former President John Quincy Adams, for not having made his accomplishments better known. "I did not hesitate to throw the blame where it belonged, and on those present and seated near me."

Calling at the White House uninvited, he found President John Tyler "seated in the center of a semicircle of the messiest-looking fellows, all squirting their tobacco juice into the fire....I have very great doubts if the President knew who I was; he continued his talks and jokes with those boorish visitors. As soon as I could I made my escape, glad to get beyond the vulgarity and boorishness of this squad of politicians."

When he died in 1877 at the age of seventy-eight, *The New York Times* obituary did not even mention the United States Exploring Expedition of 1838–42. But Wilkes had left a legacy of charts both accurate and beautiful, and a collection of artifacts, specimens, reports, and data now preserved at the Smithsonian Institution. And all those familiar names.

Mary Richardson Walker: a
feminist without knowing it

54

EIGHT ON HER HONEYMOON

MARY RICHARDSON WALKER (1811–1897)

NANCY WILSON ROSS

Although Mary Richardson Walker traveled west in 1838 with three other brides, in a honeymoon party of eight, she is considered the "third woman to cross the Rockies," two years after Narcissa Whitman and Eliza Spalding. There is no proof that Mary actually reached the summit and started down the western side of it before the other three women in the honeymoon octet, but after reading her journal one somehow believes that this must surely have been true.

To tell the story of this pioneer bluestocking's trip from Maine to Oregon and her life in the wilderness, we have to go back to the war that broke out in the 1830s between two African Zulu chiefs named Dingaan and Moseltktze. The timing of these chieftains' war helped Mary and Elkanah Walker decide that God was calling them to Oregon instead of the Africa they had originally intended as a mission field.

It is certainly our good fortune that Mary Walker's quick eye and trenchant tongue were employed in comment on life in early Oregon rather than in details of existence on the remote coast of Africa. Like Narcissa Whitman, who had preceded her across the Rockies, Mary was faithful to her pen through all hardships and vicissitudes. Unlike Narcissa's letters, however, her diary was not written for a family far to the east, but was intended for her eye alone. Although she left careful instructions that it be destroyed by any stranger who chanced upon it in the event of her sudden death, her western descendants decided otherwise, sharing with Clifford Merrill Drury, who made her story public, the opinion that she and her diary "belonged to history."

Mary was not so glamorous a figure as that other missionary to the Indians, Narcissa Whitman, nor so self-effacing and humble as gentle Eliza Spalding. She was sharper, plainer, keener-edged, a true product of the state of Maine. Mary was a feminist without knowing it, and certainly without admitting it. She began her diary at age twenty-two, and thus we are enabled to follow for many years the course of a searching female mind of the American nineteenth century operating in a world designed exclusively for men. What is more, we are privileged to observe the unflagging activity of this mind in a western environment so desolate and primitive that all the native ingenuity of the female was called into

A searching female mind of the American nineteenth century operating in a world designed exclusively for men.

play to make it livable—endurable even.

While she was still a student at Maine Wesleyan in the early 1830s, measuring herself against the world around her, she asked a professor how her papers compared with those of the men students. "Better, much better," the professor replied, and then he added with wry irony: "Aren't you ashamed of yourself, Mary?"

It is easy to believe that Mary swung regularly between the two poles of pride in herself and shame at her forwardness. Born in East Baldwin, Maine, in 1811, she was a rare combination of introvert and extrovert, given to inner struggle and vague dreams while holding to life with a grasp that was both practical and realistic. When from her parents' farm in East Baldwin, Maine, she first applied to the American Board for Foreign Missions for a post in a foreign land, she evaluated herself with unusual objectivity: "I have succeeded in combining the intellectual and domestic in a great[er] degree than I ever knew anyone else to attempt...I am aware that I possess an aspiring mind. But I have endeavored and I hope with some success to cultivate a spirit of humility; to be willing to do something and be nothing if duty requires."

Life in the Oregon wilderness as a missionary wife was to exact from Mary a good many years of doing something and being nothing. Though she was perhaps by temperament better fitted to contend with the wilderness and the Indians than her husband, Elkanah, her place was in the home. Here on occasion, however—with joy and mental stimulation—she had a chance to display publicly her native powers. Once, when in her husband's absence she had to trade with the Indians on behalf of members of the important Wilkes Expedition, she made note in her diary that an Indian chief complimented her highly on her eloquence: "said I talked as forcibly as the men would have done and that the gentlemen would not have got the horses but for me."

But, even as Mary rode across the plains toward the western world that was still legendary in the American mind, she had become more woman than adventurer—she was already heavy with child. "The minerals are interesting but I have to ride over most of them without picking them up. If I could only mount and dismount without help how glad I would be." She was then carrying the first of a family of eight—seven boys and one girl—to whom she was to be a loving yet detached mother. The story survives and is told by a grandchild that, after Walker's children were grown, a woman in Forest Grove, Oregon, said to her: "Mother Walker, you have raised seven sons and they are all good Christians and useful citizens, what were your methods? How did you do it?" And Mary replied: "Yes, I have raised seven sons and they are all Church members and good Christians." Then she paused and added: "But that's about all I can say for them."

Although Mary had determined at the early age of nine on the life of a missionary (the most exciting career open to women at this period), as she grew into her teens she found herself seesawing erratically in her religious life. She longed for a final experience of "grace" that would lay to rest forever any doubts and uncertainties. To her embarrassment the Spirit saw fit to enter her forcibly at a Methodist revival. Later, to her relief, this somewhat hysterical experience "stood the test of orthodoxy," and she united with the staid Congregational church in Baldwin. When as a grown woman and a successful schoolteacher in her twenties she finally decided on a missionary career, she tried first for a post in Siam, to teach the families of missionaries—the only post open to unattached females. When the position went to someone else Mary was left in complete uncertainty about her future. She knew only that she wanted to go to foreign lands and convert the heathen, or at least to associate with those permitted by virtue of their sex or their marriage to lead lost souls to the Lord. Such a life seemed the only possible outlet for an inquiring mind, a bold spirit, and boundless energy.

Before Elkanah Walker entered her life, she had had an ardent non-Christian suitor whose feelings for her, and hers for him, led to prolonged, tormented heart-searchings. Could she or could she not marry an infidel, one who did not possess in her opinion "knowledge and piety"? Should she "to escape the horrors of perpetual celibacy settle down with the vulgar"? It seems likely that, in the end, Mary would have done just this had not some shrewd maneuvering on the part of friends produced Elkanah Walker, a pious young man from Bangor who wanted also to be a missionary but did not want to set off wifeless on a reinforcement mission for the cause of Indian conversion in the West. The mission board urged *all* missionaries to take wives with them. Not for them was cohabitation with the Indian girls as the fur traders did.

Elkanah came to East Baldwin to look over Mary as a prospective bride. In two days they were engaged. Afterwards, with the passing of time, judging from their letters and Mary's diary, they really fell in love. But not before Mary had had many painful and disturbing scenes with the mysterious "infidel" whom she identified as "G." in her diary. His presence seemed able always to shake her faith. And G. was not inclined to spare her feelings: "I would rather have seen you pass on a bier than in a chaise with W," he told her, adding, "He does not love you as well as I do." He tried to sting her by letting her know that people did not think she was "cutting any great cheese" in taking Elkanah.

In March of 1838 at the age of twenty-seven, Mary announced the news of her marriage and imminent departure to Oregon, occasioning such tart Maine comment as: "Now isn't that just like Mary Richardson to go galloping off across the plains on a wild buffalo." Perhaps this remark came from the same source that set village gossip buzzing about her some years before when, as a guest in a house, Mary scandalously sat down on the floor on a skin stretched before the kitchen fire. Impulsive Mary was often shocking people. She frequently made Elkanah uneasy. On their way up the Mississippi the bride made note of a resolve: "Tomorrow I will not if I can possibly avoid it, do anything that will displease my dear. I wish he would try to make me at ease instead of embarrassing me by continual watchfulness." And later: "If I stir, it is forwardness; if I am still, it is inactivity...I am almost certain that more is expected of me than can be had of any one woman."

And much later from Oregon: "I am almost in despair and without hope of his ever being pleased or satisfied with [me]. I do not know what course to pursue. I can never, with all my care, make myself what he would like me to be."

Similar entries are sprinkled generously throughout Mary's revealing private journal. Her anxiety to establish a steady and adult relationship with her husband is one of the qualities that endears her to history, particularly her revealing statements about life with a moody man whom, she sometimes felt, she could never really know or be close to.

As a wife of some years Mary made a desperately sincere entry in her faithful journal, obviously addressed to Elkanah, whom she suspected of reading her secret jottings:

> I find it in vain to expect my journal will escape your eyes and indeed why should I wish to have it. Certainly my mind knows no sweeter solace than the privilege of unburdening itself to you. It frequently happens that when I think of much that I wish to say to you, you are either so much fatigued, so drowsy or so busy that I find no convenient opportunity, till what I would have said is forgotten. I have therefore determined to address my journal to you. I shall at all times address you with the unrestrained freedom of a fond and confiding wife. When therefore you have leisure and inclination to know my heart, you may here find it ready for converse.

But all these entries lay on the other side of the great journey.

Before Mary Richardson set out for the "riddlings of Creation" she crowded into her life all the experiences possible in the civilized world of the East. In going to Oregon she was, after all, facing no less of an ordeal and no shorter a journey than had it been Africa that claimed her. All that people knew about the Oregon Country in those days was blood-chilling. In congressional debates on "the Oregon Question," those senators who were opposed to admitting this wild country beyond the Rockies turned many a fearful and flowery phrase about cannibalism, wild beasts, endless deserts, impassable mountains, and unfordable rivers. "The whole country is the most irreclaimable barren waste known to mankind except the desert of Sahara. As to healthfulness the ravages of malaria defy all history to furnish a parallel." This was a typical statement. The story of the overland trip of Lewis and Clark, spurred on by Thomas Jefferson and accompanied by Sacajawea, was little known and few people were aware of its significance.

Both the Walkers had mild qualms, though Elkanah, who had once experienced the horrors of seasickness on a short coastal excursion, was relieved to feel that the hazards of water travel were at least not to be theirs. As for Mary, her appetite for experience kept her days too crowded for serious misgivings. Before heading west with Elkanah, she visited and was feted in Boston and New York. She took her first ride on a railroad train—at some ten miles an hour. She rode to the end of the line at Chambersburg in Pennsylvania and there took stage to Pittsburgh—this last a tedious journey enduring from Thursday to Monday morning. From Pittsburgh she and Elkanah went down the Ohio River, stopping at Wheeling, Marietta, and Cincinnati.

In Cincinnati they called on the famous divine Dr. Lyman Beecher, head of the Lane Theological Seminary, father of the great evangelist Henry Ward Beecher and the illustrious Harriet Beecher Stowe, whose *Uncle Tom's Cabin* was later to rock a nation. In Cincinnati Mary's path also crossed that of the most daring and outspoken feminist of her time. Fanny Wright was there in 1838 on a tour speaking publicly in support of her shocking theories on equal rights for women, birth control, a more equable distribution of property, and marriage as a moral rather than a legal obligation. Mary reported in her journal that Dr. Beecher was replying to Miss Wright in chapel on the subject of "infidelity."

We could wish that Mary had defied Elkanah and gone alone to see Frances Wright, who in 1818 had abandoned the life of luxury to which she had been born in Scotland in order to embrace the freedom of the New World. In her lifetime Fanny Wright was to give herself to many causes, including Robert Owens's socialist Utopia at New Harmony, Indiana. She devised a plan for the freeing of slaves by purchasing them, placing them in a community in Tennessee, teaching them independence and useful trades, and eventually colonizing them in Haiti. Fanny Wright was too far ahead of her time to influence it lastingly, but she, like Mary, stands as a prototype of an emerging female. The two should have met.

We are safe, however, in assuming that Elkanah would not have approved of a woman of Frances Wright's caliber, since he did not even approve of women praying aloud in the presence of men. There was, indeed, a little storm later in the Whitman mission, located seven miles west of present Walla Walla, over this very point. Mary, waiting at the mission during Elkanah's first exploring trip away, prayed aloud in public as both Mrs. Whitman and Mrs. Spalding were accustomed to doing. She then immediately noted in her diary: "I wish I knew whether my husband likes to have me pray before folks or not. When he comes home I will ask him." Elkanah was not of two minds about it. His answer was a positive no, in which he enjoyed the backing of no less an authority than the Apostle Paul, who, without mincing words, had set it forth in First Corinthians: "Let the women keep silence in the churches; for it is not permitted unto them to speak." Mrs. Whitman remarked (with some spleen) in a letter home that men of the missionary reinforcement "found it wrong and unseemly for a woman to pray where there are men." She found the distinction insulting—St. Paul or no St. Paul.

By the time they reached Cincinnati, Mary and Elkanah had joined forces with two of the other honeymooning couples who were also dedicating their newly joined lives to the cause of Indian conversion in the Far West. Knowing what lay ahead of them in the

Mother Joseph

Upon her arrival in Washington in 1856, Mother Joseph first constructed a home for other incoming nuns to Vancouver, Washington Territory. She then proceeded to establish schools, hospitals (St. Joseph's Hospital in Vancouver, Washington, was the first among many), and orphanages throughout the Northwest.

From "A Hammer in Her Hand," by Margaret Romeo, Seattle Post-Intelligencer, *February 24, 1980. Courtesy: Sisters of Providence Archives, Seattle, Washington.*

On December of 1856, five nuns from Montreal arrived in Vancouver, Washington Territory, a primitive village whose bishop, A.M.A. Blanchet, had requested their presence. They had traveled 6,000 miles by sea—sailing south to the Isthmus of Panama, which they crossed by narrow gauge railroad, and then sailing north on the western side of the continent and into the Columbia River—to reach their new home.

Through some misunderstanding, that home was not ready. Before the sisters had time to become discouraged, however, their 23-year-old leader Mother Joseph had unpacked her hammer and saw and started to build them a home in a 10- by 16-foot addition to the bishop's house.

In the years that followed, Mother Joseph, a hammer hanging from her belt and a saw in her hands, was a familiar sight around Vancouver, a village that had grown up around one of the largest of the Hudson's Bay fur trading forts. By the time she arrived, the fort had been relocated and replaced by a U.S. Army post.

Mother Joseph remodeled a small building abandoned by the Hudson's Bay Company. No sooner had she and the sisters moved in than a woman left a three-year-old child on their doorstep. "Her name is Emily Lake," she said as she hurried away. Thus, the sisters welcomed their first orphan. Others followed in quick succession.

Things happened fast after that. Besides the orphanage, the sisters established a school, hospital, mental asylum and a home for the aged.

Mother Joseph personally supervised and inspected the construction and did much of the building herself. She used skills she had learned from her father, a carriage maker, architectural designer and wood carver from Quebec.

She usually made her inspection rounds accompanied by a group of orphans. She bounced on high crossbeams to test their strength, her black habit flying in the wind. She crawled underground to inspect foundations. If anything failed to meet her high standards, she tore it apart and rebuilt it herself.

The workmen recognized her as a skilled carpenter and architect. They had a healthy respect for both her know-how and her temper. Only with children did she have infinite patience. She enjoyed having them around her and knew they could learn by watching and helping.

Mother Joseph helped tame the raw unsettled land that was Washington Territory in the mid-19th century. Building was only one of her contributions. She fed the hungry, nursed the sick, cherished the orphaned and the elderly and educated the young.

To finance her many projects, Mother Joseph with another sister and a priest or an Indian guide made trip after trip to the mining camps in the area to beg money. They rode horseback over hot, dry prairies infested with rattlesnakes, through treacherous swamps and along slippery mountain paths. They traveled by canoe over dangerous rivers. They climbed down into mines, disregarding their own safety. The miners admired their courage and gave liberally from their diggings. There were narrow escapes from bandits but nothing to fear from the Indians who soon learned that the women wearing the black robes and silver crosses were their friends.

When the nuns' small collection of wooden dwellings became overcrowded, Mother Joseph drew plans for Providence Academy and supervised its construction. She created a beautiful, symmetrical structure three stories high, all of bricks made by Lowell Hidden, a local man who had once worked in a brick yard. Each of the orphans lifted one shovelful of dirt.

The chapel is the academy's most inspiring feature. Slender curving arches soar three stories to the ceiling, past two balconies. For this area, Mother Joseph

made statues, carved benches, the molds for scrolls at pillar tops and the five carved altars.

The academy opened its doors in September of 1874 and remained in constant use for nearly a century. It is still standing—bought and preserved by Robert Hidden, a grandson of the man who made the bricks.

Mother Joseph died in 1902 after establishing 11 hospitals, seven academies, five Indian schools and two orphanages. Many of them are still flourishing in Washington, Oregon, Montana, Idaho and British Columbia.

While the work Mother Joseph began goes on, people have begun working to increase recognition for her contributions. Spurred by the Clark County Historical Society, the Daughters of Pioneers and other interested groups, the Washington State Legislature selected her to be the state's second representative for the Statuary Hall Collection in Washington, D.C. Each state is entitled to two statues. Marcus Whitman was Washington's first.

Mother Joseph

company of the blasphemous men of the Fur Caravan—a medley of itinerant traders who would serve as their mountain guides—they put to the Reverend Dr. Beecher the solemn question of their observance of the Sabbath. Dr. Beecher undoubtedly startled them, and perhaps even shocked them a little, by the eminently sane—though faintly flippant—attitude he took on the matter. Said the great divine, if he were crossing the ocean he would certainly not consider jumping overboard on the seventh day in order to avoid the onus of Sunday travel.

Myra Eells, another bride among the famous group of eight honeymooners, left an entry in her plains diary that sets forth the spiritual dilemma that the question of traveling on the Sabbath posed for the scripturally exact missionaries: "Our Sabbaths have always been the hardest day's work. This has led me very much to question the duty of going to the heathen in this way. I cannot tell how it is consistent for us to break one of God's positive commands to keep another."

The man who was ostensibly the leader of this group of missionary recruits to the Far West was W.H. Gray, who went out with the Whitmans in 1836 and immediately made a hot-foot trip back to the States for reinforcements. He represented the Indians as panting for salvation and he managed to recruit, within a few whirlwind months, three honeymooners and a single man—Cornelius Rogers of Reverend Beecher's congregation—besides getting a wife for himself.

The town of Independence, Missouri, was the last civilized stop for the four couples. Here they made all arrangements for the journey, including the very important matter of tent-sharing. Not without what Mary called a "mighty big fuss," it was finally settled that the Eells and the Grays would share a tent at night, and the Smiths and the Walkers another, each tent divided in half by a curtain. Thus for months by a flickering tallow, with Elkanah beside her urging her to put out the light, and the Smiths "sleeping loudly" on the other side, Mary made her faithful entries.

From the outset it was plain that there was going to be trouble.

From the outset it was plain that there was going to be trouble. "We have a strange company of missionaries," wrote Mary in her outspoken way. "Scarcely one who is not intolerable on some account."

W.H. Gray, who published in 1870 a two-volume *History of Oregon,* shared Mary's views—excepting himself, of course. In his *History* he managed to insert not a few sharp licks at his fellow workers in the vineyard of the Lord. He didn't trouble to analyze the women—they were just women—but he found Cushing Eells guilty of a "superabundance of self-esteem, great pretensions to precision and accurateness of statement and strictness of conduct." In Gray's opinion, he lacked "all the qualities requisite for a successful Indian missionary." Walker was "faithful as a Christian" but "inefficient as a preacher," with "no positive traits of mind." Finally, he found Smith a man of "strong prejudices" who was without Christian forbearance.

This is the same Mr. Smith with whom Joe Meek, the genial mountain man, had an adventure of which he left an account in his biography, *River of the West*. Meek came upon Mr. and Mrs. Smith separated from the other missionaries not far from the fur trappers' annual summer Rocky Mountain trading rendezvous at which Meek had first seen them. He found the couple all alone in the midst of a vast, hot, and dusty plain, the woman still on her feet, with the two horses, but Mr. Smith prostrate on the ground and sure that he was dying. Joe, not without malice, one feels certain, offered the missionary the succor of his bottle of alcohol. It was righteously refused. When Joe saw that the stubborn man might really die if he continued to lie on the earth in the sun, he made—so he reported to Mrs. Victor, his biographer—the following speech:

> You're a...pretty fellow to be lying on the ground here, lolling your tongue out of your mouth and trying to die. Die, if you want to, you're of no account and will never be missed. Here's your wife, who you keep standing here in the hot sun; why don't she die? She's got more pluck than a white-livered chap like you.

Having delivered himself of these remarks without any apparent effect on the prostrate man, Meek then informed him that hostile Indians were riding hard on their trail. Finally, in desperation, he lifted the terrified Mrs. Smith to her saddle and ordered her to ride. She rode. "Mrs. Smith can find plenty of better men than you," was Meek's parting shot. This final threat struck home. When he looked back from down the trail, Joe saw the dying man sitting up, and that night he rode into camp. After this experience it is not surprising to learn that Smith wrote back to the American mission board saying that the more he thought about it, the more improper it seemed to him for females to travel across the plains.

Mary had a good eye for the scenery and was particularly enchanted—as all western travelers have always been—by the architectural fancies of the American dry lands. "The bluffs resemble statuary, castles, forts...as if Nature, tired of waiting the advance of civilization, had erected her own temples." When they encamped on the plains near Independence Rock in today's Wyoming, Mary chipped a piece from it and then wrote one of the first descriptions of this great landmark. It was this rock in the "dry sea" that was later to become a register on which hundreds of weary immigrants paused to scrawl their names—thereby revealing a single act of self-assertion after weeks of the exhausting, dusty anonymity of the overland trail. The piece Mary chipped from the rock may now be seen in the Oregon Historical Society in Portland, along with the little antique sidesaddle in which she rode so many cramped and tortuous miles.

When, finally, they reached the Whitman mission at Waiilatpu in August of 1838, their trials were still not at an end. Living-quarters were woefully inadequate. Mary had no chance for the privacy for which she, as an expectant mother, now longed. She wrote to

Elkanah, away on a scouting trip looking for a site for their own mission, that she dreaded the coming of cold weather, when she could not stay in her unheated room any longer and must beg a place beside Mrs. Whitman's stove.

The Walkers and Eells chose to settle together among the Spokanes (also known as Flatheads) in the idyllic little valley called Tshimakain, named by the Indians for a spring that bubbled there. Mary's description of this untouched Tshimakain countryside that would also be her home for nine years—and perhaps in a sense forever her spiritual home— manages to convey the unawakened quality of a land where man has not yet intruded:

This is a beautiful country,
Still a kind of gloom seems to pervade it
As if nature were asleep,
Or rather the face of the ground.
The whole country might be supposed to be
Enjoying a long Sabbath.

It was here that Cyrus, the Walkers' firstborn, was taken shortly after his birth at the Whitman mission in December, where Mary had remained until her confinement. She was not sorry to leave the Whitman household for a place of her own amidst the Spokanes, though it was only a fourteen-foot-square log hut with a grass and dirt roof (which leaked mud in every rain), a dirt floor with pine needles strewn on it, and the skins of animals tacked at windows and doors.

There was a persistent undercurrent of strain and bad feeling among the missionary wives when around Narcissa Whitman. Indeed, through Mary's sharp yet essentially kind eyes, we get another view of the martyred Narcissa's high-strung, emotional temperament. We see her not eating her breakfast, going down by the river to have a good cry; spending long hours in prayer alone, coming impulsively afterwards to ask forgiveness for her faults; "in a worry about something; cross with everyone"; so that she "went out and blustered around and succeeded in melting over her tallow." Yet Mary also saw the other side of the matter; that the presence of so many strangers was a burden to Mrs. Whitman, and that she had "less help from the other ladies than she ought."

Mary's delivery, for a first child, was not a difficult one. Her phrases about it, written in immediate retrospect, have a rather dry humor: "About nine I became sick enough; began to feel discouraged, felt as if I almost wished I had never been married. But there was no retreating; meet it I must." After the delivery she endured a kind of suffering of which one can hardly bear to read. She had, according to Mrs. Whitman, "no nipples." She undoubtedly had milk fever. To nurse her child was an agony so terrible that she says herself

Elkanah had to hold her and the babe too: "The pain I experienced was so intense that my hands would be clinched and a paroxysm produced much like a fit. I think I can say with truth that I never knew what pain was until then." But little Cyrus had to be fed, and there was only one cow at the mission, going dry. Mrs. Whitman helped nurse for a while, then an Indian woman was found. It must have been strange indeed for Mary Richardson Walker of Maine to see her firstborn nursed by one of the heathen people she had come to save.

In spite of this terrible postbirth experience, Mary went right ahead and had her other seven children with courageous spirit and few complaints. Sometimes the doctor got there and sometimes not. Once Mary met him at the door with her babe in her arms. The courage of these missionary wives in their childbirth experiences never ceases to amaze a modern reader; partly because all of them were old for childbirth by nineteenth-century standards. They were in their late twenties or thirties. Poor Myra Eells, who was always sickly, was thirty-six at the birth of her son, Edwin, and we read of a Mrs. Hill who was so ill with a disease of the spine that she could not ride horseback or sit upright in a canoe and yet she produced a child.

In spite of the drudgery of Mary's life, she made time for the little extras that give a child pleasure. She wrote about sitting up late to make a "rag baby" for little Abigail—her only daughter— and then not being able to resist going to the child's bed and waking her to see her look of joy. She worried for fear she might force the children too fast for their natural development and warned herself by recalling an impatient childish habit of hers of picking open the buds of roses to hasten their blooming. Her detachment on the whole seems admirable. She wrote once of an altercation between Elkanah and little Cyrus in which the child refused to yield an inch. He was put to bed as punishment, but when Mary tiptoed in to look at him she was pleased to observe: "He has gone to sleep with a smile of exultation depicted on his countenance. I hope if he is ever called to suffer at the stake, he will be as unrelenting."

There was a good deal of heartburning among the missionary mothers incident to the question of how, in the midst of an amoral race, to bring up children after the good American Puritan pattern. Mary had an Indian girl "helper" who was dismissed by the whites and condemned by the Indians for "asking young fellows to sleep with her," as Elkanah expressed it. While Elkanah was away on a trip, Mary rehired the girl to help her with the washing, but the pious Mr. Eells countermanded the order, sending Mary to her diary with Scriptural complexities beyond her own unraveling:

> I do not know what is right. I have compared her case with the example of our Saviour in
> the case of the woman taken in adultery, and of the woman of Samaria, and of his eating
> with publicans and sinners. Also what St. Paul says of keeping company with immoral

Through Mary's sharp yet essentially kind eyes, we get another view of the martyred Narcissa's high-strung, emotional temperament.

65

Narcissa Whitman

Narcissa Whitman and her friend and fellow missionary Eliza Spalding were the first two American white women to travel overland from the Mississippi River to Fort Vancouver. In 1847, tension between natives and whites boiled over to a wild massacre in the Cayuses where both Narcissa and Marcus Whitman were killed. Eight years earlier, shortly after her arrival in the Walla Walla Valley Narcissa writes to her mother from Waiilatpu (seven miles west of Walla Walla) of her two-year-old's death.

From The Letters of Narcissa Whitman, *by Narcissa Whitman, Ye Galleon Press, 1986.*

Waiilatpu, Walla Walla River, Orgon Territory, October 9, 1839.

Dearest Mother:—I have written a whole sheet to father talking about our dear little daughter, and have just arrived to the scene of her death. It was half past two when we gave directions for supper, thinking to have it some earlier than usual because husband had not eaten anything since breakfast, when I sent Margaret to look for her. Mungo went out with her at the same time and went to the river, but came back immediately and said there were two cups in the river. This started us at once and as I made the inquiry, "How did they come there?" husband said "Let them be and get them out to-morrow, because of the Sabbath." I asked again how they came there and what cups they were. He said "I suppose Alice put them there," and immediately went out and took some poles to get them out. Why I was not alarmed in an instant is to me astonishing. It was doubtless owing partially to my confidence in the girl I sent for her, because she did not come and tell me she could not find her. I trusted she had and had taken her with her to get radishes, etc. I looked to see if she was with her, husband at the same time going to see about the cups. I went to the other side of the house and inquired for her, but no one had seen her. Then it was pretty plain in my mind where she was, and by the time I got to the river's brink, it flashed across my mind like a dream, that I had had a glimpse of her, while sitting and reading, entering the house and on seeing the table set for supper, she exclaimed with her usual animation, "Mamma, supper is almost ready; let Alice get some water." She went up to the table and took *two cups* that set by her plate and Margaret's (for we drank water instead of tea) and disappeared. This was like a shadow that passed across my mind, passed away and made no impression. Strange as it seemed to myself, I did not recollect it until I reached the place where she had fallen in. And now where is she? We thought if we could find her immediately she would not be dead entirely, so but that we could bring her to again. We ran down on the brink of the river near the place where she was, and, as if forbidden to approach the spot, although accessible, we passed her, crossed a bend in the river far below and then back again, and then in another direction, still further below, while others got into the river and waded to find her, and what was remarkable, all entered the river below where she was at last found. Dear mother, you cannot tell what our feelings were at that time. . . . By this time all hopes of her life were given up for she had been in the water too long now to think of saving her. As we were coming towards the house, we saw an old Indian preparing to enter the river where she fell in. I stopped to see him swim under water until he passed me, and just a little below me he took her from the water and exclaimed "She is found." I ran to grasp her to my breast, but husband outran me and took her up from the river, and in taking her into his arms and pulling her dress from her face we thought she struggled for breath, but found afterwards that it was only the effect of the atmosphere upon her after being in water. We tried every means that could be used to bring her to life, for a long time, but to no effect. Her spirit had been called to rise to worlds before unknown, and I could only say, "Lord, it is right; it is right; she is not mine, but thine; she has only been lent to me for a little season, and now, dearest Saviour, thou hast the best right to her; 'Thy will be done,' not mine."

I cannot describe what our feelings were when night came and our dear child a corpse in another room. We went to bed, but not to sleep, for sleep had departed from our eyes. The morning came, we arose; but our child slept on. I prepared a shroud for her during the day, and before evening Mr. Pambrun came, but was ignorant of her death until he arrived, although we had gone to inform him. Mr. Hall arrived on Tuesday evening, got the news Monday noon and started immediately. Mr. and Mrs. S. came down the river to Walla Walla because he had broken his ribs and was unable to ride. They arrived Thursday noon and we buried her that afternoon.

We kept her four days. She did not begin to change in her appearance much for the three first days. This proved to be a great comfort to me, for so long as she looked natural and was so sweet and I could caress her, I could not bear to have her out of my sight; but when she began to melt away like wax and her visage changed I wished then to put her in so safe, quiet and desirable a resting place as the grave—to see her no more until the morning of the resurrection.

Although her grave is in sight, every time I step out of doors, yet my thoughts seldom wander there to find her. I seem not to feel that she is there. I look above and with unspeakable delight contemplate her as enjoying the full delights of that bright world where her joys are perfect and she does not now, as formerly, need the presence of her much loved parents to make her happy. Her little prayer used to be: "O Lord, bless little Alice; may she be Thy child, may she love Thee, and when she dies, may she go to heaven and live with Jesus, and sing his praises, forever and ever. Amen."

Narcissa Prentice Whitman

persons. I cannot determine exactly how we should treat the present case or whether Paul would have us not to pay any regard in our worldly transactions as to whether they are moral or not.

There spoke the true Yankee realist who knew that the world's work must go on—washings must be done regardless of the private sins of the laundress.

The missionary wives of the reinforcement became members of the Columbia Maternal Association, which Narcissa Whitman and Eliza Spalding had established the first year they were in the West. Each mother spent the anniversary of the birth of each child in fasting and prayer with the charge whom she felt God had personally placed in her care. The rules of the Maternal organization contained, among subjects for discussion by the women at their rare meetings together, the following: "The importance of the aid and cooperation of our husbands in training our children in the way they should go." These pioneer women had almost as difficult a time as modern ones in interesting their work-tired men in the problems of a growing family. Certainly Mary had to handle her children single-handedly. Elkanah was much away, trying to wrest a living from the wilderness, learning the Indian tongue, and teaching them the white religion and civilized habits. This necessitated going with the natives to their fishing grounds and on their hunting and root-gathering expeditions.

He must have found it difficult to understand why a woman surrounded on every side by wildlife should persist in her effort to bring it dead into her crowded house.

Though there were long days of solitude for Mary in the lonely countryside, there was, always, endless work to be done. Just to read the chores enumerated in her wilderness journal makes the back ache. Her workday averaged sixteen hours. Sixteen hours of washing, ironing, sewing, mending, painting, carpentering, baking, repairing roofs and chimneys, helping the invalid Mrs. Eells ("cleaned Mrs. E's earthen ware. Cooked for both families"), milking six cows night and morning, making soap and butter. Even making cheese was added when the ingenious Mary at last hit on the use of a deer's rennet in place of the calves' rennet that she could not get. She also made all the family's garments and their shoes: "cut out eight pairs of shoes." She salted beef, cleaned tripe, wove carpets, churned, tried tallow, dipped candles: "sat up all night...dipped twenty-four dozen"—and all this labor was accomplished without even the primitive equipment that at the time passed for conveniences among more favored American women. But somehow one cannot pity a woman who can write (after she has lived for some time with a dirt floor): "Find it pleasant to have a floor to wash again," even though she could also remark: "Sometimes I wish there was a way to live easier." Perhaps this note of discouragement crept in on one of the occasions when a newborn infant was proving "very tendful."

Mary was accustomed to sit up late, either working or reading. Her lively mind allowed her no rest. Although, in order to help her husband with his work among the Indians, she had to learn the Spokane language, she frequently chided herself for making so little progress in the translation of hymns into the Indian tongue. This was a difficult task, as the sounds the Spokanes made in speech were like nothing so much as the sounds of husking corn. Mary had to teach the Indians white ways by constant precept and example and also give them some knowledge of the world outside by direct educational means; thus she set out to teach them geography with the aid of eggshells painted to represent the globe. She kept up a correspondence, as a part of her obligation to the Columbia Maternal Association, with a Maternal Association in Capo Palmas, Africa. (The other missionary wives also reached out from their wilderness hideaways to remote parts of the world: Mrs. Smith wrote to Constantinople, Mrs. Gray to "Singapoor," Mrs. Eells to Holden, Massachusetts, and Mrs. Spalding to Prattsburg.)

In Cincinnati, on their way west, when they were buying necessities for their wilderness life, Mary's journal had noted: "Think I shall prevail at last in having a botany, geology and mineralogy." She made good use of this limited library. When, as a joyful interruption to her months of solitude, men of learning came to the little hidden valley of Tshimakain she had something to share with them besides domestic chitchat. Indeed, she was so impatient with wasting time when there were fresh minds to tap that she commented tartly on Mr. Eells's monopoly of the conversation during the visit of the great western explorer Peter Skene Ogden: "We had a very pleasant visit, except there was too much trifling conversation and Bro. E.'s ego was quite prominent. When a man of such extensive information is present I regret to have the time occupied with trifles." Probably Mary was not at all sorry that both husbands were away when members of the Wilkes Expedition, surveying the still unclaimed West for a rather indifferent United States government, came to spend the night. She sat up after midnight talking and has left a picture of herself offering a "stirrup cup" of milk on their departure. These were the men for whom she bargained with the old Indian chief, winning his praise for her handling of the situation. She reported also that one of the men "took a specimen of the soda and several minerals that I happened to have."

A wandering botanist came through and we find Mary writing: "Spent most of the day arranging dried plants. Find my collection is becoming large." An artist named Paul Kane also came along, and although she called him "an ungodly man of not much learning," she noted that "he gave me considerable information about birds." He also made the only genuine portraits of the Whitmans. Another artist visited also, John Mix Stanley, who painted Elkanah and little Abigail—portraits still in existence. All in all, it is surprising how many signatures Mary collected for the combination autograph and guest book that she kept in her lonely log house.

But surely the most touching section in Mary's diary is her account of experiences in taxidermy, an occupation that fills a number of entries in the year 1847:

August 1847 Tues. Purchased a bow and a trout and salmon skin and spent half the afternoon stuffing and fixing them.

Wed 4. Bought a mocking bird.

Thurs 5. Stuffed a sparrow skin and bought a rattlesnake skin ready stuffed, except that it wanted fixing a little nicer.

Fri 6. Purchased a duck skin and stuffed it, also a cross bill. Mr. W. gets out of sorts not liking my new trade of stuffing birds, etc.

Tues. 10. Purchased a few stuffed skins but think I will wait until I can procure arsenic before I collect more.

Wed 18. Bought four partridges.

Sat 21. In the afternoon skinned and stuffed a small bird.

Wed 25. Spent the afternoon in skinning a crane; think I will not undertake another crane soon.

Although entries indicate that Elkanah did not share Mary's enthusiasm, he did at least allow her to proceed. "Got permission to continue collecting objects in natural history." For once we feel that Elkanah may have been at times a sorely tried man. He must have found it difficult to understand why a woman surrounded on every side by wildlife should persist in her effort to bring it dead into her crowded house. Perhaps, however, this was one way of establishing a subtle dominance over the all-powerful world of nature on which man here had made so little impression.

It was John Mix Stanley, the painter whose visit Mary had so greatly enjoyed, who sent the letter that was to alter the course of the Walkers' lives. He dispatched his Indian guide, Solomon, to report the terrible massacre of the missionaries at the Whitman mission on November 29, 1847. This meant that the Walkers and the Eells and their children would have to leave the gentle green valley that had been their home and go to some place where there would be protection from hostile Indians. Though their own Indians were friendly and grieved to have them leave—feeling that by this act on the part of the missionaries they, the Spokanes, lost face as protectors—there was nothing to do but follow the advice of the military men.

Mary wrote a poem for her children to keep as a remembrance of their birthplace. It reads the way an old sampler looks:

Tshimakain! Oh, how fine, fruits and flowers abounding,
And the breeze, through the trees, life and health conferring.
And the rill, near the hill, with its sparkling water
Lowing herds and prancing steed round it used to gather.

And the Sabbath was so quiet and the log house chapel
Where the Indians used to gather in their robes and blankets.
Now it stands, alas! forsaken: no one with the Bible
Comes to teach the tawny *skailu* [people] of *Kai-kó-len-só-tin* [God].
Other spots on earth may be to other hearts as dear;
But not to me; the reason why, it was the place that bore me.

Even in the dark days that followed their departure from the home in the valley she had learned to love, Mary was true to character. In walking around Fort Colville, where they had gone to await further orders from the army or the mission board, Mary regarded the scene with her usual observant and analytical eyes: "Took a long walk by the river. The stone stratified. I should think felsparic rock. Very nice for building, very brittle."

They could not go back to Tshimakain. The future was shapeless and uncertain. All the whites were under a fresh burden of fear, not knowing what the Indians were plotting. Yet, wrote Mary, in a phrase of simple strength: "I am afraid to fear."

When finally they left for the valley of the Willamette with a "rescue party," she made the most of this new trip. One of the guides, writing an account of the journey for the *Oregon Spectator,* particularly mentioned Mary:

> Passed the day quite agreeably in the company of Madam Walker, conversing on the natural history of the region, character of the natives, their manners and customs, volcanic eruptions, tertiary or igneous or aqueous geological formations. An intelligent and virtuous woman, her price is above rubies.

Not long after leaving Tshimakain, Mary and Elkanah took up their residence in a typical Willamette Valley community, Forest Grove. Mary's journal has less to record from this time on, and there are also fewer letters. She took her place in the more prosaic existence of a western village as her children grew up and went out into the world.

The slow tempo of her life was quickened once by a trip to Maine on the early railroad. Here she was pointed out as a curiosity, the first local woman to ride across the plains. (In all probability the buffalo myth had gathered the weight with the passing of the years.) Mary enjoyed herself enormously on this journey and exhibited her usual independence of spirit by junketing off alone, without Elkanah, to visit relatives. This upset and exasperated him and finally brought him to her.

Mary is said, by a descendant, to have once signed a letter: "Your loving but not always obedient wife." When in 1877 Elkanah, on his deathbed at the age of seventy-two, tried to extract from her a promise never to remarry, she refused on principle, although she certainly had no intention of marrying again. She did, indeed, mourn her husband deeply and confided to her journal with characteristic simple expressiveness: "I feel so lonely.

Think of so many things I want to tell Mr. Walker. I realize more and more how much more I loved him than anyone else."

Mary lived on for twenty years, dying in 1897 at the age of eighty-five. In her latter years her mind failed. From this period comes the story of the hours she would spend in the old sidesaddle, placed on a chair, rocking, with her traveling cape about her, dreaming perhaps of the young bride who was one of the first to see, in all their untouched freshness and beauty the green valleys, the far-stretching plains, the varied streams, and unscaled snowcaps of the American continent.

Why the strong mind of so remarkable a woman should abruptly fade in its force and clarity is an interesting speculation. Perhaps it is not too fanciful to find the answer in the pages of Mary's diary. Here was a woman of the liveliest intelligence: a human creature so interested in the world around her that she could not find time enough in a sixteen-hour waking day to satisfy her curiosity about rocks, birds, flowers, trees, animals, vegetables, minerals, fish, Indians, human beings, God, the Bible, her children. There were not many minds comparable to her own in a pioneer society—or, for that matter, in any society. What happens when you cannot find other minds with which to share your questions and your findings? Must not the overardent seeker in time turn in loneliness and feed upon himself, finding elsewhere neither stimulus nor response equal to his own?

If Narcissa Whitman's sacrifice in going to the Indians was that of the body—a blood sacrifice—Mary Walker's sacrifice was surely that of the mind. Her appetite for knowledge and for the tools of knowledge—books, scientific instruments, exchange of thought—was forever unappeased. Narcissa gave her life, Mary gave her mind, to the great experiment that made it possible for white women by the thousands to follow after them, daring the solitude and the deprivations of pioneer life. ◼

BIG LITTLE MAN

ISAAC STEVENS (1818–1861)

DAVID M. BUERGE

All day the party had ascended the mountain valley. They followed a stream that spilled over innumerable beaver dams. The sky darkened with an approaching storm, and by midafternoon the wind had risen to a gale, pelting the horsemen with hail and rain. The rush of air was accompanied by flashes of lightning and blasts of thunder echoing from summit to summit. By 4 p.m. they had reached the divide. The stream, now reduced to rivulets fed by the rain itself, flowed eastward into the rivers they had ascended; in half a month the product of the storm would enter the Gulf of Mexico, commingled with the waters of half a continent. Westward it flowed toward a different ocean.

Just beyond the crest of the divide, the wind died into the mists. Rising to the historic occasion, the small horseman in the van reined his mount to one side, pulled a paper from beneath his cape, and addressed the group. He proclaimed a civil territorial government extended and inaugurated over the new Territory of Washington as created by the Congress of the United States and signed into being by President Millard Fillmore on March 2, 1853. That done, he welcomed the members of the exploring party "very cordially and heartily" to the Territory now under his administration.

The scene was Cadotte's Pass, at the Continental Divide, on September 24, 1853, in what is now Montana. Isaac Ingalls Stevens had brought the mandate of federal authority into the far northwestern corner of the Union. Fewer than 50 years had passed since Lewis and Clark had extended the young nation's reach into this region, then so remote and unknown that Thomas Jefferson thought it might still be home to prehistoric mastodons.

In the history of the American West, individuals often played a more decisive role than usual in shaping events. In 1843, the adult white males in the Willamette Valley did not number more than four hundred. In all of Oregon, then described as the land reaching from Spanish California to Russian Alaska and from the Pacific Ocean to the Continental Divide—almost four hundred thousand square miles—there were fewer than one thousand whites. But in that same year the Willamette Valley pioneers set up a provisional government for the entire region. Of those pioneers who gathered on the oak-studded Champoeg Prairie on that bright spring morning in 1843, fifty-two voted for provisional government,

On the stage of history Stevens sought to be a hero, but his life ultimately had a pathetic end.

two votes more than the opposition. Those fifty-two, mostly American settlers and some French Canadians, had a profound impact on the subsequent history of the region, for they succeeded in creating a rival government to that maintained by the venerable British Hudson's Bay Company and thereby helped lay American claim to the region. In that same region there were perhaps as many as one hundred thousand native inhabitants, but at the time they were politically inert and had much less to say about events than the impatient fifty-two.

Nine years later, when a group of settlers met in 1852 in the little clearing called Monticello at the mouth of the Cowlitz River to draft a petition asking Congress to create a new territory north of the Columbia, the entire white population in what was to be Washington Territory did not exceed seventeen hundred. The native population in that region exceeded twenty thousand, but, for all practical purposes, they were politically insignificant. At Monticello, forty-four men convened and debated and prepared a memorial that would powerfully affect the lives of all, native and white, who inhabited the territory-to-be.

Things were happening quickly in the Northwest in those years. When the settlers met at Monticello, the American population south of the Columbia had grown to thirteen thousand; eight years later, the white population of Oregon and Washington Territory approached sixty-five thousand. Clearly, a momentous migration was taking place. These small clusters of individuals were on the cutting edge of history, and the arm that drove them through time and space was long and powerful.

The Northwest was the focus of national rivalries over that part of the continent called Oregon, a realm no less fabled than Cibola or El Dorado. Five nations—Spain, Russia, France, Great Britain, and the United States—claimed parts of it at one time or another, and the definition or annulment of these claims produced several international crises. From the sixteenth century to the nineteenth, the claims and counterclaims could be depicted in broad strokes. By 1840, however, there were many actors in the drama and motivations had become increasingly complex.

For fifty years, Americans had been drifting in and out of the region, but none became permanent residents until 1840. John Kendrick and Robert Gray, Yankee traders seeking riches in trade with the Orient, were the first ripples from the revolutionary fountainhead welling up along the Atlantic Coast. Lewis and Clark represented another pulse that flowed and ebbed across the continent; the Astor Party came after them and the mountain men after them. By 1840 the waves were coming in rapid progression and pooling in Oregon. In 1842 more than 100 people came in the first wagon train over the newly reconnoitered Oregon Trail; in 1843, 875 came on the "Great Migration"; in 1844, 1,400 came; in 1845, 3,000. Great Britain recognized the dimension of the tide and withdrew its claims to a more reasonable boundary at the 49th parallel. Mexico watched its northern provinces swept away in the flood. The native inhabitants, too, were overwhelmed.

Isaac Stevens recognized the power of this historic tide, and as the first governor of the Territory of Washington he sought to take advantage of it, to use it as an engine to animate his career and his vaulting ambitions. He came at the critical time when the pressures produced by the first great influx of settlers into the region were ready to erupt into violence. Ironically, Stevens's attempts to manage and exploit these pressures produced their eruption. On the stage of history Stevens sought to be a hero, but his life ultimately had a pathetic end. He was an enthusiastic exponent of westward expansion, a willing instrument of those forces that empowered it; but finally he was their victim.

That Isaac Stevens made his way westward, like so many of his contemporaries, is not surprising, but that he chose to go so far west was a measure of his abilities and his ambition. Like most of those who came to the Northwest, he was born neither to wealth nor in poverty. The Stevens family had been yeoman farmers in England until John Stevens left Oxfordshire in 1638 with his wife and members of her family to take up land in the Massachusetts Bay Colony. Chafing under the restrictions there, he and others moved north and founded the town of Andover in 1642. For two hundred years they remained there—farming, taking part in local government, ministering in its church, fighting its wars and its revolution. When Isaac Ingalls Stevens was born in 1818, the first son of Isaac and Hannah Stevens, the family, if they were not rich, were at least comfortable.

Isaac did not walk until he was three, and at maturity his diminutive stature, large head, and stumpy legs suggest he suffered a mild form of dwarfism. He was commonly fatigued and at twelve he ruptured himself severely while pitching hay. Isaac senior was a stern, abstemious, and strict father who believed children had to be hardened for life. As a child, young Isaac was pulled from his warm bed every morning and plunged into a hogshead of cold water.

When he was seven, Isaac's mother was thrown from a carriage, which his father always drove at a furious rate, and injured seriously. A few months later she gave premature birth to a stillborn infant and fell into a profound depression. She attempted to throw herself from the second-story window of their home and was kept from doing so only by terrified young Isaac. Soon thereafter, Hannah Stevens died. The event wreaked havoc on the family. The elder Stevens became moody and harsh to his son, who must have blamed his father for the accident. Later, Isaac senior married a woman the son came to dislike.

One of Isaac's few avenues of escape was in study, particularly mathematics, in which he appears to have been an actual prodigy, mastering all the problems presented to him by his astonished teachers. He attended public school until he was ten, and then went to the Franklin Academy, a private school that had been founded by his grandfather. When he was fourteen he shifted to Phillips Academy, where he excelled in mathematics, engineering, and surveying. The success Stevens enjoyed in the world of the abstract led him to apply these skills to the solution of more complex and vexing human problems. He had, for example, suffered from extreme bashfulness throughout his boyhood. He identified its cause as the feeling of discomfort he experienced in the presence of certain people and solved it for himself by initiating conversation with those who made him feel this way.

His sense of being able to dominate problems by creating solutions, combined with the inflexible determination he learned from his father, produced in Stevens a formidable will. His ability to break problems down into their parts and organize their solutions was to serve him well as governor and planner. But they were to cause him grief in less tractable human situations where resolute determination had the effect of stubborn intransigence.

Stevens grew up in a world that did not extend more than ten miles from his home. The rolling, elm-studded farmland of western Essex County had long been domesticated. The hills were low, the hollows shallow; the soil had been tended for centuries, and the forests were set discretely behind fences. Each vale had its elongated village punctuated with the narrow steeple of a simple church. It was a landscape that inspired tranquility rather than romance and one from which the last vestige of mystery had been assiduously harrowed out. In his first seventeen years the longest trip Stevens made from this circumscribed world was to Boston, forty miles down the road, where he had gone at age twelve, alone, to seek medical help for his rupture.

For a young man increasingly aware of his determined character and considerable gifts, such a world became a place of confinement. His family took pride in his educational accomplishments and nurtured in him the faith of firstborn sons, that some mighty destiny awaited. Farming was out of the question; the ministry and business had little appeal, and he was counseled against taking up the law because of his introverted character—and, possibly, his unprepossessing physique. In 1835, upon the advice that his abilities might best be developed at the military academy at West Point, Stevens received an appointment as a cadet.

In the well-regulated world of West Point, Stevens flourished and in 1839 graduated first in his class. The academy brought him into contact with a larger world and with people from other sections of the country. A lifelong Democrat who nevertheless supported the abolition of slavery, Stevens met many who did not share the ideas the young New Englander assumed were universal. Characteristically, to cure his habit of speaking too rapidly, he joined a debating society.

Stevens gleefully participated in the fights, carousing, and petty theft that enlivened the cadets' otherwise Spartan existence. He took pride in wearing the large shako scorned by the other cadets because it added several inches to his diminutive frame. He endured dance lessons in a not-too-successful attempt to overcome the acute embarrassment he felt at social functions. His earlier education made him chafe at the absence of liberal arts, so he sought to add texts to the library and he determinedly spent his free time reading in

Governor Stevens: a visionary for
the northern route to Asia

77

history and literature. He started an underground literary magazine in order to improve his writing style.

Stevens left West Point supremely confident in his abilities. He mentioned to a fellow classmate that he believed men like Milton and Napoleon had achieved their greatness through hard work and study rather than inherited genius. But he also left with no illusions about a military career. The United States in the early 1840s was a decidedly unmilitary nation. Stevens had entered the academy for its education, not from any love of the military life. It was a place where one could make a good beginning, especially as an engineer.

Upon leaving West Point, Stevens moved speedily into a responsible position in the Corps of Engineers. He overhauled the antiquated coastal defense network in the New England and mid-Atlantic states, displaying a reputation for competence and an ability to carry out several tasks at once. Three years later he married Margaret Hazard of Newport, the daughter of Benjamin Hazard, a prominent Rhode Island lawyer. The restless Stevens now decided to leave the military and take up the practice of law; with the help of his prospective father-in-law he had been about to enter into a prestigious law firm, but the untimely death of Hazard prevented Stevens from resigning his commission.

At once, Stevens became intoxicated with the militant nationalism of the time.

Stevens's marriage to Margaret Hazard was a happy one. This sensitive, loving woman provided him with the emotional warmth and stability he had long desired. As they made their home in various New England towns and began having children, he imagined himself settling down in his career and sinking roots into the old, familiar community. But his ambition would reassert itself, and he would eagerly assume new responsibilities.

On April 25, 1846, an American force encamped provocatively on the Rio Grande was attacked by a detachment of the Mexican army, and the event provided President James Polk with a handy pretext for declaring war on the unstable Mexican Republic. Stevens was anxious to participate in the conflict for patriotic and professional reasons. He accompanied Winfield Scott's force on their march from Vera Cruz to Mexico City where, in the battle of Chapultepec, he was wounded in the foot. Stevens did well by the war: once again he demonstrated great competence and his courage won him praise and appointment to brevet major. More importantly, he had had an adventure. He had walked through the shattered and deserted streets of Vera Cruz on moonlit nights entranced by the Oriental beauty of its Moorish architecture. He had marveled at the exotic flowers of Jalapa and the immense, snowcapped volcanoes of the cordillera. He had witnessed the thrilling spectacle of troops charging up the hill at Cerro Gordo in the face of withering fire—the American flag carried in the van to be raised triumphantly at the summit. He had seen the bloated corpses of the enemy dead, the straggling bands of defeated soldiery tended by their women. He had shed his own blood.

At once, Stevens became intoxicated with the militant nationalism of the time. The idea that the nation had a manifest destiny to dominate the continent seemed only logical.

Stevens voiced no qualms about fighting in the most imperial of America's wars, even though many New Englanders were opposed. But there were few critics after the victorious army returned, and certainly none among the Americans who were poised to pour into the western interior of the continent. Nine months before Stevens landed with Scott's forces at Vera Cruz, American settlers in the province of California had declared it a Republic, and before Mexico City fell, the first Mormons had entered the valley of the Great Salt Lake to prepare for the foundation of Zion, an American theocracy in what was then the province of Nuevo Mexico. Americans were taking northern Mexico apart piece by piece, not as agents of the federal government but as representatives of a cultural and demographic phenomenon.

Stevens's exuberant nationalism sprang from his logical mind. America had the benefit of a superior army, a superior economy, and a superior governing system. All this bred a corresponding religion of self-confidence and zeal. But underlying the arrogance was as much fear as a sense of mission. In the 1840s America had three great fears—two from without and another, the greatest, from within.

The greater external fear was British power. Stevens's improvement of coastal defenses was done with Great Britain in mind, for by 1840 only twenty-six years had passed since British troops had burned the capital. Intense anglophobia arose from the fact that Great Britain was still a threat in Stevens's day; and if it was doubtful that British troops would ever again march against America's eastern cities, she certainly had the power to land on the Pacific coast and deny huge sections of the continent to the grasp of national ambition. That fear inspired the Willamette Valley pioneers to organize their provisional government in 1843. If the United States would not or could not accept them, then they would, like Texas, declare their realm independent. Much the same fear would inspire the California settlers to set up their Bear Flag Republic.

The second external fear was Catholic Spain, or more generally, Catholic power. Spain had been expelled from the North American mainland in 1821, but the Spanish heritage lived on in the Mexican Republic where Catholicism had been retained as the national church. As the nation subsumed northern Mexico and its Catholic population into its imperium, and as Catholic immigrants began to pour into the country, many came to fear for the purity of the national soul and joined nativist movements like the Know-Nothings. Stevens himself was not a bigot, but as governor he was willing to manipulate bigotry to his advantage.

But the greatest fear was engendered from within the national community by its "peculiar institution": slavery. The architects of the expanding union had sought to control the growing animosity by ensuring that the Congress would contain an equal number of slave and free states. The drive to acquire Oregon and the northern Mexican provinces had been inspired partly to provide slave and free sections room to expand laterally across

Ezra Meeker

Medicine Creek Council of 1854, the first Indian treaty that Governor Isaac Stevens hastily engineered, produced many misunderstandings and ultimately proved to be one of the causes of the Yakima and Puget Sound wars of 1855-56. Ezra Meeker of Puyallup wrote a history of the Indian War in which he took Stevens's leadership to task.

From Pioneer Reminiscences of Puget Sound, *by Ezra Meeker, Lowman & Hanford, 1905.*

The ground selected for holding the council is a small wooded knoll on the right bank of the She-nah-nam Creek (known locally as the McAllister Creek), about one mile above the mouth, where the waters of the creek fall into and mingle with the tides of Puget Sound.

The Squa-quid (Medicine Creek), falls into the She-nah-nam nearly a mile above the treaty grounds, and is lost in the former, which is very much the larger. Hereafter these creeks will be referred to as the McAllister and Medicine Creeks respectively, for convenience, and their Indian names dropped, as has been done locally by the settlers. . . .

Into these creeks the happy Indians in times gone by used to float their canoes in countless number, laden with the shell fish and other products of the salt inland Sound. As I recently drove down the right bank of the McAllister Creek to the treaty ground not an Indian was to be seen, not a canoe; but the grinding wheels of our wagon uncovered great beds of shells, the remains of the feasts of the primitive race in by-gone days.

When the treaty making party started from Olympia bringing presents and food for the Indians and with a small army of attaches of near twenty persons, it was expected an easy victory would be gained, as the Governor had been told, as before mentioned, the Indians would sign anything presented to them. The party, however, were doomed to meet with disappointment. The first day was passed in anxious solicitude as to what the morrow would bring forth. From Indian testimony we know that the Governor was nervous and uneasy all day, walking back and forth with his head down and hands behind his back, as the fact dawned upon him that he could not have everything his own way without a struggle. All of the Indians had not arrived, although it is recorded over six hundred were present, men, women and children, though we have no certain intelligence that any material accessions to their number were made during the continuance of the council. The Indians from the up-river districts came with their horses as usual, and in considerable force. That class of the tribe, or so called nine tribes, though not numerous, were on the alert to know what was going to happen. They had heard all sorts of rumors, even that the Government contemplated shipping all the Indians out of the country to the land of perpetual darkness (Alaska). This idea became real when it was discovered the intention was to huddle the whole tribe on a small tract of land convenient to salt water, where they could not possibly live or keep their horses or even have a potato patch, or so much as a place to be out of reach of the forest and tides. Plausibility of this story became fixed in the Indian mind when an attempt was made to explain in jargon, the right was reserved to remove the Indians at the will of the Government to some unknown point.

In a recent interview Colonel B.F. Shaw (who was at the time a young man and acted as interpreter on this occasion, and who, I may say, is yet of vigorous mind), said, the intention, as he understood it, was to make the reservation allotted temporary, and remove all the Indians in the whole Sound country to one large reservation further north. Be that as it may, it is certain no progress could be made with the Indians the first day of the council.

Every effort was made by the assembled attaches to create diversion from the serious work in hand during the evening of the first day by story telling and other means to create good humor in the minds of the Indians, but with slight success. The second day developed a very

Ezra Meeker

stubborn opposition, and resulted in the spectacular action of Leschi . . . when he tore up his commission as sub-chief before the Governor's eyes, and left the council grounds.

With Leschi out of the way, and with the accession of the Olympia Indians headed by John Hiton . . . and with the assent of the Squoxons, upon whose land one of the reservations was to be located, together with the urgent solicitation of at least a part of the Governor's suit, some progress was made on the second day to induce the reluctant Indians to subscribe, but only such, as has been said, that would sign anything presented to them, gave their assent. On the third day the presents were distributed, but these did not, as expected, create a favorable impression and in fact, the opposite, when it became known how small the value allotted to each person, two yards of calico here, a yard or two of ribbon there, and of like value all around.

And so ended the first treaty council held by the new Superintendent in the new Territory, that wrought ruin not only to the Indians, yet likewise to many of the pioneers and to Governor Stevens himself, for in its injustice inflicted upon the natives came the war that followed within a year, and the season of so many years of strife among the citizens long after the Indians had been pacified by the tardy justice of larger and suitable reservations. . . .

In my recent visit to the Medicine Creek Treaty ground, an old time acquaintance and friend, the sub-Chief Steilacoom, accompanied the party and showed us the exact spot where Leschi stood, and where the Governor stood and walked to and fro, and told the words and acted the part of each with vivid reality.

I first met Steilacoom in the summer of 1853, at the then most important town of all on Puget Sound, that bore and still bears his name. He was then in the prime of life and was considered an important personage of the community in which he lived. In our last meeting referred to, I questioned Steilacoom closely, and found that he was a married man when the Hudson Bay people first landed at Nisqually in 1830, and conclude he is certainly at this time (Jan. 1905), over ninety years old. Upon this occasion the hospitable Mrs. Hartman placed a feast before the antiquated Chief and myself which she joined, where, over the cups (of tea), we three lived our old time lives over again. It was indeed pathetic to see the old Chief shed tears of anger at the thought of his fallen condition, which he contributed solely to the treaty.

the continent, but these efforts only heightened the conflict by forcing the question whether the new territories ought to be slave or free. The underlying problem of slavery could not be solved by national aggrandizement, so after a short euphoria from the Mexican War, it resumed its dominance in American politics.

Stevens quickly realized that the road to power and influence lay in politics rather than the military. After coming home to a hero's welcome in 1848, he resumed his duties administering improvements on the coastal forts, but he found opportunities for advancement limited in an army now surfeited with officers. He was rescued by an invitation to help administer the US Coast and Geodetic Survey in Washington DC, a remarkable institution whose work included the mapping of shores and navigable rivers, the siting of lighthouses, and conducting scientific research on problems related to navigation. With the acquisition of so much new territory, the Survey's work increased dramatically. Stevens's administrative genius and his ability to organize solutions to problems soon brought the survey to high levels of productivity. The work also brought him into professional contact with a great number of gifted scientists and engineers as well as the most prominent politicians of the day. Lobbying for appropriations for the Survey gave him an understanding of how the machinery of government worked.

In the election of 1852, the lifelong Democrat Stevens actively campaigned for the Democratic candidate, Franklin Pierce, against the Whig candidate, Stevens's old commander, Winfield Scott. Stevens's role in defending Pierce's record as a commander during the Mexican War was crucial, so when Pierce won, Stevens was due a political reward. He was eager for a change. His participation in a victorious episode of westward expansion and his contact with western issues in the survey gave him a feeling for the possibilities that lay in the trans-Mississippi West. There, a small number of actors could play significant, almost Napoleonic, roles on an immense stage.

The gold rush in California had been under way for two years, and already there was talk of surveying a route for a transcontinental railroad. Things moved fast in the West. A man with ambition could gain for himself in a year what it might take decades or a lifetime to accomplish in the East. Stevens had no doubts about his ambitions, but he had been struggling to find a field of action broad enough to realize them. In 1849 he had written to his brother, Oliver: "You and I both do best by taking bold, self-relying courses. I never once failed in my life from the boldness of my course."

He studied the problem and organized its solution. He applied for the governorship of the newly organized Washington Territory. This should pose no problem: at the Survey he had administered more people than there were settlers in the Territory. The governorship carried with it the Superintendency of Indian Affairs. The Indians, too, should pose no problem: like the Mexicans, they could only benefit from the American presence, and if they threatened trouble surely a few American soldiers could scatter them. Governorships,

This most remote of continental frontiers attracted individuals of Renaissance interests and dash.

83

especially those in remote territories, were not popularly perceived as roads to advancement: Abraham Lincoln had turned down the governorship of Oregon Territory when he was still an Illinois lawyer, judging it to have little benefit for his future. So it was not surprising after Stevens garnered testimonials from several of his influential and somewhat mystified friends that on March 17, 1853, President Pierce appointed him governor. It was a fateful decision for the history of the Northwest.

The real plum Stevens hoped to get was command of the northern transcontinental railroad survey. Four surveys were planned, and with the eye of a trained geographer Stevens noted that of all the roadsteads in American possession on the Pacific coast, Puget Sound was the one closest to the ports of Asia so the northern route looked to be the most promising. The more exhaustive the survey, the more likely it was to be selected for the railroad; and no one was more confident of his abilities to survey and engineer a route than Stevens. As surveyor of the route and governor of the territory in which it was to have its terminus, Stevens would stand to exercise enormous influence over the development of the Northwest and the great American trading hub of the Pacific. As master of that equation, the dimensions of his political future would be enormous. With the sectional controversy heating up, Stevens's dominance in a swing region of great economic potential would be a steppingstone to national prominence. It was a continental ambition worthy of Napoleon.

Stevens organized his drive to capture the Northern Survey with the thoroughness of a military campaign. Friends were enlisted to provide support; masterful proposals were engineered, all potential obstacles were outmaneuvered, political strings were pulled with finesse. On March 25, the Secretary of War, Jefferson Davis, awarded Stevens command of the Northern Survey. It was one day after Stevens's thirty-fifth birthday.

He plunged ahead with preparations for the survey, which he had promised Davis would be completed by the end of 1853. He read virtually everything that had been written on the Northwest, requisitioned supplies, obtained all the scientific and engineering personnel available, and analyzed almost every detail of the expedition. On June 7, after having said yet another goodbye to his family, he readied his party at the staging camp in Minnesota. With supplies packed and raw recruits and mules broken into service, Stevens, dressed as a frontiersman with a slouch hat and red flannel shirt, led his expedition westward out of their encampment as the sun tilted past the meridian.

While Isaac Stevens was certainly one of the more notable immigrants to the Northwest, he shared a number of characteristics with many others who entered the region. Contrary to the region's mythmakers, this type was not a lawless renegade or misfit. The image of the Northwest pioneer dressed in homespun is also false. This most remote of continental frontiers attracted individuals of Renaissance interests and dash.

Like most, Stevens had been born into a Northern farming family of moderate means. He was well educated and had a profession. He was still young, fairly healthy, and though

Gustavus Sohon's sketch of the Flathead Treaty Council, July 1855 near Missoula, where Governor Stevens negotiated cession of twenty-three thousand square miles of Indian land

he was married, he had left his wife and family behind. He was, for the most part, a self-made man who relied more on his own abilities to further his career than he did help from his friends or his station. He went west to seek the opportunities he believed the East could not offer.

Three years earlier another New Englander, David S. Maynard, had traveled west to seek his fortune and relief from debt. He too was well educated, a doctor. He had run a medical school until he went broke, and like Stevens he left his wife behind (though under less amicable circumstances). He was to gain fame as one of the founders of Seattle, and for a time he served Stevens as Indian subagent for King County.

Another large group of pioneers came from the Midwest, which was in many ways still a frontier march. One of the earliest settlers on Puget Sound, Isaac Ebey, was a lawyer. He was one of the leading citizens in the frontier community and was one of a group who advised Stevens when he first arrived at the Territorial capital. Because they were after the land, many brought their families with them. Arthur Denny, who led his family and Carson Boren's out of Illinois in 1851, was a rural farmer and a surveyor. Although he and his family had little formal education, they entertained themselves on the prairie by reading aloud from a translation of Horace. Ezra Meeker was another midwesterner who came out with his family in 1852. He had little formal schooling, but was one of the brightest minds in the frontier community and one of its most prolific writers. His lucid accounts of the territorial period were sharply critical of Stevens's tenure as governor.

The poor did not go west; they could not afford to. Of the two routes one could take, the overland one required the purchase of a wagon, an ox team, and supplies; by sea around the Horn and up the Pacific Coast cost several hundred dollars. Some, like Michael Simmons, a Kentuckian and the first permanent American settler on Puget Sound, were illiterate. But Simmons was also intelligent and worldly from a life of experiences on the frontier. The people who came to Oregon were also sober-minded individuals for whom the wild, get-rich-quick mania of the California gold fields held little allure. Settlers in Oregon and Washington were made up of people who were tough, resilient, knowledgeable, and independent. They had come west for its opportunities, not to work under someone's thumb. They represented a society very different from that found in the East—more egalitarian, less impressed by background, more democratic, and inclined to obey authority by choice, not custom.

Stevens may have been typical, but this was not a society he was suited to lead. At home, at school, at West Point, in Mexico, and at work for the government, he had obeyed, and as he advanced in rank and position, people obeyed him. He thrived in a military environment where relationships were governed by a rigid etiquette. The insecure Stevens responded to independent minds or differing opinions with impatience or intransigence. Not surprisingly, difficulties in dealing with such people first manifested themselves during the Northern Survey. This was essentially a civilian operation drawing personnel from many government departments as well as the private sector.

The survey was divided into several groups, each with its own itinerary. Preparing the way for the main party led by Stevens was an advance party, sent west from St. Paul to Fort Union on the upper Missouri. A western party, led by Captain George McClellan, was to explore the passes of the Cascade Mountains and to meet the main party at Fort Colville on the middle Columbia. Stevens sent a fourth group off from Fort Vancouver to set up a supply depot at the Flathead mission of Saint Mary's in the Bitterroot Valley west of the Continental Divide. Stevens's party made good progress, arriving at Fort Union on August 1 and crossing the Continental Divide on September 24. The adventure of following in the footsteps of Lewis and Clark and of passing through immense herds of buffalo and exotic native encampments was marred for Stevens by the painful reappearance of his old rupture.

Soon there were other problems. Several of the military members of the survey took umbrage over the fact that they had to take orders from civilians. Simple tact and compromise were required, but Stevens appreciated neither virtue. He thought it simple: he was

Simple tact and compromise were required, but Stevens appreciated neither virtue.

the commander and it was the duty of those under him to obey. Not surprisingly, his attitude generated discord.

Another problem was his inability to delegate authority: typically he gave instructions regarding minute details of an operation and disallowed the exercise of professional prerogatives. In the beginning of the adventure, Stevens's zeal for command inspired one member of the expedition to describe the governor as "a smart, active, ubiquitous little man, very come-at-able," yet by the end of it many shared the frustration of McClellan who fumed, "I will not consent to serve any longer under Governor S. unless he promises in no way to interfere—merely to give me general orders and never say one word as to the means, manner, or time of executing them."

By November 18, 1853, Stevens and the main party arrived at Fort Vancouver, and the survey was counted as complete. (The final report was not published until 1859.) Although the Northern Survey was the most thorough of all the routes surveyed, Stevens's hopes for it were never realized in his lifetime; in fact, the northern route was among the last to have tracks laid over it. The political need to tie California more firmly to the Union during the Civil War prompted construction of the Union Pacific and Central Pacific from Omaha to Sacramento in 1862, so it was not until 1883 that the tracks of the Northern Pacific were completed from the Mississippi to Puget Sound.

The Northern Survey was nevertheless a magnificent achievement. It completed the work of Lewis and Clark begun a half-century earlier and provided the most complete description of the territory possible at the time, in order to promote its orderly settlement. Stevens's wideranging interests ensured that it would be as much a scientific as a surveying expedition, and it had a full complement of naturalists and geologists. Beyond description, the survey also attempted to evaluate the utility of the phenomena it described. Plants and animals were collected, treated, and sent back to museums, and their edibility was judged, as was how they might be propagated, husbanded, and harvested. Soils were examined for their agricultural potential; the region's geology was probed for minerals. The resource inventory the survey provided served as a powerful stimulus to immigration.

Today, perhaps the most important parts of the survey are those sections that describe the native peoples of the Territory. Credit for this goes primarily to George Gibbs, one of the survey's ethnologists. The son of a prominent New York family, Gibbs came west in 1849 to take part in the gold rush, but ended up in Astoria as assistant collector of customs. He had studied law at Harvard but decided on a literary career and worked for a time as librarian of the American Ethnological Society. In Oregon, he helped draft treaties with native groups in the Willamette Valley. His interest in linguistics led him to compile invaluable dictionaries of several native tongues, and his skill at cartography enabled him to produce the first accurate map of the valley. In 1853, thirty-eight years old, he was hired by McClellan, a friend of Gibbs's family, as geologist and ethnologist for the Northern Survey.

Stevens seemed well on his way toward the creation of a North-western empire that would further his grand ambitions.

Gibbs's 1854 report to McClellan on the Indians of Washington Territory was the first comprehensive survey of the native groups of the region, and as such it provides an incomparable window on their societies before the treaty period. Stevens retained Gibbs's services to aid in the preparation of the treaties and sent him on a survey of Puget Sound to collect more information about the native groups and carry out a census. His numbers, when compared with earlier censuses carried out by the Hudson's Bay Company, show the native groups to have suffered a decline, evidence that confirmed in many minds the theory that the native peoples were a dying race.

Another fascinating part of the survey is the art included with it, in particular the landscape and group scenes. Stevens selected John Mix Stanley as the chief artist of the survey. Stanley was a thirty-nine-year-old painter, part Cherokee, who had spent several years painting western scenes and had his work displayed at the Smithsonian Institution. His tinted lithographs, while small, convey the broad sweep of the prairies and the brooding immensity of western lands. His best-known work, *The Dalles,* a romantic, moonlit scene of stark beauty, has been reproduced innumerable times.

The most gifted artist on the survey was Gustavus Sohon, a Belgian immigrant who served with the expedition as an army private for a year before his abilities as an artist and linguist caught Stevens's attention. Sohon was part of the group that journeyed overland to the Flathead mission west of the Continental Divide to establish a supply depot, and he spent the winter of 1853–54 at a meteorological station set up by Stevens in the Bitterroot Valley. While there, Sohon, who had a gift for languages, became fluent in the Flathead and Pend d'Oreille tongues and was thereby able to make friends with many native people. When he was not interviewing his native hosts, he was sketching them. Thanks to Sohon we have beautifully expressive portraits of many important native leaders of the period. Sohon also produced accurate and vivid scenes of native life and landscape sketches, which included the first panoramic view of the main chain of the Rocky Mountains in Montana and the earliest known drawing of the Great Falls of the Missouri. He also produced drawings of western settlements, scenes of western life, and panoramas of several of the treaty councils.

On November 25, Stevens arrived at Olympia in a drenching rain. An apocryphal story of his coming told how when he arrived at the Washington Hotel, a small, tired man in worn frontier clothing, he was told he would have to wait outside because the people assembled there were waiting for the governor. Stevens was not one to wait outside. He quickly organized the Territorial government with his usual energy and dispatch. At the hotel, he declared: "I have come here not as an official for mere station, but as a citizen as well as your chief magistrate to do my part toward the development of the resources of this territory." On December 19 he delivered a lecture describing the Northern Survey and his sanguine hopes for speedy construction of the railroad. "Little Rough and Ready" he was soon dubbed. He became an instant favorite with the pioneers. They could only dream of development, but the governor seemed determined—and able—to bring it about. Stevens started impressively. He set the wheels of the government in motion and strengthened his Democratic political base by transforming the only newspaper, the *Washington Pioneer*, into a Democratic mouthpiece, renamed the *Washington Pioneer and Democrat* in February 1854. He got his Democratic nominee, Columbia Lancaster, elected as the Territorial delegate to Congress by a wide margin.

During his first four months in Olympia, Stevens managed to accomplish most of his gubernatorial objectives. He brought the work of the Northern Survey to completion. He settled the issue of Hudson's Bay Company claims in the Territory by justly compensating them for their losses; despite the anglophobic protests of many settlers, this statesmanlike act retained the good will of the Company, which was to prove of great value during the Yakima War. He began work on an emigrant road from Fort Steilacoom over the Cascade Mountains to Fort Walla Walla—a route ultimately to prove impractical. He set as two of the Territory's goals the organization of a militia and the development of a broad educational system. He requested the legislature memorialize Congress for land for a university, and he spent five thousand dollars purchasing a wide range of books for the Territorial library.

More fatefully, Stevens also plunged into his responsibilities as Superintendent of Indian Affairs. Of all the issues on the settlers' minds, the most important was title to land. Congress had enabled settlers to file claims on public lands, but it had not yet succeeded in transferring the right of ownership from the native people who inhabited the land to the settlers who hungered to possess it. Moreover, the lands most desired by the settlers—rich prairie and river-bottom lands—were also those most valued by native groups. The natives who possessed such lands were often those most likely to resist encroachment by force. By the time Stevens arrived, the relations between American settlers and the native people had become tense. Several killings had taken place, and neither side trusted the intentions of the other. Stevens waded in in his logical fashion: he divided the Territory into several districts, appointed Indian Agents for each, and sent them out to select native spokesmen with whom he could treat in order to settle the issue.

Having set all these wheels in motion, Stevens left the Territory and its dazzled citizenry to return to the Capital to lobby Congress for the Northern Survey and for appropriations for roads and improvements and for the upcoming treaty negotiations. It had been an extraordinary political debut: the man seemed to thrive on furious activity, and to many—chief among them himself—there seemed little he could not accomplish. Up to this time all obstacles had been surmounted, and Stevens seemed well on his way toward the creation of a Northwestern empire that would further his grand ambitions. He was soon to find that the vast new realm that seemed to yield so agreeably to his grasp could respond with a fearful power of its own.

Stevens and his associates had created a tinderbox.

In December 1854, Stevens returned to Olympia with his wife and family. He had succeeded in getting most of what he asked from Congress. But there were signs of trouble. The trip across the isthmus of Panama had not been easy: the family contracted yellow fever which nearly killed one child. When she arrived at the rough little Territorial capital that was to be her home, Margaret Stevens burst into tears and refused to leave the house for two months, not even to attend a ball the citizens gave in honor of the governor's return.

Governor Stevens was not one to fret over his wife's despondency. A great deal of work awaited him in Olympia; in particular, preparations for the impending treaty councils. During his absence, Stevens's agents had been hastily visiting most of the native groups, selecting spokesmen from their ranks, and setting up a schedule of council gatherings. Not only was the timetable reckless; the whole enterprise was organized in profound ignorance of native society, culture, and history. The twenty-thousand-odd aboriginal inhabitants, who were assumed to be in rapid decline, were given a brutal choice: they could adapt to white society or they could disappear. It was a simple choice for presumably a simple people, a Darwinian calculus that many, including Stevens, believed realistic and even humane. Indeed, Stevens and those involved with the treaty process occupied a moderate position between the small minority who believed the native people should be accorded the same rights enjoyed by whites and the larger and more vocal groups of citizens who believed they should simply be eliminated.

Given patience and finesse, the elements for a peaceful resolution were there. Most native people accepted the fact that they would be living with increasing numbers of whites and only wished to be treated equally. Many sought to have settlers live among them to trade with, agreed to sell much of their land, and even sometimes fatalistically assumed that they were a dying race. But white and native concepts of land use were too different, and the settlers' demands for explicit title to the land too adamant for either group—so widely scattered over the Territory—to come to any acceptable agreement in the time that was made available. If the treaties themselves did not produce the violence that followed in their wake, the haste with which their terms were pressed upon the people made violence inevitable. The impatient Stevens, in many ways so invigorating to the Territory, was fatally miscast for these other roles.

Between December 25, 1854, and February 26, 1855, Stevens and his associates held four treaty councils west of the Cascades. Each lasted about four days, during which time the governor would distribute cloth, trinkets, and tools, read out the treaty terms in Chinook Jargon, allow a short period for comment, and then call the chiefs and subchiefs forward to sign the documents. Few native people were familiar enough with the ideas of land title and treaty negotiations to understand fully the irrevocable nature of their signatures, and those who had such an inkling muted their displeasure out of politeness or fear of the governor's armed escort. Stevens's brusque handling of the negotiations and complaints about interruptions did not invite discussion.

Stevens pressed on. He traveled east of the Cascades, and between May 21 and October 17 held three more treaty councils. The negotiations proved long and difficult, but the governor managed to cajole and coerce the native leaders into agreement. Even before the last council was finished, war between native and white had erupted in the Yakima country.

Stevens and his associates had created a tinderbox. Soon accidents conspired to add to the tension and neither side was able to control the events that followed. A major provision of the treaties was that land reserved for native use was to remain off limits to whites; in the Yakima Valley, several miners who trespassed on reserved lands on their way to a gold rush near Fort Colville were killed. Indian Agent Andrew Bolon, who was sent to investigate, was himself killed in late September. Ironically, the murder of Bolon appears to have had little to do with either the treaties or the miners, but was done by a young Yakima warrior who wanted to increase his prestige by killing an important white man.

The murder of the government official could not be ignored in the same way as were the miners' deaths. Brevet Major Cranville Haller led a force of 102 men into the Yakima country to apprehend those responsible. On the way they met a large Yakima force; the chiefs, embarrassed by Bolon's death, wanted to talk, but before they could, firing broke out and Haller was driven out with five dead and seventeen wounded. As reports of the disaster spread, the militia was called out and panic invaded native communities as whites clamored for the extermination of the Yakimas. West of the mountains, native fighters killed two members of a force that was attempting to link up with Haller over the mountains. On October 28, three white families living on the White River near Seattle were attacked and nine people were brutally killed.

The same day this calamity occurred, Stevens left the Blackfoot council grounds and began his return to Olympia one thousand miles distant. Dispatches about the growing conflict had been reaching the governor, who determined that the native perpetrators should be punished severely and their people chastised as an example. Unable to make contact with the regular army, Stevens organized a number of miners and settlers in the interior as his personal bodyguard and began a forced march to Olympia. It was his moment of truth.

There were enormous logistical problems in carrying out a military campaign against the tribes, but Stevens also had to deal with Brevet Major General John Wool, commander of the Department of the Pacific. The army was responsible for maintaining peace between a multitude of native groups and the growing number of white settlers. Wool and many of his officers believed that most of the hostilities in their region were the results of actions taken by white groups, particularly volunteer militias like those called out during the Cayuse War of 1847, which butchered groups of innocents when they could not find the

Isaac I. Stevens, first governor of
Washington Territory, 1853

perpetrators of the Whitman massacre. Through reports from subordinates like Major Gabriel Rains, the commander at Fort Dalles, Wool had come to expect a violent outbreak in Washington as the Governor's treaty negotiations proceeded. Haller's defeat indicated the uprising was of considerable magnitude but also one precipitated by circumstance rather than design. In November Rains led a force of regulars and volunteers into Yakima country and fought a pitched battle with a hostile force, succeeding in driving the Yakimas across the Columbia but not in defeating them. With winter coming on, General Wool, who had come up to Fort Vancouver from his California headquarters, determined that no large-scale movement against the hostiles should take place until the spring. In the interim he hoped things would settle down to the point where the chiefs east and west of the mountains would sue for peace and yield up those responsible for the murder of Bolon and others.

It was a thoughtful plan and one later events suggest was wise. It was unacceptable to Stevens. He had, after all, had his great effort to solve the native-white land issue blow up in his face. It was hardly a testimonial to his negotiating prowess, and he understood that a raging race war was not a particularly effective inducement to lure emigrants and railroad builders into the Territory. He had vastly overreached himself and he had blundered. Now his frustration was expressed as passionately as his earlier enthusiasm. The Yakimas and all other hostile groups would be crushed as an example to others of what they could expect if they thwarted him.

Deeply agitated, Stevens sent off a long letter to Wool outlining his plans for a winter campaign: "Occupy the Walla Walla Valley in January; establish a large depot camp in the Touchet; hold Fort Walla Walla; get up supplies by a line of barges on the Columbia; have an advance post on the Tucanan.... In February cross the Snake; attack the enemy on the Palouse; establish a depot camp at the first wood; occupy the forks of the Snake; establish the line of barges up the Snake to the mouth of the Palouse, and push forward a column to the Okanogan." Wool replied sardonically that "I have neither the resources of a Territory nor the treasury of the United States at my command."

Stevens was furious. He called out the volunteers for longer enlistments, ordered blockhouses built, and attempted to dissuade settlers from joining the exodus out of the Territory. But on December 4, Lieutenant Slaughter and several troops had been killed on the White River, and there were rumors that there were going to be attacks on settlements on the Sound. Stevens made a quick trip down Sound to calm frayed nerves. By now the velocity of events in the West was working against him. His statement to the worried citizens of Seattle that their town stood in less danger of attack than New York or San Francisco was made a day before the attack came. The embarrassed Stevens responded by vilifying Wool in the *Pioneer and Democrat* and bullying those who refused to carry out his grandiose plans.

Nothing worked. The volunteers made matters worse. Some preferred to shoot women and children rather than meet warriors in battle; a native spy who had given valuable information to white authorities was shot by volunteers who assumed he was just another damned Indian. When the Walla Walla chief Peupeumoxmox and a party of his followers appeared at a volunteer camp under a white flag to parley, they were taken prisoner. Shortly afterward the chief was murdered, scalped, his body mutilated and skinned, and his ears cut off and preserved in alcohol. Some of the grisly artifacts showed up later in Portland where volunteers were reported to have toasted one another's bravery with the specimen's alcohol.

Things were getting further out of control; Stevens began to grasp at straws. He convinced himself that the war was not being won quickly because the army under Wool was being uncooperative and because the hostiles were receiving aid and comfort from the mixed-blood population of the upper Sound, the employees and ex-employees of the Hudson's Bay Company. Stevens concocted the baseless charge against Wool that the military had abandoned the governor in the interior when the war began and left him to get back to Olympia on his own. He sought to undermine Wool's authority—the very thing he accused Wool of doing to him—by seeking support for military adventures from Wool's subordinates. Once more, he failed, but he did not pause to reassess his ruinous course. His failure simply added to his reservoir of bitterness.

The action stunned the legal community, as well as many of the pioneers.

Against the mixed-blood settlers of Pierce and Thurston counties, Stevens now leveled the charge of treason. Because of their kinship ties with the native people, most remained unmolested during the war. When it became obvious to the hostile forces in the spring of 1856 that their cause was hopeless, they sought to make contact with the government to obtain terms for surrender. The initial feelers were made through these settlers, but Stevens was set upon a policy of extermination and turned against the settlers the fact that many were Catholics. While Stevens did not swallow the accusation that Catholic priests had instigated the war, he did nothing to lessen the effect bigotry had in strengthening his charges against the old settlers.

That March, Stevens ordered them removed from their farms and their property confiscated, an order carried out by a squad of volunteers. When sympathetic lawyers went to Territorial Judge Edward Lander to procure a writ of habeas corpus, Stevens declared martial law in Pierce County. A month later Judge Lander prepared to open court in Steilacoom and resigned his commission in the volunteers, but Stevens refused the resignation and demanded that Lander comply with his declaration. Lander refused, and when he attempted to impanel a grand jury to determine whether the governor had honored his writ, a group of volunteers stormed the court and arrested him. The action stunned the legal community as well as many of the pioneers. Meetings were held and resolutions were dispatched to Congress and the president protesting the action. In one, George Gibbs and

Old Fort Walla Walla, as sketched by John Mix Stanley on Stevens's 1853 expedition

several of Stevens's old associates wrote: "The sole object of the Proclamation [of martial law] was to get half a dozen obscure individuals into his absolute control and to demonstrate that he, Isaac I. Stevens, could on the field offered by a small territory enact at second hand the part of a diminutive Napoleon."

On May 12, Judge Lander, who had been released from custody, opened the Second District Court at Olympia and issued another writ of habeas corpus on behalf of the accused settlers. Stevens responded by extending martial law to Thurston County as well. Lander then issued an order for Stevens to appear in court and explain his actions. The subpoena was met at the governor's office by an armed force of volunteers who prevented its being served. The server was followed back to court by the volunteers, who called upon Lander to surrender. The courtroom door was locked, but the volunteers smashed it in with rifle butts and once again hauled Judge Lander away.

After these lawless actions, the storm of protest against the governor reached such a magnitude that he was forced to rescind his order. Pressure was brought in Washington DC to remove Stevens from office; President Pierce refused but issued a stinging reprimand. Meanwhile, General Wool returned to the Territory from the capital, having been exonerated of all of Stevens's charges. The war appeared to be winding down. The army, not the governor, received—and deserved—the credit.

Stevens was not mollified. He was convinced that the native groups in the interior were still unchastened. After a Klickitat force attacked settlers along the Cascades of the Columbia, causing considerable loss of life, Stevens decided to steal a march on Wool and send a force of volunteers into Walla Walla country. There, they butchered some sixty-five members of the native encampment, most of whom were women, old men, and children. The so-called "Battle of the Grande Ronde Valley" poisoned the atmosphere of the area and was one of the prime causes of the renewal of hostilities in 1858.

To the volunteers it was a great victory, and the news convinced Stevens that the time was ripe for holding another treaty council at Walla Walla to consolidate his accomplishments. Predictably, the council held there in August and September was an utter disaster, during which the native chiefs barely restrained their rage and bitterness. As a dejected Stevens left the council grounds for the Dalles, his party was attacked by nearly 450 angry warriors. Only by running to the safety of a nearby encampment of regulars did Stevens and his volunteers manage to save themselves. After this disgraceful affair, General Wool ordered the Territory east of the mountains closed to settlement.

Stymied in the East, Stevens now vented his wrath in the West, pressing vengefully for the punishment of hostile leaders and the execution of Leschi, who was a Nisqually and the most famous and respected of the warriors. Leschi's hanging was a squalid ending to a tragic and bloody period. Stevens's most careful biographer, Kent Richards, concludes from Stevens's record as Superintendent of Indian Affairs from 1853 to 1857 that he was "the wrong man, in the wrong place, at the wrong time."

The record of Stevens's superintendency is sobering to contemplate, but the actions of many of the Territory's citizens are even worse. The history of this period is dark, but it is not without its heroes. Many volunteers were decent, honorable men. Judge Lander and others resisted despotism admirably. While the governor and many of his associates sought to suppress native discontent with a stupid use of force, there were individuals like Ezra Meeker who rose at no little risk to themselves to defend the natives.

If Stevens's Indian policy had been a disaster, in other areas he had enjoyed great success. Stevens's proven ability to press the Territory's interests and the likelihood of his being able to obtain pay for the volunteers' efforts in the war enabled him to win election handily as Territorial delegate in 1857 and 1858. In 1860, however, the influence of the Republican party in the Territory during the election of Lincoln combined with the secessionist odium attached to Democrats. Stevens was forced out of the race.

Once again, his grand ambition had been thwarted. Having lost his political base, Stevens also discovered as the Civil War approached that the enemies he had made in the military prevented his regaining his commission. But after the Union debacle at Bull Run, he was needed badly enough to win a colonelcy in the 79th New York Highlanders. He hurled himself courageously into the new challenge. His troops did well, and Stevens participated in several successful operations. In April 1861, he was promoted to the rank of brigadier general, at forty-four apparently the youngest of the North. At Chantilly, Virginia, in the Second Battle of Bull Run, Stevens took a bullet in the temple. He was leading a charge, the colors held high in his hand, when he died. ▰

The history of this period is dark, but it is not without its heroes.

The only known portrait of Chief
Seattle

96

THE MAN WE CALL SEATTLE

CHIEF SEATTLE (1786–1866)

DAVID M. BUERGE

Who was Chief Seattle, and what kind of a man was he? Seattle is the largest city in the nation named after a Native American, but few of its citizens know much about the man or his people, aside from some cultural projections.

The best biography of him, a monograph written by Clarence Bagley in 1931, is not widely known, and the author did not have access to much reliable ethnographic material. Another problem is that most of Seattle's life stands outside of history. The earliest reference to him was made in 1832 by William Fraser Tolmie, a surgeon assigned to the new Hudson Bay Company post abuilding on the Nisqually Prairie and later its factor, but by that time Seattle was already forty-six.

Nevertheless, enough material is available now for us to glimpse a complex individual living in a catastrophic age, a vigorous pragmatist who was awed but never blinded by white culture.

The man we call Seattle was born about 1786, probably in a house on Blake Island constructed by his father, a noted headman and war leader called tshwee-YEH-hub. He was born the son of a slave, a concubine called she-LAH-tsah whom his father had either purchased or taken in a raid from the winter village of choot-uh-PAHLT-hw, "Flea's House," on what is now the Green River west of Kent. So he was considered to be of low birth. In time, however, many villages would claim him as their native son.

The world into which this infant was born was in a state of shock, for in that year or the one preceding it, the people of the Puget Sound region suffered what may have been their first encounter with Western disease—smallpox. Entire communities were virtually wiped out, and the depopulation necessitated social readjustments. We do not know if this increased the level of conflict between the surviving groups, but among the men of Seattle's father's generation and his own, war leaders were the most prominent, and the people's memories of the battles they fought do not seem to have gone back very far.

The smallpox epidemics presaged a cultural revolution whose nature the people could describe only in mythic terms. At about the same time the pestilence swept the land apparitions were seen off the coasts. Some thought they were whales with trees growing on them,

The end of another world was at hand.

or great seabirds with huge white wings. The plague and the visions seemed to portend a great change of the type that had transformed the world at the end of the mythic age, when the primordial reign of titans gave way to the human era. The appearance of humanlike creatures in strange clothing—and some with hair the color of the sun—suggested that the prophesies about the return of the Changer—the demiurge—or his son had come to pass, and the end of another world was at hand.

In 1792, a few weeks after the moon of pah-DAH-ko-ku, the "time of butterclams," what we would call May, such an apparition appeared off Restoration Point on Bainbridge Island. Some thought Hat Island off the mouth of the Snohomish River had gone adrift, but others recognized Vancouver's ship, *Discovery,* as a vessel much like those seen farther north, and they came out to trade. According to folklore, the young Seattle witnessed the arrival of this ship, and if so he was probably among those at the camp on the point, drying fish and clams and harvesting the wild onion. For a child of eight, the days the British anchored offshore must have been momentous indeed, and the awe of of the West never left him.

An interesting difference among the native people appears in Captain George Vancouver's log. Those on the point, most likely members of the historic Suquamish, were described as ill-made, besmeared with oil mixed with red ochre and shining mica, and adorned with ornaments including some made of copper. Later, however, a group of nearly eighty visited the ship in several large canoes from the eastern shore of the Sound. These were described as being infinitely more cleanly and rather more bold although possessed of the same civility as those on the point. Moreover, their canoes were not the high-prowed "nootkan" craft seen on the western shore, but were flat, snubbed nose, and larger—the riverine type. The people in these canoes were probably members of the historic Renton-area Duwamish, an ethnically distinct people of considerable wealth and influence.

The respect the young Seattle and his contemporaries had for Western technology increased as they endured attacks by raiding parties from the north armed with muskets. Raiding may have been a regular part of life on the Northwest coast. After 1800, its intensity increased with the introduction of firearms and the desire of northern nobles, whose influence reflected the size of their families, to increase their depleted numbers by capturing children and women who could bear them. Raids on the Puget Sound region were also undertaken by groups like the Yakima from east of the mountains who carried off captives and sold them to the depopulated groups on the lower Columbia.

To defend themselves, the Puget Sound peoples turned to their war leaders, bellicose men who had demonstrated their bravery and skill. Seattle's father had made a reputation for himself raiding the Duwamish of the lower Green River and the Skokomish people near the head of Hood Canal, but the most prominent war leader of the central Puget Sound region in these early days was the Suquamish headman, Kitsap. In 1825 he led a combined

It was after this Green River victory that Seattle became chief of the Suquamish and the Duwamish.

force of warriors from most of the local groups in a great raid on the Cowichan peoples around Victoria Harbor on Vancouver Island. Two hundred canoes were said to have been involved, and the raiders killed many Cowichan men and took many women and children prisoner. On the way back, however, they met a Cowichan force at sea, and the Puget Sounders escaped with barely forty canoes. Nevertheless, the raid appears to have achieved its purpose by ending attacks from that quarter, and Kitsap remained influential until his death in 1845.

The native people ran down to the beach waving blankets and knives and filling the air with shouts and gunfire.

Spurred by the taint of low birth (even after his death, noble Duwamish from the Renton area still referred to him sneeringly as "Kitsap's slave"), the young Seattle excelled his brothers and companions in audacity and ingenuity. By the time of Kitsap's raid, in which he no doubt took part, he had already gained fame as a war leader. About 1806, the year Lewis and Clark sojourned at the mouth of the Columbia, Seattle succeeded in destroying a raiding party of upper Green and White river people and their Yakima kindred. At a rapids on the Green River near what is now Longacres Racetrack, he had a tree felled across the channel so that it rested but a few inches above the water. Since attacks were usually carried out in the dark hours before dawn, the raiders coming down the river were unaware of the obstruction until they ran into it, and as they struggled ashore from their upended canoes, they were dispatched by Seattle's warriors hidden on the banks.

It may have been after this triumph that he assumed the name see-YAHTLH, the name of his father's father, at a grand potlatch. The house in which this was held may have been the one whose enlarged version we have come to call "Old Man House" after the Chinook Jargon word "Oleman" meaning "large," a five-hundred-foot-long structure built on Agate Pass at the place called du-SUH-kwub, "clear salt water," from which we get the word Suquamish.

According to Samuel Coombs, an early pioneer from whose reminiscences we derive much of our knowledge of the man, it was after this Green River victory that Seattle became chief of the Suquamish and the Duwamish, ensuring his dominance over the groups on the east shore of the Sound by taking hostages from among them. Duwamish informants recalled no such hostage-taking, and Coombs may actually have been describing the process by which a wealthy young man like Seattle would have taken wives from several families in order to maintain and extend kin connections. Around 1811 his first child was born, a daughter whom the settlers knew as Princess Angeline. In all, Seattle is known to have owned eight slaves, some of whom may have been concubines.

Seattle took part in several other raids: he himself claimed that while still young he had killed a great chief and stolen a fathom of fine hiqwa—shell money—from the Clallams. In 1841, at fifty-five years of age, he led an attack upon the winter village of ee-LAHL-ko at the confluence of the upper Green and White rivers, and at some unspecified time, he is said to have helped lead an attack on a Chemakum stronghold near Port Townsend. Few headmen in the Puget Sound region are known to have participated in as many raids as Seattle, and his reputation was widely respected.

As a prominent man it was inevitable that he would gain the attention of the whites as they began to enter the region. In 1832, construction began on the new Hudson's Bay Company post on Nisqually Prairie, and the first systematic record of events in the Puget Sound region was begun, first in the diary of Dr. Tolmie and later, in the *Journal of Occurrences* at Nisqually House. Early on the Suquamish appear as one of the more vigorous trading groups, and barely two months after work on the post commenced, Seattle strides into history in an entry in Tolmie's diary that describes him as "a brawny Suquamish with a Roman countenance and black curley hair, the handsomest Indian I have ever seen."

Company supervisor Francis Herron had with Tolmie sought to provide the native people with Christian instruction, and after a conference with several notables, Herron made them promise to end the practice of revenge murder. A document was prepared with the promise and the names of the men who had agreed to it. Seattle placed his mark beside his name along with the rest, participating for the first time in that strange white custom whereby marks on a piece of paper were deemed more trustworthy than a man's word.

Maynard had the town change its name from Duwamps to Seattle in honor of his patron.

Christianity of a kind had preceded that introduced by Herron and Tolmie, largely through the activities of Catholic Iroquois employees of the Hudson's Bay Company and the old North West Company who had entered the Pacific Northwest in the late seventeen hundreds. As heralds of the new dispensation, the ideas, rituals, and chants brought by these individuals were believed by the native people to be possesssed of great power, and they learned them by rote. The seriousness that attended this labor astonished the Catholic priests when they later entered the area and found that as they intoned their hymns for what they thought was the first time, the people joined in, repeating both the melody and the words accurately.

One of the first successful missionary efforts among the native people of the Puget Sound region was carried out by Father Modeste Demers in 1841 when he traveled down Sound as far as Fort Langley on the Fraser River, making several stops during which he baptized some 765 individuals. Seattle may have been one of these, taking as his baptismal name Noah. In the practice of the time, the prominent men who were baptized were given instruction so that they could return to their villages, set up chapels, and instruct their own people. Among the Suquamish, Seattle inaugurated the practice of morning and evening prayer, and he instructed them according to the teachings he had been given.

While Seattle's conversion was no doubt sincere, it had many practical advantages. Through it he was able to cultivate relations with the whites who were the principal dispensers of metal, cloth, and guns. Many native leaders, however, were opposed to the activities of the priests and the presence of whites altogether, so Seattle's support of both was not without risk.

100

Seattle's character had changed from the bellicose war leader who was banned from Fort Nisqually for a time because of his violent outbursts to the pacific leader we are more familiar with. Some historians credit Christianity for the change. Possibly so. Seattle was always sensitive to the wishes of the British and American authorities—he freed his own slaves on the event of Lincoln's Emancipation Proclamation in 1863. But his character change may have had more to do with his gradual emergence as an elder amongst his people, a position in which tact and diplomacy were valued more than the arts of war. As Seattle advanced in age to this status a new generation of vigorous young men arose, from whose ranks war leaders like Patkanam of the Snoqualmie, Nelson of the Muckleshoot, and Leschi of the Nisqualli would acquire prominence.

By the time the white settlers landed on Elliott Bay, both Kitsap and Seattle's father were dead, and Seattle had become the most prominent of the Suquamish headmen. A census carried out by the Hudson's Bay Company in 1828–29 numbered the Suquamish at 576 individuals of which 72 were slaves—the greatest number of any Puget Sound group and one that underscored their reputation of being warlike. They also possessed 21 guns and 119 canoes.

In the summer of 1850 a party of American explorers led by Isaac Ebey and Benjamin Shaw landed at the winter village of dzee-dzuh-LAH-lich on the east shore of Elliott Bay. They met with a wild reception. The native people ran down to the beach waving blankets and knives and filling the air with shouts and gunfire. In the midst of this display, a large, middle-aged man with a wide head came out of a house, stood on a log, and made a speech in the native tongue that was translated for the benefit of the terrified whites into Chinook Jargon.

My name is Sealt, and this great swarm of people that you see here are my people; they have come down here to celebrate the coming of the first run of good salmon. As the salmon are our chief food we always rejoice to see them coming early and in abundance, for that insures us a plentiful quantity of food for the coming winter. This is the reason are hearts are glad today, and so you do not want to take this wild demonstration as warlike. It is meant in the nature of a salute in imitation of the Hudson's Bay Company's salute to their chiefs when they arrive at Victoria. I am glad to have you come to our country, for we Indians know but little and you Boston and King George men know how to do everything. We want your blankets, your guns, axes, clothing and tobacco, and all other things you make. We need all these things that you make, as we do not know how to make them, and so we welcome you to our country to make flour, sugar and other things that we can trade for. We wonder why the Boston men should wander so far away from their home and come among so many Indians. Why are you not afraid?

This speech was written down by Shaw, who was later to be Governor Stevens's interpreter during the treaty councils, and was said to have been a master of the jargon and to have been able to speak the native language as well. His is then probably the most accurate translation of Seattle's remarks in English that could be made after they had passed through the jargon. In tone it differs considerably from the more famous speech written by Dr. Henry Smith purportedly from notes taken from Seattle's address to Governor Stevens in front of Doc Maynard's store in 1854. In Shaw's translation Seattle is direct and blunt, not given to ornate embellishment. This version is more in accord with what we know of the native speaking style.

As Seattle said, his people wanted the whites among them to supply them through trade, and the great prize was to have a trade outlet in their own territory. When the Denny party landed at Alki in 1851, about one thousand native people gathered around them, setting up their houses next to the settlers', arguing and fighting with each other. Some even sought to win the hand of Louisa Boren, the daughter of Carson Boren. These attempts by the contending groups to gain advantage over one another were stymied, however, when Arthur Denny, the acknowledged leader among the settlers, and several other whites moved across the bay to the site of dzee-dzuh-LAH-lich, at present-day Pioneer Square. The headman of this settlement then was a man named tsah-KWAHLH, whom the settlers called "Curley." Seattle had many kin among Curley's people and often stayed with them, but while Curley was respectful, he does not appear to have taken orders from Seattle.

By removing themselves to the eastern shores of the bay, Denny and the rest withdrew from the orbit of the Suquamish, who commonly camped near Alki Point, and entered more firmly into the realm of the Duwamish. This connection was made stronger still when kwee-AHKH-tid, the aged chief of the Renton-area Duwamish—the most powerful of the Duwamish groups—visited Arthur Denny at his home and asked him to name his three sons. Denny agreed, giving them names of chiefs famous in the East: Tecumseh, William, and Keokuck. This act of naming, very important in the native culture, appears to have been done in order to bind the two men and their respective followings with ties of friendship that neither men nor their sons ever repudiated. A close economic relationship developed between Denny's party on the eastern shore and the Duwamish. The new settlement was named Duwamps, after the tribe.

Seattle appears to have been outmaneuvered by these events, but he moved quickly to reestablish his ascendency by enticing Dr. David Maynard to move from Olympia and open a store at the site of the new town. Maynard agreed and quickly became the most enterprising member of the white community. To seal his victory, Maynard had the town change its name from Duwamps to Seattle in honor of his patron. This tribute did not please Seattle since it violated the native custom forbidding the use of a person's name

The Indians' night promises to be dark.

An 1864 photograph of the Suquamish on a trip to Olympia to discuss reservation boundaries. The tall figure to the left with the cross on his chest is believed to be Chief Seattle.

while he was still alive. The influence Seattle gained, and a goodly payment, improved his humor on the subject.

Seattle was aided in his maneuvers by the death of kwee-AHKH-tid early in 1852, and the fact that the three sons of the Suquamish chief were not as influential as he was. But the rivalry between the two groups did not end there. It appears to have derived from and perhaps even exacerbated the feud between Denny and his followers, including Henry Yesler, who were associated with the Duwamish, and Maynard and his brother-in-law, Michael Simmons, who were friends of Seattle and his Suquamish. These rivalries became especially bitter during the time of the Indian War.

In 1853, the new territorial governor, Isaac Stevens, began the long-awaited process of getting the native peoples to sign away their land to the settlers in exchange for government aid. By January of 1854, Stevens and his aide set out on a flying tour through the Puget Sound region to meet with the major native groups and their leaders.

On the 10th they arrived in the town of Seattle, and after several days, during which time the Duwamish and Suquamish assembled themselves on the town waterfront, Stevens addressed them through an interpreter in Chinook Jargon. He gave them greetings from President Pierce and told them of his desire to make treaties with them that would provide justice for all, to purchase lands from them for settlement, and to provide for their protection on reservations. Until that time, he urged them to keep the peace and deal justly with their white neighbors.

After that, Seattle rose and spoke. His remarks were translated for the benefit of Shaw, Stevens's interpreter, from the native tongue into the jargon. Dr. Henry Smith, from whose notes the speech emerges, had been in the Territory barely a year, and had picked up

Chief Moses

"I fear the ruin of my people is coming," lamented the last of the great chiefs of the Eastern Washington tribes to an Indian agent at the Okanogan River, on June 30, 1870. Chief Moses councilcd peace between his people and the white men— even while maintaining his integrity.

W hen the soldiers had left the mid-Columbia, the young warrior Quetalican returned there in 1859. Shortly one of his wives, the delicate Quemollah, died. Grief for her kept him from his lodge and his young wife, Shantlahow, for long periods of time. He remained away for another reason—to gather war-scattered remnants of Columbia bands to his standard to escape confinement on a reservation by the white man. To symbolize his new mission, he assumed his father's name—Sulktalthscosum, the Half-Sun. . . .

On September 1, 1861, as the Half-Sun Chief and his band were camped on the east side of the river between Rock Island and the Wenatchee Flat, a Canada-bound party with cattle appeared on the other side of the river. The camp buzzed with excitement. The Chief, now a large, powerful man in his thirties, untethered the blue roan staked by his lodge, plunged into the river, and rode "like a centaur" to meet the strangers. Any crossing of the Columbia on horseback was dangerous, but in the low water of late summer he accomplished the feat quite easily; had there been high water, he would have swum, holding his horse's mane on the downstream side, keeping his body from the animal so as not to impede its movement. Coming out of the river, he rode across the rocky beach to a group of white cattlemen and some Indians, including Nanamkin of the nearby Entiats, who had met them on the trail and offered his services as guide. Not least among the party was a sixteen-year-old drover, Jack (A. J.) Splawn, who would never forget this meeting. The Chief asked him to whom the cattle belonged, and the lad pointed out a tall cattleman, Major John Thorp. As the big Indian turned his roan toward the Major, Splawn interrupted to ask his name. Looking down at his young interrogator, he replied, "Sulk-talth-scosum, but better known to white men as Chief Moses." *"Nika Moses"* ("I am Moses"), the tribal leader would say many times thereafter to introduce himself to white men.

From Half-Sun on the Columbia: A Biography of Chief Moses, *by Robert H. Ruby and John A. Brown. Copyright © 1965 by the University of Oklahoma Press. Reprinted by permission.*

After speaking with Thorp, Moses, as he would have the white man call him, rode back to the east side of the river. He was at his lodge only a short time when Nanamkin appeared to tell him that he had overheard some braves plotting to massacre the party and steal its cattle. The Indian Moses had come to respect Thorp in their brief meeting, and the thought of his men's killing the cattleman and his to-wheaded helper filled him with anger. Quickly, he and Nanamkin rode across the river to the party's camp at the mouth of the Wenatchee. By then, night had fallen. A full moon revealed to them the plumed-and-painted braves on a hill preparing to rush the little group. Immediately, the Chief rode between the hostiles and the party and waved the attackers back until the hill was cleared. Moses had saved the lives of the little group and, because of his dramatic action, had strengthened his leadership among his own people as well.

Chief Moses

enough of the jargon to understand the interpretation. Thirty-three years later, the embellished version appeared in print.

THE INDIANS' NIGHT PROMISES TO BE DARK

Yonder sky that has wept tears of compassion upon my people for centuries untold, and which to us appears changeless and eternal, may change. Today is fair. Tomorrow it may be overcast with clouds. My words are like the stars that never change. Whatever Seattle says the great chief at Washington can rely upon with as much certainty as he can upon the return of the sun or the seasons. The White Chief says that Big Chief at Washington sends us greeting of friendship and goodwill. This is kind of him for we know he has little need of our friendship in return. His people are many. They are like the grass that covers vast prairies. My people are few. They resemble the scattering trees of a storm-swept plain. The great—and I presume—good White Chief sends us word that he wishes to buy our lands but is willing to allow us enough to live comfortably. This indeed appears just, even generous, for the Red Man no longer has rights that he need respect, and the offer may be wise also, as we are no longer in need of an extensive country.

There was a time when our people covered the land as the waves of a wind-ruffled sea covered its shell-paved floor, but that time long since passed away with the greatness of tribes that are now but a mournful memory. I will not dwell on, nor mourn over, our untimely decay, nor reproach my paleface brothers with hastening it as we too may have been somewhat to blame.

Youth is impulsive. When our young men grow angry at some real or imaginary wrong, and disfigure their faces with black paint, it denotes that their hearts are black, and that they are often cruel and relentless, and our old men and old women are unable to restrain them. Thus it has ever been. Thus it was when the white man first began to push our forefathers westward. But let us hope that the hostilities between us may never return. We would have everything to lose and nothing to gain. Revenge by young men is considered gain, even at the cost of their own lives, but old men who stay at home in times of war, and mothers who have sons to lose, know better.

Our good father at Washington—for I presume he is now our father as well as as yours, since King George has moved his boundaries further north—our great and good father, I say, sends us word that if we do as he desires he will protect us. His brave warriors will be to us a bristling wall of stength, and his wonderful ships of war will fill our harbors so that our ancient enemies far to the northward—the Hydas and Tsimpsians—will cease to frighten our women, children, and old men. Then in reality will he be our father and we his children. But can that ever be? Your God is not our God! Your God loves your people and hates mine. He folds his strong protecting arms lovingly about the paleface and leads him by the hand as a father leads his infant son—but He has forsaken His red children—if they really are His. Our God, the Great Spirit, seems also to have forsaken us. Your God makes your people wax strong every day. Soon they will fill all the land. Our people are ebbing away like a rapidly receding tide that will never return. The white man's God cannot love our people or He would protect them. They seem to be orphans who can look nowhere for help. How then can we be brothers? How can your God become our God and renew our prosperity and awaken in us dreams of returning greatness? If we have a common heavenly father He must be partial—for He came to His paleface children. We never saw Him. He gave you laws but had no word for his red children whose teeming multitudes once filled this vast continent as stars fill the firmament. No; we are two distinct races with separate origins and separate destinies. There is little in common between us.

To us the ashes of our ancestors are sacred and their resting place is hallowed ground. You wander far from the graves of your ancestors and seemingly without regret. Your religion was written upon tablets of stone by the iron finger of your God so that you could not forget. The Red Man could never comprehend nor remember it. Our religion is the tradition of our ancestors—the dreams of our old men, given them in the solemn hours of night by the Great Spirit; and the visions of our sachems, and is written in the hearts of our people.

Your dead cease to love you and the land of their nativity as soon as they pass the portals of the tomb and wander way beyond the stars. They are soon forgotten and never return. Our dead never forget the beautiful world that gave them being. They still love its verdant valleys, its murmuring rivers, its magnificent mountains, sequestered vales and verdant-lined lakes and bays, and ever yearn in tender, fond affection over the lonely hearted living, and often return from the Happy Hunting Ground to visit, guide, console and comfort them.

Day and night cannot dwell together. The Red Man has ever fled the approach of the White Man, as the morning mist flees before the morning sun.

However, your proposition seems fair and I think that my people will accept it and will retire to the reservation you offer them. Then we will dwell in peace, for the words of the Great White Chief seem to be the words of nature speaking to my people out of dense darkness.

It matters little where we pass the remnant of our days. They will not be many. The Indians' night promises to be dark. Not a single star of hope hovers above his horizon. Sad-voiced winds moan in the distance. Grim fate seems to be on the Red Man's trail, and wherever he goes he will hear the approaching footsteps of his fell destroyer and prepare stolidly to meet his doom, as does the wounded doe that hears the approaching footsteps of the hunter.

A few more moons. A few more winters—and not one of the descendants of the mighty hosts that once moved over this broad land or lived in happy homes, protected by the

Princess Angeline, Chief Seattle's daughter

Great Spirit, will remain to mourn over the graves of a people—once more powerful and hopeful than yours. But why should I mourn at the untimely fate of my people? Tribe follows tribe, and nation follows nation, like the waves of the sea. It is the order of nature, and regret is useless. Your time of decay may be distant, but it will surely come, for even the White Man whose God walked and talked with him as friend with friend, cannot be exempt from the common destiny. We may be brothers after all. We will see.

We will ponder your proposition and when we decide we will let you know. But should we accept it, I here and now make this condition that we will not be denied the privilege without molestation of visiting at any time the tombs of our ancestors, friends and children. Every part of this soil is sacred in the estimation of my people. Every hillside, every valley, every plain and grove, has been hallowed by some sad or happy event in days long vanished. Even the rocks, which seem to be dumb and dead as they swelter in the sun along the silent shore, thrill with memories of stirring events connected with the lives of my people, and the very dust upon which you now stand responds more lovingly to their footsteps than to yours, because it is rich with the blood of our ancestors and our bare feet are conscious of the sympathetic touch. Our departed braves, fond mothers, glad, happy-hearted maidens, and even our little children who lived here and rejoiced here for a brief season, will love these somber solitudes and at eventide they greet shadowy returning spirits. And when the last Red Man shall have perished, and the memory of my tribe shall have become a myth among the White Men, these shores will swarm with the invisible dead of my tribe, and when your children's children think themselves alone in the field, the store, the shop, upon the highway, or in the silence of the pathless woods, they will not be alone. In all the earth there is no place dedicated to solitude. At night when the streets of your cities and villages are silent and you think them deserted, they will throng with the returning hosts that once filled them and still love this beautiful land. The White Man will never be alone.

Let him be just and deal kindly with my people, for the dead are not powerless. Dead, did I say? There is no death, only a change of worlds.

Undeniably majestic as it is, Seattle's speech does not conform to what we know of the native speaking style of the Puget Sound region. That style was laconic to the point of bluntness, as are the other utterances of Seattle that are recorded by other writers. While the speech before Governor Stevens probably contains the gist of Seattle's remarks, it seems partially a product of Smith's romantic, literary mind. Almost certainly another of Smith's creations is a letter from Seattle to President Franklin Pierce written in 1854. In the following excerpt we can see many of the ideas and stylistic elements that appear in the speech, but also many striking new ones.

We know that the White Man does not understand our ways. One portion of the land is the same to him as the next, for he is a stranger who comes in the night and takes from the land whatever he needs. The earth is not his brother, but his enemy, and when he has conquered it, he moves on. He leaves his fathers' graves, and his children's birthright is forgotten. The sight of your cities pains the eyes of the Red Man. But perhaps it is because the Red Man is a savage and does not understand.

There is no quiet place in the white man's cities. No place to hear the leaves of spring or the rustle of insects' wings. But perhaps it is because I am a savage and do not understand, the clatter only seems to insult the ears. The Indian prefers the soft sound of the wind darting over the face of the pond, the smell of the wind itself cleansed by a mid-day rain, or scented with a pinon pine. The air is precious to the Red Man. For all things share the same breath—the beasts, the trees, the man. Like a man dying for many days, he is numb to the stench.

What is man without the beasts? If all the beasts were gone, men would die from great loneliness of spirit, for whatever happens to the beasts also happens to man. All things are connected. Whatever befalls the earth befalls the sons of the earth.

It matters little where we pass the rest of our days; they are not many. A few more hours, a few more winters, and none of the children of the great tribes that once lived on this earth, or that roamed in small bands in the woods, will be left to mourn the graves of the people once as powerful and hopeful as yours.

The whites, too, shall pass—perhaps sooner than the other tribes. Continue to contaminate your bed, and you will one night suffocate in your own waste. When the buffalo are all slaughtered, the wild horses all tamed, the secret corners of the forest heavy with the scent of many men, and the view of the ripe hills blotted by the talking wires, where is the thicket? Gone. Where is the eagle? Gone. And what is it to say goodbye to the swift and the hunt, the end of living and the beginning of survival? We might understand if we knew what it was that the White Man dreams, what he describes to his children on the long winter nights, what visions he burns into their minds, so they will wish for tomorrow. But we are savages. The White Man's dreams are hidden from us.

However the words may be embellished by Smith, Seattle's biting irony succeeds in reaching us, and his warnings seem uncannily suited for our own age.

In March of 1854, Stevens appointed Michael Simmons as Indian Agent for the Puget Sound region and, at a meeting of assembled headmen in the town of Seattle, appointed Seattle as chief of the Suquamish and Duwamish tribes, and several other headmen sub-chiefs.

Because of his proven abilities, Seattle was respectfully regarded by members of both

David S. Maynard

D.S. Maynard was appointed Indian agent by Mike Simmons in 1855 just before the White River massacre near Auburn, Washington. Maynard was responsible for maintaining control of the Indians in the central Puget Sound. He attempted to remove the Duwamish to Bainbridge Island; however, only some of them went. Maynard describes his work in a letter to his son.

Reprinted by permission of Chris Maynard Braaten.

Seattle March 30, 1856

Dear Son,
You have doubtless formed ideas of the existing wars in this our boasted land. Also of the whereabouts of your father, exposed as he has been. I am yet alive, although I have been through some narrow passages. . . . Last fall just before the war broke out I went to San Francisco for goods. On my return I found the whole country in a great degree of excitement. Many of the citizens had been massacred by the hostile Indians. . . . I was immediately after my return thereupon appointed Indian Agent . . . This outbreak of the Indians has so completely upset all previous arrangements in this country that no one knows what calculations to make for the morrow. I would be glad to dispose of my town property in some way, let my land lie and leave the country until peace is restored. But at this time no one dares to invest with any shade of advantage to me. . . . I assure you there is little comfort in living in this state of war and confusion, continually watching these devils lest they *tote* off your scalp. Notwithstanding the uncomfortable position I have occupied for the last 5 or 6 months, I feel amply paid when I witness the expression of the public to this effect. That although I have occupied the most dangerous post of any in the field, I have succeeded in quelling the spirit of war and established a friendly feeling with the determination to remain so with over 700 Indians, which number if added to the hostiles in the field would long ere this have cleared our country of pale faces.

I will here describe to you in detail that you may form an idea of my situation during past 5 months. Accompanying my appointment I was instructed to take to my aid such assistance as I from time to time considered necessary and proceed without delay to gather together all Indians found in my district not at that moment engaged in aggression against the whites and place them upon the opposite side of Puget Sound away from any white settlers. I in vain tried to procure such assistance. Money would not hire a man to go with me. I succeeded in getting together 354 and went across with them as instructed. My wife the only white person in sight of us. I succeed in bringing them to the belief that it was for their good that they remained neutral. We remained with them entirely by ourselves for the first two months. We were in the woods upon the bank of the Sound without even a tent to sleep in until the Indians were so far reconciled that I ventured to send off to a sawmill for some lumber of which I built us a camp. This was during the rainy season & the sun was seldom seen for weeks . . . These Indians soon became much attached to me & my wife. . . . After geting into my cabin I learned from my friendly Indians that some of the hostile Indians were in the bush nearby watching an opportunity of killing me and my wife & requested us to keep in door, which we did unless guarded. Until one verry dark night they were discovered trying to get a shot at me through a crack in a board of my camp. They were driven to the bush again by my friends. The next morning I offered $100 a piece for their scalps. The consequence was they were driven across the Sound to the enemy's camp. I have now the whole Suquamish tribe on terms of peace and pledged not to join or assist the enemy. . . .

Affectionately,
Your Father
D.S. Maynard

Museum of History and Industry

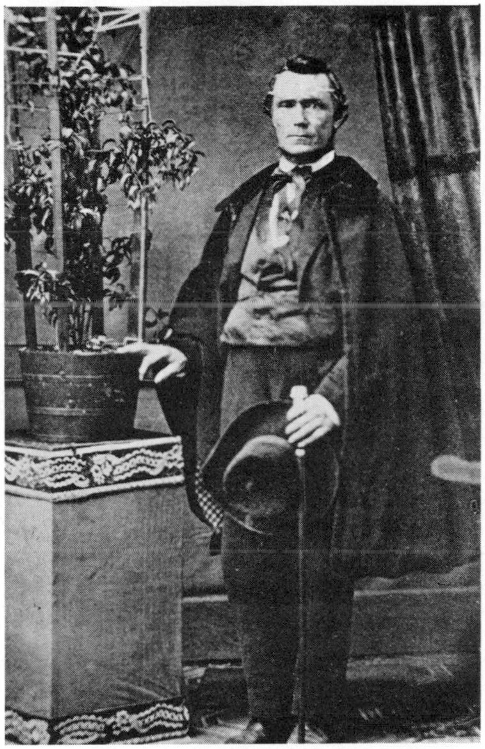

D.S. Maynard

groups as first among equals, but by imposing a hierarchical system of leadership upon the people, Stevens institutionalized what had been essentially a form of social etiquette. At first, Seattle's superior title did not seem especially threatening: chiefs mostly just received more money from the government than did subchiefs. But as the treaty-making got under way, the threat to the Duwamish manifested itself. Seattle received a reservation for his people in their territory, while the Duwamish, who were represented only by sub-chiefs, got none in theirs.

The Duwamish were not the only ones displeased by the outcome of the treaty, and elsewhere this anger led to the outbreak of hostilities. The friendly relations between the Duwamish and Denny's party prevented most of them from taking up arms. After the White River massacre in September of 1855, Acting-Governor Mason (Stevens was east of the mountains negotiating still more treaties) on the advice of Simmons directed that the native people on the east side of the Sound be removed to the west side in order to prevent their association with hostile forces.

Maynard was appointed subagent for King County to oversee the removal of the Duwamish, but the Duwamish refused to go. In this they were supported by Denny, Yesler, and most of the other residents of the town, who needed native labor to continue running Yesler's sawmill since the white settlers had been mustered into the volunteer militia. At one point Adjutant-General Tilton directed Christopher Hewitt, captain of Company H of the Territorial Volunteers, to use force if necessary to prevent the residents of Seattle from blocking the removal of the native people. Simmons threatened to place in irons anyone who interfered with his task.

But Simmons and Maynard were unsuccessful. The Duwamish retorted that if Seattle wanted to go to the western shore that was fine with them; after all, he lived there. As for them, they would as soon be shot as leave their homeland. By late November Maynard had succeeded in removing only eighty people to Bainbridge—those who wished to go, and barely a fraction of those gathered at the town. Seattle had retired to Old Man House on the new Fort Kitsap reservation where, along with Maynard, he waited for the storm to break.

On January 24, 1856, Seattle received word from Te-at-e-bush, one of his spies among the hostiles, that a large band of warriors was about to attack the town. Together with Maynard and several other Suquamish headmen, he crossed the Sound to deliver this information to Captain Gansevoort who commanded the naval sloop of war, *Decatur,* then in anchor at Elliott Bay. This information was not new; similar word had been given by Curley to Yesler, who forwarded it to Gansevoort. The captain had sent out a native scout to examine the Lake Washington area, but since he had not yet returned, Seattle's alarm was treated as just another rumor. After all, Governor Stevens, who had left the *Decatur* barely an hour before Seattle arrived, had that very day assured his listeners that New York and San Francisco were more likely to be attacked than the settlers in town. It was not until the

He was buried in the village of Suquamish—from the grave, you can see the towers of downtown Seattle.

112

afternoon of the next day, when Gansevoort's scout returned accompanied by Tecumseh and more than one hundred Duwamish fleeing their Renton-area houses, that the reports of the hostile force massing on the lakeshore prompted action. Soldiers and marines were posted to await the attack that came at 8:30 the next morning.

After the day-long fight that followed, the settlers no longer opposed the removal of the native people from town. Even the Duwamish appear to have been anxious to leave the combat zone for the western shore where Seattle awaited them. Even so, Curley and several others remained in town, and by the fall of 1856, the Duwamish had returned to their river homes.

Seattle succeeded in gaining a reservation for the Suquamish, but the Duwamish got nothing, and after the war many of them had little use for him. For the remainder of his life Seattle sought to protect what rights the treaties promised his people, but he saw promises degenerate into poverty and despair. Whites were not immune to the poverty endured by the native peoples, for excepting the brief flurry of the Fraser River gold rush of 1858–59, the economy of the region remained stagnant until after the Civil War.

At his last potlatch in 1862, Seattle distributed what few possessions he had: old clothes, a horseshoe, a muleshoe, fishhooks, gunny sacks, tin cans, boxes, food, and knickknacks. When he was not at Old Man House leading his people in prayer or petitioning the reservation agent for their needs, he could be seen in Seattle acting as a judge in tribal councils or visiting friends. He was generally accompanied by his children or grandchildren, and he commonly wore old pants, a shirt, and a Hudson's Bay blanket. On special occasions, he added a worn frock coat and a tall stovepipe hat.

As he neared the end of his days, Seattle must have despaired of his inability to save his people from the scourges of poverty, drunkenness, disease, and the indifference of the government he had tried to appease. Born amid a plague of smallpox, he ended his life amid other scourges. Still, until the very end, he retained the great physical strength in which he had gloried in his youth, and he never lost the dignity that seemed to have been a natural part of his character. His people clung to him as a protector, although he could protect them but little, and as a nostalgic reminder of days when his fortunes and theirs seemed much brighter. Many of his white friends were still alive, but like him they also aged, and as the town and the region began to fill with newcomers, and new generations arose to direct the destinies of the things they had created, the chief's circle retired from the center of the stage and began to feel irrelevant.

When Seattle died on June 7, 1866, his funeral was attended by a great throng of grieving kinsmen and sympathetic whites who mourned at his death the passing of a world. He was buried in the village of Suquamish—from the grave, you can see the towers of downtown Seattle—and the Latin initials I.H.S. were later inscribed on the tombstone. His kinsmen interpret the letters *(in hoc spiritus)* for "I have suffered."

At the time of Seattle's death, the white population of King County had only just exceeded that of the native peoples. Soon it would dwarf their number entirely. But while his people virtually disappeared from the stage of history, Seattle remained a potent figure in the town's life because his image was writ large in the memories of the pioneers. Although the settlers owed at least as great a debt of gratitude—if not a greater one—to Duwamish leaders like Curley, Tecumseh, and William, who helped and protected the white community, as they did to Seattle, nevertheless, he had been the most imposing native personality in the area at a time when whites desperately needed native help and good will.

As long as Seattle, the city, draws strength from its history as a struggling frontier community and inspiration from its earliest leaders, the image of Seattle, the man, will continue to intrigue and trouble its collective mind. The image is largely the product of cultural projection. The settlers could not—and probably would not—understand the culture Seattle represented. Their understanding of him probably never rose above the level of sentimentality. Like all famous men about whose heritage and personal life little is known, he became a malleable symbol. In the hands of a relentless romantic like Dr. Smith, Seattle's speech to Governor Stevens became a valedictory for one race and a prologue to the ascendancy of another.

But if the speech is a paean to the progress of the American State, it contains within it a powerful undertow of criticism of social progress and an eloquent caution against the hubris that attended its westward expansion. Today, the prophetic nature of his words serves the purposes of those who preach an apocalyptic form of environmentalism. In each period we have used the man to serve our purposes, and in so doing, we have created a new image of him.

Schoolchildren are taught that he was the chief of the Duwamish, Suquamish, and allied tribes; that he was a friend of the whites, a man who counseled peace, and that he gave one of the most famous orations in the region's history. Historical analysis brings many of these points into question and reveals, not surprisingly, a man far more complex and coming from a far more complicated world than our images of him suggest. ◾

RIVER OF LEGENDS

COYOTE AND SMOHALLA (1815–1885)

DAVID M. BUERGE

The Columbia is a river of superlatives: 1,264 miles long, the largest flowing directly into the Pacific, the second largest in the United States in volume. It is cold, swift, and purposeful; it rarely meanders in its valley. Like all great rivers, it has many faces, many characters. In its upper reaches, it is a mountain river flowing through deep, forested valleys, draining ice caps and the glaciated spine of the continent. It traverses its lower reaches as lordly as any river in the world. Wagner would have loved its romantic gorge crowned with cliffs, gorgeted with forests, and tasselate with waterfalls. Below are the storied valleys pioneers marched thousands of miles to win. The Columbia rolls by grandly, a mile wide in places, and then it broadens to embrace the sea in a last show of mighty turbulence.

Nothing about him is subdued. Everything about him—his actions, abilities, and appetites—is made prodigal and Homeric in the stories.

It is in its middle reach that the river assumes its most compelling identity. Here it passes through a landscape unlike anything else on the planet, a brutal world of volcanic rock riven with profound chasms—desolate, exhilarating in scale, oppressively dark. In this steep, rockbound channel, this gaunt reach, echoes of primordial chaos may still be heard.

The dark, layered cliffs rising above the river record a history of unimaginable violence. The layers represent a succession of tremendous lava flows that flooded the land millions of years ago with thousands of cubic miles of seething rock. Who can visualize the scene? Nothing remotely comparable has occurred within human memory. Each new surface, flat as an iron skillet from horizon to rippling horizon, flashed red hot and resounded under an incandescent sky.

The land was stone-cold when humans first appeared on the earth, and the river cut a channel along the margins of these monstrous outpourings. But the violence was not yet done. During the Ice Age, the continental ice sheet rested heavily on the northern edge of the Columbia Plain, diverting the river from its old course and impounding huge lakes behind ice dams. Periodically, these dams would fail, and the water behind them sweep across the land with such force that it tore huge coulees out of the basalt. The most remarkable of these is the Grand Coulee, a diversionary channel, but the floods also tore off the top of the central plain, creating the weird channeled scabland, and reamed out the Palouse-Snake River canyon as well as the great Columbia Gorge itself. During the last and greatest of the inundations, the Spokane Flood, five hundred cubic miles of water ponded in glacial Lake Missoula took several weeks to surge across the land in a flood so immense that the broad outlet at Wallula Gap near the Tri-Cities was too small to accommodate the outflow. The backed-up waters created huge temporary lakes in the Pasco basin, the Walla Walla Valley, and the Yakima Valley.

The legends and myths associated with this central section of the Columbia and its tributaries suggest that there were people present who witnessed and survived that deluge. Several of these tales can be read in Ella Clark's *Indian Legends of the Pacific Northwest,* and in other sources. An interesting Spokane legend describes a huge lake in the Spokane area that drained suddenly—an intriguing story, because Lake Spokane was one of those huge reservoirs impounded behind an ice dam. A composite Colville legend tells how Coyote cut Steamboat Rock away from the side of Grand Coulee in a fit of rage and diverted the Columbia into its present channel by splitting a high ridge with a stone hammer.

A group of American explorers that traveled into the Columbia basin in 1841 as part of the Wilkes Expedition collected a legend about Aputaput (Palouse Falls) that described a struggle between the four huge brothers of a giantess and a colossal beaver that lived on the banks of the Snake River. The four surprised the beaver near the mouth of the Palouse River and attacked him as he fled upstream. At each place where they struggled a rapids formed, and the place where the beaver died became Palouse Falls. A more complete version told by Sam Fisher, a Palouse man, has Big Beaver fleeing downriver from his attackers, tearing out canyons on what had been a smooth riverbed as he goes, and leaving the marks of his claws along the canyon walls.

Clark also presents a legend she says was told by many tribes in the Columbia basin that describes a battle between Coyote and a monster beaver called Wishpoosh that lived high up the Yakima River in Lake Cle Elum. Wishpoosh hoarded all the lake's fish and killed those who tried to catch them, and in their distress, the people asked Coyote to help them. Making a huge spear, Coyote went to the lake and attacked the monster. In their struggle, the two adversaries tore holes in the mountains so that the lake water poured out, carrying the combatants with it. The flood poured into the Kittitas Valley, making a lake there until the two cut a canyon into the Yakima Valley, where another great lake formed. Battling their way through Union Gap, they were carried by the flood into the Walla Walla Valley, where yet another lake formed.

Finally, turning west, the waters bearing the thrashing titans, as well as trees Coyote attempted to grasp hold of, poured through the lower river valley, widening the Gorge as they headed to the sea. (Like biblical exegetes who ascribed mountaintop fossils to Noah's

flood, native storytellers may have identified the petrified logs found high above the river as those dragged down by Coyote.) Utterly exhausted, Coyote turned himself into a tree which was swallowed by the monster, but once inside, Coyote changed back into his original shape and hacked at the beaver's heart until he died. Exiting the huge corpse, Coyote hauled it ashore near the mouth of the river with the help of his friend, Muskrat, and cut Wishpoosh to pieces.

These legends have been translated out of their original language and have, no doubt, been altered to suit the style of white authors. Possibly, other more localized phenomena could have provided the bases for the legends. Taken together, they seem to recall a catastrophe of inhuman dimension that changed the face of the land and the character of the river in such a traumatic manner that the memory of it was passed down through hundreds of generations.

In these tales, as in others about the great river, the figure of Coyote looms large. The

The Dalles before flooding: sacred places inundated, as the natives foretold

Chinookan peoples who lived from the mouth of the river to The Dalles called him Talapus, the Shahaptin peoples upstream called him Spilyay, but for both he was the culture hero, and a paradigm of humanity. Nothing about him is subdued. Everything about him—his actions, abilities, and appetites—is made prodigal and Homeric in the stories. He is greedy, venal, cowardly, sexually rapacious, sometimes cruel, but also compassionate, brave, resourceful, and ultimately wise. He did not create the world, the Old Creator did that, but in several myths Coyote creates people. After he cut up Wishpoosh at the mouth of the river, the story goes on to tell how he threw the parts to the four directions where they became the peoples of the land. From the legs of the monster came the Klickitats, great runners and horsemen. From the arms, the Cayuse, powerful warriors. From the ribs he created the Yakimas, the defenders of the poor. From the head the Nez Perce, wise in council. And from the hair, blood, and waste he made the Snakes, the hostile nemesis of those on the lower river.

As their creator, Coyote took special interest in his progeny, and like the Changer in Puget Sound mythology, he made the world habitable for them and taught them how to live. He wandered up and down the river experiencing the world and changing it, sometimes for ill but mostly for good.

Coyote's adventures during his perambulations along the river make up a great part of its native folklore. Much of its character derives from his labors. Besides killing Wishpoosh, he also destroyed a witch who would tie people to baby boards and send them out to sea to their deaths. Once, he came across two women who had imprisoned fish in a pond. Turning himself into a baby, he tricked them into thinking him abandoned, and they took him home. While they were out working, he made digging sticks and wooden bowls. With the digging sticks he tore at the barrier separating the fish from the river. Just as he was about to free them, the women returned and began to beat him, but he put the bowls on his body and they protected him until his work was done. Once they escaped into the river, the fish became food for the people; to punish the women, Coyote transformed them into swallows which fly up the river when salmon are running. In similar myths, Coyote teaches people how to catch and prepare the salmon to ensure their return. These directions form the heart of the first salmon ceremony carried out subsequently by the people to honor the salmon for their beneficent sacrifice; farther upstream, the figure of Coyote is closely associated with the Salmon Chief, the person who organized and directed a group's fishing activity.

Having created abundant food, Coyote later met a man near Cape Horn, a promontory on the Washington side of the river between Washougal and Skamania, who could not eat because he had no mouth. Out of pity, he gave the man a mouth by cutting his face with a flint knife. He did the same thing to all the people in the man's village, and they became big talkers ever after.

Ribald tales about Coyote seem concentrated just below the Cascades, the first great rapids and natural fish trap on the river, whose name was extended to the mountain range flanking the river. In one legend, two sons of Coyote fell in love with a girl who had beautiful hair. She enjoyed the attentions of both and would not choose her favorite, which caused them to quarrel with each other. Growing weary of their incessant bickering, Coyote asked the girl to choose, but she haughtily rejected them both. He thereupon turned her into a waterfall (Horsetail Falls), and when he found his sons still quarreling, he turned them into Rooster Rock on the south bank and Beacon Rock on the north.

Forty miles upstream from the Cascades, the river raced through long, narrow channels cut through a giant's staircase of dark basalt slabs that French-Canadian fur company men called Les Dalles. As the Cascades were to be drowned behind Bonneville Dam, The Dalles were drowned behind The Dalles Dam, and we are not likely to see this grand spectacle in our lifetime, but John Muir left one of the best descriptions of it:

> At The Dalles the vast river is jammed together into a long narrow slot of unknown depth cut sheer down in the basalt. This slot or trough is about a mile and a half long and about 60 yards wide at the narrowest place.
>
> At ordinary times the river seems to be set on edge and runs swiftly but without much noisy surging with a descent of about 20 feet to the mile. But when the snow is melting on the mountains the river rises here 60 feet, or even more during extraordinary freshets, and spreads out over a great breadth of massive rocks through which have been cut several other gorges running parallel with the one usually occupied. All these inferior gorges now come into use, and the huge, roaring torrent, still rising and spreading at length, overwhelms the high jagged rock walls between them, making a tremendous display of chafing, surging, shattered currents, counter-currents, and hollow whirls that no words can be made to describe. A few miles below The Dalles the storm-tossed river gets itself together again, looks like water, becomes silent and with stately, tranquil deliberation goes on its way, out of the gray region of sage and sand into the Oregon woods.

This was the greatest fishing station on the river. Until it was submerged in The Dalles reservoir in 1957, it was where native fishermen with dip nets gathered to scoop salmon from the thundering cataract. For at least ten thousand years people have lived here, sustained by the river's largess. During the height of the fish runs, thousands made their way along trails leading down the brave riverscape to fish, to bargain and trade, to socialize, and to immerse themselves in the exhilarating vitality of the place. It became the great trade mart of the West.

At numerous places along The Dalles, rock faces were covered with petroglyphs and pictographs marking familial fishing spots and the haunts of particular spirit beings. Given

Tsagigla'al, watcher of the river

the importance of this stretch, it is not surprising that virtually every landmark, pool, and plunge was celebrated in myth and legend. Many of the legends had to do with Coyote. Features were celebrated as Coyote's cooking pot, Coyote's fishing place, Coyote's footprints, and Coyote's canyon—which he cut to allow the poor to have access to the fishery—and there were a host of beings he had frozen into stone. A ledge of rocks on the north bank of the river near Mosier was said to be a screen he erected for privacy while he fellated himself. When the rocks told the people what he had done, the derisive laughter made him cringe with shame. It was an infamous story, apparently celebrated in sculpted figures identified coyly as flute players, but writer Rick Rubin believes it was far more than an obscene tale. From his experience Coyote learned that nothing is secret, that ultimately, everyone will be accountable for all of his or her deeds. After that, Coyote became less wanton and more a mature hero.

Near the head of the Long Narrows, the village of Wakemap rested atop its mound, the Northwestern version of a Middle Eastern tel. The name came from a monster who lived in the pool above the narrows. According to Emory Strong, author of *Stone Age on the Columbia River,* the monster was an ogress who destroyed amorous men with sharp stones in her body, an apparent reference to what in other legends is more graphically described as a vagina toothed with flints. Elsewhere, she is described as having reddish hair that hung to her waist as she rose above the water. Coyote broke her teeth by surreptitiously using a stone pestle to copulate with her. In another version, the monster is identified as a swallowing monster who consumed people in his lair in their canoes—an image of the way people perished in the rapids. As at Lake Cle Elum, the people here were afraid to go near the water, and so they asked Coyote to help them. He asked his huckleberry sisters who lived in his stomach what he should do, but they refused to tell him, claiming that he would take credit for their idea. He threatened to send rain and hail down on their kin if they did not tell him what he needed to know, so they relented and told him he would need five sharp knives, pitch, and dry wood to defeat the monster. "Yes, my sisters," the ever-wily Coyote said after extorting this information, "that is what I thought. That was my plan all the time."

Entering the pool, Coyote teased the monster by calling him names; that made him so angry that he swallowed Coyote, knives, pitch, and firewood. Inside, Coyote found the monster's victims about to expire from hunger and cold. With his wood and pitch he built a fire beneath the monster's heart, and with his knives he slashed at the cord that connected it to the rest of the body. Four knives broke in his furious work, but the fifth one succeeded in severing the cord, and the heart fell into the flames. With a great cough, the monster spewed out its victims. The monster was not dead, only weakened, but Coyote declared that henceforth he would not swallow travelers with impunity; only once in a while could he take victims.

The wonderful folklore of this section of the river has many themes, and two aspects

A chaste maid or bashful suitor are not appropriate symbols for a river tumescent with fish.

seem to evoke the river itself. The riotously obscene tales, told without euphemisms and with a relish that embarrassed many early recorders, appear to celebrate the riotous fecundity of the river; they may have been told in much the same way lewd tales were told at sowing time in Europe. A chaste maid or bashful suitor are not appropriate symbols for a river tumescent with fish, and given the desire of the people to flourish in the world rather than simply survive, what seemed licentious to many may have been more of a profound affirmation of life.

The second aspect is the destructive capacity of the river, as symbolized by the monsters that lived within it. The earth might shake and send slides to block the channel, but rock was never a match for water. The defeat of Wishpoosh may recall memories of a catastrophic flood, but the legends also provided a means for the people to understand in religious terms the river's rampages and its constant toll of lives. Coyote had tamed the river monsters, so the river's fury would spend itself before destruction was complete. This was the hope, anyway.

Once again he entered the beast, lit a fire, and forced it to disgorge its victims.

Before he changed into the small animal he is today, Coyote went into the burnt land behind the mountains where the river rolled heavily through dark canyons. There were plenty more monsters that needed taming. Where Hanford is today, Coyote acted as a judge in a contest between Winaawaya'y, the warm South Wind, and Atyaya'ay, the cold North Wind. In the Yakima collection of legends, *The Way It Was*, the story is told how North Wind and his brothers had taken over the Chawnapam land and killed all the sons of Tick and Louse except Warm Wind, who escaped to the west and married the granddaughter of Pityachiishya, Ocean Woman. He returned to fight North Wind and was killed, but not before his wife bore him a son, Winaawaya'y, South Wind, who later revenged his father and uncles.

North Wind had defeated the sons of Tick and Louse by freezing the ground and making them slip on it as he wrestled them. Ocean Woman therefore prepared a grease for South Wind from the oil of ferocious sea monsters, and it kept him from slipping. As South Wind traveled east of the mountains, leading the way for Ocean Woman who carried five containers of the sea-monster grease, the tremendous winds he produced tore the tops off mountains and gouged out canyons and the beds of deep lakes. (In Pleistocene times, fierce winds blowing eastward across the Pasco basin scoured out immense quantities of silt and deposited them in thick layers of loess on the basalt plateau, creating the Palouse Hills.) Finally, he arrived at the Chawnapam land and met North Wind in an epic battle during which the sea-monster grease was poured out onto the frozen earth. South Wind prevailed and cut North Wind into pieces that were cast into canyons and gullies. Coyote decreed that North Wind could blow for only a little while and not as murderously as before. Coyote had bet heavily on South Wind; counting his winnings, he headed up the river.

Farther up, near where the Wenatchee River enters the Columbia, Coyote came to a

121

spot where a huge doglike monster was swallowing people, helped by a family of sandpipers who tipped off the monster when people were coming. With the help of his huckleberry sisters, Coyote made a plan to kill him. He climbed a steep cliff west of the river and rigged up a trap out of vines. First he tried to kill the sandpipers, but when one managed to let out a warning cry, he promised the others beautiful robes and decorations if they would remain quiet. They agreed, but the monster had heard the warning cry and was clambering up the cliff after Coyote. Near the top he became entangled in the trap. Coyote cut the vines, and the monster tumbled down the cliff, crushing himself on the rocks and leaving his blood splattered over the surface—still to be seen as red streaks on Ribbon Cliff near Entiat. Descending to the river, Coyote freed those who had been imprisoned in the monster's stomach and gave the sandpipers their reward. That is why they sport handsome necklaces and colors.

This brutal imagery is repeated again in the Grand Coulee, where the dark streaks on the cliffs produced by water seeps are said to be the hair of women Coyote crushed against the walls after they refused to marry him. Downriver, the hair of women who die or are killed in the course of legends becomes the wispy waterfalls that grace the Gorge. The differences reflect the different moods generated by these disparate sections of the river.

Coyote's luck with women on the upper river had a profound impact on its character. Where groups on the main stream granted his requests for a wife, he created rapids where they could catch salmon more easily; on tributaries where his wishes were granted, he called the salmon to spawn. Where he was refused, he built no rapids and told the salmon to stay away. Lake Chelan was one of those places that he kept the salmon from entering, although they have since been artificially introduced. Wilkes Expedition members traveling through the interior recorded other examples of his caprice:

> On one occasion, being desirous of a wife (a common circumstance with him), the Wolf, or the divinity so called, visited a tribe on the Spokane River and demanded a young woman in marriage. His request being granted, he promised that thereafter the salmon should be abundant with them, and he created the rapids, which gave them facilities for taking the fish. Proceeding farther up, he made of each tribe on his way the same request, attending with a like result. At length he arrived at the territory of the Skitsuish (Coeur d'ale'ne); they refused to comply with his demand, and he therefore called into existence the great falls of the Spokane, which prevented the fish from ascending to their country.

Coyote brought the fish all the way up to Kettle Falls, building all the rapids in the process that were a blessing to fishermen but a terror to travelers. On one last trip down the river he encountered another swallowing monster near the old town of Sundale. Once again he entered the beast, lit a fire, and forced it to disgorge its victims, but not before many were singed and smudged by the flames. This is why Coyote's coat is yellowed and spotted. It was presumably after this episode that Coyote, whom the Klickitats likened to a Northwestern sphinx, describing him as having the body of an animal and the head of a wizened old man, was turned into a shaggy dog. According to one legend, it happened because Old Creator was displeased with his performance. Like Moses, he had tapped his rod once too often.

When the white people began arriving on the river in the 1830s, the native people of the Columbia endured a new cataclysm. In two generations these people had suffered calamities and endured changes greater than they had known in the previous five hundred years. Amid wholesale devastation, the survivors sought desperately to regain their cultural and spiritual balance. Observing that the whites suffered less, had more possessions, and seemed to enjoy the favor of the god they worshipped, many turned toward the white ways. They dressed like them, talked like them, learned to till the soil, and developed a relationship with the white god. There were advantages in assimilation, but there were also liabilities. Whites introduced hard liquor along with their plagues; they could be capriciously cruel, and, while they stoutly demanded that the native people pay severely for crimes committed against them, they rarely returned the favor.

During this chaotic time, the Columbia basin was the scene of profound religious ferment. Native prophets arose who promised the destruction of the world and the return of the dead. A belief in the return of the dead may have had ancient roots in the culture, but with the precipitous destruction of so many, it took on an urgent new meaning. Prophet cults, as ethnographers term them, sprang up throughout the basin, and the people danced to hurry the end of their troubles, the return of the beloved dead, and the inauguration of a new age.

Historians have seen many of the appurtenances of Christianity in these cults, such as honoring the Sabbath, praying on one's knees, and the use of bells. But at their heart was a message that was as old as the land. The people were to turn away from the evildoing that brought the calamity—as it had always done—and turn to the right way of living. The missionaries understandably tried to capitalize on this sentiment. For some of the people, the right way was very like the Christian way, but for others it was something much closer to their ancient experience of the world.

That old wisdom was given passionate voice by the greatest of all the Columbia River prophets, Smohalla. In the 1880s, when the army was rounding up native bands and escorting them to reservations where they could be "civilized," Major J. W. MacMurray was sent to Priest Rapids, north of the river's confluence with the Snake River, to bring in Smohalla, the Wanapam prophet, and his people. He received a stirring rebuke:

You ask me to plow the ground! Shall I take a knife and tear my mother's bosom? Then when I die she will not take me to her bosom to rest.

You ask me to dig for stone! Shall I dig under her skin for her bones? Then when I die I cannot enter her body to be born again.

You ask me to cut grass and make hay and sell it, and be rich like white men! But how dare I cut off my mother's hair?

...My young men shall never work. Men who work cannot dream, and wisdom comes to us in dreams.

Smohalla was born, sometime between 1815 and 1820, a hunchback in the gaunt country near Wallula Gap where the ancient flood had torn a gap through the mountains. On a nearby sacred mountain he received visions and became a twuteewit, an Indian doctor. The dissension among powerful chiefs forced him out, and in time he led his followers to the fishing station at Priest Rapids where the Wanapams lived. The name was given to the rapids by Alexander Ross, an employee of the North West Company, an energetic rival of the Hudson's Bay Company, who visited the fishing village there in 1811 and was greeted by a shaman dancing ceremoniously on the shore. In the middle of the river lay an immense slab of basalt the Wanapams called Chalwash Chilni, "One-legged Abalone Man," the sacred island.

In his book *Drummers and Dreamers,* Yakima newspaper editor Click Relander relates the events of Smohalla's life as they were dictated to him by Puck Hyah Toot, Smohalla's nephew. Smohalla, he writes, lived at Priest Rapids in the village of P'na, where he was attended by his many wives in a long mat lodge and where he attracted a large following by his call to return to the ways of the ancestors and shun those of the whites. He established a ceremonial regimen to strengthen threatened traditions. He developed a calendar that enumerated ceremonial seasons, and he dramatized the symbols of the Washat, the native religion, by adorning ritual objects with them. A cult flag, drums, and ceremonial clothing were decorated with images of the sun, the moon, the North Star, and the sacred colors. As in an older time, the most important ceremonies were those held to offer thanks to the salmon and to the roots of the prairie for giving their life to the people.

According to Relander, Smohalla's life entered a critical period with the death of his firstborn, a daughter whom he held in deepest affection. Devastated, he fell into a deathlike swoon. Believing he had died, his grieving followers prepared him for burial. They were astonished when he stirred, and even more amazed when he claimed that he had in fact died, had spoken with the spirits, and had received from them a message for his people. To hear it, he had them assemble downstream at Coyote Rapids. There, he told them they must sing every seventh day a song he had been taught by the spirits. It was to be accompanied by a dance. In a time to come, he said, the world would experience a turning-over, a

cataclysm, and those that remained true to the traditions would survive to live in a new and happier world.

Relander's book provides one of the more detailed accounts of Smohalla's life and work, but many among the Yakima, where the Washat is still observed, disagree with much of it. As Cecelia Eli, a traditional Yakima educator, points out, Relander did not speak the language and relied heavily upon interpreters, which resulted in some substantial misinterpretations. For example, he and other writers describe Smohalla as the leader of a cult; according to Eli, Smohalla was only restating traditional beliefs and practices.

The content of the Washat was distinct from the myths and legends that told about the land, but Smohalla appears to have drawn upon the myths' often apocalyptic tone. This is powerfully expressed in the Wanapam legends about the sacred island. These were long and complicated, and Relander's version of them tells of successive ages of creation end-

Dipnetting in the old wild Columbia: a trademark along the brave riverscape

125

Lewis and Clark

Thomas Jefferson sent Meriwether Lewis and William Clark to explore the Louisiana Purchase and to strengthen American claims in the Northwest. They became the first Americans to travel through the interior. From 1804 to 1806, they gathered information on the local tribes and geography of the Northwest. By descending the Columbia River from the middle regions to the sea, they succeeded in confirming that the "river of the west" was indeed the one Robert Gray crossed and named—Columbia's River.

From The Journals of Lewis and Clark, *edited by Bernard De Voto. Copyright © 1953 by Bernard De Voto. Copyright © renewed 1981 by Avis De Voto. Reprinted by permission of Houghton Mifflin Company.*

October 31st Thursday 1805

A cloudy rainey disagreeable morning, I proceeded down the river to view with more attention [*the rapids*] we had to pass on the river below, . . . the two men with me. Jo. Fields & Peter Crusat proceeded down to examine the rapids . . . the Great Shute which commenced at the Island on which we encamped continued with great rapidity and force thro a narrow chanel much compressd. and interspersed with large rocks for a mile, at a mile lower is a verry considerable rapid at which place the waves are remarkably high, . . . and proceeded on in a old Indian parth 2 miles by land thro a thick wood & hill Side, to the river where the Indians make a portage, . . . from this place I Dispatched Peter Crusat (our principal waterman) back to follow the river and examine the practibility of the canoes passing, as the rapids appeared to continue down below as far as I could See, . . . I with Jo Fields proceeded on,

the mountain which is but low on the Stard. Side, leave[s] the river, and a leavel stoney open bottom suckceeds on the Said Std. Side for a great Distance down, . . . the mountains high and rugid on the Lard. Side . . . this open bottom is about 2 miles . . . a Short distance below this village is a bad Stoney rapid and appears to be the last in view . . . I observed at this lower rapid the remains of a large and antient Village which I could plainly trace by the Sinks in which they had formed their houses, as also those in which they had buried their fish. from this rapid to the lower end of the portage the river is crouded with rocks of various sises between which the water passes with great velociety createing in many places large waves, . . . an Island which is Situated near the Lard. Side occupies about half the distance the lower point of which is at this rapid. . . . immediately below this rapid the high water passes through a narrow chanel through the Stard. . . . I could not see any rapids below in the extent of my view which was for a long distance down the river, which from the last rapids widened and had everry appearance of being effected by the tide [*this was in fact the first tide water*] I deturmined to return to camp 10 miles distant, . . . a remarkable high detached rock Stands in a bottom on the Stard. Side . . . about 800 feet high and 400 paces around, we calle the *Beaten [Beacon] rock*.

One of the men shot a goose above this Great Shute, which was floating into the Shute, when an Indian observed it, plunged! into the water & swam to the Goose and brought in on shore, at the head of the Suck, [*great danger, rapids bad, a descent close by him (150 feet off,) of all Columbia River, current dashed among rocks, if he had got in the Suck—lost*] . . . as this Indian richly earned the goose I suffered him to keep it which he about half picked and spited it up with the guts in it to roste.

This Great Shute or falls is about a mile, with the water of this great river compressed within the space of 150 paces in which there is great numbers of both large and Small rocks, water passing with great velocity forming [foaming] & boiling in a most horriable manner, with a fall of about 20 feet, . . . below it widens to about 200 paces and current gentle for a Short distance.

November 1st Friday 1805

A verry cool morning wind hard from the N.E. The Indians who arrived last evening took their Canoes on ther Sholders and carried them below the Great Shute, . . . we Set about takeing our small canoe and all the baggage by land 940 yards of bad slippery and rockey way. The Indians we discovered took ther loading the whole length of the portage 2 miles, to avoid a second Shute which appears verry bad to pass, and thro' which they passed with their empty canoes. Great numbers of Sea Otters, they are so cautious that I with dificuelty got a Shot at one today, which I must have killed, but could not get him as he Sunk.

We got all our baggage over the Portage of 940 yards, after which we got the 4 large canoes over by slipping them over the rocks on poles placed across from one rock to another, and at some places doing partial Streams of the river. in passing those canoes over the rocks &c. three of them rec[ei]ved injuries which obliged us to delay to have them repared. Several Indian Canoes arrived at the head of the portage, Some of the men accompanied by those from the village come down to Smoke with us, . . .

Meriwether Lewis and William Clark

ing in catastrophe: fire burning the land, floods, and terrible windstorms. At the end of the age preceding this one, at the end of eons of darkness, life returned to the world. Before the animal people lived, before Coyote walked the land, two men lived on the sacred island—Anhyi, the Sun Man, and Chalwash Chilni, One-Legged Abalone Man. Sun Man had two wives, Pahtoe (Mount Adams) and Lalac, a small mountain between Prosser and the Columbia River. Lalac would have been as large as Pahtoe, but Sun Man killed her and tore her to pieces. On Lalac, a sacred mountain and the corpse of Sun Man's wife, Smohalla received his first vision.

Sun Man and One-Legged Abalone Man were friends until they quarreled about how to fish in the river. Abalone Man killed Sun Man, cut off his head and threw his parts into the river where they became islands next to the sacred island. When this happened, Nami Piap the Earth Keeper, the Old Creator, grew angry and filled the land with fire and ash, driving Abalone Man down the river to his kin in the sea.

A new people was created and the world was made into a paradise lit by Sun Man, whom Nami Piap had resurrected into the sky. But over time the people forgot the traditions with which they had been entrusted, so the Old Creator hid the sun behind a hill and filled the world with cold. Eventually, a few survivors remembered the chant that brought food and sang it. The Earth Keeper relented a little. He released the sun, but only let him shine during the day. To help guide the people at night, he put the moon and the stars in the sky. The people would have food to eat, salmon in the rivers, and roots in the ground, but only if they took care to honor these and live as they were taught. This was the last warning. If they should forget their way again, they would be lost.

With these legends in mind and the recollection of the calamities they had suffered still painfully fresh, many accepted Smohalla's call to return to the old ways, and the movement spread throughout the region. Smohalla also made a prophecy that there would come a time when the people would see changes greater than what they had experienced, when Chalwash Chilni, the sacred island, would be drowned beneath the river. When that happened, they should know that the great turning was at hand.

Smohalla brought hope to many, but he could not restore the Wanapam's land. Many went to live on reservations, others died, and fewer and fewer lived on at the old village at Priest Rapids until they were finally evicted in the 1950s. By then, Smohalla, who died in 1895, was long gone; his son, Yoyouni, had also died, and only Puck Hyah Toot survived to lead the remnant band in their ceremonies.

Those who had got hold of the land had transformed it even more than had Coyote in the old days. Like the mountain demons farther downstream, they raised a dam across the river at Rock Island rapids in 1933. That same year saw work begun on Bonneville Dam, below the Cascades, and above Rock Island on the greatest one of them all, Grand Coulee.

The monstrous power of the river, which could yield prodigal abundance, had given rise to a new creation that consumed a prodigality of victims.

Ten years later, a mysterious new complex was rising in the desert south along the bend of the river near Hanford.

Here the government evicted some two thousand people from six hundred square miles of land, and sent in sixty thousand workers to build a top-secret facility. The complex was unlike anything built before. Huge amounts of power hummed in from Grand Coulee, and the water piped from the Columbia into several enigmatic buildings came out steaming hot. The secret of what was being produced was made public on August 6, 1945, when the Japanese city of Hiroshima was destroyed by a new type of bomb. Three days later, Nagasaki suffered a similar fate. The plutonium for the bomb had been produced at Hanford. The monstrous power of the river, which could yield prodigal abundance, had given rise to a new creation that consumed a prodigality of victims, swallowed them up in a ball of volcanic fire.

The river's old legends taught that the universe has a moral aspect. Abundance freely given must be freely shared. Violation of that law engenders violence, and violence on earth will draw down the wrath of heaven. This is an old lesson, but each generation has to learn the truth of it. Now that we have come into this land, the river has taught us another. The great changes we have wrought do not change the nature of life, they only extend its range. We face the same problems and challenges that the native people did ten thousand years ago. Life is good, but it is difficult. There are monsters in the world, and they can be met only through shrewd resourcefulness and heroism.

In the 1950s few save Click Relander gave the followers of Smohalla or his prophecy much thought. In 1955 engineers visited the sacred island and began drilling cores to lo cate the foundations of a new dam. By 1960 Priest Rapids Dam was built, and the waters of its reservoir covered Chalwash Chilni exactly as Smohalla said they would.

Today a white train leaves Hanford and makes its way down the river, bearing weapons-grade plutonium, adding substance every trip to a monster as bedeviling and violent as any that haunted the river in Coyote's day. Now might we all cry out for the resourceful and wise Coyote to save us, but where is he? ◣

David and Louisa (Boren) Denny's
first home: hacking a settlement
out of the jungle

SEATTLE'S PIONEER WOMEN

A GALLERY OF PORTRAITS 1850–1870

DAVID M. BUERGE

April 10, 1851, is not a date that stands out in the minds of many in Seattle, but it has a special significance. On the afternoon of that warm spring day, four covered wagons left the northern Illinois hamlet of Cherry Grove and joined the long columns heading west. These four wagons carried the seven men, four women, and four children of the Denny and Boren families who, seven months later, disembarked from a lumber schooner onto the cold, rain-swept beach at Alki Point.

There are two recollections of that April day. The first appears in the *Journal of the Route to Oregon* kept by twenty-nine-year-old Arthur Armstrong Denny, the leader among those who landed at Alki. The entry reads simply: "April 10, 1851, left home at 3 o'clock pm." The second recollection comes from Mary Ann Denny, also twenty-nine, and four months pregnant, and was eventually preserved by Roberta Frye Watt, her granddaughter, in her history of Seattle's beginnings, *Four Wagons West*.

For most the move west was a source of ambivalence and grief.

> I have been told how, when the travelers were ready to start, my grandmother walked through the empty, echoing rooms of her home for the last time with a strange feeling of un-reality. For months all had worked and planned for this time of departure, which was always in the future. But now the hour, the very minute, had come when she must turn her back upon her old home, old scenes, old friends—and she was unprepared. She went from room to room—out into the kitchen where she had spent so many busy hours. But there was no time to linger. She gave one tear-blurred look about the old, familiar, homely room and then passed out into the April sunshine. The barnyard was empty; the chickens were gone; even the dog was perched up on the wagon. All that was left was her flower garden, neglected of late. The very air was filled with suppressed emotion and sadness.

Arthur Denny probably felt many of the same things his wife did, but he never gave voice to them, and the differences between the recollections bespeaks the differing attitudes toward the experience. For pioneer men, departure was a time for fresh starts, but the pioneer woman bore the sundering of her world as bravely as she could.

Louisa Boren: "the sweetbriar
bride"

Seattle's pioneer women are generally elusive figures, but when they reveal themselves it is often with a richness of feeling rarely matched by their men. The westering experience had profound, even traumatic, effects on both men and women, but among women it worked to initiate a radical transformation of their social position. They left their homes in the East essentially as chattel, unable in many cases to own property, to testify in court, and nowhere able to vote in anything other than school elections. In the labor-starved West, many encountered the opportunity and, perforce, the necessity of doing work and assuming responsibilities normally carried out by men. In Washington Territory this rough, working party was legitimized to a degree and for a time when women were enfranchised in 1883. Although the women's suffrage movement began in the East, voting rights were first granted in the West, a phenomenon that had much to do with the pioneering experience.

Fundamentally it was an experience of change. Although Illinois was still a frontier march in 1851, it had experienced a half-century of settlement, and possessed flourishing farms and towns connected by an ever-growing network of roads and railroads. In the nascent cities of Springfield and Chicago, there were colleges and academies, and even a rural hamlet like Cherry Grove had a "subscription school" where the Denny and Boren children received a primary and the beginnings of a secondary education.

American society in 1851 was predominantly rural, and life in Cherry Grove was fairly typical. Women's roles were familial ones: daughter, sister, wife, and mother, all dependent upon the men in their lives. A woman could exert considerable influence upon the life of the family and, indirectly, the community, but outside the home there was precious little opportunity for expression. Indeed, the idea of a woman as an independent personality, an autonomous individual, had only recently been entertained on a popular level. Such ideas surfaced first in the cities, where the familial bonds that gave the traditional roles meaning broke down, and more and more men and women were forced by necessity into autonomous lives.

But in rural America the family remained strong, and the enormous amount of labor necessary to sustain it prevented most women from even contemplating an independent role for themselves. Nevertheless, education provided many a connection with the larger world beyond home and family. Louisa Boren, Mary Ann's younger sister, developed a special love for the sciences, in particular chemistry, logic, botany, and astronomy. After finishing her schooling, she taught in the same school for several years. But valuable as they were, teaching and nursing, the only other careers open to women outside the home, were essentially extensions of women's sisterly and motherly roles, and they were not well rewarded.

The decision to pull up stakes and move west was almost always the man's. The march to the frontier was for land. When a family carved a farm from a verdant wilderness, they could make a good life for themselves, and the land could be counted on to yield surplus. As the population grew, so did the hunger for land. And as the market economy developed, the abundance of the land—its grain, its cattle, and its cotton—produced wealth.

Until the 1860s it was generally assumed that the best farmlands were those that had been forested, and that regions like the Great Plains would be forever waste. The only land west of the plains known to resemble the forestlands of the East was that mysterious realm called Oregon. If the nation was to realize its providential destiny, it had to command both coasts, and the migration to Oregon loomed large as a popular conquest. When a doctor from Ohio, David Swinson Maynard, began the journal of his trek across the continent, his first entry, "Saw a large eagle on the prairie," was much more than a casual observation.

A few white women eagerly took up pioneering. Narcissa Whitman heeded the "Macedonian cry" of the native peoples and offered herself to minister to those seeking the Word of God. Winning their souls to the national faith was seen as a preliminary to winning the land. More went because they were expected to, and for the same reasons as their men: the opportunities afforded by cheap, rich land, to get there before everyone else, for the healthful climate, for the adventure.

For most, however, the move west was a source of ambivalence and grief. The severing of the bonds to the sorority of mother, sisters, and friends, and their support, was much harder than it was for men. When Louisa Boren met her beloved friend, Pamelia Dunlap, in her father's sun-dappled garden a few hours before she was to depart, each realized they might never see each other again and were too overwhelmed to speak. To commemorate their friendship, Louisa promised to make a garden wherever it was they settled and plant the seeds of the sweetbrier rose Pamelia gave her.

Louisa was lucky to make the trip while she was young, strong, and single. Besides being pregnant, her elder sister had to take care of two little girls. Their own mother, Sarah, who had married Arthur Denny's father, John, and who was in her forties, was caring for her six-month-old daughter. Mary Boren, the wife of Carson Boren, Sarah's son, had also just given birth to a daughter.

These women left everything behind but what they could carry in their wagons; anything worth less than a dollar a pound stayed. The longing they felt for home is revealed poignantly in that for the first few weeks the women spread a white cloth on the ground and set places for the evening meal. In tents they made neat beds for each family member as they always had, and turned back the clean sheets. During the evening they made sure all undressed for bed and were given clean nightshirts. But the familial cocoon began to come apart when the wagons left the pale of settlement and entered the terrible immensity of the Great Plains. The little rituals were maintained until they crossed the Missouri River and a violent storm blew down the tents and drenched everybody. After that, the exhausted travelers tumbled into their blankets in haphazard fashion.

The only land west of the plains known to resemble the forestlands of the East was that mysterious realm called Oregon.

133

Bit by bit, home receded and life on the trail became the new reality. A style of living was shed with the cumbersome clothing. Mary Denny's shoes wore out early in the trip and she wore a pair of Indian moccasins for the remainder of the journey. Clothes turned the color of the turbid water in which they were washed. Alkali dust and grime became commonplace; hair became tangled. The discomfort of riding sidesaddle was dispensed with, and women rode the same way as the men.

Added to the dirt and discomfort was privation. Supplies were rationed; baked bread was a rarity, and women learned to mix biscuit dough by watering the flour at the top of the sack and mixing it by hand while the wagon bumped and groaned along. Decades afterwards, Mary Denny recalled with great distress the sad faces of her children when the last peaches of home, saved for a special treat long after the dried fruit gave out, were cooked into a fragrant cobbler, placed upon the wagon tongue to cool—and accidentally spilled into the sand.

Above all there was fear. The land was alien, its emptiness forbidding, and it spawned unheralded terrors. Violent storms sprang up out of nowhere, wagons could be swallowed up by quicksand, and the prairie soil could erupt with vicious ants that swarmed over children's bodies. Even more terrible was the anticipation of the savagery of its nomadic inhabitants. Anticipation was generally much greater than realization, but native men had easy fun frightening the emigrants, and they were wont to steal horses or, more alarmingly, seek to trade them for emigrant women. Near Fort Hall, a native man brought up a string of ponies to be exchanged for Louisa Boren, who was dark and attractive. Only with great difficulty was he convinced to give up his suit.

As the ordeal under the prairie sun lengthened, the conventions that had distanced the sexes fell away. In another wagon train, the Ward family had the misfortune to drive right into the midst of a native village. There, one man took an interest in a young white woman who drove a two-horse light wagon. He and his friends crowded around her as though to abduct her, but thirty-one-year-old Hester Ward joined in a rescue party, shoving the would-be abductors aside, and successfully managed to retrieve the girl. (Some years later, Hester would marry Thomas Mercer in Seattle.) Such spontaneous acts of courage on the parts of unarmed women were not uncommon. Once, when a native man reached into her wagon to seize a rifle, Mary Denny unhesitatingly took up a hatchet and swung it at his outstretched arm, which was hastily withdrawn.

Nothing was more wrenching for the pioneers than to leave their dead buried in places they knew they could never visit again.

West of Fort Hall, the Denny Party was attacked by a native band in a ravine. John Denny, the leader of the party, wanted to stand and fight, but Sarah convinced him otherwise, took the reins of their six-horse team in hand and cracked the whip, while the men took up firing positions in the wagon bed. In the last wagon, Arthur Denny seems not to have been as energetic as his mother-in-law, for while his wagon careered down the trail, Mary, in the back with her daughters and Louisa, called out for anyone to hear, "O, why don't they hurry! If I were driving I would lay on the lash!"

As their confidence grew, many women became enchanted with the unfamiliar world around them and joined more fully in the adventure. Louisa, walking or riding beside the wagon, delighted in the natural phenomena: the new plants and animals, the hot springs and bizarre mineral formations. One old pioneer recalled with wonder his chance encounter out on the plains with a beautiful, high-spirited young woman from another wagon train. She was a crack shot with a rifle from atop her horse, and with her long and magnificent head of red hair trailing behind her, they galloped madly across the dew-spangled prairie one morning, hunting antelope.

In another train a man was attempting to lead cattle across a swift stream by pulling a tethered calf through the current with a rope secured to his own waist. When the current swept man and calf downstream, a horrified observer rushed with the news to the wagon where his wife watched with her weeping children. "Well," she responded dryly, "there is plenty more of men where he came from."

The greatest danger on the trail was accident or sickness. Children fell into campfires; men were crushed beneath wagon wheels, or were thrown from their horses. Women died horribly of childbirth or its aftereffects, and whole trains fell victim to cholera. Nothing was more wrenching for the pioneers than to leave their dead buried in places they knew they could never visit again. Hard soil, few tools, and lack of time kept graves from being deep, and they often had to be obscured so that they would not be dug up by scavengers, animal and human. Emigrants were continually passing graves freshly filled or, worse, those whose contents had been turned out and devoured. Most heartbreaking were the little graves of infants and children. Roberta Watt wrote movingly of one such solitary burial:

> One pioneer woman of Seattle, of another train, tells of passing a tiny mound with a little pink sunbonnet hanging on a stick at the head of the grave. Even after the passing of so many years, our eyes are dimmed at the thought of that mother, sitting in the back of the covered wagon, watching the tiny bonnet grow smaller and smaller—like a pink anemone waving in the breeze—until at last it passed out of her sight forever.

Some women, bone-weary from exhaustion and unable to sustain such a terrible loss, ultimately went mad with grief. The Denny Party was lucky. Although Mary Denny suffered a difficult pregnancy, the worst sickness that befell them was whooping cough contracted by her daughters, it was said, when they ran to kiss their playmates goodbye while passing out of Cherry Grove.

Other Seattle pioneers had more harrowing stories to tell. In 1850, Catherine Broshears and her husband Israel left their Illinois home with several other family members and headed west. Near Fort Kearny, in what is now Wyoming, Israel Broshears and six

Mary Ann Boren (Denny): a tearful farewell to Illinois

May Arkwright Hutton

In the fall of 1910 the Washington State equal suffrage amendment was passed by a handsome majority through the combined efforts of the Washington Equal Suffrage Association, the College Women's Suffrage Clubs, the Woman's Christian Temperance Union, and May Arkwright Hutton's league, the Washington Political Equality League. Hutton's unassuming and folksy manner was key to easing passage of the bill.

From Spokane Story, *by Lucile F. Fargo. Copyright © 1950 Columbia University Press. Reprinted by permission.*

May Arkwright Hutton was Spokane's other feminine crusader. Unlike Elizabeth Gurley Flynn, she did not arrive from the Atlantic coast but from the mining camps of the Coeur d'Alenes, where, in the early 1880's, as she liked to relate, she had disembarked from "the hurricane deck of a Cayuse" to woo fortune as a cook. Concerning events prior to her arrival there and her marriage to Levi (far better known as Al) Hutton, locomotive engineer, she had little to say. . . .

"My first hobby is the suffrage question," had been May's immediate announcement upon arriving in Spokane. Before coming, she had followed with a keen sense of outrage the later vicissitudes of the movement in the state of Washington so distressfully long drawn out. Beginning in the 1850's, and intermittently thereafter, bills permitting women to vote on any and all questions had been presented in the territorial legislature. Some had become law, only to be rescinded by court decisions. Thus, in 1881, the right of suffrage extended to the women was enjoyed by them during several elections before the law was declared unconstitutional as exceeding the powers of the territorial legislature. Later, in connection with the adoption of the state constitution, a suffrage proposition was defeated by popular vote. A similar amendment was voted down in 1898. Meantime, national leaders like Susan B. Anthony and live-wire Oregon editor and suffragist Abigail Scott Duniway had periodically toured the state or appeared before the legislature. May Hutton had met and traveled with them and at the conventions she made a point of attending had eagerly absorbed campaign techniques and platform methods. . . .

In Spokane the opportunity soon came. The best-organized state movement yet was under way. It was guided by Emma Smith DeVoe, paid national organizer from Illinois, who also acted in the capacity of president of a rejuvenated Washington Equal Suffrage Association with headquarters in Seattle. May saw herself heading up the campaign east of the mountains.

She had known Mrs. DeVoe in Idaho, and at first supported her in Washington with tongue, pen, and cash. But presently the traditional East-West rivalry awoke. Even more effective in causing trouble were the violently opposed personalities of the two women. Like most of the campaign leaders both national and state, Mrs. DeVoe was cultured, well-educated, and committed to a program of education, dignified persuasion, and well-organized pressure on the state legislature looking toward submission to the voters of a constitutional amendment. To this program May gave willing lip service; but her suggestions for carrying it out tended to meet with a polite but frigid reception in Seattle. Also her well-meant initial activities. Her proposals were put down as stunts; they shrieked personal publicity.

For a time May ignored the snubs, continued her financial support of the state organization, and joined with its leaders in maintaining a suffrage lobby with headquarters in an Olympia mansion. This adventure she enjoyed to the full. It was something to write home about, and there was nothing May loved better than to write. The lobby, she reported to the Spokane press, mixed sweet reasonableness and feminine appeal with the cleverest of legislative tactics. The ladies attended the combined inaugural ball and housewarming at the Governor's mansion en masse, but "out from the secret recesses of Saratogas and suitcases we brought forth our finest apparel and brightest jewels to bedeck our most charming member for the conquest of the . . . chairman." . . .

Passage of the bill by the House was responsible, wrote May, for great elation on the part of some members of the lobby, "but the old warhorses knew bills had been passed before . . . by one branch of the legislature only to be killed by another."

May Arkwright Hutton

So the lobby went to work again, indignantly refused subtle attempts to buy them off, and emerged triumphant. Submission of the amendment to the electorate was approved by the Legislature, and the ladies returned triumphantly to kitchens and parlors to continue the fight from the home base.

others fell ill with cholera. As they lay dying, family members pleaded with passing trains for help, but none wished to linger at the scene of contagion. Shortly after Israel Broshears died, a doctor rode by on a mule and stopped for the night to help. By dawn, Israel's brother William had died, as had the mother of the widowed Catherine. The three others died shortly thereafter and, taking pity on the rest, the doctor left his own party and joined what remained of theirs. More than pity may have been at work, for the widow now possessed five yoke of oxen, two of cows, and a large and well-outfitted wagon. She was handsome besides, and the doctor, David S. Maynard, would soon propose marriage to her.

The overland route to Oregon grew more and more arduous as it approached its end, and the pioneers grew more and more exhausted. They left their homes in the spring when the prairie grass was green and sweet, but west of the 100th meridian, midway across the country, they entered what was called the Great American Desert, and in the summer's heat it was a hostile place indeed. Filled with a corrosive, alkaline dust, the air shimmered strangely, and farther west the phantasmagorical landscape added to the unreality. Oxen began to die and furniture was dumped from the wagons to lighten the load, each item another piece of cultural ballast left on the trailside. After the desert came the ascent of the Rocky Mountains. Having never seen a mountain, the Denny women—and probably the men as well—assumed that this range, "America's backbone," was simply a single ridge from whose top one might see the Pacific Ocean. They were to be surprised.

Once astride the South Pass, they waved their hats and bonnets and shouted, "Hurrah for Oregon!" They were indeed in the southeast corner of that territory, but the Willamette Valley, the true Oregon Country, still lay seven hundred miles farther to the west. They had yet to cross the sagebrush barrens of the Snake River Plain and then the most formidable barrier of them all, the Blue Mountains. Fort Hall at the eastern end of the Snake River Plain was surrounded by acres of abandoned goods and wagons left there by emigrants who had lightened their loads even more for the final push.

The morning after the Denny Party was attacked west of Fort Hall, they joined up with the wagons of John Low, his wife Lydia, and their four children. By the time the emigrants reached the Blue Mountains, they were so tired out and their nerves so frayed that camaraderie fell victim to dispute and contention. The last of the furniture, the most precious, was hurled despairingly from the straining wagons. David Maynard even cut up and shortened Catherine Broshear's wagon here to keep from killing their enfeebled animals. If there were words or exchanges of temper among the Dennys, Borens, and Lows, no one made mention of them, but it remained for Lydia Low to observe the buildup of clouds and to admonish her preoccupied husband to whip their oxen across the stream before the flood came, saving them and the rest a delay of several days when the hailstorm lashed the wagons that evening, safely corraled on the opposite bank.

It would not be the last time a woman saved the party from disaster. On August 1, after

The pioneer experience was nothing less than a baptism, a second birth, and the rest of their lives bore its imprint.

eighty-seven days of travel over two thousand miles of trails, the weary travelers reached the wild, cliff-hemmed banks of Columbia River, the "River of the West." At The Dalles, the wagons and part of their baggage—or "plunder," as it was called—were sent on over the Barlow toll road, and the families and the rest of the baggage traveled to Portland on various river vessels. As they were nearing the Cascades, the great rapids of the Columbia, the women and children on one boat, the men on the other, their great venture nearly came to an end.

To escape the wind that commonly howled down the great gorge during the day, the boats often ran at night. On the night of August 16, just above the Cascades, Louisa Boren could not sleep. The men manning the sweeps were taking long pulls from a bottle they called "Blue Ruin," and caterwauling verses from the song "Keep 'er goin' " into the resonant night air. Above the revel and the susurration of the river Louisa thought she could hear a deeper sound rising in intensity. As the boat nodded in the current, the sound grew louder, and Louisa realized they were entering the rapids. She called to the boatmen but they paid her no heed. Frantic, she woke the other women and the children, and clambered over the plunder to where the boatmen stood, to tug at their coats and beg them to head for land. "What's all the fuss about, Miss?" one responded, bemused; "there ain't no danger—keep 'er goin'!" Exasperated, she grabbed his shoulders, shook him, and shouted into his face over the din, "Oh, man! Don't you hear the falls? Look!" She shoved him to look at the leaping froth. "Turn the boat to shore! Hurry or it will be too late!" Breaking out of his stupor, the man got the others to bend their sweeps, and they managed to put the boat up on the bank, its contents drenched with spray.

A week later, the party reached their destination, Portland. Exhausted, Arthur and Mary Denny suffered a recurrence of malarial fever, the "ague," the scourge of the Midwest, that caused them to burn with fever and shake with chills on alternate days, and twelve days after their arrival, Mary gave birth to a boy. But they had survived. And like all of those who lived through the ordeal of the overland passage, they were transformed. They had helped make history. They had put themselves into the immense winnowing fan of the American land. The pioneer experience was nothing less than a baptism, a second birth, and the rest of their lives bore its imprint.

Mary Denny rapped the knuckles of a man who tried to take the fish she was cooking out of her pan.

Portland was an anticlimax. All were possessed by a desire to move on again. The patriarch, John, who inspired the trek and led it, settled in the Willamette Valley as all had intended to do, but the eldest and the youngest sons moved on. In November, members of the Denny family, the Borens, the Lows, and another family they met in Portland, the Bells, bought passage on a lumber schooner headed north.

The women do not appear to have been pleased. On a cold and rain-swept November morning, the schooner anchored off a brushy point of land. The tide was out; everything the people brought with them had to be hauled over shifting cobbles and slippery mats of

The Felker House: Seattle's first hotel and Madame Damnable's fortress

seaweed to the shore where a roofless cabin stood. One woman passenger, a Mrs. Alexander, recalled their departure:

> I remember it rained awful hard that last day—and the starch got took out of our bonnets and the wind blew, and when the women got into the rowboat to go ashore they were crying every one of 'em, and their sunbonnets with the starch took out of them went flip flap, flip flap, as they rowed off for shore, and the last glimpse I had of them was the women standing under the trees with their wet bonnets all loping down over their faces and their aprons to their eyes.

Alki was as far as they could go, and the utter remoteness, its wild unfamiliarity and rawness, shook even Arthur Denny's iron resolve. Years later in an interview he recalled his feelings at the time:

> When the goods were secured I went to look after the women, and found on my approach, that their faces were concealed. On a closer inspection I found that they were in tears, having already discovered the gravity of the situation. But I did not, for some time, discover that I had gone a step too far; in fact it was not until I became aware that my wife

and helpless children were exposed to the murderous attacks of hostile savages that it dawned upon me that I had made a desperate venture.

At Alki, twenty-four people gathered in a cabin that likely did not exceed sixteen by sixteen feet: twelve adults and twelve children, fourteen females and ten males. For several days, until a second cabin could be built, all lived in the one shelter, beneath a roof of canvas and mats, warmed by Mary Denny's stove in the center of the earth floor.

Though they had reached the end of their journey, the pioneering had only begun. The thin thread of social fabric that had become unraveled on the overland passage had now to be gathered up and laboriously rewoven, but the pattern was not the same. Once in a house, the old division of labor reasserted itself: the men working the land and the women cooking, sewing, and tending to the children. But each group had to adapt their skills to new surroundings and conditions, and their ingenuity was taxed to the limit. The men discovered that cutting timber on Puget Sound was not the same as in Illinois, and on at least one occasion the hapless fallers dropped a behemoth on one of their own cabins.

Women dealt with extraordinary privation. Mary Denny, still weak from the trip, the ague, and childbirth, was unable to nurse her infant, and there was no cow within fifty miles. She experimented—successfully—with a formula of clam nectar. Every bit of the women's sewing skill was put to work mending and adapting garments, and Mary and Louisa made quilts stuffed with local duck down to fend off the damp cold. Supplies came by canoe from the Hudson's Bay Company post at Fort Nisqually, or from Tumwater at the head of the Sound, or from the lumber schooners that brought goods up from San Francisco.

A more anxious problem was large numbers of native people—they outnumbered settlers twenty-five to one. Within a few weeks, more than one thousand had gathered at Alki, building their longhouses right next to the settlers' cabins. And if the native camp was not hostile or particularly murderous, it fairly boiled over with activity, energy, and strife. Pioneer women dealt with the native people as much as did the men, but because the men were often away working in the woods, the women's relationships were more immediate. The native people were curious about the whites, particularly the women and children, rare commodities on the Sound. They were especially fascinated with the pale skin and golden locks of Mary Denny's baby. Stoically, she allowed them to cluster around and stroke her child, but their constant, wondering murmur, "*Acha-da! Memaloose!*" ("Too bad! He die!"), must have been unnerving once the Chinook Jargon was translated for her.

The native people marveled at the homelife of the settlers, and were usually underfoot, following the women about as they tried to cook and maintain their homes. The fact that many were unclothed did not lessen the women's anxiety. No matter how ingenious the latch on the Dutch-style cabin doors, the people always managed to find a way to release it

Asa Mercer

White men feared that mixed marriages with the native women would create racial suicide. So hundreds of white men paid Asa Mercer handsomely for his matchmaking services; he returned to the East to recruit over five hundred women to Seattle. The legendary trip was more of a comedy of errors, for Mercer returned to Seattle in 1865 with a mere twenty-eight eligible women.

From "The Mercer Girls," by Walter Evans, Seattle Post-Intelligencer, *September 7, 1975. Reprinted by permission of* Seattle Post-Intelligencer.

As early as 1860, Charles Prosch, Seattle resident and publisher of the *Puget Sound Herald,* suggested bringing single girls out from the east to fill the void in the male-dominated area. He suggested that not only were wives needed, but dressmakers, laundresses, cooks and schoolteachers were in great demand.

Asa Mercer, who moved to Seattle in 1861 and was named president of the University the following year, went east on a privately-financed expedition in 1864 and succeeded in bringing 11 young ladies, ranging in age from 15 to 25, to Seattle. Their arrival here on May 16, 1864, was the signal for a gala celebration, a celebration that lasted all night. . . . Mercer's success in bringing single women to Puget Sound, most of them teachers, resulted in his unanimous election to the territorial senate. . . .

Mercer said the success of his first venture inspired the second and he hoped to bring 500 women back to the Puget Sound country with him. But the journey started out in tragedy and ended in fiasco.

"I planned to call on President Lincoln, tell him of our situation and ask him to give me a ship, coaled and manned for the voyage from New York to Seattle," Mercer said. "I was confident he would do this. Having sat upon Lincoln's lap as a five-year-old lad and listening to his funny stories and knowing the goodness of his heart, not a shadow of doubt existed in my mind as to the outcome."

However, the morning after his arrival in New York and while he was making preparations to leave for the nation's capital on the morning train, Mercer learned the President had been assassinated the night before. . . .

Initially he had a great deal of success in finding young women to join the expedition, Mercer said. He enticed them with his descriptions of the area, saying: "The climate of Washington Territory is marked by two seasons only, winter and summer. From the first day of April until the middle of November no other spot on this green earth boasts such a mild, equitable and delightful climate as does the valley of Puget Sound. Refreshing showers visit us every few weeks and all nature breathes of purity and healthfulness . . . "

Had he been able to sail immediately, there is a likelihood that he could have brought a contingent of 500 women, but the delays and an unfavorable press took their toll. . . .

Only about 100 persons, all told, were on the *Continental* when it finally left New York harbor January 16 [1866]. Thirty-six of the passengers, including 11 unmarried women, remained in San Francisco rather than continue on to Puget Sound. . . .

It is not known how many men signed a contract with Mercer for $300, for which he agreed "to bring a suitable wife of good moral character and reputation from the East to Seattle." But certainly there were some disappointed swains in the Sound country.

Miss Stevens, one of the more articulate young women in the party, said matrimony was not the first reason the "Mercer Girls" came west. "It is impossible that the lovely girls of the party should have left the East because their chances of matrimony were hopeless," she said. "One must look for some other motive. I would say it is the love of adventure, the ardor and romance of youth." . . .

Asa Mercer did not remain in Puget Sound very long after he married his Mercer Girl. He took her to Oregon, where he engaged in trade promotion; then to Texas where he became a newspaperman, and finally to Wyoming in 1892, where he had a ranch and a publication, *The Northwestern Livestock Journal.* He also wrote a

Asa Mercer

book about the Wyoming cattle war entitled, *Banditti of the Plains.* Mercer died in Buffalo, Wyoming, Aug. 10, 1917, survived by three sons, two daughters and a number of grand-children and great-grand-children. Perhaps it is fitting that the obituary carried in Seattle papers repeated the error that he had brought "several hundred brides" to the area.

and troop in. They were not above pilfering items behind a turned back or even openly. The women were scrutinized in their most private acts, and eventually they became exasperated. Mary Denny rapped the knuckles of a man who tried to take the fish she was cooking out of her pan. Lydia Low prevented another from taking a cured ham by smacking him on his bare buttocks with a spoonful of boiling mush. Farther south on the Cowlitz River, Mrs. James McAllister became outraged at the temerity of native men who thought they could steal clothing off a line when there were only "white squaws" about. Jerking up a tent pole, she went after the astonished men, beating them about their heads and shoulders until they ran off. The next day an elderly headman of the group returned to the McAllister house, apologized for the conduct of the men, and offered her husband five hundred dollars for his courageous wife.

The native people admired courage, particularly among women, and such displays were received in good humor. There were times, however, when tensions between natives and whites were such that the former could not conceal their resentment for the intruders, no matter how eager they were to trade with them. One evening there was trouble up the Duwamish River at the native encampment near Jacob Maple's homestead. Nisqually Jim came angrily to the Denny cabin where Mary Denny was standing just outside the door and Louisa just inside it. Rising up from behind the low beach bluff, he silently pointed his gun at Mary Denny, and then lowered it. She exhibited no fear, and Jim went away. When she was later asked what his motive might have been, she replied, "I suppose he did it to show that he could shoot me if he wanted to."

Despite these antagonisms, the pioneer women actively forged working relationships with the native people. If the men found native men valuable as laborers and buyers of goods, the women cultivated relationships with both the men and the women who brought game, fish, clams, roots, and berries for the settlers' pantries, as well as pitch wood to start fires and duck down to fill quilts. Louisa Boren drove a hard bargain trading cloth for potatoes. Her firmness won admirers, and for a time several native suitors leaned poles against her cabin to signify their desire to marry her. The local flora and fauna were unfamiliar ingredients in the settlers' diet, and the native women were invaluable in identifying what was edible and when. Still, considerable experiment was necessary before many local foods became acceptable to the settlers' palate. On their own, pioneer men were known to boil up skunks, and some even developed a hankering after that animal's scent.

Women's life in the Oregon Territory was profoundly affected by the Donation Land Claim Act of 1850, which brought many west in the first place. Initially, it offered 320 acres of free land to any man who would settle on it and an equal amount for his wife, in her name. Later the amount for both was reduced to 120 acres, and eventually the wife's share was eliminated, but it was the first time in history women were given the right to acquire public land.

She became known as the "sweetbriar bride" in literature, and her luxuriant gardens were an oasis of color in an otherwise somber, monochromatic world.

144

Because there was not enough good land to go around at Alki, Arthur Denny, Carson Boren, and William Bell staked claims on the east shore of Elliott Bay in February of 1852. Louisa Denny and another woman, possibly Mary Boren, hired native paddlers to take them across to the eastern shore in the early spring, taking with them a supply of food and tools and a large dog to protect them from wild animals. They landed and beat a trail through the dense underbrush to a spot the men had earlier marked. There they cut several fir logs and laid the foundation for a cabin, probably Carson Boren's at what is now the northwest corner of Second and Cherry streets. Later the men built other cabins, and in April the three famililes moved to their eastern claims, leaving the Lows and Charles Terry, another early settler, at Alki.

It took years for the pioneers to hack a settlement out of the wild, and for a long time their cabins were lost in the boreal jungle. Because claimants had to reside on their own property, the cabins were necessarily built far apart from one another. Until the great trees were felled and the floral understory beaten back, the only way to travel from cabin to cabin was along the beach. Daylight in the forest was fleeting at best, at night the darkness was profound, and in this primeval setting, the greatest burden the women had to bear was their isolation.

For a time the most isolated of the women was Lydia Low at Alki. When Charley Terry and John Low were away at the logging camps, she was left alone with her children in the original cabin and in the midst of a large native camp. Terry kept merchandise for his store he built nearby in the cabin, including a keg of whiskey, and she was terrified the native people would break in, get drunk, and kill them all. To protect herself she had her husband teach her how to use a Colt revolver, and when he was gone she would practice shooting at the sides of trees. She became a good shot, but her very public practice was probably a greater comfort to her.

Roberta Watt preserved the recollection of the pioneer woman's terrors inspired by their dark, claustrophobic isolation.

This fear of unseen foes was probably the hardest thing in her life, for what is more terrifying? The forest about her might at any time send forth a crouching beast or a stealthy Indian. The children were never allowed to wander far from the cabins and were taught to blow out the candle at any unusual sound after dark so that they might not be too easy targets for arrows. Paradoxically, the silence of the forest and the stillness of the night were filled with a thousand sounds many times magnified; the falling of a leaf, the fluttering of a bird, or the soft tread of a furry foot might be a creeping Indian. Little wonder that the pioneer woman's nerves were often tense and her ears strained as she worked with her gun by her side.

Louisa Denny's daughter Anna: born on the frontier

Such fears may have been exaggerated, but there were enough unpleasant incidents to warrant caution. Shortly after Louisa Boren and David Denny were married in January 1853, Catherine Bell walked a mile down the beach from her cabin. She had found some pheasant eggs and decided to share them with Louisa, whom she found ill in bed. While the two were talking, two native men appeared at the half-door and, after looking in awhile, departed. Later John Kanem, a Snoqualmie, told David Denny that the two planned to kill Louisa, but, seeing another white woman there, assumed their husbands were nearby.

The women's household chores were lessened somewhat by their hiring native women to do the wash or act as nursemaids to their children. The work provided the native people with a firsthand look at how a white family lived. Pioneer women coached their native peers in the sewing of unfamiliar fabrics and the use of unfamiliar tools, and in a host of ways helped them understand and adapt to the culture and society of their white neighbors on an intimate and nonthreatening basis.

But if home chores were slightly eased, the women worked in their long dresses and aprons beside the men, hacking at the forest undergrowth and dragging it and the limbs of giant trees to the ever-burning slash piles. They dug earth from around the roots of stumps, chopped at the roots, and drove the straining oxen as they pulled them out of the ground like the huge bones of prehistoric monsters. It was wearying work, but exciting, too, for they were literally changing the face of the earth.

And adding to it, too. When Louisa and David Denny finally chopped out enough of the forest for a beam of light to penetrate to the earth, she planted the seeds Pamelia Dunlap had given her and cultivated a garden. She became known as the "sweetbriar bride" in literature, and her luxuriant gardens were an oasis of color in an otherwise somber, monochromatic world. Plants that many believe wild and native were in fact brought in by pioneer women for their gardens. The Scotch broom that brightens roadsides and sandpits was brought to the Northwest by the Sisters of Notre Dame de Namur at the St. Paul Mission on the Willamette River in the 1840s. The ubiquitous dandelion was introduced by Catherine Maynard for her medicinal garden, and other pioneer woemn brought red clover and the Himalaya blackberry.

Gradually the number of women in town increased. On January 15, 1853, Catherine Broshears officially became Catherine Maynard. Five days later, she and the doctor moved to the settlement on the east shore of Elliott Bay, only recently named Seattle, where he ran the town's first store, the Seattle Exchange. Three days after that, carrying out another job as justice of the peace, Maynard married Louisa Boren and David Denny. Catherine Maynard helped run the store, and she was the town's first nurse, assisting the doctor in his work and in a small infirmary over the store.

Henry Yesler's new sawmill attracted other men to town, and some brought their families. The lawyer George McConaha and his wife, Ursula, came, and she shortly thereafter gave birth to their daughter, Eugenia, the first white child born in the town. Hillory Butler, Daniel Bagley, and Dexter Horton all brought their families in 1853, the same year Thomas Mercer brought his four daughters to his claim north of Bell's, his first wife having died when their party reached The Dalles.

The names of many of these women are often difficult to document; historians are generally content to identify them as Mrs. Daniel Bagley, Mrs. Dexter Horton, and so on. Their obscurity is not simply the result of the fact that their descendants did not write histories about them. Once the pioneers had settled and developed a community of sorts, the social conventions that had been abandoned on the journey west reasserted themselves. Women once more assumed the roles they had in the East, and once again there was little to distinguish them in history.

Still, the very nature of the frontier community prevented women from becoming entirely invisible. The creation of a town was a social as well as a physical process, and it was marked in the early years, when women were scarce, by the intermarriage of pioneer families. Of the original twenty-four who landed at Alki, ten belonged to the single Denny-Boren family. George Frye, who came in 1853, married one of Louisa Denny's daughters, and all of Thomas Mercer's daughters married Seattle men, Daniel Bagley's son Clarence being one. The same was true for many others who came to town during this period, and this closeness was to have two important effects.

First, it created a cohesive community whose members felt the town's interests were largely their own. Secondly, it put women in an influential position. Women tended not to marry outside the community, and families tended to stay longer in town than did unmarried men. So even though women represented a small part of the total population in town, they made up a considerably larger percentage of the long-term residents. They played an important role in community opinion, and when they got the vote, they became a potent political force.

Marriage to local women was one way to attain membership in the first of Seattle's elites, "Old Seattle," a group that was distinguished by its pioneering experience and its kinship connections. Had Seattle remained a village, this group would undoubtedly have calcified into the proverbial "upper crust" or reactionary old fossils, but Seattle's destiny was far more cosmopolitan, and its society was continually enriched by new people with different ideas. Old Seattle became a kind of social ballast that kept the community trim.

One of the town's most influential members arrived with her husband in November of 1853. This was Catherine Blaine, the prim and intelligent wife of Seattle's first minister, the Reverend David Blaine of the Methodist Episcopal Church, the ancestor of today's Seattle First Methodist Church. Five years earlier, in her hometown of Seneca Falls, New York, Elizabeth Cady Stanton, Lucretia Mott, and several other women organized the first women's rights convention in American history. There, Stanton submitted a resolu-

Catherine Blaine: thin-lipped propriety

tion on "the duty of the women of this country to secure to themselves the sacred right to the elective franchise." It caused great debate and barely passed, but it marked the birth of the women's suffrage movement. The ensuing storm of derision caused many supporters of suffrage to disavow the resolution, but Catherine Payne appears not to have been one of them. Still, religious work and education absorbed her energies, and in August of 1853 she married David Blaine, a young missionary who had been seeking a wife to accompany him to his field of work in distant Oregon. Two months later, they left New York on their voyage to the Northwest via the Isthmus of Panama and San Francisco.

Catherine Blaine looked the very image of thin-lipped propriety, but had a keen sense of humor, and she adapted quickly to the rigors of the frontier. A firm temperance advocate, she found it difficult to entertain an Episcopal bishop for lunch because he drank wine. In 1854, Arthur Denny submitted a bill in the first session of the Washington Territorial Legislature that would have given women the vote. It failed by a margin of one, apparently over whether the vote would have been given to the native wives of the French Canadian employees of the Hudson's Bay Company who had been duly enfranchised. Catherine Blaine was too aware of her social position as the parson's wife to give vent to her opinions in public, but she expressed herself very clearly in letters home.

> They have passed a law permitting the half-breeds to vote. It will be no difficult matter to get any number of Indians to pass as halfbreeds at election and in this way any man can get as many votes as he may desire. A question immediately arose in my mind as to whether we women ought to congratulate ourselves that we were not associated politically with such a set or whether we ought to feel aggrieved that the highest privilege that can be conferred on citizens should be proffered to the most degraded and abandoned race possible to be imagined and withheld from us.

No stranger to work, she decided against hiring a native woman to help around the house. "You talk about the stupidity of the Irish," she wrote. "You ought to have to work with one of our Indians and then you would know what these words mean." She often accompanied her husband on his walking trips to outlying settlements, and helped him cultivate their garden. She also acceded to the settlers' wishes and opened a subscription school in her house soon after their arrival, the first school in town.

Catherine Blaine was one of the first women in Seattle to work in a profession other than homemaking. Another was Mary Ann Boyer, known to locals and sailors up and down the coast as Madame Damnable. She operated a hotel and Felker House, at one time Seattle's grandest building. Besides providing meals and lodging, her establishment also employed the town's first prostitutes. By all accounts, Mary Boyer was a formidable person, possessed of an extraordinary temper and the ability to fill the air with streams of the

Catherine Blaine was one of the first women in Seattle to work in a profession other than homemaking.

most pungent billingsgate—though no one seems to have complained about the service. In a painfully remote community where each day's hard labor could subside into one long monotony, even the slightest eccentricity was bread to a famished people, and Mary Boyer was a thick loaf. The Felker House was the setting for court sessions, and when the Madame presented the prosecutor with a steep bill for room and board, he huffily demanded a receipt. Fixing him with a baleful glance she instructed him to wait while she went to get one. Returning with an armful of stovewood, she advanced menacingly. "You want a receipt, do you?" she thundered, ripping the air with a fusillade of curses. "Well, here's your receipt! I'll larn you for asking me for a receipt!" Racing the wood to the door, the prosecutor never ventured to ask for a receipt again, nor did anyone else. She was a figure on which one with literary pretensions could hone his skill. In one fabulous story she successfully holds off an entire ship's company and a detachment of marines for several days, with a raking fire of stones, wood chips, and terrifying invective, supported by a pack of snarling dogs.

Although they lived within sight of each other, no reference to Mary Boyer appears in any of Catherine Blaine's letters, nor is it likely a woman of Blaine's self-conscious temperament would have admitted her existence in polite discourse. To a well-bred woman from the East, particularly a parson's wife, propriety meant a great deal; to acknowledge was to accept, and Catherine Blaine's zeal for reform was fortified by a considerable measure of intolerance. If she did not take aim at Mary Boyer, it was because she was hunting a different animal.

Few things absorbed her attention more when she lived in Seattle than sexual commerce between the races. She judged the native people to be noxious creatures and was appalled that men would cohabit with squaws. It was a common theme during the time that such liaisons degraded white men, yet it was generally the native women who suffered most. A sad proof was the marriage of Betsy, daughter of Angeline and granddaughter of Chief Seattle, to a pioneer named Foster. David Maynard had married them, but according to Catherine, Foster had bought Betsy from Angeline and her husband. Foster was wont to get drunk and beat Betsy, though after she bore him a son he treated her more kindly. They moved into town, but one morning, before he left for work, they argued, and after he left, she hanged herself from a rafter inside their house.

Foster asked David Blaine if he would read the prayers over her grave, but he refused, protesting that to do so would give sanction to their mode of living. Instead, her native kin conducted her to the town's burial ground, and after they laid her to rest they chanted a dirge for her in her house. Catherine Blaine wrote out the tale in response to her young nephew who had asked her to write about the Indians. Through her pen it became an object lesson on the evils of miscegenation. Roberta Watt echoed her grandparents' somewhat more tolerant view: "As the story came down to us who were children of the pioneers, sympathy was always with Betsy, and her drunken husband was condemned...." Foster eventually left the area, leaving his infant son, Joe Foster, in the care of Angeline.

It may be possible to glimpse in this episode the beginnings of a change that was to dominate women's social and political agenda in subsequent decades. The pioneer view was relatively pragmatic, a rough-hewn kind of tolerance that sought to judge situations by their own merits. In Catherine Blaine's words, we can observe the arrival of a more modern, didactic view of things. It was modern in the sense that it distrusted sentiment and sympathy and fixed its gaze on the larger idea of social reform for the common good. In time, the drive for legal and political equality for women, a logical outcome of pioneering, would be wedded to the drive for social reform, and that union was to wreak havoc on both.

Any examination of this period must include the native women of Seattle. All historical accounts emphasize the small number of women in town, but this must be judged by the fact that native women are never included in the count. Until the late 1860s, pioneer Seattle was a white enclave in a much larger native village whose numbers fluctuated during the year from one hundred to five hundred people. Probably half of these were women, and many of them found employment at the settlers' households just as the men found work at Yesler's mill. Native women virtually ran the dogfish oil industry in town, rendering the shark livers in cauldrons and skimming the pungent oil from the boiling surface with ladles. This was used to grease the skids of the skid roads that directed logs down from the outlying hills to the bay. A number of native women were married to or lived with white workers, but such liaisons were rarely regarded as legitimate.

The lives of native women are even more obscure than their white sisters', and only a few like Angeline or Betsy are known in any detail. Sally, a relative of Chief Seattle and the wife of Dick, the headman of an important village in what is now West Seattle, was the child of Kitsap, a powerful Suquamish headman who was of the same generation as Seattle's father. A noblewoman who maintained an aristocratic bearing, she would not work like Angeline did or trade with the settlers' wives, but often brought them pails of berries as gifts. On Sundays she could be found worshipping at the Methodist Episcopal Church in a bonnet and shawl and with conspicuous piety.

As native-white troubles increased after the Treaty of Point Elliott, many native people suffered the agony of loyalties divided between their own persecuted people and settlers whom they had come to trust. One early historian, Frederic Grant, wrote feelingly of Sally's predicament as it was described to him by Sally's friend, Abbie Holgate Hanford.

> Once, in the summer of 1855, she came, and after wearily bringing in her customary present, sat down on the floor and began to sob and weep.
> "What is it, Sally?"
> It was all very bad—a shadow of the coming war.

She had learned, she said, from the white men of the great Socalee Tyee, the white man's God, and her heart was toward the white man and the white man's God. But her heart was also toward her people, yet the heart of her people was against the white man; and the white man would be against her people and kill them. Her heart was very sick.

When the Indian War came, women were singled out by both sides as special targets. The raiders who massacred the White River settlers in October 1855, made a point of killing the women to heighten the terror of their acts. On the white side, volunteers, particularly those who participated in the butcheries on Meshall Creek near Eatonville and the Grande Ronde River in eastern Oregon, seemed to take special delight in raping and mutilating their female victims. For both sides, dead women were the ultimate insult.

The war was a terrible blow to Seattle: population declined, and the economy stagnated for a decade. Many left with their families for safer parts, among them David and Catherine Blaine and their son who took up residence in Portland.

The years between the landing at Alki and the Indian War were regarded as the pioneering period by early residents, and after about ten years of languor, Seattle finally began to experience the growth for which its founders had so fervently wished. The accomplishments won by its men and women during the pioneering period were not negated by the war and its aftermath, but it was to be a long time before they bore fruit.

Gradually the familial, semirural society of Old Seattle evolved into a more complex and stratified community, and the freedom and social mobility that had characterized the pioneer period was replaced by a class system. Increasingly, the restrictions that marked social roles farther east began to manifest themselves in Seattle.

The latter half of the 1860s saw the arrival of Seattle's first modest boom, and the community began its slow but ever accelerating rise toward its emergence as the regional metropolis. The pioneer period had passed, but most of the pioneer women remained and, in league with new arrivals, they worked as they always had to nurture and invigorate the life of their community. They had given up too much and labored too long and hard to accept anything less than an equal role in directing its affairs. Neither could many stand by to see the town, their town, dominated by groups that undermined the values for which they had walked through the valley, the plains, the mountains, and the deserts of death to realize. Through their efforts the concept of the frontier was enlarged to include social and political as well as geographical vistas. ▪

All excerpts from *Four Wagons West*, by Roberta Frye Watt used by permission of Binford and Mort.

VISIONARIES

COMING
OF AGE:
1900–1945

VISIONARIES

For all its earlier history, Washington in 1900 was still far removed from the rest of the world. Ninety years ago, the world was probably more familiar with Tibet. By 1945, Washington had become an important part of the world and its unfolding history.

With a population barely over the half-million mark in 1900, Washington was one of the most isolated states in the Union. To come by sea from the East Coast, one still followed the track of Gray and Vancouver around the horn of South America, a voyage that normally took three months. One could still travel by wagon over the Oregon Trail. The quickest way to get here was by train, and since the completion of the first transcontinental railroad, the Northern Pacific, in 1883, most had entered the region in Pullman cars.

Heading west from Minneapolis in 1900 on Jim Hill's Great Northern Railroad, the newest of the transcontinental roads, the traveler would have passed through parts of North Dakota and Montana still identifiable as frontier even though the government had declared that closed a decade earlier. Coming down from the Bitterroot Mountains into Idaho, one passed through the Coeur d'Alene mining district. This district received the bulk of its supplies from the youthful city of Spokane, emerging as the hub of the Inland Empire from the pines along the Spokane River. Spokane had become the nerve center for lumbering, mining, agricultural, and commercial interests in the area, and its most important ganglia, the banks, wore impressive armors of brick and granite.

Once out of town and the surrounding forests, however, the train entered a region only recently put under the plow, and there were still long stretches of quivering bunchgrass and gray-green sage. Dryland farmers took a gamble putting a crop in the dusty soil of the Big Bend country. Experience advised that they did so only every second year, for a crop failure here meant four years without income.

At Wenatchee the train rumbled on a trestle across the Columbia. The grand river was still much as it was in the days of the fur trade, wild and unfettered with no dams in its way and few bridges to cross it. In the river valley one could see the first ranks of fruit trees marching up the tawny slopes before the train entered the rupestrine folds of the Cascades. Down the western slope, the timber rushing darkly past the windows broke periodically

Washington had joined the world in a bang, and dramatically come of age.

155

into clearings holding farms or lumber camps where logs lay heaped at sidings awaiting transport to tidewater. And then, smothering the first tang of saltwater, were the rank plumes of Everett, clamoring to earn its claim as "The City of Smokestacks." From Everett the train moved out along the shore of Puget Sound, its waters furrowed by steamers trailing palls of smoke. The air was redolent of evergreen and the stink of tideflats. Passing through smoldering Ballard, the rails angled past Lake Union and entered the boxy sprawl of Seattle, portal of the North Pacific and rich in gold.

The land had been transformed. Washington had become a busy place, complicated and not especially happy. In the old days a man and his wife could come west and claim as much as 640 acres, if they would only work to improve it. Soon, however, the best lands were claimed, and those who followed the pioneers had to buy land at increasingly higher prices or work in the mills, camps, and mines for the money to buy it. The pioneers earned a pretty penny for their land, but soon the profits from speculation were reserved to those who had access to small fortunes. A pioneer might open a store, operate a forge, or dig a mine, but if he wanted to develop his holding, he needed capital. Eventually, ownership of the region's wealth passed into the hands of the few who had it, many of whom lived outside the region. The promise of the land appeared to shrink.

In the 1870s, the government that granted pioneers their homesteads granted the Northern Pacific millions of acres of land along its proposed right-of-way to attract investors. In 1900, a syndicate led by the St. Paul timber magnate Frederick Weyerhaeuser bought nine hundred thousand timbered acres of the land grant for six dollars an acre. In aggregate the acreage amounted to an area comparable in size to Pend Oreille County. By 1914 the Weyerhaeuser Timber Company had accumulated lands in the state which exceeded the size of King County, were larger than several European countries and eastern states, and quite possibly worth more too. It made its owners wealthy and powerful men.

Much of this wealth was kept within families, producing dynasties some of whose members, such as Roland Hartley and Norton Clapp, are described in this section. They might become amiable benefactors, but their wealth represented an imbalance in society. The rustic egalitarian society of the pioneers fractionated into a class system composed of many laborers, fewer middle-class professionals, and very few owners and managers.

As the West industrialized, young men came out to find work, to support themselves, and—if they could find wives—have families. The disparity between the numbers of men and women was not set right until the 1920s. When times were good, jobs went begging; pay was high, and it did not take a great deal to buy a lot, a house, even a small farm and become a proprietor and family man. Among the middle class, the rising value of land and an expanding economy enabled the energetic to advance to the front of their professions and lead comfortable lives. When times were good, class lines could be crossed with a hop, but when they were bad, they yawned as impassable chasms.

For all its smoke and noise, Washington's economy was fragile, and bad times were never far away. With millions of acres in its hands, the Northern Pacific still went bankrupt. Major industries such as lumber, mining, and fishing were labor intensive and expensive to run, and the prodigal abundance of the state's resources could be a curse as well as a blessing since with improved technology it was fatally easy to glut the markets. Mill and mine owners and cannery operators depended upon slim profit margins in the best of times, but when the national economy went into one of its periodic slumps and markets dried up, companies went broke. The inevitable might be postponed by lowering prices and slashing wages, but in the end the unemployed tramped the woods and roads, families scrimped, and children went hungry.

Out of this distress came Washington's powerful labor movement and its radical reputation given voice by figures such as Anna Louise Strong, who called for revolution. Our train rider out of Minneapolis passed through the Coeur d'Alene mining district at the height of labor unrest; radicals had blown up buildings and the governor had to call out troops to put down insurrection. There was trouble in the mines at Roslyn and Newcastle and in the forests and factories. In 1916 the state would recoil at the horror of the Everett Massacre; in 1919 there would be more bloodshed at Centralia and a general strike in Seattle.

This was the most tumultuous period in the state's labor history; there would be sporadic outbreaks of violence in the decades following, but nothing so severe. Part of this was due to such labor leaders as Dave Beck, who created unions so powerful that businessmen had to negotiate with them or face crippling strikes, but no less important was the fact of Washington's increasingly developed economy. The older extractive industries gave way to manufacturing and retail, and in the Boeing Aircraft Company, the state led the way into an entirely new field of enterprise.

Boeing was as much a product as it was a leader in this more developed economy. It depended upon the availability of aluminum produced in smelters along the Columbia that were powered by electricity generated by dams at Bonneville, Rock Island, and Grand Coulee. The dams also made possible the irrigation of thousands of acres in the Big Bend country, eliminating the greater part of the farmers' gamble when they sowed their crop. Washington's agriculture developed along with her industries, narrowing the gap between classes and making a decent life available to many.

Coming of age can be a difficult process, and Washington's adolescence was as rawboned as any. To many, the pollutants belching from the stacks of its mill towns were the exhalation of progress, but to others they cast a deadening pall. In sullen drizzle, heavy with coal smoke and the reek of its port, Seattle was an unlikely Emerald City. In Bertrand Collins's *Rome Express*, the heroine, Greta Pendrick, could only think of her return from Europe to "Chinook" as a mistake.

These people beheld their visions from an older landscape, and their dreams created new landmarks.

157

Yet, its very isolation and rough, unmolded character were exactly what attracted many to Washington. Vernon Louis Parrington could find Seattle an acceptable refuge, a fertile middle ground between the dry earth of his Kansas boyhood and the thin air of Harvard. To Henry Suzzallo, Washington was malleable clay, ready to receive the imprint of progress. Like Parrington, he had grown up in poverty and had gone east to make his way in the academic world. As president of the University of Washington, Suzzallo harnessed his abundant energies and ambitions to the task of pulling a mediocre school out of the provincial mire. But he was blocked in his path by Roland Hartley, a product of one of those lumber dynasties whose members were determined to destroy anyone who attempted to pry their fingers from their trove. The Suzzallo-Hartley battle is revealing of a parochialism that is one of the more noisome fruits of isolation, an attitude that surfaces whenever a brash newcomer with new ideas runs up against those who have been here a year or two longer and like things just as they are.

Fortunately, Washington was still large enough and new enough that the gloomy denouement of this episode did not become typical. Rough and depressing as Seattle may have been to Bertrand Collins, his model for Greta Pendrick, Guendolen Plestcheeff, came back to it in high spirits after a sojourn in Europe and made it her home. The very pace of change here seemed to retard the development of limiting preconceptions. Historically a man's town, Seattle elected Bertha Landes mayor in 1926, the first woman mayor of a large American city. A dispirited music teacher, Nellie Cornish, could found a school that went on to achieve international acclaim. An heiress to wealth, Dorothy Stimson Bullitt, could command that wealth and use it innovatively in the field of broadcasting. The place changed rapidly, but the ways it did so did not cut too deeply into the fresh earth. Others could cut new channels of their own.

These people beheld their visions from an older landscape, and their dreams created new landmarks. Although Henry Suzzallo's proud tower was never built, his great library was, symbolizing the soul of his university of a thousand years. The Wobbly dream also failed, but their ideas for better working conditions took root.

The greatest landmark of vision is that greatest of dams, Grand Coulee, worthy of the older landscape in its majestic scale. In his book *The Dam,* in the section aptly entitled "Credo," Murray Morgan tells of a fellow student at the University of Washington in 1935, a philosophy major named Carl, who explained why he was quitting college to work on the dam: "There are parts of our culture that stink with phoniness. But we can do some wonderful things too. That dam is one of them. If our generation has anything good to offer history, it's that dam. Why, the thing is going to be completely useful. It's going to be a working pyramid. I just want to help build it."

It was the kind of sentiment that inspired Woody Guthrie to sing for the Bonneville Power Administration. He was the troubadour of the new creators, the simple working people who, like Coyote, were transforming the land, making it habitable. His songs of hope came to a dry land at a hard time. His hopeful mood was shared by many here during the Great Depression. In a temperate clime, surrounded by rich earth and deep rivers, it is difficult to believe in stark failure. Privation brings one closer to the land and puts one in a philosophical mood. "No longer a slave of ambition," sang Ivar Haglund, "I laugh at the world and its shams, and think of my happy condition surrounded by acres of clams." His innocent enthusiasm was but one aspect of a flurry of artistic creativity that gained international reputations for painters such as Morris Graves, Kenneth Callahan, and Mark Tobey.

The creative flux of those years was overwhelmed by the war. The mood of innocence was swept away by the punishing rips of prosperity and destruction, excitement and horror. Drawn ever more intimately into the national embrace, Washington shared in the power and purpose, along with a growing sense of anxiety. Farther down the great river from Grand Coulee, another landmark was rising at Hanford, feeding off the dam's energy. Its enigmatic aspect and monstrous power were a prefiguration of the future. Whatever innocence remained as the war drew to its climax vanished in a flash when the plutonium manufactured in the desert released its energy over Nagasaki. Washington had joined the world in a bang, and dramatically come of age. ◼

David M. Buerge

Suzzallo's imaginary library
crowned by a 310-foot bell tower
that was never built

160

THE UW'S PROUD TOWER

HENRY SUZZALLO (1875–1933)

DAVID M. BUERGE

When Governor Isaac Stevens prompted the first Territorial Legislature to memorialize Congress for a university land grant, he added another plum to the contest over placement of public institutions. The chief prize was believed to be the capital, but Methodist minister Daniel Bagley convinced the citizens of Seattle that the university would ultimately prove a greater benefit. In 1860 the decisions were made: Olympia got the capital, Walla Walla the penitentiary, and Seattle the university.

Immediately the townsmen set to work building the great white box atop a small rise—Denny's Knoll—north of the town's commercial heart, where the Olympic Hotel now stands. For more than thirty years it remained one of the town's more prominent structures and a symbol of its pride. In September 1861 its doors opened to its first classes, but if the Territory had little problem producing politicians and criminals, university students were another matter. That fall the university's enrollment consisted of one freshman; the rest were elementary and secondary students. It did not award its first degree until 1876, and its classes did not become exclusively postsecondary until 1895.

But growth accelerated as Seattle boomed. By 1895 the university had left the wooden box atop Denny's Knoll and moved into the solid stone elegance of a new building, Denny Hall, on an extensive campus overlooking Union Bay. The development of a college of mines and engineering and a law and graduate school marked the emergence of a true university, and by the middle of the new century's first decade, the number of registered students exceeded one thousand. Moreover, the development of a marine science station at Friday Harbor in the San Juan Islands and a department of Oriental history and literature was evidence of the university's increasing involvement in the region's maturing sense of itself and its position on the rim of an emergent Pacific community.

This first flowering of the university coincided with Seattle's emergence as the dominant city in the Pacific Northwest. In 1909 the city's celebration of the Alaska, Yukon, and Pacific Exposition on the campus announced its arrival to the world and its confident expectation of greater things to come. By association, the university was making similar claims.

The first flowering of the university coincided with Seattle's emergence as the dominant city in the Pacific Northwest.

161

Once the Alaska, Yukon, and Pacific Exposition closed, many of its buildings were used by the growing university, but most of them deteriorated rapidly. By 1914, with the university's student population nearing three thousand, many buildings had been condemned, and classes were held in overcrowded rooms, attics, and a motley collection of shacks. This decaying physical plant, however, was not the only problem generated by growth.

When it had resided in its white box atop Denny's Knoll, the university was a homespun institution whose poverty appealed to the tender instincts of Seattle's citizens. The fact that it was primarily a grade school strengthened sentimental ties, for many residents received their education there. Presidents of the university like Daniel Bagley and George Whitworth, who were also churchmen, were revered; teachers like Asa Mercer and Edmond Meany, who went out into the lumber camps in search of scholars, were regarded with genuine affection. It was not uncommon to see a trustee like Arthur Denny patching the roof or a president fitting a new stovepipe.

As the school grew, however, it shed its precollege classes and the gap between it and the rest of the community necessarily widened. As students from elsewhere in the state arrived in increasing numbers, Seattle's complement declined; by 1914, it represented little more than half of the student body. The natural estrangement of town and gown grew. Then, at the turn of the century, other factors aggravated the problem.

The Northwest's prospects for the future seemed limitless, and the university's supporters felt it was on the eve of greatness.

In the early years, it had been natural to look upon the university as Seattle's school. Even as it grew more independent of the city, that view remained in force in outlying areas, especially east of the mountains. The establishment of a state college and agricultural school at Pullman and normal schools at Cheney, Ellensburg, and Bellingham created rivals for state funds, and the university's appetite for public funds became a cause for complaint. As the populist spirit of the times matured into progressivism, rural groups increasingly looked upon cities as threats to their well-being. In the cities, too, discord grew between groups of citizens and what they believed to be corrupt business interests and municipal officials. There were calls for reform, and the university was a focus of debate.

The university first came under attack when it sought to negotiate a dispute with the Northern Pacific Railroad over a right-of-way along the southern margin of the campus. Both parties were satisfied with the agreement they reached, but critics called it a sellout to a hated corporation that historically had been Seattle's nemesis. Another issue involved the university's original ten-acre site downtown, which had increased in value as the city grew around it. Rather than sell the land, the board of regents decided to lease it, and they agreed to a system of fixed rents to encourage building by the lessee. When land values soared, the rents came to appear ridiculously low, and it was not hard to imagine the regents in cahoots with the builders. Heeding their critics, the regents sought to maximize income by selling agricultural land in Eastern Washington at full value. This only added fuel to the

162

fire, because farmers believed they should be able to buy state land at low prices. The regents were now accused of being greedy speculators.

On the other hand, spirited arguments for progressive reform emanating from professors such as J. Allen Smith drew charges that the university was teaching socialism. There were calls for Smith's dismissal. Noisy political debate on campus and student requests to hear candidates for public office prompted the regents to ban such speakers. President Thomas Kane was forced to ban a speaker he had previously invited, Joe Smith, candidate for Seattle City Council in 1912. Whereupon a group of students threatened to invite him to speak on their own. In turn, Kane promised to expel any students who were involved.

The students later revenged themselves. They protested the acceptance of a gift of chimes from Alden Blethen, a regent and editor of *The Seattle Times*. Blethen's cordial relationship with Seattle's chief of police during an administration tolerant of gambling and prostitution was at issue, so the students claimed that accepting a gift from such a figure would tarnish the university's image. They threatened to publish a petition in the *The Daily* protesting the gift on the day of the acceptance ceremony. Kane had the presses shut down, but the students printed their petition off-campus and distributed it anyway.

Such antics turned critics purple, dismayed the university's friends, and saddled Kane with the reputation of being too weak to discipline his students. In 1913, the board called for his resignation. He refused, accusing the board of being reactionary; they in turn accused him of being inadequate for the job. The sorry business played loudly in the press. After charges of politics were hurled back and forth, on January 1, 1914, Kane was dismissed.

It was obvious that the university was at a critical juncture and that strong leadership would be required to restore morale and give it direction. Newly elected Governor Ernest Lister replaced four of the regents he regarded as too political and directed the reconstituted body to search for a new president.

Between 1900 and 1914, Washington's population jumped from 518,000 to 1,408,000. Apart from a brief recession in 1907, its economy boomed. The Northwest's prospects for the future seemed limitless, and the university's supporters felt it was on the eve of greatness. But who could they get to come to a tatty campus to take the reins of an institution that had been roundly accused of being at once a tool of big business and a hotbed of socialism? Considerable excitement attended the arrival in Seattle of University of Chicago Dean James Angell, but after a long hard look at the campus and its problems, he took the next train east. At this point Frank Graves, who had been president before Kane, lobbied hard for the man he thought best for the job, a bright young professor of education at Columbia University, Henry Suzzallo.

Anthony Henry Suzzallo was an outstanding example of that ideal of the time, the self-made man. His father, Peter Suzzallo, had been born of Italo-Slavic parents in Ragusa

(Dubrovnik) on the Dalmatian Coast of what is now Yugoslavia. He went to sea at an early age and landed in New York in time to hear of the 1849 gold rush. Signing on as a mate on a ship bound for California, Peter arrived there in 1852 and started mining in Placerville with some success. Eventually he returned to Ragusa and married a distant cousin, whom he brought back to Placerville. Illness and poverty forced them to move to San Jose where, on August 22, 1875, a son was born, christened Anthony Henry. He was the eighth of nine children, of whom only four survived to adulthood.

He was a frail child, prone to illness. His record of work at public schools was distinctive for its lack of promise. Two San Jose clothiers, Emil and Jesse Levy, employed him as a clerk in their store and encouraged him to get an education beyond high school. With money they loaned him, he entered the state normal school and graduated two years later in 1895. In the fall of that year he entered Leland Stanford Jr. University, which had opened its doors in Palo Alto ten years before.

At Stanford, Suzzallo came into his own, drinking deeply of the spirit of academic life and progressive reform. To pay tuition, he took a year off in 1896 to teach in a rural school in Alviso, where he was fired when he refused to join a political club. At Stanford, law and medicine beckoned, but his own experience of the tribulations of education, and the opportunities it offered people like himself inspired him to go further in that field. Working part-time as a principal of an elementary school in Alameda, he graduated from Stanford in 1899 and worked toward an advanced degree at Teachers College at Columbia.

From principal he became the deputy superintendent of San Francisco's public schools, and his work at Columbia was of such promise that he was made a lecturer before he received his doctorate in 1902. After that, he moved with ease to professorships at Stanford, Yale, and Columbia. He became the protégé and friend of Columbia's president, Nicholas Murray Butler.

This part of Suzzallo's life could have been written by Horatio Alger. Its progress was as neat as an ascending curve, but its apparent simplicity is deceptive. Along the way, Suzzallo made some important breaks in his life. Politically he went his own way, becoming a liberal Republican while his father remained an ardent Democrat. Born and raised a Roman Catholic, he left the church and later attended Episcopal services regularly, although he never became a member of that body. He became a Mason and attained high rank in the Scottish Rite, southern jurisdiction. The move from Roman Catholicism to Freemasonry might suggest a desire to distance himself from an uncomfortable immigrant background, but it more accurately reflects his profound faith in the secular institutions that had rescued him from an anonymous poverty. Toward the end of his life he addressed a luncheon of the Pilgrims Society in London and caught his listeners' attention by telling them that he did not have a drop of Anglo-Saxon blood in his body. He added that he did not have a thought in his mind nor any aspiration in his heart that came from other than the

Education was a kind of fourth branch of government by which the other three could be made more effective.

Anglo-Saxon tradition transmitted through the American system of public education.

Typical of his time, and rather like John Dewey, he developed an extremely broad view of education, seeing it as far more than simply a means of training students to be useful citizens. Through it, he believed the economic, social, religious, and political disputes troubling the nation could be mediated and the life of the Republic made harmonious. Education was a kind of fourth branch of government by which the other three could be made more effective.

Such ideas put him in the vanguard of educational and social reform, and his eloquence made him a natural spokesman for progressive ideas, as well as a popular lecturer and teacher. In 1907, friends urged him to run for mayor of San Francisco as a reform candidate, but he was unable to satisfy the residency requirements. In 1909 Columbia's President Butler appointed him to the new chair of educational sociology, and he occupied a seat in the faculty of political science as well. His work brought him into national prominence, and it is said that President William Howard Taft would have appointed him to the US Commission of Education had Taft not needed to appoint a Southerner to that post.

In 1912, he married Edith Moore, a young Chicago woman who was the niece of a prominent Seattle family, and a frequent visitor to this city. When it became known that the University of Washington was looking for a new president, he and Edith signaled their interest. On Frank Graves's suggestion, the board sent a committee to Columbia to interview Suzzallo. Butler was loath to lose a man he counted among the best and most promising of his faculty, but he endorsed Suzzallo warmly. "I assume," he wrote, "that it will be the ambition of the people of the state of Washington to strengthen and support their university in a way that will make it the center of enlightenment, culture, and intellectual leadership for the whole Northwest country. To guide and inspire the university in such an undertaking, no man in America seems to me to possess more qualities, both in mind and of character, that are of the first rank and of the highest importance, than Professor Suzzallo."

Word of the board's action met with local approval save for a few, like the editor of the *Seattle Sun,* who worried that Suzzallo's connections with Columbia might carry a desire to impose eastern ideas on a western institution, and he urged the regents to "investigate him a bit." However, in May the board invited Suzzallo to Seattle for further interviews, and he spent the evening of the 17th at the New Washington Hotel in conference with Governor Lister and the assembled regents. The next morning they announced his unanimous election as the sixteenth president of the University of Washington.

The regents congratulated themselves on getting such a man, and Suzzallo returned their enthusiasm. "I have caught the Washington spirit," he said in his first remarks to the university. "It is the opportunity...to develop a university which will take its place with the best in the country, and which will stand, backed by the community, a vigorous and

President Suzzallo: qualities of the first rank.

responsive expression of the community's desire for the best in life, that has brought me here," he said later.

In the bright spell cast by these words, Suzzallo appeared on campus on July 7, 1915, in the company of Professors Edwin Stevens and John Condon and, tray in hand, took his place in the lunch line at commons. He was short, stocky, and dark, but his unprepossessing build failed to mask the impression of energy. "The thin black hair," wrote an observer from the *Seattle Post-Intelligencer,* "stands high above a prominent forehead. The small gray-green eyes are very much alive. Dr. Suzzallo speaks in a somewhat high-pitched voice of light quality and he answers and propounds theories without hesitation. His manner gives the impression of conviction without dogmatism."

He discovered an institution rife with problems and riven with bitter factional disputes. He moved quickly to end the rancor, resolving the disputes he could and inviting those who would not be reconciled to leave. Within a few weeks observers noted a marked improvement in the university's temper.

Next, he worked to improve the school's image within the state. Within a few months he had traveled eight thousand miles and delivered about one hundred speeches. "In this state," he said at one stop, "I find there is a great shortage of the razor clam. There is also a great shortage of the Dungeness crab.... There has also been a great shortage of sockeye salmon on the Puget Sound.... What does this suggest? The need of a school of fisheries, equipped to investigate the causes for this shortage by biological research and by other lines of investigation, and to equip men for one of the greatest industries of Washington."

This emphasis upon serving the economic needs of the state was bold for its time. Within a year he called for the creation of schools of fisheries, marine engineering, commerce and business, and architecture. He also worked to educate the public that the university was not like a business or a government body: its members could not be treated like employees or subjected to the vagaries of public opinion. While a university could be administered with an eye to fiscal economy, a different kind of economy obtained in the realm of intellect and creativity. At the same time, he appointed advisory boards made up of representatives from the outside world who would act as consultants to keep the various departments in touch with the community's needs.

With great enthusiasm, he inaugurated a long-overdue building program. A master plan drawn up by the distinguished local architectural firm of Bebb and Gould described a vast new campus made up of two quadrangles, one devoted to the schools of home economics, commerce, the liberal arts, and education, and the other to natural sciences. The axes of these quadrangles, angled like the wings of a great bird in flight, met at a central point in a wide plaza dominated by a monumental library, a cathedral of learning.

The breadth and depth of Suzzallo's vision was captured in the phrase with which he liked to describe his institution, "the university of a thousand years." It conjured an image of magnificent aspect. Perhaps because of that, challenges to its ambitious scale were not long in coming.

The first came from the state college at Pullman. In Suzzallo's mind the university rested at the pinnacle of the state's educational system with all other schools subservient to it. Pullman was an agricultural school; it might become a great agricultural school, but it should aspire to no more than that. "If we are going to have two institutions of higher education," he wrote regent William Perkins shortly before his arrival in Seattle, "we do not want two mediocre colleges; rather one great university and one great vocational college for agriculture." The people at Pullman thought differently. Their school derived from an act of Congress different from the one that had given birth to the University of Washington, and they saw no reason why the eastern part of the state should not have an institution equal to that in the western part.

In November of 1916 Ernest O. Holland, a student and roommate of Suzzallo's at Columbia, was made president of Washington State College. It was hoped that the friendship the two men shared would help ease the longstanding dispute. At first, such hopes seemed reasonable as the two men publicly proclaimed their mutual affection. At a luncheon given in their honor at Seattle's College Club in February 1917, Suzzallo addressed the problem posed by the American spirit of individualism in the West. In its extreme form he believed it degenerated into provincialism. "Thus we have selfish rivalries. Cities, institutions, and individuals have quarreled and cherished small jealousies. Cooperative endeavor should succeed provincialism, and the two state institutions should lead the way."

Very soon it became clear to Holland that Suzzallo's idea of cooperative endeavor was simply for Holland to agree with him. To Suzzallo duplication of curriculum was wasteful and inefficient. Pullman was an agricultural school; if its students wanted other classes they could come to the university. Of course, this view was resisted fiercely at Pullman and by Eastern Washington newspapers. The battle was soon joined over who would teach what.

A legislative survey committee determined that, given the differences in historical and economic development between East and West and the needs of each region, duplication of curriculum was not necessarily inefficient. It concluded that liberal arts courses should continue to be taught at Pullman, but that the school of engineering Pullman coveted should remain at the university. The survey's report was a compromise that both schools accepted, but it did little to quell the debate. Suzzallo kept up the pressure against duplication by appealing to the governor, but the report was written into law with only minor changes. Things remained almost precisely where they were before the issue blew up, but the animosity between the two schools burgeoned. The presidents who had once been warm friends now eyed each other coldly as adversaries. For Suzzallo this falling-out

The rabid anti-unionists...never forgave Suzzallo for the role he played in their defeat. Suzzallo now had his most dangerous enemy.

167

Vernon L. Parrington

Vernon Louis Parrington, an obscure but devoted English professor at the University of Washington from 1908 to 1929, influenced a generation with his Pulitzer Prize-winning, three-volume work, Main Currents in American Thought. *It climaxed an era's social and cultural thought, particularly in the frontier universities.*

From Seattle Past to Present, *by Roger Sale. Copyright © 1976 University of Washington Press. Reprinted by permission.*

Vernon L. Parrington's background . . . was poor and bleak, from what he taught a whole generation to call the Middle Border. [His school was] Emporia College in Kansas. . . . His roots lie in a populist time. . . . After leaving Emporia College he went to Harvard and he hated and feared it in ways that shaped him as much as his home had done. He went back to Emporia, taught for three years, then moved to the University of Oklahoma, where he was the English department and football coach. He was fired in 1908 because, apparently, Parrington had been to Harvard, and those who fired him hated and feared it as much as he did. It is hard to think where he could have gone, since he had had enough of Eastern pretensions and Midwest know-nothings, other than the odd, quiet school in Seattle, the University of Washington. It was barely a college then, and decidedly not the university it was later to become. In 1908 Seattle was still populist enough to give Parrington a sense that he knew where he was, but it was a city too, though unlike the behemoths of power that had put him off in the East.

From all accounts, the University of Washington in Parrington's time was a pleasant, benign, and undemanding place. College was still possible only for a quite small number of students, the faculty tended to be badly underpaid, and most departments consisted of one or two professors and a large number of young instructors. One probably should not inquire into how good the university was, though it is clear that a few faculty and a few students were very good indeed. The children of the wealthy did not go to the University of Washington, but to Stanford or the East, yet there were enough who came from more modest or more intellectually ambitious families to keep the university growing until the middle-class high schools began feeding students there as a matter of course.

It was perfect for Parrington. He had plenty of privacy and time to work on his own, he had enough good and demanding students, he had an intellectual atmosphere, insofar as it existed at all, that was liberal, radical, progressive—the words are never accurate when lifted from their normal political moorings and placed down on a college campus. Parrington taught carefully and quietly but in ways students found exciting, filled with the conviction that the students had been raised in a tradition wider and deeper than they knew: Jefferson above all, but Jackson and Lincoln and John Ruskin and William Morris as well. . . . It was partisan teaching, because Parrington could not but convey his contempt for the powerful, the

Eastern, the Federalist. But his kind of partisanship could instill a desire to know the great patterns of a culture, the good and the bad, in order to enforce the partisanship with warmth, learning, taste, humanity. The result was not just a generation of adoring students—Edmond Meany had had that just by being narrowly chauvinistic about the Northwest—but *Main Currents in American Thought*, written over Parrington's years in Seattle, three volumes published between 1927 and 1930, just before and after he died, and still the best book to come out of this city.

It happened that the publication of Parrington's book coincided with the arrival of the liberal intellectuals of the thirties, so that it gained a quick and powerful popularity throughout the country. "His book now stands at the center of our thought about America" wrote Lionel Trilling in a very critical assessment in 1940. As often happens, however, the book that stands in one decade at the center of thought stands in succeeding decades very much in the shadows. *Main Currents in American Thought* will never again be read as it was by the eager liberal young throughout America in the thirties, but it is a vastly better work than its subsequent detractors have tried to realize, one that people who share none of Parring-

ton's bias can read with admiration and pleasure. . . .

Most of what is best . . . is in his second volume. The first, dealing with colonial America, comes too close to Parrington's prejudices and covers a period he did not know enough about, while the third, dealing with America after the Civil War, is sadly unfinished, though often superb in places, as in the section on the Great Barbeque that ends with a typical excellent gallery of folk heroes: Ulysses S. Grant, Jay Cooke, and Charles A. Dana. Later, after the decade of the thirties when Parrington was adored, critics began complaining that he had slighted the "literature" of America because he was vitally engaged in political and social issues. Thus, it was often alleged, he gives only two pages to Poe and a dozen to William Gilmore Simms, a minor and almost totally unread literary figure in pre-Civil War Charleston. Parrington did this not because he thought Simms was six times better than Poe, but because Simms can tell us more about the ante-bellum South; put Simms together with Alexander Stephens and John C. Calhoun and we see the "mind of the South" moving from Virginia to South Carolina at a time when Charleston could hold sway only briefly over the more rapacious spirits that were turning the gulf states into the Black Belt.

Vernon Parrington

When Parrington has the feel of a period in his fingertips, then every trait of every individual portrait, every event, every ironic play can be both an individual characteristic and a generalization for a whole period and region. . . . For thirty and forty pages at a stretch Parrington gathers and folds a variety of figures and groups in a way that is both clarifying and grand. Parrington's own aloof and somewhat stubbornly naïve temperament is expressed in a prose that is always American in its idiom and English neoclassic—like Gibbon's or Johnson's—in its structure. His critics have not produced anything as good to take its place. . . .

Seattle in the years of Parrington's maturity still had its own populist tradition, a thwarted one to be sure, but more vital than it could still be farther east. Seattle was not mean and drab, but lush, green, quiet, filled with beautiful houses and invitations to formality and seclusion. That it was static may have been part of its appeal. Here he could settle, and feel both the thwarted romanticism of his frontier populist belief and the quiet formality of his temperament gain strength, direction, flexible life. He lived on 19th Avenue Northeast, in a comfortable house a few blocks from the university, where he worked on his garden and in his greenhouse and on his great book all in the same spirit, quietly and slowly. He did not need what Seattle could not have given him: the abrasiveness or constant challenge of one's peers, the visible signs of an older culture. But from here he could look backward into American history and find more than a buttress for his own thwarted populism, though he could find that too. . . .

There is no evidence that Parrington was in any sense a city person, but only a city like this one could have provided what he then needed. He did not enter into the populist arena as did his friend and colleague J. Allen Smith, but he needed the sense that such an arena might still exist. He did not need a city of high culture because he was both too shy and too much a frontier man to be susceptible to that kind of thing. Grand, formal, quiet, stubborn, naïve—it seems an odd combination of qualities, but they express, at least in part, both Parrington and the Seattle he found a home in. Had he been born or come to Seattle earlier, the city undoubtedly would have been too crude and bustling; had he been born or come much later, the city undoubtedly would have seemed too much the creature of capitalistic industrialism. But in the static period in between, Parrington came and found himself, and quietly wrote his book.

crat Ben Hill was the man who had it in for Henry Suzzallo and who served to focus the discontent against him and his university: Republican Roland Hill Hartley.

Both men resembled one another more than either would have cared to admit. Like Suzzallo, Hartley had been born into poverty as the son of an itinerant Baptist preacher in rural New Brunswick, Canada. In the 1870s Hartley and his elder brothers moved to Brainerd, Minnesota, where he worked briefly as a hotel clerk, a cookee in a lumber camp doing odd jobs, and then as a logger hauling timber with a horse team and working rafts of logs down the Mississippi to St. Paul during the spring flood. In the summer months he hired out as a laborer and teamster on the North Dakota prairies. His schooling was spotty, but he was able at one point to attend business classes in a Minneapolis academy. He did well enough to become secretary to the mayor of Brainerd, getting his first taste of politics. The hunger never left him.

Eventually, Hartley became bookkeeper and private secretary to David Clough, a timberman-politician in Minnesota who eventually became its governor. In 1888 he married Clough's daughter, Nina. Hartley was a short, spare man with hard blue eyes and thin hair. Later photographs of him display a stern if studied rectitude, not without vanity. During an 1898 Chippewa uprising, he was the governor's representative to a military detachment that got involved in a shoot-out with some drunken Chipeweyan men. Hartley ever after styled himself Colonel and formed a lifelong fascination for the military.

In 1900 Clough moved west to establish a lumber mill at Everett, a town boomed into existence by his St. Paul friend and associate, James Hill. Hartley accompanied the migration of Clough's relatives and in-laws to Hill's barony and helped manage Clough's interests. He did it well enough so that Clough's company became the Clough-Hartley Company. They built the largest shingle mill in Everett, a feudal bastion in which bloody-handed workers toiled like serfs and unions were anathema.

In 1909 Hartley ran for mayor of Everett and won. His tempestuous single term was marked by his slashing the municipal budget after the town voted out saloons—the major source of revenue—in a spasm of moral righteousness. He was elected state representative in 1914—Hartley was now fifty—and he worked to reduce government and expenditures, themes dear to his heart and sure vote-getters in hard times. On one occasion he sought to amend an appropriations bill in order to prevent the university, which he labeled a hotbed of socialism, from teaching political economy. This amendment was easily dismissed by the university's friends, but Hartley did not forget. He may not have been present in Everett on the day the *Verona* tried to land at the city dock, but his response to the massacre seems to have been a hardening of his attitudes against unions. In 1916 he ran for governor on the single issue of the open shop and industrial freedom; he lost, but not by much.

During the war the Colonel enlisted in the National Guard, obtained a commission as captain in the regular army, and would have been sent to Europe had not peace spoiled his

Governor Hartley: a tide of popular discontent with government

plans. In 1920 he ran once more for governor on a broader platform than before, hoping to capitalize on the fears generated by the labor unrest that erupted in the Seattle General Strike and the Centralia Massacre the year before, but he lost again. During this period, however, he made his first million from a lucrative contract stripping trees off the Tulalip Indian Reservation. In *Mill Town,* the historian Norman Clark records a wonderful story Hartley himself told about walking into David Clough's office, slapping the evidence of his fortune down on his desk, and shouting, "There, you old son-of-a-bitch, I told you I could do it!"

The third time Hartley ran for governor, 1924, he won. Part of his success was owing to his colorful sense of style. Hartley was never one to use a fly swatter when a sledge hammer was available. He gleefully branded his opponents "goggle-eyed jackasses," "bolshevists," or—a favorite—"pusillanimous blatherskites." Hartley also drew support from the profound discontent that troubled the state and nation in the early 1920s. War, the Russian Revolution, economic crisis, and social change had come so fast and struck with such force that the national mood of confidence before the war was replaced by a sense of fear, individual helplessness, and an anger that lashed out at real or imagined dangers. The 1924 campaign was a particularly grotesque one in Washington politics, with the Ku Klux Klan fomenting hatred against Catholics, Jews, foreigners, and blacks. Government intervention in private life during the war had fostered a backlash. Even though many of the national programs disappeared with the armistice, many still believed government was too big and unwieldy. Sensible of this, Hartley ran as the Republican nominee on a platform in which he promised to carry out a "business survey" of state government to cut out waste and reduce taxes.

His inaugural address told his audience what they wanted to hear:

> We may as well face the fact, and face it squarely, that we are too much governed. The agencies of government have been multiplied, their ramifications extended, their powers enlarged, and their sphere widened until the whole system is top-heavy. We are drifting into a dangerous and insidious paternalism, submerging the self-reliance of the citizen, and weakening the responsibility and stifling the initiative of the individual. We suffer not from too little legislation, but from too much. We need fewer enactments and more repeals. We need to call a halt until the majority's pocketbook catches up with the desires and clamor of the minorities for more government and increased appropriations.

Cheers greeted these words. Groans attended his call to reduce the money spent on highways or his plan to end state support of reclamation and seed loans to farmers, or his caustic denunciation of child welfare programs and education. But while legislators, reformers, and editors fumed, Hartley enjoyed real public support.

As Hartley drove his program through the Legislature, he moved toward a confrontation with the university and its president, whom he came to regard, with some reason, as a political threat. As a leading figure in the circles of Progressive reform and an exemplar of cosmopolitan values, Suzzallo had the support of many urban leaders. But his style and the very nature of his institution, grossly characterized as a haven for reds, foreigners, and sneering fops, rendered him suspect in rural areas and among ordinary folk. In 1925 more than 55 percent of the state's people lived in urban areas, but the shift in population from a rural to an urban base had been recent. Those in the eastern and southwestern parts of the state feared and resented the loss of their power and influence to the cities of Puget Sound.

Duncan Dunn, a Yakima sheepherder, state representative, and regent of Washington State College, was Hartley's campaign manager and political confidant. With the help of Washington State College President Ernest Holland, whose bitter resentment of Suzzallo found a receptive ear in the new governor, Dunn labored mightily to cut the university's appropriations in the 1925 Legislature. Dunn's activities drew a protest from Suzzallo, who accused him in a speech of being the worst enemy of the university in the state. Dunn responded by calling attention to Suzzallo's annual salary of eighteen thousand dollars, the highest paid anyone in the state and almost double Holland's.

Well regarded as he was in academic circles, Suzzallo now had little public following.

The politically wise saw Suzzallo's attack on Dunn as an oblique attack on Hartley, and Dunn's reply as Hartley's response. Concerned over where this might lead, the university's regents adopted a resolution of confidence in their president, asserting that the "continuance of Dr. Suzzallo in the presidency of the university is a matter of vital importance to the state as well as the university." Dunn attacked Suzzallo again in a speech to Grangers in Yakima. He stroked the rurals' xenophobia by alluding to the president's Italian background, identifying him at one point as "Knight of the Garter of Italy or some other title of nobility by virtue of the favor of the fascist government of Italy."

Spurred by the attack, Suzzallo undertook a statewide tour before the November legislative session, to rally the university's supporters. He openly attacked the administration, putting him squarely against the governor. Hartley responded by refusing to attend and speak at the celebration honoring Suzzallo's tenth year as president.

On November 10, Hartley introduced a measure to the Legislature that produced audible gasps of amazement. He had long been displeased by the practice of the university and other schools of constantly approaching the Legislature with requests for special—and in his mind, hefty—appropriations. To him, such practice was inefficient and evidence of budgetary indiscipline. To solve the problem he proposed to abolish the boards of regents of the University of Washington, Washington State College, and the normal schools, to abolish the state Board of Education, and to pass a constitutional amendment abolishing the office of state superintendent of schools. He would replace these with a single superboard made up of his appointees, who would manage the budgets of all state educational institutions from kindergarten to graduate school. "Don't misunderstand me," he sought to assure the stunned legislators. "I am not contending for less education, but for more education for less money."

The proposal was met with outrage from educators as well as legislators. It was quickly tabled. It split the Republican party, but its public support would not evaporate. In a revolt actively supported by the university, the Legislature voted to increase funding for higher education. Hartley vetoed the bill; the veto was overridden. In this massive repudiation, Hartley believed he saw Suzzallo's fine hand.

The university was now under the microscope, its long march to distinction called into question. As evidence of the university's overindulgence, its critics pointed to Suzzallo's salary, which he received in spite of the fact that the faculty was underpaid. Critics also pointed to the library, now nearing completion. It was extravagant, they claimed, for the university to use tax money to build that big empty room: what was needed was space to store books.

If Hartley could not get his superboard from the Legislature, he resolved to get it by gaining control of the various educational boards. The only resistance he encountered in this effort lay in Seattle. He overcame it in stages, first by filling in vacancies on the University of Washington's board of regents with his own men. A second opportunity came when he forbade the regents to spend the monies the Legislature had appropriated over his veto. When the university board voted to spend it anyway, the governor dismissed two regents and replaced them with his supporters.

The massacre of the regents was done on May 5, 1926. That evening, Hartley sought to head off the outcry by delivering a ninety-minute tirade against educational "waste and extravagance" to a crowd of two thousand people in Seattle's Eagles Auditorium, the largest auditorium of the day. Following the speech, a group of anti-Hartley people met at the Olympic Hotel to organize a recall campaign.

Hartley's dismissals were challenged in court but ruled legal. In late May the governor attacked Suzzallo in an interview in Spokane. "Mr. Suzzallo does not know me. I was born in America and not Italy, and if they want to put the head of this state government at the University of Washington, all right. But until then it will remain at Olympia, one man will run it, and that will be me." The "Dago Interview," as it was dubbed, embarrassed Hartley. Editors also delighted in pointing out that Hartley had been born in Canada whereas Suzzallo had been born in California.

The university regents meanwhile voted to keep the president for another year at the same salary. Then, in August, Hartley replaced another member, which gave him a majority. In September a dispute between the state and the University Alumni Association led Hartley to suspect that this body was being organized by Suzzallo as a quasi-political party to work against him, possibly in league with the recall movement. The war was now total. On October 4, 1926, the Hartley-dominated regents voted to demand Suzzallo's resignation. He refused, and he was dismissed.

That evening, several faculty members gathered in the president's house to plan the next move. Outside, three thousand students demonstrated support and called for a strike if he were not reinstated. To quiet the situation, Suzzallo stepped out onto the porch, thanked the students for their support, and asked them not to strike. "I deeply appreciate your coming here tonight. I have devoted my life to the upbuilding of the university and I want you to devote your lives to it. Don't do anything that will reflect discredit on your alma mater. If you are tempted to do anything that might injure the university, I advise you to go to the front of our library building. Look up at it. That will be your inspiration to refrain from doing anything that might reflect on it."

Suzzallo hoped that public outrage over his dismissal and the recall movement would work to reverse the regents' action. But his battle with Hartley had reached the point where it was one he could not win. Well regarded as he was in academic circles, Suzzallo now had little public following. He could count on little support from organized labor, less from business, and real antagonism in the rural areas. Even among his own faculty, few came forward to help. According to the late Theresa McMahon, professor of economics at the university, a vote to support Suzzallo in a faculty meeting died for the lack of a second.

His dismissal, however, was not a personal disaster. Suzzallo became a kind of educational hero, especially in New York, where he was named chairman of the board of trustees and later president of the Carnegie Foundation for the Advancement of Teaching. A 1927–28 trip to Europe became a triumph, during which he and his work were lavishly praised. More honors followed. In 1929, President Hoover named Suzzallo executive director of the National Advisory Committee on Education. His influence on the formation of public policy on education remained strong.

As fate would have it, it was on a trip in connection with his duties with the Carnegie Foundation that Suzzallo stopped in Seattle on September 18, 1933. He felt tired, and when his wife requested that he be examined by a physician, he was rushed to Seattle General Hospital. During the evening of September 24 he suffered a heart attack, and early the next morning he died at age fifty-eight. Eulogies were printed in newspapers and journals across the nation.

Roland Hartley survived the recall. Somewhat chastened by the experience, he was easily re-elected governor in 1928. If the library became Suzzallo's monument, the massive capital at Olympia was Hartley's. It was an ironic one, given his loud denunciations of government expenditures, but one in which he took genuine pride. His second term in office coincided with the onset of the Great Depression, when his platitudinous bombast about individual initiative and the dangers of too much legislation eventually infuriated the electorate. He ran again in 1932 and was swept away in the Roosevelt landslide. A try in

1936—his *sixth* gubernatorial campaign—ended similarly. He retired from public life adamant, irascible, and forgotten. After he died in Seattle in 1952, his children ensured his anonymity by destroying his personal papers.

The real victim in the drama was the University of Washington, which Suzzallo's dismissal left a shambles. The destruction of higher education in Washington was the subject of essays in *The New York Times* and *The Nation,* and the university became for years a pariah among schools. When a search was made for Suzzallo's successor, no one of stature stepped forward, apparently not even Ernest Holland. The regents finally appointed Matthew Spencer, dean of the journalism department and a Hartley supporter. For eight years the university endured direct rule from the governor's office. The faculty's acceptance of the situation was eased by a comfortable pay raise, and most found Spencer a more approachable figure than Suzzallo. But the damage would last for decades.

During the Depression and World War II, the school mostly concerned itself with survival. While a few other premier state universities were growing, assembling first-rate scholars, and establishing their hold in the hearts of the state voters, the University of Washington was still recovering from the near-fatal blow Hartley had delivered. It is heartbreaking to consider what the school might have grown into without all those missed decades. In time, of course, it regained its aspirations, particularly with the arrival of Charles Odegaard; but then the catch-up game ran into the periodic cutbacks imposed by the state's economic cycles.

Perhaps Suzzallo had pushed too fast and too soon; perhaps he had foolishly neglected to build a base of political support. But his vision and his contributions were not forgotten. After his death the library that came to symbolize all those aspirations was named in his honor. In 1935, Bebb and Gould's south wing was completed, and a modern concrete-and-glass addition finished the triangle in 1963.

And the work goes on. The university plans a massive final addition to the library, now one of the nation's largest. The new addition, by the distinguished national architect Edward Larabee Barnes, will be costly and impressive—recalling the days when Suzzallo's own architectural standards became a state issue. And included in the design is a small tower that evokes the memory of the bell tower that was to be the crowning element of Suzzallo's library. The great bell tower itself was never to be built. It remains only an idea of what might have been. ◄█

EMPEROR OF THE SKIES:

THE BOEINGS (1881–)

CYNTHIA H. WILSON

In 1932 the infant Charles Lindberg III was kidnapped and murdered, and America's most prominent families were terrified. Many of them took extraordinary measures to protect their heirs from the same fate. Four years later in Tacoma, kidnappers grabbed nine-year-old George Weyerhaeuser as he walked home from school, left him handcuffed for days in a pit in the woods, dragged him across the state in the trunk of a car, and locked him in a closet. Though the child was ransomed and survived unharmed, his ordeal drove the fears of the wealthy in the Pacific Northwest toward paranoia. None were immune, including William E. Boeing, Sr., who for a time during those years secluded his only son aboard the *Taconite*, the family's palatial yacht moored just off Seattle. Young Bill, Jr., heir-apparent to one of the world's largest aircraft-industry fortunes, was allowed ashore only to go to school; after class, he was whisked back to his floating keep. "He didn't spend his whole childhood in isolation," recalls an acquaintance, "but I believe that period of his life left him with a permanent feeling that the world is made up of guards and suspicious strangers, rather than friends."

In some ways William Edward Boeing, Jr., never has come out of hiding. Though he now heads the family that bears Seattle's most visible name, Boeing has never maintained the high public profile America has come to expect of its leading families. "His name is magic," muses a local politician, "but the luster comes from the outside, from people who expect the Boeings of this generation to wield the same kind of power and leadership his father did. If anything, these Boeings have hidden from prominence." A shy, private, almost self-effacing man, Bill Boeing, Jr., has been phenomenally successful at keeping his name, his activities, and his family off the pages of the local press. He has achieved this near anonymity by avoiding the overt civic and social leadership that would have attracted publicity, by insisting that his family do the same (especially shielding his son William E. Boeing III), and by deflecting attempts to draw him out with the polite but impenetrable reserve that has earned him the sobriquet, "Seattle's own Howard Hughes."

But Howard Hughes was more than a recluse—and Bill Boeing, Jr., is far more than the elusive son of a famous father. Behind the opaque public persona there operates a

Behind the public persona there operates a philanthropist, a shrewd financial investor, and a ubiquitous power.

179

philanthropist, a shrewd financial investor, and what foes as well as friends agree is a nearly ubiquitous power in conservative Republican politics. For years Boeing has played a key if unelected role in the course of King County and Washington State government. With the rise to eminence of his old friend Ronald Reagan, Boeing's political advice is regularly sought in national circles as well. To this extent, he has taken his place within the tradition of other prominent families, but he has done it, says a political observer, "quietly, with an air of self-doubt." And Boeing has camouflaged his business activities and philanthropy so carefully behind a screen of surrogates and foundations that a host of legends portray him—falsely—as the hidden manipulator of nearly every large corporation in Seattle.

What lies behind Bill Boeing, Jr.'s ambivalent relation to prominence? Why does he have no connection to the company that bears his name? How, in fact, do any of the heirs of Bill Boeing, Sr.—the dynamic entrepreneur who pioneered a major industry and brought prosperity to Seattle—cope with the burdens of their birthright?

Bill Boeing, Sr., may have faced the same question himself, for he was born, in 1881, the son of a wealthy Michigan timber baron. His answer was to strike out on his own. At the age of twenty-one, Boeing withdrew from Yale's Sheffield Scientific School without completing his engineering degree. He left what could have been a comfortable niche in the family iron-ore and timber empire to start his own, independent timber operation near Grays Harbor. The business flourished and Boeing moved to Seattle in 1908, where his wealth and courtly bearing soon won him a prominent social position.

Wealth also allowed him to take his "hobbies" very seriously. At a 1910 air meet in California, he contracted a fascination with flying that would never leave him. Five years later, the thirty-four-year-old Boeing learned to fly at Glenn Martin's aviation school in Los Angeles, where he bought his first aircraft, a Martin hydroplane. On the homeward flight from Los Angeles, he miscalculated the approach to Puget Sound, hit the water too hard, and sheared off his new toy's pontoons. When he discovered that spare parts would not reach Seattle for months, the engineer in Boeing decided that he could build his own pontoons, and, with the help of his friend G. Conrad Westervelt, design a better airplane as well. That was the first Boeing aircraft. Christened the "B & W Seaplane," it was assembled in 1916 on the shores of Lake Union by shipwrights, carpenters, cabinetmakers, and seamstresses using piano wires, linen, and light spruce. It was also the beginning of the Pacific Aero Products Company, the rich dilettante's hobby shop that would burgeon into the world's largest aircraft manufacturing firm.

The company found its first home on the Duwamish River in the Red Barn, a two-story wooden shipyard Boeing had bought "for ten dollars and other considerations" to have his yacht built in. Despite the public's indifference to aviation, Boeing envisioned his fledgling shop as much more than a spare-parts factory, and he immediately began acting as a self-anointed pioneer who would arouse the country to the airborne future he believed lay

First flight at Meadow's Race Track in 1910 (now site of Museum of Flight); Airmail pioneers Eddie Hubbard and Bill Boeing, Sr.; Boeing's historic "Red Barn"; Yacht *Taconite*, once the family's floating keep

181

ahead. Concerned that America was not responding to the exigencies of World War I, for example, Boeing flew over Seattle dropping missile-shaped leaflets advocating military preparedness. Coincidentally, the war gave his company its first big orders—military contracts for training, observation, attack, and pursuit planes. By 1917, the name was changed to The Boeing Airplane Company.

The end of the war, however, nearly brought the end of the company. During the postwar doldrums, Boeing kept his factory open by manufacturing speedboats and bedroom furniture and by meeting the payroll out of his own pocket. It was a bleak time, but instead of giving up, Boeing took off in an uncharted direction: international airmail. In 1919, he and pilot Eddie Hubbard made the first private, international airmail flight from Vancouver, British Columbia, to Seattle in a Boeing-built B-1 Flying Boat.

Aggressive engineering of new plane designs brought an increase in military contracts and kept the factory busy during the early 1920s, but it was Boeing's even more aggressive development of airmail and passenger-flight routes that opened aviation to the public. With characteristic boldness, Boeing won a contract in 1927 to carry the mail between Chicago and San Francisco, then the longest such route in the world; he did it by undercutting competitive bids so severely that his firm had to put up a five-hundred-thousand-dollar bid guaranteeing that it would complete the contract. It did—by mass-producing twenty-five new Model 40 planes designed to withstand the distance and freezing temperatures the route would involve. That also marked the beginning of commercial passenger flights over long distances. The airmail venture became Boeing Air Transport; by 1928, the passenger operation would be called United Air Lines. Its classy flights offered tea service, embossed napkins, restrooms, and the first stewardesses, who also were registered nurses.

Nothing, it seemed, could stop Bill Boeing, who in photographs from that period resembles a taller, bolder Franklin Roosevelt. By 1930 his empire had expanded with the acquisition of several other aviation manufacturers, including Pratt & Whitney, Sikorsky, Standard Steel and Propeller, and Chance Vought. Bill Boeing actively embraced his role as an industry leader. "I've tried to make the men around me feel, as I do, that we are embarked as pioneers upon a new science and industry in which our problems are so new and unusual that it behooves no one to dismiss any novel idea with the statement that it can't be done," he said in a rare interview. "We are trustees of a veritable revolution that is taking place once more in the economic, social, and political fabric with the advent of this new speed medium."

But in 1934, Boeing's eighteen years in the industry—years he felt were "filled with real romance"—ended in bitterness. A wave of federal antitrust legislation prohibited airmail carriers from associating with aircraft manufacturers. As a result, the United Aircraft and Transportation Company was split into Pratt & Whitney, United Air Lines, and the Boeing Aircraft Company. At about the same time, the government canceled the airmail contracts it had with private airlines and gave the routes to the army. After twelve army pilots crashed in two months, the contracts were hastily returned to the airlines, but because Boeing had attended route-planning meetings before the Postmaster General, his company was ruled ineligible to recover its routes. Disgusted by the government's intrusions, Boeing resigned from the company. Ironically, that was the same year in which he received the prestigious Daniel Guggenheim Medal for his "pioneering achievements in aircraft manufacturing and air transport."

He never again took an active role in managing the company he had founded; ultimately he would sell off his entire financial interest in it. Retiring, however, did not mean leaving behind the seriousness with which he pursued his "hobbies." When he was not at the enormous family estate in The Highlands where he lived with his wife, Bertha, his son, and two stepsons, Boeing was aboard his elaborately equipped yacht. There he invented the polar-bear hair fly that came to be used widely for salmon fishing in the north. An expert fly fisherman, he would cruise to British Columbia and southwest Alaska, then fly to remote inland lakes to fish. At the end of each day, he would don a coat and tie for dinner.

By 1936, Boeing had built a stable of thoroughbred horses and raced them all over the country, following them about in his private plane. He also was interested in cattle breeding; after donating his Highlands estate to Children's Orthopedic Hospital, he and his wife settled on their three-hundred-acre Aldarra Farms near Fall City, where he developed new methods of cultivating farmlands and improved the beef stock of the region. Even as he grew older, Boeing would inspect his working farm on foot, trailed by the pet Pekingese he called General Motors.

Boeing died aboard the *Taconite* of a heart attack in 1956 at the age of seventy-four. He left behind what was thought to be the largest financial estate in the history of King County. Though the bulk of the $22 million estate consisted of blue-chip stocks and bonds (none in The Boeing Company), it also included extensive real-estate holdings, $2 million in cash, and a $10,000 collection of books. Equally significant for his descendants, Seattle's first Boeing left a legacy of inventiveness, imagination, and sheer energy unsurpassed by any other family patriarch in the Pacific Northwest.

The role Boeing played for years was "financial godfather" to King County's conservative Republicans.

Because they are so reticent, it is difficult to gauge just how the heirs of that legacy have defined their own lives in relation to it. Bill Boeing, Jr., declines to speak for himself. But people who know him describe him as a man who inherited his father's gracious manners and moral fiber but little of his father's drive or ambition. In 1938, Boeing, Jr., was sent to the Webb School in Claremont, California, one of the most exclusive private boys' schools in the country. After graduating in 1942, Boeing, Jr., had to cancel his plans to attend the Boeing School of Aviation; the army took over the school, but sinus trouble kept the young Boeing out of the army. Instead, he studied for a time at the Boeing Aircraft Engineering School, then worked in the company's motion-picture department making

Bill Boeing, Jr: a hidden
prominence

films of tours through the Boeing plant. He also worked for the King County Sheriff's office. Years later he would tell a *Journal-American* reporter that the company "was something [my father] achieved and built and I didn't feel I was going to add much to it, and so I became interested in other areas."

On his father's death, management of the Boeing family's financial interest fell to Bill Boeing, Jr. Many of these assets were included in a family-trust corporation called Mesabi Western, which held radio and television stations in Portland, Seattle, Longview, and Boise. According to Jim Davidson, a former employee at the Boise station, the family pulled out of broadcasting in 1977 in order to consolidate its holdings into real estate and industrial development around the Seattle area. Today, Boeing, Jr., heads the Tri-Land Corporation, a real-estate investment firm. Until 1979 he was a director of Seattle's Pacific National Bank, and he is still a regent at Seattle University, a school his financial aid helped to save from ruin during the recession-plagued early seventies. And he frequently makes other anonymous, philanthropic contributions through the Seattle Foundation.

But Boeing's deepest interest, say those who know him, is his unique brand of "shadow politics." "He's been a figure on the outside of life in many ways," muses a former Republican campaign manager, "but politics, the way he plays it, gives him a way to be important and listened to without being visible."

The role Boeing played for years was "financial godfather" to King County's conservative Republicans, underwriting their debts in return for access and consultation. He was the chief financial supporter of Charles O. Carroll, county prosecutor from 1948 to 1970, at a time when county politics were largely controlled from the courthouse. In the early sixties, he extended his support to Ken Rogstad, whom Boeing helped to elect as county chairman of the party. Those were years of bitter struggle for control between Republican conservatives and Dan Evans moderates; Rogstad's victory added to the bitterness, and Boeing's close alliance to the Rogstad camp earned him a reputation for divisiveness.

But other party insiders say that by 1970, Boeing grew tired of financing the endless conflict and began to shift his attention to national politics. He had been drawn to Ronald Reagan since the mid-sixties, entertained the California governor on the Boeing yacht when Reagan came to Seattle, and moved easily into the group of wealthy businessmen who constitute Reagan's oldest friends and advisers: California moguls Holmes Tuttle and Justin Dart, and Boeing's own old pal, the Colorado beer magnate Joseph Coors. Boeing was Reagan's finance chairman for Washington State during the 1980 election, was near the top of the national finance committee, and helped select Reagan-administration appointees in this region.

Boeing's increasing involvement with national concerns did not mean that his influence over county and state matters waned. His interests remained keen in property taxes, what Boeing considers to be the excessive power of the teachers' lobby in the legislature, and land use.

The land-use issue, in fact, propelled the reclusive Boeing into the most public leadership role of his life. Angered over King County's growth-management plan, Boeing founded a group called Property Owners of Washington (POW) in 1980 to oppose what he considered unfair government restrictions to the rights of private citizens to develop their property on the plateau east of Lake Sammamish. Aldarra Farms, the Boeing family's three-hundred-acre cattle ranch is there, and so is Bill Boeing's own fifty-six-acre B & B farm, with its baseball diamond "Boeing Field." But even his opponents on the issue admit that Boeing's interest goes beyond himself and his own property. To defend the principle of private property rights, Boeing even appeared in person at county hearings.

That was highly uncharacteristic. Except for his chairmanship of POW, Bill Boeing, Jr., had never taken an activist role in any cause. His personal style makes this tall, pleasant-looking man a sort of misfit among the powerful. "I was shocked when I first met him," recalls a Republican fund raiser. "Walking into a meeting of [prominent men] is like entering a tank full of barracudas. They're competitive, aggressive, and if you don't have your act together, they'll nail you to the wall. But Boeing isn't like that at all. He makes himself fade into the wall."

Within his immediate family, Boeing's authority is not in question. His daughters portray him as the loving head of a close-knit clan, consisting of his wife, Marcella, Gretchen Boeing-Clough, Mary Rademaker, Susan Hayward, and William Boeing III. "At home he was just Dad, and he roughhoused with us just like 'normal' dads do," laughs Mary, a six-foot-tall blonde who remembers her father dragging all four children across the floor with two clinging to each ankle. Mary describes her mother as "a go-ahead person," an energetic woman. Gretchen calls their mother, a former stewardess and nurse, "a basic mom." In fact, the Boeings grew up just about as children of any other wealthy Seattle family might: paying slightly stiff Sunday-afternoon visits to their grandparents' estate, yachting, attending private schools, coming out as debutantes. While their brother was sent to Overlake, the three girls went to Forest Ridge for a Catholic education (their mother is Catholic). There, according to Mary, the nondescript uniforms helped to blur social distinctions.

Except for Susan, whom Mary dubs "the best cook in San Francisco," the clan has stayed in Seattle, living in an arc along Lake Washington. "We're all different," says Mary, whom the family calls Bebe. "Susan is the social bee, heavy into lacquer and the Chinese stuff. Gretchen is the artist. Billy has Dad's dry wit and is a very private person. I'm the mother of the group."

Children are Mary Rademaker's first love. She dropped out of Seattle University during her freshman year and worked first at Fircrest School, then at the Seattle Children's

A replica of Bill Boeing's first plane, the B & W, is among the suspended exhibits.

185

Tex Johnston

The Boeing test pilot's surprise exhibition flight at the 1957 Gold Cup Races took place above the nation's leading engineers and scientists. His famous stunt didn't necessarily accelerate the sales of Boeing's 700-series jets. But soon the big gamble in the flight was matched by the extraordinary gamble Boeing won in launching commercial jets.

In the morning [of August 7, 1955] Tex Johnston and his co-pilot, Jim Gannett, cranked up the beautiful Dash Eighty and set out to do a little testing. Aboard were Bill Whitehead, a Boeing flight test engineer, and Bruce Mengel, the flight engineer, who sat in behind Tex and Jim Gannett. By now, Gannett had a pretty good idea of what Tex had in mind to titillate the huge crowd down on Lake Washington.

Tex took the Dash Eighty up to 25,000 feet over Bremerton and Hood Canal, all the time keeping a close check on the time. As the moment grew near for the Blue Angels to move out of the Gold Cup course, Tex dropped down to 20,000 feet. Then he looked over at Jim Gannett and said, "Hey, Jim, I'm going to roll this airplane over the Gold Cup." Gannett said, "Jeez, they're liable to fire you." Tex said, "Well, yeah, but I don't think so."

Then Tex brought the Dash Eighty right down to the deck, no more than 500 feet above the water in close proximity to the huge crowd and a barge full of airline power hitters. Tex raised the nose above the horizon, kept his feet off the rudder pedals, cranked in left aileron, and did a smooth, elegant barrel roll, gaining about 1,200 feet in the process.

"Hey, what're you guys doing up there?" yelled Mengel. Meanwhile, Bill Whitehead was floating around back in the plane snapping pictures. By now, as Tex put it later, "I figured I had their attention, so I did it again." He took the Dash Eighty out in a lazy chandelle and came back down along the race course and rolled it again.

Several stories have surfaced about what happened on the barge. One story is that Bill Allen [president of Boeing], now ashen-faced and shaken, turned to a friend who had heart problems. "Give me about 10 of your heart pills," he said.

It didn't take long before Tex's phone rang on Monday morning. He arrived to find Allen and five other Boeing officials waiting. One of them said, "What in the hell were you doing yesterday?"

Then, in his low-key Kansas drawl, Tex launched into his speech. The maneuver wasn't all that risky, he told them. No strain was put on the airframe, it was only a one-G maneuver, and airplanes fly all the

From "Tex Johnston," by Emmett Watson, The Seattle Times, *August 3, 1986. Reprinted by permission of* The Seattle Times.

time at one G, which is the weight of the plane while it's sitting on the ground—that's what holds you on the ground, and, in fact, you walk around at one G. The only control that is used is the aileron and a slight amount of elevator, and besides that, Tex said, he knew the audience.

"I've always sold airplanes by demonstratin' em," Tex told them, "and I knew the audience was the IATA [International Air Transport Association] and all the leading engineers and scientists. There were the airline people, rival manufacturers, everyone who meant anything in aeronautics. Never before has that quality of talent been assembled in one spot to see anyone's airplane, and probably never will be again. So I just had to do it. It was not a risk and I would never do anything to risk myself or the company's equipment."

"All right," Allen said. "You know that, now we know that. But don't do it anymore."

[That 707 prototype was] the most beautiful, the most revolutionary airplane ever built, and for a few brief, wondrous moments, it lit up the skies over Lake Washington. It was a symbol of how the world was going to change, as it did change, in time and space and distance.

Tex Johnston

A 747 in the final body-join
position at Boeing's Washington
assembly facility in Everett

Home, with emotionally disturbed children. She is still on the Home's board. "I don't have the credentials the other board members have," says this commonsensical Boeing, "but I've worked downstairs." In 1975 she married lawyer William Rademaker; he is now Bill Boeing's in-house counsel and shares his father-in-law's conservative views.

With its enormous kitchen and football-field-sized backyard, Mary's Broadmoor home looks like a place for children. But a few blocks away, Gretchen's multigabled blue house, with its iridescent, fuchsia-colored apple tree in front and its panoramic view of the lake, is like a museum filled with Boeing memorabilia. Many of its pieces are antiques from her grandparents' Highlands estate: a massive English cherry-wood armoire built in 1740;

a Tiffany grandfather clock made at the turn of the century; an array of antique Oriental carpets; and a Bengal tiger skin.

There are more contemporary objets d'art of the family's own making. After two years at the University of San Diego College for Women, Gretchen, the artist of the Boeing clan, studied photography at the Brooks Institute in Santa Barbara. She returned to Seattle to do a photo book for the Sierra Club, but decided that she "loved people too much to spend my life in a darkroom," so she turned to printmaking at Seattle's Cornish School and glassblowing at the Pratt Fine Arts Center. A lovely glass vase she made stands on a table beside a plaster sculpture her husband made of his hunting dog.

In a photograph Gretchen took of him standing on a mountain slope, Max Clough could be mistaken for the young Ernest Hemingway. "Macho Max," as the family calls him, could have served as the model for Hemingway's Nick Adams stories, minus the post-World-War-I angst. A soft-spoken, southern Virginia gentleman, Clough played football for the College of William and Mary, was once president of a sled-dog association in Alaska, and takes sports—especially fly fishing—as seriously as Nick Adams and Gretchen's grandfather did. Gretchen is a fishing aficionado, too; she and Clough spend a good part of their summers flying up to Alaska and British Columbia to fish where William Boeing, Sr., did, and she treasures a collection of her grandfather's bamboo fishing poles.

But if Gretchen Boeing-Clough is the keeper of many private family antiques, she also has a trove of memorabilia that will be opened to the public. Gretchen has been part of the drive to build the Museum of Flight, which opened in 1987 on the west side of Boeing Field, alongside the restored original Red Barn. A replica of Bill Boeing's first plane, the B & W, is among the suspended exhibits. A four-engine B-17, though not owned by the museum, sits across the field and can be seen through the museum windows.

Seattle is the ideal site for such a museum because the city contains repositories of aviation memorabilia scattered about in the memories of its people—many of them industry old-timers—as well as in its attics. And Gretchen Boeing is an advance scout: to collect artifacts and information, she traveled to Alaska to interview old bush pilots and is in touch with many who now live in the Seattle area. These men, she hopes, will one day tell their tales in the "Oldtimers Room" of the museum. She also is seeking aviation artifacts among 124 boxes of her grandfather's effects, where she has discovered such treasures as a photograph of her grandparents with Amelia Earhart, standing before a plane that will hang in the Great Gallery. The work has led this Boeing deeper into family lore than she has ever probed before. "Working with these archives is like reading a novel," she muses. "Only I'm involved in this one."

Her father has contributed significant financial support for the museum, but, characteristically, he prefers to keep that quiet. Even so, it is no secret that Bill Boeing, Jr., is a cochairman of the museum foundation, and that he is a final judge of which of his father's effects should be shared with the public. "It's the kind of public gesture, as a Boeing, that he has never made before," observes a King County politician. "Possibly it's a way of coming to terms with his name."

Perhaps. The concept of a family birthright is still somewhat foreign to American experience, and that can make an inheritance like Boeing's as much a burden as a privilege. We treat our leading families as stereotypes, expecting people born with prominent names to carry some symbolic burden of achievement for us all. Bill Boeing, Jr., may have been a victim of that expectation, a man forever judged in relation to the power of his name, no matter how he tried to distance himself. But those who admire him and wish him well—and there are many—hope that he may now be accepting that heritage with a new ease, that in helping to build the Museum of Flight, he is freeing himself from the weight of his name by allowing the public to recognize the achievements that name represents. ◼

PORTRAIT OF A LADY

GUENDOLEN PLESTCHEEFF

JOHN S. ROBINSON

A faint fine reek of cocktails floated through the rooms on clouds of cigarette smoke." That sentence begins *Rome Express,* a 1928 novel by Bertrand Collins, and to read it today is almost to feel that one has passed through some kind of time warp. The setting is a post-World War I party on First Hill in a booming Northwestern port city the author calls Chinook. In the year it was written, the sentence was undoubtedly intended to startle. The Eighteenth Amendment, banning the sale of liquor, was in force, and not all of that smoke came from cigarettes in the hands of men. This was a period when many people still found smoking by women unacceptable, though not for the same reasons they might object to it today. It was thought "fast."

On page one, we are introduced to the novel's heroine, an independent young woman who, though *in* Chinook, is not completely *of* it: "Greta Pendrick, whom one had known always. A child of one of those families known as Pioneers. The old Pendrick house on Duwamish Street, with its cupola, its iron fence and hedge of lilacs. Greta as a slim, vivid child flitting about the maple trees around her mother's tennis courts. That episode of the mad Pole...."

Though, to my knowledge, the mad Pole has never been identified, contemporary Seattle readers of *Rome Express* had no difficulty in recognizing Chinook as their hometown, First Hill as Seattle's First Hill, Duwamish Street as Madison, the cupola'd house as the home of the city's leading contractor, Morgan J. Carkeek, and Greta Pendrick—with her "fine-cut olive profile, absinthe-green eyes, straight blue-black hair"—as his only daughter, Guendolen.

Despite its familar locale, *Rome Express* was greeted in Seattle with something less than wild applause. Collins, the Thatcher-Middlesex-Harvard-educated son of John Collins, Seattle's first mayor, had an inborn flair for upsetting people. After the appearance of one of his novels, some outraged citizens were even heard to suggest that "he ought to be horsewhipped."

Today's reader of *Rome Express* —particularly if unfamiliar with the Seattle milieu it describes—may well wonder what all the fuss was about. Collins's treatment of his

"She's the most elegant woman in Seattle."

*"It's like having Isabel
Archer...right here, walking down
the street."*

protagonist, at least, seems wholly sympathetic. The book follows the general course of Greta Pendrick's life, much as Guendolen Carkeek's early years actually unfolded. Greta marries the Italian consul in Chinook/Seattle, lives for a time with his family in Rome, and then travels to Estonia, where his country has sent him as its minister. The post-World War I period in Estonia proves unusually exciting, especially as its capital, Reval, is crowded with White Russians fleeing the Bolshevik revolution.

Greta's husband becomes ill, and he and Greta return to Rome, where he dies while she is in Paris. Following his death, the book (never a wholly factual history) departs significantly from the real life of its model. Rejecting a Russian prince, Greta accepts a proposal of marriage from a titled Swede, and presumably abandons Chinook for upscale life in Europe. The real Guendolen, after living for several years in Paris, married Theodore Plestcheeff, an exiled Russian aristocrat she had first met in Estonia. Until his death, they commuted between Paris and Seattle, which, with a lot of time out for extraneous travel, she essentially continues to do.

For, though novels come to an end, real life goes on. "You mean, she's still *around?*" asked an impressed reader of *Rome Express* the other day. "It's like having Isabel Archer"—the American heroine of Henry James's *The Portrait of a Lady,* whose fictional career has some parallels to Greta Pendrick's—"right here, walking down the street."

Indeed, Guen Plestcheeff is still around, and very much part of the current scene. For the half-century since the era of *Rome Express,* she has remained a formidable Seattle force, providing proof by her own example that, at any age—at least, if one's physical and financial resources hold out—it's possible to live one's life with verve, panache, and purpose.

"She's the most elegant woman in Seattle," says her friend Anne Grosvenor Robinson, using the present tense quite naturally—although some might suppose that a woman who achieved much of her elegance in the Paris of Hemingway's Lost Generation would long since have retired from this competitive field. It's not among Guen's goals, however, to look like Whistler's Mother. Retirement is not on her agenda. More sensitive than most to the values of the past, she yet lives wholly in the present, and speaks of the future as readily and easily as any thirty-year-old.

In the Pacific Northwest, she divides her time between a country reteat on Bainbridge Island and her Seattle town house, which was built in 1909 to entertain a future king of Belgium. Annually, if circumstances permit, she departs for a sojourn in Paris, where, for thirty-five years, she has been a regular guest at the Lotti Hotel. There, in deference to her late husband's family—Paris visitors since the nineteenth century of Napoleon III—she is addressed as the Princess Plestcheeff. In plain Chinook, where few can properly pronounce her married name ("Pless-tscheff," with a slight stress on the second syllable, is close enough), she is widely known simply as "Guen"—her preference—or "Guennie"—

nearly everyone else's. Most of the time, she needs no further identification. There are certainly many Gwendolyns in Seattle, and even, possibly, a few spare Guendolens, but, among her friends, associates, and numerous fans, there is only one Guennie.

Like most founders of fortunes, her father, Morgan James Carkeek, was brainy, tough, energetic—and lucky. He was born in England, in Redruth, Cornwall; Guen has visited Penventon, his ancestral house, a graceful, eighteenth-century, neoclassic edifice, today a hotel. To his family, long resident in the same place, his transatlantic move, undertaken in 1863, seemed quite daring. A worn Bible in Guen's possession is touchingly inscribed, "Presented to Mr. Morgan Carkeek on his leaving for a foreign land."

Yet, as a man with talent, ambition, and the inborn instincts of a developer, he found he had come to exactly the right place at exactly the right time. In the frontier Pacific Northwest, there were no pesky government regulations, no bothersome zoning laws, and no niggling environmental-impact statements. The Indians were by and large friendly, and the land went on forever.

Already an accomplished stonemason, Carkeek built Port Townsend's first stone building (the Fowler Building, which today houses the *Port Townsend Leader)* and later moved to Seattle, where he went into business with his brother, Will, and built many more. Although few of these still stand, many Seattleites will recall some of them—like the pillared public library at Third and Spring, or the tall, brick Burke Building at Second and Madison, both since razed and replaced.

Carkeek's real forte, though, seems to have been the acquisition of promising real estate. At one time, he owned the whole of what was to become Boeing Field. "It's your nest egg," he told his daughter.

As things turned out, that particular nest egg never hatched. Much of the land was condemned for the airfield, while the rest was sold. However, this was by no means his only property. While Guen and her brother were growing up, he owned some thirty-five acres on the Lake Washington shore at Sand Point. The Carkeeks would go there each summer with their friends, the Goodfellow family, which included eleven children. "They were English and we were English," the mature Guen explains, recalling with special pleasure that "Mrs. Goodfellow made wonderful scones."

"From her father, Guen gets good business instincts," says Seattle writer Bill Alpert, who has studied the Carkeek family history. "It's from her mother that she gets her interest in life." Emily Gaskill Carkeek was English, too; she came from Bath. In 1863, Carkeek returned to England to bring her back to Seattle. The frontier city she found on her arrival was very different from home, and very different from the Seattle of today. In the words of Bertrand Collins, ostensibly writing about Chinook, what the newcomer was likely to notice when venturing downtown were "the slag fires of the droning sawmills; the wharves; the white-washed cottages, meandering dirt streets and wooden sidewalks;...the

Guendolen Plestcheeff at home:
retirement is not on her agenda

194

Chinamen in blue denim, baskets of vegetables strung across their shoulders on wooden yokes; and the Indians in bowler hats and bedroom slippers, or lace pantalettes and Hudson Bay blankets, who would wander into town from their shanties on the tide flats at the south end of the Bay."

Today, when such scenes are no longer to be seen anywhere, most people would find them picturesque, pure milk and honey for the Sunday travel section. Collins plainly thought them repellent, and it may have been partly because of a wish to escape them that Emily Carkeek was such an avid and discriminating reader. She particularly enjoyed English history and biography. In *Rome Express*, Edith Pendrick, her fictional alter ego, is pictured with "Greville's *Memoires* on her knee." Today, in Guen Plestcheeff's library, Emily Carkeek's copy of *Greville's Journals of the Reign of Queen Victoria, 1837–1852* may still be seen.

"In her own generation," says Olive Lambuth, a childhood friend of Emily's daughter, "there weren't many people with the same enthusiasm she had for the world of literature. Not all the ladies on her calling list were interested in the books that interested her."

Although Mrs. Carkeek may not have been wholly comfortable with every aspect of Seattle, her contribution to her adopted city was considerable. On November 13, 1911, the sixtieth anniversary of the landing of the schooner *Exact* bearing the first pioneers to Alki Point, she and a group of friends founded the Seattle Historical Society. It is an organization that continues to flourish, and one which she, her husband, and daughter were all later to serve as its president.

In 1885, many years before Guen's birth, her parents built the "grand new house" described in such detail in *Rome Express*. Its location, on the southeast corner of Madison and Boren, was well chosen; this was the commencement of First Hill's brief but shining hour as Seattle's prime residential neighborhood. Like other houses soon to rise nearby, Carkeek's was wooden, drafty, and, by today's standards, lavish in its use of space. All the ceilings were fourteen feet high, and the woodwork of the staircase and reception hall was mahogany and redwood. Overlooking the staircase was a stained-glass window, containing a striking figure of a white knight with blue eyes. As a child, Guen found it rather scary, but it became locally famous. In later years, it was dubbed "The Playboy of 819 Boren" by Everett Earling (an uncle-by-marriage of Seattle attorney James Ellis, and something of a *bon vivant* himself).

Outside the house were a tennis court and garden. "We had fruit trees there," Guen says today; "cherries and plums and wonderful peaches. The flesh was white and the outside was pink. I never see these peaches now." Still standing in the garden was a huge alder, said to be left over from the original forest that formerly covered the area. Once, when some workmen tried to cut it down, Emily Carkeek stopped them just in time. The whole property was enclosed by the iron fence mentioned in *Rome Express*. It was the first such fence

After all this, it was confusing to return to Seattle, where her peers were enrolled in places like Broadway High School.

in the area, and was widely considered undemocratic.

"What did your father think about that?" I asked Guen.

"He didn't care," she said. "He was English."

The Carkeeks had two children. Their son, Vivian, was a graduate of the first (1901) law-school class at the University of Washington and later practiced in Seattle. Guendolen was born not long after 1890. (Guessing exactly how many years after is a popular Seattle diversion; the princess herself is disinclined to shed any light on the subject.) Although she began her education in company with her First Hill peers at the Pacific School—about a mile away, across Broadway—when she grew older her parents sent her abroad, first to school with her cousins in England, later to a Swiss convent in Lausanne. Possibly to Emily Carkeek, Seattle still seemed a kind of colonial city like Nairobi or Hong Kong, where, even today, British children are seldom entrusted to local schools, if their parents can at all afford to send them home.

Unhappily, Europe utterly failed to prepare her for the stresses and strains of teenage social life in western America. Even before she left, her artistic inclinations set her somewhat apart ("I don't remember her playing hockey in the street with a tin can and a bent stick," says one contemporary), and her unusual education only widened the rift. In her convent, girls didn't "go out" with boys. When they were permitted to leave the premises, it was only with other girls, walking in a file, two by two; their headmistress would accompany them, running back and forth to make sure no girl of wobbly morals cast too warm an eye on some passing soccer player. Once, when a friendly young Turk dared to sing a serenade under her window, Guen was confined to quarters and forbidden to join her classmates at a circus.

After all this, it was confusing to return to Seattle, where her peers were enrolled in places like Broadway High School. All they wanted to talk about was proms and football. She'd never been to a football game, and didn't know what a prom was. Her conversations with boys tended to fade off into long, hopeless silences. They didn't understand her, and she didn't understand them.

In the long run, such experiences seem to have strengthened what many of her friends consider one of her outstanding qualities: her continuing desire to better herself, to make the most of her potential. She hoped to become a portrait painter—she has enjoyed sketching most of her life—and Europe seemed to her the place to accomplish this.

It was true that by World War I Seattle could no longer be considered part of the frontier. The Indians in bowler hats had long since gone the way of the Indians on the warpath. But in many ways the city was still a very Klondike place. For the most part, the business of the men was business, while women took care of the arts, usually in a somewhat amateur fashion. To Guen, despite the restricted life she had led in her convent, Europe appeared much as Henry James's heroines saw it—as the fount of civilization, of culture, and, for that matter, of better-quality fun and games. Certainly the attraction she felt for the Continent influenced her in choosing her first husband, Paolo Brenna, who appears in *Rome Express* as Piero Lequio.

Brenna, the scion of a Roman diplomatic family, had been his country's Seattle consul. Set down amidst First Hill's insular WASP society, this well-born Latin Catholic had seemed a highly exotic plant, or, in the words of one of Guen's contemporaries, "a foreigner in our midst." On the other hand, he was handsome, dashing, intellectual, and admired by most of Guen's friends. They thought she had done well to attract him. Only her conservative father had little enthusiasm for him, particularly as a prospective son-in-law. In *Rome Express,* the narrator asks what Greta's father thought of Piero Lequio.

"Piero and papa never had enough in common to find a mutual question on which to disagree," Greta replies.

Nevertheless, they were married—in Europe—and, for a time, were very happy. At first, they were based in France, where Brenna served as a member of an international body formed to aid in the reconstruction of countries devastated by war. Guen's lifelong love for Paris really began at this time. She and Brenna enjoyed all the city had to offer—museums, plays, the ballet, anything that was new. "It was all gala," as Guen puts it. At the theaters, one could buy inexpensive standing room, and some nights they went to three of them, one right after the other.

Not long after, Brenna drew a promising new assignment. He was posted as his country's top diplomatic representative—its minister—to a new European nation, the Republic of Estonia. To prepare for this, in June 1921, the Brennas traveled briefly to Rome.

Since Rome was Brenna's native city, their short stay was packed with social life. One afternoon, they visited the palace of Prince Colonna to watch the king drive by to open Parliament. Trotting along beside his carriage was the young Benito Mussolini, as yet no dictator, simply an ambitious and rising politician. He had been wont to appear in public accompanied by a lion cub, until Paolo Brenna's mother, a Hungarian countess, had written him suggesting that this was perhaps a bit tacky; whereupon—as Guen tells it—the poor beast vanished, carted off, no doubt, to the nearest zoo.

"[We] got a special salute and wave from the king, who passed in a wonderful old coach with six white horses and footmen in red and plumes," Guen wrote her mother. "The dowager queen leaned out of her coach and she waved up to the balcony. We were opposite the royal palace, so when they went back I came out on the balcony. We saw all the demonstration. The people came for blocks. The fascisti followed the carriage like an army, and when the king came out with the Duke of Aosta and two princesses (dressed in black, white hats), they yelled for hours. If you see this country, you realize how little chance there is of Bolshevism."

There was much more than a mere chance of Bolshevism taking over in Estonia. This was one of those unhappy countries so weak and so badly placed geographically that the only predictable thing about any conflict in their area is that they will certainly lose. For seven centuries prior to World War I, the Switzerland-size nation lying on the Baltic coast and right next to Russia had been ruled by neighbors: Germans, Danes, Poles, Swedes, and finally the Tsars. In 1920, while Russia still struggled with revolution, Estonia broke free. For twenty happy years, it was independent; in 1940, the Russians moved back, and today, as the Estonian Soviet Socialist Republic, it is part of the Soviet Union.

The Brennas arrived at its capital, Reval—now known by its Estonian name of Tallinn—just at the outset of independence. It was a truly bizarre period. Dignified, many-spired Reval, one of the best-preserved medieval towns in Europe, was stumbling blindly into the modern age. I know of only one work of fiction which in any way deals with the city at this time. That is Anthony Powell's *Venusberg,* where the unnamed Baltic port, which is the site of the action, is apparently a combination of Reval and Helsinki. Powell's fictional capital seems largely peopled by a dizzy crew of loonies and dingbats, careening through a terminally boring round of dinners and receptions, chasing floozies with names like Countess Clothilde de Mandragore, and uttering crackbrained profundities such as the one the author hangs on an American diplomat: "The tongue of Shakespeare and the *Saturday Evening Post* is good enough for us...and you can take it from me, Colonel...if people are worth talking to, they talk *English."*

Incredibly, after reading *Rome Express* and talking things over with *Madame la Ministre,* I have concluded that Reval/Tallinn must actually have been something like that. "Graustark," she calls it, referring to the fictional country of Viennese operetta; "it was like *The Merry Widow."*

There were certainly a lot of parties. "It was the first time I've ever heard of a 'rout,' " says Guen. "We didn't have cocktail parties, we had routs." The Estonians gave them. The diplomats gave them. Refugee Russians (some of whom still owned hunting lodges surviving from the imperial era) gave them. If the food all seemed to be prepared with burnt butter, still it was generally good, and there was enough first-rate caviar to satisfy Peter the Great. In winter, they skated on the frozen Baltic. In summer, it was light all night, and the Russians would play their balalaikas and dance. Sometimes all this action proved a little overwhelming for the statesmen of the new republic. Most had only lately risen in status, and few were used to so much social life. "They would hire deafening brass bands for dancing," says Guen. "All the men would sit in a row, with the women in a row opposite them, like sparrows on a telephone wire."

By contrast, most of the foreigners in Reval were in their twenties and thirties, lively, vigorous, and fun-loving. At times, the scene must have been more Camelot than Graustark. Once, Prince George, the future Duke of Kent, came out from England on some kind of official business. "He was at a formal reception," Guen recalls, "and he got bored.

She wrote home to Seattle of people being bayoneted and chopped to pieces in their homes.

So he stole the president's car, and we all went out to somebody's house. He played the piano, and we danced to 'Yes, We Have No Bananas.' "

If such scenes seemed to belong to the musical stage, they were being played out adjacent to real-life Greek drama. Across the border, in the newborn Soviet Union, awesome changes were under way. To John Reed, the ten days that shook the world meant progress; to the Russians Guen met in Estonia, they signified utter disaster, the end of all that was meaningful in life, if not of life itself. She wrote home to Seattle of people being bayoneted and chopped to pieces in their homes; Morgan Carkeek, a product of the innocent nineteenth century, told her to play down such horror tales. "No one will believe you," he advised.

Fantastic valuables, once possessed by the exiled Russian nobility, appeared in Reval for sale. There were enormous, sterling silver champagne coolers, as well as four-foot-high sterling silver candlesticks that seemed to have come out of some Land of Oz, but which actually once belonged to the powerful Orlov family — one such candlestick formerly stood behind each guest at dinner. Such bulky items as these were usually melted down; otherwise, it would have been too difficult to transport them.

Much more common was jewelry. Precious stones were highly portable and fairly easy to hide. For some reason, the Soviets permitted those refugees they allowed out to take a bed with them; often it was brass, and sometimes its hollow tubes were used to conceal diamonds. Occasionally, border officials detained passengers and fed them laxatives, because people often tried to save their diamonds by swallowing them.

One of the more dramatic chapters in *Rome Express* describes Greta's excursion into the deep Baltic forest to visit a dealer in smuggled treasures. Like so much of the book, this incident is loosely based on fact. "You'd go out in a sleigh to a little hut in the woods," Guen says today. "There would be a man there, wearing old clothes that looked like pajamas. He'd have beautiful ermines and sables that reached down to the ground. Or he'd show you a lot of parasol handles encrusted with jewels. He'd open a drawer, and it would be full of emeralds."

Refugees, of course, were constantly escaping, though sometimes only with great difficulty. On the train out of Petrograd—as the city of Leningrad, formerly St. Petersburg, was then known—Soviet police would study the hands of passengers to see if they disclosed the hardness or callousness caused by manual labor. If they turned out to be the soft hands of members of the upper class, their owners could be taken out and shot.

Among the Brennas' friends in Reval was Count Paul Kotzebue, a lineal descendant of the Estonian-born navigator who, in 1816, discovered Alaska's Kotzebue Sound. One night, the Count brought to their house a tall, slim Muscovite, but lately out of Russia; Guen recalls their arrival together, by sleigh. The newcomer was Theodore Plestcheeff, a member of an old, Moscow-based boyar family.

Rome Express seems largely the product of Collins's thorough study of the detailed letters Guen sent back to Seattle.

199

Nellie Cornish

The founder of Cornish Art Institute in Seattle spent the first twenty-four years of her life in Tennessee on her father's sheep farm. At the turn of the century she moved to Blaine, Washington, where she bartered her piano skill for meals. Twenty years later she founded—without any initial support from Seattle— an art school that was the focus of an extraordinary collection of artists.

From Miss Aunt Nellie: The Autobiography of Nellie C. Cornish, *by Nellie Cornish. Copyright © 1964 University of Washington Press. Reprinted by permission.*

Although it was April 9, 1900, I arrived in Seattle in the midst of a light snowstorm. I took a horsedrawn cab to my new address. I have always been more or less a lone wolf, but that day, with snow falling and the clomp-clomp of the horse's hoofs, I felt it was a terribly big world and I its only occupant. I admit to a little wave of loneliness when I stood at the railway station and saw other passengers being greeted by loving friends. However, my landlady was warm-hearted and made me welcome. My room was large and airy, but furnished with scraps.

For the first time I met Seattle face to face. It was a far cry from the splendid city of today. The population then numbered 80,691. The final "1" has always intrigued me. I wonder, did it mean me? All the elements whose fusion contributed to Seattle's character and importance were already present. The blue waters, lush evergreens, and snow-capped mountain ranges on the horizon were to a great extent the font of what the inhabitants hail as the Seattle spirit. I felt that my life was caught up in it. Those new faces, young and old—artists, musicians, businessmen, and dreamers alike—seemed carried along by the same stream of pulsating energy. But, of course, the first necessity was to make a living. . . .

When I arrived in Seattle in 1900, the Holyoke Block was already established as a building where artists, especially musicians, worked and where many lived in their studios. Up one flight of stairs was a large court with solemn-looking doors lining three sides. Each of these doors opened into a two-room suite consisting of a small dark reception room, which led into a large room with high ceilings and four tall windows. Sliding doors separated the two rooms and, when open, gave enough space to seat thirty or forty people. Studio recitals were frequently given there. Near the head of the stairs was a water tap and washbowl. Next door to the tap was a "co-ed" toilet. . . .

Now that I needed a studio, my thoughts naturally turned to Holyoke. But it had a waiting list. I was on the verge of discouragement when Harla Sloan invited me to share her Holyoke studio. I moved at once, bag and baggage, as she permitted me to live there. It was sparsely furnished, and I had no money to spend on decoration. Fortunately, a friend loaned me a valuable collection of Indian baskets and several Navajo rugs, which immediately gave our studio a western air and made me quite happy.

My earlier barter technique now came in handy. Holyoke was lacking in many necessary conveniences. There was, for instance, no bath. So, once again, I obtained the use of a bathroom nearby, up the hill, in exchange for lessons. And teaching Karl, the talented little son of Mrs. Presley, paid for my daily meals. Thus I established myself in the Bohemian atmosphere of Holyoke.

One of the first tenants of this artistic community was Louise Coman Beck, who was the wife of a minister. (Their two sons, Broussais and Dillard, later became active in the business and civic life of Seattle.) Mrs. Beck, tall and majestic, spoke with a definite Alabama accent. She was one of the earliest pioneers of musical life in Seattle. Long before the days of Holyoke, she had opened a girls' school in her home in Ravenna Park, where she and her husband owned a large tract. The park is now a residential district with a small island of trees, but then it was filled with tall Douglas firs. Mrs. Beck named the largest tree for Paderewski, and once, when he was playing in Seattle, she invited him to attend its dedication.

Nellie Centennial Cornish

Through his mother, Plestcheeff was related to the Stroganovs, powerful landowners of the old regime, who had been ennobled as a result of their part in opening Siberia. (Their St. Petersburg palace, designed in 1754 by the Empress Elizabeth's architect, Carlo Rastrelli, once contained works by Van Dyck, Perugino, Tintoretto, and Donatello; around 1800, when a craze for French cuisine took over in Russia, Beef Stroganoff was invented in their kitchen.) Plestcheeff had spent much of his youth on a Stroganov estate at Tambov, south of Moscow. Later, he had been close to the inner circle of the court of Tsar Nicholas and Empress Alexandra. Through the influence of the Grand Duchess Elizabeth, the Empress's sister, he had held the position of official host for the Tsar at the Moscow Ballet, a ceremonial post usually given to a much older man.

Some of his friends had been involved in the successful plot to kill Gregory Rasputin, the sinister, power-mad monk who had convinced the Empress that he had the God-given power to cure her small son's hereditary hemophilia, and had thereby attained what many Russians believed to be dangerous power over her. Plestcheeff had actually been invited to a dinner of the conspirators that preceded Rasputin's murder, but had declined. His mother, who was widely thought to possess powers of extrasensory perception, and whom people listened to for that reason, persuaded him to stay away.

During World War I, Plestcheeff had served in the Carpathian Mountains, and had been several times decorated. After the Tsar was overthrown and he and his family were murdered, Plestcheeff had tried four times to leave the country. Once, when taken off the train, he had managed to elude his would-be captors and walk back to Moscow. He had finally succeeded in crossing the Estonian frontier, using the identity and passport of one Metz, a friendly Moscow policeman.

Once safe in Estonia, he found he had many friends who were willing to help him. Guen quickly discovered that he shared many of her own tastes and interests. Because a Stroganov uncle had owned one of the largest collections of Russian antiquities in the world, he knew a great deal about Russian art, particularly the highly specialized field of Russian porcelain. Through him, Guen came to know the work of the Imperial Porcelain Factory at St. Petersburg, and of the great Moscow houses of Francis Gardner and Ivan Popov. Following his advice, she bought a number of pieces, which she still owns.

Paolo Brenna's tour of duty in Reval was destined to be brief. He became seriously and chronically ill, and eventually had to leave Estonia. Guen took him to several European cities in the hope that he would recover, but he did not, and eventually they returned to Rome.

Curiously, Italy seems to have made little lasting impression on her. Though her Seattle house is filled with memorabilia from Russia and France, it contains little or nothing to remind the visitor of her first husband's homeland. Paolo Brenna's family belonged to a society as rigid in a wholly different way as that in which Guen had been reared. In Rome, even though married, she lacked the freedom that, as an American woman, she naturally took for granted. Proper matrons in the Rome of that era had very little to occupy their time. They lived what they called a *vie mondaine,* a worldly life, but in some respects it was not all that worldly even though they wore spectacular clothes and gossiped a lot. (When Britain's Queen Mary visited Rome, her appearance caused some amusement among the local gentry; she was not so much dressed, they thought, as *upholstered.)*

Of course, none of them worked. They seldom traveled. Instead of going to restaurants, they dined at home or with friends. Guen found many of them quite limited. Each afternoon, she would take a formal drive with her husband's family through the Pincio, the great Roman park. That was often the extent of her daily outings, though she sometimes attended the theater with her sister-in-law (who, as *Rome Express* suggests, disapproved of her independent American ways). She remembers a concert at which new music by Darius Milhaud was played. It was far too innovative for the Roman audience, which stomped and booed, greatly distressing the composer, who was present.

After an extended illness, Paolo Brenna died, the doctors said of encephalitis. His death was a watershed for his widow, who was forced to make one of the major decisions of her life. Her family was anxious for her to return to Seattle. But Guen had had enough of domination by families. Instead, she decided to live in Paris. She took an apartment on the Ile St. Louis, and, to help support herself, found a job buying antiques for Macy's in New York. Here, at about the point where the story of her *Rome Express* counterpart comes to an end, Guen began a wholly new life, concerning which a second Greta Pendrick novel has yet to be written.

Meanwhile, Bertrand Collins was working on the first, which he was to publish near the end of the twenties. Except for the portion set in Chinook, *Rome Express* seems largely the product of Collins's thorough study of the detailed letters Guen sent back to Seattle. Such an absentee method of producing fiction involves risks for an author, particularly for one writing about a time and place many of his readers already know.

Collins was not overconcerned about this danger, as I discovered for myself on the one occasion when I met him. I told him I had read all three of his books.

"Oh," he said, deprecatingly, "I thought everyone had forgotten those."

"I read *Moon in the West,"* I told him, referring to his third novel, which is set partly in Austria; "I've just been to Vienna, and I thought it gave a good picture of the place."

"I've never been there," said Collins shortly. When, some time later, I told this story to a group of his friends who had known him since youth, they laughed and said, "That's Bertie!"

However, *Rome Express* was not rejected in Seattle for the reason that Collins had never visited Estonia. Few Seattleites had. Nor did the book include anything really scandalous. The problem was that it was a true *roman à clef* containing several thinly disguised but recognizable Seattle people, about whom its author was none too kind, nor apparently always too accurate. Even worse in the eyes of many in Seattle was his second novel, *The Silver Swan*. The swan, though named Claire and supposedly a native of the Midwest, was widely thought to be an unflattering portrait of Elspeth McEwan, a celebrated beauty with whom Collins had grown up.

The resentment engendered by these two books probably kept their merits from being more widely recognized. *Rome Express* is the best of his novels. Largely because of details drawn from his own observations, its opening Chinook chapters effectively evoke the spirit of the town. They give the reader as good an idea as can be found anywhere of what Seattle looked and felt like in the early 1920s.

On the other hand, all three of his books take place mostly in Europe, and, in differing degrees, fall prey to the hazard of Collins's limited knowledge. Never much of a psychologist, he didn't understand Europeans deeply enough to portray their inner life, or even to present their exteriors convincingly. Those chapters of *Rome Express* set in Italy fail to ring true, while *The Silver Swan* seems even less persuasive. Much of it is an attempt to depict upper-class English life—both the real Elspeth and the fictional Claire married Englishmen—but, just as few English authors seem able to draw believable American characters, so few Americans can create authentic-sounding Englishmen. Collins was not among those few. Writing in the shadow of Henry James, whose plots were similar, and who understood Europe far better, Collins just couldn't compete.

During World War II, Collins joined the United States Merchant Marine. For *The Seattle Times,* he wrote a series of articles describing life aboard ship as he actually experienced it. One can only wish he had forgotten about Europe and done something similar with a novel about Seattle. As a mayor's son, close from childhood to the city's movers and shakers, he was far better placed than most authors to produce such a book.

Perhaps, indeed, he did. A retired lawyer who knew him has told me he is sure that at one time Collins wrote a novel entitled *The White Knight* after the Playboy of 819 Boren in the window of the Carkeek's First Hill house. If so, it has never been published, and this is surely Seattle's loss.

Guendolen Carkeek Brenna's life in Paris was very different from the one she had led in Italy. The decade of the 1920s was among the liveliest in the city's history, and not only in the realm of the fine arts. The young Maurice Chevalier was appearing in the music halls. At the Folies-Bergère, the American Josephine Baker—fascinating to the Parisians merely because she was black—pranced about the stage, nude save for a few strategically placed tailfeathers. Great restaurants like Maxim's and La Tour d'Argent flourished. In the afternoon, there was tea at the Ritz, and, in the late evening, dancing at Le Perroquet.

Couturiers like Worth, Paquin, and Callot Soeurs turned out the best-dressed women in the world, while their successor, Gabrielle Chanel, was becoming as famous for her per-

"How are you going to pay for it?" Plestcheeff asked. "Pay for it? Pay for it?" said his aristocratic mother.

204

sonality as for her distinctive clothes. Guen became acquainted with her, and, some years later, with a group of Russian friends, spent a New Year's holiday at her country house. (As always, Guen took careful note of the decor. "Beige was Chanel's color, and her house was decorated in beige. I think she was the person who introduced the idea of all-over beige carpets that cover the floors and stairs.")

The Russian influence was everywhere. Fyodor Chaliapin, the finest singing actor of his time, lived in Paris, where he made many of his last public appearances. Serge de Diaghilev was producing majestic works like Stravinsky's *Les Noces* at his famous Ballets Russes; exiled grand dukes attended regularly, and the first public perfomance of *Les Noces* was given to benefit a Russian charity sponsored by the exiled Grand Duchess Marie.

Among the many émigrés in the city was Theodore Plestcheeff, whom Guen had known in Estonia. Unlike the grand dukes—who, being by definition descendants of Tsars, had many connections outside Russia—but quite like most of his less exalted compatriots, he had few funds to spare. When his refugee parents arrived, they immediately rented an attractive Paris house. "How are you going to pay for it?" Plestcheeff asked. "Pay for it? Pay for it?" said his aristocratic mother. This daughter of the Stroganovs had never handled money or paid a bill in her life. In Russia, a manager, an *intendant,* had taken care of such mundane chores for her. "You'll be sleeping under bridges," said Plestcheeff, and moved them out.

Luckily, he had aided a rich Russian merchant to escape the Revolution with some of his capital intact. By posing as a ship's stoker, the man had managed to smuggle out a fortune in pearls hidden beneath his clothes. Plestcheeff received five thousand dollars for his part in this successful venture. The money had helped him get started in France, and he was able to supplement it by selling American-made White automobiles. This was not, perhaps, the easiest possible line of work for a man whose grandfather, according to Guen, had once offered to give the Tsar a battleship. Still, he was apparently fairly competent at it, and the job carried certain fringe benefits. Among his customers was the celebrated Mistinguett, she of the eternal youth and unforgettable legs. Mistinguett not only bought a White, she invited Plestcheeff to a party and gave him her picture.

Guen, meanwhile, accompanied him to many events, notably the Russian Ballet, where he knew many of the personnel from his days in Moscow. He continued to advise her about Russian arts and crafts. When there came on the market a cigarette case made by Fabergé, the celebrated jeweler to the Russian nobility, he suggested she buy it, which she did.

The effect of her Paris years on Guen's *persona* is strikingly evident in her portrait, which appears near those of her parents on the lower floor of Seattle's Museum of History and Industry. Morgan Carkeek, wearing a superb walrus mustache, a wing collar, and a

Guen in Russian costume for a
party in Estonia in 1922

dour look, seems every inch the no-nonsense nineteenth-century businessman. Emily Carkeek, in a tight-waisted, high-necked gown, appears much as Edith Pendrick is described by her daughter in *Rome Express*—"a mid-Victorian figurine with a lavender velvet ribbon in her hair." Guen, on the other hand, seems almost to have dropped down from a different planet. Clad in a sleek, dark dress from the Paris house of Vionnet, she's the last word in *entre-deux-guerres* French chic, with bobbed hair, bee-stung lips, and an impersonal, Art Deco expression that would have made Lorelei Lee of *Gentlemen Prefer Blondes* envious. It's not your garden-variety generation gap; it's a yawning Columbia Gorge.

Emily Carkeek died in 1926, and Morgan Carkeek in 1941; they left their daughter a considerable estate, including their First Hill house. In 1929, Guen married Theodore Plestcheeff. They moved to Seattle, but, for a number of years, traveled often to Paris, spending almost more time at sea than many of us do today on the I-5 freeway. As Plestcheeff's wife, Guen came to know the international Russian community far better than before, and to feel a strong sense of empathy with it.

To her, the word "Russia" connotes something quite different from what it does to most other Americans. It has nothing to do with the Soviet Union, whether seen as a nuclear threat or wave of the future; nothing to do with the stone-faced members of the Politburo or Winston Churchill's "riddle wrapped in a mystery inside an enigma"; nothing even to do with General Secretary Gorbachev and *glasnost*. Russia to her is Act I of *Swan Lake*. It means a small group of interrelated families, whose ancestors Tolstoi described in *Anna Karenina*—charming and cultivated men and women, not all that different from Guen herself, brought low by malign winds of fate in a kind of Old World version of *Gone with the Wind*.

What happened to many of these people in the years following the Bolshevik takeover was quite beyond the emotional grasp of most Americans. There was first the violence of revolution. Plestcheeff's patron, the Grand Duchess Elizabeth, having refused to seek shelter in her native Germany, was taken to the Ural Mountains and thrown down a mine shaft, where she lived with a number of other victims for several days; when their bodies were discovered by White Russians, the head of an injured boy was found to have been bound with her handkerchief.

Those who fled into exile often faced insurmountable problems. By no means all of them were lucky enough to find a means of support. Many died of undernourishment or what Guen calls "consumption"; many others killed themselves. Having been reared in what was still, in many respects, a feudal society, few had much more knowledge than Plestcheeff's mother of how to cope with the capitalist world. Often they emerged with a single divisible asset, say a string of valuable pearls. Instead of selling all of these together and investing the money for the future, they would dispose of the pearls one by one, until all were gone. Yet, surprisingly, over the years, many survived, made a place for themselves, and even prospered. Guen came to have great admiration for their courage and resilience.

Oddly, though Paris was filled with Russian compatriots and old acquaintances, Plestcheeff (most of whose American friends called him by his wife's nickname of "Teddy") much preferred to live in Seattle. There were, of course, White Russians in the Pacific Northwest as well, most of whom had reached the United States via Siberia and Harbin. They had endured the same privations in the Seattle area as elsewhere. One of my own family stories involves the two daughters of one Dr. D., who, in his native Russia, had been Prince D. The two young princesses had jobs in American factories, but their father thought they would learn English better if they worked in private homes. My mother considered hiring one of them, but felt squeamish at the prospect of having someone working in our kitchen whose name she recalled from *War and Peace*. "Overqualified" seemed much too weak a term.

It wasn't the presence of other Russians in Seattle that caused Plestcheeff to want to stay there. He simply liked the Northwest way of life—or so it seemed. As was natural for someone from Russia's Tambov District, a rural area of mixed forest and wooded steppe, he much enjoyed field sports; Guen recalls his hunting pheasant with future Congressman Tom Pelly along the tracks of the interurban railway that once ran through the Green River Valley to link Seattle and Tacoma. The Plestcheeffs spent many pleasant days on the Redmond farm of their friends, Neal and Janet Tourtellotte. She would pick berries and he would fish.

Like the Russian noblemen in Tchaikovsky's opera *The Queen of Spades,* Plestcheeff liked to play cards, and Seattle offered plenty of opportunities for that. His closest friends were men like the late banker Cebert Baillargeon, who shared his cosmopolitan outlook; still, for a man who, in Europe, had been so closely involved with the ballet, he didn't seem to miss the kind of metropolitan cultural life which, until very recently, Seattle lacked. "Ze symphony!" a friend of Guen's, attempting to reproduce his accent, recalls him saying; "eet ees expensive noise!"

He never lost that accent, and, indeed, there were some who felt sure that he kept it on purpose. Women, however, liked it, and they liked him. "I think 'debonair' would be a good word for Teddy," mused one of them recently. He made a powerful impression on most of his friends' children, partly because he paid attention to them and often brought them small gifts. One of them recollects some friendly advice he once gave her (a down-home Tambov proverb?): "Before you make ze coat, you must catch ze bear."

Seattle stockbroker Peter Rawn, whose great aunt married Guen's uncle, Will Carkeek, and whose mother traveled through Europe with Guen in their youth, well remembers when he first met Plestcheeff. At the time, Rawn was a small boy selling *Saturday Evening Post* on the streets of First Hill. A big, black car drove up, with his mother's old

"Ze symphony!" a friend of Guen's, attempting to reproduce his [Theodore Plestcheeff's] accent, recalls him saying; "eet ees expensive noise!"

207

friend and her new husband inside. Plestcheeff jumped out. "He had a warm, friendly smile, and I liked him right away," Rawn recalls. "Besides, he bought a *Post.*" Plestcheeff had raised some eyebrows in workaday Seattle, because, unlike most of the husbands of Guen's friends, he didn't go to an office every day. Yet such matters didn't seem to disconcert him; he possessed an unflappable self-assurance, perhaps to be expected in a man who could boast the sixteen quarters of nobility necessary for membership in the Knights of Malta. He helped his wife in the management of her real estate. One friend remembers that he rented a warehouse to some fellow Russians, only to have them complain that hungry rats were gnawing at the insulation around some of the pipes.

"You're the tenants," he told them. "It's your space. Why don't you feed your rats?"

The year 1934 proved to be a seminal one for the Plestcheeffs. In Paris, Leon Blum's Popular Front government took charge, finally ending what remained of the Gay Paree of the 1920s, and ushering in a new era of austerity. In Seattle, Guen decided to sell her parents' First Hill house, which the Standard Oil Company wanted to demolish and replace with a service station.

Today, preservationists would greet the proposed demise of this grand period residence with cries of outrage. Half a century ago, attitudes were very different. Port Townsend, for instance, was not then seen as an architectural monument of the past, still less as an attractive set for contemporary films, but rather as an economic disaster area, a barely surviving ghost town. (Guen's father had left her some Port Townsend properties, and her bankers were blunt about what she should do with them: "Get rid of those cats and dogs.") As central heating was now nearly universal, and cheap, few home buyers wanted to take on a house like the Carkeek mansion, with all those out-of-date fireplaces.

Like the trees in Chekhov's cherry orchard, the alder that Emily Carkeek had gone to such trouble to save was finally chopped down.

More important, the First Hill of Guen's childhood seemed to be dying. The venerable trees once lining the street had mostly disappeared, the old lilac gardens were only fragrant memories, and a daily rush of noisy commuter traffic was steadily eroding the peace and quiet and home-town neighborhood feeling. The children of Guen's generation were grown and gone, and few new ones had come to take their place. As one newspaper article put it, the area was "declining."

Characteristically, Guen chose to celebrate the forthcoming sale with a spirited rite of passage. On February 27, the Plestcheeffs were hosts at a memorable dinner dance, designed to evoke the past. As a guide to decorating the house, Guen copied a picture of a Christmas celebration her family had held there in 1896. The old-fashioned sitting room became for the evening a bar. Guests were asked to wear costumes of their parents' generation. Facial hair being out of fashion in the 1930s, many of the men sported fake handlebar mustaches, together with high collars and top hats. (Plestcheeff wore a fake moustache too, but somehow lost it between the *P-I* and *Times* photos.) The women seemed to relish the chance to appear in the styles of the *belle epoque,* and sharp-eyed reporters took in every detail—particularly one from the *P-I* who respectfully referred to the hosts as "M. and Mme. Plestcheeff." ("Mme. Plestcheeff's gown was a lovely yellow satin one, which had been worn by her mother in 1880; she herself wore it very gracefully, and its huge puffed sleeves and flowing skirt looked striking. Her hair was done with frizzed bangs and a chignon low at the neck.")

The guest list included several names like that of Mrs. W. E. Boeing, which any newspaper reader of today would recognize. Others might be less familiar—such as that of Prescott Oakes, whose father had been president of the Northern Pacific Company during the period when Seattle and Tacoma struggled for supremacy. The senior Oakes had been the best-known promoter of Tacoma, and, when he eventually moved to Seattle, it had the significance of a general surrendering his sword at the end of a battle. Everyone knew Seattle had won.

Standing at the head of the staircase, the hostess said to Mrs. Neal Tourtellotte (later Mrs. J. Lister Holmes), "Janet, I think my party's a failure." Mrs. Tourtellotte—who was reported as wearing "embroidered batiste with a number of starched frills and a picture hat"—knew better.

"Guennie," she said, "this is the party of the year."

She was right. It may well have been the party of the decade. The guests stayed until 3 A.M. dancing to such tunes as "A Bicycle Built for Two" and "After the Ball Was Over." As the end of the party approached, a crisis impended. Janet Tourtellotte's embroidered batiste, having been locked in the closet for decades, began slowly to disintegrate. After the ball was over, she went home and stuffed it in the furnace.

In due time, the great house was razed, White Knight and all. Like the trees in Chekhov's cherry orchard, the alder that Emily Carkeek had gone to such trouble to save was finally chopped down. The property was sold—for a sum not announced, but reported by one of the papers to have been all of twenty-five thousand dollars. Today it's occupied by a gas station. Though not everyone realized it at the time, First Hill's golden age was over.

One might have believed it nearly impossible to find a house as historically intriguing as the one the Plestcheeffs had sold—but, in 1939, they managed to do just that. Among the least characteristic and most thoroughly un-Seattle-like of the city's notable houses was a thick-walled, five-story stone fortress on Capitol Hill, which looked down across a wooded ravine to Lake Union below. Unlike most of its neighbors, it had no inviting lawn or garden, no transparent plate-glass window giving onto the street. This house was aloof, reserved. In its design, it suggested a European town house; in terms of physical security, a Moroccan Kasbah.

Indeed, it was a kind of dream castle, one of those unique structures in which the builder's inner personality seems to have taken tangible, physical form. It had been erected in 1909 by a singular visionary, among the most remarkable men in Washington State's

While the house was in its finest flower, Guen, like Sam Hill, entertained royalty there.

The Morgan Carkeek residence, 918 Boren Avenue, now a gas station

history: Samuel Hill, son-in-law of that James J. Hill who had brought the Great Northern Railway to the Pacific Coast.

Sam Hill was a powerful but enigmatic figure about whom much contradictory information is available. Many, including Guen Plestcheeff, consider that he was far ahead of his time. He was a great road builder in an era when few others foresaw the coming importance of highways. A thoroughgoing pacifist, he conceived and largely paid for the Peace Arch at Blaine to celebrate harmonious relations between nations. He created Maryhill, that massive, Valhalla-like chateau improbably set atop the wild Columbia River cliffs, which today serves as a historical and fine-arts museum. Hill was oddly obsessed with the crowned heads of Europe, perhaps because he identified with them. He had built his Capitol Hill house for the sole purpose of receiving Crown Prince Albert of Belgium, who twice planned to visit Seattle and twice was forced to cancel his plans.

In 1939, Hill had long since died. Eloquent testimony to the vanity of worldly ambition, his Capitol Hill stronghold was vacant and falling into decay. Ivy covered it and had even crept inside and over its floors. It was for sale. Standing on its front steps, Guen said, "I don't want it." To her surprise, Plestcheeff, to whom it doubtless suggested a kind of provincial Stroganov outpost, said, "I do." They bought it and moved in.

Guen put her decorating talents to work, enlarged its windows, lightened its walls, installed a skylight, redesigned its rooms, and filled the whole place with European antiques. The change, in the view of her one-time neighbor, Eulalie Merrill Wagner of Tacoma, was spectacular. Guen lives there today, occupying the first floor, while the two above it form a separate apartment. After her death, the entire property will pass to the University of Washington as headquarters for the Plestcheeff Institute for the Decorative Arts.

While the house was in its finest flower, Guen, like Sam Hill, entertained royalty there in the person of Grand Duchess Marie of Russia, cousin of Roumania's Queen Marie, daughter of the Tsar's uncle Paul, and sister of the Grand Duke Dmitri, one of the pre-revolutionary Rasputin conspirators. It was Grand Duchess Marie whose Russian charity had benefited from the initial public performance of Stravinsky's *Les Noces*; but at the time of her Seattle visit—1940—she was best known in the United States as the author of a popular book, *The Education of a Princess*.

Indeed, among the Russian exiles, she was an outstanding survivor. She had grown up with Plestcheeff in Moscow; when they were little more than children, they had been partners at a court ball. In adversity, she had displayed many of the strengths that presumably brought her Romanov forebears to prominence. After escaping from Russia, she had found work in a Paris dressmaking shop, since needlework was one of her few skills that was of value in the job market. In time, she had become a successful designer, and was visiting Seattle at the invitation of Best's Apparel (now the downtown store of Nordstrom) in order to display her line.

At the dinner Guen gave for her, she wore a giant Romanov sapphire, exclaimed over the view from the Sam Hill house, and blew the press completely away. An unnamed "socialite" was later quoted as saying that the event was "the most beautiful party Seattle has ever seen." Sam Hill could hardly have wished for more.

Despite many temperamental differences among the Carkeeks, there was one interest that all of them shared—Morgan, with his dedication to business, Emily with her devotion to books, Vivian with his law practice, and Guen with her other life in Paris. This was an absorption in the history of Seattle. In Guen's case, this interest surfaced rather late. During her childhood, her father would tell her stories of early-day Seattle, to which she paid little heed, as, at that age, she found tales of Indians and pioneers terminally boring. Yet, together with the projected Plestcheeff Institute for the Decorative Arts, her chief monument may well turn out to be Seattle's Museum of History and Industry. As a longtime member of its board puts it: "I would say there would be no Museum of History and Industry were it not for Guennie."

Almost since the days when her mother founded the Seattle Historical Society, the organization had been seeking a permanent home. Many of the items that had been granted or willed to it were stored in the Plestcheeff basement. In 1938, Guen, who had become Society president, began raising money for a new building. She persuaded Philip G. Johnson, then head of the Boeing Aircraft Company, to donate five thousand dollars, and, with his backing, other contributions were easier to pick up. When it came to selection of a proper site, though, difficulties arose. Eventually, these plunged Guen into a jungle of politics, a wilderness from which many another idealistic neophyte, promoting a worthy cause, has emerged torn to shreds and wondering what happened. This did not happen to Guen.

A few years before, Morgan Carkeek had given his thirty-five Sand Point acres to the City of Seattle for use as a park; he and his wife thought it would be an ideal summer playground for Seattle's children. It was a major disappointment to him when, in 1926, the federal government condemned the property for use as a naval air station. A clause in the original deed provided that the land would revert to him should it ever be used for anything other than a park. Instead, he was paid thirty-five thousand dollars. He used this money to buy land on the Puget Sound shore, which he later gave to the city, and which is today known as Carkeek Park. It was there that he thought the Historical Society might best locate, and, in his will, he bequeathed a section of the area for this purpose.

No doubt Louis XIV would have been delighted with the result, but it proved very expensive.

Trustees of the museum, however, after consulting with the Seattle Park Board, had decided that a site more suitable than remote Carkeek Park would be a parcel just off Lake Washington Boulevard then occupied by the University of Washington. Unfortunately, the university's board of regents declined to release the property, preferring instead to expand the adjacent Arboretum.

At this point, Mrs. Frederick Swanstrom entered the scene. As the daughter of Eugene Semple, the next-to-last territorial governor of Washington, she remembered that many years before, the property had been set aside by federal fiat for the Lake Washington Ship Canal. A little research confirmed that the university was indeed a squatter; the US government was the true owner.

Immediately, Guen flew to Washington, where she sought aid from a well-known member of Congress. She couldn't get past his secretary, who told her that, since the university wanted the land, nothing could be done. But Guen's husband's forebears had been among those Russian nobles who had chosen the first of the Romanov dynasty to be Tsar; she was not about to be put off by a mere Washington State Congressman. She went straight to the office of Senator Hugh B. Mitchell, then in the midst of his brief senatorial tenure. "He arranged it in half an hour," she says. The property was declared surplus and deeded back to Seattle.

One roadblock yet remained. Seattle City Council member Mrs. F.F. Powell didn't want to release the Arboretum property unless the city got the Carkeek Park land in exchange. The Historical Society agreed to this, and the transfer was completed.

Inevitably, more money was needed. When Philip Johnson died, the Boeing Company donated fifty thousand dollars in his memory to be used as an aviation wing in the projected new building—with the condition that if an additional two hundred thousand dollars were not raised by January 1, 1951, the gift would be forfeit. Led by Emil G. Sick, president of the Rainier Brewery, and a museum trustee, a successful fund drive was begun. In 1952, the new Paul Thiry-designed building was dedicated. At a formal ceremony, Guen presented its key to Seattle's then mayor, William O. Devin.

"It was *she* who persisted," says one longtime board member, "even though she'd never done anything of a public nature before." Her efforts were recognized in 1950, when she was among the women honored at the annual Matrix Table banquet of the women's national journalism honorary, Theta Sigma Phi.

Guen remained president of the Historical Society for a total of seventeen years. Meanwhile, she was active in other areas. In 1946, she was one of the hostesses who established Seattle's annual debutante party, the Christmas Ball. When someone intimated that in the mid-twentieth century, a debutante ball seemed rather an anachronism, she had a ready reply: "I have no children myself, and I want to do something for the children of my friends."

She was chosen to decorate the Olympic Hotel's Spanish Ballroom, and she did her job almost too well. Using as a guide an old print of Versailles, she imported a couple of scenic but bulky statues from a Capitol Hill garden, and hired a skilled nurseryman to create a leafy indoor bower, complete with hedges and espaliered trees. No doubt Louis XIV would have been delighted with the result, but it proved very expensive; her cohostesses were a bit taken aback. After a few years, not wishing their party to escalate into a prerevolutionary Stroganov fete, they suggested that Guen assume other responsibilities.

A wholly successful project was the rejuvenation of yet another interesting house that she and Plestcheeff bought a few years later. This was a one-story waterfront cottage in that section of southern Bainbridge Island known—with an irony that somehow epitomizes the difference between a city like Seattle and a city like Los Angeles—as "Poverty Flats." The house was basically a sound one; Seattle architect Carl Gould, Sr., had designed it in a somewhat Mediterranean style, enclosing a sheltered garden. But it had been painted dark brown and had deteriorated a bit, as Puget Sound beach houses will do if given half a chance.

Sensing the possibilities inherent in its architecture, Guen transformed it into a small summer villa, shunning standard Pacific Northwest earth tones, and painting it inside and out in bright blue and white, the colors (though she says this is pure coincidence) of many

Just prior to the Gorbachev era, she paid her first visit to the Soviet Union.

213

of the palaces of imperial St. Petersburg. She tore out the formal garden and replaced it with a pool, in which she still swims. As a final touch, she took the iron gates from her parents' old First Hill house, painted them white, and placed them at the entrance to the property.

With the end of World War II, the Plestcheeffs resumed their regular voyages to Paris. Their hotel, the Lotti, was a high-style, low-profile establishment just off the Place Vendome. It had originally been financed by one of Gabrielle Chanel's many lovers, the Duke of Westminster, who had reserved an entire floor for himself. As always, Paris proved stimulating. Guen came to know Louise de Vilmorin, a novelist and poet, whose perceptive comedies of manners have numerous followers in France, and through her met a number of notables like the painter, Salvador Dali—"a wonderful artist, but a professional show-off."

A new set of couturiers had succeeded those of her prewar years—men like Balenciaga, Hubert de Givenchy, and Jacques Fath. Guen regularly attended their openings, and particularly those of her favorite, Christian Dior; she was present in 1948 when he launched his New Look. She not only viewed their collections, she bought their clothes, many examples of which she has stored in her Capitol Hill house.

Once, when walking down a Paris street, she passed a woman dressed exactly like herself, even down to the shoes. As she had assumed that what she was wearing was hers and hers alone—why else patronize Dior instead of Frederick & Nelson?—she glanced back after she had passed to see who this sartorial pirate might be. It was the Duchess of Windsor.

In 1967, Theodore Plestcheeff died of a heart attack. Though he had become an American citizen thirty years before, those who attended his funeral at Seattle's Russian Orthodox Cathedral of St. Nicholas, in which he had been active, realized that in many ways he remained very much a Russian. His body lay in state, and some mourners kissed him. Others saluted.

One wonders if he favored Seattle over Paris solely because the Pacific Northwest offered superior hunting and fishing. Some of his more perceptive friends believe that, like the novelist Vladimir Nabokov, he regarded the obliterated Russia of his youth as a Paradise Lost, and that visits to Paris, where he knew so many people associated with his past, brought only painful memories.

In any case, his influence on his wife's development had been great. His expert knowledge of Russian art and particularly of Russian porcelain, had sharpened her taste for such things as far back as their days in Estonia. Today, her extensive collection includes such unique items as a pair of gilt-edged, footed platters, which were given by the city of Vienna to Tsar Alexander I in gratitude for his help in freeing their city from Napoleon.

Some of her pieces have special family significance. One of these is an unusual teacup, sky blue, with a frieze of roses around its rim. It belonged to Alexander II, to whom Plestcheeff's grandfather was aide-de-camp. When he was about to marry, he asked the

Tsar's permission, as was the custom of the time. Alexander granted it, and as a memento of the occasion, gave him the teacup from which he had just been drinking. Such pieces will form the core of the collection of the Plestcheeff Institute for the Decorative Arts.

Today, Guen's life goes on much as before. She remains an honorary trustee of the Museum of History and Industry. In her Capitol Hill home, she lives surrounded by mementos of her past: photographs of old Russia, showing lavish costume balls, where the guests are dressed in the style of an eighteenth-century French court; hunting parties, where everyone looks like a Tolstoi peasant; Romanov empresses hung with pearls the size of quails' eggs. There are nineteenth-century Russian prints of such subjects as Napoleon's soldiers, as well as all manner of porcelain. She continues to follow New York auction catalogs, and she still picks up books she finds intriguing, particularly those dealing with the decorative arts. Her phone rings constantly, and though she keeps Whiskey on hand for visitors, she herself is probably the only person in the galaxy who drinks vodka and soda.

"I've got a new Russian piece," she said not long ago. It turned out to be a small ceramic figure of a woodcutter in a white blouse. Princess Galitzine, whose wedding she had witnessed in London, had passed through Seattle a few days before and had brought it to her.

"She's never stopped reading and learning," says Bill Alpert.

In Italy, her Brenna in-laws used to call her a "leaf in the wind," and even today, when she's well past ninety, her travel schedule continues to boggle the minds of her younger friends. It's not only a matter of regular, wardrobe-replenishing flights to Paris, (When complimented on a black-and-white summer outfit she wore to a Bainbridge Island party in 1988 she observed, "It's the only Givenchy I bought this year"); each year, she tries to visit some new place. She's been to Lebanon, to the French Dordogne, and to Budapest. Once, on the spur of the moment, she flew to Sitka, where the Russian-built St. Michael's Cathedral, which burned in 1966, had been restored with the help of money donated by her old friend, Paul Kotzebue. Just prior to the Gorbachev era, she paid her first visit to the Soviet Union. (She didn't like it; the people seemed unsmiling and dour, quite unlike the convivial expatriates she'd known in her youth.) Not long ago, she asked me about Africa. Should she go there? I could think of no reason why not. No reason at all.

A large, sit-down luncheon she recently gave to honor a European visitor was a typically smoothly organized and upbeat Plestcheeff event. She produced it at her blue-and-white Bainbridge Island house, and Poverty Flats never seemed livelier. It was a gentle day, near the end of a brilliant summer; light from the Sound filtered through feathery locusts to fall on pale blue hydrangeas, just starting to fade with the first touch of autumn. Cheerful clusters of blue and white balloons flew everywhere. Almost the only note of contrasting color was supplied by a huge, world-class beach ball, orange, white, yellow, blue, and green, that drifted freely with the wind on the surface of her pool.

No grand dukes were present, no itinerant Balkan queens, but among the guests sampling Guen's East Indian curry were several who had attended her farewell to First Hill half a century before.

Greta Pendrick, whom one had known always—with her memories of driving with her Roman in-laws in the Pincio, dancing to "Yes, We Have No Bananas" on the edge of the Baltic, taking tea at the Paris Ritz with contemporaries of the Lost Generation—Greta Pendrick was back in Chinook, home for a time on the familiar shores of Puget Sound, but thinking ahead to Africa. ◢◣

THE QUEEN OF KING

DOROTHY BULLITT (1892–)

JOHN S. ROBINSON

The year was 1970. Charles Royer, later to be mayor of Seattle, had recently been hired as a commentator for KING-TV, the Seattle television outlet of the KING Broadcasting Company. One day, working at his desk, he was startled to see standing in his doorway an awesome presence: KING's founder, principal owner, ex-board chairman, ex-president, resident figurehead, and company symbol.

"May I come in, Mr. Royer?" asked Dorothy Bullitt.

"What have I done?" thought Royer. When his visitor began talking of the Alaska oil pipeline, he felt he had the answer. He'd recently delivered a piece on that very subject and suspected that some VIP had been enraged by something he'd said. Twice before, he'd left other television jobs because of similar incidents.

"I was sure I'd blown it," he said not long ago. "I kept waiting for the other shoe to drop."

It never did. Mrs. Bullitt hadn't come to complain, but to learn more about the pipeline, a project that intrigued her. Though a mere two years from her eighth decade, she had lately made a trip to Prudhoe Bay, in the deepest Arctic, with a group of three US senators. It quickly became obvious to Royer that she had wasted little of her time.

"I exhausted my knowledge of the pipeline in about fifteen minutes," he said. "I ended up asking *her* questions."

As she talked, Royer found himself more and more intrigued. Here was a woman of almost eighty whom age seemed unable to slow down. "I could just see her up there," he said, "wearing her thermal underwear, stomping around in the snow," at a time of life when many of her contemporaries were wholly content to sit at home, hugging the radiator, and watching—yes—television.

"God, it must have been *cold,*" he said to her.

"Well," said Mrs. Bullitt in her famous, throaty voice, which has sometimes been compared to that of Tallulah Bankhead, and sometimes termed merely a "gentle baritone," "we had a little bourbon."

The long life of Dorothy Bullitt—in many respects, a quintessential Northwesterner—

"What other woman would be inspired to go into the broadcasting business because of some article she'd read?"

comes close to spanning the history of her city. As a young girl, she remembers the aged Princess Angeline, favorite daughter of Chief Seattle, selling Indian baskets on the corner of Second and Madison. Even in those years, Angeline was an almost legendary woman, who was said to have once paddled across Elliott Bay to warn early settlers that hostile Indians were descending the forest-rimmed Duwamish River to attack—thus giving the pioneers time to drop trees across the stream and block passage to their fledgling village.

Time has since moved on. Not long ago, Mrs. Bullitt took off from the roof of the monumental, state-of-the-art KING Broadcasting Building, to fly in a brand-new KING helicopter over the same Duwamish, transformed today beyond all recognition—cleared of its warlike Indians, but as industrial, as polluted, as thoroughly *civilized* as any river in old Europe.

Dorothy Bullitt has lived many lives. Once married to a politician of national stature, she was a friend of Franklin and Eleanor Roosevelt. She has been deeply involved with her church (St. Mark's Episcopal Cathedral), with the University of Washington, and with charities almost without number. She has reared three successful children. Before World War II, when women were thought incapable of business leadership, she was a dominant figure in downtown Seattle real estate. In middle age, she bought the Northwest's first tiny television station and supervised its explosive development into a broadcasting empire. Her influence persists. Today, more than three decades beyond what many people consider the age of retirement, she continues to drop in often at her downtown office.

Yet, somehow, after all this, she has kept her youthful zest for life, even in its smaller aspects. "Look," she said, taking me to the window of her officed when I called on her there. Outside, I could see a gravel-covered rooftop, and a seed-filled cup, but no more. Then suddenly I spotted a small bird, brown and pepper-and-salt in color, resting quietly on the gravel—almost perfectly camouflaged against the rocks.

"It's a nighthawk," she said, with obvious affection for the sturdy little visitor. "She used to fly off when the helicopter went over, but no more. We think she might be sitting on her eggs."

How did it all come about?

Some, says the poet, are born great. Certainly our ancestors matter, and Dorothy Bullitt began by choosing hers well. Her paternal grandfather, Thomas Douglas Stimson, made a fortune in midwestern timber. When the forests in Michigan and Minnesota began to give out, his son, C.D. Stimson, moved west with his wife and their small son, Thomas. They arrived in Seattle early in the year of the great fire of 1889. Stimson bought an old Ballard sawmill, and began at once to expand it. In a few years, his Stimson Mill Company grew into a giant; its shingle-manufacturing arm was, for a time, the largest such facility in the world. Dorothy was born in 1892 in the Stimsons' first house, on Queen Anne Hill.

Though C.D. Stimson was destined to become a powerful business figure in Seattle,

218

his boyhood had been marred by a crippling tragedy. As a result of an accident, his right arm was amputated just below the elbow. Before going into surgery, he said, "If they cut it off, I don't want to come back." But he did come back, and perhaps it was this misfortune that produced in him an uncommon ambition. His strong-willed mother refused to pamper him because of his infirmity, and, seemingly driven to succeed, he not only multiplied his inheritance, but became an expert golfer, hunter, and all-around sportsman.

He owned the first gasoline-powered car in Seattle. "In the summer of 1903," writes Tom Bayley, grandson of Dorothy's elder brother Thomas and his wife, Emma Baillargeon Stimson, "he made a trip to Tacoma and back in one day, a feat considered so remarkable that it was played up in the newspapers." Most of all, he was an accomplished yachtsman; he enjoyed sailing in his big yawl, often with small Dorothy secured by a leash to its mast. It may have been those early voyages that inspired in her a lifelong love of the water.

In 1900, the "C.D.s"—as they were known within their family—moved to a splendid new home at Seneca and Minor on First Hill, a half-timbered structure with stables in the rear, now called the Stimson-Green Mansion, and preserved for the future through the efforts of the Historic Seattle Preservation and Development Authority. First Hill was then the heart of a now-vanished subculture, almost impossible for today's hurried motorist to envision as he roars up frenzied Boren Avenue, past ever-expanding hospitals and ever-higher-rising condos. For many years following the turn of the century, this highly urbanized district remained a peaceful, quiet enclave of unpaved, treelined streets, where lily ponds flourished, rose gardens bloomed, and children could safely ride their ponies at full gallop.

It is said that she didn't so much invite guests to her parties as order them to come.

Here, in vast, drafty wooden houses, which they had begun to build after the fire leveled most of the town below, lived the city's ascendancy. Though little remains of this period—Trinity Episcopal Church, the Sorrento Hotel, the Men's University Club, a mere handful of the old houses—its survivors look back on it with great nostalgia, and often return from The Highlands or Bainbridge Island to take up residence in one of the beetling condos.

In the years before automobiles, people moved in a much smaller orbit. Families knew each other almost too well, and such a tightly knit neighborhood emerged that even today many middle-aged grandchildren of these families remain close friends. It was a slow-moving life of tennis parties and Sunday night buffet suppers; occasionally there was a picnic at far-off Madison Park, or even a boat trip to savage Laurelhurst, where only a few decades before there were more bears in swimming than people.

For the children, there were no video games, no MTV—but Dorothy McEwan Black, a slightly younger friend of Dorothy Bullitt's, recalls hurrying through dinner so she could run down the street to the house of her uncle, Alec McEwan (whose great-grandson, Alec Fisken, founded the late *Seattle Sun*), in time to hear him read chapters out of *Nicholas*

Nickleby to his two daughters.

On the other hand, First Hill's was a somewhat rigid society, where tribal conventions were strictly observed. Protesting little boys wore white gloves to Mr. Christensen's dancing school—but, as they grew out of childhood, they ceased to protest. One Seattle matron told me that when her father, a promising young lawyer, arrived in Seattle just after World War I, he was denied admittance to the most prestigious local dance club because his parents had been divorced.

Women, of course, stayed home, receiving friends on special days engraved on their visiting cards. The general view of their participation in serious affairs was well summed up by C. T. Conover, a journalist of a slightly later period. In *Mirrors of Seattle,* a sort of up-with-people eulogy of such civic leaders as Harold Preston, lawyer-grandfather of novelist Mary McCarthy, he wrote:

> The administration of the schools is a great big business proposition, pure and simple, and that is why one woman on the board decreases its efficiency just 20 per cent. I don't care who the woman is, she can't grasp big business matters like Nathan Eckstein, Ebenezer Shorrock, William Pigott and men experienced all their lives in the management of great business enterprises. Sentimentally, women should serve on the school board; practically, absolutely not.

Young Dorothy Stimson is very well remembered from her First Hill years, always as a strong, decisive personality. In a 1957 memoir in Seattle's Junior League magazine *Puget Soundings,* her contemporary, the late Gladys Waterhouse Minor, termed her "the only girl who could climb, hand over hand on a rope, up the steep sides of the [Waterhouse] stable to the loft above. A power even then to be reckoned with." Always devoted to animals, she was much envied by her Minor Avenue peers because she owned a horse. Josiah Collins, former husband of her daughter Patsy, recalls being told how, when a couple of neighbor boys began teasing it, feisty Dorothy picked up a buggy whip and drove them off.

She didn't spend all her hours outdoors. From the time she could sit at a keyboard, her mother saw to it that she studied piano. Harriet Overton Stimson, at least in her mature years, was reportedly a rather regal presence. It is said that she didn't so much *invite* guests to her parties as *order* them to come. On the other hand, she was devoted to music and was herself an excellent pianist. A friend of Nellie Centennial Cornish, she at least twice rescued that famous arts educator's budding Cornish School from financial ruin. Mrs. Stimson also helped found the Seattle Symphony Orchestra. Dorothy Bullitt remembers the Symphony's initial Moore Theater concert in 1908, for which many men in the audience appeared in rented evening clothes, having lent their own to the musicians.

"She had tears in her eyes," says Mrs. Bullitt of her mother's response to the concert.

220

The redoubtable Dorothy Bullitt:
queen of KING

Bertha Landes

In 1926, Bertha Landes, a competent and progressive woman, rode a popular antivice campaign into the mayor's office. The city was not settled on the question of vice or women, however, and two years later she lost her reelection campaign.

From "What Happened in Seattle," by Julia N. Budlong, The Nation, August 29, 1928. Copyright © 1928 The Nation Company. Reprinted by permission of The Nation magazine/The Nation Company, Inc.

Bertha K. Landes came into political life by the logical though unusual avenue of the woman's club. Her life had been spent as a university professor's wife, with home and school her major occupations and her husband's students as her hobby, until her own children were grown and she found herself left with her hands freed for less personal labors. She joined the social-service department of the Century Club, one of the largest women's city clubs, and became, in rapid succession, her department's chairman, the club's president, and president of the City Federation of Women's Clubs. . . .

When the war came Mrs. Landes was made chairman of her club's Red Cross department and endured for two years the incessant strain which broke many a conscientious man and woman. It did not break Mrs. Landes. The war over, agitation for "a woman on the City Council" brought a demand that she run for the office. The idea seemed ridiculous to her at first, but the insistence of her friends and the pressure of city-wide appeals eventually persuaded her to permit her candidacy to be filed. She and her teammate were elected by a large vote on a non-partisan ballot. Three years later she was reelected by an even larger vote, though her teammate was snowed under. She was made president of the council.

Then came Mrs. Landes's big chance and she met it like a Puritan and a general. The mayor was journeying eastward to a convention in New York. As president of the City Council, Mrs. Landes was to preside at the City Hall in his absence. "Well, there won't be much to do," he said, as he inducted her into his swivel chair behind the mahogany table. "But keep your eye on the Chief here," and he indicated the head of the police force, present for the ceremonies. . . .

Mrs. Landes was not a politician. She was a housekeeper and a clubwoman. She had been given power. She believed in God. She lay awake all one night thinking about it, she tells us. She felt like a martyr. "Oh, I didn't want to do it!" But in the morning she wrote the Chief of Police a letter, calling to his attention certain glaring defects in his administrative force and directing him to correct them immediately. The Chief's reply was saucy. In effect he said: "The charter gives you authority to take over the police forces of the city and run them yourself. Why don't you do it?" So she did.

The next limited train leaving New

York for points west had Mayor Brown of Seattle on board. Five days later he stormed into the office where Mrs. Landes sat in his swivel chair. His month's visit had been cut to three weeks. It was the wrong gesture on the Mayor's part, and the next election found Mrs. Landes established in his swivel chair by a 6,000 plurality.

But two years later found her defeated for reelection by a plurality of 19,000. Had her administration been a failure? Far from it. Her knottiest problem had been the street-car tangle. Seattle, insisting upon a five-cent fare, had taken over its street-cars under a tremendously inflated condemnation appraisal. The five-cent fare had had to be raised to ten cents and during three months of the year the employees of the system were on a voucher basis. This tangle Mrs. Landes inherited. She wrestled manfully with the problem and each year of her incumbency the city was less in debt than the year before. But, midway of her term in office, in December, 1926, the banks suddenly refused to honor the city's vouchers. Investigation revealed that, under the State law, the city could not transfer funds from one department to another to meet an emergency. It looked as if the city would have no funds with which to pay its employees, and Christmas was at

Bertha Landes

hand. Then the character of the allegiance which Mrs. Landes is able to command became evident. Every one of the vouchers was redeemed—by private citizens, by downtown department stores, by small, outlying banks. . . .

The only reason for her defeat which

Bertha Landes with Will Rogers

game of politics. And this Mrs. Landes has steadfastly refused to do. She has contended that politics has no place in municipal government; that political parties should be national organizations concerned with national policies, while the governing of a city was a matter of civic housekeeping—of buying stores and repairing streets and keeping the city clean and well and beautiful and as good as possible, efficiently, smoothly, and economically.

To this end she made all her appointments on the basis of efficiency and fitness, and not from the standpoint of political sagacity. . . . This is no way for a politician to act. It is puzzling, and irritating to the old guard. It is impossible for the politicians and bosses and grafters to catch step—to understand the rules of the game. Moreover, Mrs. Landes had what she characterized as an immense advantage over a man in her position. Having no family dependent upon her, she was in a position to ignore caution and self-interest. This is the unique contribution which, she believes, the woman with a grown family may make to wise governing. . . .

It is strongly to be doubted that Mrs. Landes will ever seek office on her own account. . . . Certainly in politics one must stoop to conquer, and she, no doubt, will choose never to stoop.

anyone has ever given is her sex. Seattle is sensitive to its reputation as a he-man city. It did not like to be teased about its mayor. It was just as irritated by the taunt: "What's the matter with you folks out there; haven't you got any men in Seattle that you have to have a woman for mayor?" as was Texas by the gibe: "The great open spaces, where men are men and women are governors." No one, not even a city, not even an honorable woman, can stand up against a campaign of ridicule. . . .

There is a deeper moral to the story, however, and a sadder one. No one can be successful in politics without playing the

It included the overture to Wagner's *Tannhauser,* and one recalls that this period was close in time to the preradio epoch of Willa Cather's story *A Wagner Matinee,* in which an elderly woman, long exiled on a pioneer Nebraska farm and starved for good music, is overcome with emotion on hearing the same overture performed in New York.

Dorothy loved learning piano, and her early enthusiasm was not destined to fade. KING-FM fans almost certainly owe the existence and format of their favorite radio station to the determination of a woman of whom they may never have heard, that her sports-minded daughter should know something of serious music. Indeed, it may well be that without those First Hill piano lessons, today's whole mammoth KING Broadcasting Company would never have come into being.

As a young girl, Dorothy Bullitt's education was not markedly different from that of other girls of her First Hill circle. It was not designed to produce an original thinker, or even a woman equipped to fend for herself; she was never taught to cook, and cannot do so to this day. She attended an eastern boarding school—Briarcliff Manor—but, bright and talented though she clearly was, it was not expected or intended that she should continue on to college. Instead, she studied voice at The Juilliard School in New York.

Meanwhile, her father, increasingly successful, branched out into real estate. His philosophy was to buy property and sell it fast. In burgeoning Seattle, which grew explosively after the Klondike Gold Rush, that was exactly the right approach. In 1913, he moved his family to Norcliffe, a Spanish-style mansion he had built for them in The Highlands—a residential suburb north of the city, carved out of land to which he had once held full title.

In later years, his grandchildren seem to have regarded this house chiefly as the locus for long, tiresome Sunday breakfasts with critical older relatives. It was eventually sold to the late Paul Pigott of the Pacific Car and Foundry Company, and today belongs to his widow, now married to former CIA Director John McCone. A few years ago, one of Patsy Collins's sons told his mother that he was going out that evening to a party in The Highlands—"somebody named McCone." "I was born in that house," she told him.

In 1918, Dorothy was married to a somewhat older man she had met while serving as maid of honor at a wedding—Alexander Scott Bullitt, a Princetonian lawyer who came from a family quite as remarkable as hers. Its origins were in Virginia and Kentucky. A Philadelphia offshoot produced William C. Bullitt, once Franklin D. Roosevelt's ambassador to France and the Soviet Union, who was briefly married to Louise Bryant, heroine of the film *Reds.* Scott Bullitt had studied under Woodrow Wilson. His lifelong passion was politics, which, to his wife's friends, was all right—but his party was the Democratic, which was not.

It would be misleading to suggest that Democrats were wholly beyond the pale in pre-Depression Seattle. The animal dislike between the parties that marked the New Deal years had not yet developed. Still, many middle-class WASPs saw the Democrats as an unwholesome gaggle of unwashed immigrants and scheming union members, prone to corruption and likely to threaten the foundations of the Republic by their support of wholly unjustified strikes.

There were a few well-known Democrats in Washington public life—like J.T. Ronald, for many years the patriarch of the King County Superior Court—but, for the most part, they reached their status not because of their party, but in spite of it. A far more usual type was the upwardly mobile young Democrat, who arrived in the city, saw he was not on the winning team, quietly switched parties, and joined the Rotary Club.

Scott Bullitt, as an old-time Southerner and admirer of Wilson, was not about to switch. He is remembered as a highly gregarious, popular man—"He'd move into a building, and in three days the mailman was his best friend," says Dorothy Bullitt—and, had the times been different, he might well have succeeded in his political ambitions.

In 1926, he ran for the United States Senate, and lost to the incumbent, Wesley Jones. Two years later, he tried for governor. This time, his primary opponent was another distinguished Democrat with southern connections: Stephen J. Chadwick, whose wife was a granddaughter of President Tyler. Amid cries that the Bullitts had "bought" the election, he defeated Chadwick but lost the general election to the Republican, Roland Hartley. That year, 1928, was the peak year for Republican power. I recall in a straw vote on the presidential candidates taken in the first grade at Madrona School, the only kid who favored Al Smith over Herbert Hoover was Stephen J. Chadwick's loyal daughter, Mary Tyler.

Meanwhile, Scott Bullitt became Democratic national committeeman, and a friend and supporter of the rising young star Franklin Delano Roosevelt. In 1932, he persuaded the Washington State Democratic Convention to endorse Roosevelt's bid for the presidency; James A. Farley, Roosevelt's postmaster general, once stated that in the event of Democratic victory, it had been planned to make Bullitt the secretary of the navy. But the victory came too late. Prior to the national convention, at which he was scheduled to put Roosevelt's name in nomination, Scott Bullitt, then fifty-three, died of cancer of the liver. He was survived by his wife and three children: Charles Stimson, known as "Stim" to most of his friends; Priscilla, who has never lost her childhood name of "Patsy"; and Harriet.

In this crisis, the party turned to his widow, who took his place as delegate to the national convention in Chicago. Dorothy Bullitt recalls waiting up all night in the stifling summer heat—no air-conditioning then—for the arrival of the candidate to accept his nomination, at dawn.

Later, when Franklin and Eleanor Roosevelt came to Seattle, Mrs. Bullitt asked them to visit Children's Orthopedic Hospital (now Children's Hospital), so that the handicapped children there would see for themselves what Roosevelt—crippled by polio—had been able to do with his life. As they were riding up the hill from the Olympic Hotel, the future President touched her deeply by turning and saying, "Scott knows about this."

But politics were never to be her main line of endeavor. She had other and more immediately pressing concerns. Her father had died in 1929; her only brother, Thomas, in a 1931 airplane accident (himself leaving a wife and four small children). These three sudden deaths not only profoundly affected her; they left her in a very insecure position. Her upbringing had perfectly prepared her for a role in Washington, DC, as the wife of a cabinet member. Instead, at forty, she found herself not only the single parent of three minor children, but charged with the sole responsibility for managing her share of a large estate—work for which she had had no previous training whatsoever. Needless to say, wolves waited in the offing; the widow no doubt appeared easy prey.

"I didn't know the difference between a lease and a permit to go swimming," she says today. "I didn't even have a lawyer. Can you imagine?"

That particular lack was soon remedied. At a Princeton reunion, she had met the late Raymond Wright, and she called him at once. But even a good lawyer couldn't solve all her problems. In 1932, the Great Depression had hit bottom. The downtown Seattle real estate that provided the core of her holdings (the Stimson Mill having been largely left to her brother) showed signs of becoming a liability. The lessee of her Coliseum Theater had broken his lease, and some of the office tenants in her 1411 Fourth Avenue Building were moving out. More than one came up to her and said, "We're broke. Here's your lease. Goodbye. You can keep our furniture."

She went to work at once. A reliable lessee was obtained for the theater. Losing confidence in the manager of her office building, she dismissed him and took over its management herself. In her old First Hill house—which had since been bought by banker Joshua Green—her name "Dorothy" remained by a bell in the kitchen, placed there so she could communicate with the servants whenever she needed them. But in the 1411 Fourth Avenue Building, she herself learned to do such down-to-earth chores as inspect bathrooms in order to make sure they had enough towels, or ascertain that the janitors had a proper place to sleep.

She learned about balance sheets, and became well known for her ability to memorize them. She entered with enthusiasm into the perpetual downtown battle for tenants—then aggravated by the grim state of the economy—and, says her friend Frances Owen, never forgot those who stuck with her. The wolves soon slunk off in search of weaker prey.

Just as had been the case with her father, it almost seemed as though adversity had released in this properly bred First Hill lady hitherto unsuspected reserves of talent and power. When Children's Orthopedic Hospital needed a new site, Frances Owen, as hospital president, called on Dorothy Bullitt for help in locating one; she was amazed at her friend's shrewd knowledge of real estate. Again, when the hospital's governing structure needed revision, Mrs. Bullitt suggested that it be set up like a bank headed by a president

She began a wholly new career, the one in which she was to achieve her greatest fulfillment.

Mrs. Bullitt on the roof of the
futuristic KING building

and board of directors. That remains its basic organization today.

Such extracurricular efforts, coupled with her evident expertise at her work, soon earned her a widespread reputation. "Best businessman in town!" the late *Argus* publisher Philip Bailey—no mean businessman himself—was wont, many years later, to say of her to his new reporter, Shelby Scates. That some might consider this remark less praise than old-style male chauvinism surely never occurred to Bailey, nor to the many others who made it—so many of them, indeed, that it soon attained the status of a Seattle cliché. At least, it marked a quantum leap from the views of C.T. Conover.

One of the fascinating things about Dorothy Bullitt is that for all her business shrewdness, for all her intuitive understanding of people, for all her affinity for the new, both in science and politics—none of them qualities usually associated with Edwardian heiresses—she retains the appearance, manner, and many of the conventions of behavior of the period and class in which she grew up. When it came to her children's education, she proved as traditionalist as any Boston banker. All went east, Stimson to Kent and Yale, Patsy to Ethel Walker and Vassar, and Harriet to Chatham Hall and Bennington. (Harriet later graduated from the University of Washington and Stimson from its law school.)

While this early education in a different part of the country certainly broadened their world view, and may well have strengthened them by placing them in situations where they were unable to coast on family and connections, it may also have increased their separation from most western contemporaries. One of Stim's chief boyhood aims was to appear a tad more *average*. During a teen-age summer, he and I worked for a time with a state highway department crew at Chinook Pass. When he dropped by in his family's station wagon to drive me to work, I apologized for our modest Denny-Blaine house, feeling that to one used to the splendors of his home turf—which I knew from taking out his cousin—it must look like some gatekeeper's cottage.

"It's a nice house," said Stim tactfully (actually, he was quite right, I wish I could afford to buy it back today). As yet, I didn't know him well enough to realize that of all the boys in Seattle, the one who would probably care least about the size of his friends' houses was Stimson Bullitt. His worry, only a few years before, had been that he might be spotted by fellow Boy Scouts as he passed them in his grandparents' chauffeur-driven Rolls.

As the 1930s drew to a close, Dorothy Bullitt discovered that real-estate management no longer presented its once-formidable challenge to her. After a lease had been signed, there was little more for the lessor to do. A natural extrovert, she sought activity that involved more daily contact with people. She found it in the world of broadcasting. At an age when many men, feeling their options for the future are rapidly falling away, face up to a serious crisis of spirit, she began a wholly new career, the one in which she was to achieve her greatest fulfillment.

She had always been interested in FM radio; before World War II, she had heard it demonstrated in a New York laboratory, and it seemed to her the ideal medium for broadcasting the kind of music she liked. She was about to submit an application to start the process of obtaining an FM license, when Arch Talbot, one of her tenants, said, "It's silly to bring in another station. I have a station nobody listens to. Why not buy it?"

It seemed a good solution. In 1947, the newly formed KING Broadcasting Company, of which she was president, bought KEVR, which had both an AM and an FM outlet. She wanted the call letters KING because they spelled the name of the county; learning that they already belonged to an East Coast merchant ship, she was able to acquire them. It was next necessary to find a station manager, and here she displayed a quality that nearly everyone mentions as one of the principal keys to her success.

"Her great ability was in picking the right person for the right job," said her longtime associate, the late John Leffler, retired Dean of St. Mark's Cathedral. "She has an uncanny sense of personality and ability. If she thought someone was the right man, she'd do anything to get him."

In this case, Henry Owen, the husband of her old friend, Frances, was out of military service and considering offers. He joined the company and remained with it for many years, later becoming its vice president for business.

"The morning we moved into the office, Henry took the manager's desk," she says. "He looked at the mail. A check fell out of the first envelope he opened. The letter was from Hooper, the first man who measured ratings. Hooper said, 'We've just made a survey of the Seattle situation, and we didn't find any audience listening to your station. Here's your money back.' "

From that point, there was nowhere to go but up. The station was located in the Smith Tower; Mrs. Bullitt took a desk in the hall and came down each day. One liability was promptly converted into an asset. Seattle's harbor lay just below, and, precisely at noon, all the boats blew their whistles, drowning out whatever program happened to be in progress. The whistles couldn't be silenced. So they were put to good use. "Set your watch by our whistles," urged the station and offered the time for sale. "We had them standing in line for that," says Mrs. Bullitt.

Her involvement with television was to come years later. Before World War II, she had seen a photo in a copy of *Life* illustrating a piece which told how—as she puts it—"you could have a box in your house which would show moving pictures." The novel concept appealed to her scientific turn of mind. In 1939, she went to New York where she observed the possibilities of the new medium. ("What other woman," asks Frances Owen, "would be inspired to go into the broadcasting business because of some article she'd read?")

Meanwhile, one P.K. Leberman, a bright, young toiler in the Seattle vineyard of Merrill Lynch, had been even more captivated. This enthusiastic amateur had gone so far as to acquire Channel 5 from the federal government and build himself a station, using an old butcher shop for its headquarters and surplus property for its tower. On Thanksgiving Day, 1948, it went on the air. Its first broadcast was a high school football game.

"It was full of bugs," says Mrs. Bullitt. "Engineers didn't know a lot then." Leberman's employers saw his station as a distracting toy, something like a large, backyard telescope. They offered him the chance to head their *Family Circle* magazine if only he would move to New York and "get rid of that thing you're playing with out there on the Coast."

Leberman knew of Mrs. Bullitt's interest; she had been the only person to send flowers when his station opened. "He asked if I would buy it," she remembers. "I said, 'We're running in the red with our radio station now, and I don't know if I can afford it,' " (a characteristic response). Leberman offered the station to radio stations KIRO and KOMO. Both turned it down, feeling there weren't enough sets in the area—a mere six thousand—to justify its cost, especially since it only broadcast from 4 A.M. to 10 P.M. Much of the really wise money chose to avoid television altogether, seeing it as a diversion that might titillate the rich, but would never, as they say, play in Peoria.

Chicago's Marshall Field, however, was interested enough in buying Leberman's station to send the head of its broadcasting division west to Seattle with a broker. In the negotiations that followed, Mrs. Bullitt was represented by Andrew Gallagher Haley, an outspoken lawyer who had left the Federal Communications Commission for private practice (his daughter, Delphine, became well known to readers of *Pacific Northwest,* the magazine later founded by Harriet Bullitt, for her environmental articles).

When Haley proposed a price for the station, the broker, his competitor, said, "That's an insult!" Haley said, "You keep out of this, you Arab rug merchant." Mrs. Bullitt was charmed. "Where did you get that epithet?" she asked. "I just made it up," said Haley. "What I wanted to say, I couldn't in front of you."

The Marshall Field representatives held off, hoping the price would go down. Meanwhile, Mrs. Bullitt moved in and bought the station—with an FM station thrown in—for $375,000. Field's agents lost out, though they had been authorized to offer up to $500,000.

"I'd have hated," says Mrs. Bullitt, "to go back to Chicago and explain that someone else had bought it for only $375,000."

Today, of course, $375,000 seems a paltry figure, the price of a comfortable house in some of Seattle's lakeshore neighborhoods—a mere fraction of KING's current annual budget for news alone. To Dorothy Bullitt's advisers, though, it sounded enormous: "375,000 round simoleons!" exclaimed one of them when he heard the news. Then he considered for a moment and remarked with great prescience, "Being you, I think you'll probably make it go."

Almost immediately, the number of television sets owned by the public began to proliferate, and not only in mansions. Antennae sprouted from unkempt cottages faster than the crabgrass in their lawns. It became clear to the most skeptical that the new medium would have much of its appeal precisely for those who could not afford to buy a boat or make a trip abroad.

Then came the freeze. Because certain transmittal problems had developed that no one had yet been able to solve, the FCC placed a temporary ban on the establishment of any new stations. For KING, this proved a bonanza. Being the only television station west of the Mississippi and north of San Francisco, it had a monopoly. For a time, it carried programs from all three networks.

Though the freeze eventually thawed, and KING today is affiliated with NBC alone, it continued to prosper. Like her father in the post-Klondike years, Dorothy Bullitt found herself in exactly the right business at the right time. Some years later, when Channel 8 in Portland became available, things were going so well that Haley urged her to acquire it.

The Blethens

Like many publishing dynasties in America, the Blethen family has gone from flamboyant founders to sober scions. In the process, **The Seattle Times** *became the dominant paper in the city and the state. Here's the story of the first two generations, and a powerful editor, who shaped the paper into its ultimate character.*

From "Behind the Times," by David Brewster, Seattle Magazine, *November 1969. Copyright © 1969 David Brewster. Reprinted by permission.*

The *Seattle Times*' traditional formula was established by three very strong men, each of whom ruled the paper for about 20 years. The first of these, Colonel Alden J. Blethen, arrived in town in 1896, a victim of the Panic of 1893 which had ended his newspapering in Minneapolis. A native of Knox, Maine, Blethen blew into Seattle at the age of 40, possessed of a blunt manner of speaking, a leonine head, a strictly honorary title (he had never been in uniform), and several impressive talents, among which was a gift for invective. When he played pool at the Arctic Club, the Colonel hit every shot as hard as he could. The same aggressiveness soon characterized the *Times*, which he resurrected from a lingering death in 1896. Soon he was a familiar sight in the young city, recognizable by his strutting walk and his heavy gold-headed cane. This last item he carried for protection, since the Colonel had a lot of enemies.

Chief among these enemies was the *Post-Intelligencer*. After reading the competition, he would come on full-bore against whatever the *P-I* favored, whether it was a slate of candidates, municipal ownership of utilities, or an "open-city" policy toward vice. At the time, the *P-I* was an organ of the Republican party, and the Colonel, who argued he was a "true" Republican deserted by his party, soon tore

into government by party regulars. He fought for the blanket primary, a device for weakening party control (and strengthening the paper's influence over elections). He advocated frugal business principles as the way to run a city, and launched a campaign against R.H. Thomson, the visionary city engineer of the day. (Thomson fought back in a very practical way: he repeatedly sent his men up to fine the Colonel for illegally watering the lawn of his Queen Anne home, at 519 W. Highland Drive.) . . .

Despite the paper's erratic track record, it was forming solid alliances with the downtown interests and the upper crust of the city. Other habits of the paper were also being set: its love of playing politics and being a part of coalitions; its advocacy of low taxes; its preference for prudent businessmen rather than for politicians who aroused the populace and often took bribes; and a noisy patriotism mixed with boosterism.

The Colonel died in 1915, shortly after his last, most extravagant campaign, which was waged against the I.W.W. The Colonel, who was an admirer of William Randolph Hearst, elevated a fist-fight into a full-scale riot—and just about had a real one on his hands the next day—in order to inflame his readers against the Wobblies. It didn't work, partly because the *Times* had become too closely identified with the chamber of commerce and shipping interests. . . .

When the Colonel died, his son, Clarance B.—known as "C.B."—had been managing editor for a dozen years, and there was no doubt where the paper's allegiance still lay. . . . Editorially, solid Republicanism set in at the *Times*—except for the few months in 1932 when the paper, to everyone's astonishment, supported F.D.R. Apart from some of C.B.'s idiosyncratic judgments—he opposed the first floating bridge, which he claimed would sink (later he wrote an editorial headed, "I eat Crow"), and the Aurora bridge, claiming traffic it carried would asphyxiate the animals in the zoo—he was a steady supporter of the downtown point of view. He was also a fanatic supporter of all things military; unlike his father, he was a real colonel (in the Washingtton National Guard), and was eventually promoted to general.

The second-generation Blethens lived in ostentatious wealth. Their summer home was in Medina (later to be owned by the Norton Clapps), and their winter quarters were in the "bungalow," which was nothing less than the entire top floor of the Olympic Hotel, for which they paid $700 a month rent. . . .

The Blethens had five boys. They

Nick Gunderson

The Blethens: (left to right) Will, Bob, Jack, Frank, and Buster

grew up to be very polite, somewhat distant and shy men who lacked their father's verve or love of fame. The youngest son, John Alden, who later became a relativlely unknown publisher of the *Times*, has only a few close friends and does not publically articulate any strong views. His oldest brother was the one son with a strong personality. He stood up to his rather domineering father, and even bolted the paper to work for the Seattle *Star*, a spunky, workingman's paper that folded in 1947. Everything he wrote for the competition had a large, needling byline, "By Clarance B. Blethen 2d." Eventually "Judge," as he

Alden J. Blethen

was called by reporters who were fond of his spirit, had trouble with the law, was disinherited, and finally joined with the Ridder family—who in 1930 had bought 49.5 per cent of the paper's stock—to try to regain his inheritance and turn over control of the paper to the Ridders. . . .

C.B., meanwhile, had one consuming interest: to make the *Times* a mass-circulation paper. In this endeavor, C.B.'s right-hand man was one of the legendary figures at the paper, Harry Cahill, a red-faced, affable man whose manner is reminiscent of George F. Babbitt. . .

Together, C.B. and Cahill devised the "clean-editing" policy of the *Times*. They decided Seattle was going to be something more than a raw port city, and also that if they went after home-delivery sales by producing a paper no man would be ashamed to have around the house at night, they would soon overtake their more sensation-prone competition. Thus, crime news was banished from the front page; such unwholesome words as "gun" and "blood" were prohibited; the upper-class orientation of the paper was altered to attract the more cautious middle-class, and an emphasis was put on heart-warming local news and "correct" editorial policy that would offend almost no one. "We wanted a down-to-earth newspaper that is welcome in every home and of interest to each member of the family," explains Cahill, who retired in 1970 after 44 years of service. In short order, the *Times* became the best-selling paper in the city.

Probably no man has been more responsible for the *Times*' financial success than C.B. He knew the business cold. His formula for keeping ahead of the competition was to pick out a superior batch of comics, to contract for good wire services and features, and to initiate a variety of mechanical advances. Above all, he followed the lead of most American publishers, dishing out daily helpings that were big but bland, digestable but forgettable. The day had passed when Joseph Pulitzer's *New York World* would have adopted as its motto, "The *World* Has No Friends." As far as anyone can remember, the *Times* lost its last libel suit when it poked fun at an embassy party in the late 1930's; indeed, the sum of *all* libel settlements paid by the paper throughout its existence is less than $25,000. . . .

After C.B. Blethen died in 1941, the paper seems to have become primarily a business, with the three active sons sharing an interest in separate aspects of the paper: Frank in the mechanical side, Bill in advertising (these two brothers died within a month of each other in 1967), and Jack, the present publisher, in editorial. The fourth brother, Clarance Jr., remains disinherited and lives in New York; the fifth brother, Alden, was killed in a motorcycle accident at the age of 20. . . .

The third editor, Russell McGrath, is still a powerful influence at the *Times*, even though he departed, dramatically, in 1960 in a policy row. "Mr. McGrath," as he was called, was a self-educated man who grew up in Pittsburgh and joined the *Times* in 1919. He wore a green eyeshade, arm garters and an out-of-date green tweed suit. He was very fastidious, eating his sandwich with a knife and fork, and very *gallante*, always standing when a lady entered the newsroom. But he wrote his reporters thousands of withering notes that revealed an extravagant concern for the purity of the English language. Once a headline writer tried to get away with "Blue Skies for Seafair!" McGrath shot back: "There's only one sky."

McGrath put together an excellent staff and proceeded to turn the paper into a "journal of record." He started the practice of meticulously detailing local events in a concise, flat style, convinced that Seattle needed a local paper which future historians could refer to, much as they do the *New York Times*. . . .

In one field, however, McGrath often encouraged boldness, and this was investigative reporting by two-man teams. Many well-known *Times* men—Paul Staples, Stanton Patty, Ed Guthman, Don Duncan, George Meyers, and John and Marshall Wilson (who are not related)— worked on various crusades, the most famous of which was Guthman's exposure of the Canwell committee in 1949. "The investigations played no favorites," recalls a writer under McGrath, "and the paper gained heightened respect. Now, I'm afraid too many *Times* investigations have obvious political motivations." Yet it was his fondness for exposés, says this *Times* veteran, which led to McGrath's downfall, for he refused to lay off when advertising or circulation interests might be jeopardized. (The reason usually given for his departure is that McGrath, who favored emphasizing local news, let the *New York Times* news service lapse—to be picked up at once by the *P-I*.)

McGrath retreated to his home on Queen Anne, and an era of much smoother relations between editorial and business interests set in. Yet McGrath's impact remains strong. If the paper today has a high reputation for accuracy, it also has a high one for stodginess; if it covers a lot of territory, it also concentrates on the standard sources; and if it still has a sharp nose for corruption, it also appears oblivious to subtler, less sensational, but enormously important failings in our society.

"Your application will be fought," he said—by this time, the box showing moving pictures had found its way into a majority of homes, and eager competitors for an available channel were everywhere—"but even if you don't get it, you'll still have Seattle."

"So we headed for the contest," says Mrs. Bullitt, "and it was one of the bloodiest situations I've ever gotten into."

The resulting FCC hearing, held in Washington, DC, lasted a grueling eleven weeks in the winter and early spring of 1953. "I was in court every day," says Mrs. Bullitt; "I never even saw the cherry blossoms." She was accompanied by Haley and by Gloria Chandler, an expert on children's programs at KING (she had brought in Ruth Prinz, creator of the immensely popular "Wunda Wunda").

Chief rival suitor for the Portland channel was the powerful Westinghouse Corporation. Its representatives were totally confident of victory—particularly when they saw their opposition, two nice ladies wearing hats and white gloves, "looking," as Harriet Bullitt puts it, "as though they were going to a meeting of the garden club."

Luckily, the Westinghouse group presented its case first, and the KING faction was able to profit from their errors. "We made some mistakes," says Mrs. Bullitt, "but they made more." Though the hearing was conducted before an administrative law judge, the leading Westinghouse lawyer, accustomed to trial practice, behaved as though he were trying a jury case.

To the astonishment of their opponents, the garden club ladies ultimately triumphed.

"Each time a witness gave an answer he didn't want," she recalls, "a pained look would come over his face, as though he were thinking, 'That's a lie!'" Without twelve good men and true to impress, such tactics proved, in the end, counterproductive.

During the hearing, Mrs. Bullitt spotted a wheeled platform bearing a huge load of documents apparently pertaining to the Hearst Corporation. The importance of these was immediately clear. At that time, Hearst owned a 25 percent interest in KING, having bought it when the television station badly needed money for new equipment. It seemed apparent that Westinghouse would seek to prove that Hearst's nationwide record of public service was not such as to warrant awarding it the new channel. Mrs. Bullitt wasted no time. She promptly went to New York and bought back Hearst's 25-percent share. Now Hearst lacked any interest whatever in KING, and when counsel for Westinghouse sought to introduce the supposedly damaging documents, they were no longer relevant.

When the time came for Mrs. Bullitt and Mrs. Chandler to testify, they were ready. "They'd done their homework," says Harriet Bullitt. "They spoke without reading notes."

During a discussion of KING's financial condition, Mrs. Bullitt was asked, almost as an afterthought, if she could contribute anything. "I said I would try," she says. "That was one thing I did know." It was soon clear to everyone in the courtroom that she understood KING's financial affairs down to the last nickel.

A crucial factor that emerged in the testimony was KING's strong commitment to

236

community service. Mrs. Bullitt and her staff had queried all sorts of groups and agencies in Portland to learn what they thought a television station might be able to do for them. When they couldn't reach a local rabbi, they went to his synagogue to get his views. KING's Seattle record was also helpful, particularly the testimony of Gloria Chandler concerning her children's programs.

To the astonishment of their opponents, the garden club ladies ultimately triumphed. At the time, Westinghouse was advertising, "You can be sure with Westinghouse." When Mrs. Bullitt returned to New York, the clerk at her hotel asked, "Have you seen *Variety?*" Across the front page of the show business periodical was a banner headline reading "Westinghouse Is Not Sure." Soon after, the victors took over Channel 8 and began broadcasting as KGW-TV.

Having secured its second television channel, the KING Broadcasting Company was well on its way to becoming the regional giant it is today, with additional stations in Spokane and Boise, cable holdings in California and elsewhere, and AM and FM radio outlets located as far south as San Francisco. Dorothy Bullitt retired as company president in 1962, replaced by her son, Stimson (who, in turn, left KING in 1971 to practice law and manage the family real estate, and was succeeded as president by the recently retired Ancil Payne). For several years, she functioned as board chairman; later she stepped down in favor of her daughter, Patsy. As a director, she continues to exert a strong influence in company affairs—though nowadays usually in concert with her two daughters. Around KING, the Bullitts are spoken of collectively as "The Family," in much the same way as Mount Rainier is spoken of as "The Mountain."

Outside of KING, Dorothy Bullitt's reputation within the industry has long been well established. "In the mid-sixties," says anchorman Mike James, "I was a student at Washington State. She would come in as a speaker to address students in radio and television. The whole notion you had of this woman was of a real pioneer in broadcasting. KING was the station you wanted to be associated with."

For years, KING-FM was carried by the company with no expectation that its classical music format would ever make money. Essentially, Dorothy Bullitt subsidized it, in much the same way the late Dr. Richard E. Fuller underwrote the annual deficits at the Seattle Art Museum. Eric Bremner, now president of KING's broadcast division, tells of a time during those dark ages when a particularly gifted AM salesman actually sold a commercial for the FM station. This was such a novelty that the announcer forgot to read it. "On the FM station," says Bremner, "a commercial was a foreign beast."

This is no longer true. "A few years ago," he adds, "we faced the question of whether to keep the station as a classical juke box operation, or to work toward the day when we could have an improved facility with better equipment and staff and sell it to advertisers." The latter option was chosen. The station's equipment was updated and its original signal

When it was over, her response was succinct. "Of course you should show it," she said.

237

Brother Tom and Dorothy, age 3

strengthened. Today, as its listeners know, KING-FM sells plenty of advertising, without having to sacrifice the quality of its programming to do so.

Dorothy Bullitt's influence on the development of regional television has been equally profound. As the area's bellwether station, KING-TV inevitably became a trend-setter. In many ways, it helped determine the manner in which the rest of the industry would grow—and most observers feel that, relatively speaking, Pacific Northwest television now stands fairly high. "Technically, it's as good as anything in the country," says John Carmody, Seattle-born television columnist for *The Washington Post*. "I think KING had a lot to do with that." As for the standard of its programming, Seattle television is usually seen as comparing favorably with that of such highly ranked cities as Boston—and few would dispute that over the years, KING has had much to do with *that*.

From the outset, the company has tried to pursue multiple goals. Education mattered and quality mattered, particularly in the coverage of news. Dorothy Bullitt has always had a strong feeling of identification with the Pacific Northwest. "It's almost a separate country to her," says her daughter Patsy. Past programs on KING-TV have dealt with such controversial local issues as pollution on Puget Sound, and the station has initiated "space bridge" programs in which Seattle residents talk via satellite with people in the Soviet Union. In many cities, there is open war between commercial and public television. Not in Seattle, says Jean Walkinshaw of KCTS-TV. KING has given this public station cameras and other equipment and often shares news clips with it.

As for its commentators, KING's policy has always been to select capable people and give them their heads, an approach that Mayor Royer, as a new man at the station, found particularly refreshing. "Consistently," he says—speaking of stations where he previously worked—"bankers or owners of used car lots called the shots in the newsroom. At KING, there was a commitment to be independent."

Critics of KING have frequently charged it with reflecting the political philosophy of the Bullitt family. Some of this feeling may well date back to the 1960s, when Stimson Bullitt, as company president, spoke out editorially against escalation of the Vietnam War before this position became popular. "There are many people who won't have anything to do with us because of some of the stands we've taken in the past," says a company executive.

Dorothy Bullitt's personal politics, though, do not appear to diverge very far from the concern for First Amendment rights displayed by the United States Supreme Court. "She's an old-fashioned, civil-rights civil libertarian," says Ancil Payne. "Those are the areas where she comes through very strongly. She's very conscious of education in all its forms, and social security—taking care of the poor, and those who can't help themselves. Beyond that, she's not doctrinaire at all. She wouldn't care about high interest rates. I don't know what she thinks about Reaganomics. But if there's a free speech issue, I can tell you how she'll respond."

238

Dorothy riding Jester in 1911

During part of the 1950s, Mrs. Bullitt was a member of the Code Board of the National Association of Broadcasters, which was charged with the duty of setting standards of ethics for the industry. The issue arose of whether or not to televise Eugene O'Neill's play *The Iceman Cometh*. Today, no one would seriously object to this classic, but attitudes were very different then. At a special preview showing, many broadcasters' wives were so offended by it that they walked out. Payne recalls that Mrs. Bullitt was the only board member who sat through the entire three and a half hours of the play. When it was over, her response was succinct. "Of course you should show it," she said.

Religion has always been of great importance to Dorothy Bullitt. On acquiring her first radio station, she at once announced that she would sell no air time to religious organizations, and this injunction is still in force at KING stations. On the other hand, she has given away much such time without charge. Dean Leffler, who first knew her as a parishioner at St. Mark's, later suggested to her the possibility of televising the Cathedral's Christmas Eve midnight service, and this has now been broadcast for thirty years. Each Sunday evening, St. Mark's compline service is aired over KING-FM. Sunday mornings, a special broadcast of the Eucharist is presented on KING-TV with clergymen of different denominations participating. In a small circle at the bottom of the screen, the service is translated into sign language for viewers unable to hear it.

Dorothy Bullitt has served on the boards of directors of several businesses, and in 1958, Governor Albert D. Rosellini appointed her to the University of Washington's board of regents. Charles Odegaard, then university president, notes with amusement that she was immediately put on the finance committee and never taken off it. "Best man on the Board!" it was—inevitably—said of her.

"When a subject of importance would come up," the late attorney and former regent Harold S. Shefelman once observed, "the men on the board would plunge in and begin arguing. For ten or fifteen minutes, Dorothy wouldn't say a word. Suddenly, we'd hear a very quiet—almost timid—voice, saying, 'Gentlemen, of course I don't know very much about this subject, but I wonder whether *this* might not be a solution...'

"Then she'd express herself in a very few words. It was amazing how many times her suggestion was better than anything anyone else had thought of."

One of her chief memories of her years as a regent involves the bitter battle—in that pre-Kingdome era—over a heavily lobbied proposal to allow professional sports teams to play in the university's football stadium. Resisting intense pressure to permit this, the regents turned down the plan. Mrs. Bullitt feels that then-Governor Albert D. Rosellini has never received proper credit for his courage in supporting their decision, which, she believes, harmed him politically.

Despite her intense involvement with the growth of her broadcasting company over the years, Dorothy Bullitt has always found time for recreation and fun. In her case, this has usually meant going out on the water. She would heartily endorse the famous philosophy of Water Rat, expressed with such feeling in *The Wind in the Willows:* "Believe me, my young friend, there is *nothing*—absolutely nothing—half so much worth doing as simply messing about in boats."

In 1960, she carried out an ambitious project she and her husband had planned many years before: nothing less than a trip across North America *by water.* Accompanied by a skipper, and a woman cousin of approximately her age, she took a powerboat from Brownsville, Texas, around Florida, up the East Coast, down the St. Lawrence River, through the Great Lakes, down the Mississippi, up the Missouri, and—after a portage overland to the Snake—down the Columbia and up around Cape Flattery into the Straits of Juan de Fuca and Puget Sound.

It was far from an easy trip. There were some bad storms. But it not only fulfilled a recreational purpose, it served a practical function as well—the boat was afterwards used by KING for gathering news.

Several years later, she discovered in Lake Union an abandoned hulk, the wreck of an old tug once used to barge lumber from her father's Ballard mill out to the three-masted schooners waiting for it in the harbor. When its price came down far enough, she bought it, had it restored, christened it the *Stimson,* and in time took it all over the Sound. Once again, this enterprise served more than one end. In the mid-seventies, when the trees on a small Canadian island she owned blew down in a storm, she sent the *Stimson* up to help salvage them. She flew to the site and in freezing, snowy weather, joined in the operation.

She has continued to mess about in boats. A few years ago, at age eighty-five, she rode down the Colorado in a rubber raft, the oldest person known to have made the trip; she insisted on riding in the bow, in order to experience the full effect of the waves. "You should try it," she advised me with the enthusiasm you might expect to find in a teenager. "It's the greatest thing going."

At an auction, she was high bidder for a trip around Lopez Island (in the San Juans) via a Haida-style war canoe, a craft carefully designed and built to traditional specifications by the noted Northwest Coast Indian expert Bill Holm. The voyage took all day.

"Do you remember anything you saw?" I asked her daughter Harriet, one of several *pro tempore* Haida who accompanied her. "Whales?"

"We were too busy paddling," said Harriet. "We sang a Haida paddling song."

"What about your mother?" I asked Patsy Collins, who was also along.

"We handed her a paddle," said Patsy, "and she paddled."

So much did she enjoy the experience that she repeated it the next year.

Certainly the worst disaster to befall the Bullitt family in recent years occurred in 1982 when Ben, twenty-four, the much-loved, if wayward, son of Stimson Bullitt and his ex-wife Kay, drowned in Lake Washington after falling from his boat at night under highly suspicious circumstances, which have never been fully explained. His family's reaction seemed characteristic. KING's reporters covered the event like any news story, making no attempt to conceal his troubles with drugs, his unwise borrowing of money, and the doubtful nature of some of his associates. His father aided in the investigation, while his mother, displaying what many thought an admirable surface stoicism, continued with her active civic life.

Others among Dorothy Bullitt's grandchildren appear to have inherited many of her interests and abilities. Her namesake Dorothy, elder daughter of Stimson and Kay Bullitt, is an articulate lawyer who works for her father's real-estate company. And one of Mrs. Bullitt's most striking qualities, her all-embracing ardor for life, seems shared by many of her descendants. When Harriet's daughter, Wenda, was married to James O'Reilly, the locale she chose for her wedding was a sunny expanse of lawn at a mountain lodge Mrs. Bullitt built before World War II in the Cascade Mountains near Leavenworth. Many guests brought tents and slept outside.

It was a doubly happy occasion; at lunch, news came through that the bride's mountaineer Uncle Stimson, at sixty-two, had safely reached the peak of Alaska's 20,320-foot

Mount McKinley. Later that afternoon, for the ceremony, Wenda wore her mother's formal white wedding gown—while a sudden Cascades wind whipped down from the surrounding mountains, and bemused Peruvian llamas browsed in the middle distance. Earlier that day, her friends had set up a wedding night camp for her in the pinewoods across a nearby creek, with a cache of food hung high in a tree to protect it from marauding bears. En route to the camp, the bride fell in the creek, but this failed to dampen her spirits, and the bears thoughtfully kept their distance.

These days, Dorothy Bullitt remains very much a part of her community. "I saw her walking down Fifth Avenue," Mrs. Sheffield Phelps, a Vassar classmate of Patsy Collins remarked recently. "She was wearing a good tweed suit and a pretty hat. You know, I saw her first in 1946, and today she doesn't look any different. I walked up and said, 'Hello, Mrs. Bullitt. I'm Patty Phelps.' 'How are you, Patty?' she said, in that deep voice. 'I'm fine,' I said, 'and I don't *need* to ask how you are.' "

She keeps in close touch with affairs at KING, and enjoys reminiscing there with such friends as her bookkeeper, Clara Stenstrom, who has been with her for forty-nine years. A rare but characteristic newsroom appearance occurred a few years ago when promoters were demonstrating a new supergadget there. This was a high-tech information retrieval system that would enable reporters to press a button and have instant access to everything *The New York Times* —and several other papers—had ever printed about, say, Winston Churchill. The woman who had once bought a television station "because of an article she'd read in a magazine" was scarcely about to miss a chance to inspect an item like that.

Not long ago we sat in her KING office surrounded by many mementos of her astonishingly active life—like the oversize loving cup she won for driving, riding, and jumping at Seattle's first horse show held in 1909. While we talked, the KING helicopter clattered off its pad, providing further proof, if more were needed, that her original investment of 375,000 round simoleons had been wholly sound. The machine failed to disturb the nesting nighthawk, which sat fearlessly on her nest, quietly refusing to budge.

Briefly, I wondered what Princess Angeline might have thought of this exotic aircraft—that Princess Angeline whose father, Chief Seattle, as a boy of six or seven, is said to have accompanied his own father out to meet Captain Vancouver, first visitor from a world whose existence no one on Puget Sound had even suspected. Certainly, this was a meeting that must have seemed to these Indians as baffling, as wholly awe-inspiring as any imaginary Close Encounter of the Third Kind.

For them it was a peak, a watershed. It marked the end of a prehistoric age when the Northwest Coast was the center of the cosmos and all beyond was spirit-haunted darkness and mystery. History has since moved swiftly. A bridge of but three overlapping lives— Dorothy Bullitt's, Angeline's, Seattle's—links that almost unimaginable era with our own.

NORTHWEST DYNASTY

NORTON CLAPP (1906–)

NICK GALLO

Hobbies: boating, surveying, shopwork." This from *Who's Who in Washington*. A Northwest history buff, a paper in a company archive reveals. A fan of ham radios as a youth, a rare newspaper clip informs us.

Such are the trivialities, scattered randomly, that one pores over in hopes of finding some key element of character, a moment of revelation, an utterance—"Rosebud." In the end, these fragments are as meager and unrevealing as the lists of awards and achievements bestowed upon Norton Clapp. He remains virtually unknown, glimpsed recently when he succumbed to a spate of estate planning to benefit his heirs. He is one of the state's most influential and wealthiest people—to the point of ridiculousness, rich enough to be different, rich enough to be anonymous.

Called fifteen years ago "perhaps the region's most important backstage economic and political presence...an Olympian presence of Seattle business" in a list of the *Seattle Post-Intelligencer*'s 'Ten Most Powerful People in Seattle, his activities nevertheless have commanded only the spottiest of media attention. "Norton Clapp, a Tacoma-Seattle financier, is reportedly being considered by the White House for appointment as governor of Alaska," a bulletin blurts out. Clapp: "the single most influential man associated with the University of Puget Sound in this century," exclaims another. Clapp: "the region's greatest philanthropist." Clapp: "the able executive of Weyerhaeuser Company and grandson of one of its founders." But who is he?

Clapp, a man who has had tremendous impact on the Pacific Northwest, has rarely articulated his vision publicly.

Flip through a half-century of history-making and you piece together a résumé—and an incomplete one. For starters, he is the Weyerhaeuser Magnate, with 1.8 million shares of the company's common stock in 1974, says a proxy report; at one point during that year that would have meant he was worth $82 million.

He is also a Lord of Lakewood, a title given to members of wealthy timber families who lived in Tacoma's Lakewood District. It is particularly appropriate since Clapp chose Lakewood as the site to develop one of the Northwest's first suburban shopping centers, in the process steering land development to that previously sparsely populated area.

He is also the Real-Estate Tycoon with a Midas touch who people joke "owns half the state of Washington—or is it just one-quarter." He is the University of Puget Sound Angel, a board member at that university for more than fifty years, who donated countless hours and big bucks—$7 to 10 million, according to one published estimate. He is the Patron behind the Medina Foundation, a regional philanthropy that dispenses more than eight hundred thousand dollars in grants every year.

But flip through the pages more slowly for a private statement of purpose, for a personal reading of the significance of all this sound and fury, and you come away empty-handed. Clapp, a man who has had tremendous impact on the Pacific Northwest, has rarely articulated his vision publicly. He almost never gives interviews, and most family members say they could not talk about him without his permission.

Once Clapp was burned by an editor whose fearlessness—fearlessness that came in a bottle—extended to publishing sometimes scandalous social doings of the wealthy. The details are vague but the hateful experience only reinforced a passion for anonymity typical of old wealth. Clapp, a descendant of nineteenth-century millionaires, exemplifies classic, traditional old wealth—staid, patient, quietly overpowering wealth. It is so quiet that it is only fitting that until 1987 Clapp's empire escaped *Forbes 400* listing of America's wealthiest. *Forbes* estimates the family fortune to be at least $300 million. Because much of his wealth is tied up in family-controlled, privately held companies, few details are publicly reported.

Obscurity has long been a matter of personal style for Clapp, now eighty-two years old and living in Medina. At six feet four inches and upwards of 230 pounds, he is a massive man. Few would think him a timber baron. Placid, with a large head and thick-rimmed glasses, he looks as if he spent his life behind a plough. Private and unpretentious, he dressed the part. Over the years, he won few awards for sartorial splendor, occasionally even wearing unpressed clothes. For a period of time he wore a torn raincoat and carried a beat-up briefcase. Once, while walking in the rain with a friend, he was forced to wad up a piece of paper in order to cover a hole inside his shoe. For a while he drove a Buick Special, which was not only not a Rolls-Royce, it wasn't even a top-of-the-line Buick.

Such behavior is *de rigueur* for old wealth—after all, it isn't they who have to impress anyone. But in Clapp's case, it also reflects a certain vulnerability. "There is a whole class of people here who do not like the limelight," explains one multimillionaire who prefers to remain anonymous. "They haven't forgotten the days when George Weyerhaeuser was kidnapped. Windows were barred, kids were driven to school by chauffeurs, it was a very traumatizing thing. The Patty Hearst thing and the publicity over the Weathermen hit lists, which had the names of corporate executives on them, stirred up bad memories." That particular obsession understandably extends to Clapp.

Fred Baker, a longtime friend, says, "A while ago, we were going to throw a testimonial dinner for Norton that would end all testimonial dinners. But the FBI put its foot down.

Norton Clapp: a real estate tycoon
with a Midas touch

245

They told us to forget it. He's too vulnerable. He's got too many children and grand-children."

Clapp has a brood. He has been married four times, has fathered six children, ac-quired six more in marriages, and has enough grandchildren, sons-in-law, and nephews and nieces at work in family businesses to fill out nicely a cast for Northwest Dynasty. His fourth marriage took place in 1984, to Jacqueline Hazen, the widow of his first son. He previously divorced Jane Bumiller Henry, widow of Horace Henry, who came from an old Seattle family that goes back to early railroad days and the subsequent founding of Safeco and Seafirst Bank. That marriage has been referred to as a merger.

In 1940, Clapp's marriage to Mary Davis, his first wife, ended in divorce. Five years later, Clapp's four sons and ex-wife were inside a car involved in a head-on auto crash in California. His ex-wife died; one child, a ten-year-old, also was killed; another never fully recovered.

A year after his first divorce, Clapp remarried, inheriting two young children, Gail and Booth Gardner. On April 6, 1951—ten years later—Evelyn Booth Gardner Clapp and her daughter Gail boarded a plane bound for Santa Barbara, where she was to accept a prize at an orchid show. The airliner went down in the Santa Ynez mountains and both perished.

The personal misfortune is even more haunting. In 1944, Clapp's half-brother was killed when a tractor overturned on him in Pasadena. A son died of cancer at twenty-four. Another son, who drank heavily, died when he was forty-three. Clapp's mother died when he was a teenager.

Some people say Clapp never broke stride during what borders on Kennedy-like trag-edy, that he was often in his office on the day following a funeral, more determined than ever to charge forward as far as he could go. Never an extrovert, he buried his private thoughts and feelings even deeper, revealing himself to few, if any, people.

Clapp is the stepfather of Booth Gardner, current governor of Washington. Gardner's wealth—a portion of it is from his mother's estate, most of it is part of Clapp's fortune—is the center of political speculation.

In the early seventies, Gardner was a state senator who resigned to head Clapp's fam-ily businesses. At that time, he placed his assets in a trust managed by a Seattle investment broker. In sworn statements to state officials, he has maintained he does not know its cur-rent assets, or what goes in or out of the trust. When he returned to political life in 1980, state officials administering a state law requiring candidates to reveal financial assets granted him an exemption. Since there was no provision for how to handle "blind trusts," they sided with Gardner, who had claimed that his ignorance of the holdings guaranteed his personal assets would have no influence on his decisions as a public official. Sub-sequently, Public Disclosure Commission officials demanded that Gardner supply con-

Frederick Weyerhaeuser led his band of millionaire lumbermen into the West with one of the largest single land transfers in the nation's history.

tents of the fund when it was formed in 1972. Gardner complied, but even then, the value of items was only reported by "value category," with the highest category being twenty-five thousand dollars and over.

There are few topics that whet the American appetite like vast wealth. It is the stuff of fantasy and legend—and also suspicion. How did Norton Clapp get to the top? Like the famous millionaire Malcolm Forbes, he was born there. Like Forbes, who attributed his own great fortune to "sheer ability and inheritance," Clapp was born atop a mound of wealth, which he then turned into a mountain.

Born in Pasadena in 1906, Clapp was the answer to a prayer. In the mid-1850s, two brothers, Matthew G. Norton and James Norton, left Pennsylvania to head west for the land of opportunity: Minnesota. They joined their cousins, the Lairds, in the frontier town of Winona to start a lumber business. While it suffered setbacks at first, it soon thrived. Following the Homestead Act, which opened the plains to development and expansion, the Laird Norton Co. grew to run the biggest, most modern sawmills in the region.

Meanwhile, the lumbermen joined a group of other sawmill owners along the Mississippi River to form a remarkable cooperative that would bring riches to all involved. At first, the owners pooled efforts to run logs downriver from the pineries to the north, but eventually they joined forces to purchase vast stands of timber. The leader of the consortium was Frederick Weyerhaeuser. For the remainder of the century, Weyerhaeuser, the Lairds, and the Nortons, and more than a dozen associates maintained their loose association.

The Nortons were transplanted Scots, a group of pioneer settlers described in *Timber Roots,* a history of the Laird Norton Co., as "dour, with a harsh, ascetic religion (Calvinist Presbyterian), which disciplined their unruly instinct and appealed to their intellect.... They relished two-hour-long sermons devoted to theological exposition."

Though they lived in one of the town's largest houses, the Nortons are described as characteristically thrifty, practical, and unassuming. Little display of wealth accompanied their rise to the top. In 1900, the *World Almanac* published an item that shocked townspeople. In their midst were millionaires: the Lairds and the Nortons.

That year, Frederick Weyerhaeuser led his band of millionaire lumbermen into the West with one of the largest single land transfers in the nation's history. Weyerhaeuser's next-door neighbor in St. Paul was railroad magnate James J. Hill, who had some land to sell. The Weyerhaeuser syndicate purchased nine hundred thousand acres at six dollars each from the Northern Pacific Railway and opened an office in Tacoma. Weyerhaeuser and his partner put in the largest share $1.8 million. Laird Norton contributed $1.2 million. Three others added $350,000 apiece and nine others offered smaller amounts.

It is hard to believe now, but the purchase was a gamble. Some rivermen refused to venture into the unknown Northwest, just then booming because of the Alaska gold rush.

Many of the timber lords drove modest brands of cars.... Parties went on, but privacy was guarded tenaciously.

247

However, with timber stands in the Midwest decimated, lumbermen had only two choices: the South and the West. The Weyerhaeuser group staked its future on Douglas fir, a decision that proved sound; the enterprise has grown to become the world's largest timber-products firm. It owns 5.9-million acres of land in the United States and controls millions of acres of timberland in Canada.

Because Weyerhaeuser Company was named after Frederick the Great, who had four sons to carry on his ambition to expand the timber fortune and also his name, few people associate the name Laird Norton with the company. There was a serious lack of male heirs in the families. Laird had no sons. James Norton had one boy with no inclination for business. Matthew Norton had two sons who died early.

Thus, when Dr. Eben Clapp, a practicing physician, married one of Matthew's daughters and produced young Norton, the elder Norton celebrated with a message: "I pray God's loving care will be over you always and that you will be a comfort to your Father and Mother, and to all of us and a blessing to the world."

Matthew Norton, the best educated of the older Nortons, was six feet three inches, big-boned, quiet and reserved, deliberate and cautious in business affairs, and appreciative of education (he was a prominent benefactor of Minnesota's Hamline University). All these traits would surface eventually in Norton Clapp.

Young Clapp graduated from high school in Pasadena, went to Occidental College for one degree, then added degrees in law and philosophy a year later from the University of Chicago in 1929. He returned almost immediately to Tacoma to practice business law. "Norton was like any other struggling young lawyer," remembers one neighbor, "except that every few years a rich aunt would die and leave him a few million."

Clapp practiced law until 1942, saying later his study of law was a way to train his mind. Originally, he intended to become a minister, claims one longtime friend. Others say this is highly unlikely, but he did marry a minister's daughter. With his wife Mary's help he started a project in 1937 originally dubbed "Clapp's Folly," later acknowledged as a brilliant piece of land development.

In the middle of a sparsely developed settlement at the junction of Gravelly Lake Drive and Steilacoom Bridge Road, ten miles south of Tacoma, the Clapps designed and developed Lakewood Center on fourteen hundred acres of land Clapp had reportedly acquired for one hundred dollars an acre. One of the region's first suburban shopping centers, Lakewood boasted a hall for elite social dances, a ritzy dining room, theater, grocery store, butcher, barber, doctor, dentist, and beauty parlor—pedicurists, manicurists, masseuses included. Imagine imported wood paneling, crystal lamps, and expensive furnishings, then include incongruous colonial architecture as icing—colonial-style columns and facades set on a prairie—and it is little wonder this city under one roof seemed like a flight of fancy, especially in the Depression decade. The original dentist, Dr. Edward Klopping, who still practices at the center, confesses he thought he would be extracting teeth from chickens.

The area boomed. McChord Air Base and Fort Lewis grew. The suburban exodus began. By 1941, six thousand people inhabited what had been a summer colony for a few hundred residents. Today, the suburb is sixty-five thousand strong; the center is still in family hands.

The center, unlike today's malls, was intended to be more than a plaza for merchants. As homes, schools, and churches sprouted around it, it became a social hub. The Clapps were shaping a town—the Perfect Country Life, they advertised. "Make no little plans," counseled one ad. "They have little power to stir men's blood."

Mary Clapp, the minister's daughter with a talent for doing business—"This is all Mary's doing," Clapp once explained the center to a friend, not all in jest—also boasted a streak of wildness and a taste for a grandiose lifestyle that suited her husband less and less. The end was fiery. A lawsuit was filed, according to a *Post-Intelligencer* story, and it was later settled out of court. The lawsuit charged Clapp with defrauding his wife of between $14 million and $26 million in divorce settlement. A year later, Clapp married Evelyn Booth Gardner, a former New York model and daughter of Lawrence Booth, president of Washington Title Insurance Co. Her marriage to Bryson "Brick" Gardner, who ran a Tacoma car dealership, had fallen apart. Years later, Brick Gardner left for Hawaii. Gardner was to die in Hawaii in 1966, after a fall from a hotel window. The whole episode produced a social scandal, since the controversy was taking place in the close-knit Lakes District.

Homes in the Lakes District, like Clapp's brick house, were gracious, but hardly architectural pacesetters. Many of the timber lords drove modest brands of cars. Wives shopped out of town. Parties went on, but privacy was guarded tenaciously.

Clapp was a fixture in this world, but he was awkward and slow-moving, well-meaning but not charismatic. Quiet and cool, he maintained his distance. When others tried to be intimate—perhaps undeservedly so in social encounters—he clammed up faster than a razorneck. His social instincts were gentlemanly—with an occasional failing. Once, at a dinner party, he realized his fly was open. Rushing to correct the problem, he caught the dinner napkin of the hostess in the zipper of his pants, causing considerable commotion.

But he was rarely embarrassed in the business world. Following a break during World War II, in which he served in the navy and was stationed in Seattle and Alaska, directing convoy and routing tasks, he turned his attention to empire-building.

Behind the placid image, Clapp had a bright, thorough, disciplined brain. "He was a great collector of data," one associate remembers. "He always wanted to know what X and Y were doing before he made up his mind. He was never unprepared."

A former speechwriter for him recalls, "He has a penetrating, logical mind. There were times I'd write fuzzy things, but let them go, thinking no one would notice. Well, Norton Clapp *always* noticed."

If he had patience for detail work, he also had a sixth sense for developable land and reliable people. The late Bill Speidel, Seattle historian and a fund raiser who worked with Clapp, said, "There is a certain feeling of residual power to him, and it isn't just his money. He has great judgment. I'd rank him among the most forward-looking financiers of his generation."

Clapp always asked questions, mounds of them. Says one observer about Clapp, "The men at the top always have the ability to ask the right questions. It's essential to running a company. You can hire anyone to go find you the answers."

In the late forties and early fifties, Clapp, with the aid of his general manager Al Link, took up the business interests of his father, now old and ailing and retired to Pasadena, which spread across banking, insurance, real estate, construction, and lumber.

Clapp had joined Weyerhaeuser Company as corporate secretary in 1938, but now he replaced his father on the board. He became president of a Salt Lake City building-materials company, a seafoods company, a lumber company, and chairman of the board of Laird Norton Trust Co., a holding company for the families' investments that has now expanded so greatly that a banking magazine recently claimed it controls "hundreds of millions" in trusts.

Clapp was also chairman of the board of Metropolitan Building Corporation, which managed (none too aggressively, by most accounts) the University of Washington's prime ten-acre downtown tract now supervised by UNICO. He also held the future site of the thirty-nine-story Federal Office Building, which he traded to the government for land developed into Lakewood Industrial Park. The Federal Office Building, which replaced a fine old office building and was questionably sited—too far from the freeway—may have gone through because of Clapp's political clout. If so, it was a rare exercise of direct influence. Until the late seventies, Clapp held two major downtown buildings—the Exchange Building and the Medical Dental Building. He also built and owns the Norton Building.

Today, the seventeen-story Norton Building, built at a cost of about $11 million and completed in 1959, seems like an unremarkable glass box derived from the International School of Architecture. It sits on Second Avenue and Columbia Street, dwarfed by the glitz and height of nearby towers. It was one of the first major buildings erected downtown after the war, and it helped peg the financial district and downtown development. It used contemporary design from a distinguished firm, quality materials, and placed art in a plaza long before laws began requiring such things. "Norton set a good example," says Seattle architect Fred Bassetti. "He spent more than he had to. It was relatively innovative and carefully done. In hindsight, we criticize all-glass buildings, but it was a first-class job."

The risk had been large. It paid off, though: the Space Needle eventually returned to its investors a handsome profit.

Clapp sank some money into another profitable enterprise that would become a civic landmark: the Space Needle. Prior to the Century 21 Exposition, a few idea men, inspired by a tower in Germany, advanced notions of a restaurant in the sky. Failing to win support from the city or county, they turned to various financiers. One was a recent arrival named Bagley Wright, another was Ned Skinner, and the third was, in the phrase of one of the principals, "the man whom everyone went to with a financial package": Clapp. The three each took a 25 percent interest, leaving a fourth share to be divided by others. With a deadline staring them in the eyes, they secured the necessary bank loans for eventual construction. The risk had been large. It paid off, though: the Space Needle eventually returned to its investors a handsome profit.

Clapp joined the group when it formed Pentagram Corp., but did not play a major role. He was part of a later deal that put up 50 percent interest in the Bank of California Building. Since then, his influence downtown has drooped. Besides the Norton Building, the family firms hold only one well-known property: the Marsh & McLennan Building at 720 Olive Way, formerly the Daon Building. Real-estate sources say they are much more active outside the office-building market.

The family businesses that operate out of the Norton Building, however, include holdings spread out so far and wide that few know the extent of the empire. They include building-supply stores throughout the Northwest and Midwest, lumberman's stores in this region, shopping centers, and vast acreage on the Olympic Peninsula and in the San Juan Islands, where Clapp has a summer home on Orcas Island—built on a mountain with a 360-degree view. He owns Samuel Island, a horseshoe-shaped island in British Columbia. Business articles say Lanoga Corp., another of the family enterprises, acquired 110 stores in Rocky Mountain states in 1982 and twenty-three building-materials stores in 1984, doing an annual business of $300 million.

At various times, Clapp ventured to Alaska, running steamships there through his Alaska Transportation Company, operating radio station KFQD, actually owned by his son, Matthew, and maintaining cold-storage plants.

Bob Atwood, longtime publisher of the *Anchorage Times,* recalls: "He was behind the scenes a lot, one of the courageous ones who came up when no one wanted to invest in our little colony. He had a hotel in Juneau, one in Anchorage. He was part of a bunch of guys fooling around with oil leases, but I don't know if anything ever came of it."

A more publicized venture occurred in 1971 when Clapp was part of a group that acquired the famous Halekulani Hotel, built in 1917, a $4 million Waikiki Beach preserve where the rich went and were rich. Part of "old Hawaii," it was popular with Seattle bluebloods, but Clapp eventually succumbed to real-estate pressures and sold it to developers who erected a high-rise.

On the Eastside, there is the story of Clapp, the Overlake Golf and Country Club, and

Opening an executive portrait gallery with George Weyerhaeuser (left): demanding boss

two bottles of Scotch. He had moved to Medina in 1946—into the former home of Colonel C.B. Blethen, publisher of *The Seattle Times*. In 1950, he purchased property that had been used during the war years for running Hereford cattle, the J-Bar-J Ranch. After Clapp acquired 187 acres at one thousand dollars each, he was at a barbecue with six or seven prominent Eastsiders to kick around the idea of a golf course. Two bottles of Scotch later, the group agreed to proceed. Clapp leased 132 acres to the club for a nominal fee and made available an interest-free fifty thousand dollar loan. That's how Overlake Golf Club was reborn.

Above the golf course, in Medina, Clapp developed the hillsides with expensive view homes a few years later, selling them quickly. He also donated seven acres nearby to rebuild St. Thomas Episcopal Church and headed the finance committee for the church.

In his only other widely known venture on the Eastside, he developed the Newport

Shores area, an exclusive residential project that turned out to require lots of work. It did not move fast, and though two hundred thousand dollar (and up) homes inhabit the area now, it is possible Clapp did not do well there. Some financiers think Clapp also made a rare miscalculation in Medina, selling off land before prices soared.

What kind of businessman was he?

He was tough as nails, says one businessman who had experience with him. Others say he could have been tougher, given his immense resources. One story circulates that he once paid $5 million for a piece of property insiders believed could have been had for $3 million. Crazy, everyone thought. Years later, he resold the property for $27 million.

One of his relatives calls him the model of prudence. "His business advice to me was to look at the people first, then the terms of the deal, and if I had any hesitations, to wait. He believes there is always another opportunity, another chance."

Clapp himself has said, "We take fewer risks, and if you take fewer risks, you miss some opportunities. But our decisions are informed."

He could have been referring to his own business instincts, but he was discussing Weyerhaeuser Company, the corporation he headed from 1960 to 1966. When he became the company's eighth president, the timber giant had been conservatively managed. Some had called it the Bank of Tacoma, a reference not only to its vast resources but to its determination to conserve them. The sleeping giant was awakening when Clapp assumed the top post.

The first few years of his tenure coincided with unfavorable trends in the industry, but by 1965, the company was quite wide awake. Between 1957 and 1965, the work force doubled, the number of shareholders tripled, and the corporation had gone from a regional forest products company to a national and international firm. It had consolidated its position in pulp and paper, found new markets, and expanded into Europe, Canada, the Caribbean, and the Pacific.

While Clapp headed Weyerhaeuser, it became fully public, listed on both the New York Stock Exchange and Pacific Stock Exchange. It also launched its first major borrowing effort—$150 million. It initiated its relocation to Federal Way and began moves into real estate, now a prominent subsidiary.

Clapp was only the third of the company's eight presidents who was not a member of the Weyerhaeuser family. He had joined the company as secretary in 1938 and succeeded his father in 1946, but had been an outside director until 1955, when he was named a vice president and chairman of the executive committee. In 1960, when he rose to the top position of presidency, Weyerhaeuser Company was in a leadership bind. J. Philip Weyerhaeuser, a dynamic leader, succumbed to leukemia in the mid-fifties. F.K. Weyerhaeuser, a grandson of the original Frederick, filled J. Philip's shoes and then he retired several years later. That left a void, or more precisely it created an interregnum. The young George

Party leaders turned to Clapp, who quietly rounded up the right people to wipe out the debt.

253

Booth Gardner

Norton Clapp's stepson, Booth Gardner, parlayed his limited public service record, good management credentials, and vast financial resources into an impressive victory over incumbent Republican John Spellman in 1984. The family, and its role in Gardner's administration, remained an issue in the campaign and through his first term in office.

From "Young Booth Gardner," by Rebecca Boren, Seattle Weekly, July 18, 1984. Copyright © 1984 Rebecca Boren. Reprinted by permission.

William Booth Gardner was a 5-year-old preschooler when his "model and housewife" mother Evelyn divorced Bryson Gardner to marry Norton Clapp. Young Booth remained with his father, only joining the Clapp household for two years during World War II, when the senior Gardner went away to war.

Gardner today describes growing up in a middle-class household. His father ran a local automobile dealership and remarried; Booth attended Tacoma area public schools, Park Lodge Elementary and Clover Park Junior High. Church was a regular part of life. He says, "Because I was raised by my father and stepmother, I had a normal upbringing. I wasn't around a whole lot of wealth and when I was, I didn't notice it, because I had my own friends."

By 1951, life was changing. Booth's mother and sister died in a plane crash, and the 15-year-old inherited a million-dollar fortune, which was placed in a trust for him. Booth says his father "got sick" (those close to him say alcoholism was a factor), so Gardner lived with guardians in Seattle while attending the exclusive Lakeside School. Clapp's role in his life then, says Gardner, was limited, but important. He explains, "After my mother died, he called me in and said, 'If you ever need anything, I'm here.' He always let me know I was welcome to ask him for anything."

Gardner adds, however, that he rarely availed himself of the privilege, insisting, "I had my own life to lead." That course took him, in the '50s and '60s, to the University of Washington, and to time working with the minority youth of Seattle's Central Area. He soon established a consistent pattern of ignoring, one is tempted to say denying, his position. Old friends like Emory Bundy, for many years public affairs director at KING television, still shake their heads over the day — sometimes after knowing Booth for years — they realized this self-effacing fellow claimed membership in one of the state's most influential clans. . . .

In the 1960s, Gardner seems to have stayed on the fringes of the Clapp family circle, occupying himself with an academic career (including a stint as head of the business school at the University of Puget Sound). He took legal control of his inheritance at age 25; at the end of the decade he broke Clapp family tradition by winning a state Senate seat from Tacoma under the Democratic Party label. In another in-

Booth Gardner

stance of his sense of distance from the GOP clan, Gardner explains: "I really wasn't aware of the family political activities until I started to get involved." Despite reports of flaming rows between Gardner and Clapp, he says the two rarely discuss politics, while adding the patriarch "would have been happier had I been a Republican. But the fact that I was willing to be involved and have done well pleased him." . . .

In the early '70s, Booth, as it were, took up his family responsibilities. . . . At age 35, with little beyond academic experience, he became president of Laird Norton Company, which embarked on a major expansion program to today's estimated $300-million-a-year building-supply firm. He also plunged into a collection of boards of directors, including seats with Weyerhaeuser and Puget Sound National Bank.

That's when he really got to know Clapp as "an extremely bright man, intellectually. He's also extremely meticulous in his work habits and he's very analytical" and enjoys detail. Like everyone else who worked for Clapp, Gardner adds he found out the hard way: "All of us that went to work there, the first time you ever turned in a report, it came back so you wouldn't recognize it" on account of all of Clapp's changes, comments, and questions. After the first time, he continues, "you learned to try to anticipate" Clapp's thinking. "And no matter how hard you tried to anticipate, he'd find something." . . .

Much of what Gardner says about Norton Clapp could apply to Booth Gard-

ner as well. He is a private person, as well as a shy one, and one of the few politicians around who quotes the Bible completely unselfconsciously. He too talks of life in terms of family, and of community obligations, to the extent that he has several times been accused of exercising *noblesse oblige* in running for public office. And neither Gardner nor Clapp, with their separate public awkwardnesses, fit the mold of political power and business tycoon.

So how does Booth Gardner think of Norton Clapp? As a second father, an uncle, a distant relation, a friend? "I can't answer that," replies Booth. "It's an unfair question. I just think of him as Norton Clapp."

Weyerhaeuser would burst onto the scene in less than a decade.

Thus, the company turned to Clapp, who was not an operating executive at the time, but in many ways was a perfect match for its corporate personality. In those years, Weyerhaeuser Company promoted "planned permanency." Its basic resource—timber—took sixty to eighty years to develop, therefore its focus was long-term planning, and, consequently, conservative management. "We deal not only in terms of decades, but we must also project our thinking for nearly a century," Clapp once told *The New York Times*.

Clapp was a good fit for Weyerhaeuser then. They needed his financial skills and his deliberate nature to steer the company along a sound, steady course. He was the last of the conservators, the last of the great guardians, the last of the Bankers of Tacoma. Around the corner would come George Weyerhaeuser and his hard-charging gang of Harvard MBAs to push the company in new, bold directions. And yet it was Clapp who, with an eye to the future, established Weyerhaeuser training schools to prepare its future leaders and then willingly yielded the reins to the newcomers.

"When Clapp came in, the company had been so conservative that anyone with new ideas looked like a river pirate," says a former Weyerhaeuser director. "He wasn't any swashbuckler, but he was open to new ideas. He got professionals in all the departments, he upgraded management, and then he basically put the company in the position for its big growth surge when George took over."

Outside the company, Clapp served as director on the boards of Safeco, Seafirst, Univar, Puget Sound National Bank, and a host of smaller companies. He served in numerous civic and industry organizations, such as heading the chambers of commerce in both Seattle (1970) and Tacoma (1939). He was president of Pacific Basic Economic Council, an industry group that worked to accelerate investment in the Pacific's developing nations. Following the Boeing recession, he sat on various councils to push for new industry and development.

Not surprisingly, his speeches during those years reflect a free-enterprise, free-trade businessman. He lambasted wasteful government, claiming it stifled productivity and creativity. He compared government structure to a nineteenth-century stagecoach unprepared to take us into the twenty-first century and urged creation of a Metro-like "megacity" to replace the patchwork of bureaucracies in the Puget Sound area.

Politically, he supported mostly conservative Republican causes. Yet, during the sixties when Young Turks like Dan Evans, Slade Gorton, and Joel Pritchard were rising up against Goldwaterites, Clapp and several other Weyerhaeuser leaders opened their checkbooks for the newcomers. One insider remembers that upon Evans's election for governor in 1964, the Republican party inherited a debt of one hundred and fifty thousand dollars that was difficult to erase. Party leaders turned to Clapp, who quietly rounded up the right people to wipe out the debt.

"He's a pragmatist, not an ideological warrior," says one Republican party big-dollar contributor, explaining Clapp's alignment with moderates. "The Evans wing was a practical group. Clapp was a pragmatist who liked to win, not toot his ideological horn."

Another source close to Evans says: "Clapp was like one of those Great Pyrenees dogs—those big, even-tempered ones. He didn't snap or bark for favors. He didn't have to. He didn't have that kind of need."

In 1984, he found himself backing—of all things—a Democrat: stepson Booth Gardner in his bid for nomination for governor. A friend of Gardner's says, "They're not in the same political world. They're in the same business world, but they have fundamentally different views on the role of government. Booth is a Democrat—he sees a much more active role for government. Clapp is a classic Republican. They've had some tremendous fights over it."

Clapp has also made his social vision felt through his leadership at Medina Foundation, a philanthropy with assets exceeding $19 million in 1982. Begun in 1948, it dispensed $835,000 in 1982. The family foundation focuses its grants on feeding the poor, getting jobs for the mentally and physically handicapped, private education, and programs to promote efficiency in organizations and in government. Medina has a reputation for a tough-minded approach to giving away money. It has goaded both agencies that receive its money and other foundations in the area to become more businesslike in keeping books. It's "accounting for the bleeding hearts," says Medina's Greg Barlow, who was a leading force behind the formation of the Northwest Grantmakers' Forum, a regional association of philanthropies.

It is an America we don't quite believe in anymore, but Clapp does.

"During the sixties every fool in the world solved the unemployment problem by setting up his own job development company and applying for a grant," says Barlow. "It was silly money." The tough approach extends to restricting funding to no more than 10 percent of an agency's budget, enough to start the job but not take it over.

A glaring omission is the category of arts and cultural activities. The Seattle Repertory Theater and Tacoma's Pantages Theater are two groups that have gotten a little—each was granted twenty-five thousand dollars in 1981—but they are exceptions. Medina pushes self-improvement, not symphonies and ballets, an orientation said to reflect quite closely the tastes of Clapp.

Environmentalists also need not apply. One conservationist claims he was introduced at a party to Clapp, who turned around and walked away. The Laird Norton Foundation, another family philanthropy that many say reflects more diverse opinions, however, has made awards to conservation groups. One Medina Foundation insider claims Clapp has come to regard the philanthropy more and more as a force for social good, but that early on he viewed it mostly as a tax dodge.

Clapp's deeper enthusiasms are the University of Puget Sound and the Boy Scouts.

He joined the UPS board of trustees in 1932 and was elected chairman of the board in 1967. The law school, founded in 1972, was named after him when it moved and expanded into its $11 million quarters in downtown Tacoma.

"Without Norton Clapp, the law school would still be nothing more than a nice idea," Judge James M. Dolliver once said. Clapp once told a reporter he turned down a chance to be a University of Washington regent, believing that private education was more flexible. He has backed up those thoughts with $7 to 10 million, according to one published estimate, calling his donations "an investment in America."

Not surprisingly, some of his biggest fans are at the school. President Philip Phibbs has said, "No one has been more responsible for the University of Puget Sound's growth in size and stature than Norton Clapp, who saw it go from a small and struggling college to one of the premier private universities in the Northwest." Clapp is what one UPS trustee calls "the quintessential board member. He reads everything, probes for answers, and can issue forth a withering cross-examination."

A rival for his attention is the Boy Scouts. He joined at age twelve, became a scoutmaster in Tacoma—an austere one, remembers one person in his troop, no sneaking beer on overnighters—and served on the national board for much of his life. He held the top volunteer position in the country in 1971 and 1972. He has a boxful of major awards, and he has donated a large sum of money, though no estimates are available.

In a talk in Eugene, Oregon, he once said, "We know all boys are going to be voters some day. Better scouts will be better voters, and it's that simple. So what we're trying to do is make better people, isn't it? To make them a little more thrifty, a little more brave, a little more loyal."

A little more thrifty, a little more brave, a little more loyal. This is the closest glimpse Norton Clapp will allow into his private universe. One can imagine the next words: duty, honor, valor. Why the Boy Scouts? The right leadership. Why UPS? The right education. The right stuff for success. It is an America we remember from civics textbooks. It is an America we don't quite believe in anymore, but Clapp does.

What else do we know? He is something of an Old World figure. He has little patience for idle chatter. He does not suffer fools gladly. A Weyerhaeuser manager discovered this when he tried to win points with Clapp one day complaining about his long hours; when that didn't work, he mentioned his dismay that his son had chosen to become a pilot instead of getting a master's degree in business. "My son's a pilot," Clapp shot back, "and I'm proud of him."

As a Weyerhaeuser executive he was cool, even icy. Employees rarely cracked jokes around him, unless they were certified funny in seven languages. He rarely got angry, but he was demanding. "You didn't want to disappoint him," one employee remembers.

Outside the business world and left to himself, he is a tinkerer, someone who loves

Painting of Norton Clapp, patriarch of a vastly influential clan

259

nothing more than to play in the engine room of a boat. One friend recalls visiting him at his home on the night of an eclipse. Clapp had pieced together a telescope out of old parts, mirrors, string, and tape.

At parties, Clapp likes to drink and enjoys the company of women. Yet, he would no sooner wear a lampshade on his head than light cigars with one-hundred-dollar bills. He is old wealth, often cited as someone with the best instincts of that class—the obligation to repay society for its good fortune, rather than to flaunt it, dissipate it, or hide it away. Clapp certainly has given some back, and not only money—philanthropy, to the very wealthy, is like discarding surplus overcoats in July, one wag has written—but time. He served on committees and boards long after most people retire. Thus, it is fair to presume that through the Medina Foundation, the Boy Scouts, UPS, and the like, he genuinely desires to make the world a better place. It is also fair to surmise that has not been his overriding mission. His goal has been turning that mound of millions into a mountain.

Once a year, he brings together the family clan—135 people showed up at one recent meeting.

"Norton was painfully aware of being born into so much money," one of his friends says. "He entered many ventures when he didn't really have to, but he wanted to show he could make it."

Would he have made it without his inheritance? His capacity for work, his even-keeled nature, his judgment of talent—all say he was bound for success. His cautious instincts suggest he may not have been a likely candidate to have founded Weyerhaeuser Company, but perhaps he was a good one to have run it.

A better question might be: could he have done more? Here is a man who lacked for little: money, power, connections. On top of that, he has a rigorous mind that feasts on details and an intelligence that generates solutions to problems. He is also, however, afflicted by shyness, a trait in the wealthy that has its admirable side. It translates to lack of ostentatiousness—to that kind of sober, hard-working ethic of the Midwest, where modesty is a candle to merit. No displays of omnipotence in downtown Seattle for Clapp, no Columbia Centers to shout his worth. He is too restrained, too secure.

The flip side to this old-shoe, subdued, timorous style is the matter of aspiration. With his resources, Clapp could have brought something great to the Northwest. Instead, his conduct has been to preserve, to hold back, to go forward, but not to leap forward. He invested in the Space Needle, but did little to build any community resource that could be a showcase to the world. He played the loyal and decent sugar daddy for the Republican party, but he could have served as powerbroker. He inhabits an expensive and gracious, but architecturally unoriginal, waterfront home. He endowed no remarkable cultural organization. He chose to put his might behind the University of Puget Sound, not Evergreen State College; the Boy Scouts, not the Gray Panthers. Admirable as these institutions are, they represent little risk commensurate with his wealth. Clapp rarely gambled his money or his reputation. With his resources, he could have boldly dominated the Northwest and perhaps even transformed its business leadership.

All that might have been. But today, Clapp has settled into his role as aged patriarch. Once a year, he brings together the family clan—135 people showed up at one recent meeting—that now includes fifth and sixth generations of Lairds and Nortons. At the offices of family businesses, such as Lanoga Corp., Matthew G. Norton Co., Pelican Cold Storage, Northwest Building Corp., Northwest Management, and a host of others, members of the family keep the dynasty going.

Two who play vital roles are Bill Clapp and Gary MacLeod. Bill Clapp, born in 1941, was the first of two boys Norton Clapp had with Evelyn Booth Gardner. Bill went to Alaska, ran a school for bush pilots, then returned to head many of the enterprises Booth Gardner managed before he resumed political life. Bill Clapp replaced Gardner on the board of Weyerhaeuser Company, in 1981. He has been listed as owning 552,818 shares of common stock. He also sits on the boards of Alaska Airlines and Laird Norton Co. MacLeod is the husband of one of Norton Clapp's stepdaughters by Jane Henry. He replaced Clapp on Univar's board of directors in 1974 and plays an important role at Laird Norton Trust Co.

Clapp's brood includes others involved in the family businesses at one time or another. His first son, Jim, built and owned turbine-powered hydroplanes and raced sportscars, more inclined to seek thrills than run multimillion-dollar businesses. He was wild, flamboyant, drank heavily, and died at forty-three. His first wife, Jacqueline Hazen, married Norton Clapp, creating the odd situation in which Clapp's granddaughter from that marriage is now his stepdaughter. Another son, Matthew, has drifted in and out of family businesses and lives in Hawaii. Clapp also has a son, Stephen, by Evelyn Gardner.

By all accounts, Clapp has been very generous with his family, both in terms of support and financial backing. He is ultimately a family man, say friends. It extends outside bloodlines, also. When he married Jane Bumiller Henry, he took in three more children. Arthur Henry practices real estate in Issaquah. A second, Linda Henry, owns a nursery on Orcas Island and serves as fire commissioner; a Democrat, she served as a controversial and admired county commissioner during the mid-seventies, pushing for strong land-use laws. A third child, Michela, is married to Gary MacLeod, active at Laird Norton Trust Co.

According to one downtown financial source, the entire operations of the family are growing more aggressive. Out of town, their large purchases of stores and shopping centers are capturing attention. "They've got some people over there now who want to get more active," he says.

Much of the activity is now the province of Bill Clapp, who is in his mid-forties, down-to-earth, low-key, unpretentious, and talented. There is also activity, of course, outside the bloodlines in the person of Booth Gardner. Gardner lived in the Clapp household for only a short period of time, and he clearly represents a different political school, a different style of devoting energies—coaching sports in Seattle's Central District, for instance, versus heading the Chamber of Commerce. And yet there appears to be in Booth Gardner some of that same reticence.

Norton Clapp himself is in declining health. His eyes are going; his hearing is not good. He has a raspy respiratory problem that causes him to wheeze. Not long ago, a UPS administrator told the story of delivering a presentation at a board meeting in which Clapp, who was chairman of the board, appeared to be dozing. Slumped, stoop-shouldered, eyes closed, he would have been easy to underestimate. As the administrator flashed chart after chart of figures related to a development campaign, running through rows and rows of numbers, she was suddenly cut short. "The figure there," said Clapp, his head rising, "in the third column in the fourth row. It can't be right. It doesn't add up." And it didn't. ◀■

THE BLACK CAT

THE WOBBLIES (1905–1925)

DOUG HONIG

The Wobblies have acquired a near-mythical status, standing as romantic symbols of a rebellious past that still fascinates Washingtonians. The term "Wobbly" itself has come to serve as a generic handle for any old-time activist, to be credited—undeservedly— with everything from the Seattle General Strike to FDR adviser James Farley's reputed toast to "the Soviet of Washington." But the real legacy of the Wobblies—their flesh-and-blood accomplishments and failures—is rarely understood.

So let's get some facts straight. The *Industrial* Workers of the World is a labor group founded at a convention in Chicago in 1905. Its guiding principle was "industrial unionism," the notion that all workers in a given industry should be organized in the same union. These groupings would someday join together in One Big Union of all workers, skilled and unskilled, men and women, black and white alike. The One Big Union would run society as a Cooperative Commonwealth, thereby ending the reign of greedy capitalists. The IWW's founders were a bit vague as to how this remarkable transformation would come about, but their message of worker solidarity was unmistakable. The preamble to the IWW constitution got right to the point. "The working class and the employing class have nothing in common," it proclaimed.

As for the nickname by which they are best known—"the Wobblies"—no definitive account exists of its origin. A popular IWW tale holds that a Chinese restaurateur, sympathetic to the union but tongue-tied by the letter "w," could only manage "Eye-Wobbly-Wobbly." A variant ascribes the naming to the group's many Scandinavian immigrant members, who similarly tripped in pronouncing "Wobble-You."

Whatever one calls them, the Industrial Workers of the World flourished for a ten-year period—before the rise of the Communist Party—as the most dynamic, most feared radicals in America. They organized workers and won victories in places no other union had reached. In turn, they were targets of as intense a campaign of repression as any domestic political group has faced. The IWW continues to exist today in skeletal form, a reminder of the passion that once fired America's labor movement.

The Wobblies were not the first group to talk of uniting all producers and abolishing

IWW's notion of industrial unionism formed the heart of the campaigns of the 1930s.

263

A typical gathering of Wobblies: a
potent blend of songs and sabotage

wage labor. Their unique genius lay in expressing class politics in terms clear to any working person. They put Marxist ideology in an American idiom. Toilers in Tacoma's sawmills cared little about distinctions between bourgeoisie and petit bourgeoisie. But when Wobs lambasted the police as "the slugging committee of the capitalist class," the lowliest sawyer knew what they meant.

Most Wobbly literature displayed a dramatic verve, a biting wit, a smirk in the face of authority. New recruits could peruse the union's press for reports from the frontlines of class warfare, written in the salty language of rank-and-file fighters. Habitués of freight trains and employment offices would find thousands of small IWW stickers with pungent advice to the downtrodden: "The hours are long, the pay is small. So take your time and buck them all."

The spirit was best captured in the union's celebrated songs, rendered with gusto and frequency. Most were simply clever parodies of dance hall and religious tunes of the day; the likes of "Take It to the Lord in Prayer" would emerge born-again as "Dump the Bosses Off Your Back."

The IWW purported to speak for all the toiling masses, but their main appeal was to those on the lowest rungs of the economic ladder: the unskilled, immigrants, women, and racial minorities. In the West, the Wobs drew support from a large reservoir of migratory laborers—loggers, harvest hands, miners, and construction workers. These were mostly young, single males without home or family ties, who wandered from job to job.

Membership was open to all wage earners, regardless of race, sex, or trade.

These workers had been neglected by the established unions of the American Federation of Labor (AFL), which represented the labor aristocracy of skilled craftsmen. By contrast, the IWW was specially suited to the outcasts of the labor movement. Membership was open to all wage earners, regardless of race, sex, or trade. Initiation fees and monthly dues were low, and the Wobblies' red card of membership—a little booklet with spaces for dues stamps—was transferable when a worker switched jobs. One had only to agree to abide by the IWW constitution and rules and to study diligently its principles to be welcomed into the ranks.

One stronghold of the Wobblies' appeal was the Pacific Northwest. With an economy dependent on migratory musclemen in timber forests and harvest fields, with cities where hoboes gathered in cheap hotels to spend the winter, the region was a natural breeding ground for the IWW's brand of radicalism. Orators denouncing the depredations of "the master class" became fixtures on Skid Road corners. Within a couple years of its founding, the organization was boasting of several hundred Puget Sound members at branches in Seattle, Ballard, Tacoma, and outlying mill towns.

Wobblies from the Northwest played an important role in shaping the identity of the national union. It had begun as an amalgam of organizers and ideologues bound together only by a belief in industrial unions and contempt for the AFL. Early national conventions turned into factional donnybrooks.

A major dispute at the 1908 convention gives the flavor. This battle was over political strategy. Socialists like Daniel DeLeon supported electoral politics, while other members scorned the ballot box in favor of "direct action"—battling bosses right on the job. A key bloc of votes in the direct-action camp came from a crew of migratories assembled in Portland by organizer James H. Walsh. Clad in denim overalls, black shirts, and red bandanas, this twenty-person "Overalls Brigade" embarked on a twenty-five-hundred-mile odyssey by boxcar, holding street meetings and selling IWW literature along the way. Their itinerary included an unscheduled overnight stop in the Seattle hoosegow after

armed railroad guards sidetracked them in Auburn. In Chicago, DeLeon scornfully dubbed the Overalls Brigade "the Bummery" for their fondness for singing the hobo anthem, "Hallelujah, I'm a Bum." But the western hoboes helped boot DeLeon from the union and establish direct action as its *modus operandi.*

The Wobblies first stirred the public imagination in the Northwest with their energetic direction of a 1907 sawmill strike in Portland. In many ways the affair was a model of IWW agitation. It was a walkout of previously unorganized workers over which a few Wobblies assumed leadership. The organizers used militant tactics to spread the strike, with roving squads of picketers surrounding mills to call out twenty-three hundred fellow workers. Observers found the conflict surprisingly peaceful and orderly, as leaders prudently counseled workers against violence. Wobblies were hardly pacifists, but they normally stressed passive resistance from a hardheaded calculation of who stood to suffer most from spilling blood.

As usual, the Wobs exchanged verbal fire with their AFL antagonists. To these mainstream unionists, the IWW's were Irresponsible Wholesale Wreckers bent on disrupting the labor movement. When a state AFL leader opposed the sawmill strike, the radicals retaliated with a leaflet blasting him as a liar and "labor faker." Support for the strike ebbed, and organizers called it off after a few weeks and some small wage gains.

The size and speed of the 1907 shutdown sent shock waves through employer and labor circles alike. "The suddenness of the strike and the completeness of the tie-up are quite unprecedented in this part of the country," remarked a writer in the *Oregon Journal.* "Wherever the Industrial Workers of the World are organized, they can paralyze industry at almost the snap of a finger."

Wobbly agitation involved a lot more than finger-popping. A campaign in Spokane in 1909–10 provided a powerful demonstration of tactics for mobilizing supporters. Under the direction of James H. Walsh—fresh from shepherding the "Overalls Brigade"—the union leased a spacious new hall with the standard free reading room, a cigar and newsstand, and an assembly hall offering movies and lectures four nights a week. The Spokane branch also began publishing its own weekly newspaper, the *Industrial Worker,* which established itself as the voice of Wobs throughout the West.

At the hub of the Inland Empire, Spokane was a magnet for harvest hands, lumberjacks, and miners looking for a warm room between jobs. The Wobblies located their hall on Front Street (now Spokane Falls Boulevard) near the "slave markets"—employment agencies where migrants paid a fee to receive a job. Workers often complained that employment "sharks" sent them to nonexistent jobs or split fees with foremen after a quick firing. A standard joke was that sharks had devised a perpetual motion system: one man going to the job, one man on the job, and one man leaving the job.

Under the slogan "Don't Buy Jobs," Wobbly street speakers urged a boycott of employment agencies. The agencies fought back, convincing the city council to ban street meetings. (This ordinance was later amended to exempt religious groups such as the Salvation Army—a move which incensed the irreligious radicals.) The union men regarded the right to address workers in the street as an essential organizing tool. So they challenged the ban with a "free-speech fight," a classic form of civil disobedience that was a precursor of civil-rights organizing fifty years later. The Spokane fight was the first large-scale test of its effectiveness.

Wobblies did not originate the tactics, but they refined civil disobedience to a political art, even before television. Men responded by the hundreds to the call for "footloose rebels" to pack the jails of Spokane. Speakers would mount a platform, deliver the salutation, "Fellow Workers!" and get out a few other words before being dragged off to prison. Crammed into dirty cells, subsisting on bread and water, sometimes drenched with icy water or bathed in scalding water, they showed a dogged willingness to endure brutal conditions.

Elizabeth Gurley Flynn, a fiery orator who would later be canonized as "The Rebel Girl" in a Joe Hill tune, joined the men. Pregnant at the time, Flynn chained herself to a lamppost to delay arrest, then shamed officials with revelations that guards were engaging in sexual relations with female inmates.

Their jail overflowing and their treasury drained, Spokane officials caved in after five months. They revoked the ban on street meetings and released all prisoners. In addition, nineteen of the most notorious sharks lost their business licenses.

The Spokane scenario was replayed in thirty free speech skirmishes throughout the West. Results varied, but press accounts spread the Wobblies' reputation for tooth-and-nail defiance. While such persistence won the admiration of working stiffs and some liberals, it aroused the deepest anxieties of the middle class. Historian Robert Tyler, author of *Rebels of the Woods,* a study of the IWW in the Northwest, termed this "the Hobo in the Garden" syndrome—a fear of rootless vagabonds swarming into a community to flout accepted standards. That fear eventually doomed the Wobblies.

Business and professional interests soon resorted to extreme measures to combat the Wobbly menace. In Aberdeen in 1911 and Everett in 1916, armies of citizen deputies patrolled the streets, pummeling intruding Wobblies with ax handles and wagon spokes. In Aberdeen the feisty radicals forced their opponents to back down. But in Everett strong-arm tactics by business interests and the Wobblies' stubbornness resulted in tragedy.

The free speech fight in Everett had begun, typically enough, with Wobs from Seattle offering unsolicited support to a dying strike by AFL shingle weavers. After a particularly vicious beating of Wobs via a gauntlet, the Seattle supporters resolved to return in larger numbers. On November 5, 1916, more than two hundred singing union men sailed from Seattle on the steamship *Verona*. Awaiting them on the Everett dock was a large

Speakers would mount a platform, deliver the salutation, "Fellow Workers!", and get out a few other words before being dragged off to prison.

267

Anna Louise Strong

Anna Louise Strong arrived in Seattle in 1915 and quickly gained prominence as the editor of the Seattle Labor Paper. *She was the first woman elected to the school board; however, she was recalled in 1919 for her 1918 public support for Louise Olivera, a self-proclaimed anarchist. After her flaming editorial on the general strike was picked up in papers across the nation, she decamped to China where she eventually became good friends with Mao Tse-tung.*

From I Change Worlds: The Remaking of an American, *by Anna Louise Strong. Copyright © 1979 The Seal Press. Reprinted by permission.*

The Seattle to which I came in the second year of the World War rated as a progressive city. The populace invariably voted against the "reactionary interests" who represented capital imported from New York. There were two organizations of business men. The Chamber of Commerce was composed of big business, the "interests," by which we meant the great timber and power companies. There was also a cheerfully democratic Commercial Club, of the young and progressive business men. They organized excursions and beach parties and clam-bakes to get acquainted with the surrounding farmers; together with these farmers they demanded municipal ownership of docks, warehouses, power, street cars, in order that independent business and farming might thrive under the shelter of cheap and benevolent public utilities. They were supported in these demands by the equally progressive Central Labor Council, the delegate body representing the trade unions of the city, whose slogan was a city of high wages and sound homes.

In every hard election fight, when the populace was really aroused, it was certain to beat the interests. Other cities might settle down under corrupt government, but not we. Political candidates always refused endorsement from the Chamber of Commerce and from its spokesman *The Seattle Times*; to accept financial contributions from the interests was a sure path to defeat. The population of young business men and respectable American skilled workers achieved one venture of municipal ownership after another; City Light was successfully competing with the power trust, the municipally owned docks were out-distancing in spectacular size the privately owned docks. Seattle was becoming a paradise of public ownership, visited by delegations from other cities. . . .

The progressive forces asked me to run for the School Board; for many years they had wished to have a woman on that board, which had been for two decades a self-perpetuating committee of bankers and business men. The chief plank in our platform was the wider use of school buildings for all sorts of public meetings, a demand close to the heart of all small clubs, societies, cooperative organizations, liberal and radical associations, which wished a respectable and inexpensive place in which to meet.

Fresh from my work with the U.S. Children's Bureau, with the degree of doctor of philosophy and two or three books to my credit, I was easily the most acceptable candidate in town. University clubs supported "a really educated woman against those self-made men of business."

Labor organizations supported "schools run by teachers and mothers, instead of by capitalists." I was not a little helped by the wide popularity of my father. He had induced the Ministers' Federation to exchange fraternal delegates with organized labor, and had supported certain local strikes. The school election was at that time a sleepy affair attended by a few citizens and usually controlled by the self-perpetuating board through their pressure on the teachers. I easily captured the election. . . .

Among the conservative members of the School Board I was already marked as a radical. My election to the board against the clique of business men, my articles for the [New York *Evening*] *Post* on the Everett trial, my increasing visits to the I.W.W. headquarters and championship of their leaders—were listed against me. We progressives resented the term "radical"; we were not digging anything up by the roots; we were merely continuing the good old American tradition of inevitable progress, a country getting better and better forever—a tradition which the interests had attacked.

Towards the end of 1916 it became evident that strong forces were pushing America towards the battle trenches of Europe. . . . I threw myself into the Anti-Preparedness League, the Union Against

Anna Louise Strong

Militarism, the Emergency Peace Federation—all that rapidly shifting galaxy of organizations with which pacifists, liberals, radicals and progressives fought America's advance towards war. These organizations sprang up in the East, New York, Washington or Philadelphia, with varying and perhaps conflicting leadership: socialists, bourgeois, pacifists of all kinds. We of the Pacific provinces never distinguished between the different leaderships. We all met together—all who opposed war, and of these there were a goodly number—in regular luncheon meetings once a week in a cafeteria, and in occasional Sunday mass meetings enthusiastically attended. We accepted speakers, campaigns, pamphlets from any national society that chose to send them. . . .

Then this America whose populace protested war and whose profiteers desired it, left us and marched into the war with all of Europe. As the war approached, our local branch of the Anti-Preparedness Committee, the American Union against Militarism, the Emergency Peace Federation, dwindled; the respectable members were turning to war work. The presidents of women's clubs were "swinging in behind the President"; the head of the Parent-Teachers organizations, who spoke so valiantly for peace in the mass meeting which featured the flag, found other duties now.

The weekly cafeteria meetings grew smaller. . . . The fight was lost, and forever! "Our America" was dead! The profiteers, the militarists, the "interests" had violated her and forced her to their bidding. I could not delude myself, as some did, that this was a "war to make the world safe for democracy"; I had seen democracy slain in the very declaration of war. The people wanted peace; the profiteers wanted war—and got it. There had been a deep mistake in the whole basis of my life. Where and how to begin again I had no notion.

I turned like a wounded beast to the hills for shelter. Like the pioneers of old I fled to the simpler wilderness from the problems of human society that I could not face. Week after week on the high slopes of Rainier I was busy with problems of pack-trains, commissary, cooking, hikes. Eight or ten hours a day I led parties on the glaciers. Few newspapers reached me; I did not read them. I shrank from every mention of the war. I drugged myself with forests, cliffs, glaciers. I exhausted myself with twenty-four-hour climbs. It was the end of youth, the end of belief, the end of "our America." I could not face the ruins of my world.

contingent of gun-toting deputies. A shot rang out—from where was never proven—and a lengthy volley ensued, leaving five Wobs and two deputies dying, several Wobs drowned, and fifty men on both sides wounded. The Everett Massacre was the bloodiest outbreak of labor violence in Northwest history. The subsequent trial of the first of seventy-four Wobblies charged with first-degree murder drew national headlines. With an astute defense led by Seattle attorney George Vanderveer, the self-described "Counsel for the Damned," the radicals scored a rare victory in the courtroom.

Everett turned out to be the last of the tumultuous free speech fights. Wobbly organizers had already realized the limits of soapbox campaigns. For all the attention they brought, they were essentially sideshows, distractions from the long-term task of building a permanent union structure. As Wobbly editor Ben Williams lamented in 1913, "We are to the labor movement what the high diver is to the circus: a sensation, marvelous and ever-thrilling.... As far as making Industrial Unionism fit the everyday life of the workers, we have failed miserably."

Throughout its heyday, the IWW was plagued by an inability to consolidate victories, to form stable, ongoing local chapters. In part this reflected the migratory lifestyle of its members. Novice organizers tended simply to tell off the boss and move on, sending the warning "Bum job, stay away" to the *Industrial Worker*. Meanwhile, the labor movement as a whole was in a weak state, with scant public acceptance or government support.

Virtually any transient Wobbly was empowered to act as an organizer in the field.

Another problem stemmed from the IWW's split personality: it was a labor union striving to improve wages and conditions on the job, and it was a revolutionary cadre working to overthrow capitalism. In theory the dual functions were compatible, as Wobblies believed that job actions for short-run gains served as drills for the ultimate task of dumping the bosses. In practice, the two were hard to reconcile. The radicals at times seemed hostile to the nuts and bolts of union operation, as when they derided sickness and death funds as "coffin benefits."

A distinctive feature of IWW strategy was opposition to signing contracts with employers. These agreements were the bread and butter of AFL unions, but the radicals regarded union contracts as unholy alliances with mortal enemies, "death warrants of labor," in the phrase of organizer Big Bill Haywood. The reasoning ran that since the strike was the crucial weapon in the ongoing class struggle, workers should make no bargain to restrict its use.

This revolutionary stance naturally made employers loathe to deal with the IWW. In businessmen's eyes, Wobbly organizers seemed utterly unreasonable since—unlike their AFL counterparts—they could not be relied upon to provide a disciplined work force. "Their policy is to demand more and work less until industry is ruined," ran a typical complaint in a lumber-industry journal. Yet the Wobblies' most lasting impact on the Northwest came precisely from trying to function as an everyday union in its lumber industry.

Wobblies in Everett, in front of the IWW Hall, 1916: Dramatic verve, smirks at authority

Organizers were active in mills where wood was processed, but their greatest strength was in the forests where timber was harvested.

Northwest wages in the forests were relatively high compared with elsewhere in the industry, so disputes more often raged over the terms of the work. To some extent, harsh conditions were unavoidable. Logging was strenuous physical toil performed outdoors in the rain and far from the comforts of city life. Conditions in logging camps were typically primitive. After a ten-hour day in the woods, lumberjacks trudged back in wet clothes to crowded, boxlike shacks with neither showers nor drying rooms. Warmth came from wood stoves around which the woolen garb was hung. "The sweaty, steamy odors of a bunkhouse at night would asphyxiate the uninitiated," wrote Rexford Tugwell.

The lumberjacks' biggest gripes concerned sleeping conditions. Camps often provided neither blankets nor mattresses, but simply hard pallets with perhaps a bit of straw. So migratory loggers had to carry their possessions rolled up in "bindles," or bedding, from camp to camp, with lice and bedbugs frequent companions. The men were "timber beasts," said the Wobblies, a virtual subspecies of humans in the eyes of employers and city dwellers.

To lonely bindlestiffs in the deep woods, the Wobblies offered the fellowship of a common cause—a community of shared songs, literature, and exhortations to get up and do something to improve their lot. The union gave a means of political action on the job and a focus for social life off the job. It provided a sense of self-respect and hope. As Marxists, the Wobblies believed that bosses were parasites living off the labor of people who actually produced the wealth. Their gospel taught that by organizing together workers could reclaim their just deserts—and their proper place in history.

By 1912 the IWW had enough followers among timber workers to form their first industrywide union. It was an exemplar of the Wobs' egalitarian philosophy, aiming to represent everybody from woodchoppers and sawyers to game wardens and collectors of bark and sap. A notable success came with a strike of five thousand men around Puget Sound that won clean blankets and mattresses with springs in some camps. Yet the new union was defunct in a year.

A major handicap lay in giving practical aid to men who worked far from headquarters in cities. So the Wobblies devised a system of "job delegates" that brought the union directly to workers. Virtually any transient Wobbly was empowered to act as an organizer in the field. Carrying a mobile office of dues books, membership cards, and pamphlets, they could sign up recruits right where they worked and deal with grievances on the spot.

The owners who ran the industry provided the union with rugged adversaries. Logging was a cutthroat, boom-and-bust enterprise, and the lumbermen who succeeded were harddriving, self-made apostles of laissez-faire who regarded unions as hindrances to the natural laws of the market. To such men, Wobblies were incarnations of chaos and Wobbly strikes were the handiwork of a few outside agitators intimidating loyal employees.

Especially odious to the employers was the Wobblies' frequent advocacy of sabotage. The black cat—the IWW symbol for the tactic—was a regular adornment of cartoons in the *Industrial Worker.* To lumbermen the "Sabo Tabby Kitten" conjured images of deranged anarchists heedlessly destroying property: a common charge was that Wobs drove spikes into logs to wreck saws. The radicals claimed that sabotage was merely peaceful noncompliance—"the conscious withdrawal of the worker's efficiency," explained the pamphlet "Sabotage" by Elizabeth Gurley Flynn. But Wobbly rhetoric, such as the reference to sticking a pitchfork through the cogs of a machine in a Joe Hill ditty, did little to calm fears.

Lumbermen's journals were full of warnings about "The Wobbly Plague." Ridding the woods of the disease became an obsession. Employers adopted a simple solution: any

Dave Beck

Seattle's labor leader believed in a common cause between management and labor. As he rose to national head of the Teamsters, Beck used tough tactics to deradicalize the unions after the 1919 General Strike and turn Seattle into a middle-class union town. His enforced truce captivated the town's oligarchs for a time, until Beck fell into federal legal problems and was toppled.

From "Labor's New Men," by Daniel Bell, Fortune, *June 1953. Copyright © Fortune. Reprinted by permission of Fortune Magazine.*

To the power-hungry Dave Beck the successful businessman is a shining American image; Dave Beck is a businessman himself. He once told an interviewer: "I run this place just like the Standard Oil Co. or the Northern Pacific Railway. We sell labor. We use businesslike methods. And business people have confidence in us."

Dave's father, Lemuel, spent an unsuccessful lifetime in the carpet business. "I guess he had no business ability," Beck once remarked. "We were very, very poor." Mother Beck had to work in a laundry to make ends meet. Dave, born in 1894, left high school in Seattle at the end of his third year to work full time.

But he was an ambitious boy and bookish. "I never smoked," he once recalled, "never drank [he still doesn't], never played a game of pool; I used to go off alone and read." He still reads. "I've read the autobiography of every successful man I could get my hands on." Between 1920 and 1928 he took extension courses at the University of Washington. His language is flavored with such highbrow euphemisms as "we perfected the organization," meaning he signed up everybody in sight. "Perfected" is, in fact, his favorite verb.

Although Seattle before and shortly after World War I was the center of turbulent radical activity, Beck remained untouched by these movements. In 1917 he started driving a laundry truck. Shortly after, he enlisted in the Navy, and became a machinist's mate, first class. After the war he returned to his truck. . . .

By 1925 Dave owned his own truck, and apparently was on his way, when he was confronted with an important decision. The law firm of Schwellenbach and McFarlane (which later represented Beck's Teamsters) had merged several laundries into a chain and asked Beck to become general manager. At the same time Dan Tobin offered him a post with the Teamsters as an organizer. Dave had an overwhelming desire to become a respected businessman. He had joined the Elks and had met men who were rising in the world. "I was making fine friends there," he recalls. "There were judges, attorneys, and businessmen, many of whom I number among my best friends." . . . But, perhaps because he was still a little unsure of himself, it was Tobin's offer that he took.

His province was the Pacific Northwest. Organizing the area was a tough job, and Dave Beck went at it in a tough way. A top Seattle businessman recalls those days: "Beck practiced all the rough stuff there was in the game, tipping over farmers' trucks—for which he incurred the farmers' everlasting enmity—stink-bombing, breaking dry cleaners' windows, using goon squads. He followed completely relentless methods." . . .

About 1937 Beck changed his methods. Instead of terrorizing business he decided to work with it, displayed a cooperative attitude, and won a reputation as a man who kept his word.

His new philosophy was simple and matter of fact: by assuring him a profit the employer could be made to pay a higher wage. Beck's system, like John L. Lewis', was to "stabilize" industry by limiting competition and maintaining prices. "The government regulates railroad rates. It doesn't permit each line to run berserk underbidding competitors for business. If fares between Seattle and Spokane can be stabilized," Beck asked himself rhetorically, "why can't we apply the same principle to the prices charged for rye bread and chocolate pies?"

The Pacific coast business community breathed a sigh of relief. It feared the rising power of Harry Bridges and the C.I.O., and decided, as one observer put it, "If businessmen were going to have to deal with unions, they would rather deal with Dave Beck, because he kept his contracts."

Seattle Post-Intelligencer Collection

Dave Beck

In order to "stabilize" thoroughly, Beck helped organize the boss too. Employer associations were set up in the laundry, cleaning and dyeing, and other fields, and some of them were staffed by former union officials. Beck sought to limit the number of gasoline stations in Seattle. And, in a spectacular battle, he managed for five years to keep Californian and eastern beer out of the Seattle area. . . .

The year 1937 . . . marked the beginning of Beck's expansion from his Washington base, a drive that took the Teamsters' membership in eleven western states from 60,000 to almost 400,000 [in 1953].

His tactics were to solidify first in the cities, then to utilize these unions as bases from which to leapfrog out into the surrounding towns. In this fashion, he advanced down the Pacific coast, and finally, as one of his men said, by the implied threat of Teamster boycott power, "organized Los Angeles from outside of Los Angeles." Once unionized, the various Teamster services were grouped into "trade divisions" such as baking, cannery, garages, etc., which cut across the local and metropolitan lines and allowed Beck to centralize control at the top. . . .

In 1940, Beck persuaded the A.F. of L. Council to award the Teamsters national jurisdiction over all "warehousing" operations. In practice it meant a claim on all workers who handle goods between the factory bench and the retail stores—a stupendous grant over the entire distribution world. Beck staked it out before other A.F. of L. unions realized what was up.

These achievements made Beck the heir apparent to the presidency of the union. Patiently he waited for Dan Tobin to retire. To "Uncle Dan" he was sweet talk itself, but he cut down all possible rivals, including Tobin's sons. Beck became president in December, 1952, when Uncle Dan, at seventy-seven, finally stepped down.

Dave Beck plugs hard the line that the distribution industry should understand the great asset it has in his Teamsters union. "My slogan," says Beck, "is the sanctity of contract above the sanctity of the picket line."

He can see an employer's side. In

December, 1946, the Retail Clerks in Los Angeles closed down 1,500 groceries in a wage strike, which, as a Los Angeles union official explained, "would have pushed the whole wage structure out of line; other unions would have been prompted to strike for more money too."

The Los Angeles central council was sympathetic and there was talk of a general strike to back up the Clerks. Beck fired off a telegram to Joe De Silva, the Retail Clerks' representative in Los Angeles, saying the strike must end or the Teamsters would sever relations with them. De Silva's answer was to call Beck "the No. 1 strikebreaker in America." The Teamsters then moved in, took over publicity for the grocery employers' association, and generally ran interference for the association. The strike was broken.

Beck also believes in joint action with "his" employers in fighting competitors. Recently he announced that the Teamsters union was uniting with trucking companies and truck manufacturers to protect the industry against "governmental and legislative discrimination." With Roy Fruehauf, president of the Fruehauf Trailer Co., and B.M. Seymour of As-sociated Transport Inc., Beck visited President Eisenhower to charge that the ICC was biased in favor of the railroads and to ask the President to appoint some truck-minded commissioners to the next vacancies.

Beck sees this cooperation as a new stage in U.S. unionism. That it may result in a coalition against the consumer is a possibility that Beck does not discuss.

Other union leaders fear Beck's ruthlessness, they resent his new self-righteousness regarding racketeering in the labor movement, they charge him with making "sweetheart deals" with employers. Beck does not appear to mind his lack of popularity. He has no open political ambitions, and in national politics he stays strictly neutral. He is far less concerned over who gets elected than he is over whether some political figure may try "to destroy my relation with the businessman."

suspected Wobbly was fired on the spot. To help identify agitators they relied on a network of labor spies who supplied names for blacklists.

Determining how many adherents the radicals had was always problematic, considering the union's rapid turnover of members. Precise figures were beside the point anyway, for the IWW's influence reached far beyond its core of supporters. A prime example was its most widespread campaign in the Northwest, the timber strike of 1917.

Wartime orders for lumber to build railroad cars, cargo ships, and army housing had rescued the timber industry from a cyclical slump. Buoyed by the demand for labor, Wobbly representatives met in Spokane in March to revive the industrywide union and plan a large-scale drive. The time was evidently ripe. Loggers and mill workers began walking off their jobs in advance of the projected strike date. A new AFL union also called out its men, and by early summer timber production was crippled.

The key issue was reduction of the working day to eight hours, a coveted goal of American labor since the previous century. By now many lumbermen were willing to grant the eight-hour day as a reasonable reform which would not harm productivity, but none wanted to concede to any demand if doing so would appear to mean giving in to the despised Wobblies leading the strike. After several weeks of unbending employer opposition, the Wobblies resorted to a wily stratagem they called "transferring the strike to the job." The men returned to work, but engaged in sabotage. They would follow orders to ridiculous extremes or waste time waiting for obvious instructions. The slowdown tactics hamstrung production, with workers getting their paychecks to boot. "Much against their will, the companies were forced to run the commissary of the strike," crowed organizer James Rowan.

With Uncle Sam fighting "the war to end all wars," federal officials fretted about the lagging supply of Northwest spruce needed for constructing airplanes. So the US War Department dispatched Colonel Brice Disque, a former prison warden, to the scene. A fair-minded, shrewd operative, Disque devised an ingenious solution. First, he established a special army unit—the Spruce Production Division—to work in mills and camps at his direction. Secondly, he set up a joint employer-worker body—the Loyal Legion of Loggers and Lumbermen, known as "the 4-L"—to run the industry under a no-strike pledge. With a federally sanctioned army of twenty-seven thousand strikebreakers and an industrywide company union in place, spruce production surged ahead.

Disque also took away the rallying cry of the strike by imposing the eight-hour day on lumbermen in early 1918. Through the 4-L he instituted such reforms as providing bedding and regular changes of linen in logging camps. Wobblies celebrated, declaring May 1 a day to burn all bindles, but lumbermen would have the last laugh. Their acceptance of reforms was conditioned by a most desirable tradeoff—a wholesale crackdown on Wobblies in the Northwest.

Just as Seattle had been a focal point for the IWW's growth, so it became a national leader in suppressing the union.

As the bogeymen of employers and the middle class, Wobblies had often felt the wrath of both public officials and vigilantes. The radicals' scorching rhetoric made it fatally easy for the popular press to distort their ideas and actions. In Seattle in 1913, for example, a mob of sailors, egged on by *Seattle Times* assaults on "red flag anarchists," had wrecked the IWW headquarters on South Washington Street.

America's entry into the war in Europe in 1917 had greatly intensified fears of radicalism at home. Though Wobbly leaders judiciously avoided taking an official stand on the conflict, their literature had long denounced warfare and militarism as the devilish work of capitalists. Patriotic zealots cited such propaganda to accuse the IWW of being un-American agents of the kaiser, of being "Imperial Wilhelm's Warriors." The Reverend Mark Matthews, scourge of sin and sedition at Seattle's First Presbyterian Church, wrote the United States Attorney General to warn that the city was prey to a cabal of "pro-German forces, IWW fiends, and vice syndicate agents."

Just as Seattle had been a focal point for the IWW's growth, so it became a national leader in suppressing the union. Throughout the war years police raided its hall and arrested its adherents. The Minute Men, a two thousand-member veterans league, assumed the privilege of spying on and detaining suspected Wobs. Another mob of sailors smashed the plant of the Pigott Printing Concern, printer for the *Industrial Worker* (then based in Seattle).

A committee of federal officials in the city determined that deporting alien radicals was the easiest way to dispose of the Wobs. The United States Immigration Bureau began rounding up men by the hundreds for merely possessing IWW pamphlets or supporting the union's ideals; the crusade was a test run by the notorious Palmer Raids held after the war. Secretary of Labor William Wilson eventually clamped down on the roundup by insisting on evidence of overt illegal acts. Undaunted, the Washington Legislature passed one of the nation's first "criminal syndicalism" acts, a measure outlawing the mere advocacy of political change through intimidation or sabotage.

Anti-Wobbly hysteria reached a climax with the Armistice Day clash in Centralia in 1919. When parading American Legionnaires tried to rush the union hall, Wobs—in an unusual show of force—defended it with gunfire. Four Legionnaires were killed, and a Wobbly was later lynched. In the legal battle that ensued, the verdict showed how sharply public sentiment had turned against the radicals since the prewar Everett Massacre. This time seven Wobblies were convicted and received lengthy sentences; the final prisoner was not released until the late 1930s.

Despite all the persecutions and prosecutions, some Wobblies remained politically active. During wartime, thousands of migrants had drifted to Seattle to work in the shipyards. While IWW theory frowned upon "boring from within" the established unions, the lure of a steady paycheck produced many "two-card men"—holders of the IWW red

Remember!

WE are in HERE for YOU.
You are out THERE for US

card who also took up membership in AFL unions. They joined with independent radicals to provide a noisy left-wing presence in Seattle's Central Labor Council. Some two-carders got themselves elected delegates to the body, and comrades attended meetings to cheer passionate speeches and belittle conservative leaders as "Labor Kaisers."

Among the Wobblies' dearest dreams was a general strike—a single, coordinated blow in which wage earners would lay down their tools and bloodlessly topple the capitalist system. Oddly, the first mass tie-up of an entire American city, the Seattle General Strike of 1919, found the AFL in command. Two-card men had pushed vigorously for the action, and some thirty-five hundred other Wobs walked out in sympathy, promising to abstain from provocative rallies. However, Wobblies were excluded from the strike's governing committee and even had to argue to gain acceptance of red cards as tokens for cheap meals at strike feeding stations.

For all its discipline and unity, the five-day general strike did nothing to improve the position of organized labor. The wartime boom collapsed like a pricked balloon, and the city's industrial work force shrank by two-thirds in two years. Youthful, familyless Wobs, as was their custom, simply drifted on to the harvest fields of eastern Washington or the mines of Montana. "The IWW's are pretty well scattered now in Seattle," observed a Wob talking unwittingly to a labor spy. "But I don't believe our membership has gone down any, for once a Wobbly always a Wobbly. You can't make a capitalist out of him."

Unlike old soldiers, the battling radicals refused to fade away. They continued to agitate in the woods, sparking a 1923 strike that idled camps from British Columbia to Chehalis. Citizens in Seattle were treated to a 1923 IWW campaign against "dehorn" (bootleg whiskey), as allegedly lawless Wobs enforced prohibition by smashing kegs and overturning bars. "A direct action squad of more than one hundred men went through Chinatown like a devastating cyclone," reported an amazed UPI correspondent.

But the wave of repression had taken its intended toll. Many an organizer spent long months in jail, and those on the outside fell into bitter wrangles at conventions. By the mid-twenties the Industrial Workers of the World had fallen apart as an effective national organization. Its energy was sapped by legal defense work and its appeal to radicals had been superseded by the Communist Party.

There were a few local last hurrahs, such as a 1932 hop-pickers' strike in the Yakima Valley that culminated in a clash between picketers and several hundred armed farmers. But when the labor movement revived with massive organizing campaigns during the Depression, it was the new Congress of Industrial Organizations that led the way.

Most individual Wobblies kept their radical faith, though often in new arenas. Big Bill Haywood fled to Russia. Elizabeth Gurley Flynn joined the Communist Party. Ralph Chaplin, the Wobbly writer who composed "Solidarity Forever," came to Tacoma to edit the local AFL newspaper and ended up rather tamely—working for the Washington State Historical Society.

In Seattle, wet-behind-the-ears radicals could still visit the Wobbly hall near Pioneer Square to read the latest *Industrial Worker,* pick up a *Little Red Song Book,* or soak up tales of yesteryear's struggles. The hall closed without fanfare in 1965, though small IWW branches still meet around the state.

It would be simplistic to think that the IWW would have achieved its aims if only world war and repression had not come. Organizational weaknesses and the balancing act between unionism and revolution would have remained in the way. Historian Irving Werstein hit the mark in calling Wobblies "good fighters but bad builders."

Yet it would also be a mistake to treat the radicals as simply historical curiosities. Their notion of industrial unionism formed the heart of the campaigns of the 1930s, which ultimately shaped the modern labor movement. Later generations of activists have continued to build upon their tactics of passive resistance. Above all, the Industrial Workers of the World provided a sense of vitality, an ability to inspire masses of working people, a very American belief in themselves, and a vision of the future from which today's labor organizers could learn much.

Woody Guthrie: quintessential folk poet

282

ROLL ON, WOODY

WOODY GUTHRIE (1913–1967)

ERIC SCIGLIANO

I magine him: the wiry, wizened little self-proclaimed "dust bowl refugee," feeling the dry winds that swallowed the empty middle of America and the venal compromises of its commercial capitals. Imagine him standing wide-eyed before a promised land of prosperity and freedom on the Columbia River. It was May 1941 and Woody Guthrie had made it to the Northwest.

Bound for Glory, Woody's so-called autobiography (he called it a novel) written in 1941, begins far from here, atop a speeding freight train in Illinois:

> My ear flat against the tin roof soaked up some of the music coming down from inside of the car.
> This train don't carry no rustlers,
> Whores, pimps, or side-street hustlers
> This train is bound for glory,
> This train.
> Can I remember? Remember back to where I was this morning? St. Paul. Yes. The morning before? Bismarck, North Dakota. And the morning before that? Miles City, Montana. Week ago, I was a piano player in Seattle.

By the book's end, after a hallucinatory flashback through his life from Oklahoma to California, narrator Woody is on his way back to Seattle, where his journey began. "About a dozen cops" have dragged him and his companions of the road off the train. As they shake the travelers down, a westbound train pulls up.

> An old gray-headed hobo trotted past us in the dark, swinging his bundle up onto his back, splashing through the mudholes and not even noticing the patrol men. He got a glimpse of all of us guys there under the light and yelled, "Plenty of work! Building ships! War's on! Work, boys, work."…
> "Seattle! Seattle! I heard the old man holler back through the rain. "Work, worrrrk!"

"I slep' under every bridge in Seattle."

283

"Crazy!"

"Yuh know, men, there ain't work out a Seattle. Hell's bells, that's more'n fifteen hundred miles west uv here!"

"Out toward Japan!"

"Th' old man had th' letter right there in his hand!"

"Reckin' he's right?"

Three more men tore loose through the dark.

"I know them Seattle people. You cain't beat 'em. Mighty purty women. An', by God, they don't write letters, less they mean what they say!"

"I slep' under every bridge in Seattle! That's a working town!"

Two refrains rise as the book ends: "This train is bound for glory/This train," and "This train's a-goin' ta Seattle! Fifteen hundred miles!"

Why the big deal about this town? There's no evidence Woody had ever ridden a freight train here. The documented record shows him passing through the Northwest just four times, twice in 1941 and again in 1947 and 1954. How many times was he here? "Beats me," he told Portland writer Ralph Friedman, an old buddy from farm-camp organizing days. In the Depression, recalls Friedman, people (especially Woody) traveled far looking for work or a change, without much noting where they were or saying where they had been. Old-timers here recall other encounters in other years with Woody—in labor halls, on the road, in their own living rooms—as early as 1935, before Woody ever left Texas. Sort the tales with a grain or two of salt; as Guthrie scholar Guy Logsdon at the University of Oklahoma says, "People knew Woody who never even met him."

It's fitting that Guthrie's comings and goings should be shrouded in legend and foggy remembrance. He was America's quintessential and greatest folk poet, who exerted an influence on music, culture, and even politics that still rolls like a slow avalanche far beyond the lives he touched personally. Guthrie was at once larger than life and a nondescript little guy, a bum, not the sort the television cameras turn out for. Woody did his own bit to muddy the details and mythologize himself. Ramblin' Jack Elliott, his partner and protégé in his last rambles, says, "Woody's numbers were always arguable. His favorite number was 'a jillion.' "

What's certain is that though the times Guthrie spent in this corner of the country were brief, they were pivotal to his progress as a populist visionary. It was here that he wrote his most extraordinary series of songs, here that he broke with his wife and family, here that he came to heal after his most devastating personal tragedy. And it was here that he gained visions, which he cherished all of his life, of immeasurable riches, of government actually working to bring those riches to serve *all* people, and of people working on their own, in high good fellowship, for the just society. "You could say Woody was inspired by Seattle

Campground for dust bowl
refugees, 1938: ballads of hard
knocks and hard sights

and the Pacific Northwest," recalls his premier musical comrade, Pete Seeger. Never
mind the personal disillusionment that came later, or the tarnish that the Washington Public Power Supply System's nuclear boondoggles put on the promised millennium on the
Columbia; whenever the Northwest was mentioned, says Jack Elliott, Woody would ex-
claim, "Best country!"

In early 1941, writes Joe Klein in his comprehensive biography, *Woody Guthrie: A
Life,* Guthrie was "languishing in Los Angeles." At the age of twenty-eight, he'd already
packed in a full life: drifted through sign painting and soda-jerking; schooled himself
through wide, eclectic reading; fled the dust-bowl winds that swallowed towns like his native Okemah, Oklahoma, and Pampa, Texas; ridden the freights; followed the great Okie
migration to the dismal farm camps of California; and been radicalized by hard knocks on
his head and harsh sights in his eyes. He had written enough "Dust-bowl Ballads" and

other songs to fill volumes—songs to make people feel good and rise up angry. Some have endured as anthems of their eras, classics forever: "This Land Is Your Land" (originally written as an ironic parody, "God Blessed America For Me"), "Union Maid," "Tom Joad," "So Long, It's Been Good to Know You."

Like the migrant workers he immortalized, Woody was again and again "gone with the wind." He struck lucrative radio gigs in Los Angeles and New York, but impulsively cashed them in when he felt compromised or claustrophobic. It took him only a month to ditch his crassly commercial national show for CBS and the Model Tobacco Company, at Christmastime 1940. He put his first fat check down on a shiny new Pontiac, loaded his long-suffering wife Mary and three kids in, and banged his way back to California.

Woody loaded the family into the Pontiac and set out for Portland.

There, writes Klein, Woody found little to return to. The Okies, "my people," had drifted from the farm camps to new war industries, and the old union organizing movement he'd served had disintegrated. In Los Angeles, his old job on radio KFVD wasn't waiting for him. He settled next door to Ed Robbin, his buddy and mentor on *The Daily People's World* (the San Francisco-based Communist paper Woody wrote a column for till he grew too commercial and respectable). Woody pounded at his typewriter and watched his money run out.

Meanwhile, up on the Columbia River, a fledgling federal agency was trying to build dams as no one had built them before, to bring the seeming miracles of irrigation and electricity to the arid, unwired rural byways. The Bonneville Power Administration (BPA) proposed to plug everyone in the region, even the private utilities, into a grand web of public power. But so far it had only built one dam, the 518-megawatt Bonneville Dam that gave the agency its name. Now the electrical New Dealers were building the biggest dam of all—the 5,463-megawatt Grand Coulee—and running into trouble.

The BPA prodded cities and counties to establish their own public utility districts. Not surprisingly, such a campaign alarmed the existing power utilities, which swung their civic influence like a club from Spokane to Portland. They and their allies denounced public power and rural electrification as socialist boondoggles (though wartime industrial demands suddenly offered more use for the big dams' juice). In March 1941, Portland, Eugene, Tacoma, and Spokane all elected not to go public power. A Republican backlash was building.

These times called not just for engineering, but for propaganda. In 1939, Bonneville's acting information director, Stephen B. Kahn, had written and produced a rousing documentary film, *Hydro.* Shown to granges and town meetings throughout the state, it loudly touted public power as the cure to everything from dust-bowl misery and prohibitive electric rates to boom-and-bust timber cycles and the job drain of log exports to Japan. (Some things never change.) Now Kahn and *Hydro* director Gunther Von Fritsch contemplated making a new, feature film. They hit on an angle that might reach the proverbial little guy

286

where thundering rhetoric had failed: a folk singer.

Alan Lomax, since the 1930s the seminal archivist and impresario of the folk music revival, recalls, "The Bonneville Power people called when I was working at the Library of Congress, where one of my appointed functions was to try to get folk singers a real hearing. They asked me if there was anybody who could come and make songs for the campaign for public power. I told them Woody was the one they wanted. Woody was a born genius. He was capable of really sitting down and tackling a whole subject. They said, 'If Lomax says he's good, he's good.' They got him on a plane, and flew him up there."

Actually, Woody's landing a job with BPA was not all that simple. "He came up on his own," recalls Kahn, now retired in California. "He heard about the earlier film, *Hydro,* and thought there might be work for him up here." There's truth to both accounts.

In early April director Von Fritsch, apparently on Lomax's recommendation, visited the Guthries in Los Angeles to explain the planned film and listen to Woody sing songs and tell stories. "I could see he had the kind of talent I was looking for," Von Fritsch told Klein. "But I hadn't made up my mind—Guthrie was one of several possibilities I was looking at." Woody apparently got a more definite idea from their meeting, or was too desperate to care. He later told friends he got a registered letter from BPA telling him to come on up. (Von Fritsch said he wrote to say the job still wasn't definite.)

Mary Guthrie also gathered that prospects were more certain in Portland. She recently wrote, in response to an inquiry from BPA media specialist Bill Murlin, "I remember meeting Steve Kahn who hired Woody in Los Angeles. He arranged for a photographer to come to our home and take pictures of all the family. The one of the three children on our front porch is my favorite picture. The idea was that we would or could all have a part in this special project of the dam."

In late April or early May, Woody loaded the family into the Pontiac and set out for Portland. Perhaps it was his own personal straits that lent special poignancy to "Washington Talking Blues," one of the most engaging of the songs he would write for the BPA. Never published, it was only recently rediscovered in Murlin's search for lost Guthrie songs:

Long about 1929
Owned a little farm, was a-doin' just fine;
Raised some row crop, raised a little wheat,
Sold it over at the county seat,
Drawed the money. Raised a family...

Well, the hot old rocks and the desert sand
Made my mind run back to the dustbowl land.

Bing Crosby

Harry Lillis "Bing" Crosby's lighthearted Spokane youth gave little indication of his meteoric rise soon after he left Gonzaga University in Spokane and went to California in the late twenties. It wasn't long before all nights were silent and all Christmases were white. Crosby's talents extended into other mediums as well. He and Bob Hope formed one of the great comedy teams in motion picture history. In 1944, while on his own, he won an Academy Award for his starring role in **Going My Way.**

From "Happy-go-lucky Spokane Beginnings of an American Legend," by William Stimson, Spokane Magazine, *Vol. 1, No. 9, December 1977. Copyright © William Stimson. Reprinted by permission.*

The house at E. 508 Sharp [in Spokane] was painted yellow then and faced a dirt and sawdust street. Otherwise it is the same: a bulky turn-of-the-century structure with a roomy front porch and lots of bedrooms. The Crosby family was large (with seven children), and like most other families around, Irish and Catholic. . . .

People who knew Bing as a young kid say you wouldn't pick him out of a crowd—or, more appropriately, a gang. Like the other kids in the [neighborhood], he was tough, mischievous and addicted to pranks—rather like the good-hearted hooligans that gathered around Bing's robes in *Going My Way.*

People who remember him confess now they never noticed his voice. Margaret Emahiser, who has lived in the Gonzaga [University] neighborhood all her life, sang with Bing in various parish functions and recalls, with a shrug, "He could sing, but so could lots of kids in the neighborhood."

Only in retrospect do people recall that he was usually humming, singing or whistling as he ambled about. Bing himself attributed it to a kind of total immersion in music he underwent at home. His father, a modestly paid bookkeeper, always spent a little more than the family could afford on recordings of the latest popular tunes. "I had a constant succession of them in my head," Bing said. "And I had to whistle or sing to get them out."

He entered Gonzaga High School in 1916 (which tends to confirm his birth year as 1901, not 1904). A natural loquacity led him to excel in elocution, something Gonzaga stressed. He spoke at his high school graduation and won a debating award his first year of college. This, and his later ambitions to become a great trial lawyer, were consonant with a life-long savoring of anything that involved performing. In his last few years in Spokane he tried not to miss any of the good vaudeville that came through town. Since he didn't have much money, this usually required a short-cut through the theater's rear exit. . . .

Bing entered Gonzaga University in 1920 and in his freshman year played B-squad football, varsity baseball and was a yell-leader at the all-male school.

His would-be career in music was going nowhere. In high school he took up the drums in a casual way and for a short time played with an amateurish band. Then, in the spring of 1921, a fellow student at Gonzaga by the name of Al Rinker came looking for Bing. Rinker had started a little band and was in need of a drummer. Part Coeur d'Alene Indian, and handsome a la Burt Reynolds, Rinker would be Bing's partner for the next ten years. Like Bing, he had a genius for music but no training. The others in the band were Al's brother, Miles, Bob and Clare Prichard and Jimmy Heaton.

None of them could read music, and this presented a problem in building up a repertoire. The Musicaladers, so they were called, solved this problem by going to a music store—Baily's near the northeast corner of Riverside and Post—and listening over and over again to records until each member of the band had memorized how to play it. Ralph Goodhue managed Baily's for the owner in those days. "Skinny" Goodhue knew the Musicaladers as friends and as deadbeats of the first order. In the hundreds of hours they spent at the store he can't recall them ever having bought a record. . . .

Nearly everyone who remembers Bing at this time uses the words "casual" and "easy-going" to describe him—precisely his public image. He was glib and witty in an arched-brow spoofing sort of way. Bing's wit depended less on punchline than on quick and ironic language—as in the attachment of a humorously appropriate nick-name. The Rev. Arthur Dussault, a life-long friend of Bing's and later

vice president of Gonzaga, remembers working out with the basketball team while Bing, typically, provided from the sidelines an unsolicited, needling, but humorous commentary. . . .

In Spokane Bing dressed casual to

Bing Crosby (far right) with Phil Harris and Bob Littler

sloppy, though not noticeably worse than most other students. The hair was light brown and parted near the middle. The famous summer-sky eyes notwithstanding, he was considered just an average looking guy. Father Dussault remembers him always, "with a smile just about breaking out on his face." Even back in those days, says Father Dussault, "He had a mellow voice that came out to you. Not necessarily soft but resonant." . . .

In his last couple of years in Spokane Bing acquired a taste for bootleg liquor, and that could easily lead to problems in prohibition days. Once [Dutch] Groshoff [one of Spokane's best known musicians], having just finished playing a dance job, was walking down Sprague around midnight when he came upon Bing— dressed in his band uniform of a striped jacket and bowler—and a policeman. The two were attached at the wrists by handcuffs and the policeman was on a callbox requesting a paddy wagon. Groshoff never did determine exactly what Bing's transgression was—it may have been only that he had been drinking.

A small crowd gathered around to appeal for leniency, but the policeman wasn't listening. When the paddy wagon arrived he opened the doors, climbed in and pulled Bing up after him. As Bing hopped up, he turned, doffed his hat with his free hand, and executed a grand bow for the audience. The policeman jerked the handcuffs and Bing disappeared into the dark of the wagon. . . .

One morning in the fall of 1925 Bing and Rinker loaded all their belongings (and some of their brothers') in the Model-T. They said hurried goodbys to their families. None of their friends had been alerted, so there was no great send-off.

The $8 car put-putted down Sharp and to a service station at Boone and Division run by a friend, Lavilo Curry. Curry filled the car's tank and agreed to catch them later for payment.

Then Bing put the old flivver into gear and maneuvered it down the curb. The last Curry saw of them they were headed south on Division and out of town.

That was the last anyone ever saw of Bing Crosby, the kid next door. Two years later he and Rinker made a triumphant stopover in the hometown as they were on their way east to appear with the most famous orchestra in the country. In another four years Bing was both a radio and movie star.

But my hopes was high and we rolled along
To the Columbia River up in Washington.
Lots of good rain. Little piece of land.

Grow something.
We settled down on some cutover land,
Pulled up brush and the stumps by hand.
Hot sun burnt up my first crop of wheat
And the river down the canyon just 500 feet.
Might as well of been 50 miles.
Couldn't get no water....

I struck a lumber town and heard the big saw sing,
And when business is good, why lumber's king;
I went lookin' for a job but the man said no,
So we hit the skids on the old Skid Row.
Traipsing up and down. Chasing a bite to eat. Kids hungry....

Now what we need is a great big dam
To throw a lot of water out acrost that land,
People could work and the stuff would grow
And you could wave goodbye to the old Skid Row.
Work hard. Raise all kinds of stuff. Kids too. Take it easy. ©

The Guthries arrived at the BPA offices like latter-day dust bowl refugees, tired, dirty, and hungry from the road. Woody stepped out munching an apple from what Kahn recalls as "a battered old car—no a battered *new* car...I thought, 'What are we in for now?' He looked very disreputable, dirty clothes, a beard, strictly out of the Oklahoma Panhandle. But as soon as he pulled out his guitar and started singing, it was different. He touched people. He was a real troubadour."

What with civil service regulations, says Kahn, "we had a real problem hiring him. I was a little hesitant risking my neck for a guy like Woody, who might do all sorts of things. But I said I'd love for him to work with us, but the only possibility would be if [BPA administrator Dr. Paul] Raver would intervene. Raver was a pretty conservative guy, from Illinois, a professor. Woody went in there with his guitar and came out an hour later, and lo and behold Raver agreed. He said, 'I think we should use this fellow. He'll get across to people.' " Just the thing the Communists in Los Angeles and New York said of Woody, even as they worried about his unpredictability and uncertain dedication to Marxist theory.

Bonneville signed Woody on as a "narrator-actor" in an "emergency temporary appointment" for a maximum one month, at an annual rate of thirty-two hundred dollars. His duties were "to narrate designated sequences of documentary motion picture…to appear in designated scenes of film and accurately depict human experiences of man engaged in construction on Bonneville and Grand Coulee dams…to assist in writing narration, dialogue, and musical accompaniment." Kahn recalls that "when his application asked 'Sex?' he wrote, 'Very good.' "

"All of us beat ourselves down every day yelling and singing little snatches of songs we was too hot and too busy and too tired to set down with our pen and pencil."

Thus began one of the most fruitful episodes of artistic patronage since Pope Paul III summoned Michelangelo to Rome. Some of the time Woody goofed off in inimitable fashion. "He'd park at some secretary's desk and serenade her till you dragged him away," recalls BPA co-worker Elmer Buehler. "He was really putting that guitar to work." Other times, says Kahn, "he'd hang out on Skid Row, at the Hooverville under the bridge on Grand Avenue." Kahn sent him "all over the Northwest, to see the dams, the logging camps, the farms, the skid rows, to get some background, understand the people."

Woody himself later wrote, "I saw the Columbia River and the big Grand Coulee Dam from just about every cliff, mountain, tree, and post from which it could be seen. I made up twenty-six songs about the dam and about the men, and these songs were recorded by the Department of the Interior, Bonneville Power Administration out in Portland. The records were played at all sorts and sizes of meetings where people bought bonds to bring the power lines over the fields and hills to their little places."

That magic number twenty-six—"I wrote twenty-six songs in twenty-six days for $266," Guthrie also said—has since bedeviled lesser souls who pick up the scholarly pieces. Kahn remembers Woody producing "about thirty" songs. Bill Murlin has managed to track down twenty-one in BPA files and in the attics of friends around the Northwest for whom Woody cut private homemade records as gifts. But two, "New Found Land" and "Grand Coulee Powder Monkey," recorded for Mo Asch's Folkways label in New York, do not show up in BPA records, though they certainly reflect what he saw on the Columbia. Others—"Hard Travellin,'" "The Talkin' Blues," "Ramblin' Round," and "Ramblin' Blues"—do not seem especially specific to the Northwest, though Woody presented them to the BPA. He freely transplanted themes and even lines from one song to another, and later rewrote many Columbia songs for private publication and recording. He never recorded commercially his most famous Northwest song, "Roll on, Columbia," which became the anthem of Henry Wallace's 1948 presidential campaign on the Progressive party ticket.

However lousy his record keeping, Guthrie was a naturally gifted reporter. He speedily summed up the dilemmas of his "new found land"—as in his unpublished, recently uncovered "Lumber Is King":

I'm tree-top Tom, I'm a tree-topping man,
I top the tall timber all over the land.
It's bucking 'em up, and it's snaking 'em down,
'Cause lumber is king in a lumbering town...
Times are better, the paper it shows,
Cutting the timber twice as fast as it grows;
The trees will be gone when the years roll around,
'Cause lumber is king in a lumbering town...
What you gonna do 'bout these hard-working men,
Whole families and women and kids pouring in,
Looking for land and there's land to be found;
But lumber is king in a lumbering town...
King lumber might live for 100 years, too,
If when you cut one tree you stop to plant two;
But boys, if you don't, he's on his way down;
'Cause lumber's just king in a lumbering town. ©

Sometimes Elmer Buehler drove Woody around the Willamette and Columbia valleys in a 1940 Hudson, taking him along to grange meetings (where Buehler often pitched for BPA by showing the *Hydro* film). "The poor guy had BO so bad you could hardly stand it," recalls Buehler. "A lot of people just couldn't. He was referred to as kind of a pitiful Okie. But he said some profound things. He was kind of a wit. He could call you a liar without saying the word 'liar.' "

One night Woody gladly opened an Oregon grange meeting with some songs. But when the Spokane Chamber of Commerce heard Guthrie was in town, says Buehler, "one of the members thought it would be kind of nice to have him play in the background for their dinner meeting. He said, in his Okie way, 'I wouldn't be in the foreground for any chamber of commerce, let alone in the background!' "

Chambers of commerce might be the same everywhere, but the wild Columbia country was like nothing Guthrie had seen before. He later wrote:

These Pacific Northwest songs and ballads have got all these personal feelings for me because I was there on these very spots and very grounds before, when the rockwall canyon stood there laughing around me, and while the crazybug machines, jeeps, jacks, dozers,

Woody left the BPA a song titled "It Takes a Married Man to Sing a Worried Song" that seems to speak to his uneasy conjugal condition.

mixers, trucks, cars, lifts, chains, and pulleys and all of us beat ourselves down every day yelling and singing little snatches of songs we was too hot and too busy and too tired to set down with our pen and pencil right then while the thing was being built. This is the main thing I have tried to get across in these Pacific Northwest songs.

Everything to him seemed *bigger* in the Northwest: natural grandeur and human aspiration meshed into one. Woody's awe peeks through the stately chorus of "Roll On, Columbia":

Roll on, Columbia, roll on,
Roll on, Columbia, roll on.
Your power is turning our darkness to dawn,
So roll on, Columbia, roll on! ©

In "The Grand Coulee Dam" his awe explodes in cascades of rhyme, alliteration, and imagery, matching the river itself. Even outward oxymorons like "misty crystal glitter" seemed perfectly fitting:

She bends down the granite canyon and she bends across the lea
Like a dancing, prancing stallion down her seaway to the sea;
Cast your eye upon the greatest thing yet built by human hands,
On the King Columbia River, it's the
Big Grand Coulee Dam.
In the misty crystal glitter of that wild and windward spray,
Men have fought the pounding waters and met a watery grave.
Well, she tore their boats to splinters but she gave men dreams to dream
Of the day the Coulee dam would cross that wild and wasted stream.
Uncle Sam took up the challenge in the year of thirty-three,
For the farmer and the factory, and all of you and me.
He said roll along Columbia, you can roll down to the sea,
But river while you're rambling you can do some work for me. ©

Was it all just a lark for Woody, or did the public-power campaign strike a deeper chord? "He was an adventurer and always wanted to see how people lived," says Kahn, but "I think he was inspired by the things he saw and what was intended for the power." And just as Kahn and Raver expected, Woody *could* translate grand irrigation and electrification schemes into terms that mattered to the people who needed them. Though he was never much at either manual labor or home-building himself, he identified instinctively with the Okies and other hard-times refugees who had flocked to the Columbia seeking a job or piece of land worth calling their own. And he projected himself—sometimes as a farmer, sometimes as a "Grand Coulee powder monkey" or "jackhammer John"—into songs of their arrival in this promised land as in "Columbia's Waters":

I'd like to settle down but I'm forced to ramble all o' my time,
I'd like to settle down with this wife and kids of mine...
I said I like to work, I don't like to beg and steal.
The harder I'm a-workin' the better it makes me feel.
But my wife and kids get juberous
Every time they miss a meal...
Columbia's waters taste like sparklin' wine.
Dustbowl waters taste like picklin' brine. ©

Or as in "End of My Line":

Oregon State is mighty fine
If you're hooked on to the power line.
But there ain't no country extra fine
If you're just a mile from the end of the line. ©

Even huggin' and lovin' ("Sex: very good") somehow fit into the ecstatic Grand Coulee equation of "Eleckatricity and All":

I love my longshoreman, I do, mamma!
I love that longshoreman, I do, ha ha!
We're bound to get married, but don't you tell pa!
And we'll have eleckatricity and all
We'll have eleckatricity and all.
I kissed his lips, I did, mamma!
I kissed his lips, I did, ha ha!
I told him I'd kiss him about six dozen ways
When we get eleckatricity and all
When we get eleckatricity and all. ©

Ironically, Woody's own life was taking just the opposite course in Portland. Mary Guthrie Boyle recalls in her letter to the BPA, "I stayed home with the children while Woody went to work. I was never out to the river with him.... It was a normal thing for

Woody to write wherever he was. I was happy to be there with him and enjoy a rather normal standard of living, at least for a while."

Willard Johnson, then a Bonneville graphic artist who also worked under Kahn, formed a simple impression of Woody: "He thought more of himself than he did of his family. She came in the building several times. They didn't seem to be especially close."

Woody left the BPA a song titled "It Takes a Married Man to Sing A Worried Song" that seems to speak to his uneasy conjugal condition, though it bore at the bottom of the page the inscription "December 20, 1940, New York City":

> Well, you single boys can ramble
> And you single boys can roam,
> But it takes a married man, boys,
> To sing a worried song.
> It was once I used to ramble
> And I sung a single song.
> But it's now that I am married, boys,
> I had to change my tune. ©

Meanwhile, the finance company tracked Woody to Portland and repossessed what was left of the Pontiac. He was not fazed; when his magic month on the federal payroll ended, he rode a cattle car back to New York. Mary and the kids stayed in Portland till September, then returned to Los Angeles. There she met up with Woody, who was back on the road (and on his way to Seattle) with Pete Seeger. She declined to rejoin him, went home to her family in Texas, and eventually divorced him and remarried.

Woody had hardly arrived in New York before he was on his way west again. While he was in Los Angeles and Portland, three eager young writer/musicians—Pete Seeger, Millard Lampell, and Lee Hays—had started singing for social change under the moniker The Almanac Singers. Their loft, and the rousing rent parties they held to support it, became a nexus of the febrile New York folk/political scene. When Woody arrived, Lampell was organizing a cross-country tour to play at strikes and union organizing drives. Woody quickly made the group a foursome.

The Almanacs earned a two hundred and fifty dollar advance cutting two albums of nonpolitical songs in one night. The next day they set out in a car that Seeger still remembers well: "We had a real gas-guzzler...a 1932 Buick limousine that burned a quart of oil every seven miles, with two jump seats that could hold seven people. We could sleep on the floor of it—which Woody and I did."

It was an exciting, even triumphant, journey, as the Almanacs sang and marched their way across the country. By early September, Hays and Lampell had dropped off the tour, and Seeger and Guthrie pushed north from California alone. In Portland, they visited Woody's BPA friends but, in Klein's words, "couldn't find any unions to organize." Seeger wrote Lampell: "Portland is a pretty poor union town, full of factional strife, but it is a lesson to us. We hear in Seattle that we are already booked up for a while there, so we are cheered up a bit. But right now we don't feel too good, what with being broke in a boss's town..."

The welcome was warm and times were hot in the state that Roosevelt's campaign manager James Farley called "the Soviet of Washington." Farley may have been thinking of the Washington Commonwealth Federation, Guthrie and Seeger's host, when he said that. The WCF was founded in 1935 as a coalition of labor unions, granges, United Builders, Technocrats, the predecessor Commonwealth Builders of Washington, and progressive Democrats. It worked (quite successfully) as a statewide front for the New Deal, supporting legislative and congressional candidates pledged to Roosevelt's program (including congressmen Warren Magnuson and Henry Jackson). One of its most conspicuous victories was the first state-guaranteed old-age pension plan in the nation.

"Its purpose was to work within *and* outside of the Democratic party," recalls Terry Pettus, who with his wife Berta published the WCF's lively weekly newspaper, *The Washington New Leader*. Nevertheless, admits Pettus, the federation became the progressive, policy-setting wing of the party; much of its success stemmed from its savvy willingness to coexist with established county officials and blink at their patronage systems.

"It was a little bit like the Labour party in England," says Hugh DeLacy, the WCF's president through most of its history and also a longshoreman, Seattle city councilman, and one-term congressman, who now lives in Cleveland, Ohio. "It was directed more at gaining particular objectives."

Practical programs, not ideology: that described Woody Guthrie's politics as well. But like Guthrie, the Commonwealth Federation was always burdened with allies that tried to infuse it with, and enemies that accused it of, more radical purposes. Its first convention in 1935 refused to seat the Communist party. "There were of course Communists in the federation," says DeLacy. "But the Communist party was never permitted to send delegates. I don't think *any* party, Republican or Democrat, was represented." Still, various squeamish unions—the Federation of Labor, Auto Mechanics, and Newspaper Guild—eventually withdrew. *The Seattle Star* raked the WCF for its Communist connections in 1938 and endorsed the Republicans opposing its candidates.

Nevertheless, recalls Seeger, in 1941 "we were very much impressed with the Washington Commonwealth Federation. It was one of the few clubs in which people tended to work together. One of the big problems with radicals throughout history is we tend to speak

But like Guthrie, the Commonwealth Federation was always burdened with allies that tried to infuse it with, and enemies that accused it of, more radical purposes.

297

to each other, get caught in our own little sectarian traps. The Washington Commonwealth Federation seemed to have broken out of that, and had relations with all sorts of people and groups."

And had a hell of a good time in the process. "We were pretty ignorant of the history of Seattle," says Seeger. "We just knew there was a gang of good people there that would hang along. And we were inspired to do our best." Where the good people hung out was at the hootenannies started by the WCF as fund-, consciousness-, and hell-raising parties in the Polish Hall, at Eighteenth and Madison. Terry Pettus remembers the hoots vividly: fueled with beer and Polish sausages, the guests would schmooze, dance, listen, and perhaps sing along to music by everyone from a Calypso singer named Sir Launcelot to native son Earl Robinson, already famous for writing "Ballad for Americans."

The highlight of a hootenanny was often a satirical skit by the Topical Players, an after-hours offshoot of Burton and Florence James's Seattle Repertory Theater. Some of the Topical Players went on to become household names on Seattle radio: Lloyd Bloom, under the radio name Freddie Lloyd, on KOMO, and Dick Stokke of KOMO and KJR, who introduced rock 'n' roll to Seattle by lampooning it. But the mastermind of the troupe, said Stokke before his death in the fall of 1987, was free-lance newscaster Johnny Forrest, an incomparable improvisational wit and lady killer, who would make up newscasts in rhyme, accompanying himself at the piano.

On September 20, 1941, the Topical Players shared the hootenanny stage with "the famous Almanac Singers from New York." "We made a lot of friends there," recalls Seeger. "To fill out the ranks of the Almanac Singers, we recruited local people to help out on the chorus." As Stokke said, "It didn't matter if you could carry a tune. People just sang along."

Seeger thinks he taught Ivar "Acres of Clams" and thus gave Seattle a household word.

On the other side, "We were just fascinated by Woody," recalls DeLacy. Offstage, the Seattle hosts were startled at the wide personal differences between their two guests. "Pete was really a great guy," said Stokke, but Woody was more withdrawn and unpredictable—"a redneck, really"—and not the sort you'd want to leave your girlfriend with alone. Seeger was sociable and easygoing, says Jean Ashford, whose family put him up, but "Woody was—let's say—more irreverent. He didn't talk much, he was usually singing. He was impatient with people and things." He spoke of the songs he had just written for Bonneville, but "he seemed to think it was a big joke that he'd sold those songs, that he'd put one over on them."

One of the most striking differences between the two buskers was their way with drink. Guthrie liked his beer (sometimes to outrageous excess), but Seeger never touched the stuff. As Jean Ashford recalls, he didn't abstain just from principle: "he said alcohol affected his nose, the blood vessels." By chance, her husband, University of Washington professor Paul Ashford, had put together an anthology of traditional drinking *and* temperance songs titled *High and Dry*. Seeger gulped down this lode of musical material with typical enthusiasm. Even today, while remembering Seattle, he bursts suddenly into one of the songs he learned from the Ashfords: "Cold water, cold water for me. There's nothing so pure and free..."

Pete and Woody found luxury digs at the big West Seattle home of an erstwhile folk-singer who'd made good: Ivar Haglund. Haglund's wife, Margaret, was a WCF leader, and Ivar supported the movement, but he was mainly busy with a more mercantile venture: a small waterfront aquarium that later blossomed into a seafood empire. Seeger still remembers Ivar's "little radio program, where he sang funny little songs about fishes" to promote the aquarium. Haglund described their meeting as "one of the most interesting times in my life. I think I got 'em on the air on a couple of stations." And they swapped songs: Ivar remembers teaching Pete "Acres of Clams" and James Stephens's "The Frozen Logger," which Pete later recorded with the Weavers. Seeger thinks he taught Ivar "Acres of Clams" and thus gave Seattle a household word.

During their stay, Haglund left for a Mexican vacation; when he returned, he found his guests had left a parting gift: a record of "Columbia Talking Blues" and "Jackhammer John," which they had cut on his home recording machine. For Terry Pettus, they cut "Roll On, Columbia" and the old Wobbly song "Overalls and Snuff."

Seattle was indeed a fertile swap meet of songs, stories, and sayings. Seeger and Guthrie learned an odd term that they would make a household word nationwide: hootenanny. They borrowed it to describe their own rent parties in New York, and eventually "hootenanny" became a magic slogan for the whole folk revival. The original inspiration was Terry Pettus's: when the WCF was fishing for a label for its fund raisers that would not sound like fund raising, he remembered it from the country slang of Terre Haute, Indiana, where he grew up. There, hootenanny meant two things: an informal front-porch get-together, where someone might pick a tune or crack a jug, and "an outhouse."

Beyond that, the word has perplexed philologists. But Seeger himself stumbled on a beguiling explanation: some French friends said, "Ah yes, *nuit de l'année* (night of the year), when a newly married couple was shooed into the fields to spend their married night."

Seeger and Guthrie picked up more useful lore from Hugh DeLacy, whom Seeger salutes as "one of the great storytellers of the 20th century." He recalls two stories in particular that "Woody loved so much he kept repeating all the next year." One is self-explanatory: "These two rabbits were being chased by a dog and hid in a hollow log. The log was too small for the dog to get in, but the rabbits couldn't get out. The boy rabbit says to the girl rabbit, 'Honey, what do we do?' And the girl rabbit says, 'Honey, we stay here till we outnumber them.' "

"The other story," says Seeger, "is about a woman whose husband had died. Then she

Terry Pettus, 1984: inventing the hootenanny

James J. Hill

Intelligence and business savvy set Jim Hill apart from other railroad tycoons. He succeeded in constructing the Great Northern Railroad without any government grants and built one of the best engineered lines ever. The Japanese wanted cotton from the East Coast, and his former St. Paul neighbor Frederick Weyerhaeuser wanted to ship his Washington timber east, so Hill made sure his trains would be full to capacity, round trip.

From "Jim Hill Built An Empire," by Stewart H. Holbrook, The American Mercury, Vol. LXV, No. 283, July 1947. Reprinted by permission of Comstock Editions.

First came the blizzards. Then came the droughts, then the grasshoppers and hard on the leaping legs of the parasites came the greatest curse of all—James Jerome Hill. Jim Hill was the Little Giant, the Devil's Own of the northern plains, the prince of the Great Northern, King of the Northern Pacific, emperor of the Burlington—the man who *made* the Pacific Northwest, the Empire builder, the man who wrecked Minnesota, wrecked the Dakotas, Montana and all Puget Sound, the prophet of northern wheat, the Evil One of Homesteaders, the shaggy-headed, one-eyed old so-and-so of Western railroading.

In his lifetime Jim Hill was each and all of those things, a legend while he lived, a legend still in death. . . . What old Corneal Vanderbilt had been to the tight little kingdom of the New York Central, Jim Hill was to the vast empire that ranged unbroken from the Great Lakes to Puget Sound, from the Canadian border to Colorado and Missouri, and on across the Pacific to China and Japan.

Jim Hill was vindictive: because the mayor of small Wayzata, Minnesota, objected mildly to all-night switching in the village, Hill tore down the station and set it up more than a mile away. Jim Hill was loyal: when he had used his own, not his stockholders' money, to speculate in ore lands and the speculation turned out to be a magnificently wonderful investment, he let his stockholders, who had risked nothing, into the deal, to their enrichment by millions of dollars in dividends. Jim Hill was down to earth: he would grab the shovel from the hands of one of his laborers to spell him off, meanwhile shoveling snow from the Great Northern tracks as though he were a steam-driven plow. He had delusions of grandeur: he built a castle in St. Paul and considered himself as the builder of empires, on a plane with Genghis Khan and Napoleon. . . .

When he was eighteen years old in 1856, Hill arrived in the settlement on the Mississippi that was beginning to dislike its original name of Pig Eye and was calling itself St. Paul. He had been born in Ontario of parents who meant him to be a doctor. The loss of one eye from accidental discharge of an arrow seemed to preclude medicine; and anyway, young Hill wanted to be a trader in the Orient, like Marco Polo. He struck out to approach the Orient from a Pacific American port, his first thought being to join one of the brigades of trappers who covered the country between the Mississippi and the west coast of America. From San Francisco or Portland, he believed, he might get passage on a ship across the great ocean. In 1856 St. Paul was a jumping-off place for trappers, but young Hill arrived there just a few days too late to join the last brigade of the year, a fact that undoubtedly changed the course of his life. . . .

Hill's first job was clerk for an outfit that operated packet steamers on the big river. He saw the first shipments of Minnesota grains go down-river. With his own hands he cut the stencil for the first label on the first barrel of flour made in Minnesota. He noted the increasing number of immigrants. . . .

In 1865 he set up for himself as a forwarding agent and general transportation man, acting for the St. Paul & Pacific, a political football of a railroad that had never got anywhere, but by state appropriations managed somehow to keep a few trains moving. He also had one eye on the Red River of the North, a large and muddy stream that rose in Dakota Territory to flow north into Lake Winnipeg in Canada. . . .

Hill traveled a good deal in the region, much of it on horseback. He noted the rich black soil and the vast expanses of a virgin region. He watched the steady decay of the St. Paul & Pacific railroad. If he could but lay hands on that haywire pike, he believed, he could extend it into Dakota and make it a paying line. . . .

[In 1873], Hill, barely forty, started to perform a miracle with the dismal remains of the grandiosely named St. Paul & Pacific. For very little cash and a lot of credit, he laid hands on rails, rolling stock, locomotives and laborers. Directing the job in person, much of the time at the railhead or in advance of it, Hill drove his construction crews at a furious rate, laying one mile of track every working day, sometimes more. When he reached the Canadian border he reorganized the road into the St. Paul, Minnesota & Manitoba. The Canadian Pacific, building west in the Dominion, ran a line down from Winnipeg and the two roads met. It was destined to be a busy line.

The organization of Hill's new railroad could not have happened at a more opportune time. Two thumping great harvests followed. What had been a trickle of immigrants from Norway and Sweden now rose to a full flood. There were homesteads for the taking, or Hill would sell them good land at from $2.50 to $5.00 an acre. From the first day of its operation Hill's railroad was a highly profitable carrier; and now he wanted more of it. In 1879 he told friends that he was going to push his line across the continent to reach Puget Sound. A few may have believed that he could and would. The others jeered at the idea. . . .

When Hill announced his intention to build to Puget Sound, many of his

James J. Hill

stockholders were aghast. No other company had attempted such a thing without a subsidy from the government, in land grants and sometimes in cash as well. Hill could get no grant. And even if he did by some quirk manage to get to the Pacific, how then could he hope to compete with the old subsidized lines? The majestic railroad he planned was promptly labeled Hill's Folly.

Hill's Folly moved swiftly westward into Dakota, putting out short feeder lines as it went, for Hill had studied the country and knew, as no other did, where a branch might blossom at once because of ready traffic; and presently the road started on the long and difficult haul across Montana, running well north of the Northern Pacific but an encroachment, to the minds of NP officials, wherever it went. That unhappy road, now rejuvenated somewhat and in the hands of Henry Villard, was carrying on construction at both ends of its line, east and west. Hill ignored it, other than to set his own rates uncommonly low in territory where he could compete with the NP. He had designs on the Villard road, true enough, but he was content to run his own line for the present and to let time and the sheriff catch up with the overcapitalized Northern Pacific. . . .

Hill always protected his rear, too, having grain elevators built and attracting by steady advertising still more and more immigrants, chiefly from northern Europe, to come and farm along his line. Hill would haul a healthy immigrant half way across the United States for $10, if he'd agree to settle on Hill rails; or, if it were an entire family, complete with household effects and perhaps a few farm animals, he'd rent them a freight car for little more. Nor did Hill, despite much loose writing to the contrary, gouge his new settlers with high rates. He told his partners again and again that it was to their best advantage to give low rates and to do all possible to develop the country and increase traffic as they pushed the rails westward. . . .

What Jim Hill wanted was a through line from the West Coast to Chicago and St. Louis and for a very good reason. He knew that for many years his Great Northern's eastbound traffic would be lumber, or nothing. He knew that the Midwest was potentially the greatest lumber market in the country. Very well, then, he would supply the lumber and deliver it so cheaply that the near-at-hand Southern pine people could not compete. But it would not do to haul empty cars back to the Northwest. In Jim Hill's sight nothing was quite so loathsome as an empty Great Northern freight car. The Orient had always appealed to his imagination, and now he sent agents to Japan and China, and other agents to New England, into the Atlantic states, into the South, with instructions to find out what each region had to exchange for products of the other regions. . . .

Japanese industrialists crossed the Pacific to meet Mr. Hill, and Mr. Hill prevailed on them to try a shipment of American cotton to mix with the short-staple article they were getting from India. From that time onward Great Northern cars carried a steadily increasing amount of Southern cotton over Burlington and GN rails to Seattle for shipment to Japan. It proved to be a big business. So did the export of New England cotton goods to China. Minnesota flour went across the Pacific. So did metals from Colorado. Thus did Jim Hill's imagination build a trade route from New Orleans and Boston to the Orient. And meanwhile his line laid Puget Sound and North Idaho lumber down at sidings in the American midwest at prices which encouraged the building of the rugged houses and barns and silos and fences that still mark that region.

While this was going on, Hill was making spectacularly successful efforts to populate the so-called wasteland between the Great Lakes and Puget Sound. He imported the finest cattle and gave them away free to farmers. He advocated Dry Farming Congresses. He set up whopping prizes for the best exhibits of grain grown on dry farms within 25 miles of his railroads. To Europe he sent scores of agents armed with wonderful photographic slides depicting Western farming, to be thrown on screens to amaze and seduce Scotsmen, Englishmen, Norwegians and Swedes. The effects were startling. In 1909 homesteaders took up more than one million acres in Montana. In 1910 still more homesteaders settled on 750,000 acres. Between 1910 and 1922, almost half of the entire area of Montana was settled by homesteaders, virtually all of them induced to come there by the enthusiasm and perseverance of Hill (who died in 1916) and his inspired agents.

The tragedy was that at least 80 percent of the area settled was unfit for crop agriculture, even though the wheat acreage increased from nothing to 3.5 million acres in ten years. This, as it turned out, was the mere laying of groundwork for the disaster that followed. Deep plowing brought erosion. The wind, which in Montana never stops blowing, blew the soil out and disaster into the region. Thousands of small personal tragedies followed. The homesteaders gave up and moved away. It was the one portion of Jim Hill's magnificent dream that did not pan out.

died herself and went to the pearly gates and told St. Peter, 'I'm looking for my husband.'

"St. Peter said, 'Well, what's his name, I'll look it up.'

" 'John Smith.'

" 'We have all sorts of John Smiths here...short John Smith, tall John Smith, butcher John Smith. Don't you remember anything about him that would help us identify him?'

" 'Well, he did say if I ever looked at another man, he'd roll over in his grave.'

" 'Oh, you mean *whirling* John Smith!' "

Biographer Klein dismisses this as one of several stories that "inexplicably tickled his fancy" after Woody's halcyon Almanac tour that made "even the worst jokes funny." But Seeger explains that Woody loved the joke because it *was* so pointed, "kind of a joke on ourselves." Until that year, Communists and many other leftists had urged America to stay out of the European war. Then Hitler broke his pact with Stalin and invaded Russia, and the left screamed for Nazi blood. Leave it to Guthrie to laugh at ideological flipflops that tormented his comrades.

But Hugh DeLacy explains that "whirling John Smith" had another origin, of special meaning to Seattleites. He believes he first heard it from Mayor John Dore when DeLacy was on the Seattle City Council. Dore had won his seat in the Depression on a cut-costs-and-taxes platform, but then lost the next election when his business support withdrew. So Dore ran and won twice as the candidate of labor, especially of Dave Beck's Teamsters. " 'That's why they call me Whirling John Dore,' " Dore said. "We called him Johnny the Revolving Dore," laughs DeLacy. "You had to be captivated by the guy."

Years later, in a less euphoric time for the left, Seeger ran into DeLacy at Daffy's Bar and Grill in Cleveland, where DeLacy led the local Progressive party campaign. A crew of Cleveland "red squad" cops were tailing the former congressman. "Hugh said, 'They're watching me to see who I talk to,' " recalls Seeger. "And he went around shaking the hand of everyone there, people who loved him and people who hated his guts. The red squad had no *idea* what was going on! I learned an important lesson from that: reach out to *everyone*."

Guthrie and Seeger's Seattle stay was an idyll and a schooling the two young singers would never forget. "Woody never lost his love for the Northwest," says Seeger. "It's the most beautiful part of the country—I can still remember waking up and seeing that big red strawberry ice cream cone, Mount Rainier, hanging up there. I hope people who live in the Northwest realize how precious it is. I got a whiff of the Seattle spirit there, and I think it's the spirit of the far West, of a freer way of life—the ability to test new things and make them work." Three decades later, when Seeger built the sloop *Clearwater* and launched his famous campaign to clean up the Hudson River, he took the cleanup of Lake Washington as inspiration and a model.

As winter approached in 1941, Seeger and Guthrie gathered their busking take—"five dollars here and ten dollars there, enough to start east"—and limped over the frozen passes in their ailing car. They sang for miners in Butte and dour loggers in Duluth, finally making it to New York, where Woody plunged into writing *Bound for Glory*.

Pete Seeger returned to Seattle several times—first as a private first class in the army. In 1944, he was drafted and stationed at Seattle's Fort Lawton before being shipped to Saipan, and would show up at the Ashford's for dinner on Sunday. Did Woody return during the war? According to Klein he was fully occupied until the end of 1945 courting his soon-to-be wife Marjorie in New York, getting torpedoed in the Merchant Marine, and getting mired in red tape in the army. But his roamings were always mysterious.

Del Castle, who was secretary of the Seattle Ship Scales Union from 1942 to 1946, distinctly remembers Woody playing at his union hall in that time. Jo Patrick, a veteran farm-camp organizer and Seattle's first woman union welder, recalls that Woody stayed with her and her husband "in 1945, just before the war ended. We had a big seven-bedroom house on Capitol Hill," an international way station for "French seamen, Russian seamen, almost anyone." Folk singer Bruce "Utah" Phillips of Spokane, who knows the freight-train circuit well, says that he has heard that Woody and his 1940s singing and traveling partner, Cisco Houston, "used to ride the trains from Portland to Seattle."

If Woody didn't come to the Northwest, the Northwest came to him. In 1942, BPA's Steve Kahn showed up in New York. He planned to go ahead with the feature film, "to be titled, *Roll On, Columbia* or some such name." Woody would not appear on camera. Instead, a professional actor would play the archetypal Columbia-country immigrant/worker and mouth Woody's renditions of his songs. Kahn recorded Woody singing "six or eight" of his best Bonneville songs, plus Earl Robinson's "Our Hope and Strength." (Robinson's "Ballad for Americans" was to be the film's chorus.) "We were on a very tight budget," recalls Kahn. "We only paid him twenty dollars. I pulled ten dollars of my own money out and gave that to him too."

But the feature film project was pushed aside amid more pressing wartime exigencies. In 1948, with an additional news peg—the great flood that destroyed Vanport, Oregon— the BPA decided to make another documentary to promote the taming of the river. *The Columbia,* released in 1949, contained much of the same message and even footage as *Hydro,* but with an added human dimension. Four of Guthrie's songs—"Roll, Columbia, Roll," "The Grand Coulee Dam," "Pastures of Plenty," and "The Biggest Thing That Man Has Ever Done"—were used as background music, giving its scenes a startling new poignancy.

Meanwhile, Woody swam as best he could through the uneasy postwar period. Despite the soaring inflation and unemployment triggered by the return of millions of servicemen, the fire seemed to be dying out in the labor unions. They grew entrenched, cautious, and more concerned with consolidating bread-and-butter gains than with sweeping social change. Many purged their Communists. Churchill intoned against the "Iron Curtain"

"I like the Pacific Northwest more every time I see it. The folks out here got a good shot of the old free and easy pioneer spirit in them."

Jo Patrick, 1984: memories of
Woody, and Washington's radical
past

in Europe, Stalin likewise warned of the American threat, and the World War II alliance disintegrated. The American Communist party responded by becoming more dogmatic, sectarian, and irrelevant; hard-liner William Z. Foster overturned the more moderate Earl Browder as chairman. The Washington Commonwealth Federation dissolved in 1945, confident that it had worked itself to successful obsolescence; its legislative program had passed, and its purposes were coopted by the Democratic party. Soon after, when the Canwell Committee started hunting Communists at the university, and officials the federation helped elect underwent ideological sea changes, Commonwealth leaders wished they hadn't been so quick to disband.

Woody meanwhile stuck up for the Communists, and even for Joe Stalin. Mostly, however, he was busy building a new life with Marjorie in Coney Island. He started, but never finished, new novels. Matured and less footloose, he threw himself ecstatically into rearing the first child of his new family, Cathy Ann, nicknamed Stackabones.

Then tragedy struck Woody—just as it had in his youth, when various fires destroyed his family's house, killed his sister, and nearly killed his father, and just as flames would nearly kill Woody himself six years later. In February 1947, four-year-old Cathy Ann was fatally burned after "a no-good wartime radio" shorted. A few days later, the devastated Woody got a telegram from the BPA asking if he would like to sing Columbia River songs at the National Rural Electric Cooperative convention in Spokane in April: "Good chance your songs might come into their own out here where they were meant to be sung. Might arrange other appearances. Are you interested? How much besides expenses?"

The trip seemed like just the ticket to Woody's recovery from the tragedy. He offered to come to Spokane for a very small fee and then, as he wrote, "took my airplane money and bought a railroad ticket."

The telegram was written by Ralph Bennet, who went on to become editorial-page editor of *The San Diego Tribune* but was then a flack for the BPA. "It was my idea to bring him to the convention," recalls Bennet. "I asked him because I wanted to meet him. The songs were there, recorded and all that. I thought Woody Guthrie was the greatest. It turned out to be something of a disaster."

Woody arrived by bus, after stopping off in Oklahoma and Pampa to check up on family and old haunts in Texas. He arrived in Spokane in high spirits. "This is an awful nice hotel," he wrote Marjorie, "just a little too fascisti to satisfy my higher ideals. But Spokane ain't that way at heart. I like the Pacific Northwest more every time I see it. The folks out here got a good shot of the old free and easy pioneer spirit in them. They still ride the tough grass and dig in the hills."

"We'd gotten a room for him in the Davenport, the fanciest hotel in town," recalls Bennet. But when he went up to meet Woody, his charge wasn't there. "He'd obviously been there, because somebody hadn't flushed the toilet, and there were some dirty shirts lying on the bed. Woody didn't believe much in washing. When his clothes got dirty, he'd just get some new ones." Apparently what he did was stop at the hotel and then go down to the skid row and sing some songs in the bars—he had a good time."

The Rural Electric convention was about the hottest thing to hit Spokane since wheat—or, as Spokane's *Spokesman-Review* called it in the first of a week of front-page stories, "the biggest event in Spokane to date." Senators Magnuson and Milton Young led the mile-long list of dignitaries presiding. *The Spokesman-Review* even noted that "entertainment will feature Woody Guthrie, nationally famous folk singer, who as a wandering troubadour will sing and play his songs wherever groups gather to listen." The same article also promised an "Indian show" and vaudeville performances.

Woody returned from skid road in time to meet Bennet for his first appearance, at the kickoff luncheon. And, says Bennet, "things went from bad to worse, because we didn't know how to use him. He was not a performer really, he was a poet. He'd forget his music, make mistakes. Woody is kind of a respected figure today—we see him as an authority. He wasn't like that in life at all. He was a wild one. Just a natural-born kind of genius, a complete individual. That kind is very hard to work with."

By chance, *The Daily People's World* had written Woody in Spokane asking him to resume his long-dormant column and even offering to *pay* him. His first installment, dateline Spokane, told the story of the convention fiasco: "First place he [Bennet] took me was to the padded room where the gents of the press was having a banquet. I had to sing before they got started eating, but their knives and forks drowned me out. I took the old runout powder." (He told another Bonneville friend, Michael Loring, "I got tired of them asking me to sing 'Deep in the Heart of Texas.' ")

Bennet next "tried to get a mike so's I could sing around on the mezzanine, but the big boss said no loud speakers was allowed....Then he looked at me with that newly wedded light in his eye [Bennet had left his bride in Portland to meet Woody] and said he would stay over here in Spokane if I figured I needed him to be my guide.

"I told him to guide it on out across them mountains to finish his honeymoon. By the time I got my last word spoke he was over half way back to meet his wife."

Woody sang the next day in a display booth at the Masonic Temple: "Every time I said a cussword it leaked out into the loudspeaker." The following day he evaded a request "to sing for a busload of ladies going up to Coeur d'Alene.... And I didn't go back to that display booth. (They turned my booth into a coffee bar, I hear.) Trying to thaw out these Roosevelt democrats."

The "disaster" left no hard feelings: Woody later visited and corresponded with Bennet, and cut for him a homemade record of several Bonneville songs that would later fill some pieces in the musical mystery of the twenty-six songs.

Woody stayed on for two or three weeks in Spokane with someone he described in the

"He didn't so much hate the other side as he loved his side, and he was blind to its faults."

People's World as "a little, boney man, said his name was Cummings, Bill Cummings, the organizer for the Communist party in this territory." That man was in fact Bill *Cumming,* the painter who moved to Seattle, quit the Communist party in 1957 in disgust at its "dangerous bullshit," and is now revered as a living master of the Northwest School. "I was bony, but I towered over him," says Cumming, still smarting genially at Woody's description. "There were snapshots taken of us together to prove it!"

Cumming persuaded Guthrie to play for a couple of fund-raising parties. "He was anxious to know it wasn't for wealthy liberals," says Cumming, "because if it was wealthy liberals he'd have to charge 'em. I assured him it was just raggedy-ass people." At home, wrote Woody, "Bill sat on my bed and I paced the floor and told him how tangled up my life had got to be." Cumming remembers him as "a very restless guy," but still firm in the leftist cause: "He didn't so much hate the other side as he loved his side, and he was blind to its faults."

Just as in his old rambles, Woody dabbled in trouble himself. From San Francisco soon after, he wrote a bitter, ambivalent love letter to Marjorie that ended suddenly, "I met one girl in Spokane who—" Bill Cumming fills in some of the mystery: "He developed a relationship with a friend of ours named Evelyn, all very hush-hush, and spent a lot of time going out with her—an unexpected human note amid all that dogmatic piffle."

Still, Woody closed his column on his Spokane sojourn on a rousing dogmatic note: "Multiply this [experience] by the forty-eight states and you can see what I mean when I say that the Communists everywhere are the only people I know of that know how to make the right use of our own American folk lore, folk culture, folk songs, and folk singers. And folks."

Guthrie was rising to the spirit of six years earlier, when he and Seeger and the Almanacs sang across the nation in the good fight. It was the last time he would try to repeat that busking tour. Invitations had poured into Spokane to sing for sympathetic groups up and down the coast. He was in San Francisco on May Day and singing the next day in an Oakland telephone workers' strike that the police broke up.

Then he headed up for Portland and dropped in on an old New York political buddy and singing partner, Michael Loring, then BPA's assistant public affairs director. "I sang the songs, but I wasn't really a folk-singing man," says Loring, who became a cantor at a synagogue in Fresno. But Loring can boast of a notable contribution to folk song nevertheless: he wrote two verses which Woody, never one to scorn borrowing, incorporated in "Roll On, Columbia," those that begin "Tom Jefferson's vision would not let him rest" and "These mighty men labored by day and by night." The contribution was reciprocated: Loring has six Hanukkah songs written by Woody, who was always ecumenical in his spiritual enthusiasms and had his son Arlo bar mitzvahed.

In Portland, Loring arranged a concert at Reed College. Guthrie "should come on like a fresh cool breeze in the academic cloister," proclaimed the *Reed College Quest,* adding that folk singing "is enough to make a man hopeful, despite the fact that being hopeful is strictly subversive and is bound to land you on J. Parnell Thomas's [red-baiting] list."

In his *People's World* column, Guthrie saluted these "young folks...that do more good honest thinking in a couple of minutes than these boggy brain landholders and owners do in ninety-nine years and ninety." Otherwise, he found:

> You see big chunks of this world's best scenery here around Portland right about this time of the year. When it comes to greens and pretty scenes, Oregon, you've not got to go begging of nobody....
>
> Portland is a place where rich ones run away to settle down and grow flowers and shrubbery to hide them from the massacres they've caused. Portland is the rose garden town where the red, brown, blackshirt cops ride up and down to show you their finest horses and saddles and gunmetal. Mentally, Portland is the deadest spot you ever walked through. She's a good fifty years behind Seattle.
>
> As long as our rich ones can buy and own your prettiest valleys these beauty spots will be our deadest holes....

Sure enough, a leftward native son stood up for "the real Portland." Earl Payne wrote *People's World* to complain of "the sectarian, egotistical, and ignorant article about Portland, Oregon, by Woody Guthrie" and list the town's virtues as the home of 122,000 good union brothers and sisters and of "a growing Oregon Communist party."

But by then Woody had pushed on to Seattle, where he performed for the Pacific Northwest Labor School, a short-lived but vigorous collaboration of some two-dozen local unions and other labor groups. One of its organizers, Johnny Daschbach, recalls that Woody still carried blazoned on his guitar his famous wartime slogan, "This Machine kills fascists." And he was still "sharp-tongued, no question about that. He wasn't going to go downtown to sing in the big hotels. He was one tough hombre."

Ship Scalers Union secretary Del Castle, who knew Woody from the 1941 hoots, bumped into him the day of the concert and invited him home to dinner. Afterwards, he and his wife drove him to the fund raiser. "We weren't invited because we didn't have much money," says Pearl Castle. Woody invited them to stay, but one of the Castles' children began to bawl as he sang, so they tiptoed sheepishly toward the door by the stage. Woody stopped in midsong, turned from his upscale audience, and said amiably to the Castles, "Thanks for the beans."

Pearl Castle, herself an actress in the Seattle Repertory Theater, invited Guthrie to sing in a benefit for the local Artists for Action, a cultural wing of the Progressive party campaign. Woody promised to return in the fall. The Artists printed up a "terrific poster,

"Roll On, Columbia" or not, Henry Wallace's 1948 presidential campaign fizzled pathetically.

with lots of red," designed by itinerant artist Bill Mutch. But Woody never showed up. "Subsequently we found out he was ill," says Pearl Castle. "He was having a hard time keeping to schedules."

"Ill" was an understatement. Though he still assiduously concealed it under the guise of drunkenness, Woody was starting to show the signs of Huntington's disease (or chorea), the paralyzing hereditary degeneraton of the nerves and brain, inevitably fatal, that would send him to the hospital for the last time eight years later. When he played at Reed, says Loring, "the kids loved him, but I was greatly troubled. He was having a great deal of difficulty remembering the words and carrying it off." Jo Patrick remembers him nervous and agitated, unable to sleep, pacing the floor all night strumming his guitar.

Woody's miseries paralleled the disintegration and oppression of the left nationwide. America built atom bombs, fought Communism in Korea, and chased un-American activities at home, but the Soviets' butchery and duplicity offered no alternative or consolation. From Greenwich Village to Hollywood, blacklisting and congressional subpoenas brought Woody's old friends to ground. The Weavers, the successors to the Almanac Singers and a national sensation, disbanded, unable to get gigs. Pete Seeger traveled playing for the only audience that would hear him, kids in schools and summer camps. When he toured Seattle with his wife Toshi and tried to visit Vancouver, they were turned away by Canada's Oriental-exclusion laws.

In Seattle after the war, left-wing institutions left after the Washington Commonwealth Federation crumbled. The cash-starved Labor School and the *New Leader* folded. When its director, Burton James, was hounded by the Canwell Committee and killed by a heart attack, the Seattle Repertory Theater went dark and was snatched up by the University of Washington's Glenn Hughes. Terry Pettus and Johnny Daschbach starred on the defense stand in Washington State's notorious Smith Act trials in the fifties, and Daschbach was hauled up before the House Un-American Activities Committee. The two were sentenced to not only five years for "conspiring to advocate the overthrow of the United States government," but three years for contempt of court because they would not name names. (Their convictions were overturned by the United States Supreme Court.) "Roll On, Columbia" or not, Henry Wallace's 1948 presidential campaign fizzled pathetically. After it, Hugh DeLacy, who had never been overly politic about his principles while a congressman, could not find work except as a carpenter. "High executives wound up [bridge] toll-takers," recalled Stokke.

Even public-power visionaries were backed against the wall. When Guthrie resumed writing for *People's World,* with fond notes for his old agency, Bonneville administrator Raver was in the capital fighting for appropriations. The BPA honchos had Loring chase down Woody and "insist" he stop mentioning BPA in his columns. Woody consented.

In September 1950, with war raging in Korea, the Bonneville dams were closed to the public for national security. Distribution of *Hydro* and *The Columbia* was also squelched because the films showed this "newfound hydroelectric defense system."

The same year, Republican Douglas McKay, a staunch critic of public power, defeated public-power booster Austen Fiegel for the governorship of Oregon, dooming further expansion of public utilities. In 1953 McKay was appointed secretary of the interior in the new Eisenhower administration. The populist New Deal rhetoric of the two films, even a softened re-editing of *Hydro,* hardly suited the new regime, which had drastically chopped budgets for federal documentary films.

BPA staffing was shaken by layoffs and political upsets. Elmer Buehler, Woody's guide, was demoted to custodian at the Ross substation. There he was given "thirty or forty films with orders to incinerate them": prints of *The Columbia* and the master print of *Hydro* —the same films he had shown all across the region.

Buehler, still a passionate partisan of public power, laments: "Can you imagine it was *my* bad fortune that I had to destroy those films?" He nevertheless managed to save prints of both—and eventually conveyed them to the National Archives. He admits he never saw *written* orders to burn the films and the literature, dioramas, and media miscellany sent over with them. Nor was he told outright the purpose was to suppress the propaganda of the past. But he claims "it was common knowledge that the orders came from the top. Douglas McKay gave orders to dispose of all the exhibits. I think it's just a deliberate attempt to eliminate those films by people who were opposed to any development of the Columbia. The very fact that the films weren't available later proves it." Two of Buehler's coworkers at Ross substation, Jess Sitton and Vern Taylor, say they know nothing of the film-burning. No one else from the old BPA has emerged to confirm or deny Buehler's account.

For all their historic fascination, the films are now forgotten. But Woody Guthrie's stature and myth have only continued to swell. He received official sanction in 1966 when Secretary of the Interior Stewart Udall presented him with the United States Conservation Service Award. What wry response might Woody have made to such an unlikely turn? He had been for years too enfeebled to speak. In October 1967, the year Guthrie died in a Brooklyn hospital, Bonneville quietly opened the new "Woody Guthrie Substation" in Hood River, Oregon. The American Legion squawked, and *The Hood River News,* never a big public-power fan, inveighed against the "sick joke on the Hood River Valley" of naming its facility after "a 1930-vintage beatnik who was lately idolized by the folk-singing set." The president of the Hood River Chamber of Commerce asked, "Who was Woody Guthrie?" And "What did this Mr. Guthrie ever do for our Hood River Valley?"

What did Guthrie do? He transmuted it, and all the Northwest, into enduring poetry. The Northwest was the apogee of many journeys for him—even the farthest stop on his last sad trip, when he passed like a ghost in the night. In 1954, Guthrie left his dismal situation in New York for a hasty drive across the country with Ramblin' Jack Elliott. With a final hop on a freight, they landed in Los Angeles, at his old would-be Topanga Canyon homestead. "He only stayed there overnight and disappeared the next day," says Elliott. "I went out to buy some beer—Olympia, ironically—and when I got back he was gone.

Woody hitched up the coast as far as Olympia, Washington. "I heard he wound up in jail there for the night, for loitering," says Elliott. "He was really great at accepting jail-house hospitality." Lurching under a disease that made even those who knew him think he was drunk or psychotic, Woody rode the rails and roads across the country, landing again in jail in Montana, Ohio, and who knows where else. After a few weeks, he made it back to New York. Three days later, he checked himself into the hospital where he would die thirteen years later.

Jack Elliott worried about Woody out somewhere on the loose, but reassured himself: "He had an amazing though wizened sharp head. He couldn't be conned. He had a wonderful way of letting people and cops know he was a beautiful old bum that you wouldn't want to hurt. Everyone seemed to feel a profound respect and compassion for him."

Likewise, it's sure. In 1960, Pete Seeger ran across a note Woody had scribbled to himself on their halcyon visit to Seattle nineteen years before, a little reminder that Seeger still takes as inspiration:

The worst thing that you can do is to cut yourself off from people. And the best thing is to sort of vaccinate yourself right into the big streams and blood of the people.

To feel like you know the best and the worst of folks that you see everywhere and never to feel weak, or lost, or even lonesome anywhere.

There's just one thing that can cut you to drifting from the people, and that's any brand or style of greed.

There is just one way to save yourself, and that's to get together and work and fight for everybody. ◼

THE KING OF CLAMS

IVAR HAGLUND (1905–1985)

DAVID BREWSTER

There he was again, his captain's cap jauntily in place, a little stunt for the cameras (putting a bronze "Ivar's" above the words in the plaque, "Smith Tower, 42 Stories"), a quip about historic preservation ("I think it means replacing all the johns"), and in due course a bad pun (Ivar-y Tower).

Ivar Haglund was pulling off another *coup de media*, transforming his purchase of the Smith Tower into a widely perceived act of civic benefaction (which it is), launching his new restaurant on the front pages before he had the foggiest idea what it would be like, and prompting columnists to trot out once again those shaggy stories of Ivariana: yet once more Two-Ton Tony Galento boxed the octopus (who died), and Joe Gagnon set all over again the world record in clam-eating at 371 (a feat, Doug Welch once figured out after inspecting the tiny clams, amounting to twenty-three ounces of clam meat).

"He created a public image of himself as simply the corny sea captain," muses Kenneth Callahan the painter and one of Ivar Haglund's oldest friends. "But of course he was much better, much more serious than that." Back behind the carefully cultivated zaniness that made his restaurants famous and made Ivar into a millionaire and the operator of the largest seafood houses in the country (more than a million persons a year eat at Ivar's three restaurants combined) was a shy, pensive man whose real roots were in the 1930s, when Ivar lived the life of a bohemian and a folk singer, and was part of a fascinating circle of artists and writers.

Ivar was born in 1905 at Alki Point, where his family had purchased about four hundred acres of land including, suitably enough for the future history buff, the original Plymouth-Rock land owned by David Denny. "It was an elegant place to grow up in," recalled Ivar. "In the summer people would come over in little boats and rent land from us and live in tents—the Bainbridge Island of the day." His mother, a Norwegian woman named Daisy Hanson Haglund, died when Ivar was two, so he was brought up by his Swedish father, Johan Ivar Haglund. Johan came from Stockholm, jumping ship at Port Townsend, where he went to work at the Eisenbeis Pilot Bread and Cracker Factory, later moving to Seattle and continuing to work as a baker. Ivar was the only child.

"...I had turned down my chance to go to New York for a show. I decided I'd rather stay here and be a small-time celebrity."

313

It was an interesting family. "Dad loved to read, and he was also a theosophist and a vegetarian. And there was always music around the house—violins, guitars—which we would often play." Ivar picked up the ukulele and the guitar and he developed his light tenor voice—he sang in the Burl Ives manner—while at the University of Washington. "I became the first guy to do folk songs around here, fifteen years ahead of the time. I got ahold of things like Carl Sandburg's 'Song Bag,' and I would sing around town at places like the Junior Girls' Vaudeville."

Ivar graduated with a degree in economics in 1928 and then launched into "ten years of delightful bohemian life. I did nothing. Just lived like a hippy on the one hundred dollars a month I had from eight houses I'd rent at Alki."

"When there's a depression there's not much else to do besides culture," recalled Guy Williams, a writer and publicist who was a close friend of Ivar's since college days. Ivar soon fell into a bohemian circle of artists and writers, who appreciated Ivar's songs, his sense of humor, and his ready good hospitality (among other things, Ivar made an annual batch of wine). The friends would meet at Ken Callahan's house at Cherry and Broadway, or at Jim Stevens's little house on Randolph Place in Madrona (Stevens was an Idaho logger who worked up the Paul Bunyan stories and formed a group of lumber mythmakers), or at the Club Mauve on Broadway near Cornish, where the owner, Ted Abrams, ran a little restaurant popular with Mark Tobey, another friend of Ivar's, who liked to talk theosophy with him.

"I knew Mark quite well, though I didn't understand his painting," Ivar recalled. "We'd often seen each other at Ray and Eloise Wardall's, where I'd sing a few songs and talk about mysticism, and then maybe go to the Metropolitan Theater to see some ballet and wind up the evening at the Pig and Whistle. Mark lived in a cabin in West Seattle, and sometimes I'd give him a lift into town or to the Market. One day I told him I was going to open a restaurant on the waterfront and I showed him the spot. 'Ivar,' he said—he pronounced it that way, EE-var—'You're not. What about your folk music? You'll lose everything.' By then I knew I was not vocally adequate to be a folk singer and I had turned down my chance to go to New York for a show. I decided I'd rather stay here and be a small-time celebrity."

Seattle in the 1930s was in a terrible depression, but the life was stimulating. "There was a simple good feeling then," recalled Kenneth Callahan. "We were all in the same boat economically and none of us had a reputation to be jealous about." There were several circles, and Ivar was part of each of them. One was *The American Mercury* crowd of Mencken contributors, some of them cultivating (and making up) the last logging stories: Stewart Holbrook, Stevens, Harold Davis, Glenn Hughes, Archie Binns, Betty MacDonald—all wonderful storytellers. Ivar, while properly aware that folk singing in the Northwest is a very thin tradition, nonetheless tried to find some old songs. When Burl Ives

Ivar in front of the Smith Tower

Mark Tobey

Mark Tobey came to Seattle during the 1930s, and he soon became fascinated with Seattle's Pike Place Market. For a book that celebrated his Market paintings, Tobey described his fascination with the Market and protested its modernization.

The sketches in this book show my feeling for the Seattle Market perhaps much better than anything I can say about it. And yet there seems to be a need to speak, today, when drastic changes are going on all around us. Our homes are in the path of freeways; old landmarks, many of a rare beauty, are sacrificed to the urge to get somewhere in a hurry; and when it is all over Progress reigns, queen of hollow streets shadowed by monumental towers left behind by giants to whom the intimacy of living is of no importance. . . . And now this unique Market is in danger of being modernized like so much processed cheese.

The Market will always be within me. Established back in 1907 by the farmers themselves—not for the tourist trade, but as a protest against the high prices paid to commission men—it has been a refuge, an oasis, a most human growth, the heart and soul of Seattle.

In the twenties, after many years in New York, I walked down this fabulous array of colors and forms. So many things are offered for sale—plants to be replanted; ropes of all kinds; antiques; Norwegian pancakes made by an old sea captain, to be eaten on one of four stools on the sidewalk looking in. I hear the calls to buy—"Hey, you, come over here for the best tomatoes in the Market." Across the street are open shops under long burnt-orange-colored awnings.

The L-shaped Market is alive with all kinds of people, from everywhere, dressed in all kinds of garments, walking under the long shed studded on either side with little cafes, restaurants, and stalls. One man could be from the Black Forest in Germany, and the woman just passing the cucumber stall walks with the stateliness of an Italian princess. Among the men darting here and there is one unsteady on his feet, just dodging the green posts placed at intervals.

Gathered in small groups like islands in the constant stream of people are the men for whom the Market is more than a place of a gathering, almost a home. They live in furnished rooms and rundown hotels, some of them habitués of Skid Road at night and the Market in the day. From the many faces I picked out one man as someone I would like to know. He had looked at me with his friendly eyes—I felt he knew me, so why not speak? "What is your lineage?" But I did not expect the answer I got. "Adam and Eve, just like you, my son."

From Tobey: The World of a Market, *by Mark Tobey. Copyright © 1964 University of Washington Press. Reprinted by permission.*

Mark Tobey

317

came to visit, or Pete Seeger and Woody Guthrie lived with Ivar for a month in 1940, they would go over a few songs worked up by Stevens (like "The Frozen Logger" Seeger picked up) or discovered by Ivar at the University of Washington library (like "The Old Settler" with its last stanza, "I think of my happy condition surrounded by acres of clams").

Another circle mixed leftist politics, mysticism, and the arts, and this circle was of most interest to Ivar's first wife, Margaret Raffenberg, an intense, small, dark-haired woman who dressed in peasant clothes, favored health foods, and was much more bohemian and political than Ivar, whose residual Swedish socialism and feeling for the proletariat never got him much further than support for the New Deal. (Ivar's first marriage lasted twenty-five years; typically, he made a generous settlement at the time of divorce and always treated his first wife with kindness.)

Then there was the Seattle Press Club, holding forth at the Eagles Club, where slot machines and the best bar in town nourished a generation of taproom philosophers and jokesters. Here Ivar was to befriend people like Eberhart Armstrong, the influential drama critic of the *Seattle Post-Intelligencer*, Ross Cunningham, Nard Jones, and others.

318

It was the last vibrant time for the provincial Seattle Spirit—tinged with political radicalism, in touch with the world capitals of art through Cornish (in its financial decline during the 1930s), sociable, intellectual, jolly, still rooted in lumber traditions, fond of tall tales and American-style humor. "There was a magic then," recalled Guy Williams. "We were all very unself-conscious, never giving a damn what some eastern critic might think of us and protected from the trendy thoughts and problems of elsewhere. Why then you could even fill Meany Hall to hear a novelist talk."

In 1938, Ivar opened his tiny aquarium on the waterfront at the foot of Madison. "It wasn't much but it was the first." His friends thought it a reasonable thing to do, since Ivar knew the Swedish boat captains who could bring him specimens, and he also knew a thing or two about promotion. He had once come up with the idea of putting advertisements for stores on a large drum, which he wheeled through town on a cart with a thumping mechanism.

"For two years I lost my shirt. Then I discovered that it takes two minutes to do an order of fish and chips."

At first the aquarium did not go any better than the lanolin hand lotion Ivar had once concocted and tried to sell. ("It worked fine," remembered Callahan, "but it was the most repulsive looking stuff you ever saw; it had all curdled.") Ivar would catch fish himself, throwing them in a garbage can for transport to the aquarium. He made up a title for himself: "aquarist."

Then one day in 1941 he called up a friend at KIRO, Tubby Quilliam, and asked if he could put on a radio show. KIRO slotted Ivar at 9:30 Sunday morning, "between two shows, both cultural as hell." Thus was born Ivar's long radio career, a show called "Around the Sound." "Good morning friends around the Sound, and cheerful clam-happy greetings to you," he would start, and then sing some folk songs and plug the aquarium. The effect was instantaneous. Ivar made so much money at the aquarium that he promptly bought a new DeSoto and went to Mexico for three months. Later he would stop by KRSC to do a five-minute show at 8 A.M. on his way home from working the graveyard shift at Boeing during wartime, and then he graduated to KOL and KOMO-TV.

And so, in the ripeness of time (1946), Ivar came to his calling as a restaurateur. "We thought it a fine idea," said Callahan, "as long as Ivar was not going to do the cooking." But Ivar's boon companions convinced him that Acres of Clams should be a first-class fish house complete with a French chef. "I soon learned that it takes thirty minutes to produce an order of oysters Rockefeller or lobster thermidor," said Ivar. "For two years I lost my shirt. Then I discovered that it takes two minutes to do an order of fish and chips. We shifted and started doing fine."

Ivar was always a completely honest person—as long as his tongue was not seven inches into his cheek, as it was on his television commercials. He once told Mark Tobey his white writing looked like "viscera." He was no less honest about his restaurants. "Let somebody else have the best and the biggest: we'll be the most successful."

Vic Meyers

According to hoary legend, the MC of Club Victor was talked into running for mayor of Seattle in 1930 by an assistant editor at the Times who, late one night, needed a story for the next day. It all began as a joke, and it remained one. Vic Meyers gained such popularity that two years later he won the position of Lieutenant Governor, where he sat for five terms.

From "His Majesty the Jazz King Who Enjoys the Last Laugh," The Literary Digest, Harper & Row, Publishers, Inc., December 24, 1932. Reprinted by permission.

S natch the derby off the trombone and toss it to the ceiling in honor of Victor A. Meyers, the Seattle jazz-band leader who ran for lieutenant-governor of the state of Washington. . . . [Meyers] was coaxed into political life as a roaring joke, a burlesque, a satire on the ballyhoo methods of the day, a harlequinade on electioneering—and stayed in it to capture the second highest post of executive authority in the state.

A little band of practical jokers— newspaper men stretching and yarning "after the last edition is put to bed"—are credited by the Seattle *Argus*, a weekly journal, with having started band leader Meyers on his conquering political career. His election, *The Argus* says, according to the Associated Press, is the "aftermath of a jest," thus:

"Last January, *The Seattle Times*, as a protest against the inferiority of candidates for municipal offices, decided to view the campaign lightly, and make sport of its absurdities.

"*The Times* decided to enter its own candidate in the mayoralty race, and Meyers was called on the telephone and told:

" 'If you'll hurry down to city hall and file for Mayor, we'll spread your name all over the first page of our last edition tonight.'

"Then for the next thirty days news-paper readers throughout the land were amused and entertained by *The Times's* sardonic jest.

"Nine other candidates cringed as they saw their extravagant campaign promises parodied in a series of daily articles appearing under the by-line of Vic Meyers (but actually written by able reporter Doug Welch).

"Almost a promise a day was forthcoming from the Meyers's camp. Samples: hostesses on streetcars; flower-boxes on water hydrants; cracked ice on midnight streetcars.

"*The Times* 'jokesters' found their candidate tractable, eager to lend himself to any and all farcical plans to 'build up' the jest.

"To a business-club luncheon went Meyers, dressed as Mahatma Gandhi. In a street parade Meyers rode on an old-time beer truck."

But although the Meyers candidacy remained a joke throughout the campaign as far as *The Times* was concerned, it was not so with Bandmaster Meyers, we are told. On the contrary:

"Infected by the bite of the political bug, the harmony candidate, as he was then called, began a series of campaign speeches, mastered a number of three-syllable words, and begged the electorate to make him Mayor of Seattle.

Vic Meyers and his band

"He received a handful of votes.

"Despite his defeat, the virus of the political 'bug' remained strong, although *The Times* dropped its interest in him.

"Last summer, Meyers filed his widely-known name for lieutenant-governor, ran in the primaries against little-known Democratic opponents, and won a comfortable plurality of the Democratic primary vote.

"Thereupon followed the aftermath of the jest, at election time.

"Thousands of voters, intent on the election of Democrats to major State and national offices, voted a straight Democratic ticket. Meyers was swept into office with a small but adequate majority, to the confusion of, among others, *The Seattle Times*.

The formula was fairly simple. The fish was usually fresh, although when you are buying three hundred thousand pounds of salmon a year it is not quite the same thing to have fresh fish as it was when Ivar used to walk next door on the pier and pick out the day's purchase.

The second part of the formula was a happy staff, which Ivar assured through his marvelous personal touches and a profit-sharing plan for employees around more than ten years. Waitresses were very good, and they had been around an average of eight years. "I'd look for women, " explained Mrs. Eleanor Hill, for years Ivar's manager, "without much makeup, neat, with good English, age twenty to thirty, fast, size ten to fourteen." One reason Ivar's was so popular with families was the waitresses were very good at handling children who were themselves distracted by the amazing clutter of nautical knickknacks and junk Ivar was never able to resist strewing around.

The corny decor was the secret formula. "Certainly I don't want anyone to come into a restaurant and feel inferior to it," Ivar smiled. Added Guy Williams, "I used to write ads for Ivar that were very classy. Ivar would reject them, saying, 'I want people who read my advertising to feel superior to them.' "

Ivar himself marveled at the financial returns from vulgarity. "I once left up the Christmas decor for months. People would say, 'Geez, they're stupid. They left the Christmas lights up till June.' I don't know why that works so well!" All this meant that Ivar was constantly being shown carvings and flotsam brought around by hopeful craftsmen, much of which Ivar bought. He had a virtual warehouse full of unused seagulls, one crony reports. And the ideas kept coming, despite numerous rebukes by the city fathers, who turned down his plan for a seagull fountain on Pier 54 (it might attract rats, the city sneered), and for putting up a replica of the David Denny cabin in Pioneer Square as part of a popcorn concession.

Ivar did have his limits, however. Once, after his Salmon House on Lake Union had won an architectural award for its authenticity and carvings (by Duane Pasco, Bill Holm, and Bill Neidinger), Ivar let himself lapse. He opened a drive-in portion complete with garish signs. A local paper unloaded on him, and Ivar tore down all the signs and put up a simple one in their place: "Sorry."

The final element of the formula was promotion. "We were camp before the word was invented," said Guy Williams, and many of the stunts had a marvelous quality of the put-on about them. There was the time Ivar rushed out and set up a pancake stand when a molasses car overturned. (He was in business only as long as the cameras were present.) He launched a parody campaign to get a clam stamp and then buried the printed sheets in Elliott Bay to the strains of "Bye-Bye Bivalve." His own songs were largely spoofs, such as "Hail, the Halibut": "When I say hail, I don't mean but." Best of all were his clam-eating contests, with Ivar holding forth as executive secretary of the International Pacific Free

Ivar and his gulls

Style Amateur Clam Eating Contest Association (IPFSACECA), flooding the country with bogus crowd estimates and the name of his restaurant.

In recent years, Ivar's promotions unfortunately became more straightforward. He put on the Green Lake fireworks, and he plunked down twenty-two thousand dollars to sponsor seventy-eight broadcasts on KCTS of the Monty Python show (a good investment in publicity, by the way, and Ivar insisted that the names of his restaurants be used—all of them). Only his television commercials, for which he rehearsed carefully at home a full week, still had the proper spoofy style.

Before he succumbed to being a port commissioner, Ivar had been casting about for some new project to get the blood beating again. He considered a new salmon house in Kirkland or in Honolulu (where he had a condominium), and thought about buying a building uptown since his properties (three restaurants and an apartment house on Queen Anne) had exhausted their tax-depreciation advantages. Along came the Smith Tower, which Ivar bought in a twinkling for $500,000 down and $1.3 million balance from a North Carolina investment company.

The new property brought out a new side of Ivar. His collection of Chinese stuff, looking for a home, went into the lobbies and the refurbished Chinese observatory, then in sad repair. The Tower itself got a washing in mild detergent and the brass a polishing. Ivar always showed a reverence for past craftsmanship—when he opened Ivar's Fifth Avenue at the site of the former Rippe's, he was careful to save the pressed tin ceiling—and could therefore be trusted not to automate the Tower's elevators.

It was always a very good life for Ivar, who had the knack of infectious enjoyment. In his last years, he lived in an elegant home in Magnolia, rising each morning at 5 A.M. to take a swim in his covered pool, and then spending two or three hours reading and thinking. (His voracious reading was mostly in science and the arts.) Then he went to his crowded, small office atop the Acres of Clams to talk with his cronies and launch his schemes. He adjourned for lunch to the Captains Table, where a couple of drinks got him going with some more pals. The face was still ruddy as ever, and as he had been balding, the old description of him, "a wistful walrus just emerging from a storm," got more apt. Surprisingly, he did not have a large circle of close friends, and evenings were normally spent at home with Opal, his wife, who finally induced Ivar to do a lot more traveling—the most he had done, in fact, since a semireligious trip to India just after college.

What made it such a lovely life was its steadfast individualism. Ivar never drifted into the golfing set that his money entitled him to, never went "uptown." Instead he kept his friends among captains and writers and restaurant people. He gave away a lot of money, usually with no fanfare, such as the time when a girls' basketball team needed money for travel to a tournament and Ivar, asked for a part, funded it all. He became, in the words of his friend, the writer Mack Mathews, "the natural voice for the region's homespun corn," and he never pretended that the region was old enough to have a culture worth getting all Arty about. Nor did he pretend that business is a religion: "I owe my success to ambition, myopia, and greed."

"There is," Ivar liked to say, "nothing pre-fab about me."

It is tempting to think of Ivar, who died in 1985, with his Alki birth and Scandinavian roots, as kind of a presiding comical spirit of Seattle. In many ways he was such a spirit, happy in paradise, tolerant of the city's international style, amused by popular tastes, jesting and earthy, fond of risks. I imagine him in his hideaway apartment atop Pier 62, which he had outfitted in parvenu grandeur with porcelain doorknobs, an electric organ, a copper-crowded kitchen, and a rococo bathroom. (It burned down one day and Ivar told the builder, Rudi Becker, to take all that he could salvage.) Or I see him with his guitar in the 1930s, when Skid Road was thriving with people and good restaurants and good talk and good vaudeville. "How are all the bums we used to love?" Warren Magnuson asks his old pals from that era when he meets one. That was the time that formed the city's individualistic taste and verve, and it is going away. ◼

CONTEMPORARIES

MODERN
TIMES:
1945–1989

CONTEMPORARIES

Trying to understand postwar Washington is a lot like rowing a boat in fogbound surf: the sense of it is immediate; we feel the currents, but we cannot tell where we are going. But wherever we are, Washington today is a much different place than it was. Since 1940 the population has increased from something over one and one-half million to over four million, and with all that growth, the land that seemed limitless has shrunk dramatically under urban sprawl. The Evergreen State is much more a part of the nation than it used to be, and it takes much less time for trends or fads to arrive here. The anguished query that surfaces now and again—whether there is anything unique about the Northwest besides its scenery—is a measure of just how intimately we have become bound to all that is outside of us.

This is not to say that we have been digested in the belly of the beast. Most who live here were not born here, and those who are natives are not especially different from the rest. It is remarkable, for example, how many residents have family or know someone in Brainerd, Minnesota, or Duluth. But we live here, in this land; we respond to the way things are here; and the ways we respond have changed along with our common history.

Since the war, for example, the building that was once so noticeable when there was little built is now pretty much taken for granted. John Steinbeck could shake his head at all the earthmoving equipment tearing things up in the early sixties when he traveled through with his dog, Charley, but now, unless construction levels a good portion of downtown Spokane or Seattle, we rarely notice how much building is going on. Things that used to impress us no longer do. Timber is now a crop like wheat and potatoes, and some of the second-growth trees that Frederick Weyerhaeuser planted to restock his timber bank are nearly as impressive as the original virgin growth. The cutting of logs is called harvesting and is no longer considered heroic. There is little romance attached to railroading, either, since utilitarian diesel has replaced the glory of steam. There is a certain wry irony in the fact that a number of people plan to celebrate the state's centennial by riding in covered wagons down an abandoned railroad grade known as the John Wayne Trail. It will be as though a chapter had been excised from our history. Doing things on an epic scale no

Maintaining a balance here amid powerful currents still requires what it always did—devoted individuals.

longer seems to excite the popular imagination. Huge projects that in an earlier time would have had editors drooling are now greeted with skepticism and loud citizen protest. For many, keeping the rolling steppe east of the mountains in sage and bunchgrass is just as important as planting it in wheat. The Columbia has been dammed for all but a short stretch near Hanford, and the fight to keep it free is nearly as intense as the earlier crusade to build Grand Coulee Dam.

Similarly, brawn and swinging gait are less attractive as personal traits now than imagination and subtle insight. The field of action is smaller and the competition keener. The idea of the frontier still exists, but it has been internalized and made a personal quest. Coyote is still an interesting figure, but those parts of his stories that are most likely to touch us now are not when he waylays the girl or slays the monster but when he feels compassion or experiences a flash of tragic illumination.

We can see this inward drift in the art from our region. The big four of the Northwest School—Morris Graves, Mark Tobey, Kenneth Callahan, and Guy Anderson— were by no means the first artists to paint here. The Northwest has been the focus of western artistic endeavor ever since ship captains began sketching our coastal landmarks in the seventeen hundreds. That first art was didactic, as in the case of the shore profiles or in the sketches done to illustrate the life of native peoples. Later, it developed an epic quality as painters depicted native encampments along the shore, particularly those beside city wharves, as emblems of one culture fading before the triumphal march of American civilization. There was an epic quality too in paintings of the virginal land, the railroad passes, and Mount Rainier at sunset. The newer artists were less concerned with representing what they saw than in expressing their private vision conjured out of the land and their experience in it. The influence of Asia began to internationalize the regional focus.

Of course, the Asian influence had been here long before critics discovered it in our art. There is a wonderful story, worthy of an epic, about Japanese fishermen who were shipwrecked on the Olympic Peninsula in the 1830s. They were ransomed from captivity among the Makah people by the Chief Factor of the Hudson's Bay Company at Fort Vancouver, Dr. John McLoughlin. During their stay at the fort, he taught them English and introduced them to Scripture. He sent them to London, where they had an audience with Queen Victoria, after which they took passage on a ship bound for Macao. All dreamed of returning home to their families, some of preaching their newly acquired Christian faith, and at Macao they worked with a missionary translating the Bible into Japanese. Finally, they took ship to Japan, where officials prevented them from landing. During their absence, the fishermen had been given up for dead, and as "ghosts" they fell into the category of foreign intruders and were not permitted entry. Devastated, some of the "ghosts" returned to the Olympic Peninsula where they lived out their lives among their former captors. One was believed to have made it back to Japan after that country was opened to the West in 1853.

For a long time, Asians in the Northwest were looked upon as foreign intruders and lived like ghosts, forbidden from owning property, having wives, and becoming citizens. The Chinese were the first to come in large numbers, eager like other immigrants to earn a better life working on farms or building the railroads. When jobs were plentiful, they were praised for their hard work and respect for authority, but when jobs became scarce, they were branded as slaves who stole bread from the mouths of white children. No calumny was too gross to smear them with, and in towns throughout Washington in the late 1880s, white workers rioted against them, beating them and shooting them and demanding their removal.

The Japanese began to appear in large numbers shortly afterwards, but unlike the Chinese, they were permitted to bring over wives and start families. The Japanese community grew while the Chinese languished, but the xenophobia of the 1920s bore down heavily upon them. The Exclusion Act of 1924, which sought to end Japanese immigration, was only one example of legislation that created a gulf and made it much easier to drive them from their homes during World War II into internment and relocation camps.

In spite of this long history of harsh treatment, most Asian-Americans refused to be defeated, and many succeeded in rising to positions that commanded respect in both cultures. Ruby Chow overcame her limitations as a woman in Chinese society and a Chinese in American society to attain prominence and influence in both. Bruce Lee passed through town, brilliant as a peacock, opening doors upon a culture of whose novel richness few here had even an inkling. Wing Luke's brief career leaves us wondering what had been lost during all those years when Asian immigrants were treated as foreign intruders.

There had been attempts by the churches to help bridge the gap separating Asian immigrants from the rest of society, but it was through art, the other doorway to the soul, that both cultures were able to meet upon a common ground of appreciation and begin to borrow from one another. Seattle Art Museum founder Richard Fuller, who was fascinated by Asian forms, could amass a wonderful variety of objects here. His dedication introduced us to entire new worlds of form and had a profound effect upon individuals like Mark Tobey. Coming out of the traditions themselves, artists such as George Tsutakawa have made these forms an indelible part of our own cultural landscape, strengthening the ties that bind us ever more firmly to Asia.

The art of Jacob Lawrence provides a similar opening to the black experience. Lawrence may not be of the Northwest, but his paintings evoke the difficult, often luminous reality that was the fate of black Americans here as it was elsewhere. Like Asians, blacks were here early on, accompanying white settlers in exploration, settlement, and de-

Like Asians, blacks were here early on, accompanying white settlers in exploration, settlement, and development of this land.

velopment of this land. George Washington Bush helped lead the first American settlers north across the Columbia and was a constant source of help to those who followed him. But as the land filled, black Americans were increasingly excluded from its promise. Resolutely ignored, they emerged from their isolation in the 1960s when many worked successfully to deflate the conceit long and lightly held that Washington had no racial problems. It was an ambivalent triumph, however, and the persistent struggle it required—and still requires—finds powerful expression in Jacob Lawrence's paintings.

Every group to come to Washington had its own story, not necessarily so bittersweet as those of Asian and black Americans. The Scandinavians who came here have done quite well for themselves, spectacularly so in the case of the Nordstrom family, but immigrants who did not speak English during World War I and its aftermath often felt the heat of hysteria. Eventually, however, the populist-progressive politics of Scandinavians at home and abroad exercised such an influence here that some claimed it was the rare person who could be elected to office in Washington whose name did not end in "sen" or "son."

The lives of nearly all Washingtonians experienced a relative improvement after World War II. Even that most tormented of all minorities, the native Americans, have by dint of persistent effort managed to emerge partway from the hole of oblivion into which the pioneers thrust them. They have had help in the efforts of archaeologists like Richard Daugherty, whose discoveries at the Marmes Rock Shelter and at Ozette provided us with a new perspective of the human presence in this land, on the enormous length of occupancy, and on the concept of wilderness itself. Was it a wilderness the pioneers won, or a garden lovingly tended by others for thousands of years?

That question is of more than historical interest. As more and more people come to Washington, attracted by jobs, the land's beauty, and its quality of life, the Evergreen State has become a garden that requires constant care. In the art of politics, Washingtonians have staked out a pragmatic middle ground between extremes. It is a place that produces liberal Republicans like Dan Evans and conservative Democrats like Henry Jackson, or where historically conservative areas like Yakima and Spokane give rise to a William O. Douglas and Tom Foley. And the tilth required for this propagation is not restricted to cities; it is widespread, thanks to individuals such as Baker Ferguson and Henry Gay, who regard cultivating excellence in a small place preferable to harvesting mediocrity in a larger one.

As with politics, Washington has come to occupy the middle ground of American states: twentieth in size and population, with its largest city, Seattle, hovering around twentieth in size among major American cities. It also occupies a middle position between the heartlands of Asia and America, and between California and Canada. The state is in the thick of a world economy. But while Washington may be an integral part in an expanding

Pacific-American system, it retains its historic measure of isolation, keeping the distance apart that the middle ground offers.

It is an undeniably attractive situation. It attracted novelist Tom Robbins here, a place as far from Richmond, Virginia, as he could get, but still recognizable enough to afford him images of a mythic landscape. The cultural critic Vernon Parrington came for perspective and calm. But it is a tenuous position, too, with its own brand of tensions. Being in the middle means trying constantly to maintain a balance between opposing forces. The divisions that marked Washington before the war did not magically disappear after it, even as they were muted by postwar prosperity. Catholic Archbishop Raymond Hunthausen reactivated these forces when his liberal views and his decision to withhold part of his taxes to protest the arms race very nearly resulted in his removal. They can still explode into violence, as with Seattle's Wah Mee massacre.

It is still a volatile place, a volcanic landscape. Maintaining a balance here amid powerful currents still requires what it always did. More than rich soils, abundant timber, and deep water, it requires devoted individuals. This land, with its outsized landscape and heroic challenges, has brought forth such adventurous individuals for decades. Will it continue to do so, now that the land has been tamed? Will the Washingtonians of the future recognize much in common with the inhabitants of *Washingtonians* ? ◼

David M. Buerge

Baker Ferguson at home in L'Ecole 41: Whitman overseer, bander, professor, civic activist, and wine maker

Paul Gregutt

332

VINTAGE
WALLA WALLA

BAKER FERGUSON (1919–)

PAUL GREGUTT

Lowden, Washington, a one-blink town on the highway to Walla Walla, is a cluster of grain elevators and a handful of wood-frame houses. A three-story schoolhouse—the one-time Lowden Schoolhouse Number 41—sits at the eastern edge of town, looking south across the highway to the Walla Walla River and the Oregon hills beyond. Closed and abandoned in 1974, it stands today trim and stately, set back in tall trees behind a broad expanse of lawn. A dozen new French oak barrels, scattered about the front yard, offer the only clue to its new identity as L'Ecole 41, a recent addition to this state's growing ranks of wineries.

From its oddball location to its child's-art label, from its full-blown Merlot to its ripe Semillon, L'Ecole 41 approaches the business of making and marketing wine with a quirky insouciance. To those who know owner Baker Ferguson, retired bank president, community activist, and longtime member of the board of trustees of Whitman College, that quixotic flavor comes as no surprise.

"There's no way to predict what he'll do next," admits Jean Ferguson, his wife of thirty-seven years and L'Ecole 41's wine maker, "but ever since I met him I've known that sooner or later I was going to end up in a winery." When his retirement neared, in the late seventies, they began vineyard hunting. "He's not the kind of person who's going to sit down and watch television," she explains. As has frequently been the case in his life, Baker let his instincts guide him and his intellect justify the results. The old schoolhouse loomed larger every time he set out to find vineyard land. "I kept driving by and looking at it," he recalled, "and after a while it sort of forced itself on me." Good-bye grape-growing, hello wine-making.

It makes all kinds of economic sense to do a winery rather than a vineyard, he will tell you. But economics aside, it is the idea of a schoolhouse as residence and winery that appeals to this dedicated eccentric. Baker Ferguson has devoted a lifetime not so much to breaking molds as to recasting them. A creative iconoclast and vagabond intellect, he is, in the words of Whitman College former president Robert Skotheim, "the ultimate searcher." The winery is the most recent harbor for his restless energy.

Baker's interest in winemaking extends to tracing its history in the Walla Walla Valley.

333

At sixty-nine, he has already led a life rich enough for several men. The great-grandson of Dorsey Syng Baker, who founded this state's oldest bank, the Baker-Boyer National Bank, and its oldest railroad company, the Walla Walla chartered in 1868, Baker Ferguson's path was, in many respects, preordained. It is less the road he has traveled than the detours along the way that make his story an interesting one.

In 1939 he was graduated from Whitman College (whose original campus was donated by great-grandfather Dorsey). Two years later, Harvard MBA in hand, he moved to San Francisco to work as an investment analyst for Wells Fargo Bank. When World War II interrupted, Ferguson became a navigator with the Eighth Air Force, flying B-17 bombing runs until he was shot down over Kiel, Germany. He spent two years in a German prison camp. Returning home after the war, he was pressed into service as a Whitman College economics professor, a time he recalls fondly.

"My students were mostly GIs, really my contemporaries. I wasn't qualified to teach economics, but I learned a lot of it in those two years. I don't know if it was good for them, but it was good for me," he explains in his self-effacing way. Perhaps as a result of that early experience, Ferguson has always been able to empathize and communicate with students. "He was the listening post for students in the late sixties," says Skotheim. "They'd actually go downtown into the bank president's office and talk to him about their worries about the war and so on." If such stories are more than apocryphal, they must make him unique in the annals of bank presidents.

Another story reinforces the notion. Some years back, Senator Henry Jackson, a member of the Whitman College board of overseers, had arranged a luncheon for a number of Washington DC alums. Baker Ferguson was the topic of conversation. "I've met a lot of bank presidents," Scoop is alleged to have commented, "but never anybody like Baker. I have the feeling it's a good thing Baker's president of that bank, because I don't think he could get a loan there otherwise."

Despite his eccentric reputation, Ferguson defies easy definition as a well-to-do gadfly. He's had far too much conventional success for that. From 1950 through 1965 he was vice-president of public relations for First National Bank of Oregon. During that time he also served as chair of the Alaska committee of the Portland Chamber of Commerce, director of the Portland Freight Traffic Association, and director of the Inland Empire Waterways Association. Returning to Walla Walla in 1965 to succeed his uncle as president of Baker-Boyer National Bank, he quickly undertook a civic-service workload that included membership on the Whitman board of trustees (he was its president from 1972–1983), eight years with the state highway commission, and time with the state tax advisory subcommittee, the Washington Citizens Council on Crime and Delinquency, the Walla Walla Chamber of Commerce, and the PNW Ski Association, to name but a handful. A sportsman since his college track days (he ran the hurdles), he was an avid flyer until narcolepsy grounded him, and he remains to this day an active tennis player and skillful downhill skier.

On one sunny October Saturday, Baker Ferguson greets me with his cat "Chat-O" in the entrance of the old schoolhouse. Baker is a tall, silver-haired, and mustachioed figure with a white cap perched jauntily off-center on his head. Jean is out visiting one of the vineyards from which they purchase their grapes, testing them for ripeness. The winery has been laid out so that, in Baker's words, "one elderly character and one female winemaker can do everything. Jean's the winemaker," he adds with a wink, "and I'm her flunky."

The ground level looks like any number of other mom 'n' pop winery operations, packed with fermenting tanks, barrels, and odd pieces of wine-making equipment, such as a German-built Güth "mixmaster" that mechanically stirs the fermenting grapes. Jean and Baker do all the considerable labor involved on their own, bringing in hired help only to run the bottling line. Baker credits Jean with having the distinguished palate. "I think you learn more by cooking than by tasting food," he explains, "which may be why women make such exceptional wine makers."

Upstairs, the spacious second floor holds the public rooms and winery offices. It also serves as an unofficial social center for gatherings of all four Walla Walla wineries, as well as functions involving Whitman alumni and trustees. Its centerpiece is a high-ceilinged tasting room decorated with antiques, Persian carpets, and a grand piano. Adjacent is the corporate office, lined with bookshelves and almost completely occupied by a large billiard table that doubles, he informs me, as a buffet and guest bed. In the bathroom are what may be the world's only rolltop desk/sink and armoire/Murphy bed.

The winery's French name is a nod both to the wine-making style the Fergusons hope to emulate and to the roots of Lowden, which was originally settled by French-Canadian trappers and known as Frenchtown. Baker's interest in wine-making extends to tracing its history in the Walla Walla Valley, and he contributed his research to enological historian Leon Adams for inclusion in the new edition of his classic text *The Wines of America*. Ferguson contends that wine was being made from European grapes before the arrival of Marcus Whitman in 1836. Following the Civil War a local wine-making industry sprang up in earnest, and the newspapers of the time were quite taken with the possibilities.

"Somebody would grow a tobacco plant on their front porch," says Baker, "and the next article would tell you that Walla Walla was going to be the cigar capital of the world. The same thing was true of grapes." Interestingly, despite the wine-making renaissance in Washington, the Walla Walla Valley remains the newest and smallest wine-making region in the state.

In 1986, L'Ecole 41 released its first two wines, a Semillon and a Merlot. (The Merlot promptly won a gold medal from the prestigious Northwest Enological Society judging.) There is nothing standard about either of them. "We make a very idiosyncratic Semillon,"

Skotheim labels him "the ultimate Huck Finn, marching to his own drummer"

335

Dorsey Syng Baker

The West is, of course, the land of the tall tale, delivered with a poker face that never blinks as the fantasy grows ever grander. Newspaperman Stewart Holbrook loved this tradition of the region, and few stories drew his admiration more than the deadpan rendering of the saga of a rawhide railroad, improbably constructed across the sagebrush country near Walla Walla. The story so mingled facts and fabrication that to this day many probably still think such a railroad existed.

From The Far Corner *by Stewart Holbrook.* *Copyright © renewed by Sibyl Holbrook Strahl. Reprinted by permission of Comstock Editions.*

In my occupation of newspaperman and writer of books, I have perhaps been exposed to as many liars as the next man. Of the hundreds I have heard in action, and often listened to, only half a dozen could be called masters. . . . I mean the genuine master who can relate some patently improbable story with such artistry as to daze and charm his auditors into at least temporary belief in the marvels under consideration.

Such narrators are as rare now as they were in Virgil's day. We have had only one native master of that caliber in the Pacific Northwest. He was the late George Estes of Troutdale, Oregon. I regret that I never met him in the flesh, for it was he who fashioned our one Northwest tale that appears to have the indestructible qualities of a classic. He called it *The Rawhide Railroad*. It first appeared in print in 1916, and he had to publish it himself. Book publishers and the editors of magazines and newspapers had rejected the manuscript in heartbreaking numbers. . . .

The text opens with a dedicatory paragraph that would disarm any doubter.

It has the perfect flavor of the typical amateur home-town antiquarian sending his labor of love out into the world. It is romantic, bombastic, filled with capital letters, laboriously punctuated, and ungrammatical. It is, in short, perfect. . . .

Historian Estes next goes into his Preface, and here he begins to get up a head of steam and give his readers an idea of the forgotten, though authentic and marvelous, material he has in store for them. "This," says he, "is the story of a remarkable steam railroad actually constructed and successfully operated in the beautiful Walla Walla Valley many years ago, on which rawhide, overlaying wooden beams, was used in place of iron or steel rails." . . . With these typical flourishes of the local historian out of the way the author gets on with his narrative.

Into his bucolic scene of pioneer times comes Dr. Dorsey S. Baker—an actual person—who was among the first settlers in the town of Walla Walla. He was a practicing physician who had crossed the plains from Illinois, and was easily the most energetic and purposeful figure in Walla Walla. He was into everything. No local project could get under way without tremendously bearded old Doc Baker being a party to it. Thus when on his rounds he heard grumbling against the high cost of freight to Wallula, nearest port on the Columbia, he swore he would remedy the condition. He would, he said, build a railroad forthwith. . . .

Doc Baker had looked into the matter of iron rails. They were too costly, he pronounced. His trains, said he, should run on wooden rails. These were laid, and one day soon the first train of the Walla Walla & Columbia River Railroad made a successful first round trip. Presently Walla Walla wheat was going to port for a fourth of what the despicable freighter operators had charged. It was wonderful to behold. Doc Baker was more than ever a hero.

"But," says Historian Estes, "it was soon found that the gnawing movements of the tread and flanges of the locomotive drivers quickly wore off the tops and edges of the wood rails." But do you think for a moment that Doc Baker would face them with strap iron? He would not. It cost too much. Anyhow, he had figured out the remedy. The remedy was rawhide, that renowned "metal" upon which all Western pioneers, time out of mind, relied to surmount all difficulties of a mechanical nature. . . .

Occasionally, because of rain or snow, the rawhide railroad had to suspend for a day or so; then the sun came out, the rawhide quickly became taut again, and as hard as mild steel. It was as simple as that—all glory to good Doc Baker, a man

with stout belief in the fundamentals of pioneering America.

Yet, disaster lay just ahead. It came during a winter of unprecedented severity. Provisions grew scarce. Feed ran short. Cattle were turned out on the snowy ranges to get such fodder as they might. They fared ill. Most of them froze. Wolf packs now swept down from the Rockies, devouring the frozen cattle, and at last crowded to the very edge of Walla Walla Village. One terrible night, as still another blizzard rolled over the land, two of Doc Baker's faithful Indian friends came pounding at his door. They brought hideous news of the railroad. Half frozen, they yet managed to tell the pioneer magnate what had happened: "Railroad, him gonum hell. Damn wolves digum out—eat all up—Wallula to Walla Walla."

Well, sir, old Doc Baker was understandingly shaken at this catastrophe, yet he rallied manfully, and in the spring had strap iron fastened to the top of the wooden rails. The era of rawhide had passed. The refurbished road operated successfully for many years more, and was then purchased by the Union Pacific.

Dorsey Syng Baker

booms Ferguson, proudly. "It's made to go with the spicy Indonesian food at Nettie Ray's (a favorite Tri-Cities restaurant). That's the acid test." Idiosyncratic or not, the wines are strong and attractive. The Merlot, a thick, grapey, tannic wine, was the only Merlot to receive a gold medal in the festival.

At dinner a few hours after our winery tour, Baker grumbles to Jean about the time constraints the winery places on both of them. "Maybe we should just do a vintage every five years," he offers. She herself admits that they do not know how long they will be able to manage it on their own. Besides the obvious physical limitations that their advancing ages will impose, there is Baker's always restless intellect.

Skotheim labels him "the ultimate Huck Finn, marching to his own drummer," adding, "I think the archetype he is, is out of Winesburg, Ohio, that nineteenth-century small-town America creation—Robert Ingersoll the freethinker; Gene Debs the small-town socialist. That person who seems to be sui generis—you can't explain where he came from."

New York attorney Ross Reid, a schoolmate and lifetime friend of Ferguson's, recalls that "Baker was always one of a kind. In the undergrad bull sessions he'd take a unique view—positions that were good for debate."

"He is a divided self at work," adds Skotheim uncritically, "the child of the aristocratic family in democratic Walla Walla. Time and time again he's got a foot in two camps. I think his chief intellectual anxiety has to do with the problems of governing a democratic society. He was very much affected by his time on the state highway commission. I think that Baker, as a western American, by implication democratic in his impulses, was really troubled by populism in the proceedings of the highway commission and the extent to which projects were delayed by public hearings. I think it's a dilemma because not only are his impulses democratic, but he's also very patient, process oriented—the ultimate collegial person. Yet the highway commission in miniature became what he feared was one prospect for the greater society—special-interest politics. He worries about our ability as a college to prepare students for a political world in which this is going to be a reality."

The college, which neatly transects his banker's interest in the local economy, remains a primary recipient of his time and attention and, in his words, "a marvelous and satisfying connection." Though he stepped down as president of its board of trustees in 1983, he continues to play an exceptionally active role as a board-member, and is thought to be the most knowledgeable person alive on the subject of Whitman College.

If Whitman and Walla Walla present a schizophrenic face toward the rest of the state—part isolated wheat-farming community, part New England-style liberal arts university town—Ferguson represents some extreme variation on the theme. What unites his disparate interests is a zest for living that transcends any of the particulars. He throws himself into anything that catches his attention. He loves to ask questions, the odder the better. Even his narcolepsy, a nondegenerative sleep disorder that has troubled him for decades, has become yet another avenue to explore, another opportunity to participate in a quest for knowledge. He speaks of it freely, without bitterness, and for years has been an active and willing guinea pig for the Stanford Sleep Research Institute.

The wine business, with its infinite opportunities for self-expression, its essential connection to the land and the seasons, and its unique blend of art and artifice, business and pleasure, offers him a broad palette of colors with which to paint his retirement. Along with his ongoing commitment to Whitman and its liberal arts orientation, his lifelong love of skiing, and his endless fascination with myriad intellectual pursuits, the winery brings a satisfying focus to his life.

It is a chance to play a new game, a business game to be sure, whose rules are defined by solid and familiar economics, but at the same time a business game that allows him such indulgences as a label designed by an eight-year-old. We stop in a tiny room behind the office to admire the original artwork, done by a distant cousin. In bright crayon colors it shows the schoolhouse with a tractor parked out front, and the brilliant Walla Walla sun poking out from behind a blue cloud. Off to the right a hot-air balloon, in the shape of a purple grape cluster, floats lazily in the sky.

"Like Château Mouton we thought we ought to have original art for our label," he says with a grin, popping the cork on a bottle each of the Merlot and Semillon. Beaming with obvious satisfaction, he fills some glasses, inhales deeply, and tastes. "I don't consider this a hobby," he volunteers in response to my unasked question. And then, to place it in final perspective, he adds, "I consider it a mid-life career change rather late in life." ◢

Anderson in his garden: Asian
echoes and a Gallic manner

OLD MAN
AND THE SKAGIT

GUY ANDERSON (1906–)

JOHN S. ROBINSON

Bog Tule!" answered the cheerful voice on the La Conner phone. Something was plainly rotten in the county of Skagit. "Maybe I have the wrong number," I said. "I don't want to talk to Bob Tully. I'm calling Guy Anderson."

"Maybe you want the *other* Guy Anderson," said the voice. "There's one that lives in Burlington. He's a builder."

"No," I said. "I think it's you I want. Who's Bob Tully?"

"Oh, I always answer 'Bog Tule,' " said Guy Anderson—the artist, not the builder—in a matter-of-fact way. "That's the name of this place. I call it that because I like bogs and I like tules."

Bogs? Tules? It wasn't a bad start for an interview, but off-the-wall whimsy is somehow not what one looks for from a major painter, particularly one who has been called (by Bruce Guenther, former curator of contemporary art at the Seattle Art Museum) "the most powerful artist of the Northwest School." But, as I was shortly to learn, Guy Anderson resists easy classification.

He's a highly social being, but a lifelong bachelor and essentially a loner. By nature a cosmopolitan, he years ago chose to live in what was then a remote fishing village on the road to nowhere. At eighty-one, when most artists have long since retreated into silence— or when painting has become "just a bad habit, something to keep their career going," as his friend, Wesley Wehr, puts it—he continues to produce some of the strongest work of his career.

Anderson's output is also difficult to categorize. Though many consider him almost the archetype of the regional artist, his large, dramatic paintings evoke the entire planet. Repeatedly, relentlessly, they seek out the frontiers of human experience, in our distant tribal past, in the outer cosmos, and in the mysteries of conception, birth, and death.

Several hours after our phone conversation, sitting in Bog Tule's fenced garden, I felt that the contradictions in Anderson's life and art were fully apparent. Early on, he took pains to tell me that despite his name, none of his ancestors was Scandinavian. They were English, Scottish, and Norman French. He looked French, in a *La Bohème* sort of way.

Slower to develop than the others, Guy Anderson had emerged as the recognized Old Master of the Northwest tradition.

Short and compact, with bright, observant eyes, he greeted me wearing paint-stained jeans, a blue shirt, a dark blue scarf around his neck, and a white cap. And something about his style of life suggested France. His small, sun-dappled garden—replete with fruit trees, and with bronzed pears, scarlet apples, and purple plums scattered about on tables—might have been an impressionist painting come to life. The glass of wine he served was a sunny French Sauternes.

Yet there was nothing Gallic about the art in his garden: a statue of the many-armed Hindu god Shiva, an African mask, and, dominating all else, several of his recent paintings. These were oils on reinforced brown paper, which he had hung on the fence and on walls; weathering doesn't seem to harm them. Like most of his work, they dealt with deeply serious themes. In one, a nude male figure represented Sisyphus, the character from Greek mythology eternally doomed to push a huge rock up a hillside, only to have it forever roll down again. In another, an allegorical study of the birth of the world was built around two dark blue panels—"rich, dense, and chthonian," to quote the words of La Conner novelist Tom Robbins, who has written appreciatively of Anderson's work. These panels stood for the great continental plates that lie beneath the earth's surface and strain to pass each other in opposite directions, forming stresses only to be resolved by earthquakes. It is Anderson's habit to produce such paintings in series, until he has exhausted the potential of a given theme; another painting from the same creation series hangs in the Skagit County Courthouse in Mount Vernon. With a wry smile, the artist commented that not all the officials there regard it with enthusiasm.

Guy Anderson first came to national attention with the publication in the September 18, 1953, issue of *Life* magazine of what was to become the best-known article ever written about painting in the Pacific Northwest: "Mystic Painters of the Northwest: They Translate Reality into Symbolic and Distinctive Art." Though unsigned, the piece was the work of Dorothy Seiberling, a Vassar arts graduate, who, during a long tenure with *Life,* served in turn as a writer, art editor, and senior editor.

"For more than a decade," she began her opening paragraph, "a remarkable art of shimmering lines and symbolic forms has been coming out of the northwest corner of the United States, stirring up storms of irritation and enthusiasm in the galleries of New York, London, and the Continent. Produced by a variety of artists living around Seattle, the paintings range in style from realistic to nonobjective. Yet they have one characteristic in common: they embody a mystical feeling toward life and the universe. This mystical approach stems partly from the artists' awareness of the overwhelming forces of nature which surround them, partly from the influence of the Orient whose cultures have seeped into the communities that line the US Pacific Coast. The painters of Seattle have merged these influences, creating an art that without being a limited 'regional art' is distinctive of the Northwest."

In particular, the article assessed the work of four men: Mark Tobey, Morris Graves, Kenneth Callahan, and Guy Anderson. Most of the photographs accompanying it were taken by *Life's* celebrated photographer Eliot Elisofon, who, Anderson says, postponed work on *Moulin Rouge,* the filmed biography of Toulouse-Lautrec, to shoot them. Two pictures were especially arresting. One was a full-page reproduction of Tobey's seminal painting *Electric Night,* which depicted, by means of his calligraphic white writing, "his conception of Seattle in wartime when mobbed streets and cluttered signs seemed to create a frenzied network of lines and lights." The other was an astonishing study of the young Morris Graves, which seems to prefigure, a decade ahead of its time, the whole counterculture of the 1960s. Dressed in worn jeans and sneakers, and looking mildly stoned, the bearded artist kneels in the forest, "contemplating," says the caption, in a quote from the title of one of his paintings, "new visions of the inner eye."

As for Dorothy Seiberling's text, it has been soundly trashed by a number of Northwest commentators. They have charged, among other things, that the four artists were nowhere near as cohesive as the article implied, that they were influenced by many sources other than the Orient, and that to style them "mystics" was to oversimplify their complex individual approaches to life and art. There can be little doubt, though, that Seiberling was among the first to identify and pin down a major artistic movement, one as indigenous to the soil of the Puget Sound country as Garrison Keillor is to the soil of Minnesota, or Bordeaux wine to the soil of the Medoc. Since her article appeared, few have been able to write at length about the history of Northwest painting without eventually referring to it.

Often called by the imprecise term "Northwest School," the movement persists today despite many changes in the area's artistic climate. In 1953, Graves was much the best known of the four artists, having shortly before held a highly successful exhibit at New York's Museum of Modern Art. Within a few years, Tobey had come to the fore. In 1955, an article by Janet Flanner in the Paris magazine *L'Oeil* declared that of all American painters, Tobey was of most interest in Europe, *"où bien des gens le considérent comme un maître."* By 1958, when he became the first American since Whistler to win first prize for painting at the prestigious Venice Biennale, he was well on his way to developing the considerable European following his work retains to the present.

Three decades later, Tobey and Callahan are dead, and Graves is living quietly in California. Slower to develop than the others, Guy Anderson has emerged as the recognized Old Master of the Northwest tradition, which he both embodies and transcends. In no small part, his primacy is due to his steady productivity and continuing timeliness. Already, the compelling visions of the youthful Graves—the birds singing in the moonlight, the joyous young pines, the bird wearied by the length of the winter of 1944—and the triumphant works of the mature Tobey—*Modal Tide, Forms Follow Man, White Night, Eskimo Idiom* -seem splendid artifacts from our history. By contrast, the later paintings of

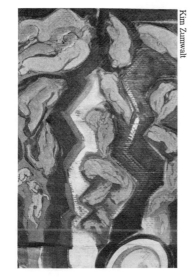

A symbolic vocabulary of deep dimensions

Morris Graves

Morris Graves defined his mystical art out of the Northwest. When his work was exhibited in New York at the Museum of Modern Art, Graves had developed a fresh vision that broke away from his contemporaries into a style all his own. He demonstrated the enduring theme of Northwest art, to be local and global at the same time.

From "The Visionary Painting of Morris Graves," by Kenneth Rexroth, Perspectives U.S.A., *Winter 1955. Reprinted by permission of Bradford Morrow.*

Morris Graves is less provincial, far more a "citizen of the world" than any of his predecessors of the visionary school. It is curious to reflect on this fact, a symptom of the terrific acceleration of the civilizing process of this continent, for Graves was born, raised, and came to maturity as an artist in the Pacific Northwest, a region that was a wilderness until the last years of the nineteenth century. Greatly as I admire Graves's work, it must be admitted that certain of its characteristics are those found, not at the beginning, but at the end of a cultural process—hypersensitivity, specialization of subject, extreme refinement of technique. Nothing could show better the essentially worldwide, homogeneous nature of modern culture than that this successor to the great Sung painters sprang up in a region that was created out of a jungle-like rain forest by the backwash of the Alaska gold rush.

People in the rest of the United States and in Europe have difficulty in adjusting to the fact that the Pacific Coast of America faces the Far East, culturally as well as geographically. There is nothing cultish about this, as there might be elsewhere. The residents of California, Oregon, and Washington are as likely to travel across the Pacific as across the continent and the Atlantic. Knowledge of the Oriental languages is fairly widespread. The museums of the region all have extensive collections of Chinese, Japanese, and Indian art. Vedantist and Buddhist temples are to be seen in the coast cities. And of course there are large Chinese and Japanese colonies in every city, and proportionately even more Orientals in the countryside. It is interesting to note that besides the direct influence of the Orient on them, the Seattle painters, Graves, Tobey, and Callahan, the Portland painter, Price, the San Francisco abstract-expressionists, have all avoided the architectural deep-space painting characteristic of Western Europe from the Renaissance to cubism, and show more affinity to the space concepts of the Venetians. Venice, of course, was for centuries Europe's chief window on the East, an enclave of Byzantine civilization, and the first contact with China. . . .

Graves was born in 1910 in the Fox Valley of Oregon and has lived in the state of Washington, in or near Seattle, all his life, except for short visits to Japan in 1930, to the Virgin Islands in 1939, to

Morris Graves

Honolulu in 1947, and a year in Europe in 1948, after his personal style was fully developed and "set." He studied at the Seattle Museum, with the old master of Northwest painting, Mark Tobey, and had his first one-man show there in 1936. His first New York shows were in 1942 at the Willard Gallery and the Museum of Modern Art. His paintings are now to be found in the permanent collections of most of the major American museums, including the New York Metropolitan.

Except for the emphasis on deep complex space and calligraphic skill which he learned from Tobey, but which he could just as well have learned from the Far Eastern paintings in the Seattle Museum, Graves's style, or styles, his special mode of seeing reality and his techniques of handling it, have come, like the spider's web, out of himself, or, at the most, out of the general cultural ambience of a world civilization, syncretic of all time and space. Therefore, influences and resemblances which seem certain to an historian of art may never in actual fact have existed. . . .

The first of Graves's paintings after his apprentice days are in a rather thick medium, often laid in like cloisonné, between broad, abrupt, dark, single brush strokes. The colors are all "local." There is no attempt to achieve deep space or movement in space by juxtaposition of color. In fact, the color is limited to a small gamut of earths, dull reds, browns, and yellows, with occasionally a slate blue. The line, however, has a great deal of snap, while the movement is very shallow, almost Egyptian. If there are receding planes in these pictures, they are kept to a minimum and the lines stick to the silhouette, never crossing from plane to plane to fill the space. The thing that identifies these paintings immediately is a peculiar, individual sense of silhouette, a silhouette defined by an eccentric calligraphic stroke.

As is well known, a highly personal line of this type comes late, if at all, to most artists. Yet it seems to have been the first thing Graves developed. I can think of nothing quite like it.

Anderson, with their obsessive concern with man's place in the wider universe, seem as contemporary as the films of George Lucas or Stephen Spielberg.

As we finished Anderson's French wine, and his orange-and-gray cat snoozed companionably beneath the anguished form of Sisyphus, the artist talked of his development as a painter. In the hip Seattle of the eighties, where the muses are heard from all sides, in books, in magazines, and on television—where the threatened removal of a difficult abstraction by Henry Moore almost set off a civic revolt—it's hard to imagine the dearth of artistic life in the much less sophisticated city of six decades past. Outside the University of Washington, almost the only informative books then available to the public—or to the young artist—were in the public library, and, Anderson recalls, many of the illustrations had been torn out of them.

Anderson was born of pioneer Pacific Northwest stock in the small Puget Sound community of Edmonds, Washington. Very early, he was aware of his vocation. Not long out of high school, he studied in Seattle with Eustace Zeigler, a talented artist who had lived in Alaska, and who, says Anderson, was "so much in love with painting," but often had to supplement his income by turning out potboilers. When he ran out of money, he'd just paint another picture of Mount McKinley. "He knew he was selling out," Anderson says, "but he had to raise a family." "Do you know anything about the lives of artists?" Zeigler once asked the young Anderson, who replied, "I know a little." "It's a long and difficult path," Zeigler sighed.

Under his master's tutelage, Anderson learned to draw the nude human figure, a skill which, as his painting of Sisyphus suggests, remains central to his vision. For the first time, he met contemporaries who were seriously interested in art, among them the young Kenneth Callahan. Money was not their primary goal. "Their ambition was to paint a good painting." They seized on new ideas from Europe. "We were concerned with Picasso and Braque, where the whole intention was to do a beautiful painting in which you couldn't recognize anything."

There were many other influences, notably from across the Pacific. In 1933, Dr. Richard E. Fuller and his mother, Margaret MacTavish Fuller, gave to Seattle the art museum in Volunteer Park. Trained as a geologist, Dr. Fuller had developed an interest in Asian art partly through his appreciation of jade. A man of many facets, he was also a shrewd businessman. Assisted by support from the lumber fortune of Mrs. Thomas D. Stimson, and the department store fortune of Mrs. D.E. Frederick, he was able to acquire at very low prices some exceptional works of Chinese and Japanese art at a time when few other museums wanted them. Anderson has said that during this period in Seattle, the museum's Asian collections were "all that was worth the seeing."

These collections were to leave their mark on Anderson's work. Though his aesthetic is in many ways different from that of the Orient—for instance, no one would ever accuse him of Japanese understatement—Asian echoes continue to resound throughout his painting. His forceful brushstrokes recall Zen Buddhist masters of old Japan, and he habitually depicts water in formalized patterns. I once commented that one of his solitary male nudes looked to me classically European. He pointed out that he had placed the figure high in one corner of the picture space, whereas a traditional Western artist would have set it right in the center.

European and Asian art provided valuable technical sources for Anderson and his group, but, as the 1953 *Life* article suggested, what more than anything else formed the unique character of their work was the special ambience of Puget Sound—the soft, gray light, the rain, the mist, the rocks and the mountains, the evergreen wilderness and the northern sea. The bogs and the tules. Anderson, whose palette suggests nothing so much as Puget Sound in November, thinks this environmental influence was of utmost importance. He compares it to the effect the austere desert surroundings of New Mexico had on the painter Georgia O'Keeffe, whose work did not attain its full power until she had moved west from New York.

Yet for all this suburban glitz, La Conner somehow hasn't lost its soul.

In 1936, Anderson and Morris Graves settled in La Conner, sixty-five miles north of Seattle in the Skagit River delta, one of the areas where the "Northwest" quality of the region seems distilled into purest form. For a time, they rented a fire-damaged cabin, at least one remnant of which endures. When they later abandoned the place, and it was about to be torn down, a La Conner businessman noticed on one wall a large Graves painting of a chalice. He sawed it out and took it to his house, where it remains today. Not all the townspeople showed equal foresight. According to one story, when Graves and Anderson moved from their cabin, they left a number of sketches and drawings scattered around the floor. Neighborhood kids picked these up and used them to make paper airplanes.

In 1940, Graves moved across the Swinomish Slough to Fidalgo Island, in pursuit perhaps of the ancient Zen ideal of a life of study in natural surroundings, remote from the cares of the everyday world. Atop a steep crag called The Rock, he built another cabin where he was to produce some of his most inspired work. Save for a few forays into the outer world to earn money, mostly by teaching, Anderson has stayed put in La Conner, where everyone knows him, and with which he is now permanently identified. Fellow artist William Cumming put it colorfully in his *Sketchbook: A Memoir of the Thirties and the Northwest School* (University of Washington Press, 1984): "Guy's soul is stuck so deep in the La Conner mudflats," he wrote, "that if he were to leave a spaceship to settle on Mars, he would still have one foot rooted at least knee deep in La Conner mud." Mud flats are scarcely all that distinguishes La Conner. It is surely the only community in the state whose two best-known citizens (Anderson and Tom Robbins) are artists. And, beneath its deceptively simple small-town surface, it's always been a complex place with long roots in prehistory.

My own first memory of the area is one I hold in common with Anderson, one that dates back to before World War II, only a few years after he and Graves had first moved there. At the University of Washington, I was taking a course on the Northwest Coast Indians from the great anthropologist, Dr. Erna Gunther. This famously charismatic teacher urged her students to visit La Conner to watch one of the three-night January dances held annually by the Swinomish Indians in their Fidalgo Island longhouse. I went. It was an awesome experience.

The longhouse was a traditional structure, about 130 feet long, with a dirt floor and three great holes in the roof, through which smoke and sparks poured into the winter night from huge log fires built inside. I remember there were big piles of sliced Wonder Bread on the tables where the performers and their friends had been dining. Somehow, that struck me as odd; in my innocence, I thought they should be eating something more *ethnic.* But when the dancing began, any doubts about authenticity swiftly vanished. An elderly native warned me about the dancers. "Don't sit so near the fire," he said. "They get excited. They don't know what they're doing. You could get hurt." Stomping to the beat of skin drums, darting and lunging, the dancers weaved around the fires, hypnotized, entranced, apparitions from some timeless Swinomish past.

Like most white residents of Puget Sound, I'd previously known little of Native American life, and that evening stimulated in me an interest I've never lost. Anderson, also a friend of Dr. Gunther, attended similar events in the same longhouse, which helped awaken him to Indian culture and exerted a permanent effect on his art.

The old longhouse has since burned down, and if such dances are still held on Fidalgo, uninvited strangers don't attend them. White La Conner has greatly changed as well. From a forgotten pioneer hamlet, dozing along its canal-like slough, it became first a haven for artists, and later a retreat for tourists and boaters. These outlanders have transformed it. Today, it's a kind of geoduck Venice.

While interviewing Anderson, I occupied the apartment of an absent friend, a two-story, San Francisco-like place overhanging the slough. Outside, lavish watercraft paraded past, landlubber skippers standing proudly at their wheels. On either side of the apartment were restaurants. Several sported view decks, built over the water, where patrons could lunch in the sunshine. Besides the restaurants, all along First Street were inviting tourist-grabbers: small boutiques selling everything from leering Mexican jungle cats to Christmas tree balls made from Mount St. Helens ash; the excellent Skagit Bay Books; a sculpture gallery, a "Cheese and Wine Shoppe," an ice cream parlor featuring folk art. On Sunday afternoon in the La Conner Tavern, where Guy Anderson has quaffed many a beer, instead of the farmers and fishermen of old, one saw well-fed, well-clad, well-coiffed retirees dancing in late 1930s style to "Ramblin' Rose" and "Edelweiss."

Yet for all this suburban glitz, La Conner somehow hasn't lost its soul. When the tourists depart at nightfall, a metamorphosis occurs, and once again it becomes the working town it used to be. A least one modern innovation has strikingly improved it. Soaring across the slough, linking the mainland to the Fidalgo cliffs, is the state's handsomest bridge, a structure so graceful and so much in harmony with its surroundings that it might have been built by environmentalist elves. In fact, it was designed by an unsung genius named Harry Powell. It seems a fitting symbol of the traditional town, where, according to painter Max Benjamin of nearby Guemes Island, "fisherman, artist, merchant, Indian chief, and farmer live and work together in mutual acceptance and understanding."

It's only beyond La Conner's city limits, though, that one feels the full presence of the Skagit Valley memorialized by so many artists. Here the delta stretches for mile on mile of rich farmland, broken occasionally by soldierly rows of poplars. In the near distance rise snowcapped peaks, the spiky Three Sisters, and Mount Baker. Tom Robbins has pointed out that this terrain is essentially Chinese, subtly suggestive of Sung or T'ang dynasty art, and it must have been full of resonance for artists recalling the paintings at the Seattle Art Museum. In the city, it's easy to ignore nature, even in Seattle, far more so in New York. In the Skagit Valley, nature seems omnipresent, omnipotent. One is always aware of slight shifts in the weather, and in the appearance of growing things. "I never tire of going from La Conner to Mount Vernon in different seasons of the year," says Anderson. "The landscape is always changing."

The day following my first interview with Anderson, in company with Art Hupy, director of La Conner's Valley Museum of Northwest Art, I hiked what seemed a mile through endless strawberry fields to reach a riverside marsh. We seemed to pass from sunny fields of Asia to the bayou country of Louisiana. We walked on narrow planks high above wetlands that were largely bogs and tules; overhanging trees shut out most of the sun. Eventually, the planks took us to a small, hand-built cottage that seemed as natural an outgrowth of the swamp as a hut in an African forest. It was embowered with bright flowers that bloom in shade, fuchsias and begonias. On the side that faced a vista of the Skagit, in a suddenly light-drenched spot, its owners had planted geraniums and other sun-loving plants. A flock of noisy geese waddled about, and on the river a small boat, a link with the real world, bobbed beside a float.

We had reached Fishtown, a tiny community of escapists whose laid-back look and relaxed style of life seemed to relate them to the Guy Anderson and Morris Graves of the post-Depression years. The cottage was one of several, unreachable by road and unserved by electricity or sewers. Somehow, these dwellings seemed anachronisms—survivals of a vanished era when, throughout the bays and inlets of Puget Sound, many people lived close to the earth like this. Hupy suggested that the bountiful Skagit delta must have been especially friendly to this way of life because it costs so little to live there. Salmon could easily be obtained from the Swinomish, and even today, when the farmers harvest their fields, they

Guy Anderson: "I only paint when I have enough energy."

leave spare corn and squash around for the taking.

Across Harry Powell's bridge on Fidalgo Island, the landscape is wholly different, though fully as exotic. Here massive rock escarpments rise sharply from thick woodland. With Bob McCracken, son of Guemes Island sculptor Philip McCracken, I drove there to visit Morris Graves's lofty Zen retreat, a spot Bob has known since boyhood. No one occupies the site today. On the outer walls of Graves's weathered cabin, traces of black and Chinese red paint still lingered; as Bob pointed out, the fading became them, as moss becomes antique walls, or dismemberment certain Greek statues. Behind the house, in the disheveled shadow of a garden, were shapely boulders chosen with a Japanese eye and placed with Japanese care. On every side, Graves's joyous young pines reached for the sky.

Most impressive was the physical site itself. The cabin stood on the brow of a precipice that fell sheer for hundreds of feet to a grassy glen. From beneath our feet rose

Richard Daugherty

Washington's archeological history is surprisingly rich, as geological conditions have often preserved material from far back in time. The man chiefly responsible for such digs, and the protection of key sites, has been Richard D. Daugherty, an archeologist at Washington State University.

From "Richard Daugherty: He's Dug Up Our Past," by Ruth Kirk, The Seattle Times, *March 23, 1980. Copyright © 1980 Ruth Kirk. Reprinted by permission.*

Prof. Richard D. Daugherty, archeologist at Washington State University, probably has done more than any other person to put this state's cultural past on the map of public awareness.

His scholarly contributions form a major base on which today's knowledge of ancient Northwesterners has been built. Also he has shown many how archeologists go about piecing together an understanding of the past.

Marmes Man, the 10,000-year-old human skeletal material from near the mouth of the Palouse River, came from a Daugherty "dig." Its discovery in 1968 disrupted a professional meeting in Tokyo, prompting a rewrite of a scientific paper on man in the New World. Ozette, an ancient Makah Indian village on the Olympic Peninsula and another Daugherty dig, also has drawn world attention. . . . It was spring, 1970, that he began the Ozette dig, which he directs on the outer coast of the Olympic Peninsula. . . . Archeologists have recovered more than 50,000 artifacts at Ozette, including wood and fiber from houses struck by a mudslide 400 years ago.

The houses—fairly complete, though flattened and buried—are an architectural treasure. They are the Northwest's oldest remaining wooden houses.

Inside are whalers' harpoons and babies' cradle baskets, woodworkers' tools and weavers' looms, decorative combs and children's toys. Such material ordinarily quickly decays, but at Ozette it has stayed constantly wet and sealed from air by the overlying clay. Consequently it has survived. . . .

Richard Daugherty is a field archeologist, a professor and an instigator of state and national programs for the protection and understanding of our human past.

The aspects intermingle. He has made archeological expeditions to Northern British Columbia's Peace River, Egypt, Sudan, Spain, and France. . . .

The Peace River work was in the 1950s and most then thought that man had migrated south from the Arctic by funneling through major passes, which were therefore the places to look for early campsites. "We didn't find much because the premise was wrong. Small nomadic bands aren't restricted that way. They move all over the landscape.

"My interest came from discoveries at Lind Coulee, in Central Washington. At the time, most archeologists thought people had reached the Northwest only about 2,500 years ago. But at Lind Coulee I found fossil animal bones and chips of flint, obviously the work of man, lying beneath volcanic ash which we supposed was from Crater Lake, Oregon. The flint's stratigraphic position prompted a 'guestimate' that man had been present 8,000 or 9,000 years ago, and carbon-14 dating bore me out. It was the first real indication of human antiquity in the Pacific Northwest." . . .

From time immemorial people have concentrated along waterways and consequently basins now flooded by reservoirs have held a detailed archeological record of our past.

In 1946 Daugherty joined the salvage work at McNary Reservoir. Two summers later he began directing summer excavation at a series of Columbia and Snake River archeological sites. That pattern continued 20 years, culminating at Marmes Rock Shelter, which produced an exceptional record of human occupation spanning 10,000 years.

One early undertaking stood out from the overall pattern. In the fall of 1947, Daugherty returned to his native west side of the state and hiked as much of the coast as time permitted, checking for archeological sites. He found 50, Ozette included. His impression? "Ozette had the biggest and highest potential on the whole coast—and the worst rain."

Since then the Ozette site has won fame. For Daugherty one of the satisfactions is having pioneered a broadly based approach.

"You need to know about environment in order to understand how people lived," he points out. "What climate did they contend with and what resources could they draw on? As far back as the Lind Coulee work, in the 1950s, I joined forces with geologists. They kept me from making stupid mistakes.

"At Ozette a geologist and a zoologist were part of the first field team and we had a plant ecologist, a soils specialist, a marine invertebrate expert, and so on as consultants. That's one of archeology's fascinations; it draws from a whole spectrum of expertise. Best of all, at this site we've worked with Makah Indian elders and students, descendants of Ozette's original inhabitants."

Richard Daugherty

tops of great trees. Hunting hawks dipped and wheeled below. Bob confided that down in the valleys, hallucinogenic mushrooms were reputed to raise their tiny heads. What use would one have for them here? Almost by itself, such a landscape could bring on dreams and visions. With its pines and its cliffs, it seemed another mirage of old Asia, a realization of some painting by a fifteenth-century Chinese master. All it lacked was the presence of a venerable sage, dwarfed by his surroundings, standing quietly with his staff near the summit of the rock.

Our sage was back in La Conner, sitting in his garden, drinking French wine. Late in the afternoon, I returned there, seeking to learn more about his painting. The evolution of his style can be traced in *Guy Anderson,* a monograph by Bruce Guenther published in 1986 by the Francine Seders Gallery, Anderson's Seattle dealer, in conjunction with the University of Washington Press. His earliest pictures were recognizable scenes from the world about him, still lifes or regional landscapes, stylish and well composed, but lacking marked individuality. Later works displayed the influence of his peers; for instance, *Sharp Sea* (1943), with its angry, rolling waves, looks very much like Tobey's *Modal Tide.* As the years passed, Anderson tended increasingly to strike out independently. His paintings of the last three decades have been indisputably his own.

"I never paint with the idea of selling or having things in a gallery or show," he told me. "I think I paint only for myself. I'm pleased if someone comes along and happens to like what I've done."

Today, most of his works are statements on the human condition, vehicles for the expression of his ideas and philosophy. In many, like *The Birth of Prometheus* (1984–1985), a realistically drawn human figure or torso, often elongated like an El Greco, broods over enigmatic forms and shapes, which serve as visual metaphors for the artist's deeper meanings. In others, like *Northern Birth* (1967), a haunting study in purplish black and a decomposed white like old snow, no human figure appears. The forms and shapes themselves carry the painting's entire message.

Though they sometimes seem wholly nonobjective, the origin of these mysterious images is quite often to be found in the external world, in objects that have drawn Anderson's eye because of their color or unusual configuration. In her *Life* article, Dorothy Seiberling noted that the youthful Anderson collected beach driftwood, and that the gray, weathered tones and floating lines of these pieces appeared everywhere in his work. While we talked, a pressed leaf fell from one of his books; he had found it under a willow across the street, where it had been flattened by a passing car. Its somber, purple-black hue was remarkably close to the color he used in paintings like *Northern Birth.*

Northwest Coast native art has also been a rich source for him. In *Primitive Forms II* (1962), which Dr. Fuller bought for the Seattle Art Museum, Anderson created what might seem to a layman almost a copy of a Haida or Tlingit tribal design. In fact, it's no more than an impression of such a design, like Chinese calligraphy reproduced by someone who has chosen to ignore the rigid rules laid down for drawing it. But the traditional Northwest Coast motifs, such as the enclosed oval representing the eye, are utilized both for their compositional effect and to recall Northwest Coast Indians to the viewer. Anderson's 1959 painting *Deception Pass through Indian Country* is a kind of abstract landscape, in which a formalized sea, surging with rhythmic energy, beats against a formalized shore where obscure patterns hint at totemic myths and legends. The effect of these allusions is to deepen the work's significance, giving it a historical dimension no realistic landscape could possess.

It is the symbolic vocabulary Anderson has developed from such sources that often enables him to paint the unpaintable, as he has done in *Father and Son* (1974), in which the infant son, imprisoned in a bubble of light, is hopelessly separated from his parent by an impassable void of turgid black. In *The Birth of Prometheus,* the ultimate mystery of birth is connoted by a great, twisted chain, an umbilical cord leading from the floating figure at the top to a great white wheel which here seems to stand for the cosmos. Anderson's use of a giant wheel or circle as a dominant image in many of his works seems to derive in part from Byzantine icons, but in his paintings, such wheels imply many things—the sun, the womb, a mandala, a seed.

Sometimes his titles give a clue to his precise intention. A reference to Galileo explains the round forms of planets and moons as seen through a telescope. *Laocoon* (1978) is one of many titles that refer directly to classic myths, Laocoon having been the priest who warned the besieged citizens of Troy not to accept the huge wooden horse, secretly crammed with warriors, that the Greeks had left outside their city as a gift. For his pains, Laocoon and his sons were attacked and killed by huge serpents, sent from the sea by an angry god. Anderson's abstract rendering of this tale is full of violence. With whipping, snakelike forms, he suggests what he has called "the great dragon forces of nature," powers he sees as constantly surrounding and threatening humans in a mysterious and hostile universe. His colors can be symbolic too. *Laocoon* contains a looping strand of geranium red. Anderson rarely uses bright colors, and I liked this red when I first saw it in his work, believing that it supplied a welcome note of cheerfulness. I later learned that I had misunderstood. Red in his paintings is nearly always used to imply violence—blood, or the trauma of birth and death.

It isn't necessary, of course, to grasp the precise meanings of Anderson's symbols in order to appreciate his work. Thus, to take one of Anderson's strongest and most beautiful paintings, *Dream of the Language Wheel* (1962), one doesn't need to know that the luminous white circle in that painting was not inspired by the cosmos, nor by the sun, but by giant, carved Mayan stones. With its spinning rhythms, its mysterious fish and bird forms, and its fascinating gradations of white tones, it reaches deep into the subconscious, to the birthplace of dreams, and transmits its message through intuition rather than through reason.

On my final visit to Bog Tule, I had looked forward to inspecting Anderson's studio, but was distracted in his garden by the easy flow of his conversation. We talked of his favorite writer, the poet and Nobel laureate Saint-John Perse, and of his favorite composer, Stravinsky (he has titled a recent painting *The Rite of Spring*). A notable raconteur, long familiar with the Seattle art scene, Anderson on this day had plenty of stories to tell.

He spoke of how Mark Tobey used to ride the bus to Tacoma to teach an art class there, coming home with just forty dollars for an afternoon's work. He told me how it came about that Tobey happened to hold his first nationally significant art show at the California Palace of the Legion of Honor Museum in San Francisco. It happened in 1951, well after Graves had been widely recognized, and it was Seattle's Elizabeth Bayley Willis, acting curator there, who talked the Californians into it. This turned out to be the show that launched Tobey on his international career, and Anderson feels that Betty Willis has never been given enough credit.

Always a sharp-eyed observer, Anderson recalled homely vignettes about even such an austere personality as Dr. Fuller. Shortly after Fuller and his mother had donated the Volunteer Park museum to the city, Anderson recalls being in the building when Fuller was down in its vaults inspecting a box of treasures. When he found something he liked, it was his habit to hum, and he was humming merrily away, when his imperious mother hove into view. "Dick!" she said, "stop that humming! It's dreadful!" Anderson said, laughing, "He just went on."

I asked to see his studio, which occupies the upper floor of his small, contemporary house. To reach it, we climbed an outside staircase, adjoining one of the delta's natural rock walls that was covered with a Northwest tangle of Himalayan blackberries. Though his studio was a disorderly chaos, it was a species of chaos that could only have been created by an intellectual. Paintbrushes were soaking on the floor, which was smeared all over with eccentric splashes of color. ("The closest thing you have to Tobey in your work is your floor," a critic observed.) One wall was lined with books, displaying his eclectic and individual taste—Hemingway, Colette, Pasternak, E.M. Forster, Paul Theroux, Alberto Moravia, Dylan Thomas. Other walls were covered with pictures and clippings, including a Picasso clown, a Ghirlandajo grandfather, and a news photo of a baseball player in the midst of an elegant pratfall. I inquired about that. What had intrigued Anderson was the unusual posture of the athlete, with his legs stretched forward, and one arm curved over his head: another source for Anderson's studies of people.

On the floor, on a large piece of reinforced paper about seven-and-one-half feet square, lay the beginnings of a work in progress. It was one of a series of paintings showing a group of barely defined human figures hurtling earthward through space, victims, perhaps, of an

No veil of comforting sentimentality softens his view of the world.... The heroes of his pantheon are nearly all tragic, doomed figures.

356

Delta country; the soul of
La Conner; La Conner and
Harry Powell's bridge
across the slough

Photographs by Kim Zumwalt

357

air disaster. There were a man and a woman locked in an embrace, a mother and child, and a mutilated torso, like some fragment of statuary dredged from the Aegean. A sky full of bodies. Anderson seems to view our twentieth-century invasion of the air as an outright challenge to the great dragon forces, and relates it to the fable of Icarus, who flew toward the sun on manufactured wings, fell into the sea, and was drowned. Similarly, one of the completed works in this series, visually among the handsomest, has been called by this lifelong pacifist *Persian Gulf.* Though little more than a sketch, the embryonic painting, with its intimations of death in the air, was already deeply disturbing. Something in such paintings seems almost to belie Anderson's Gallic heritage, for the only Frenchman they bring to mind is Pascal ("The eternal silence of these infinite spaces fills me with dread"). Whether his Anderson forebears were truly British, or, as seems likely, offspring of Viking invaders, much of his work links him to that long line of dour Norse thinkers, Ibsen, Munch, Strindberg, and Ingmar Bergman.

Here lies one answer to a question that has puzzled many of Anderson's thoughtful critics: Why is he not better known? Since the appearance of the *Life* article, he has had little notice in the national press. One reason is surely his deliberate reclusiveness, the way he has shut himself away from art centers while in his work stubbornly pursuing his own private path. But another explanation may be the profound gravity of his vision. He makes little effort to produce art of immediate appeal. No veil of comforting sentimentality softens his view of the world. His paintings will never be called "decorative," and Tom Robbins's grim word "chthonian" exactly fits many of them. The heroes of his pantheon are nearly all tragic, doomed figures: Sisyphus, Laocoon, Prometheus, Icarus. One of his earliest master-pieces, *Through Light, Through Water* (1940), was admired by Mark Tobey for its color, which, he told Anderson, was the most beautiful he had seen in any painting. But behind its subtle gradations of red, behind the seductive rhythms of its cubist construction, this lovely painting portrays a drowning man.

If more of the lightness and humor that graces Anderson's social conversation or some of the *joie de vivre* that seems to invigorate his personal life had found their way into his art, it might well have drawn a larger audience.

That one day Anderson's paintings will nevertheless find such an audience seems hard to doubt. Perhaps, as with Tobey, eventual recognition will come via Europe. In 1987, John-Franklin Koenig, a Seattle painter who has lived many years in France, curated for five French museums (Carcassonne, Perpignan, Pau, Albi, and Dunkerque) a show he called "Seattle Style." Included were four characteristic Anderson works, three of them male figures floating over symbolic forms, one of them another version of the Prometheus myth. In the accompanying brochure, which was reprinted in the French magazine *Cimaise,* Daniel Abadie, a curator of the Pompidou Center in Paris, echoed a number of Pacific Northwest critics when he wrote, "The only question left unanswered is why

Anderson's work is so little known in the United States. But, after all, it is perhaps reassuring to know that there are still some great painters to be discovered."

At least, it appears that Anderson is not destined to be a prophet unhonored in his own community. Art Hupy's Valley Museum of Northwest Art, which today occupies the second story of the restored Gaches Mansion just off La Conner's main street, features artists Hupy considers to be part of the classic Northwest tradition. Today it is very small, with limited exhibition space and a one-room gallery where works by artists like Tobey, Helmi Juvonen, and Richard Gilkey are for sale. But it is headed for a major expansion. Seattle architect Roland Terry has offered to design a new museum building, which will one day rise on the edge of the Skagit flats, hard by the bogs and the tules, at a precise site yet to be determined. Most of the Skagit artists will be represented there, Anderson among them. To see his paintings displayed in the distinctive environment to which they owe so much should be as rewarding as watching the Swinomish dance out the night in their firelit longhouse.

As we climbed down the steep stairs from Anderson's studio, I wondered how much longer this sturdy octogenarian, who has traveled so far on Eustace Zeigler's long and difficult path, could continue turning out such formidable work. He seemed no more threatened by time than if he were fifty, explaining that since he had been able to afford giving up time-consuming teaching, painting had been easier. "You have to get enough sleep and to eat properly," he said. "And when you paint on the floor, you have to keep active. I don't paint every day. I only paint when I have enough energy.

"I'll paint until dark tonight." ◼

Children at Chinese school:
memorization, recitation, and
internalization

THE THREE KINGDOMS

RUBY CHOW (1921–)

FRANK CHIN

To understand Chinatown, the Wah Mee killers, the tongs, associations, and Ruby Chow, put away your Aristotelian unities, your Bible and simplistic universals, and step into my civilization. I'm so fluent in your culture, people there declare me positively assimilated. Eat your food. Love your women. Your language is mine down to the raunch, for I know where it comes from. I went to school with your kids and know the lullabies you sang to them, the stories you told, and the Plato, the Homer, the Bible, the Shakespeare you wrap your language and literature in like fish in old newspapers. But you don't know our lullabies and heroic tales, the myth and drama that defines our sense of individuality and relation to the authority of the state. And you should know, you have to know if you're going to understand Chinatown, tell the difference between the sweet 'n' sour hoochie koochie, quality suey, and real food. To appreciate the differences between the players, you have to know how Chinatown plays. You should know our life is war.

Inside any given tong in Seattle's Chinatown are members of three to four generations. They have been established here for over one hundred years. The old men of today's tongs have skied, eaten fresh salmon steamed in black beans, bought their sons a boat for college graduation, investment property for the family legacy, and have drenched themselves in life insurance. The tongs are not what they used to be. They are not the flophouse, the life insurance, the family bank, post office, and mortician to brothers of the alliance any more. They have gone from warring on the streets for turf, to warring in the courts for corporate control and equal rights. They are no longer violent Mafiosi with blood oaths. They do not have to be. And they cannot be. Not in Seattle. Why? Because there's no biz buzzing in Chinatown. Restaurants are closing early for lack of customers.

As long as Chinatown was maintained by discriminatory laws as a preserve for the yellow, the tongs had a pie to divide and fight over: three hundred fifty whorehouses, hundreds of gambling shops, and protection for the legit business operating on their Chinatown turf filled the Chinatown pie. Not that many people live in Chinatown now. Only the old, the multiracial weary, cast-off, and worn-out people, and white winos with pensions. The whores all saved their money and bought property in better neighborhoods

Ruby began her relentless progress into white consciousness, toward local legend and mystery, from the bar in the Seattle restaurant she started—the Hong Kong.

and moved out for good. There has been nothing to fight over or divide for years, for decades. Even Ruby Chow, the driving force of Seattle's Chinese, has given up the dream of Chinatown Seattle rivaling the hustling fantasy shop of Chinatown San Francisco.

The Bing Kung Tong (Chinese Free Masons) and the Hop Sing Tong, the two largest and most powerful tongs in Chinatown, are all very old men and very young men. The old Wah Kiew, the idealistic "overseas Chinese" generation of the twenties and thirties, are the last of the bachelor society, created by discriminatory laws against the entry of women and against miscegenation. Forty years separate these old men of the tongs from the oldest of the young men joining for a place to hang out. Willie Mak and Benjamin Ng, two young men in their early 20s, were new members of the Hop Sing Tong. Mak had been in the Hop Sing for two weeks before the Wah Mee Club massacre of February,1983.

In Seattle the tongs, family associations, and district associations are dying, fading. They are mostly just names over doorways and a couple of rented rooms. The Hop Sing Tong and Bing Kung Tong of Seattle stopped growing in the 1940s and gathered dust, while elsewhere they used their kids' college educations to buy, own, and manage huge chunks of money-bearing real estate. Elsewhere the Chinatown populations swelled, and immigrants and American-born swarmed the streets and crowded by the thousands into little cluttered rooms. In Seattle the population dropped and dropped.

In all the Seattle tongs the second and third and fourth generation, middle-aged, thirty-to-sixty-year-old Chinese-Americans are missing. The American-born, English-speaking, college-educated, and talented, along with Ruby Chow, became a part of the Chinatown establishment, the Chong Wah. They rose not through the traditional route of the tongs, family associations, and district associations that sat on the Chong Wah board; the "young turks" of the late 1950s created a group of such influence in Chinatown that they had to sit on the board of the Chong Wah.

The old stranded generation of the last Wah Kiew "overseas Chinese" has never recovered from the shock of Ruby Chow, who, through her Chinese Community Service Organization (CCSO), brought American-born, English-speaking, non-Cantonese, northern Chinese, outsiders, and *women* onto the Chong Wah board. To this day, the only Chong Wah in the world where women sit down with the men to make decisions about the Chinese community is in Seattle.

The very old of the tongs look on the very young men joining, looking for friends of a common language and need, a place to hang out and show off their clothes and styled hair, and news about jobs in interesting American places, as scum, lazy bums good only for occasional old-time roughstuff. The old men of the tongs and the young do not know each other. The old have not been Chinese Chinese for forty to sixty years. The rhetorical wonders of Chiang Kai-Shek's Wah Kiew, making China great from international China-towns, have all died and died again years ago, as the China that conferred the identity fell and another China rose. Very Confucian. Very Mandate of Heaven. Very sad, these old Wah Kiew, fossilized in their legendary loyalty to what is no more.

The China they came from and mourn is ancient history to the boys from Hong Kong, who obviously did not come to Seattle to ski. Once here, they became the near side of the forty-year generation gap in the tongs. The old Wah Kiew of the two top tongs in town, the Bing Kung Tong and the Hop Sing Tong, want the young to join their tongs, for their prestige and vague power is now based on numbers of members, nothing more. In a Chinatown where once-mighty family associations—which gambled, whored, and chased opera women across the stage—are reduced to three old men and a black-and-white TV turned up loud, survival into the foreseeable is a military objective.

Remember those days the white racists were what's happening out west? Old West was getting dim. White doctors in those days didn't jep their rep by bringing Chinese babies out of Chinese wombs into Seattle's fresh air. Chances are, Mar Seung Gum was born slipping into the hands of a Chinese midwife on the San Juan Fish Company dock in Seattle. The boss of the docks for a father, and the one twin saved from a flood for a mom. Her father, Jim Sing Mar, an immigrant from the Kwangtung village of Hoi Yuen, ran the San Juan Fishing and Canning Dock. Pio di Cano, a Filipino who was Jim's bodyguard and a loyal friend, was given the docks when Jim retired. "And that," Ruby Chow says, "was how the docks became Filipino!" How does she know this story? Ruby Chow is Mar Seung Gum.

The well-gardened and cultivated creation of hair that rises and rises in the shape of a huge popover over her head, is the largest French roll ever to survive wind and snow, rain and the rest of the weather in Seattle. The hair is the most elegant, the most satisfying cliché Oriental Terry 'n' the Pirates' Dragon Lady about her. The rest of her, even stuffed inside a *cheongsam,* doesn't bring Suzi Wong to mind or satisfy your need for a Suzi Wong when you sit down in a Chinatown bar to get away from it all. That is where Ruby began her relentless progress into white consciousness, toward local legend and mystery, from the bar in the Seattle restaurant she started—the Hong Kong. Ruby Chow has come a long way.

There are at least two Ruby Chows. The Ruby Chow known through the metropolitan press, radio, television, her restaurant, and her hotseat on the King County Council. And the Ruby Chow the Chinese-Americans of Seattle know and take personally. The Ruby Chow whites know is the product of men who drank together in the bar of the Hong Kong restaurant, back in the early 1950s when television was just beginning to fence off the free air. It all came out at the Hong Kong. Ruby Chow kept their secrets, remembered their birthdays, never said a bad word about Chinatown or the Chinese, and never asked for a pay-back.

What was it about her that made her the perfect waitress and barmaid? Not her looks.

Wing Luke

Perhaps in atonement for Seattle's sorry record of racial intolerance toward the Chinese, the city became one of the first to allow Chinese-Americans to rise politically. Wing Luke, elected to the Seattle City Council in 1960, led the way, not only for Asian-Americans but in many of the issues he pioneered. Luke was killed in a plane crash in 1965, but the urban agenda was altered for many years afterward by his bold advocacy and winning manner.

From "The Many Crusades of Wing Luke," by Junius Rochester, Seattle Weekly, *January 28, 1987. Copyright © Junius Rochester. Reprinted by permission.*

Most of the West Coast Chinese came from the densely populated, tropical Kwangtung province. Known as the Chinese "Siberia" because emperors used to exile their enemies to Kwangtung, the province consists of delta paddies and the great city of Canton nestled in the heart of China's typhoon zone. Wing Chong Luke was born in Kwangtung province on February 25, 1925, the year of the ox. Neighbors and friends of Luke's family had been emigrating to America for years. Lung Sing Luke, Wing's father, was sent back from America to China in order to marry. He worked as a farmer in an impoverished region and then returned to America, leaving a wife and tiny son behind.

The 1920s in Seattle were relatively serene. Anti-Chinese sentiments had abated. Americans were celebrating the victory of World War I, booze was at hand (despite Prohibition), and Warren G. Harding and Calvin Coolidge benignly presided over tolerant, lazy national administrations. It was the calm before another tempest.

After struggling with the immigration authorities, Wing Luke's father managed to bring his wife, Lew Fung Hai, and son to Seattle. Luke's first memories were of crowded, simple quarters behind the family laundry business in the University District. It proved difficult for an immigrant Chinese family to live so far from the ethnic and cultural support of Seattle's Chinatown. Then, in the first grade, Luke discovered another disadvantage: he spoke no English. Seattle's University District, feeder area to an affluent and socially prominent Roosevelt High School, had seen few minority families. In later years, Luke recalled that the first English words he learned were "yes," "no," and "he hit me first."

Luke learned to speak English in one year, adapted to his new life, became fiercely patriotic (including, he later recalled, standing at attention in a movie theater while the national anthem played from the soundtrack), and struck a bargain with two cultures. His ethnic heritage remained a proud possession, while he enthusiastically saluted the traditions and customs of others. That "cultural pluralism" extended to amazing lengths. He sang Irish ballads with an ersatz brogue on St. Patrick's Day. He crooned Norway's national anthem in Norwegian (for the king of Norway). In school he studied Spanish, and was known to throw around a few Swedish phrases. His friends applauded the occasion (at a fundraiser) when he pranced across the Seattle Opera

House stage in Scottish kilt—playing bagpipes.

Marshall Junior High and Roosevelt High School students now came to appreciate Luke's serious efforts as a scholar and colleague. He distinguished himself as a cartoonist, even drawing his own comic books for a gaggle of eager pals. At Marshall he was elected Boys' Club president; his Roosevelt classmates elected him student body president and he served as president of the Seattle Inter-High Student Council. The immigrant from Kwangtung was already a leader among leaders.

Before his graduation, World War II broke out. Luke joined the Army, served overseas in the Philippines and Korea, and returned home wearing a Bronze Star. To some Americans during World War II, all Asians were suspect, and so, while Sergeant Wing Luke was rescuing fellow passengers from his torpedoed ship, his parents, neither of whom spoke much English, and his five US-born brothers and sisters were sporadic victims of hometown taunts and abuse. After a series of bottle-throwing incidents and name-calling, the landlady tripled the Lukes' rent, explaining, "We are at war with those people—you can't tell them apart." Wing Luke returned home on emergency leave to relocate and calm his family.

Following the war, Luke, now 21

Wing Luke

years old, became an American citizen. (His mother took US citizenship when Luke ran for public office [in 1960] so she could cast her first vote for her son.) After a brief spell at American University, Washington DC, where he got a close look at the stirrings and machinery of government, he took a BA (1950), a Master's in political science, and a law degree (1954) at the University of Washington. He was still a popular fellow, getting elected president of his sophomore class at the UW, and scribbling and drawing cartoons for the UW *Daily* and *Columns*. . . .

Luke served for five years as Washington State assistant attorney general, most of that time as chief of the civil rights and real estate divisions. He remembered when his parents had been forced to move from the University District to James and Terry when their rent was trebled, and threats against his family and other minorities were a way of life. Open housing soon became a Wing Luke crusade.

Inner-city living was to Wing Luke an ideal, not a punishment. He advocated historic preservation, kite festivals, abolishing parking meters, fishing programs for city residents, bilingual international street signs, pea patches, communal living schemes, and a healthy mix of young and old residents. Every child, he believed, should have, outside his or her family, a "grandparent." If Wing's political creed could be summarized, it might be to preserve humanism in the face of a fast-paced technological age.

Wing liked to characterize himself as "the oldest living member of the Young Democrats." He served as president of the UW and King County YDs, finding the groups a greenhouse for the germination of his dreams for Seattle. "Vote for Wing Luke" messages were put in Chinese fortune cookies when he campaigned as a delegate to a YD convention. Environmentalism, a little-known word then, was nurtured by Luke in the YDs. His City Council race was largely planned by such young political colleagues, who pioneered the first Seattle use of "coffee klatches" and political posters on buses.

Despite an anonymous smear campaign with racial overtones, Luke became in 1960 the first person of Chinese ancestry to win political office on the West Coast. Immediately after his election, he was helping his family stock the shelves in their grocery on First Hill.

If I were to cast the part of even a young Ruby Chow for the movie about her, I would pay Edward G. Robinson anything and put him in a wig. He wouldn't even have to change the way he walked or talked. There is a lot of Ma Barker about Ruby Chow. She commands. With the death of her mother, Ruby Chow became the head of ten children, and no one in her family forgets it for an instant.

The Ruby Chow Chinatown knows is internationally famous among Chinese. Among Chinese-Americans in San Francisco, Los Angeles, New York, Honolulu, Chinese from Hong Kong and Taiwan, Ruby Chow and her husband Ping are Seattle tourist attractions. She made it from the bottom, from the lowest, to become first woman in Chinatown politics, then led the Chinese community to discover itself as a political power in Seattle.

A waitress, a barmaid, a divorcée, she remarried Ping, a *hay bon low,* a Cantonese opera man (opera people were lowlife in the eyes of the self-styled merchant-class Wah Kiew). Seattle's Chinatown establishment of the 1950s ridiculed her and wished her ill when she opened her restaurant on the hill, the first Chinese restaurant outside of China-town in Seattle. It was on Broadway on a corner in a largely black neighborhood, lying in wait full of fantasy and opera for white customers hungry for Chinese. Ruby Chow's res-taurant was a hit. The Seattle who's-who discovered it and brought their in-laws.

Ping Chow, the head cook at Ruby Chow's, is good home cooking and not a great cook. But he is fast. Cooking for Ping Chow is a study in form, speed, accuracy. How fast can he get it right? Very fast. What he learns about cooking form seeps into his understand-ing of the forms of Cantonese opera. In the world of Cantonese opera, Ping Chow com-mands respect and appreciation. As a performer, as an example of the ethical and loyal art-ist, an entrepreneur, a connoisseur, an elder of the art—Ping Chow is a power. Bruce Lee did not just come to Seattle: he was sent to Ping Chow's care in 1959.

The loyalty of opera people to one another—people of different origins, births, and classes, dedicated to an art—is legendary in Cantonese culture. It is modeled on the three brothers of the "oath of the peach garden" forming a brotherhood to save China, in the Three Kingdoms period of the Latter Han Dynasty (206 B.C. to 221 A.D.). *The Three King-doms* is the most popular Chinese opera of all time, and its hero, Kwan Kung, is the most popular hero. Kwan Kung is also the patron protector of theater and opera. There are folk tales of actors who wear the mask of Kwan Kung on stage, having all the power of Kwan Kung. There are tales of opera companies invited to perform *The Three Kingdoms* at strange hours and places, discovering they have been lured into a magic spell as soon as Kwan Kung appears on stage. For he destroys all magic. Witches fall out of the sky, ghosts disappear, and royal courts turn back into the cemeteries they always were, as soon as the actor playing Kwan Kung steps on stage. Kwan Kung is the force of reality.

Ruby Chow, like many Chinatown-born who grow up speaking Cantonese, learn

English in public schools, and have no more than a high-school education, if that, does not speak English so much as she speaks English as if it were Cantonese. The Chinese Cantonese speak is an all-present-tense language. It is also very physical. Gestures of the head and chin—pointing to humiliate, snorting to ridicule—ride the flexing tones that make the difference between *gow see,* meaning "the past" or "dogshit" or "nine four." The language she spoke in the family is the language of the village haggler all small-town Cantonese speak.

In the bar at the Hong Kong, Ruby was one of the boys because she was entirely street in her talk, down and dirty and cussed them out with an authentic understanding of the art's potential. Ruby Chow speaks the same language in the bar, in the home, in the chambers of Chiang Kai-Shek, the sanctums of Warren Magnuson, and at lunch with Dorothy Bullitt. The KING-TV Baroness of Seattle lunches with what refuses to be but is passed off for the Dragon Lady of Seattle, at the same table in high society.

Ruby Chow is remarkable for moving in, being accepted among, and leading a group of Chinese-Americans more educated, more literate, and better-spoken than she. She has always moved with eye-popping, blunt-edged ease through all kinds of social situations, because she is Ruby Chow and for no other reason. Newspapers regularly front-paged snaps of dignitaries, governors, mayors, and consul generals walking up the steps toward the moon-gate entrance of Ruby Chow's restaurant. They had the look of paying a state visit, not just going out to dinner with the wife. Her restaurant succeeded, in terms of customers and money, without gambling in the back room, greasing palms, or getting on her knees, back in the days when things like that happened. Ruby Chow's made it on guts, not manners or looks, bribery or blackmail. She was always the first.

In *The Three Kingdoms*, Ping Chow is famous for his playing of the first of the three brothers of the oath of the peach garden. Low Bay, the first brother, is the outlawed pretender to the throne of the Han, a royal-blooded, high-educated, good-looking, fair-skinned High Confucian young man, born and bred to rule by his good example, not by laws and crooked men to administer to them. The second brother, Kwan Kung, is the red-faced fugitive who burst out of the room his parents had locked him in for punishment, and on his way out of town took pity on a girl being forced by her father into marriage with a greedy and corrupt bureaucrat and, unlike St. George, after killing the dragon, keeps his hands off the girl, wishes her luck with her freedom, and runs off to save China. Kwan Kung is tall, his face constantly flushed with terrible anger and rage, his rules of personal conduct and honor absolute. Of the three brothers, he is the most like the Cantonese of southern China, the most like the people who settled here. The third brother is described in the tales as having the face of a leopard with cat mustache and whiskers. Chang Fay is the least engaging, the most common, perhaps, of the three brothers. He is a man of property and money; in short, a capitalist. It is in Chang Fay's peach garden that the three different

Perhaps politics is too far into the twentieth century for her, or maybe the cloakroom and telephone are where she makes things happen.

368

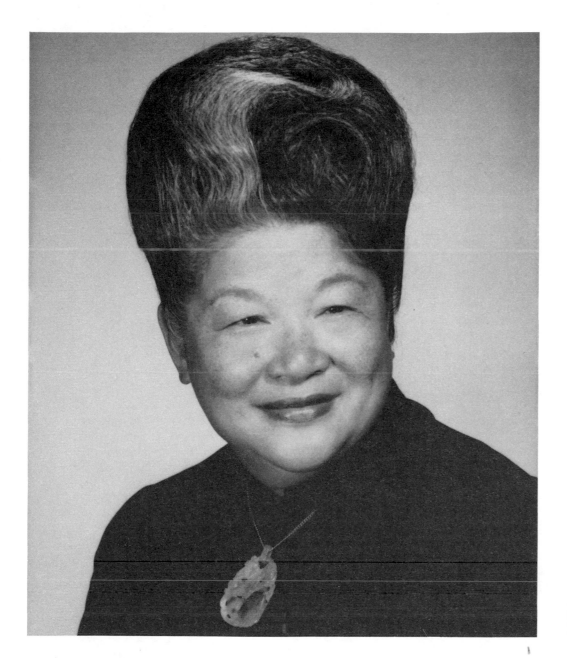

Ruby Chow: never forgiven for busting open the old Chinese male stronghold

Theresa Takayoshi

In fear of West Coast invasion, the war department set the Japanese relocation plan into action immediately after the bombing of Pearl Harbor. In days, all people of Japanese descent were forced to give up their livelihoods and spend the next few years at internment camps throughout the West Coast. Twenty-four-year-old Japanese/Irish Theresa Takayoshi spent eighteen months at Camp Harmony (now the state fairgrounds in Puyallup) with her two young children.

From And Justice for All: An Oral History of the Japanese American Detention Camps, *by John Tateishi. Copyright © 1984 by John Tateishi. Reprinted by permission of Random House, Inc.*

Evacuation took place on May 9, 1942. There was a beauty shop right next to our store, and in front of it, a young fellow bought our car for twenty-five dollars. It was a 1940 Oldsmobile, not very old. Well, he bought it for twenty-five dollars. He then drove us down to Dearborn and Seventh, where there was a big bunch of people and luggage all over. The Army had told us that all we could take was what we could carry. You can't expect a two-year-old and a six-year-old to carry very much, and we followed the rules to the letter. Then I remember getting so angry because some of those people had bicycles and everything, you know, and they had maybe six or eight things and packages. My mother came and my two brothers and some of my friends. I can remember getting on the bus, and at that time they hadn't told us about visitation or anything. I can remember thinking I would never see my mother or my brothers again.

We went to Puyallup, or Camp Harmony, which had once been a fairgrounds. When we got there, I got sick to my stomach. I really did. I don't ever remember anything having an impact on me like that. Because the first thing they did was give all the men these great big sacks, and they told them to go to the back of the camp and fill them full of straw for mattresses. Then we got these canvas army cots; and the boards on the floor had maybe about a half an inch of space between them. So eventually the grass grew up between them. Then there was not a full partition between our compartment and the people next door. So you could hear everything that went on, because I think the roof was sort of pointed and the partition ran straight across. I can still picture it. We had a door on each side, but it was very small quarters, very small.

I was a mother with little kids, but I just didn't know. Because at that time nothing had been announced about relocation centers. And so I kept thinking that this was just a temporary thing, until August. Then they announced that we were going to have to leave. Meanwhile, I had some really bad experiences because of misdiagnoses by some doctors. Once I was quarantined under the grandstand with my youngest child who had a big lump sticking out. The doctor kept saying it was mumps. My older son had had the mumps so I knew what to expect. This thing turned red; mumps don't turn red.

So anyway I was under the grandstand, and it was so damp and I couldn't leave that place and nobody could come and see me. My little boy and I stayed there for six weeks. Finally my cousin who was a registered nurse came to see me. And I told her to go and get Dr. so-and-so and bring him in here and show him this child has not got the mumps. It's something else because it hasn't gone away in six weeks. And so she did, and he came. At first he said, Well, that's Dr. so-and-so's patient; I'm not really supposed to see him. Then he said, "No, he hasn't got the mumps, he's got a swollen lymph gland." He let me out. I got to go back across the street.

Well, that was one incident. And then my older son got very, very ill, and I was afraid to call a doctor because I didn't have any confidence in them anymore. He was vomiting and I didn't know what was the matter with him or what to do. Finally the ambulance came with my cousin and the doctor. My cousin told the doctor, "I know my cousin, she doesn't get excited over nothing." So he came over, and the minute he walked in he started sniffing and said, "Acidosis, this child has food poisoning. I want him to go to Tacoma immediately to a hospital so they can pump his stomach and we can have evidence because there's been a lot of people saying they had food poisoning, but you don't know because of no evidence." So at two o'clock in the morning, this Army car came with a big black man who was supposed to be some kind of security person and my cousin, and we rode to the hospital.

I'll never forget that hospital; I've never had the guts to go back and look it up in Tacoma. We climbed stairs; I'll bet we climbed a hundred stairs to get up to the night door. When we got there, the nurse came rushing out with a wheelchair. She got my son in it and turned around. When I started in after her she said, "You can't come in. You're supposed to be in the prison camp." That's the way she put it.

Then the next morning, back in camp, my husband, who is kind of a hothead anyway, wanted to call the hospital to see how our son was. We weren't sure, at that point, what had happened to him.

Theresa Takayoshi (far right) and family

And the guard, for some reason or other, took it on himself to not allow us to use the phone. So we went and got the Red Cross contacts, Min Masuda and Sam Hokari. They asked to use the phone, and the guard refused to let them use it. So then my husband, Min, and Sam threatened him and told him that if he put down that gun and came inside, they'd show him. In the meantime, the Army guards were right across the street and a lieutenant saw what was going on, and he came over and he asked us what was going on. We told him. He relieved that guard immediately and he handed us the phone.

We were told that our son was going to be released that afternoon. So again, we drove over to Tacoma and this time they did let my husband and me in. And when we did, here's this little six-year-old kid; he was lying on his side and just crying, but silently, you couldn't hear him. And he said, "Oh, take me back to the camp. They were going to let me die last night." I said, "What are you talking about?" And he said, "Well, the nurse said, 'Let this little Jap die, don't even go near him.'" And to this day he remembers that. He's forty-five years old now, but he still remembers that.

men, born on different days, in different years, declare themselves brothers who intend to die on the same day. It was Chang Fay's black bull and white horse they banqueted on, and wines made from grapes grown in Chang Fay's vineyards they drank, to seal and celebrate their oath. It was at a forge in a village on Chang Fay's property that they forged weapons of their own design to identify themselves with, in battle together.

So the first brother was the emperor in exile. The second the god of war, plunder, literature, avengers, gamblers, and actors. And the third was a combination of John D. Rockefeller, Ernest and Julio Gallo, Joseph Krupp, and Rothschild. In this day and age, perhaps, Chang Fay is the most interesting and heroic of the three, not Kwan Kung. But Chang Fay is also known, because of his face and blotchy skin, as "The Ugly One." Ping Chow, because of his fair skin and ageless porcelain good looks, plays the Handsome One, Low Bay, the outlawed emperor, the underground king, the one who commanded and ruled by moral example.

The opera is made of the soul of the Cantonese. It speaks from and to the heart of their deepest matter. The opera people are considered lowlife, with scummy, perverted, pimping, and criminal men and slutty women. The Cantonese opera, more folk, more democratic than the high snoot and soulless Peking opera, used both real men and real women actors and performers. In early Chinese America the lowlife opera people were paid enormous salaries to come to San Francisco and stay in a permanent company, in an opera house of their own. San Francisco had three open houses blowing full time *Three Kingdoms* five to seven hours a night, for one hundred nights, performed from memory of the form, the story improvised to play the crowd of the night. The opera people entered the country at Seattle, performed at a small opera house to appreciative and enthusiastic audiences in the building on Seventh Avenue South that now holds the China Gate restaurant. On their way to San Francisco they fell in love with Seattle.

The opera people, on their way to the bucks in San Francisco, or just come to visit the adventure, invested in Seattle. They left a little money each time they left town. Money that built the building next door to the opera house, with classrooms in the basement and first floor, and a hall with a small stage upstairs, a place for a Chong Wah Wooey Goon to come into being to pull the contending tongs and family and district associations together to make Chinatown self-sufficient, a geographical entity, run without government interference. Elsewhere, in other booming and all-night money-changing Chinatowns, Chong Wah Wooey Goons ensured the wars would go on in privacy, and Chinatown would remain self-sufficient and secure from government or outside obligations, influences, or interference.

The opera people were midwife to Chong Wa Benevolent Association of Seattle. It is a gesture of mythic proportions, worthy of legends. The legends exist, and inform, and

Bob Santos: championing an International District over ethnic separateness

enrich the lore of the Cantonese opera people. It is that lore that makes opera people pleased to open restaurants in all parts of Seattle and await the call of Ping Chow to ride to the opera again. Happy to cook in the kitchen, chopping to the rhythm of battles and entrances of heroes, till the phone rings. It is that lore that made it easy for an opera master performer of Ping Chow's stature to settle down in the shadowy back in the kitchen of Ruby Chow's.

Those forty-seven years of marriage to Ping Chow may not have quite civilized Ruby Chow, but she has become more Chinese, more primitive raw Confucian art of war, more subtle and brilliant. There is no mystery about Ruby Chow and the raw Cantonese of the opera. The sky they live under is the sky Confucius looks into, when he says, "Don't leave the enemy of your father alive under the same sky with you."

Ruby Chow is the ideal of Cantonese earth mother and fighter, in the tradition of the heroic classics and operas. She is to the primal Cantonese, Hong Kong Chinaman sensibility what Grant Wood's *American Gothic*, Betty Furness, Pearl Bailey, and Ma Kettle are to the average American TV. Certain kinds of old-time and streetwise and real Cantonese and Taiwanese naturally gravitate to Ping and Ruby Chow.

In 1957 she became the first woman in the world to sit with the men and make decisions on the governing board of any Chong Wah Wooey Goon. The world headquarters of the Chong Wah, in Taipei, records the history of every Chong Wah, in every Chinatown. In 1975 Ruby Chow became the first woman to achieve the presidency of a Chong Wah, anywhere in the world. And, in no small part, due to her generalship, Chinese America in Seattle maintains its social and cultural integrity, and (when Wing Luke was elected to the Seattle City Council) held the first, and now more elective offices in Seattle and King County than Chinese in any other city in America. Seattle has more Chinese-American city council seats, judgeships, seats in office than San Francisco, Los Angeles, or New York, even with only fourteen-thousand-plus Chinese-Americans in the entire Seattle-Everett area.

Over the years, she has amassed an assortment of enemies and bad-mouths in Chinatown and two generations of Chinese-Americans. Some, like her sister, queen of Chinese frozen food in Seattle, Mary Pang, are close and blood; others are close and not blood, but marriage. It was a hard place to be a child of Ruby Chow's.

I wore my hair in a ponytail when we met. One look at me, though I wore a tie, Ruby Chow said, "What do you think you're doing with that hair? You remind me of my son. He's about your age, and I'm telling him to get a haircut right now, or I'm going to fly down there to San Jose and make him get one." She flew to San Jose. He got a haircut. When I first met him, he had a haircut and I had my ponytail. I could see it in his face. His mother was everywhere in the world there was a Chinese restaurant.

The last suey shop on the edge of the farthest Alaskan town knows Ruby Chow, the way people in the atmosphere of spaghetti westerns know Clint Eastwood is nobody to mess with, without knowing his name or having ever seen him before.

With neither the *Post-Intelligencer* nor *The Seattle Times* endorsing her, Ruby Chow in 1974 became the first Chinese-American to sit on the King County Council. In the next election the papers backed her opponent, Ron Sims, and a Chinatown faction, The Alliance of Chinese Associations, made a show of Chinese being so against Ruby Chow they would back a black man. Ruby Chow squeaked a win.

Her style on the council, in a public show, is not as effective as it is in its natural habitat, the personal face-to-face, the bar, the restaurant, the banquet. Perhaps politics is too far into the twentieth century for her, or maybe the cloakroom and telephone are where she makes things happen. But as a force in the shaping of Chinese-American Seattle, she has been most effective. Showy deeds, like putting up lanterns in Chinatown. Commercial deeds, like reviving the Chinese New Year's celebration in Chinatown. Gender-brokering deeds, like changing the shape of the Chong Wah, by being a woman.

All of Chinatown began fading. By the 1950s the tongs and associations were names over empty rooms.

She has been a first in many places in many ways, breaking Chinese-Americans into politics, women into Chinatown power. There used to be more women like her, low to the ground, stout, and stubborn, who take everything personally. My grandmother. My mother. Six aunts. Like her, but not her. Whatever greatness Chinese-Americans have as a people includes a large measure of Ruby Chow. For all her familiarity, there's never been a Chinaman woman like Ruby Chow. And, man, am I glad she's not my mother.

The ethic of private revenge is the heart of the Confucian Mandate of Heaven. The mandate says power corrupts and the most benevolent and kindly government inevitably betrays the people, and private revenge empowers wronged individuals to band together to overthrow the emperor for unredressed grievances. Kingdoms rise and fall. Nations come and go. No matter when you were born in China or Hong Kong, or how long it was before you came to an America where even the people who look like you are foreign, you are born in war. You will die in war. No one will win the war. The state cannot win the war. The honorable soldier lives forever. All nations and empires need honorable soldiers whose word is good. All arts are martial. All behavior tactical. All relations military. All friendships alliances. All form is strategy. Our life is war. Morals is a martial art. All relationships are martial alliances.

In Chinese America there are two kinds of alliances. Alliances of individuals into gangs, tongs, family associations; and district associations, guilds, and unions. All alliances of individuals are modeled on the alliance of the brothers of the oath of the peach garden that opens *The Three Kingdoms*. "Hubba Bubba Wong," the Younger Bob Wong, and Herbie the Pompadoo each in their own time joined the Hop Sing Tong, because it had a clubhouse, a pool table, a place to hang out and something to do there. After awhile, you join one tong or the other for imagined job opportunities at the restaurants owned by fellow

Nick Gunderson

Hing Hey Park with Bush Hotel in background

tongmen. The Younger Bob Wong joined the Hop Sing Tong because he worked at the Four Seas as a busboy, and hung out after hours with the cooks, who were Hop Sing, and just drifted in, with some vague notion of a good job at some Hop-Sing-owned Chinese food palace in Montana. Hubba Bubba Wong joined the Hop Sing when he took a job as a busboy at Seattle's King Cafe, owned by a Hop Sing. "I didn't know about their *gie siew fie,* the introduction fee. They took back half my first month's paycheck, so I quit." Benjamin Ng, later convicted for the Wah Mee massacre, had been in the Hop Sing Tong a little while. Willie Mak, another one convicted, had joined just two or three weeks before the night of the massacre in February 1983.

The moral influence of all the tongs and family associations is the oath of the peach garden. The central covenant that is the basis of all law in the Bible is the selling out of individual human honor to one nameless, inhuman God. The central covenant that is the basis of all law in *The Three Kingdoms* is the oath taken by three men, from different Chinas, to be loyal to each other and to save China.

For one thousand years Chinese kids grow up memorizing and trading tales of the heroes of *The Three Kingdoms* and sitting through the one hundred nights of the opera. They memorize the oath in the peach garden. Every oath they will give in Chinese, in gangs, in criminal triads, in taking office, in all of Chinese cultures, will echo and claim blood ties to the oath in the peach garden.

The oath of the brothers in the peach garden is the model for all alliances of individuals. The second brother, Kwan Kung, the fugitive, is the model of individuality, the most popular hero in Chinese folklore and opera. You should know Kwan Kung. All the kids do. Watch for him. He is all over Chinatown. Red faced. Eyes that fry. (The convention in Cantonese opera is to play him with squinting, hooded eyes, and open the eyes full and stare, only to kill.) Long black beard. Right side armored like a general. Left side robed like as scholar. Green and gold are his colors. Kwan Kung is the god of war, the god of plunder (military wealth, gambling), the god of literature, patron protector of actors, high executioners, small business. He is the god of loyalty, righteousness, and justice; the embodiment of revenge. The mention of his name dispels all magic. No ghosts or spirits can exist in his presence. He is the Buddha Who Defends the Realm to the Buddhists, and the Emperor of the Eastern Peak to the Taoists, making him the only hero to stand in both the Buddhist and Taoist pantheons.

All the first waves of immigrants from southern China's Kwangtung province who created the Chinatowns and settled in Seattle were soldiers, actors, and the other brothers of Kwan Kung. In a demonstration of loyalty and righteousness of legendary proportions, actors built Fraternity Hall, next door to the opera house in Seattle.

Fraternity Hall is where 108 bandit and rebel chiefs met inside their stronghold on

Mount Leongsahn, deep inside Leongsahn Marsh, and allied their alliances to keep harmony between their bands and armies of honorable fighters, while the armies of the corrupt state massed to destroy them outside. This tale is told in *The Water Margin,* mighty sequel to *The Three Kingdoms.* As alliances of individuals are modeled on the three brothers of the peach garden, so the alliance of the alliances, the Chong Wah Wooey Goon, composed of the heads of the tongs and associations contending for control of turf and certain biz in Chinatown, is modeled on the superalliance of righteous outlaw gangs and rebels who ride through the thirty chapters of *The Water Margin.*

Think of Leongsahn Marsh as Sherwood Forest, and the 108 chiefs as Robin Hood and his Merry Men, for a start. This Robin Hood is not a nobleman, but a model of small-town mediocrity. Soong Gong, the outlaw leader, was a common clerk of a small county located at a busy crossroads. The kind of man Peter Wong, president of the Bing Kung Tong and Wang Family Association, or Bob Santos, a righteous International District visionary, or Ruby Chow could identify with in 1988, as they look about Seattle's Chinatown, Little Manila, and Japantown moving in and out of the name International District.

Soong Gong is nicknamed *Sup Gup Yer,* "The Timely Rain," for he always offers nourishment and a few bucks to needy heroes. He is not a fighter himself, but a groupie, a fan of renowned fighters and has the mind of a great strategist and knows all the history of war. He is somebody like you and me: petty, competent, trapped, and untapped by the corrupt government bureaucracy. He is like all the Hong Kong kids. The little clerk is tricked into marriage, cuckolded, betrayed to enemies, robbed by his wife and mother-in-law, accused of treason and exiled by the corrupt government, assaulted and robbed by corrupt troops, and almost poisoned in prison by corrupt officials before he accepts the bandits' longstanding offer to join them in Leongsahn Marsh and become their leader.

The government becomes more corrupt. More of the honest and honorable are outlawed. The government armies lose their guts and desert, rather than fight the outlaws of Leongsahn Marsh. One year The Timely Rain rides against a town run by a corrupt literary critic who found treason in Soong Gong's poetry. It is the fifteenth day of the first lunar month and the last and gaudiest day of Chinese New Year. The day happy households display plenty of fancy lanterns, like Christmas tree lights. Because of the lantern show, the whole town burns as the outlaws ride away whooping and hollering.

Soong Gong leads the outlaws to subdue the north, then the south for the government, in return for amnesty, honors, and a promise of honest government, which the government will betray. The 108 chiefs include the five Nguyen brothers. All the fighting done, they want no part of China. They were loyal to Soong Gong and righteousness, not to China. They move on south, out of Kwangtung and found Vietnam, where Nguyen is a very common name. *The Water Margin* is to the Vietnamese the epic of their founding. The outlaws of the Cong who set off the Tet Offensive were using *The Water Margin* as a manual of strategy, and rode the same New Year's ride as the 108 chiefs and their armies, out of their stronghold in Leongsahn Marsh.

All of Chinese literature and language, high and low culture, schooled and unschooled immigrants, the founders of the tongs and associations, the founders of the Chong Wah, the hatchet men, the Chinamen on the railroad, the gamblers, dopers, fighters, and writers in Chinatown—all swim in the scenes and strategy of heroes of *The Three Kingdoms* and *The Water Margin*. The nineteenth-century Taiping Rebels, the Boxers, Mao Tse-tung, the writers of Hong Kong chop sockies can't speak or write of life and war without allusion or reference to Kwan Kung, *The Three Kingdoms, The Water Margin,* and the strategy of Sun Tzu's *The Art of War.*

Think of Chinatown as Leongsahn Marsh, the stronghold of the righteous and honorable against a corrupt, hostile state that outlaws and exiles Chinaman people. Think of the presidents of the tongs and associations as the 108 bandits and rebel chiefs. Think of Fraternity Hall as the Chong Wah Wooey Goon. Every Chinatown of any size in the world is modeled on the stronghold in the marsh. Inside there is a war on and power shifting between the tongs and gangs, and a high council, a Chong Wah Wooey Goon holding Chinatown, the stronghold, together against the war of extermination being waged by the Christian missionaries, wild-eyed social Darwinists, racists, and a hostile state.

From Canton, out into the seas of the world, the Cantonese went looking for opportunity and adventure, and for one hundred years, wherever they landed, in Indochina, in Chile, Costa Rica, Cuba, San Francisco, Portland, Seattle, Vancouver, New York, the adventurers from Kwangtung expected a tong, and/or a family, and/or a district association to give them a place to hang out, a quick flop, daily rice, local prestige, and a Chong Wah Wooey Goon to keep harmony inside Chinatown, and the government out.

In 1924 they stopped coming. The last loopholes were closed in the Chinese Exclusion Act of 1882. Chinese women were banned entry into the country. Fewer men. The old began to die without having reproduced. As, in San Francisco, only Christian converts would legally marry, only Christian converts were reproducing. The first generation of Chinese-Americans born of Christian converts debuted in a series of Christian conferences in 1925 with Charlie Chan.

What is now the China Gate was originally built as an opera house. The opera stars liked Seattle so much that in 1928 they contributed the money for a building next door to the opera house to house the Seattle Chong Wah. In the 1930s, the opera house became the Chinese Garden, a Chinatown honky-tonk. Dine and dance in the front. Gambling in the back.

The tongs and associations in Seattle started fading out in the 1940s. All of the Chinatown began fading. By the 1950s the tongs and associations were names over empty rooms.

378

The Chong Wah's only substantial service to the people of Chinatown was their owner-ship of three cemetery plots for indigent Chinese, at Mt. Pleasant, Lake View, and Washelli; and the Chong Wah Chinese language school, on the first floor of the Chong Wah building.

Since the "Young Turks" became a part of Chong Wah, with Ruby Chow, in 1957, the Chong Wah has added English language, naturalization, Mandarin and Cantonese classes for adults, and a senior citizens dinner and entertainment during the Thanksgiving and Christmas holiday season to its services, and bought a school bus and hired a driver to pick up the seventy Chinese-American children about Seattle who spend two hours every school day at the Chong Wah learning Chinese.

Ruby Chow's Chong Wah Chinese girls' drill team was drumming and dinging and marching in parades all over the country and winning prizes. The Young Turks were tak-ing the Chong Wah into Seattle politics with them. Suddenly Chinese-Americans seemed to be making it in American politics. And tons of good publicity were heaped on Seattle's Chinatown and Chinese-American people.

The old Wah Kiew were not impressed with the new bloom come to Chinatown in the late 1950s. The hardline old-timers of the Bing Kung Tong and the Wong and Eng family associations cooled out of the Chong Wah in a huff. In one fell swoop, Ruby Chow and the Young Turks had burst open their stronghold and become a part of the outside, American government.

The Young Turks had created organizations like the Chinese Community Service Organization (CCSO) in Chinatown to reduce the position of the tongs and family associ-ations on the Chong Wah board. The membership of the CCSO was greater than the tongs combined, and their hanging lanterns in Chinatown, their revival of the Chinese Chamber of Commerce and return of a Chinese New Year's celebration to Chinatown demonstrated to all that their influence in Chinatown was suddenly greater than any and all the tongs.

The Young Turks of Seattle's greater Chinatown broke all the rules. Instead of paying for what they wanted under the table, they walked themselves and the Chong Wah through the front door of Seattle politics. Instead of whispering in back rooms and passing black money under the table, Ruby Chow increasingly huffed and puffed and asked the city, "What's the big idea?" At last Chinatown Seattle had discovered the power of speaking English.

The Young Turks played PR with the press. They turned Chinese food and fake and real Chinese culture into political weapons. They raised so much money for Chong Wah community service projects that they had to increase the number of projects. In 1960, they elected a candidate for the city council, an immigrant son of a laundry family, Wing Luke. Ruby Chow, with the grace of Ma Kettle and the persuasive powers of George Patton, asked every Chinese restaurant in Seattle to serve fortune cookies stuffed with slips saying "It's wise to vote for Wing Luke."

It seemed, on one hand, taking unfair advantage of white naïveté. Whites work so hard to believe they have some expertise in real Chinese food. They need to believe they know and understand the food they eat, that they can really tell one pile of suey from another. The restaurants do themselves up gaudy as Hollywood sets and whorehouses to call to whites wanting out of the rat race into timeless mystery, dim lighting, and the flocked wallpaper of safe and sane exotica. A drink. Put a fantasy into your stomach and be secretly Chinese. Whites are so vulnerable in Chinese restaurants. And that's where Ruby Chow hit 'em with her loaded fortune cookies. ◼

MAN IN THE MIDDLE

TOM FOLEY (1929–)

REBECCA BOREN

A veteran congessional aid vividly recalls his first encounter with Spokane's Tom Foley. When the staffer was an infant member of Warren G. Magnuson's congressional nursery, he attended an evening meeting of various representatives. Congressman Foley arrived late, stretched his considerable length along a couch, and, to all appearances, fell fast asleep. He remained dead to the world until the gathering degenerated into pointless squabbling. Then he opened his eyes, stood up, and began to lay out for every member specific reasons, carefully thought out, why each should support the measure being discussed—and how to justify the vote back home. The congressman then resumed his nap.

Nowadays, Tom Foley keeps wide awake and on his feet. The Fifth District congressman is the acknowledged leader and widely admired class act of Washington State's DC delegation, as well as the idol of young Capitol Hill staffers. Foley is the second-ranking Democrat in the United States House of Representatives, an emerging spokesperson for the Democratic party, and a strong favorite one day to become Speaker of the House. But in his home state, Foley is still a sleeping giant who narrowly escaped defeat in the 1980 Republican landslide.

"There's an awful sense of chance in public life," Foley insists. "It's something that plays a much bigger role than anyone realizes. The other side of that is, you have to take advantage of the chances offered." Certainly the fates have favored Foley, beginning with his birth, fifty-nine years ago, to longtime Spokane County judge Ralph Foley. Foley Junior attended Gonzaga University (he is still a Roman Catholic, but pro-abortion) and the University of Washington, and in 1961 took himself and his law degree to a job as counsel to the Senate Interior Committee, then chaired by Henry M. Jackson. By 1964, the young attorney was ready to run for Congress himself.

Sort of. Actually, the ever-cautious Foley planned to wait until 1966, but a casual encounter in the Spokane Club resulted in a little goading from a friend. Foley got mad, quit his job, and made a last-minute dash to Olympia (complete with late departures, flat tires, and empty gas tanks), entering his name in the 1964 lists less than half an hour before filing

Food stamps and Foley hit Washington DC simultaneously, and he quickly adopted the program...as his own.

closed. He then upset twenty-two-year Republican incumbent Walt Horan, with a lot of help from the 1964 Johnson landslide.

Luck continued running Foley's way back in Washington DC. The state's delegation, with Brock Adams, Lloyd Meeds, et al., soon emerged as one of the best and the brightest. Foley himself did well in the seniority and committee-assignment lotteries, drawing a seat on the powerful Agriculture committee—a body whose senior Democratic members seem to have been uniquely doomed to election defeats. Foley's original administrative assistant, Richard Larsen, recalls, "We were probably as amateur a staff as was ever assembled." (Larsen himself was a *Wenatchee World* reporter who'd predicted Foley would never beat Horan.) But Foley as a Jackson protégé was able to rely on the senator's powerhouse team of the 1960s.

Foley soon took advantange of the opportunities—and the disasters. A seat on Agriculture may look mighty good to the farm folks back home, but it was scarcely a bed of roses for a liberal Democrat like the young Foley. Most members are only there because they represent farm constituencies; errant urbanites get off the roster as fast as possible. Northerner Foley not only managed to deal effectively with his largely Southern, generally conservative and occasionally off-the-wall colleagues; he turned what one former Department of Agriculture official calls "a position of splendid misery" into a fertile field for such nascent causes as meat inspection, food stamps, and the like.

Foley, as an agricultural spokesperson, became fairly well known. Much less conspicuous has been his work to "democratize" the House. Foley, according to Democratic Study Group Executive Director Richard Conlon, was one of the three members largely responsible for the so-called Watergate reforms that opened committee meetings, made the seniority system accountable to the caucus, and such. (Conlon also loses his cool if they're called Watergate reforms—he says the changes were the result of years of work by Foley, the late Phil Burton, and others, all of which was ignored when the Watergate babies got elected "and the press went goo-goo over them.")

Although Foley claims that the old tyrannies of seniority and party discipline have been greatly exaggerated, he also vividly remembers the bad old days when legislation was decided by the ranking members from each party, and the impressive occasion when his first Agriculture committee chair lectured the new class to the effect that he "hated and detested to have new members of Congress *interrupt*" the committee's business. Foley adds that any committee head who tried the same spiel today would be greeted with prolonged laughter from the rookies.

Watergate, the reforms, and agriculture came together for Tom Foley in 1975. By then he was vice-chair of the Agriculture committee, a well-respected second-in-command to Bob Poage, a thirty-eight-year veteran of Congress whom Larsen calls "an old curmudgeon, Deep South rhinoceros." In short, an ideal target for a rambunctious

Tom Foley: making the system work

383

Henry Jackson

Henry Jackson twice ran for the US presidency and was the most influential political figure ever to come out of the Northwest. He grew up in Everett, the son of a working-class Norwegian family, graduated from the University of Washington and its School of Law, and soon went off to Congress and his eventual role as a world figure. But Scoop Jackson never neglected his home base; indeed, as this excerpt makes clear, he invented an enduring style of Washington politics that made him the most popular political figure in the state.

From A Certain Democrat: Senator Henry M. Jackson, *by William W. Prochnau and Richard Larsen. Copyright © 1972 Prentice-Hall. Reprinted by permission.*

By 1960, Henry M. Jackson had developed a distinctive political style that eventually would become almost a prototype for other successful politicians in his far, northwestern state. Politically, the state of Washington is extremely loosely structured. A blanket-primary system enables Republicans to cross over and vote for Democrats and, of course, vice versa. The result is that the political parties are seriously weakened. Occasionally a politician will put together a fairly strong personal organization. But there are no machines, not even in the metropolitan area of Seattle. A big-city eastern politician, visiting Jackson's home state, would be horrified by the absolute lack of party control.

Also, Washington is diverse—often with widely conflicting political interests from region to region. It is, in some ways, as diverse as the nation itself. The eastern part of the state is conservative and generally Republican—a desert plateau of wheatlands and cattle ranches and reclaimed sagebrush prairies that have been turned into gleaming-green farms through irrigation. In the middle of the state the jaggedly beautiful Cascade Mountains bull upward into a natural, north-south barrier—the Alpine slopes dropping eastward into pine forests and grazing meadows, westward into the sweeping stands of majestic Douglas Fir that first attracted the Rockefeller money into Scoop Jackson's hometown. The bulk of the population—and thereby the political power, too—resides in the west. There, tough little logging towns dot the mountainsides and picturesque fishing villages enhance the shoreline of Puget Sound. But the western half of the state is dominated by a sprawling metropolitan area that stretches roughly from Tacoma, thirty miles south of Seattle, to Everett, twenty-eight miles north of the state's urban center. . . .

To serve the interests of such a diverse, politically fractionated state, Jackson inevitably developed a something-for-everyone political style. The federal favors that he appeared to deliver ranged from the almost comically minute to the massively impressive. He arranged for the Army to serve asparagus in its mess halls to help the farmers in the Yakima Valley. And he announced the award of $100 million bomber contracts for Boeing. He and his colleague, Senator Warren G. Magnuson, became almost classic pork-barrel politicians.

But there was another, more significant, side to Jackson's political style. He developed what came to be known as the cult of the personality—a highly personalized style that was almost nonpartisan. He delivered government goodies to Republicans as easily as to Democrats. He seemed as at ease at a Chamber of Commerce luncheon as he did at a millworkers' meeting. During a campaign he was smiling, affable, and he ignored no one. Gradually, he drew together a Jackson personality cult that included almost all the Democrats, most of the independents, and a fair share of the Republicans in his state. . . .

Jackson's recall of names and events became almost legendary. As his law professors had concluded years earlier, he was not exceptionally intelligent. But he seemed to forget nothing. He would call a shopkeeper, whom he hadn't seen for years, by his first name. He would thank a housewife for a ride to the airport six years earlier. Jackson, to be sure, had his memory aids. On the campaign trail he often had with him three bulky, black, looseleaf books filled with the names and other relevant information about hundreds of little-known people he would be likely to meet. . . .

Armed with that kind of information Jackson would be certain to thank Tak Kubota for the thoughtful present he had given to the senator's young daughter. And

Henry Jackson

Tak Kubota would be just as certain to smile broadly and spread the word around Seattle's Japanese community that Scoop Jackson was one helluva guy.

caucus eager to clean things up by throwing out a few old-style autocrats. Agriculture was first on the alphabetical list. Foley, as it happens, opposed the move to bump Poage; former Congressman Bob Bergland from Minnesota claims that, during one private meeting, Foley even offered to lead a fight on Poage's behalf. Poage declined the offer and lost his committee in the first caucus coup in modern times. Foley, still only forty-five, ended up chair, "without lifting a finger," adds an admirer. Indeed, his reputation was in the end enhanced and broadened by his defense of the committee system.

But if Agriculture-committee membership can be miserable, former Assistant Secretary of Agriculture Carol Tucker Foreman says, "there has to be a certain masochistic quality to anyone who wants to *chair* the Ag committee." Committee members, almost without exception, want higher price supports—and the highest-possible farm prices—for their constituents while Congress as a whole wants the exact opposite: cheap food for the voters. The chair has to assemble a farm bill acceptable to both. Foley succeeded, in Foreman's view, because he was "an absolute genius at getting behind the scenes and saying, 'Come on, be *reasonable* about this.' "

He also saved the Carter administration's bacon on food stamps. Food stamps and Foley hit Washington DC simultaneously, and he quickly adopted the program—complete with its tie-in as a program designed to benefit American agriculture—as his own. By the mid-seventies, however, the program was under constant attack for soaring costs, fraud, and abuse. Farm-state legislators, like Bob Dole and George McGovern in the Senate, and Tom Foley in the House, waded into the morass.

The resulting package combined genuine reform with eligibility cutbacks. None of this scored points with either conservatives who dislike welfare on principle or liberals who did not want the system touched. But without the reforms, says Bob Bergland (by then Carter's secretary of agriculture), the food-stamp program "would have collapsed. The public wouldn't have put up with the abuses." So it's no wonder that Foreman says she'd walk across the state barefoot to help Foley, and Bergman adds, "So would I. On hot coals, if necessary."

The 1980 election crapshoot that sent both Bergland and Foreman back to private life nearly cost Foley his job. Ultimately, the Democratic disaster propelled him into the Majority Whip's office. Nationwide, of course, Republican Ronald Reagan unseated Jimmy Carter; in Spokane, Foley came within a few percentage points of losing his seat to a local GOP physician. Meanwhile, down in Oregon, House Ways and Means chair Al Ullman suffered the defeat Foley narrowly missed. In the post-election carnage, Democrat Dan Rostenkowski of Illinois found himself eligible for either Majority Whip or Ways and Means chair. He took the high-profile committee; Democratic caucus chair Foley moved up to the higher-ranking whip's job.

Mind you, there have been uncertainties on the higher rungs. Foley's nonpartisan style has alienated some of his colleagues; liberals, in particular, have wanted a leader less willing to compromise on such issues as the MX missile and the Gramm-Rudman spending cuts. When Speaker Tipp O'Neill retired at the end of the Ninety-Ninth Congress, Foley nonetheless took the next step up and he was elected to the number-two post of House majority leader by acclamation. He since adopted a more partisan tone on such hot topics as aid to the Nicaraguan contras.

In late 1987 and early 1988, there was even a brief Foley-for-President boomlet. Local schemes to draft Foley as a regional favorite son were taken up by national pundits seeking a Democrat with stature. Foley, however, had signed up early for Richard Gephardt and he put an end to the talk by announcing that he was immune from that particular form of Potomac fever.

"People support Tom Foley because they like him," says a senior House staffer. "It's the most justifiable explanation there is." Similar reasoning is evinced by Seattle Republican Joel Pritchard, who calls his former colleague "proof that nice guys don't finish last." Well yes, but Foley's stature goes beyond mere geniality, or even respect for the man regularly described as one of Congress's towering intellects. (A photographic memory—luck again—helps on the latter score.)

At first glance, however, Foley offers less a picture of an ambitious and rising politician than of a gentleman and scholar who has never quite gotten comfortable within his own body. Six-foot-three, hair going white, large head, and afflicted with a tendency to fuss with his suit buttons, he has the manner of one who—as his friends regularly say—could as well be an ambassador or a judge ("and even happier as a member of Parliament").

In the Whip's outer reception room, high-ceilinged walls of deep green with gilt mirror and wall sconces and marble fireplace argue with the modern veneer desk, computer terminal, and closed-circuit television tuned to the House proceedings. The spacious inner office is a beautiful blue expanse of Oriental carpet and chandelier, decorated with modern oils and stuffed full of tables and leather furniture. Clutter ranges from carved masks to leftover towels stacked on convenient shelves. Alice, the dog, is likely to be asleep nearby.

The Foley staff is almost as odd an assemblage as the room, ranging from a Magnuson press office graduate to a former wheat growers' lobbyist to Mrs. Foley. Some have fine reputations, others provoke questions about how they have managed to hang on so long. Even more interesting in a world where politicians are often held captives of their staffs, Foley doesn't even have an administrative assistant, normally the top staff post. Instead, Heather Foley, whom the congressman married in 1968, fills the administrative assistant's job as a volunteer.

Opinions of Heather Foley vary, from the reactions of young congressional staffers who shudder when she is mentioned, to defenses by veterans like Foreman who note that she carved out a life for herself—and went to law school—in the soul-destroying days when

Foley: too many red-eye flights

congressional wives were supposed to smile sweetly and keep out of the way. She has the reputation of a holy terror (most forceful political spouses do) but has kept a low profile through the simple expedient of refusing to grant inteviews. Still, she is hard to miss around the office—charging about in a tight Dress for Success suit and gold bangles, hair pulled into braids; chewing gum and grimacing into the nearest ringing telephone; organizing everything from gifts for a departing intern to a young member's ill-timed bill.

With or without Heather, the net result is a staff Foley can conveniently evade. Dick Larsen, who enjoyed a penchant for packing Foley off to address the Future Farmers of America in Twisp during a blinding snowstorm, left after two terms (and went on to a distinguished career writing politics for *The Seattle Times*). Looking back, he says cheerfully, "I think Tom may have been quite relieved when I left."

Foley wends his way through the office first thing one typical morning, past both furniture and staff, to spruce up a bit before a KING-TV interview. On the way back, he offers the throwaway line, "Remind me to write a thank-you note to the FAA." Startled aides and gaping reporters eventually extract the information that, on the way to a colleague's New York fund raiser the previous evening, the chartered plane had lost an engine. The travelers had barely made an emergency landing in Baltimore, and Foley thought the federal flyboys had been most helpful, under the circumstances.

When the taping finally begins, Foley sits very still, and speaks very slowly, delivering measured words about bipartisanship and moderation on the budget, immigration reform, and the MX. Only after the camera is down and the notebooks put away does he lighten and brighten up, start waving his hands while telling a few of the famous Foley stories. That's when the equally well-known Foley charm at last begins to show: witty, prone to both parody and deadpan, likely to range from the state of British party politics to the state of the art in stereo systems. Self-conscious with the cameras, perhaps, but clearly at ease among the trappings of power.

Perhaps that is because he is so much at home with Congress. A moderate mid-western colleague runs through the standard pro-Foley litany: "He's bright, he works hard, he understands people very well." Then he adds, "Also, he has an institutional sense of the place that other people who are bright and hardworking don't have." More important, adds a labor lobbyist, Foley "tries to make the system work."

Making the system work might stand as a Foley motto. Congress's 1981 strategy for dealing with Reaganomics—which to an outsider looked like rolling over and playing dead—Foley defends as having "mitigated some of the damage." He estimates that the Democrats, if they had offered a strong, ideologically based alternative to Reagan, could have gotten the votes of, perhaps, half of Congress and lost everything. He emphasizes, "What many people wanted would get a majority of the Democratic party but wouldn't get anything like a majority of Congress. I have to deal with the reality principle. And the reality principle in 1981 was that the president had won an election, he claimed a mandate, and had the enthusiasm of a new administration." He concludes, "I'd do the same thing all over again."

In a moderate and bipartisan spirit, of course. The chief—indeed almost the only standard—criticism of Foley is that he is "too cautious and getting more so." Consumer activists particularly say the Whip is increasingly reluctant to tread—let alone rush in— on issues where he ought to take a stand. (To some extent the lament is applied to Congress as a whole.) Partly, the charge reflects Foley's view of himself as a plodder who sees the flaws enthusiasts miss; indeed, colleagues say they sometimes test-fly new ideas in Foley's range just to see if he can shoot them down. Along the way, he acknowledges, "once in a while I may fall into the pitfall of being too clinical."

But caution is also a basic component of the Foley character. Going slow goes hand in

Ideologically, he is either a moderate or a moderately liberal Democrat, depending upon who is splitting the hairs.

William O. Douglas

Supreme Court Justice William O. Douglas's outspoken judgments determined the outcome of such landmark civil rights cases as Brown vs. Topeka School Board. Douglas was born in Minnesota in 1898 to a very poor family; however, he spent most of his youth in Yakima. His decisions often showed his deep sympathy for the underprivileged and for the preservation of wilderness.

In the early years of the century when we first moved to Yakima, the land around town was mostly bleak sagebrush, occupied only by jackrabbits and rattlesnakes. With scant rainfall, the land had the semi-arid quality of a desert, and only with the gradual introduction of irrigation was the valley transformed into orchards and vegetable gardens. Hot, dry summers were common; there were many days of ninety-degree temperatures, and once in a while the thermometer went as high as a hundred and ten. The sun was then searing. I noticed it especially while picking cherries, thinning apples, or picking peaches. Sweat came profusely—sweat and orchard dust. But one was never soaked through, as the humidity was nil and evaporation very fast.

Though the sun was hot, the shade— where it existed—was cool. Art and I planted locust tree saplings in the front yard that eventually grew to magnificent proportions. The sweetish odor of locust blooms and the tantalizing scent of lilacs, like those that grew at the side of the house, still create a strong nostalgia. . . .

While there were many children's parties in Yakima, we were never invited to a single one, and we were far too poor to have one in our own home. We grew up never seeing the inside of another home. In the after years I thought it was a blessing that I had not. For if I had been united with the elite of Yakima even by so tenuous a cord, I might have been greatly handicapped. To be accepted might then have become a goal in later life, an ambition that is often a leveling influence. To be accepted means living in the right area, wearing the right hat, thinking the right way, saying the right thing. What it means in the law is a Dean Acheson or John Foster Dulles or a reactionary president of the Bar Association. They cause all the beauty to disappear in a pontifical emptiness.

One experience of my adolescence enforced my feeling that I had been born on "the wrong side of the railroad tracks." A prominent churchman in town, the father of one of my friends, was bent on ridding Yakima of prostitutes and bootleggers. The prostitutes were scattered in brothels along South Front Street, in establishments that advertised "Rooms" or "Hotel," most of which have now been reclaimed as "Gospel Missions," carrying luminous signs: *Jesus Saves*. The bootleggers were supposed to operate there, too. At that time Yakima, having the benefit of local option, allowed beer to be sold but no hard liquor. The bootleggers, however, brought the whiskey to everyone, including high churchmen and other members of the elite.

This particular reformer had several sons, my age and older, and he and they would have made an admirable vice squad. But as he told me, he would have none of that; he wanted to "save" his sons from being polluted by these evil people. That is why he approached me. Would I, for one dollar an hour, spend Saturday and Sunday nights "working Front Street"? My instructions were, "See if you can get a woman to solicit you. See if you can buy a drink from someone. When the night is done, check in at the office, execute an affidavit, and the police will move in."

And so a teen-age boy became a stool pigeon in a red-light district. Never did I have such a shabby feeling, and in the end, never did I feel sorrier for people than I did for those I was supposed to entrap. I met voluptuous women whose faces were etched in sorrow, suffering and fear. Their tears never seemed very far beneath their coarse laughs and dirty stories. The men who brought "white mule" in gallon glass jars for sale to these brothels were shadows respected neither by the prostitutes nor by themselves. They had hunted looks; they swore softly under their breath; their eyes never met mine. I shamefully bought "one shot" glasses full of the fiery stuff for a dollar each, putting it to my lips and then tossing it into a basket or potted plant or under a sofa when no one was looking.

In time I came to feel warmth for all these miserable people, something I never felt for the high churchman who hired me. They were scum that society had produced—misfits, maladjusted, disturbed, and really sick. What orphanages had turned them out? What broken homes had produced them? Which of these prostitutes had first been seduced by her father, causing all standards of propriety and decency to be destroyed? Which of them had turned to prostitution and bootlegging as a result of grinding poverty?

As much as my family needed the money, a few weeks of this job were all I could endure. As the evening hours passed along South Front Street, I heard stories about my employer whose sons were too precious to expose to crime and criminals. South Front Street did not know that he

Seattle Post-Intelligencer Collection

William O. Douglas

Front Street to entrap a low, petty class of criminals; I discovered on South Front Street that on the day of the final reckoning there was one high churchman who would have to make a more severe accounting than they.

From this experience two impressions burned themselves into my memory. First was the only class consciousness I ever had. Most of my own experiences prior to this one and virtually all of them subsequent to it, spelled equality as the dominant American theme. But South Front Street in Yakima made me realize that there were those even in this free land who thought that some men were more equal than others, that their sons were to be preferred over the sons of other people less worthy. Second was a residue of resentment of which I have never quite got rid—resentment against hypocrites in church clothes who raise their denunciations against petty criminals, while their own sins mount high. This feeling somehow aligned me emotionally with the miserable people who make up the chaff of society. I never sought their company, nor engaged in their tricks or traffic, nor spent my hours with them. I think, however, that I have always been quicker to defend them than I would have been but for the high churchman of Yakima.

was financing stool pigeons; it heard, however, of his other doings. He had put enterprise after enterprise together, including many orchards, in his own lawless way—ruthlessly foreclosing mortgages, ruthlessly forcing competitors to the wall, ruthlessly reducing wages. I went to South

hand with the high value he gives to reason, bipartisanship, and pragmatism. "It's sometimes said I see too many sides of the question." He promptly applies the thought to Congress generally, saying, "Our politics is sometimes accused of being Tweedledee and Tweedledum. And there is some justification to that." But, he adds, "the muddled middle is to some extent where reality is."

Sometimes, though, the middle is a pretty strange reality. Take Congress's 1983 vote to release MX missile flight-test funds. In comparison with the vocal Norm Dicks, Foley was publicly quiet, almost invisible. Nonetheless, two days after Congress released the funds, Foley mentor Jackson said his protégé "played a critical role on the MX. He made the difference, along with Les Aspin." During the weeks before the vote, Foley pulled considerable weight in swinging other moderate Democrats to vote for the missile.

In one sense, the vote was moderation and bipartisanship at its best. Congress got promises (albeit vague ones) from the president, developed legislation members of both parties could support, and promised checks to ensure that the executive carried out the legislature's wishes. But in the real world, Congress engaged in the foolish act of voting to build more, destabilizing missiles, in the name of arms reduction and stability.

The next day, Foley engaged in some remarkably convoluted reasoning to explain that his vote for the MX "reflected the underlying consensus of Congress—at least of the Democrats—that the US and the Soviet Union move forward on arms control." In those terms, he argues, "If we did not vote for the MX—and the headlines read 'MX KILLED'—I believe the net effect would have been to weaken Soviet interest in negotiations."

There has been plenty written on the faults of such thinking—the strategy embraced by Foley has not worked so far and reflects an unrealistic view of the Reagan administration's intentions. In addition, Foley's decision, mirroring as it does the collective thinking of Congress, reflects the fatal flaw in adopting moderation as a necessary virtue. Politicians and institutions that habitually aim for the center are far too likely to end up arguing illogical positions defined by the strident extremes.

The vote on the MX highlighted the chief weakness in Foley's present political position. Ideologically, he is either a moderate or a moderately liberal Democrat, depending upon who is splitting the hairs. He gets respectable-to-good ratings from unions, consumer groups, and civil libertarians, but has not feared to step outside of the liberal mainstream, opposing measures ranging from gun control to laws restricting automobile imports. Although his power base rests among the moderates, he most clearly functions as a human bridge between the congressmen of the sixties (and before)—because he was one of them and is respectful of their version of the institution—and the members of the seventies—he paved the way for them and represents the clean, urbane, and reasoned model of the media politician.

But the chief leadership gap in Washington DC right now is among the liberals, those sixty to seventy Democrats who have drifted since the death of Phil Burton of California. Those are the members whom Foley alienated by supporting the MX, and they may well turn out to be the members for the eighties.

Will Tom Foley nonetheless wind up Speaker of the House? The question, says former Agriculture Secretary Bergland, is "not if, it's when." Once Tip O'Neill stepped down, only Jim Wright of Texas stood between Foley and the speakership. Wright had the votes locked up by 1985, and, in any case, Foley-watchers couldn't envision him challenging a higher-ranking colleague. So he simply moved up a notch, and is waiting. He can afford to tarry, since 59 is not old by House standards and there's always a chance that the sometimes rashly activist Wright will self-destruct. Among the top House Democrats, members say they favor Foley because he reasons with them. Retired United Food and Commercial Workers Vice-President Arnold Mayer, who has known Foley for more than twenty years, can be more irreverent. "Foley won't run over you; he'll talk you to death," he says. By contrast, Speaker Wright cajoles and Ways and Means chair Rostenkowski bullies or calls in chits. ("One's from Texas and one's from Chicago," comments Everett's Al Swift. "And I think they're typical examples.") In addition, while party leaders from safe districts (unlike Foley's) are sometimes accused of ignoring the tough choices less secure members face, members rely on Foley for help with congressional votes. As a result, Seattle's Mike Lowry says flatly, "If there were such a thing as a straight-up vote for Speaker of the House, Tom would win easily."

But does he really want the speakership? Foley is sometimes accused of lacking a necessary "killer instinct," even though colleagues inevitably reply that O'Neill, Carl Albert, and other congressional leaders have not had one either. Although a blazing Irish temper reportedly flickers somewhere inside Foley, it is hard to imagine him burning for power or, indeed, almost anything. Foley himself pleads "partially guilty there. On the other hand," he warns, "I'm a lot more impassioned than I seem."

Close observers suspect he is running for something, while a number of friends worry that he is running himself to death. Ever since 1980's close shave, they say he is taking too many red-eye flights from Spokane, while trying to keep up with being a congressman and the man who is tracking the pulse of the House.

Foley himself discounts talk of further ambitions. Sitting on the comfortable leather couch in his office, phone lines flashing and a can of Tab in hand, he insists, "I have no interest at all in seeking the vice-presidency, or any other office in the future. Then he admits there is one position he would like to hold, if only he could discover the means to get there without any stops along the way. "The best office in the country," announces the congressional leader on whom Lady Luck has smiled so often, "is ex-President." ◼

'AN ARTIST WHO PAINTS BLACKS'

JACOB LAWRENCE (1917–)

JAMES HALPIN

A pretty blonde waitress once more interrupts my interview with Jacob Lawrence to put a few drops in our brimming water glasses. We are lunching at the Union Bay Cafe in Laurelhurst. Lawrence lives in the neighborhood—my neighborhood—so the waitress knows who he is. The other diners keep glancing at us, wondering why the waitress keeps hauling water to us.

Lawrence doesn't look like anybody special. He is dressed in a red wool sweater and khaki slacks, and his salt-and-pepper hair is cut so short that it grips his head like a shower cap. His only affectation is a push-broom mustache. I don't have the heart to ask the waitress for a little less service. Lawrence, the most courteous of men, would be offended. Besides, I too am imposing on this very private artist and for the same reason. I want to find out what it is like to talk to a Great Man.

There are not all that many of them around. Seattle has never shown much interest in becoming the Athens of the Pacific Rim. Several times during the past century the University of Washington has enticed a first-class intellect or two. Vernon Parrington comes to mind, and Theodore Roethke. And currently, Jacob Lawrence. But one inspired mind at a time does not a Renaissance make.

He started to paint in exactly the right community—Harlem—at exactly the right time.

Lawrence was brought to the University of Washington in 1970 by Professor Spencer Moseley, who regards this coup as a highlight of his academic career. I had asked Moseley, now retired, just how good Lawrence was. Could he be included in a list of the top ten American painters?

"He's right up there," he had said. "He was one of seven artists invited to paint President Carter's inauguration. Some of the others were Warhol, Rauschenberg, and Jamie Wyeth. He did something there that was typical Lawrence. All the others painted Carter being sworn in. Lawrence painted ordinary people standing on the other side of the street, watching."

By all accounts, the university not only got a great artist when they hired Lawrence but a great teacher as well. He took it so seriously and worked so hard at it that it reduced his output of paintings to about three a year, according to Francine Seders, whose gallery handles his work. Since a Lawrence original goes for $35,000 to $45,000, Lawrence was making a financial sacrifice by teaching, but he is not exactly hurting: he is always under commission to do a large mural somewhere in the country and his fourteen-color prints sell for $900 to $1,750 each.

Lawrence is now professor emeritus of the art department, an honor conferred by faculty vote. He still teaches graduate students each fall quarter and maintains an office-studio at the university, but he does almost all his painting at home.

As a teacher, Lawrence is strict and yet beloved. "He could tear you down when your work was bad and then build you right back up," recalls Barbara Thomas, who studied under him a decade ago. Thomas, now with the Seattle Arts Commission, vividly remembers turning in a painting "where I really hadn't worked out all the patterns, figuring it was, after all, abstract art and no one would notice. Lawrence caught it immediately: 'Don't bluff,' he said. 'If you paint, do it well or not at all.' The things you learned from Lawrence about how to live were just as important as any of the plastic skills he taught you."

In the Union Bay, when the waitress departs, I ask Lawrence if it bothers him to have people constantly trying to make his acquaintance. Lawrence, as he usually does, pauses before replying, taking time to get things right. Even in the most casual conversation he is as careful about what he says as if he were under oath. "I've lived with it all my life and I'm used to it," he says at last. "I was very fortunate that I achieved recognition early. It isn't like it happened last night."

In another man, this might sound vain. But Lawrence is simply stating a fact. In November 1941, one month after his twenty-fourth birthday, he became the first black artist to exhibit in a New York gallery. The show consisted of sixty panels and was titled "The Migration of the Negro." It was held in the prestigious Downtown Gallery on 57th Street, then the art center for the entire country. The same month, *Fortune* magazine reproduced twenty-six of the panels in color as part of a long article. Lawrence's career, unstoppable as a glacier, was on its way.

"It must give you a lot of satisfaction being the first black painter to break through the color barrier in American art."

Lawrence looks pained: "I don't know how to respond to that."

"Didn't anyone ever ask you that before?"

"Oh, they've asked but I just never know what to say."

"Why?"

"In the first place, I don't consider myself a black painter."

"What are you then?"

"I'm an artist who paints blacks."

"I don't see the distinction."

"If I were white and painted blacks, you wouldn't call me a black artist, would you?"

Lawrence of Seattle: the steady
gaze of a man who never backs
down

William Cumming

*The glory time of art in the
Northwest seems to have
coincided with the Depression, when painters like Bill
Cumming and Kenneth Cal-
lahan had plenty of time to
spend long evenings specu-
lating about the elements of
an indigenous style. One
such conversation is caught
in a memoir Cumming
wrote years later (1984), recalling an evening at the
home of Kenneth and Mar-
garet Callahan in Seattle.
Out of that talk a key element of the style—the
muted light of the region—
came to be seen as the defin-
ing essence of their vision.*

From Sketchbook: A Memoir of the
1930s and the Northwest School, *by
William Cumming. Copyright © 1984
University of Washington Press.
Reprinted by permission.*

Through the nurturing of Ken and Margaret Callahan, their joyous conjoining of the spectrum of world-art with the direct experiential awareness of the here and now of our Northwest, I was brought to the edge of what would be my art.

Kenneth talked in his staccato manner of the transformation of his vision after his Mexican visit, where he had been deeply affected by the monumental greatness of Jose Clemente Orozco and the intimate directness of Rufino Tamayo. Sitting there, his pert figure perched alert in his big chair, cigar curvetting like a baton, a continual smile of self-destruction bracketing his thoughts, he seemed almost apologetic about expressing these things about what to him was his sole reason for being.

And Margaret?

I see her now, long legs curled under her, her gray eyes lighting first on Kenneth, then on me, as the conversation eddies, her smile as she interjects her own observations, remembrances of someone on a Guadalajara street who lies now in her ebullient remembering.

"Oh if you had only been there with us! The Mexican people! They live in such poverty with such dignity. And Orozco catches it all in his paintings, the only one who does. He gets that direct existing with a certain real space that most people in this country seem to have lost. Maybe it's because we don't occupy a space long enough to grow into it!"

Kenneth smiles ruefully, agreeing.

I nod in eager alignment, leap into the talk, babbling with eagerness. "You know I get it now, what Margaret meant when she told me to stop trying to paint like Pascin, rather to stop trying to paint Pascin's people. I have my own people in my sketchbooks! They're different. They belong to this earth. You know they really are separate and distinct. I guess it's the mist in our air that encases them and we live our lives more apart from each other than people in Paris or New York or London, but more together at the same time!"

I paused, then plunged on. "Our color's different! The mist in the air grays the color, so that the color field is muted or soured. You know the tempera emulsion Kenneth taught me really is the perfect medium for our part of the world. And I've noticed how, when there is a field of color that's been grayed by the overcast of mist, pure colors like neon signs or traffic lights really break through, they sing out sort of like Bix's corner in the middle of Paul Whiteman's violins, or like Louis' four-bar break on *West End Blues*!"

I collapsed, embarrassed.

And, so far as I remember, that's the first time anyone ever bothered to construct a theoretical hypothesis for one of the essential tenets in the mythology of the Northwest School. Indeed, the mist in our air does even in summer lay a slight wash over local color, so that the color field shows up as grayed or muted. Within that muted field, splashes or shapes or calligraphs of pure color sing out with astonishing brilliance. All of the Northwest School painters have made use of this at one time or another, some more regularly than others.

That night [this formulation] rang out into the fire-warmed air and hung there. Kenneth eyed it speculatively a few moments, hummed morosely, squinted his eyes and assented. "Well by golly I think you're right, about the mist in the air graying colors generally!" Seeing perhaps the ranks of his paintings over the last several years. Seeing his color, selected without thought in direct touch with the world, the

pigment picked up on a flat oil brush, picking out the slate gray-blues of the Cascades, the angry green-gray, blue-gray spume and wrack of our inland Sound, specked with cobalt and cerulean, pure; how touches of pure color, a logger's red shirt, the glow of a neon sign, how these pure touches sing out in a field of gray, how they have leaped out of the real world into his painting; and now he sits mildly astonished as this baby of their circle languages what Kenneth has been doing all these years, how this is one of the things they have all been tending towards, and he remembers things Mark [Tobey] said at various times before he left for England.

So that is how I remember how something which could conceivably be called the Northwest School was born, dozens perhaps hundreds of times, in the paintings and drawings and shoptalk of a half-dozen people breathing this air on this earth in a parcel of time labeled the thirties.

Pete Kuhns

William Cumming

"So it makes you uncomfortable when they call you the Jackie Robinson of painting?"

"There were other blacks who were recognized painters before I came along."

"Who exhibited on 57th Street?"

"Well,...who had showings in Europe. Anyway, I don't think I deserve any particular credit for that first exposition. It's just that there was a general broadening of view in commercial art galleries at the time and not only for minorities but for women as well. Georgia O'Keeffe, for example."

"Everything I've read defines you as America's first and best major black artist, so you're probably stuck with the title. How would you define yourself?"

"I'm a Western painter, in that my influences come from the West rather than the Orient. I paint the things I've known and experienced in my lifetime."

The description is accurate. Probably no other major American painter has done such a thorough and honest job of depicting his own life and times. The power and extent of the Lawrence achievement were revealed in 1986 when the Seattle Art Museum put on a retrospective of a half-century of his work. The retrospective, which consisted of 147 paintings from public and private collections around the world, drew the biggest crowds SAM has had in a decade. The exhibition then went on national tour and also drew record crowds in Atlanta. Many viewers were affected so powerfully by his work that they burst uncontrollably into tears.

"I was at the Lawrence one-man show at the [New York's] Whitney in 1974," Moseley recalls. "It was the only exhibition I've ever attended that brought tears to the eyes of the viewers. There were people crinkling up Kleenex all over the place. There aren't many parallels in the history of art. Maybe the unveiling of Giotto's frescoes in the arena chapel had the same effect on the audience."

Lawrence's work is as packed with compressed emotion as the overcrowded tenements that he loves to paint in primary colors as vivid as fresh blood. The people are cubistically distorted, so that you sense a spring-steel tension. The colors, elemental and violent, convey emotions as unmistakable as the flushed face of an angry man. Lawrence refuses to discuss his paintings, though he will call himself an expressionist if you press him to define his style. He does not really need to explain what his paintings mean, since every one of them tells a story that even a child can understand.

Lawrence's biographer, Ellen Harkins Wheat, contends that Lawrence's greatest contribution may be his resurrection of art's narrative function. This has made a lot of critics ignore him as unfashionable. But this has also allowed Lawrence to attack social problems that most other painters would not touch with a ten-foot paintbrush. Lawrence has somehow managed to paint, without the slightest touch of bathos, war, riots, lynchings, sweatshops, and even the victims of Hiroshima.

Looking across the table at this tranquil man, sipping wine and inhaling unfiltered

400

Luckies with guilt-free pleasure, it is hard to believe there was ever enough anger in him to create such scathing portrayals of bestial behavior.

"Does it anger you that your family had to suffer so much, that your sister died of a disease that she could have been cured of if she had been diagnosed early enough?"

"No, that's just the way things were in those days."

"How about the Coast Guard losing those fifty-or-so paintings you made as a combat artist in World War II?"

"No, it doesn't bother me. Those things happen. All in all, I feel I've been very lucky all my life."

Lawrence means precisely what he says: he has indeed been lucky. He started to paint in exactly the right community—Harlem—at exactly the right time. He was assigned to the first racially integrated ship in the United States Navy or Coast Guard. He served twenty-six months, making repeated trips to England, Egypt, Italy, and India. This unassuming artist has been honored by presidents and a pope, Paul VI, who, given the choice of a work by any American artist, chose Lawrence. His work is exhibited in more than seventy major public and corporate collections.

In 1987, Francine Seders gave him a quiet little party in her Greenwood gallery to celebrate his seventieth birthday. His work is more in demand than ever. But the birthday passed unnoticed in Seattle.

While public and private collectors around the world scramble to acquire Lawrence's work, the Washington State Legislature has been doing everything to ensure that he not be allowed to fulfill a Washington State Arts Commission assignment to put up murals in the Capitol Building. The legislative committee had specified that the subject be about Washington's history and main industries. It also had to contain trite-and-true state symbols like apples, rhododendrons, Western hemlocks, salmon and fishing boats. Given these strictures, even Michelangelo would have produced a dud. Lawrence worked on the task on and off for six months and, incredibly, came up with something that wasn't all that bad. The Washington State Arts Commission broke into applause when Lawrence finally showed his models for the $342,000 project. He had prophetically entitled them "Debates I and II."

They were going to be big—two twenty-eight-foot-wide arcs, each thirty feet high - and they had all the requisite symbols. The central theme was legislators looking dynamic as hell as they debated, drafted proposals, and milled about with their arms full of charts and graphs. Lawrence's proposals triggered some of the most heated debates of the 1987 session. One legislator said they were "inappropriate." Another felt they were "too contemporary."

Unfortunately for Lawrence, House Speaker Joe King and Senate Majority Leader Ted Bottiger were determined that Lawrence would never be allowed to touch even the tip

Mid-1950s: determined

401

In his studio: "It's hard work and you have to keep it hard."

402

of his brush to the Capitol rotunda. They were, in fact, planning to purge their chambers of every trace of "modern" art. There wasn't all that much of it in place — just a mosaic by University of Washington art professor Michael Spafford in the House and a landscape by northwest artist Alden Mason in the Senate. Exerting all of their considerable influence, and despite strident objections from the media, Bottiger and King got their respective houses to vote for the removal of the offending works of art. Lawrence announced that if this desecration were carried out, he would withdraw his own proposal. It was and he did.

Lawrence is the least-known famous man in town. For years, I did not even know he was my close neighbor. Although Lawrence's home is only three doors down from mine, I exchanged hellos with him for more than three years without having the faintest inkling who he was. My first impression was that he was an unpretentious man with a great deal to be unpretentious about. He and his wife live in a very modest home. Whenever our paths crossed, Lawrence was invariably afoot, and as far as I could tell he did not own a car. Generally dressed in inexpensive slacks and jacket, he walked too slowly to be exercising and too aimlessly to have any particular destination. It was the gait of someone strolling to think things through. Lawrence always waited for me to speak first. I found myself calling him "sir."

When he does talk, he focuses his complete attention on you. That steady gaze belongs to men who never give up and never back down. And, as a matter of fact, Lawrence's benign outward appearance does indeed conceal an indomitable will. Otherwise, we would never have heard from him.

He was born on September 7, 1917, in Atlantic City to Jacob and Rose Lee Lawrence. Jacob, père, a railroad cook, split seven years later. This left Rose Lee to raise Jacob, Geraldine, his three-year-old sister, and William, his one-year-old brother. Geraldine would die at age twenty-five of tuberculosis, then a common disease in black ghettos. William would die at forty-four of a drug overdose. His father died in 1955 and his mother in 1968. Lawrence is the only survivor.

Rose Lee, a domestic, often left the children with foster parents as she traveled around looking for work. In 1930, when Jacob was thirteen, the children rejoined her permanently in Harlem. The reunion was not a happy one: "We had problems, we didn't communicate, and we weren't very close," Lawrence recalls. When his younger brother stumbled across their father shortly after they moved to Harlem—he was running a small corner grocery store—Lawrence resumed an uneasy relationship with Jacob, Sr.

The Depression was very bad. In Harlem, at least half the population, including Rose Lee sometimes, was on relief. It would have been hard to find a worse place to raise children, but for a black kid crazy about painting nothing could have been better.

Harlem's wealth was people. More than five hundred thousand blacks were jammed into three square miles, and there was probably more living, loving, and suffering per

At first, Lawrence used crayons and poster paints to repeat the bright patterns of the furnishings he saw at home.

403

The Gaytons

Black history in Seattle has not received the recognition it is owed, but in sagas such as the story of the Gayton clan one realizes the three-generations depth of the history and the commitment to achievement patriarchs such as J.T. Gayton could instill. Gayton left the South in the 1880s to seek genuine freedom in the Northwest. He was a bailiff at the courthouse; his daughter, Virginia Gayton, became a remarkable pioneer woman of color; and her children have done the black community and the Gayton traditions proud.

From "The Family of Two Revolutions," by Patrick Douglas, Seattle Magazine, *January 1969. Reprinted by permission of KING Broadcasting Company.*

The Gaytons are a black family whose story exemplifies in many ways the history of the modern American Negro. John T. Gayton, the patriarch, was born in the South in the final year of the first civil rights revolution—the American Civil War; after the end of Reconstruction and the rise of Jim Crow, he left the South and came to the Northwest in search of genuine freedom. Similarly, his grandsons have reached maturity during another civil rights war, and they, like their grandfather, have set out on a kind of odyssey. . . .

Born into a large family of former slaves on a plantation near Yazoo City, Mississippi, John T. Gayton was reared, after the death of his mother, by his half-sister. Since she was the child of the plantation owner, and hence a house servant, it is likely that young Gayton learned from her many of the manners of the Southern gentry. His formal education was sporadic at best; much of what he learned was acquired from a white physician named Dr. Yanal, with whom Gayton secured a position as coachman while still in his teens. During the latter half of the 1880s, Yanal determined to pull up stakes and move his family to the Northwest, and Gayton decided to go along.

The party arrived in Seattle in the summer of 1889, when Gayton was 24. After remaining with the Yanals for a year or two, the young man struck out on his own, working for a while as a house painter, then as the proprietor of a succession of barbershops (none of which was successful). Around the middle 1890s, he obtained a job as a waiter at the Rainier Club, where he soon rose to the position of head steward.

"It was while he was at the Rainier Club," says Leonard Gayton, the youngest of John Gayton's three sons, "that Pa was approached by a Judge Hanford, who was a member there. The judge said, 'John, how would you like a job as bailiff over at the federal courthouse? It wouldn't pay quite as much as the job you have now, but it would offer you more security.' Well, Pa said he didn't even need to think about it, and he accepted on the spot."

Doubtless one of the reasons Gayton decided to make the switch was that by this time he had acquired a wife—a young woman from Nashville named Magnolia, or Maggie, as she was usually called—as well as a young son, John. During this period (around the turn of the century) the Gaytons were living in an old frame house at Seventh and Madison, but in 1905, after the birth of another son, they moved into a brand new house on 26th Avenue North. There they remained until 1912, when, because of Maggie Gayton's failing health, they moved to a five-acre farm near Hazelwood, just north of the present site of Bellevue. . . . By 1917 her health had improved enough so that the family was able to return to their house on 26th Avenue.

By all accounts, this was a relatively happy time for the Gaytons, as it was for Seattle Negroes in general. Since the city's black community numbered fewer than 3,000, it was not regarded by the white majority as any kind of threat. . . . "I really think," says the present John Gayton, "that we had more fun than kids do today. Our favorite meeting place was the little wooden building at the Tennis Club [not *the* Tennis Club, of course], which is now the site of the East Madison YMCA. We had dances there nearly every Friday night—often with my dad acting as chaperone—and on Sunday night we all went to vespers at the YWCA on 22nd Avenue." . . .

Another favorite gathering place was the Gayton family home on 26th Avenue. Once a week, the senior John Gayton—or "J.T.," as he was known to most of his friends—held his regular bridge game, and on weekends the house was invariably

J.T. Gayton

crowded with visitors, especially young people. "Often there were dances in the basement on Saturday nights," recalls the younger John Gayton's wife, Virginia, "and Papa Gayton would always lead the quadrille. Then on Sunday, the Gayton children would all bring their friends to a big family dinner after church. They never had to let their mother know who was coming—she always had more than enough food to go around." . . .

J.T. Gayton was anything but a stereotypical, laughing, carefree "darky." In addition to his ebullient sense of humor, he had a strong, frequently stern sense of Protestant duty and a deep-seated patriotism. "He never talked much about the fact that we were Negroes," recalls Louise Adams (Gayton's only daughter). "He merely felt that we were Americans."

"My grandfather," adds Don Phelps, a large, expansive man who [is now chancellor of Seattle Community College], "had a strong faith in American political institutions, especially the Constitution. I remember he spent many a weekend helping Italian immigrants prepare for their naturalization exams." . . .

Naturally, J.T.'s sense of duty involved obligations to his community. Thus, he helped found both the East Madison YMCA and the First African Methodist-Episcopal Church, which quickly became the place of worship for Seattle's Negro establishment. ("The AME," J.T. told one of his sons when the church was being planned, "is where the classy people go.")

The most important institution in J.T. Gayton's scale of values, however, was the family, and it was in the home that the most important lessons were to be learned. "Time after time," recalls Louise, "he would tell one of us children that we couldn't do such and such because we were a Gayton. I know this caused a lot of people to say, 'Just who do those Gaytons think they are?'—but Papa didn't care. I remember once he walked into the living room when a girl friend and I were talking to a couple of boys. One of the boys had his hat on, and Papa glared at him for a second, then cleared his throat and said, 'Young man, if you can't show respect for these young ladies, you might show some respect for this house. You may remove your hat.' "

square foot there than any other place in America, much of it going on in full view. Jacob Lawrence had come to the right place. He would understand and paint Harlem's weddings and funerals, its preachers and prostitutes, its dancers and its drunks. He would record with special respect his people's strivings for dignity through labor and prayer and craftsmanship. Harlem and America did not know it yet, but they had themselves a Brueghel.

"Who encouraged you to become an artist? Your mother?"

"No. My mother did everything to discourage me. She wanted me to become a civil servant. It was tradition with blacks then who wanted economic success to get a degree and a government job. Blacks didn't even think about going into fields like art or architecture, because they knew that nobody would hire them."

"Whatever made you think that you could make it as an artist, then?"

"Harlem in the thirties was hard on parents, but it was an exciting place for younger people coming along like myself. It was a community full of hope, organizations, and parades. There were all sorts of groups formed for all sorts of things: socialist theater and philosophy, dance, music, art."

The early 1930s were the tail end of the Harlem Renaissance. "There were only two places to be at the time—Harlem or Paris. That's where it was all happening," remembers one artist. The greatest jazz bands of all time were playing regularly at the Savoy Ballroom. Harlem theater was flourishing, and writers were turning out hard-edged prose and poetry. Lawrence had dropped out of his second year of high school to help support the family. In recompense, he was meeting and sitting at the feet of artists from every field. He soon got a matchless education in the arts, politics, philosophy, and black history. Writers like Claude McKay, Countee Cullen, Richard Wright, Ralph Ellison, and especially Alain Locke inspired in Lawrence a fascination with black history that he made the subject of much of his work.

The artists who most influenced Lawrence were the sculptor Augusta Savage and the painters Aaron Douglas and Charles Alston. Alston, then becoming a major black artist, taught at a settlement house day-care program where Lawrence's mother left him when she was working. He became Lawrence's first teacher. Impressed by Lawrence's concentration, Alston quickly realized that the brilliant youth was already teaching himself and even developing his own style. Alston deliberately limited himself to providing encouragement and technical advice.

At first, Lawrence used crayons and poster paints to repeat the bright patterns of the furnishings he saw at home: "The furniture in our house was full of color," Lawrence recalls. "And there were bright throw rugs all over the place. We were very poor and it was an inexpensive way for us to brighten our lives." Soon, Lawrence began painting the urban scenes that would be his main subject for the next half-century. He would cut cardboard boxes so that they had three sides and a floor like a stage set. Then he painted houses and people and streets on paper that he pasted inside the boxes to create three-dimensional urbanscapes.

Lawrence continued to study under Alston when he became the director of the Works Progress Administration Harlem Art Workshop at 306 West 141st Street, a building that contained the studios of other notable artists. At 306 he met the musicians, dancers, actors, writers, and artists who profoundly influenced his thinking and art. The main current for all the arts in the thirties was social realism, and Lawrence plunged in and never really came out. He was particularly influenced by the cubistic style of the Mexican muralists, who used art to stir people into fighting for a Marxist social system.

Just how determined Lawrence was to become a painter may be gauged from his practice of walking the sixty-odd blocks from his house to the Metropolitan Museum, there to spend hours admiring the old masters. He especially liked the precise way the early Renaissance artists painted figures in water-based media.

Lawrence was also a frequent visitor at the studio of Augusta Savage, who lavished encouragement on him. Savage, who had studied and exhibited in Europe, was such a determined teacher that she would actually drag young people off the streets to join her art classes. Savage worried about Lawrence, who was so busy working to support the family that he was abandoning his painting. In 1937 she hauled him down to the WPA office and tried to get him a job on the Federal Art Project. He was not twenty-one, so they turned him down. A year later, Savage took him back and got him hired. Lawrence has often said he would never have become an artist if Savage had not insisted that the Federal Art Project take him on. "I thought it was all over," Lawrence tells me with a catch in his voice fifty years after the event. "It would have never occurred to me to go back the second time. But Augusta didn't forget." The WPA job, which paid $23.86 a week, lasted eighteen months and gave him time to start his "Migration of the Negro" series, which was to bring him dramatic recognition and success a year later at the Downtown Gallery.

Savage did Lawrence another big favor: she introduced him to one of her students, a stunning woman of regal bearing named Gwendolyn Clarine Knight. They were married on July 14, 1941. She is also a professional painter. The Lawrences both have studios in their small home just a couple of blocks from the Union Bay Cafe.

After lunch, walking Lawrence back to his house, I ask him if black civil rights groups ever grumbled about him living in a white neighborhood and teaching mostly white students."

"Yes," he says, without further explanation.

"Do you work closely with any of those groups?"

"No."

"Why not?"

Regal Gwendolyn (far left)
and the 306 Group at 306
West 141st Street: mid-1930s

"Because," he says, "they want to own you."

Both Lawrence and Gwendolyn are at home when I get there for my second interview. The interior is as austere as a monastery: a few pieces of very simple, very beautiful furniture on bare hardwood floors gleaming like a Nordstrom salesman's shoes. None of his work is on the walls, but Lawrence shows me his collection of Nigerian ironwork figurines that he got when he lived and worked there in 1962. The Lawrences go together like an heirloom salt and pepper set. I had often seen Gwen in the neighborhood though we had never spoken. She is a high-cheeked Katharine Hepburn of a woman who walks as regally as if there were books on her head. She wears even casual clothes as if Oleg Cassini made them for her yesterday.

Lawrence and I go upstairs to his studio attic. The place is just about the size of a freight car and almost as stark. The only semblance of interior decoration is some inexpensive wall paneling. There are two small windows. The north one looks on the blank wall of a neighbor's house. Lawrence once made a painting of that uninspiring view, substituting a row of Harlem tenements for the blank wall. The other window looks out at the back of a windowless commercial building. There are a few Lawrence prints leaning against the wall but no originals and no works in progress. He has brought up a jug of

Frank Matsura

Frank S. Matsura, a Japanese photographer who moved to Okanogan in 1907, captured the daily life of the Eastern Washington Indians, the ways of the homesteaders, and the development of several government irrigation projects. In 1913, Matsura met an early, yet natural, death while on an errand to notify a store owner of a prowler.

From "Frank S. Matsura: Photographer on the Northwest Frontier," by JoAnn Roe, American West, *March/April 1982. Copyright © JoAnn Roe. Reprinted by permission.*

He stood there, blinking a little in the hot summer sun, his eyes adjusting from the gloom of the stuffy stagecoach he had just left. Looking around, he soberly regarded the rough buildings and partial boardwalks of the little gold-mining town, Conconully, Washington—far from any city and so different from Tokyo, Japan, his native home. Frank S. Matsura picked up his bag, bulky camera, and tripod and set off for the unadorned square building called the Hotel Elliott.

Passersby glanced curiously at him as he went—a slight figure just over five feet tall, dressed immaculately in suit, tie, and jaunty straw hat, a sharp contrast to local ranchers and miners in flannel shirts and overalls. Setting his baggage down, not in the hotel lobby, but at the back door of the place, he announced, "I'm Frank Matsura. Please tell Mr. Dillabough I'm here to start work." He was the cook's new helper.

This is how Okanogan pioneers collectively remember Matsura's arrival in Conconully in 1903. Noticed immediately as the only Japanese person in the little community, he soon won respect for his unusual talents—not as a cook's helper (a job necessary for survival), but as a photographer. From 1903 until his sudden death in 1913, Frank S. Matsura documented the life of the hardworking people of Okanogan County, an area of over 5,000 square miles peopled by about the same number of residents.

In the early twentieth century, this county of northern Washington was a backwater of the old West, a ranching and mining region only beginning to see homesteaders vie with Indians for land. Little touched by urban influence, being about 300 miles from Seattle and at least that far from Vancouver, British Columbia, the Okanogan country attracted only the hardy. Having made the difficult journey there—usually by horseback or stage and riverboat—homesteaders and miners found an idyllic area of rolling grasslands and brawling rivers, of lakes filled with fish, forests alive with game, and towering mountains rich with valuable minerals.

Orientals were emigrating to the Northwest at the time of Matsura's arrival, but most of them were Chinese laborers. The few Japanese who filtered into the Seattle area usually stayed near the cities. It was unusual for a Japanese man to venture alone into a backwoods town like Conconully, and Matsura's presence was even more surprising because he proved to be a man of culture and education. He remains a man of mystery; his roots in Japan have eluded researchers to a large extent, and his full story can only be surmised. . . .

After performing his chores at the hotel with alacrity and cheerfulness, Matsura lugged his camera equipment to scenic spots, mines, social events, and school gatherings. The pictures he took were developed in the hotel's laundry room sinks at night. Although Matsura maintained a close relationship with the editor of the Conconully paper (O.H. Woody and then Frank Putnam), his photographs did not find a ready market there. Newspaper reproduction of photographs was an expensive technique, and Conconully was far from shops furnishing this type of engraving. However, Matsura's photographic forays were documented in the social notes of the paper with increasing respect.

Evidence suggests that Frank Matsura might have been in the Japanese Army before 1900. When the Russo-Japanese War heated up in 1904, Matsura dutifully packed up and went to Seattle, purportedly to rejoin the army. He returned to Conconully two weeks later, however, explaining that he was an American and did not need to go. The Japanese Army did summon some of its immigrant citizens from Seattle, but only a few— mostly former officers. Matsura probably checked his status and found he was not required. Often during his life, Matsura expressed the wish that American law would permit him to become a citizen.

In 1907 he moved to the newly incorporated town of Okanogan to open a studio—actually a rough board shack with a crooked awning that shielded its one window from the merciless Okanogan sun. Although he had sold photographs to Conconully residents, it was not until this move that Matsura became a career photographer. Here his photos were published regularly in the *Okanogan Independent*. Okanogan businessmen created a commercial club to promote the area and bought prints from Matsura for national advertising. Even the Great Northern Railway, laying rails northwest from Wenatchee in 1911, sent an agent to obtain Matsura's photos for use in traveling displays that promoted homesteading in the Okanogan area and emphasized the fledgling orchard industry.

Matsura's efforts were underwritten to a degree by small sums of money received periodically from an unidentified source. Some said the donor was an aunt in Tokyo, others a cousin in New York. No one really knows. Although Matsura looked for work as a cook in Okanogan at one point, he was able to continue his photography without taking on another job.

In Conconully, Matsura had conceived the idea of marketing his photographs as picture postcards, then a relatively new technique. Sent by purchasers to friends all over the world, Matsura's postcards helped to publicize Okanogan County. In 1908 Matsura bought a stamp photo camera, a portrait camera, and backdrops necessary to produce studio portraits. A fad of the time, stamp photos were small pictures collected much as today's hobbyists gather playing cards, comic books, or old match covers. The camera used a battery of small lenses, partitioned into an equal number of frames. The photographer had the option of using one lens at a time or all at a time. The resulting print has numerous small views on it similar to the proof sheets used by modern photographers. Inexpensive and very popular, the stamp photos became a steady source of income for Matsura. He and his friends had fun in the studio posing in ridiculous costumes and making funny faces.

Indians from the Colville Reservation bordering Okanogan were regular visitors to that town and mingled with townsfolk at parades, horse races, and other social events. It was a time of transition for the Indians. Bands called Moses, Colville, Okanogan, San Poil, and Kartar all lived on assigned lands sprawling from east of the Okanogan River to a point near today's Grand Coulee Dam.

While Matsura was living in Okanogan, government surveyor Bill Muldrow became his friend. When Muldrow roamed through the Colville lands on surveys, Matsura frequently accompanied him and took pictures of Indian life, welding a friendly bond with the Indians in the process. These Indians became Matsura's studio customers, sometimes appearing in ranchers' garb and at other times in their finest traditional dress. In this way, Matsura created a rich storehouse of important visual history for later generations.

The life of this remarkable man ended in tragedy before he was forty. As early as 1911 or 1912, he told acquaintances that he had tuberculosis and would not live long. At one time he remarked to O.H. Woody, "I'm glad I'm a Christian. I am not afraid to die." However, few took him seriously, as he was known for his joking manner and always appeared energetic.

Unfortunately, Matsura was gravely

ill. In October, 1912, he announced in the *Okanogan Independent* that he was closing his gallery indefinitely because of his health. He rallied, however, reopening his business in time for the Christmas season. Again in February, 1913, Matsura admitted he was in pain. This time he advertised his postcards and store racks for sale and essentially dismantled his studio. But he continued to do free-lance photography, roaming the county to take photographs of orchards, the government's irrigation project, stagecoaches, the new auto stages connecting frontier towns, and the daily life of homesteaders and Indians.

On the evening of June 16, 1913, Matsura was walking down the streets of Okanogan when the town marshal stopped him to ask for help. A prowler had entered a local store, and the marshal asked Matsura to notify Mr. Neumann, the owner. Always a fast-moving person, Matsura ran down the street. As he approached Neumann's home he was stricken with a fit of coughing and veered off toward the house of his friend Bill Muldrow across the street. He rushed up on the porch, pounded the door, then fell on the front lawn hemorrhaging from his lungs. By the time help reached him, Matsura was dead.

Shocked and sorrowful citizens bore their friend, one of the most popular men in Okanogan, to the local undertaker to await instructions from the Japanese consul in Tacoma. When the terse comment came that they were to bury Matsura where he was, residents gave him the largest funeral ever seen in Okanogan to that time. An overflow crowd of 300 people came to his service at the Okanogan Auditorium. He was buried in the Masonic Cemetery on a benchland overlooking the Okanogan valley—his adopted home so different from the lush, green lands of Japan.

Matsura's photo collection went unnoticed for sixty-two years. After his death, the dry plates and negatives were given to his good friend Judge William Compton Brown, who later donated his own papers on Indian affairs and legal proceedings to Washington State University. Some of Matsura's negatives went to WSU, as well, quite possibly by accident. The bulk of the collection, mostly on glass plates, was stored in the garage of Brown's legatee before being donated to the Okanogan County Historical Society. In 1975 the society rediscovered the excellence of the Matsura collection while preparing displays for their new historical museum.

Frank Matsura

Gwendolyn and Jacob Lawrence:
"We prefer to live simply."

Almaden Chablis. He pours us a couple of glasses. I am struck by how steady his hands are and how deftly he handles things. Inanimate objects like silverware look willing in his hands. He fondles the dozen or so antique tools he keeps on shelves in his studio. He handles words with his hands too, giving his statements an affectionate push, like sending a kid out to play.

"Why do you live so modestly?"

"We prefer to live simply. The less clutter there is, the fewer things you have around the house, the less there is to distract you from your work. Simplify everything you can. That's my philosophy."

"Yes, but doesn't it get terribly warm up here on hot summer days?"

"You bet. And really cold in the winter too." There is a slight smile on his face as he lights up another Lucky and waits serenely for the next question.

"I know you strongly believe that government should support the arts and that you were one of the members of the committee that drafted the original plans for the National Endowment for the Arts. Has the Capitol Building controversy affected that belief?"

"No, I'm still for massive intervention of government in the arts. The government, though, should represent the populist point of view. There are plenty of large companies and moneyed people to buy art that represents their tastes and views. But if the government doesn't promote art that reflects the people's feelings then who will?"

"I'm curious about why, given the limitations put on you by the Legislature, you took the commission for the rotunda murals in the first place?"

"What interested me was the challenge of working in that space. A mural has to conform to its environment and the Capitol is magnificent—very imposing, overwhelming. I studied texture, forms, and shapes very carefully. I gave it my best shot. To carry out a mural there successfully would have been very rewarding."

"What does this episode say about the level of art sophistication and education in this state and what can be done to make things better?"

"I think something is being done about it. Even the debate about the murals has been an educational process. The media have been almost universally pro-mural and so have most of the people who wrote letters to the editor. There has been a great advance in degrees of acceptance of art in this country that began with the federal art projects. Suddenly art was not just for people with money. I favor both government and private support. But remember, the private sector tends to support what's in keeping with their philosophy."

After the interview, I thought for a long time about the reasons for the battle of wills between the legislators who claimed to represent the people and the artist who claimed to paint for the people. Senator Ted Bottiger had said during the mural debates that the telephone calls and letters he was getting ran five to one for tearing down the murals. There is no doubt that art has become so abstruse that most people, including me, do not understand or like it. Now I had met and talked at length with a man who all his life had striven to paint in a way that could and did move ordinary people.

It bothered me that I was not getting as much out of Lawrence's work as some other people. I bought *Jacob Lawrence, American Painter* by Ellen Harkins Wheat, a big art book prepared for the SAM Lawrence exhibition. I spent a lot of time looking at those reproductions. I got some books on art appreciation that a painter friend of mine recommended to me. I pored over this stuff on and off for a couple of months.

One evening, I was surprised to find myself actually responding to a Lawrence casein on paper entitled *Depression 1950*. Unfortunately, I know something about depression, having suffered from it, been treated for it, and, I hope, cured of it. Only someone who had endured this affliction—this nausea of the soul—could have depicted its sufferers this powerfully and compassionately. (Lawrence entered a private Queens sanitarium in 1949 where he was treated nine months for depression. There, he painted a series on the life of psychiatric patients.) The painting that struck me shows five depressed patients in a bare-bones psychiatric ward. Three of them are standing in a hallway with their shoulders hunched in a way that makes it look as if they are trying to disappear like turtles inside themselves. Behind them are two hospital rooms. In one, a man is reading a big black book, possibly a Bible; on his bureau is a toothbrush glass with a single daisy in it. In the other room, all you can see are the bare feet of a patient stretched out on his bed; the sun-drenched room tells you that it is well into the afternoon.

Lawrence had painted a nightmare—my nightmare. As I stared at the damned thing, fascinated and repelled at the same time, I began to realize that at long last I was *seeing* a painting. It dawned on me that each man was stranded on a different level of depression, which made communication between them impossible. In the past, I had tried to understand paintings by studying them as deliberately as an oil prospector examining a geological map. This time, however, things happened too quickly for rational thought because comprehension came as unexpectedly as a breaching orca that crashes through the surface of a quiet sea and sounds, dumbfounding you with its sudden power.

The thing that triggered this unexpected insight was the reading man—remembering when he was me—reliving the exact moment when I knew beyond doubt that I was going to get well. For weeks I had been trying unsuccessfully to read. I could not concentrate long enough to finish even one full sentence. Then one day comprehension returned like a light flashes on when a fuse is replaced, and I could read again as effortlessly as I breathe.

I had repressed that luminous moment just as effectively as I had blanked out all the spirit-shriveling fears I had weathered in those seasons of despair. By refusing to remember these things I had vandalized my own existence. Lawrence had not made this mistake. He

Lawrence...had toured hell with his eyes wide open and had come back and painted its picture.

had toured hell with his eyes wide open and had come back and painted its picture. I understood then what it is that artists do and why we need them to reveal the terrible and beautiful things we cannot confront alone.

I made another appointment with Lawrence at his studio and talked to him about it. I could see Lawrence was pleased with me, so I didn't tell him that so far most other paintings, including his, still did not affect me very much. Instead, we talked about the collection of antique hand tools he keeps in his studio.

"Why have you done so many paintings of people working with tools?"

"When I was a kid in Harlem it took a long time to put up a building, so you could spend a lot of time studying and painting the scene. Besides, there was something beautiful and utilitarian about tools and people who worked with them."

"You've given your whole life to painting. Has it been worth it?"

"It's hard work and you have to keep it hard. The danger is that your stuff becomes facile. You have to keep looking for new challenges, and that's exciting. You never know when you start to paint something what's going to happen. Besides, painting is important."

"Why?"

"If we go back through history, the only way we know how people thought and how they looked at things is art and architecture. Take the human figure. It looks very different in, say, Egyptian paintings than it does now."

"It gives me an eerie feeling to think that maybe the only thing that will have survived from our time might be some of your work. What makes a painting or work of art endure?"

"It has to have clarity and strength so that it's aesthetically good. And it has to have universality so everybody can understand it."

"But who decides if a work of art has these qualities?"

"Time decides."

"Not the art buyers, the galleries, or the critics?"

"They can affect the acceptance of an artist's work for a while, but in the end time decides. The artist ultimately is in control."

"You've never had any children. Do you ever regret it?"

"No. My students have been my children. With my art, my wife, and my teaching, my life is very full."

"I don't see much Northwest influence in the paintings that you've done here."

"It's true I don't paint the Seattle scene—lakes and flowers and trees. Maybe the influence will come after I move away. In any case, I think there already has been considerable influence; for example, I'm graying my colors a lot now."

"You're planning to move, then?"

"We haven't definitely made up our minds."

"Do you hold on to some of your paintings?"

"Yes, I keep the best work within each period."

"What are you going to do with them?"

"We have a will. They'll go to a school or a museum."

"I want to thank you for the time you've given me."

"I always get something from an interview too. Listen, did I really get the psychiatric patients right?"

"You got it all exactly right," I said. ◼

Lee in his Seattle years: as brave as
flags and as convincing as poetry

418

THE LITTLE DRAGON

BRUCE LEE (1940–1973)

JAMES HALPIN

Lee Yuen Kam was eighteen years old in 1959 and washing dishes for his room and board in Ruby Chow's Seattle restaurant. They buried him fourteen years later in Lake View Cemetery overlooking Lake Washington. In the interim, he had worked hard and succeeded—succeeded beyond anyone's imagining, possibly even his. And so there were 180 mourners at the grave site, and among the pallbearers were James Coburn and Steve McQueen. It was really his second funeral. A crushing mob of thirty thousand people attended the first one held a few days earlier in Hong Kong, where he had died under circumstances as lurid and perplexing as his own brief life.

Lee Yuen Kam was, of course, the given name of Bruce Lee, the Seattle scullion who became the hottest international superstar of his time, the dropout whose movies grossed up to $100 million apiece, the 132-pound Eurasian who became the greatest martial artist of the century, the ex-juvenile delinquent who is the biggest movie cult figure of all time, revered by countless millions in every country in the world. Indeed, years after his death in July of 1973, Bruce Lee devotees continue to flock to his old reruns like pilgrims to a holy shrine. Many see each film dozens of times, watching his every move, listening to his every word.

Lee's movies pander to the considerable percentage of people on our planet who are aroused by violence. But that still does not explain why audiences flock to see them almost a generation after they were made. If you do not understand this devotion, you have never been to a Bruce Lee movie, and if you want an astonishing film experience you really ought to see one. No one, not Douglas Fairbanks, Sr., not Errol Flynn, not Gene Kelly himself ever moved from left to right across a silver screen with such effortless grace. It's like watching Fred Astaire do a number in a garbage dump, only better. "Bruce Lee makes Nureyev look like a truck driver," Bob Dylan once said.

The theme of the films is revenge. In them, Lee plays a humble Gung Fu (the word means worker) who is essentially nonviolent but whom evildoers provoke beyond endurance until he turns on them in cold fury and destroys them. In *The Big Boss,* for example, Lee avenges himself for outrages committed against Gung Fu, himself, his *sifu*

No one, not Douglas Fairbanks, Sr., not Errol Flynn, not Gene Kelly himself ever moved from left to right across a silver screen with such effortless grace.

419

(master), and all Chinese everywhere. The film opens in Shanghai around 1908 when envoys from a Japanese martial arts dojo present Lee's school with a tablet on which is engraved, "The Sick Man of Asia." When Lee, while imposing vengeance for this and other affronts, yells, "Chinese are not sick men," Chinese audiences frequently stand and howl in agreement and empathy.

It adds up to a message, particularly for Third World fans, although the last thing Bruce Lee's producers wanted in their flicks was social significance. "Bruce went beyond being a hero," Fred Weintraub, developer of television's Kung Fu series, once commented. "The blacks, Chicanos, and Chinese took Bruce as a hero because he made it. He was the first [nonwhite] hero they ever had. They felt as if he came from the same barrio that they lived in."

No other film actor ever had this *authenticity*. We know in our hearts that John Wayne was a drunken buffoon, that Clint Eastwood is about as tough as overcooked spaghetti, and that the nearest Sylvester Stallone came to answering the call to arms during the Vietnam war was work as a gym instructor in a private girls' school in Switzerland. But when we watch Bruce Lee overcome impossible odds for a worthwhile cause, there is something there as brave as flags and as convincing as poetry. And so young men still sit in dark movies and pray: "Please, God, make me like him." They stare at those movies and those moves, hoping to figure out how Bruce Lee, scullion, transformed himself into Bruce Lee, superhero. The metamorphosis took place in Seattle.

How it occurred has remained a tantalizing mystery because the half-dozen or so Seattleites who witnessed this remarkable event have heretofore refused to talk with writers about it, tired by the way the movies and exploitative books and magazines had turned a man they loved into a one-dimensional cartoon character. Many of these witnesses were part of Seattle's now-vanished street-fighting scene, which consisted of some two hundred deprived kids from areas like the projects, Lake City, and Renton who fought for turf and status with fists, knives, razors, and an occasional gun. Since they fought mostly themselves, Seattle and its police dealt with the problem mostly by leaving them alone and hoping they would go away. They did: by the early 1960s they were mostly gone, some to prison, some to the hippie movement, and some into the drug scene. While the street fighters lasted, they served Lee well. It was by matching himself against these dangerous young men that he developed the extraordinary techniques that would make him the deadliest no-rules fighter in the world.

One of these former miscreants remembers Lee with great clarity. He is James W. DeMile, now a fifty-two-year-old entrepreneur, psychologist, lecturer, author, and world-class martial artist. "Bruce Lee was the most interesting and complex human being I've ever met," DeMile said recently. "Knowing him not only changed my life but determined its course forever."

The suit, of course, hid his physique so that what you saw was this frail-looking, eighteen-year-old kid wearing thick, round spectacles.

The story of how Lee met DeMile and some of the toughest hoodlums that Seattle ever produced sounds like something that came out of a movie script rather than real life. It probably did, according to DeMile, who suspects that Lee lifted his recruiting techniques whole cloth from Kurosawa's film classic, *The Seven Samurai.* "If you've seen the movie, you know the scenes in question," says DeMile, "the ones where the hero provokes passing masterless Samurai he encounters into dueling with him so he can judge whether they have the mettle to fight against overwhelming adversity for a worthwhile purpose he has in mind."

Aside from the fact that the worthwhile purpose Bruce Lee had in mind was Bruce Lee, his first encounter with DeMile does have the hallmarks of a classic movie confrontation, though it took place in 1959 at Edison Technical School (now Seattle Central Community College) instead of the OK Corral or the Hozoin temple at Nara.

"It was something called Asian day," DeMile remembers, "and there were maybe forty students, including me, who showed up in a classroom to do a kind of show and tell on Gung Fu, which the notice on the bulletin board said was a Chinese martial art."

Lee, DeMile recalls, was "all dressed up in a dark suit and a tie and so neatly turned out that all he needed was a black book under his arm to make him look like a Mormon missionary. The suit, of course, hid his physique so that what you saw was this frail-looking, eighteen-year-old kid wearing thick, round spectacles—the stereotype of the filial and studious Chinese teenager. On top of that, he had this weird Hong Kong accent and what seemed to be a speech impediment that made his r's sound like w's, as in 'I wecently wealized I'm weally not weady to whessle.' All in all, Bruce looked about as dangerous as Don Knotts. If somebody had told me I'd spend the good part of the next two years watching him transform himself into the most lethal human fighting-machine in the world, I'd have thought he was hallucinating."

DeMile recalls that Lee began by telling his audience that they had never heard of Gung Fu because it had never been taught to Westerners. The Chinese kept Gung Fu secret, he said, so that it could never be used against them as had so many other Chinese discoveries, such as gun powder. Gung Fu, Lee went on, was a bare-handed fighting system that priests and peasants developed thousands of years ago because their warlords were in the habit of promoting the domestic tranquillity by slaying any civilians they happened to catch carrying weapons. The Buddhist and Taoist priests therefore learned how to turn the human body into a weapon by the elegant expedient of studying the ways in which animals and insects fought.

Through the millennia, priests perfected Gung Fu and gradually realized that patience, exercise, and meditation could prepare a man to face any adversary or adversity. The Gung Fu masters eventually transformed their fighting system into a full-fledged philosophy that taught its practitioners not only how to survive but how to prevail.

Jimi Hendrix

Jimi Hendrix, born in Seattle in 1942, hit the late-sixties music scene like a psychedelic comet, becoming both a rock archetype and the era's most influential musician. He shocked the music world, first with his wild looks and showmanship, the album Are You Experienced?, *and by three years of startling live and recorded performances. His innovations and virtuosity irrevocably changed the path of music. On September 18, 1970, Hendrix died suddenly at age 28.*

From Jimi Hendrix: Voodoo Child of the Aquarian Age, *by David Henderson. Copyright © 1978 by David Henderson. Reprinted by permission of Doubleday, a division of Bantam, Doubleday, Dell Publishing Group, Inc.*

In the mid-fifties there were black recording artists who were very happy to remain in the narrow race market. Hank Ballard and The Midnighters were doing very fine with their brand of "blue" material. No one would dare copy, cover, or even sell it over the counter. Yet his music spread by word of mouth like wildfire. Their first recording of "sexually frank" material, "Get It," was a big success in every black ghetto from coast to coast. Although it got virtually no airplay, "Get It" was followed by a string of singles that used "Annie" as a sex goddess [and maternal force]: "Annie Had a Baby," "Work with Me Annie," "Sexy Ways," and "Annie's Aunt Fannie." . . .

[These were] the records everyone talked about but few heard, especially the teen-agers of the Central District in Seattle. Hank Ballard wailed on, his high Texas tenor piercing the heavy raunch of The Midnighters. [These were] more pure get-down rockers than . . . risque songs to Jimmy, but his ears glowed anyway because he was not supposed to have heard [them].

Having babies and making love were normal in Seattle's Central District. The house rent parties that were given every weekend seemed to play "Work with Me Annie" and "Annie Had a Baby" continuously. Amos Milburn and his "Bad Bad Whiskey" was still popular and Muddy Waters was coming on strong with "Long-distance Blues" and "Hootchie Cootchie Man." But Hank Ballard and The Midnighters with their happy uptempo songs about "Annie," a carefree, free-loving, unattached young woman, and her subsequent motherhood, were closer to the reality of how the blacks in the project *really* felt and lived their lives. Of course, the authorities felt very differently about the joy of lovemaking among the blacks in the project, especially since the consequences seemed to make their jobs a nightmare. But the blacks had their own feelings about it that were hidden from the authorities, to be celebrated among themselves. It excited Jimmy to know that the records [were] banned, [were] secret, but sold very well anyway. And [their] popularity also gave him a new sense of the emergent underground black music. He realized that there was more happy fun where "Work with Me Annie" and "Annie Had a Baby" came from.

The first band Jimmy consistently played with in Seattle was a band formed by Fred Rollins, a high school friend, called The Rocking Kings. At first he had been terribly shy and played rather badly. But his deferential sincerity and his good ears made him a good person for the young band. He listened to every kind of musical expression and idea. When they had a gig he took what was offered with sincere appreciation, whether it was a couple of hamburgers in payment or five or ten dollars. He became the best R&B and rock 'n' roll guitarist in Seattle. . . .

Although spacey and spooky, Jimmy was a hit with the girls. This never failed to irritate the members of The Rocking Kings or the regular guys at Garfield High. When it got around that Jimmy would not engage in fist fights he began to have trouble.

One day after school, Jimmy refused to let a bully handle his guitar. He was chased across the football field in full view of the homeward-bound students, knocked down and beaten, kicked and stomped. But he never released his guitar from his protective embrace.

He stopped playing with The Rocking Kings after an intrigue with another band member's girlfriend. Jimmy did not go out of his way to attract the girl, but there was something in the way he moved and joked and jived that she found attractive. Jimmy would always go into his showtime routine onstage while he played. This would enrage all of The Rocking Kings. They thought he was making a fool of him-

self, and them too. Jimmy would always say he was sorry, but would do it again at the next occasion, afterward saying he was sorry again. But the girls ate it up. One night before a gig at Birdland, Jimmy was called into the men's room for a private conference with the band member whose girl dug him. Everyone in the band knew what was up but did nothing to stop it. As the boys disappeared behind the door the band members speculated on whether Jimmy would fight back or not. When they came out a few minutes later it looked like Jimmy had not bothered to defend himself. He had a bloody nose, his hair was messed up, and he was puffy in a few other places, but he cleaned himself up and went on and did the show anyway. Soon after that incident Jimmy ceased playing with The Rocking Kings.

Jimi Hendrix

"Bruce saw no reason to disenchant his audience by telling them that many of the fellow Gung Fu fighters he'd left behind in Hong Kong were punks and thugs who used it as a philosophical excuse for robbing and chastising those who didn't know how to fight as well as they did, sort of like Christians have been doing for a couple thousand years," DeMile recalls.

At first, Lee did not exactly electrify his audience. Nonetheless, he began to demonstrate the fighting styles named and patterned after animals. As DeMile reconstructs it, Lee first assumed the eagle stance with his hand extended in a claw. Then he transformed himself into a praying mantis with his forearms making piano-hammer strikes. Then he was a white crane with its wings spread and its leg raised in the defense position. Finally, he was the monkey stealing the peach, a euphemism for ripping your opponent's balls off. "It was a beautiful performance," DeMile continues, "sort of a cross between ballet and mime. But it sure as hell didn't look like fighting and the audience began to titter."

Lee suddenly became stock still, "Like a cat that's just seen a robin," DeMile says. "The audience got very quiet very quickly, too, and I got my first intimation right then that this guy might really not be all talk. He got some sucker to come up front, and suddenly he's all over this guy like flies on manure. He starts explaining how he would tear this guy apart like an overcooked chicken while he's miming out how he'd cave in his temples with a praying-mantis strike, then rip his muscles apart, whip his windpipe out, and tear his rib cage asunder. It was vivid and nobody was laughing anymore. Next thing I know, Bruce is looking right at me and saying, 'You look like you can fight, how about coming up here for a minute?' "

DeMile was then twenty years old and 220 pounds of gristle. He could indeed fight. He was a former undefeated heavyweight champion of the air force as well as the unscarred veteran of one hundred street fights. It took a very self-confident man to invite DeMile to fight. He was the son of a ne'er-do-well Filipino cook and a teen-aged Texas farm girl, and his earliest memories were of living in boxcars and begging with his brothers and sister in the streets of Stockton, California, for food. DeMile had never lost a fight in his life. He joined Lee on the podium.

Lee said he would now demonstrate his own system, which was named Wing Chun after the Buddhist nun who had originated it four hundred years ago. Wing Chun, Lee told the audience, had gotten her inspiration while observing a fight between a broken-winged eagle and a fox. The eagle's tactic was to keep the talons of one foot always pointed directly at the fox's face. The fox tried a dozen feints but the eagle just kept turning to face him and clawing his muzzle whenever the opportunity presented itself, until the fox slunk off with nothing to digest but the day's lesson. Now, four centuries later, James W. DeMile was about to learn the same lesson the eagle taught the fox. It would not make his day.

Lee continued that in Wing Chun you fought in close and controlled your opponent

No matter what I did, he tied me up with sticky hands and punched back at will, always stopping the blow in the last possible millimeter.

by redirecting his strikes or entrapping his arms with "sticky hand," a technique where you keep pressure on so that the friction makes him feel like he is punching under water. He now turned to DeMile and matter-of-factly invited him to hit as hard as he could, with either hand, whenever he was ready.

"I couldn't believe this guy," DeMile recalls. "It's easy to block a fast punch if you know which hand is coming first, but if you don't it's quite another matter. Anyway, I fired a straight right hoping it wouldn't take his head off in front of forty witnesses. I needn't have worried. He blocked me easily as you'd brush away the hand of a baby that's trying to find out if your eye is edible, and gave me a left that stopped just short of my nose. From then on, no matter what I did, he tied me up with sticky hands and punched back at will, always stopping the blow in the last possible millimeter. I can't tell you how devastating this was. Here I was all tied up and as helpless as if I was in some giant roll of flypaper. It was Br'er Fox punching out the tar baby and I felt like I was in a slow-motion nightmare. And it didn't help things when Bruce ended it all by knocking on my forehead and asking if anyone was home. I knew that I had to either find out what this guy knew or go into intensive therapy, so after the demonstration I swallowed what little was left of my pride and asked him if he'd teach me some of his techniques."

Thus, DeMile and another Edison student named LeRoy Garcia, who had also watched the demonstration, enrolled in an informal Gung Fu class that Bruce Lee was already teaching. Lee held it in the parking lot of the Blue Cross Clinic at Broadway and James, a place chosen because it was secluded, partially under cover, and right next to Ruby Chow's restaurant.

With the addition of DeMile and Garcia there were now eight students, a pan-racial microcosm of Lee's future worldwide audience of blacks, whites, yellows, and browns. Like a lot of Lee's fans, they were poor and mad at a world that seemed to have no place for them.

They included a very smart, very angry, black kid named Jesse Glover who became Lee's first disciple after seeing him do a Gung Fu demonstration in Chinatown during the 1960 Seafair. Glover had been studying Japanese martial arts for several years, obsessed with plans to revenge himself against an alcoholic Seattle cop who in a drunken fury had beaten him savagely when he was twelve years old.

Another student was Glover's roommate, Ed Hart, a white who had boxed professionally and was the inventor of the Hart Attack. This was a ploy that Hart resorted to when engaged in barroom brawls. Hart would sink to the floor grasping his chest and apparently gasping out his last breath. Then, when his foe bent over him, Hart would corkscrew off the floor like a goosed mongoose and knock the poor sucker out of his socks.

There was Skip Ellsworth, a handsome University of Washington student who was the Gentleman Jim of the group. Ellsworth was courteous and soft-spoken, but beneath the

Ruby believed in the work ethic: She immediately put Bruce to work washing, waiting, and busing at her restaurant for his room and board.

Bruce Lee: He invented a kind of
nuclear weapon in martial arts, too
deadly to be employed

veneer was a boy who had grown up poor in a wealthy Midwest town and had achieved status there by pounding the pie out of any rich kids who even looked like they thought they were better than he.

There was Charlie Woo who had grown up in the era before Bruce Lee when school bullies felt perfectly safe about beating up Chinese kids. Charlie's feelings of inferiority about his size had driven him to earn a second-degree black belt in judo. He was the gentlest and best-liked guy in the gang. He had trained diligently to defend himself against the huge people he saw all around him, but he was kicked to death by a skittish horse a few years after he joined the group.

There were also some whites who had studied martial arts, such as Howard Hall, LeRoy Porter, and Pat C. Hooks, a black belt in judo whose arms were crisscrossed with scars earned for wrong moves during knife practice with naked blades in Manila.

426

"None of us then had the least inkling that anything big was happening to us," DeMile says. "Being all of us about twenty years old, it seemed perfectly natural that an eighteen-year-old Chinese kid should be unveiling to us the forbidden secrets of a secret martial art in a Blue Cross parking lot. At that age, you think that is the way life is always going to be."

Why was Bruce Lee in Seattle teaching an arcane Oriental craft in a parking lot? We have to go back to San Francisco. On November 27, 1940, Lee was born to Mr. and Mrs. Lee Hoi Cheun in the year and the hour of the dragon. The lad would have dual American and Chinese citizenship, and the time would come when he would need America badly.

Show biz was part of his makeup, for his father was a famous comic star with the Cantonese Opera Company, which was doing a gig in San Francisco's Chinatown at the time the birth took place. Bruce's mother, Grace, who was half-European, christened him Li Jun Fan, which means, "Return to San Francisco." The Lees, along with their new son, returned to Hong Kong shortly after his birth and there he grew up in relative affluence.

Throughout his life, Lee would acquire new names with the frequency of a check forger. First, his parents changed his name to Lee Yuen Kam because the characters were similar to his dead grandfather's. A nurse at the hospital at San Francisco had given him his American name of Bruce. In the family he was called "Small Phoenix," a girl's name that was pinned on him to confuse evil spirits that are always on the outlook for little boys' souls. Later on, a movie director named him Lee Sui Loong, meaning Little Dragon, because of his birthday. With all these names and all these identities, with a Buddhist father and a Catholic mother, with mixed blood and dual citizenship, it is small wonder that Bruce Lee would spend much of his thirty two years trying to find out who he was and what he was here for.

No man ever tried harder, but Bruce Lee was never able to measure up to his own expectations. Some of his dissatisfaction came from his inability to become a scholar, as his father wished. His grades were terrible because he simply could not sit still long enough to study. With his metabolism, to expect him to spend his life poring over books was like expecting a hummingbird to turn into an owl. These feelings of inferiority were exacerbated by Lee's jealousy of his brother, Peter, who did wonderfully at school and went on to become a noted scientist and the fencing champion of the British Commonwealth. Peter was the eldest son, studious, filial, never in trouble; he earned most of his father's praise. Bruce was none of these things; he earned most of his father's disapproval. To vent his frustration, Lee took to the streets. His father, who was a registered opium smoker, hardly noticed at all that the kid was seldom at home.

The Lee family wanted for nothing, since Mr. Lee had made profitable investments in Hong Kong real estate immediately after the end of the World War II Japanese occupation. So Bruce was sent to private British schools, where he fought a lot because his classmates gave him a bad time for being Chinese. He also had to fight Chinese kids who taunted him for being one-quarter Caucasian. Thus, Lee was able to convince his mother that he was going to end up maimed if she didn't pay for him to take Wing Chun lessons. Both of them kept this arrangement secret from the father, who still entertained fantasies about having two scholars in the family. Bruce enrolled in the school of the master, Yip Man, an ancient and frail-looking man of less than one hundred pounds.

Lee began spending all his available spare time working out at the Wing Chun gym and training his body during virtually every waking moment—doing secret isometrics at his school desk and sit-ups while he was reading his homework, exercising one hand at mealtime while he ate with the other. He was soon one of the half-dozen top Wing Chun fighters in Hong Kong, no mean achievement in a skill that often takes decades to master.

The admiration denied him at home was richly accorded in Yip Man's school and in the streets, where he became, at least in his own mind, the fearless righter of wrongs who makes everything come out all right in the end even though it means risking getting killed or crippled to do it. In reality, he was a street punk armed with knives, chains, and knuckle-dusters who went around looking for trouble. Sometimes, he would represent the Wing Chun clan in illegal matches against the champions of other Gung Fu styles, of which there are at least five hundred. These clandestine matches were held on Hong Kong rooftops because the crown punished severely any participants it caught.

In one such combat, Lee made the mistake of littering a rooftop with the permanent teeth of a Choi Lai Fat representative. Cho Lai Fats are pugilists who harden their arms by pounding them on things until they are as hard as crowbars. In battle, they swing these lethal arms in a furious figure-eight pattern. The parents of this detoothed human windmill unsportingly lodged a complaint against Lee with the crown police. His mother offered to save the Queen boarding expenses by shipping Bruce off forthwith to his other homeland.

Lee ended up in San Francisco in 1959 with four hundred dollars in his pocket and a maternal order in his head not to return home until he had made something of himself. He migrated to Seattle, where he expected to be received as an honored guest by Ping and Ruby Chow. Ruby was the most flamboyant Chinese in Seattle. She had a remarkable talent for getting free publicity for herself and her restaurant, the Hong Kong, from the media. She later went on to become a King County councilwoman and a powerful spokesperson on minority issues. Her husband Ping was a former Chinese opera singer who had worked with Lee's father and would probably have stood still to letting the son of an old friend sponge off him. But Ruby believed in the work ethic: she immediately put Bruce to work washing, waiting, and busing at her restaurant for his room and board. This was a precipitous drop for the playboy of the Eastern world, so there was bad blood between Bruce and Ruby right from the start. Lee claimed he was being exploited under the guise of a family friendship.

Lee also missed Hong Kong. The move interrupted his career as a rising champion of

Wing Chun, for there were no Gung Fu instructors in America then. The move also terminated his career as a movie actor in Hong Kong films made for the Southeast Asia circuit. By the time Lee was eighteen, he had made twenty films, sometimes in starring roles. Usually he played the tough, wily street urchin with the heart of gold, a kind of Chinese Artful Dodger. Without a doubt, he preferred who he was in movies to who he was in real life, and this led him to try to prove himself on Hong Kong's mean streets.

Making movies in Hong Kong may have been a dirty and poorly paid business, but the actors, like gladiators, at least got attention which Lee needed as he needed air and water. His picture began appearing in the papers, depicting him in the company of ravishing starlets and looking as macho as Genghis Khan. In reality Lee was nowhere near as confident sexually as he looked. He had a defect that he kept hidden. An undescended testicle marred the symmetry of his amazing physique, and he was so ashamed of it that he undressed in the dark when he was with lovers. He took up dancing and won a contest which enthroned him as the cha-cha champion of Hong Kong. At eighteen, he was living in three crazy worlds: his crowded extended-family home, the movie scene, and the quasi-legal Gung Fu netherland of fights on high rooftops and in darkened alleys. He was beginning to get things very confused.

By the time Lee arrived in Seattle, recalls Ruby Chow's son, Mark Chow, now a tough-talking criminal attorney, "he was a self-centered asshole because he was an athlete and all athletes are self-centered assholes. One thing the guy's done, though, is that nobody takes lunch money away from Chinese kids anymore because they assume they won't fight back."

The kitchen help at Ruby Chow's restaurant tried to give the fresh-off-the-boat kid a hard time, mimicking his accent and mocking his claims to being a movie star and a Wing Chun expert. One day, Lee invited one of his persecutors, who was armed with a meat cleaver, to take a swing at him. The cook wisely backed down, and there was a hasty rearrangement of the pecking order. Bruce reinforced his social position by setting up a wooden dummy in the corner of the kitchen and pounding it to splinters when business was slow. In Seattle, at least, Lee was soon what he had never been in Hong Kong—the toughest kid in town.

"He was always the center of attraction," DeMile recalls, "and he worked hard to stay that way. He'd gotten all that early recognition as a child movie star and had gotten hooked on it and needed it like an alcoholic constantly needs a drink." A voracious eater and a nonstop talker, Bruce Lee's subject was always the same—Bruce Lee and Gung Fu.

Skip Ellsworth would introduce Lee around at fraternity and sorority parties. "He would invite people he hadn't met to try and punch him in the face, or he'd suddenly start doing push-ups in the middle of a dance floor on his thumbs. Sometimes the things he would do were dangerous—for example, blowing a police whistle at crowded downtown

Lynda Barry

*The work of Lynda Barry,
a Seattle-based cartoonist
(and most recently, writer),
is continually evolving. Her
early drawings illustrate
what it means to be a child
in a working-class neighborhood. Barry's later car-
toons shed a serious grin on
a number of issues from racism to sexual abuse to
marriage and divorce.*

From "Funny Girl: Cartoonist Lynda
Barry Draws on Her Own Experience,"
by Ella Taylor, The Boston Globe
Magazine, *December 13, 1987.*
Reprinted by permission.

he way Lynda Barry talks about her childhood and her work suggests a life defined by marginality and a feeling of not quite belonging. "One of the reasons why I allow myself to get away with doing funky work like I do and not being able to spell and making funny drawings is, I always feel like somebody's cousin from Omaha arriving at a big black-tie party." Coming from a poor neighborhood is like "a tattoo," yet the artist is proud of her origins, in particular her Filipino heritage. It's disconcerting to hear this green-eyed, freckle-faced redhead declare that as a child she was "always scared to eat at white people's houses."

Born to a Filipino mother and an Irish father, Barry grew up surrounded by Filipino relatives in the working-class, ethnically diverse Beacon Hill district of central Seattle. Most visitors to the Northwest see a clean, affluent city inhabited by tall, blond Nordics, but the *Ernie Pook* strips give us the tough Seattle of the blacks, Samoans, Cambodians, and other kids with whom Barry grew up. It's this world that interests her, yet even hanging out with street kids whose collective life is recorded in her more recent comics, she always felt like an outsider. "I could *see* the 'us,' but I couldn't feel it, I could only imagine it. The 'us' was them," she explains wryly. "I was sort of the Alfred E. Neuman girl, always nervous about whether I was a jerk. I can't remember being relaxed before I was 26."

Among her family, too, Barry was always the odd one out. Her two younger brothers, whom she adores ("I'm very close with them; I'm *extremely* close with them. They're not close with me at all!"), still live in the old neighborhood and show little interest in her work. When she told one sibling of her intention to title the strip after his childhood habit of naming everything in sight "Ernie Pook," he had no idea what she was talking about. . . .

Barry's major childhood companions came out of books, music, and movies ("Lassie was a big peer"). From the beginning she displayed an intense flair for the dramatic. "I used to sleep in ballerina poses," she says, chortling, "thinking that my mom might bring an expert in who'd say, this child has a natural talent. I always imagined that something big was going to happen some day." But although she loved to write and draw, Barry had no early thoughts of becoming a cartoonist. "In my neighborhood," she solemnly told an audience at a festival of women's humor held at the University of Washington, "a lot of us wanted to be pimps." . . .

At Evergreen State College, fine art began to attract Barry, but she began working in cartoon form only "when the guy that I was living with left me for this real pretty girl. I was going to go over to her house and just tell her off, and then it was going to turn out just great." Barry assumes the expression of bemused mirth she reserves for her own lunacies. "I knock on the door, and she opens it, and she's just this *gorgeous* woman. I couldn't sleep after that, and I started making comic strips about men and women. The men were cactuses and the women were women, and the cactuses were trying to convince the women to go to bed with them, and the women were constantly thinking it over, but finally deciding it wouldn't be a good idea."

Matt Groening, Barry's "good buddy" and author of the equally idiosyncratic comic strip *Life in Hell*, published Barry's first cartoons in the Evergreen State College newspaper, and they were quickly taken up at the University of Washington. "And from there, things just started happening," Barry says. Her strips began running on a regular basis in the *Chicago Reader* and other weeklies, and in 1983 she was picked up by *Esquire.*

Barry has been cartooning for about eight years. "When I do a comic strip, I literally have not an idea in my head when I

Lynda Barry self-portrait

sit down. I come up with a title, and it doesn't matter where I get it, out of an old catalog, or a song on the radio, and from there (this sounds a little Shirley MacLaine, you know) I let the comic strip do the work. The characters actually talk. They usually have something they want to say. It's not anything that's mystical or beautiful or mysterious. It's real practical."

431

She's aware that her cartoons are more stories than they are jokes, and finds the four-panel structure of the *Ernie Pooks* well suited to her purposes. "You can tell a really long story in four panels if you're careful." She was first struck by the narrative power of the cartoon when, in the eighth grade, she came across the work of R. Crumb, and "it hit me that you could make a story about absolutely anything." And the drawing style of Dr. Seuss, whose books also taught her to read, has found its way into her own deliberately naive, asymmetrical, decidedly uncute cartooning.

"People are really surprised when they find out I can draw representationally. It's kind of a primitive drawing style, but I try to make it sincere. One of the problems that I have in cartooning and in writing is that when anything becomes a style or when I can expect how it's going to come out, then it's not interesting to me anymore. So I try to draw as though I'm drawing for the first time." It's the unpredictability, both for herself and her audience, that excites her. "I genuinely feel I can't draw when I'm doing my comic strips." . . .

More and more, Barry's work has found a voice, a voice of ambivalence and uncertainty, of large problems cunningly embedded in the scaled-down world of the neighborhood. Her strips remain profoundly political, but the politics has become more diffuse; she draws and writes about racism and sexual abuse, but she also explores the small joys and miseries of everyday life. In a culture where the key to success lies in the quick giggle and easy endorsement of "positive thinking," that's entering dangerous territory. Indeed, it's precisely what's most exhilarating about her work—its ambiguity—that has brought the cartoonist misunderstanding and some vituperative hate mail, which still shocks and upsets her.

Barry is unsure just how wide her appeal is, and she worries that her work loses readers when it's not obviously funny, and in particular when it deals frankly with childhood. "Discussing childhood throws people off. For some it's too much to look back, particularly people from seriously dysfunctional homes. I think people want very badly to believe that childhood is as a rule a happy time, because you don't have feelings and can't be seriously depressed or affected by things. When in fact it's much harder than being an adult in certain respects."

intersections so he could see people's reactions, or potting birds from his bedroom window at Ruby Chow's with a pistol."

Despite Lee's self-centeredness and occasionally odd behavior, his tough young friends loved him and, as much as it was possible for him, he returned their affection. "I don't think Bruce ever again had friends with whom he was so open," Ellsworth says, "or who cared for him as much."

Although essentially a lonely man, Lee hid it well by putting on a nonstop, one-man show. He would grab a dime out of your hand before you could close it and leave a penny in its place. He could catch two flies in the air at the same time or kick a seven-foot-high ceiling. "He had a ten-year-old's love of disguises," DeMile remembers. "He used to get all dressed up and swagger into a restaurant surrounded by us guys as a kind of guard of honor and let it be known that he was the son of the Chinese ambassador and that we were his bodyguards."

Lee remained as serious about Wing Chun as a fundamentalist about salvation. He worked out with his students for hours every day, and he exercised relentlessly. He began to develop the beautiful physique that millions of men would envy and millions of women would fantasize about. It was mind over matter, for Lee had been so frail and sickly when young that he almost perished.

Lee's relationship with his students was generous but exploitative. He did not charge them anything, but he made no attempt to teach them the fundamentals of Wing Chun but merely the techniques in which he wanted to improve his own skills. "Bruce didn't give anything," DeMile comments. "You had to take it, and this he didn't mind, even respected, in fact. He had premonitions of an early death and so he was a man in a hurry. He'd tell you what he knew, but you had to pick it up the first time. He felt he didn't have time for people who were too slow or too lazy to learn as fast as he did."

Eventually, Bruce got his general education degree from Edison and went on to the University of Washington, although he never graduated. There he fell in love with a Nisei, Amy Sanbo, who was to prove more than an equal match. Now a ballet dancer, choreographer, and actress in Southern California, Sanbo remembers her first meeting with Bruce as one of the least suave on record. He reached out as she was passing his table at the University of Washington HUB, squeezed her arm so forcefully that it was black-and-blue for days, and informed her that this proved how much power could be exerted with just two fingers. She saw something about the guy she liked—the chip on his shoulder. Sanbo had one, too: one of her earliest memories was of armed soldiers rummaging through her mother's underwear in the Tulelake relocation camp where they had been interned with other Japanese-Americans in World War II. She had come out of the experience with the determination that no one was ever going to put any fences, real or imaginary, around her again.

He then goes to the blackboard and gives Roethke a fifteen-minute lecture on Gung Fu, complete with diagrams and an explanation of the principles of yin and yang.

Kim Zumwalt

Taky Kimura at his Seattle
supermarket

Besides being strikingly beautiful, Sanbo shared a drive to bust through barriers with her new boyfriend. She had been Garfield High School's first Nisei homecoming queen; besides studying ballet, she was working her way through the university by singing in a band, all rather risqué conduct as far as the prim Nisei community was concerned. "What I liked about him," Sanbo says now, "was that in a time where so many Japanese-Americans were trying to convince themselves they were white, Bruce was so proud to be Chinese that he was busting with it."

Another person who found this fierce pride irresistible was Taky Kimura, then, as now, the owner of a supermarket at Eighth and Madison. Kimura too had been psychologically devastated by his incarceration during World War II. "I thought I was white, until they sent me to the camps," Kimura said recently in the back-room office of his supermarket. "They wouldn't even delay shipping me off one day so I could graduate from high school. They took away my identity because if I wasn't white and I wasn't free and I wasn't American then who was I?" When I got out of the camps I was a derelict, except that I don't drink. I was walking around half-ashamed even to be alive. And then I hear about this Chinese kid giving Gung Fu lessons in a parking lot near my supermarket. And there he is, bubbling over with pride, knocking these big white guys all over the place easy as you please. And I got excited about something for the first time in fifteen years. So I started training and bit by bit I began to get back the things I thought I'd lost forever."

Kimura was thirty years old then. He would later become a surrogate father and unpaid business manager for Lee, helping him to set up and manage martial arts studios. To this day, he regards Bruce Lee as the man who saved his life and gave it meaning; he still gives free martial arts lessons to a select group of students in memory of the man to whom he owes so much.

Amy Sanbo saw him in a less uncritical light. "He had a childlike naïveté that was touching," she says. "But he also had the emotional maturity of a twelve-year-old, and he made me feel like his grandmother. For example, he insisted that I have a bodyguard of his friends when I went around Chinatown. Who in the hell were they supposed to be protecting me from? I mean, I grew up in Chinatown."

One day on campus, Lee pulled her into an open office in Parrington Hall on the pretext they could study together there in privacy. "In walks Theodore Roethke, who tells us his name and asks what the devil we're doing in his office," Sanbo remembers. "Bruce sticks out his hand, says he's glad to meet him and says that he is Bruce Lee, the Gung Fu master. He then goes to the blackboard and gives Roethke a fifteen-minute lecture on Gung Fu, complete with diagrams and an explanation of the principles of yin and yang. After it's all over, Roethke thanks him and invites him to come back whenever he wants to talk more about Gung Fu." Sanbo was less impressed. Furious, she told him, "Maybe you can impress those thugs you run around with, with this yin and yang bullshit, but we both know you don't believe a damn word you're saying."

When he was not being impossible, Lee would be wonderful. He could do anything physical with the ease of an angel making his first flight. He made a strike the first time he picked up a bowling ball and a perfect pirouette the first time Amy challenged him to try one. He was everything a girl could want—handsome beyond credulity, brave as a matador. He danced like Fred Astaire, fought as elegantly as Muhammad Ali. He was funny and fun to be with. And he was attentive. In love, as in combat, his technique was to overwhelm the target. He cooked Sanbo ginger beef every morning at Ruby Chow's and took it to her for breakfast at her nearby home where she lived with her mother.

Amy grew weary of ginger beef every morning for breakfast and of proposals pressed with ever greater insistence. She felt crowded but her repeated demands to Bruce that he give her more room were about as effective as ordering an advancing glacier to back off. There was another problem, too: Lee's attention was focused like a laser beam on making himself better at martial arts, but he had not the faintest interest in making the world a better place, while Amy, an activist, had tried repeatedly to involve him in causes she worked for.

For the first time in her life, Sanbo ran away from something. She fled to New York with instructions to her mother not to tell Lee where she was. She took a job there and did not return west until she heard that Lee had married Linda McCulloch, a pretty, blonde Seattle girl who had also been a Garfield High homecoming queen.

Around this time, Lee became as ubiquitous as the Northwest rains, giving Gung Fu demonstrations on television, at the Seattle World's Fair, at the university, at high schools. He also wrote a book grandly titled *Gung Fu: The Philosophical Art of Self-Defense.* The book was impressive only because it was written by a teenager, but it made him five thousand dollars. Copies today are worth thousands of dollars each. Lee also went around lecturing to high schools on Oriental philosophy. Lee was riding high. He had been telling people how good he was for so long that he began to believe it himself. So he went back to Hong Kong in 1961 to visit his parents and to show Yip Man how far he had progressed in Wing Chun.

"His progress was zip," says DeMile. "He came back from Hong Kong shattered." He could hit the good Wing Chun men maybe once out of every three times they could hit him. He thought seriously about giving up martial arts."

But Bruce Lee, though he lived in a world of dreams and fantasies, also could think as coldly as the computer in a cruise missile. He analyzed how he had been bested in his Hong Kong matches. "He came to a conclusion that would revolutionize the martial arts," DeMile recalls. "He concluded that Gung Fu, like any system, is set up to ensure that the top people are not threatened by talented newcomers. Gung Fu students, in other words, were trained so they would be sure to fail if they ever challenged their teachers, who

He decided that he would create a system that worked better for Bruce Lee than for anyone else in the world.

435

had held back from them the techniques that really work."

"When you think about it," DeMile continues, "this is the system that people use everywhere to perpetuate their power, whether they're businessmen, professors, politicians, police, or Mafia. They all guard the secrets of what makes things really work as though their existences depended on it, because they do.

"Bruce Lee now came up with a remarkable solution to this problem. He decided that he would create a system that worked better for Bruce Lee than for anyone else in the world—a system designed for a man of his size, his speed, his brains, and his aggressiveness." To do this, Lee began to explore the American environment—much as the old Gung Fu masters had studied the animal and insect environment of ancient China—for things that would teach him how to become a better fighter.

"There is no doubt that between 1960 and 1962, Bruce Lee entered the most creative years of his life," says DeMile. "He was driven now, more than ever, to succeed by the bitter experience of having for the first time failed at something he set out to do. Even worse, he had failed at the two things he cared most about—winning Amy Sanbo, and proving to Hong Kong that he was, or at least would be, the best Wing Chun man of them all." He could not do anything about Amy, but he could do something about traditional Gung Fu. So he now set out to purify Gung Fu, strip it of everything that was superfluous, "meaning everything that wouldn't work in a fight to the death." (After he left Seattle, Lee later named the martial arts system he was developing Jeet Kune Do.)

"He studied all the sports," DeMile says, "looking for principles and techniques he could incorporate into Wing Chun—football, baseball, basketball, the martial arts, and track, where he learned a lot about leverage from watching javelin throwers." One way he increased his speed, which was phenomenal already, was by working against timing devices. He developed what he called "the startle response" by "fighting" his television set: he would make his move only when there was a cut in the picture.

Lee also explored the arts and sciences, studying anatomy assiduously and making accurate sketches of muscle and bone structures. To study how people tapped their emotional resources, he read copiously in psychology and watched acting classes at the University of Washington. This eventually would help him master his extraordinary and perhaps unique power of summoning *chi* at will. *Chi* is the Chinese word for the adrenal force that enables a small woman to lift a large automobile off a child that it is crushing to death.

So far as anyone knows, Lee did not study wild animals, perhaps because that had already been done. But he did explore the Northwest wilderness with LeRoy Garcia, who lived in a log cabin in the foothills near Issaquah. "LeRoy hated the city," recalls DeMile. "He was kind of the last of the mountain men. He came into Seattle only because he had to earn a living when there were no more beaver pelts to trap and sell." Lee did not like to

It turned out to be the most unexpected and suspicious death of a celebrity since that of Marilyn Monroe.

shoot and hunt, but he loved to practice the quick-draw against LeRoy, using blank cartridges. Since Lee always won, and since the wads stung like hell, LeRoy after a while refused to play.

"The Northwest environment influenced Bruce a lot," says Amy Sanbo. "He loved the freedom and openness. Northwest people often accomplish tremendous things when they go elsewhere, because they haven't been taught that what they want to do is impossible, like they teach you early on in, say, New York or Los Angeles."

However he created it, the achievement was astonishing. Within two years, Lee had revolutionized the million-year-old art of murder and become the most lethal no-holds-barred fighter in the world. To the extraordinary innate quickness of his reflexes, he brought relentless training, an incredible capacity for work and exercise, and a compulsion to be without rival. What he invented, ironically, was a kind of nuclear weapon in martial arts, a technique so deadly that it could not be employed without killing an opponent. It also could not be used in his movies, for the action would be too fast to see. Nonetheless, he finally made it, finally laid the ghosts of inferiority to rest—or so it seemed.

By now, there was no way for Lee's Seattle friends to keep up, and one by one they began dropping out of the classes he had been holding in a storefront at Sixth and Weller. "We were growing up and getting jobs and wives and responsibilities and interests beyond fighting," says DeMile, "so we closed down the place on Weller and had a few farewell dinners at the Tai Tung, and broke up."

Lee, whether he had used them or not, had at least taught his students that anything was possible, and they went on to some notable achievements. Glover wrote a charmingly chatty book about the period, entitled *Bruce Lee;* Garcia became a very successful roofing contractor; and Ellsworth is now one of the world's foremost log-cabin builders and instructors, operating out of Duvall. "When Bruce told us that he was going to go to California and get back into movies, we were already so used to being amazed that it didn't seem at all unreasonable that a 135-pound Chinese kid with thick glasses and a funny accent who stuttered when he got excited should head south for Hollywood to become a movie star."

Lee remained in Seattle for a while after the gang broke up. He married Linda McCulloch, fathered a son, Brandon, and operated several Gung Fu schools here for a while. But essentially he had already made the preparations and plans for the odyssey that would make him a modern legend.

By 1964, Lee was in Hollywood working as a stuntman and giving Gung Fu lessons to celebrities such as Coburn, McQueen, Elke Sommer, and Kareem Abdul Jabbar. Though still an unknown, Lee dominated and enthralled celebrities as easily and completely as he had the Seattle gang. "In my whole life," declared Sterling Silliphant, the Academy-Award-winning screenwriter, "no man, no woman, was ever as exciting as Bruce Lee." Sil-

Lee's grave in Seattle's Lake View cemetery: the last script was the game of death

437

liphant, Coburn, McQueen, and others used their power and influence to get Lee a starring role, but to no avail. Although he finally got a part as a flunky chauffeur in the "Green Hornet" television series, Hollywood's moguls refused him any major roles, claiming Caucasian audiences would never identify with an Oriental hero.

And so, an angry Lee returned to Hong Kong and made two Gung Fu flicks that drove audiences so wild and made so much money that Hollywood was soon begging him to come back, money no object.

The attention that Lee craved insatiably was now given without stint and without letup. Hong Kong adored its gaudy boy. Crowds followed him everywhere, fools tried to goad him into fights, and once, when he lost his temper and checked some persistent provoker, the press portrayed him as a bully. Starlets vied to seduce him or at least be seen in his company.

Lee took to spending most of his off-the-job-time in his Hong Kong apartment with Linda Lee, Brandon, and their daughter, Shannon. He lamented that the freedom and openness of the Northwest he loved so much was now gone and he was, as he frequently complained, a prisoner in his own house. On the few occasions when he did go out he loved to put on a false mustache and glasses to hide his identity—an ironic switch from the days in Seattle when he disguised himself to attract attention.

Lee now worked on his films with even more demonic energy than he had on Gung Fu. He would do ten retakes on an exhausting fight scene without rest; he was badly cut in a fight scene against an opponent who was armed with a real broken bottle because the producers considered a prop an unnecessary expense.

By all accounts, he was growing physically and emotionally exhausted by the pressures. When the breaking point came, it was fatal. On July 10, 1973, Lee and a producer were in the flat of a beautiful actress named Betty Ting-pei, purportedly going over the script of a film called, chillingly enough, *The Game of Death*. When Lee complained of a headache, the actress gave him a tablet of Equagesic, a kind of superaspirin prescribed for her by her physician. Lee went into a bedroom to lie down; the producer went out to eat. Two hours later, Bruce was unconscious and could not be revived. An ambulance took Lee to Queen Elizabeth Hospital where he was pronounced dead.

It turned out to be the most unexpected and suspicious death of a celebrity since that of Marilyn Monroe. Both had the same melodramatic ingredients, drugs, sex, and dark tales of murder. According to the coroner's report, Lee had died of a swelling of the brain brought on by a hypersensitivity to the Equagesic tablet. Hardly anybody at first believed the coroner and a lot of people never would. That one of the most perfectly fit men on earth could die from taking a big aspirin seemed beyond belief. The press began circulating rumors that Lee had been given some undetectable poison by a Hong Kong film king who believed Lee was trying to take over his turf, or by Gung Fu masters who hated Lee for

438

teaching Gung Fu to non-Chinese. Many of Lee's intimates, who knew how he drove himself, wondered if he had not simply worn himself out driving his flesh and spirit beyond all human endurance.

In any case, Linda Lee accepted the medical conclusions. After the funeral in Hong Kong she took him back to Seattle to be buried, as she wrote, "where the light, fresh rain that he loved so much falls often and there are lakes and mountains and trees all around."

The pallbearers who took him to the grave site included, besides McQueen and Coburn, Taky Kimura, D. Inosanto, Peter Chin, and Bruce's brother, Robert. Coburn spoke the last words: "Farewell, brother. It has been an honor to share this space in time with you. As a friend and teacher, you have brought my physical, spiritual, and psychological selves together. Thank you. May peace be with you." Then he and the others threw their white pallbearers' gloves into the open grave.

When everyone else had gone, Bruce Lee's first student, Jesse Glover, and his brother, Mike, took the shovels away from the cemetery workers and filled the grave. It didn't seem right to have strangers do the job. ◄▌

Shelton and the Simpson Mill:
turning to page four every week to
see what ol' Henry is up to

THE SCOURGE OF SHELTON

HENRY GAY (1926–)

ROGER DOWNEY

The whole history of Mason County, Washington, is bound up with trees, and the history of Shelton, the Mason County seat, with the cutting, transport, and processing thereof. Since the 1960s, the economic base of the area has diversified—a good thing, it turned out, when the lumber slump of the late 1970s hit. The market in vacation property boomed, a state prison facility at Purdy sweetened the payroll, and bedroom annexes to Olympia, nineteen miles away by freeway, sprang up within shopping distance of Shelton.

When the family-owned, Shelton-based Simpson Timber Company announced in 1986 that it would be laying off six hundred employees—closing three mills and shutting down the last two live-in lumber camps in the Lower 48—the main line connecting Shelton and Mason County to an identity-defining past of big trees finally snapped. A lot of small towns and rural districts, when hit by similar rapid change, experience the collective equivalent of an identity crisis. Shelton, economically rocked and still reeling, has not suffered that last humiliation. The reason is not hard to locate. The town of Shelton was founded by early settler David Shelton in the spring of 1885. On December 31, 1886, a twenty-year-old Californian named Grant C. Angle published the first issue of the weekly *Mason County Journal,* and continued publishing it for nearly sixty years. Today *The Shelton–Mason County Journal,* with never a missed issue to its discredit, is still publishing, under its fourth owner, Henry Gay.

The population of Shelton proper today is a little over seventy-six hundred, with perhaps as many more people living nearby. *The Shelton–Mason County Journal* averages thirty-eight or forty pages an issue. Coverage, the editorial page apart, is exclusively and aggressively local. The eighty-six-hundred-odd paid subscribers to the *Journal* get coverage of town and country news and events on a level of detail and exhaustiveness unimaginable in bigger towns like Seattle, or even Olympia. There may well be many papers like the *Journal* in the older-settled parts of the United States: in Shakopee, Minnesota, or Waverly, Iowa, or Banks, Georgia. There is certainly none like it in the Northwest.

And look where you may, you will find it difficult if not impossible to find a publisher like Henry Gay. There is something almost ninenteenth century about the man: a Mark

Gay's tendency to accentuate the negative in his editorials is not viewed with universal approval around town, even by those whose oxen have never been gored.

Henry Gay in his office: something of Twain and Mencken and throw-the-bastards-out about the man

Twain, H.L. Mencken, throw-the-bastards-out quality to his own editorial writing, along with a stern devotion to the shopworn ideals of journalism, that breathes an air of the simpler, more straightforward days of newspapering. *Seattle P-I* subscribers, and other lucky newspaper readers here and there all over the Northwest, can get a whiff of that air once a week when Gay's page-four *Journal of Opinion* is reprinted in their local papers. Shelton folk get a big gust every week.

The front page of the February 20, 1986, issue of the *Journal,* for instance, featured such headlines as "Squaxins claim treaty rights to shellfish"; "Haller plans to run for sheriff"; "Boy, 3, drowns in Satsop Fork." There is nothing here among the immemorial topics of interest in a small community to prepare one for the "editorial" in the same issue that begins as follows:

Mildred?

Yes, Harold.

It says here there is a bill in the legislature that would prohibit state and local agencies from hiring homosexuals.

That's nice, Harold. It shows our public servants are alert to the dangers that threaten our democratic society.

That's what I think, too, Mildred. Why should taxpayers have to pay the salaries of creeps who make normal people feel nervous?

They shouldn't, Harold. Of course, there are exceptions. Edwin Meese makes me nervous. So does Caspar Weinberger.

But it wouldn't make you nervous just being around them.

No, it wouldn't, Harold. Meese may lead us into a police state and Weinberger into World War III, but I wouldn't worry if I saw them shake hands with a law student or a soldier...

Since 1966, when Gay acquired the paper, Mason County readers, some with trepidation, some with glee, have been turning to page four of the *Journal* to see what "ol' Henry" is up to this week. It was around 1967 that expulsions of high-school students with long hair produced a Gay reminiscence of another longhair so troublesome the authorities finally had to crucify Him to shut Him up. The gubernatorial term of Dixy Lee Ray, 1976–1980, was a halcyon period, with the Guv providing Gay with near-weekly material to scorn (remember her response to critics of nuclear-waste storage? "There's enough water in Lake Washington to drown all of Seattle..."). Now it's Reagan, Reagan's backers, Reagan's advisers, and Reagan's cabinet who star most often in Gay's column. Since Baltimore's Mencken and Vienna's Karl Kraus in the early part of this century, there has not been anything in journalism quite like Henry Gay's twenty-year reign of terror against stupidity, illogic, and malice in public life in *The Shelton–Mason County Journal.*

Some things you can be sure you will never find in Gay's column. One is political endorsements. State Senator Brad Owen recalls that when Wes Uhlman, beating the bushes for support for his bid for governor, came through the front door of the *Journal's* storefront offices at Third and Cota in Shelton, Gay went out the back, through the print shop. "I've never given endorsements. Never. When I went to Buckley [Washington, where Gay ran a paper before coming to Shelton], this fella I didn't even know came into the shop, came in back where I was working, and said, 'Who should I vote for?' I said how should I know? And he said, 'Well *Bob* always used to tell me.' This happened three, four times: apparently the former publisher had told these people who to vote for, so they just came on in to me, who they didn't know from Adam, 'cause I was the guy down at the newspaper and I would know." Gay subsides in his chair, fizzing and chuckling with an emotion apparently equal parts glee and outrage.

Gay's strong tendency to accentuate the negative in his editorials is not viewed with universal approval around town, even by those whose own oxen have never been gored. "About the only time Henry ever came close to me," says Senator Owen of Shelton, "he was shooting at my opponent; as I recall, Henry said that his accomplishments after thirteen-and-a-half years in the Legislature would not impede a lemming on its way to sea. I think he was extremely unfair to Dixy: She could not do a thing right as far as he was concerned. And these days, when people have so much to worry about because of the economy and all the uncertainty, I think he hurts the community by being all the time negative, always criticizing, instead of trying to bring people together."

But Gay's notions of an editor's obligation to the public are not expressed on the editorial page. "I think you develop your journalistic philosophy over a long period of time; of course it's stronger when you have some personal beliefs. Now, I truly believe that people will like and respect a newspaper that tells them what is going on, everything that's going on. People shouldn't have to go to a county commission meeting unless they want; they should be able to get what happened from their newspaper. That's what we provide: the news. Now, some people say, 'That's kind of dry, isn't it?' Well, I don't play with the news. And I don't decide what goes in and what doesn't. I don't know how you can believe what you read or know if you're getting the full story or not from a paper that picks and chooses what it's going to cover."

The *Journal's* inclusiveness is a hot issue these days, though it is cooling down. It was hot enough in 1985 to warrant a front-section story in *The New York Times.* The story centered on the *Journal's* policy of covering all felony trials in the county, including publication of names of all parties concerned in each case. The case in question was one of rape. When Gay published the name of the plaintiff in the case, he was roundly assailed by some law enforcement personnel, attorneys, rape-relief and counseling agencies, and

When Wes Uhlman, beating the bushes for support for his bid for governor, came through the front door of the Journal's *storefront offices...Gay went out the back, through the print shop.*

Edward R. Murrow

Edward R. Murrow came to epitomize cosmopolitan ease in broadcast journalism, but he sprang from humble traditions in Washington State. He was a star on the campus of Washington State University, but what really formed his style was a diminutive, beloved teacher of speech and elocution. In Miss Anderson's classrooms in the 1920s, the future fearless opponent of Senator Joseph McCarthy found his voice and his values.

Adapted from Going to State, *by William Stimson. Copyright © 1989 Washington State University Press. Reprinted by permission.*

It is difficult to imagine anyone better fitted to broadcast journalism than Edward R. Murrow. Murrow had the dark good looks and riveting eye contact for television and a voice that could make three words, "This is London," roll with all the drama of the Battle of Britain. He had a quick mind and constantly astonished people by absorbing information on the run and then stepping up to a microphone and delivering a news report that sounded like it had been revised for a week.

What made this paragon? Was he born to be the perfect journalist, or was he somehow formed for the work? Undoubtedly it was both. He credited his success to a tiny crippled woman who taught speech at the State College of Washington, later Washington State University.

Egbert Roscoe Murrow was born near Greensboro, North Carolina in 1908. In 1913, his parents moved to Blanchard, in Skagit County, where his father went to work for a lumbering company. Like his two older brothers, Lacey and Dewey, Murrow was a leader in the small schools of Blanchard and nearby Edison. In high school at Edison he played basketball and baseball, was student-body president, and was on a debate team that won the Northwest Washington championship. He was ambitious and dreamed of going to a major Eastern university. But there was not enough money, so he followed his two older brothers, Lacey and Dewey, to Washington State College in Pullman.

He started as a business administration major but switched in his freshman year. He had met Ida Lou Anderson. She was only eight years older than Murrow but had the air of one much older. Crippled as a child by infantile paralysis, "Miss Anderson," as everyone called her, was tiny, under five feet tall, and had a hump on her back. She walked with difficulty and wore dark glasses because light hurt her eyes.

To her mediocre students, those who could hardly bear to rise to give a talk, she was patient and gentle. But her unusually talented students remember that she was a perfectionist, who would make a student go over and over an "interpretation" from a poem or a prose passage until every nuance had been wrung from the words. Insincerity was the ultimate sin. "A voice, in short, is only the fine instrument of something far greater than itself, which is

Edward R. Murrow

the whole man," she wrote one student, Art Gilmore, who went on to become a national broadcaster.

In his eight semesters at Washington State College, Murrow took fifteen courses from Miss Anderson. They also spent endless hours together as Ida Lou became Murrow's adopted tutor. The six-foot-tall Murrow and the four-and-a-half-foot Miss Anderson were a familiar sight walking across campus, "he carrying her books," recalled Dorothy Darby Smith, a WSC student at the time, "she looking up at him, both of them so engrossed in their conversation." One thing they discussed was Ida Lou's favorite philosopher, Marcus Aurelius, the Roman general who preached stoic disregard for personal concerns and fearless devotion to duty.

A spectacularly successful speech started Murrow off on his quick ascent to fame. As student body president at WSC, he attended a national sudent meeting held at Stanford University in 1930. During the meeting, Murrow rose to urge the other delegates to realize their responsibility at a time when the world was in such a hazardous condition, and his speech so impressed the others that he was elected president of the organization a few days later. That took him to New York City immediately after graduation in 1930. When his tenure as president of the National Student Federation expired, he was hired to assist with a committee which rescued scholars from Hitler's Germany. That assignment ran out too, and in 1935 Murrow took a low-level administrative job with CBS Radio. Within a few years his talents and the emergency descending on Europe made him chief of European correspondents.

He was in Europe reporting crises of Munich and the beginning of World War II when he learned that Ida Lou had been forced to resign her teaching job because of failing health. He had a new radio delivered to her and asked her to listen and critique his broadcasts. In one of her telegrams to him, she suggested that a brief pause in the opening dateline of his broadcasts would underline the gravity of the times. Murrow's "This . . . is London" soon became a famous broadcast signature.

She died in 1941, at the age of 41, from the complications from her childhood disease. Several years earlier Murrow had written in a personal letter—to the woman he was about to marry—about Ida Lou Anderson. "She taught me to love good books, good music, gave me the only sense of values I have. . . . The part of me that is decent, wants to do something, be something, is the part she created. She taught me to speak. She taught me one must have more than a good bluff to really live."

Father and son, Henry and Charles Gay: journalistic principles and passion

members of the general public for doing so. Gay stood firm on his policy, even afer KOMO-TV's Ken Schram and his weekly "Town Meeting" show turned the policy into a Puget Sound basin-wide issue.

Gay refused to appear on the show, though his son Charles, since 1985 managing editor of the *Journal,* did. "When people asked why I refused, I told them that I thought a show which is mainly an entertainment program was the wrong forum to discuss such a serious issue. They still said, 'But you ought to have been on.'

"The TV people talked the same way, like 'If we want you on then you have to be on!' To me that's like someone saying, 'You come on down this dark alley with us and don't pay any attention to this sap I have in my hand and I assure you there are not more than ten or twelve other folks waiting for you down there.' And if you don't let them set the ground rules, if you don't respond to this arrogance, *you're* arrogant!"

Gay's defense of his paper's policy is devastatingly simple. "We cover all felony trials in the county. All of them. If we make an exception in our coverage in a rape case, if we conceal the name of a plaintiff in a rape case, we are bowing to the very prejudice that the case is brought to combat. We are saying, 'If an old couple in West Seattle is roughed up, we will publish their names and they will receive sympathy and offers of help and gifts from the public. But if a woman is physically assaulted and brutalized, that fact is to her *dis*credit.' It's the old macho 'damaged goods' idea in different clothes. If we bow to that, we are reinforcing prejudice, we are bowing to the reaction or supposed reaction of the weakest, basest, most bigoted mind who might read it.

"This issue is about the last vestige of the good-old-boy philosophy about sex. This is the breakthrough point: If we put a stop to concealment and the false sense of shame that comes from concealment, we can start putting a stop to the whole business. Most rape is not some psychotic jumping out of the bushes in Seattle and raping a nurse. Most rape is some high-school or college boy assaulting his date because he knows that society's attitude about the victim makes it very unlikely that his crime is even going to be reported."

Gay does not deny that public expressions of opinion on the *Journal's* rape-case reportage have been preponderantly negative, but he believes that the policy is right, and that in time, the public will come around to his way of thinking. "People are looking at the matter from an emotional viewpoint, not an intellectual viewpoint. But I believe that they'll begin to think it over in time, and one reason they will think it over is that for the last twenty years they've been reading the *Journal,* and they know that what others have said about the paper and about me because of this issue does not jibe with what they *know* from their own experience."

Some Sheltonians who are less than enamored of Henry Gay's underdog-oriented editorial stance were only too happy to make the most of the rape-case issue. Though they managed to put him on the defensive for about the first time in twenty years, they failed to affect his policy. Suggestions that subscribers and advertisers boycott the *Journal* fizzled almost before they got under way. Gay's critics say that the *Journal's* total dominance in its market is the reason. Gay scoffs: "Look at the size of this town and the number of people in the county, then look at our circulation: probably the best per capita in the state, I would imagine. Go to a lot of other towns and you'll see papers with anemic circulations and give-away shoppers with big circulations. People pay for this paper and there's only one reason they pay for it, because they want to *read* it."

Gay's publishing philosophy may be based on his long experience of the business, but it is also founded on a hard kernel of family tradition. He was born into a newspaper family in Monterey, California, where his parents published the *Monterey Trader,* a weekly in a daily town. "My dad quit his job on the daily over a matter of principle at the height of the Depression, four kids to support, started his own paper with forty dollars and an orange

Suggestions that subscribers and advertisers boycott the Journal *fizzled almost before they got under way.*

448

crate and a typewriter. Fantastic. People don't do that kind of thing any more. Well, there was no unemployment insurance then, either.

"I didn't want to be in the newspaper business when I was a kid. I was interested in art. One of the advantages of growing up on the Monterey Peninsula, you sometimes got teachers who weren't really high-school teachers, especially in the art field. Our art teacher had been a professor at Stanford before he decided he'd rather live in Carmel. Well, World War II took care of that dream; by the time I got out I didn't want to be an artist any more, I wanted to *do* something. I was full of energy.

"Still, I wasn't aiming toward the newspaper business. But you can imagine what happened to small papers during the war: no supplies, no help. My dad was really beat up, he was tired. So I jumped in to help him out for a while, and then I bought the printing side of the operation from him 'cause I'd always liked working with my hands, and just gradually worked on over to the newspaper side."

In 1953 Gay and his father, joined by Gay's brother-in-law, sold out in Monterey and bought the *News-Banner* in Buckley, Washington, a town of around three thousand just south of Enumclaw. "Why'd we move? Well, I'll tell you, Monterey was heaven on earth when I was growing up, only about nine thousand in the town, another twenty-five hundred in Pacific Grove, maybe five hundred to a thousand in Carmel. But the sardines went away and Cannery Row closed down. Five years after the war it was crawling with people; no longer a working town, it was a hustle-the-tourist town, a real-estate developer's paradise."

Why Buckley? "It was small, for sale, cheap—we didn't have any money—and it could be improved. Then in 1964 my dad decided to retire: We sold the paper, I did some consulting work for a while, then I found the *Journal,* and here I are. The circulation was about thirty-eight hundred and it ran between sixteen and twenty-four pages: just about perfect."

As owner of the one newspaper in a one-company town, Gay had his chance to join the establishment or fight it. He has done neither. "A lot of places you go you'll find there's a town power structure; maybe a country-club kind of thing, but it doesn't have to be that formal, maybe just a coffee shop somewhere where everybody drops in, in the course of the day: the millowner and the banker and doctor and the newspaper publisher.

"Now, I don't believe in that sort of thing *at tall,* but the funny thing is that there never has seemed to me to *be* a power structure in this town, apart from Simpson—and I'm sure they had 100 percent cooperation from the newspaper in the past, though as companies go they seem to have used a comparatively soft hand. But I don't consult with anybody on how I cover the news, and I've never had any pressure from them, and I assure you I react very strongly even to very light pressure."

Gay puts out the *Journal* with a full-time staff of around fifteen. That includes four full-

Behind all Henry and Charles Gay's statements of principle one senses something more primitive and immediate: a suspicion and dislike of power exerted for its own sake.

Rufus Woods

Editor of The **Wenatchee World** *Rufus Woods and contractor Jim O'Sullivan battled resistance from Spokane where many insisted it would be cheaper to produce gravity-driven electricity from nearby Lake Pend Oreille than to build the proposed—and unimaginable—Grand Coulee dam. Together, the editor and the contractor kept Billy Clapp's idea alive and by the early thirties convinced the state legislature to set up the Grand Coulee project funded by the Public Works Administration.*

From Builders of the Northwest, *by Jalmar Johnson, Dodd, Mead & Company. Copyright © 1963 by Jalmar Johnson. Reprinted by permission of the Putnam & Grosset Group.*

It was hot in the hamlet of Ephrata, Washington, even under the shade trees which set it apart from neighboring towns. Miniature dust-devils skittered along the dirt street.

Short, chunky Billy Clapp, amiable, fortyish lawyer, got out of the sun as soon as he could. He stepped into a small restaurant, wiping his brow on his shirtsleeve. Inside he found Paul Donaldson, a young mining prospector. They fell into conversation over coffee and doughnuts.

Donaldson had just returned from Grand Coulee, where he had been exploring for mineral deposits. He and Clapp got to talking about the Coulee, a deep canyon, fifty miles long, which runs southerly from the Columbia River in north central Washington. . . .

Suddenly, Billy Clapp, who was as sharp as he was amiable, was struck by an idea that was to transform a large part of the state and engage his own and the efforts of many other people for the next twenty years.

"Hey!" he exclaimed. . . . "If ice could dam the Columbia and fill the Coulee with water, why couldn't we do the same? Then we could irrigate the whole Big Bend country!"

The great expanse of land contained within the big bend of the Columbia needed water desperately. The soil of pulverized lava was rich, but not enough rain fell on it to make farming practical. Ranchers had moved in many years before and for a time produced amazing wheat crops. But the moisture in the soil was soon used up and not enough rain fell to replenish it. . . .

Possibly nothing would have come of Billy's impulsive idea, if Rufus Woods, editor of the *Wenatchee World*, hadn't come to Ephrata a few days later in search of advertisements and news. A go-getting booster for his part of the state, Woods traveled over the wide, sparsely settled area in a Model T Ford equipped with a built-in typewriter.

He happened to meet Donaldson on the street.

"Any news?" asked the eager editor.

"Nah, awfully dull around here lately," the mining man replied. Then he thought of his conversation with Clapp.

"Say, you might get a story from Billy Clapp," he said. "He's got a real big idea!"

On July 18, 1918, a headline stretched across the front page of the *World*. It read: FORMULATE BRAND NEW IDEA FOR IRRIGATION GRANT, ADAMS, FRANKLIN COUNTIES,

COVERING MILLION ACRES OR MORE.

. . . . Woods' story was ridiculed by practically everyone, except some men in Ephrata and in a few other hamlets of the arid basin. The *World* didn't print another story on the subject for several months.

The idea might well have died right there if Jim O'Sullivan had not returned to town. He first saw the Columbia River in 1906 when, as a lawyer of thirty, he came west with his bride, Pearl, to start a practice. But Seattle, where the young couple planned to settle, had too many lawyers already. So Jim turned to construction work, having had experience in that line. His father was a contractor in Port Huron, Michigan, and the tall, slim young graduate of the University of Michigan had run the business for a couple of years during his father's illness. . . .

[In 1909] he established a law office in Ephrata on the same street where Billy Clapp had his. The two men became good friends. . . . Then he bought a large tract of land at [Moses Lake] and installed a modern pumping station and irrigation system. He was $40,000 in debt when the land boom broke in 1914.

That same year, Jim's father took ill again, so he went back to Port Huron to run the business. The elder O'Sullivan died in 1915, and Jim remained in Michigan to manage the contracting firm. . . .

However, in April, 1919, when Jim O'Sullivan returned to Ephrata [to defend himself against a lawsuit arising from the Moses Lake project], the [Coulee] battle had not even begun. Few paid any attention to Billy Clapp's fantastic brainstorm. It had just flared up momentarily in the *Wenatchee World* and the *Grant County Journal* and then subsided.

O'Sullivan retained Clapp as his lawyer in . . . suit he had come west to defend. Undoubtedly, the old friends discussed Grand Coulee as well as the damage action. In any event, Rufus Woods found the contractor from Michigan full of the subject when he ran into him at Quincy.

The Wenatchee editor told O'Sullivan how he had been unmercifully ridiculed since his story on Grand Coulee appeared the previous year. He had been unable to get a contractor to say whether or not the idea was feasible. Would Jim, as an experienced builder, take a look at the project and, if he found a dam possible, write an article for the *World*? Jim said he would.

Woods, however, did not wait for

Rufus Woods

O'Sullivan's considered opinion. He hurried back to Wenatchee and wrote a story quoting the contractor as saying a dam was not only possible but "perfectly feasible," and added that a dam would "yield untold electric energy, as great as a number of Niagaras." This energy would not only pay for the dam, the story claimed, but would electrify railroads, factories and heat thousands of homes.

Even though Woods had reported his opinions before he could obtain the supporting evidence, Jim went through with his survey. Accompanied by Norval Enger, he reached the head of the Coulee and triangulated a likely site, the same one finally selected by Bureau of Reclamation engineers [in June 1935]. O'Sullivan and Enger found that the river was 600 feet below the rim of its canyon at that point and that the canyon itself was approximately a mile wide.

time reporters in addition to son Charles, and a pressroom staff of three headed by Charles's older brother Steve. In addition to the regular weekly issue appearing each Thursday, the paper puts out a massive annual supplement at the beginning of the tourist season. What the *Guide* does not include about the towns, businesses, facilities, activities, and amenities of Mason County is literally not worth knowing. For the Shelton town centennial in March 1985, the *Journal* issued a ninety-six-page supplement containing, along with a lot of ads, a book-length survey of town and county history by Berwyn Thomas, a retired paper chemist at the ITT Rayonier research labs in town, plus pages of reminiscence by sons and daughters of county pioneers, including Dick Angle, grandson of the *Journal's* founder. The *Journal* actively maintains the record of the past as it records week by week its present and future.

There is no reason to expect the continuity to be broken soon. "I can't remember ever wanting to do anything else," Charles Gay says. "I used to carry the papers to my father as they came off the press up in Buckley so he could put the address labels on them. A little later I printed my own little newspaper and my grandmother bought every issue. I was sports editor of the *Journal* when I was in high school. When I went to the University of Washington, I planned to major in journalism, but in my first year news-writing class I realized—not that I knew it all already, but that there were a lot of other things I didn't know as well as I already did the newspaper business. I majored in economics instead."

Charles Gay worked at papers all over the region, from Lynnwood to Scappoose, Oregon. "Then my father made me an offer I couldn't refuse: to be managing editor here. Nobody has ever asked me why I like to do what I do. It's just been my life. As for why I came back here, there's the factor, I guess, that on a paper this size you are able to control more of the product. And I can live with the journalistic principles this paper is based on, because they are what I grew up with."

But principles alone do not make for exciting and effective journalism. That takes passion as well, and behind all Henry and Charles Gay's statements of principle one senses something more primitive and immediate: a suspicion and dislike of power exerted for its own sake. "Two traumatic experiences, early on, made me swear never to work for any-body but myself," says Henry Gay. "When I was fifteen I had a job in a large department store. The politics of that place were absolutely fantastic. Words meant nothing. I couldn't imagine spending my life in a situation where you have an idiot in control of your destiny and no way to find a rational basis for what you were doing and why.

"Then there was the military. I was in the navy in World War II; it wasn't the highlight of my life. I recall when we got to boot camp the toilets were clogged up and we had to go in there, still in our civvies, and fish the feces out with our hands, just to show us that by God if they said to do that, you did that. So that's probably why I don't write local editorials much, but when I do, it's nearly always about somebody getting kicked around by someone else in authority. That just drives me wild." ◼

Tom Robbins: "a rebel and a
prophet"

THE SHAMAN'S GIFT

TOM ROBBINS (1936–)

ROGER DOWNEY

If someone took a survey to find out which Washingtonians were blessed with "name visibility" for the American population at large, it is likely that only four would produce more than a glimmer of recognition: Mr. Justice Douglas; Henry Jackson; Jim Whittaker, probably; and a novelist and ex-art critic named Tom Robbins.

The wild card in this hand is Robbins. The other three gentlemen were not only visible nationally, they became household words at home. But Robbins, after nearly thirty years in the Northwest, is unknown to most of his fellow Washingtonians: nearly all, in fact, except for a few newspaper reporters and readers with long memories, some painters and gallery owners, and the local chapter of a worldwide *ad hoc* fan club, for whom Robbins is the Sage of the Skagit Valley, the mushroom magician, the man who wrote the fantasy biography of an American generation by mental radar.

Since 1971, more than a half-million copies of an odd little book called *Another Roadside Attraction* have been sold nationwide. God knows how many people have read it; dogeared copies pass from hand to hand, and it is a rare one that turns up in a secondhand bookstore. And unlike most novels, popular or otherwise, it keeps right on selling. *Another Roadside Attraction* is one of an oddly assorted but select company of books that just keeps going, season after season, year after year. "The only books in recent years you can compare it to are *Stranger in a Strange Land, Lord of the Rings,* and *Dune,*" says a bookstore buyer. "It's been going steadily for five years and it'll probably go for another five."

Like the other books mentioned, *Another Roadside Attraction* has sold its hundreds of thousands mainly to young people, mainly to readers unaffected by the tastes and fashions of the literary establishment, and almost without publicity except for word-of-mouth. In the shrinking, conglomerate-ridden publishing business, where "novel" is another word for "raw material for a screenplay" and "first novel" is a synonym for "tax loss," works like these are called "cult books"; or, in other words, "We don't understand it, we don't like it, but that's no reason we can't get a piece of the action."

When in 1976, the respectable Boston firm of Houghton Mifflin published Robbins's second novel, *Even Cowgirls Get the Blues,* cult author or not, they gave it the full estab-

"My main reason for coming to the Northwest was it was just as far as I could get from Richmond, Virginia."

Somewhere out there the Robbins people were waiting

lishment treatment: a strikingly ugly full-page ad in *Publishers Weekly*, plenty of advance copies circulated to big bookstore accounts, and some high-powered lobbying to nab reviews in the mass-circulation weeklies. But it was not the department stores and *The New York Review of Books* that Houghton Mifflin was counting on to earn back the whopping fifty thousand dollar advance paid Robbins for *Cowgirls*. Somewhere out there—in dorms on the far side of the Charles, in fifth-floor SoHo lofts, in Oregon farmhouses and Colorado ski shacks, in paisley-curtained VW buses, Montana pickup trucks, and Greyhound waiting rooms—the Robbins people were waiting.

> "There are three things that I like," Amanda exclaimed upon awaking from her first long trance. "These are: the butterfly, the cactus and the Infinite Goof."
> Later she amended the list to include mushrooms and motorcycles.
> ——*Another Roadside Attraction*

Roosting on a hill overlooking the murky Skagit Valley waterscape that his book has made part of the American psychic slide show, Robbins in some ways appeared a mode of novelist-on-the-verge-of-publication: pleased by his fifty thousand dollar advance, but quickly pointing out that it is not all that much for five years of work, delighted by the fact that *Cowgirls* is already in its third printing before publication day, looking forward with a kind of horrified glee to an autograph tour.

But, like Amanda, Robbins also believes in the Infinite Goof. He has good reason to. The whole history of *Another Roadside Attraction,* from birth to best-sellerdom, provides him with ample proof for his belief that the universe has a very peculiar sense of humor.

His childhood was rich in productive contradictions. He was born in Blowing Rock, North Carolina, in the high, far northwest of the state where the Iron Mountains curve around from Tennessee into Virginia. "In the summer, it was a resort town, full of Rolls-Royces and Cadillacs; in the winter it was Dogpatch: hillbillies drinking and shooting each other. My parents were respectable folk—daddy worked for the power company and my mother was the daughter of a Baptist minister—but there was bad blood in the family, too: her brother was a disc jockey on WBT, and he was a great drinker and womanizer. One night a lady's husband came up in the elevator during "Carolina Hayride" and shot him, right on the air."

The literary gift was manifested early: "My first story was about a man who was stranded on a desert island with a brown cow with yellow spots. They were both hungry, but the man didn't want to eat the cow, so they both learned to eat sand together." Most of those years were spent in the usual way of "sensitive" children, in the cultivation of a rich fantasy life: "My heroes in those days were Tarzan and Jesus. I read a million comic books and listened to "I Love a Mystery" on the radio: Jack, Doc, and Reggie. I can still remember two of those serials: "My Beloved Is a Vampire" and "The Thing that Cried in the Night."

When Tom was nine the family moved to Virginia, where he devoted the next decade or so to slowly falling short of his family's expectations. After two years during which the College of William and Mary vainly tried to make a Virginia gentleman of him, he hit the road; then for contrast he spent a couple of years after dropping out of Air Force Officer Candidate School behind a steel door at SAC Headquarters in Omaha intercepting coded Chinese weather messages. He polished this fine grounding in weirdness with a couple of years of philosophy and art history at Richmond Professional Institute. (Those years in the boneyard of the Confederacy bear fruit in the opening chapters of *Even Cowgirls Get the Blues,* which in their way do for fifties Richmond what *The Day of the Locust* did for twenties Hollywood.)

"I left for the Northwest as soon as I got out of college in 1962," Robbins says, in a tobacco-dust drawl that years of Pacific fog have not softened. "In school I had been a budding mystic. I studied about Tobey and Graves, and got curious about a place where an American kind of mysticism could develop. Of course, I was a kind of naïve romantic then: I'd heard that Graves lived with some woodpeckers in a hollow tree. My main reason for coming to the Northwest was it was just as far as I could get from Richmond, Virginia. But I was still enough ruled by the Protestant Ethic that I needed A Reason to come, so I enrolled in the graduate school of Far Eastern Philosophy at the UW."

"I got here in the winter and school didn't start till the fall, so I got a part-time job at the *Times* filling in for the guy who did 'Ask Andy.' By the time he got back from vacation, the art critic had quit, so I went over there to help out Lou Guzzo while he shopped around for a new one. I sat there, watching Lou interviewing these ladies with their fur pieces and their Helena Rubenstein treatments, and I said to myself, 'Well, Tom, if art is ever going to have a chance in this town, somebody besides them had better take this job': so I applied for the job myself and Lou gave it to me. Lou was always like a father to me."

If that doesn't sound unlikely enough, Lou Guzzo agrees: "The feeling was mutual. Tom was *different:* I've always thought he was a genius of sorts. He was one of the first of the rebels and a prophet: why, he foresaw this present subculture—we disagreed about some of its values of course—but he foresaw it."

It was not all foresight: Robbins was picking up a little practical experience at the same time. Shortly after arriving in the Northwest, he became interested in edible mushrooms; an article in *Life* magazine brought it to his attention that there were other kinds. "I went down to Olympia where Margaret McKinney, the Mushroom Lady, lived, and said to her, 'Miz McKinney, I have heard about another kind of mushroom that makes you see jeweled castles: do you know where I could get some?' And Miz McKinney wasn't interested in that kind of mushroom, but she knew someone who was, and they knew some-

Jack Kerouac

Sixties hip generation writers such as Jack Kerouac, Gary Snyder, and Ken Kesey are normally associated with California, but many of them drew inspiration from the forest-and-mountain landscapes of the Northwest. Kerouac spent one summer at a fire lookout in the Cascades, and his little cabin became the object of a literary pilgrimage years later by a writer who kept the Kerouac flame burning in Seattle, Darrell Bob Houston.

From "Kerouac in the Cascades," by Darrell Bob Houston, Seattle Weekly, *October 18, 1978. Copyright © the Houston family. Reprinted by permission.*

Desolation Peak Summit

I shiver here in Jack Kerouac's old leather-thonged bunk, staring through the northern windows of the lookout cabin. Far off I see the cobalt strand that is Canada. I see the Lonesome Star rising between the black fangs of Hozomeen. Outside the shack's door the wind gauge rides its creaking pole. Rigging wires hum. To the east, Venus throbs blood-orange over mountains whose names I'll never know. The dot of an airliner cuts through the stars. The wind stops. Desolation lies in solitude. It is the time of hobo angels and haiku monks; it is midnight in the balcony of the world.

The pilot light of the propane stove casts a glow inside the cabin. I tiptoe across the icy floor. I bump into a table, perhaps the one on which Kerouac played his solitaire baseball game during the 63 days he spent here in the summer of 1956. Here, too, he wrote the first part of *Desolation Angels*. . . .

[The next morning] I linger by the stove where Kerouac flipped his hotcakes . . . years ago. At last, I tell myself, the pilgrimage is completed. You have stood beside the railroad tracks in Mexico where Neal Cassady, Kerouac's hero and road-pard, lay down to die. Now you have finally made it to Desolation. Pay your final respects, but keep the flashbacks short.

Recall Kerouac as he was at 34, sitting muscularly at that table in his lumberjack shirt, working away—between bouts of fire-watching, day-dreaming, boredom, and loneliness for Neal and the gang waiting down in San Francisco's North Beach—on *Desolation Angels*. Don't forget his prophecy of a rucksack revolution, and how it grew. Or his fantasy of Gary Snyder, his old dharma buddy who got him a job as a fire lookout in the first place, scaling these "vast triangular mountain walls" like a goat. Recall that, long before anybody even thought of making this wilderness a park, he enshrined the North Cascades with his words.

And before you get too damned Zenistic about it, there's one more shrine to visit. Kerouac's outhouse—the greatest john in the world.

Yep. There it sits, moon-doored and tottery, on the hell-blown edge of No-

Jack Kerouac

where, still facing across Lightning Gorge to the east. One false step and you've got a good start toward Montana.

I try, but it's hard to get nostalgic over a toilet.

I heft my mailbag. I start down the trail at a half-trot. At the first white stump I turn. The poet's frail pagoda hangs there in the fog, like a Chinese drawing on a strand of old grey silk. There is nothing left to quote, or even remember. It is time to say goodbye forever to all my Desolation Angels

one else who knew about something *much* better and safer than mushrooms, and they knew someone else who knew where to get it..."

And so it came to pass that on the morning of July the 16th, 1963, a Tuesday morning when he was supposed to be making the rounds of the galleries for the *Times,* Tom Robbins was sitting in an easy chair in the Ballard love nest of a UW professor, deep in conversation with a daisy and with three hundred micrograms of pure, fresh legal Sandoz lysergic acid diethylamide dissolving under his belt buckle.

"It was the most important event in my life. I can't even remember when my book was published, but I remember that date. I sat in that armchair for eight hours. I got up only to go to the bathroom, and that was like the voyage of Ulysses. You can't communicate the things that matter in an experience like that—I can remember looking at a picture of a lady wearing slacks and working out a whole theory of engineering based on the way the seat of the pants fit her—but the most important thing was the relationship I developed with that daisy. Looking at it, I realized that that daisy had an identity, a personality, every bit as real as my own.

"But the primary effect of that day was to make me very lonely. I had had an experience that I couldn't share. It was like I had been brought up all my life as a Southern Baptist, and suddenly I found out like Moses that I was a Jew. I was living then with a lady who liked to drink. First I gave up drinking. Then I gave up the lady and my job and everything else and went to New York, because it was the only place I knew where there were other people who had had that experience.

"Even then, I had to think up a practical reason for doing it—I was going to write a book about Jackson Pollock and abstract expressionism. But one night I was lying on a cot on the Lower East Side reading *Sometimes a Great Notion* and I heard rain falling softly on ferns: so I came home."

The postacid Robbins returned to a town that was beginning to vibrate slightly from the cultural earthquakes happening elsewhere and wasn't sure it liked the feeling. Strangers, both Ivy League and shaggy, were beginning to infiltrate its institutions. In the art world the long, icy fog of the Northwest School was beginning to break up; a new kind of rock 'n' roll was stealing the children and beginning to soften their brains for the Hard Stuff; a noisy, glossy, trendy, suspiciously East-Coast monthly magazine was making fun of Our Institutions; worst of all, it was financed by the scion of one of the Northwest's First Families, so it couldn't just be crushed like a bug.

"When Tom was writing, it was all there for the first time. Art in Seattle hasn't been much fun since."

"Practically the first thing I did when I got back was to go over to *Seattle* magazine to give them hell about butchering an article I'd sent them from New York. So I chewed them out and they offered me a job." The funky Southerner with the funny gleam behind his eyes wasn't very comfortable with the Ivy Gang at *Seattle*—"They all thought that they were in some kind of Cole Porter musical... Every time I hear 'These Foolish Things,' I see Peter

Felix watching over Robbins's desk
in La Conner

Bunzel and Charlie Michener tap-dancing in white-tie-and-tails in front of a mirror"—but as a publication, *Seattle* was just what Robbins and the hypoxygenated Seattle art scene needed.

"In those days, you painted with the palette they gave you or you didn't get shown," says Burt Garner, who arrived in town about the same time: "I mean, if you wanted to use *red* or something, forget it." Out at the University and around town there were some young artists—Trudy Pacific, Larry Beck, the Heald Gang, Don Scott—who wanted even more unreasonable things, and a few galleries trying to show them. In his *Seattle* articles Robbins criticized, cajoled, clowned, insisting there was more to art than watercolors and fifty-thousand-dollar tasteful swirls. "He helped mount some shows," remembers Garner, "including the one at the Attica with the weenies all over the place and the painted camper and the girls' marching band." He staged happenings, even managing to get modestly arrested for one he did at The Kirkland Creative Arts League. "For art to mean anything, you've got to have all the pieces; the artists, the galleries, the public, and the critics," says Jimmy Manolides, who about this time was making the transition from full-time rock 'n' roller to gallery owner. "When Tom was writing, it was all there for the first time. Art in Seattle hasn't been much fun since."

A lot of people loved Robbins's one-man critical show, but he, like *Seattle,* also made plenty of enemies in a one-museum town. Lou Guzzo recalls, "I wanted to make him a star at the *P-I;* I was going to install him as arts critic. But Tom had written some wonderfully scathing things about these housewife artists, and the wife of the publisher, Dan Starr, knew some of those ladies, so Starr wouldn't touch him. 'This guy doesn't know anything about art,' he said."

Robbins's career as Seattle's top critic would probably have lasted just as long as *Seattle,* but before the Establishment quicksand sucked it under, fate, or something, curled up in his mailbox and changed all that.

"One day I went to the mailbox, and in it there was a letter from Luther Nichols, who was the West Coast representative for a publishing company called Doubleday. And Mr. Nichols said that he had read some of my *Seattle* pieces and liked them, and when he was in town he would like to get together with me and talk about doing a book for them. A book. First time the thought had ever crossed my mind. I said to myself, well, here it is, my life is changed. So I wrote back and said, why, yes, Mr. Nichols, I would be happy to meet you.

"We got together in the old coffee shop of the Benjamin Franklin where he was staying—I was just one of a lot of appointments he had that day—and he told me that they were interested in having me write a book for them about West Coast art, or any art, right then; so I took a deep breath and told him that what I had in mind was more like A Novel. Well, he covered *his* disappointment very nicely—he even managed to fake quickening interest—and he said, well, that's nice, what's the novel about?

"Now, I'd never thought about writing a novel, let alone written one; but for several years I'd been carrying around in my mind this idea about some people who find the body of Christ in the catacombs and put it on view in a roadside museum. So I told him that that's what the book was about.

"So naturally, he said, I see, that's interesting, tell me more. At that moment, there wasn't any more, but I started talking, and what with his questions and my lying, I came up with an outline. And he said, that's very interesting, when can I see it? So I said, well, it's in awful shape right at the moment, you know, handwritten on scratch paper, it's very sloppy...

"So he said, OK, when you've got it revised and typed out, let me have a look at it. And that was it. I was very naïve about publishing. I thought that if he liked the idea they would give me some money and then I could go off and actually write it. But it doesn't work that

Robbins: the infinite goof

way. So I went home and started in.

"I'm a very slow writer: three pages is a wonderful day for me. I don't rewrite, so every-thing has got to be very clear to me before I go on. It took me so long just to get started that I realized I couldn't do it while I was working full time. So I quit my job and moved out to La Conner and took a part-time job at the *P-I* on weekends writing headlines." (For con-noisseurs of headlines, the late sixties were a Golden Age at the *P-I:* you never knew what was going to turn up when you opened your paper on Sunday and Monday mornings.)

"Finally, I finished Part One and sent it off to Doubleday. Some of the younger editors were really excited by it and recommended that the firm should take an option on the book and send me an advance. But some of the older ones said, well, it's interesting, but we can't quite see where it's going. I couldn't be much help to them, since I didn't know where it was going either. So I went to work on Part Two.

Ivan Doig

Ivan Doig, once a sheep-rancher in Montana, began his career as a novelist of the American West by reading comic books. After a brief stint in Illinois as a magazine journalist, Doig and his wife Carol moved to Seattle in 1966, where he got his doctorate in history from the University of Washington. His sensitive Montana memoir, **This House of Sky,** *was a finalist for the National Book Award.*

From "Ivan Doig," by Wendy Smith, Publishers Weekly, September 18, 1987. Copyright © 1987 Wendy Smith. *Reprinted by permission.*

The West Ivan Doig knows so intimately and writes about with such eloquence is *not* the West of legend. "I'm writing deliberately about sheepherding, because we've had too damn much cowboy West. I don't think that's what the West has been about, although we've got a guy in the White House who thinks so: too many movie sets will give you that idea. The West has been about families, schoolteachers, miners, fur trappers, town-builders, all kinds of people coming out here to try and make a living. I'm trying to write against the grain of what I call 'Wisterns,' after Owen Wister, the author of *The Virginian*. He went off from Philadelphia and Harvard and got in with some of the rich cattlemen of Wyoming. So far as he could tell, no one in the West ever had to do any work. In 'Wisterns' it's all card games and saving schoolmarms; nobody ever milks a cow or plants a spud. As best I can tell, there's got to be some kind of catering service out of Omaha that comes out and takes care of the whole damn West. It's nonsense, and I think it's harmful nonsense.

"So much of the West has been nurtured and can only be nurtured by Federal policy: the national forest, the Park Service, the Bureau of Land Management. It's an enormous, dry, fragile part of our country—what Wallace Stegner called 'a land of little rainfall and big consequences.' We've had a complex history of coming to terms with that; there's an ecologically, socially and culturally complex quilt out here from the Ohio River westward. To think that fixing it is just a matter of strapping on your chaps and six-gun is infantile nonsense. This almost tidal swash back and forth between beneficial consequences and harmful consequences interests me."

Doig's characters are always aware that actions have consequences, and the plots of his novels are often driven by the conflict between people's desires and their strong sense of responsibility. "My characters accept that in their lives they do have second thoughts, that part of what we carry around in the attic of our heads are our thoughts about the past. You feel your way along and do as much as you can, yet trying at some point to lead your own life. You're forever feeling your way along this line of equilibrium. Part of the consequence of being alive is that it's not always comfortable." . . .

His strong sense of identity as a Western writer doesn't preclude a larger feeling of kinship with world literature. "I've been very much aware of being a Westerner all my life, partly because of memories of the landscape, partly because of the way I was brought up in the West through the accident of being motherless after I was six. I have in some ways the best of both worlds: I'm halfway regarded as a Montana writer, and yet I live outside. . . .

"Montana has always had this big colonial question, part of the land question: Are we simply, can we ever be, more than an energy colony to be mined? So the West has a lot in common with writers from the old outposts of the British Empire, who are often very skeptical of government and very potent. Nadine Gordimer is one of the most potent writers extant in showing the awful naked skin under her society. Then there are books like *The Book of Ebenezer Le Page* and *Riddley Walker*, which push the language out into odd, eloquent corners of the world: the Isle of Guernsey, post-Holocaust England. I'm tending toward the idea, and I don't think it's at all original with me, that there are quite a bunch of us out here at our own centers of the universe, and they're not the metropolitan, polar centers. It seems to me that there's a new kind of eloquence that is not just an eloquence of the West, but an eloquence of the edge of the world."

Ivan Doig

"The same sort of thing happened with Part Two: the younger editors were crazy about it; the older ones who had been kicked upstairs kept saying, well, it's *interesting,* but...There was a young, beautiful Jewish lady at Doubleday who used to write me about the in-house fights going on. All this time I was going through these terrible mood changes: one day I'd read some back and say, hey, this is pretty good stuff, and the next time I read it I'd come close to burning it. But after they sent back Part Two and asked to see some more before they made up their minds, I said to myself, fuck it: I don't know if it's really good or really terrible, but it's a *book.* So I went back to work and finished it.

"They bought it. I got twenty-five hundred dollars and left for Japan. When I got back with a bad cough from the Tokyo smog, things looked pretty good. Graham Greene sent a cable from England saying the book was magnificent; Lawrence Ferlinghetti loved it, Herbert Gold loved it, the *LA Times* loved it, *Rolling Stone* loved it—and Doubleday let it die. They had a promotion budget; they never spent it. They didn't even advertise it. There was one very important thing about Doubleday I hadn't known. For many years it had been a very conservative, *Catholic* publishing house. There had been some changes, but up at the top there were all these old fellows who did not think there was anything funny about a novel concerning how a dope dealer finds Jesus's body in a catacomb under the Vatican, or about an order of assassin priests, or, well, you know. The book disappeared. After a while I got a letter that the paperback rights had been sold to Ballantine. And that was it.

"Things started to change when Theodore Sturgeon reviewed the paperback edition in *Galaxy. Another Roadside Attraction* is not science fiction, but Sturgeon liked it, and there is one thing about science-fiction fans: they buy a *lot* of books. City Lights in San Francisco and Cody's in Berkeley started to get calls for it. It started selling in bookstores in college towns and just kept on going.

"A little while after I got back from Japan I began to feel faint stirrings and I started to write another book. By this time I had an agent: a sweet, vague Gemini lady who leaves my manuscripts under palm trees and in Greyhound bus stations; but she takes care of me. One day she called me up and said, 'Hey, you're worth more than Doubleday will give you—Doubleday had an option on my second book—let's break your contract!' She went in there like a killer shark and the next six months were real hairy, but she pulled it off. She sold *Cowgirls* directly to Signet paperbacks. The hardcover publishers were not amused."

One thing disappoints Robbins about the success of *Another Roadside Attraction.* "The reviews were about 90 percent favorable—the reviewer in *Playboy* compared me to Nabokov and Borges!—but they never dealt with the questions I hoped the book would make people discuss: the question of Christ's divinity and what this has meant for the West over the last two thousand years."

Well, maybe that is a little much to expect from a jaded bunch like literary critics. A lot of people *did* appreciate just that side of *Another Roadside Attraction:* the people who wrote letters to him or Joanie, the girl who was chosen by her Arkansas commune to take a Greyhound to the Northwest and meet the author. Since his days as Seattle's first underground disc jockey (Sunday nights from 8 to 10 on KRAB), Robbins has had the uncanny ability to make people feel that he is talking directly to them alone. "I finally had to stop it. I got calls from high-school kids who said 'You're the only adult I ever thought I could talk to. Tell me what to do.' And no matter what you said, you knew that next week they'd be back. One day a kid came to the station who wanted to sing his songs on the show, and I can remember thinking, 'Everybody is talking about the hippie philosophy and here is somebody who really *believes* it: he's like a man who's discovered electricity and knows nothing about insulation.' I went off the next day on a peyote hunt in New Mexico and sort of forgot about him. When the Sharon Tate [murder] business was in the papers, something seemed familiar about it, and sure enough...I don't know if Lorenzo [Milam] ever made a tape of him singing his songs or not."

Still, even the most devoted readers of *Another Roadside Attraction* probably would not say that Robbins's thoughts on the divinity of Jesus and Catholic hypocrisy are the most important things in the book. As a matter of fact, by any kind of English 301-Art-of-the-Novel standard, *Another Roadside Attraction* is a terrible mess, full of dry lectures, dead ends and trapdoors of plot, beaver-board characters, grinding syntax, and as much superfluous verbal tinsel as a department store Christmas tree. A lot of readers who operate by those standards get stopped dead before the end of Part One. And the Ideas, valid or not, do not help one bit.

But of course, Robbins never took English 301—"I know that in a book like this I'm juggling a lot of things, and I drop some, and some roll under the couch and I never find them again"—and we're all a lot better off because he didn't. Reading *Another Roadside Attraction* is like being invited by a hairy, grinning, soft-spoken stranger to go swimming in his murky, silty backyard consciousness-pond, and discovering after the first shock that the water's fine: very much, in fact, like the one in your own backyard, the one you put up NO SWIMMING signs around.

Whether it is something the daisy taught him, or whether he had it all along, Robbins has the shaman's gift: he can make the Universe speak—not just animals or trees, but weenies and mufflers and water molecules. Lots of people can draft a clean plot and plausible characters; but there are not many others who can make Existence such an exciting place to be.

But it does make Robbins hard for critics to read—harder than most of the "new novelists": "I can't conceive of writing a book without a plot, but for me the plot is one thing and the book another, with the plot definitely secondary. My sort of writing goes by many critics. they can relate to Tom McGuane, because they can see that he's a kind of bent extension of Hemingway, and Kesey, because he's a bent extension of Faulkner. But writers like me and Ishmael Reed, for instance, don't come out of that tradition at all: if they're looking for my influences, they'll have to remember that I studied art in school and go take a look at John Cage."

Cowgirls is a lot more straightforward book—literally: maybe the saga of Sissy Hankshaw is not traditional narrative, but whatever it is, it's exhilarating high-octane stuff. And cleaning up his narrative act does not stop Robbins from doing what he does best and hardly anybody else can do at all.

Something important happened to us in the sixties. Looking around today, it is hard to tell whether it died and rotted, went away without leaving a forwarding address, or soaked in so deep it doesn't show. *Cowgirls* may affect you like a picture-postcard of palm trees and sand that arrives in the middle of winter—with a golden aura of that past around it.

THE PEACE BISHOP

ARCHBISHOP RAYMOND HUNTHAUSEN (1920–)

CYNTHIA H. WILSON AND REBECCA BOREN

If God had told a college sophomore named Raymond Hunthausen he did not have what it takes to be a priest, the young man might have become a stunt pilot flying the P-38s he loved to watch flashing across the Montana skies. His interest in chemistry might have led him toward a medical career. Or he might have inherited the brewmaster's job at his grandfather's Rocky Mountain Brewery in Anaconda. But God, Hunthausen's professors, and the young man's own conscience would not let him off the hook.

So one day in 1941, he told his father he had decided to become a priest. They were playing golf, and the senior Hunthausen, a veteran of World War I, had just been urging his oldest boy to move into officer's training, where he would have the best shot at flying. But the sudden news that his son's life had taken a different turn thrilled him, and later he was to write, "When I think of that day, my Adam's apple becomes unruly."

It is safe to say that neither father nor son had any inkling then that the quiet, deferential Raymond Hunthausen would eventually find himself one of the most controversial Roman Catholic leaders in the country, or that his unqualified opposition to the nuclear arms race—and his consequent act of civil disobedience—would unsettle the public conscience. Nor would these two staunchly loyal Catholics have imagined that Archbishop Hunthausen would end up the target of an unprecedented public investigation by the Vatican, an event with larger implications for the American church itself.

In fact, the archbishop's life at sixty-eight is full of contradictions no one would have predicted. Despite his position as head of the largest church in Western Washington, he is virtually unknown in local civic and political circles, and can walk down the street unrecognized. He had to be introduced to the Seahawks' owners at a pregame brunch, yet a few weeks later the mention of his name evoked prolonged applause at peace vigils in Washington DC and New York City. He lives in the least-Catholic American city outside the South, yet during his tenure the Archdiocese of Seattle has become known to outsiders, depending on their political stripe, as a laboratory for the evolution of a new church, or as the Berkeley of Catholicism.

What propelled a man utterly without evangelistic zeal or political ambition to take

"Becoming a bishop was the remotest thing from my mind," Hunthausen says.

such a bold step? Is he the prophet his most devoted admirers believe might save us from nuclear winter, or is he merely a "holy naïf," an impressive witness to the purest form of Christian morality, but a man unable to affect the course of history?

Anyone looking for a magisterial bearing or other tangible sign of Raymond Hunthausen's episcopal eminence will be disappointed. The archbishop does not fit the part. He has the short, compact body of a wrestler, the square hands of a truck driver, the silver gray receding hair and kindly expression of a favorite uncle. Everything about him bespeaks small-town warmth, which seems perfectly natural when he talks about a boyhood family life straight off a Norman Rockwell canvas. His parents, German stock on both sides, settled in Anaconda before World War I and married after Anthony Hunthausen returned from duty in France. Raymond, "Dutch" by age six, was the oldest of seven children whose lives were full of enormous family gatherings at the homes of their grandparents. "Those were noisy, happy times," Hunthausen says with a grin. "We recall them with such delight that my brothers and sisters and I will throw a family reunion at the drop of a hat." (That is no small project these days; a gathering of his father's clan one recent summer in Wyoming drew 140 relatives.) The Hunthausens were not immune from trouble—the future archbishop wrecked the family car as a teenager, and his father extended enough credit from his grocery store that the family had to scrape some during the Depression—but generally Hunthausen remembers "lots of comfortableness" in their home and a Rock-of-Gibraltar sense of stability. "We were more blessed than most."

No doubt that security was bolstered by an easy intimacy between his family and the church, in a town that was 50 percent Catholic. The Hunthausen children went to parochial schools during the week, trooped down the street to mass every Sunday, sang in the choir, and visited the Ursuline nuns' convent across the street from their grandparents' house at Christmas. The archbishop still drops in on his old Ursuline teachers on return trips to Montana, because "I'm their boy."

Though Anthony Hunthausen was a civic leader by temperament—big, jovial, easy with people—his son Dutch shied away from the spotlight. "I always have found it easier to follow," he confesses. But the nuns pushed "their boy" to give the welcoming speeches whenever the bishop of Helena would visit, thereby setting the pattern Hunthausen repeats to this day. "It killed me, but I did it out of duty and respect," he says. "Now I realize it was important to have been pushed. I still feel a sense of pressure about everything."

That is a typical Hunthausen statement. So is "I never had my own a-to-b-to-c agenda," and each provides a clue to why the archbishop does not meet traditional expectations of a leader. Instead of initiating action, Hunthausen's lifelong habit has been to respond. He seems always to have set out in one direction, only to have been steered another way—by people, by events, and ultimately, he says with a faint smile, by God. Thus, despite his interest in pursuing chemical engineering at Montana State University, he went

St. James Cathedral

Hunthausen: a prisoner of his own
bureaucracy

to Carroll College in Helena, a small school known for its religious education, because "my local priest would be happy." There he met Father Bernard Topel, later bishop of Spokane, who strongly influenced him to enter the priesthood. "Humanly speaking, I didn't want to be a priest," Hunthausen recalls. "I was attracted to marriage and family life, and I wanted to fly airplanes. I'd have been relieved if Father Topel had said, "Don't, you aren't cut out to be a priest." "Humanly speaking" is another characteristic expression for a man who often describes his life as the road not taken.

The road he did take led next to the St. Edwards Seminary in Kenmore, Washington, where he found the 7:00 A.M. to 11:00 P.M. regimen, rigorous but not onerous, despite the fact that he arrived only minimally equipped to read the Latin texts. "The real struggle was over whether or not I should be there at all," he says. Yet he kept his doubts about his vocation mostly to himself, airing them only in his correspondence with Father Topel.

Seminary training did not make Hunthausen a scholar or a theologian. "I wish I avidly sought challenging theological materials," he says frankly, "but I'd honestly rather read books on the peace movement, women's roles in the church, or *US Catholic*. I'd rather know what *people* are reading." He did not see himself as a leader at St. Edwards, either, but he was chosen head sacristan. Preparing the chapel for the liturgical celebration was an honor in the seminary world, but Hunthausen points out wryly that when the students joked about who among them was "ecclesiastical timber," his name never came up. Even if no one thought he would be a bishop, Hunthausen was well liked for what former classmate Father Joseph Oblinger calls "his genuine manliness. He was deeply spiritual, but never pious."

Hunthausen was ordained June 1, 1946. "At the moment of ordination, when I heard

472

myself promising a life of prayer and celibacy, all my doubts were resolved, even though other choices were finally cut off." He went back to Helena with a sense of peace in his heart and expectations of running a parish, but he was soon returned to Carroll College as a chemistry professor. Though "being a teacher had never entered my mind," he loved working with the intense premed and predental students he found there, and he fell accidentally into coaching, his second great love.

Dutch Hunthausen had played football (back), basketball (guard), and baseball (shortstop) as a student at Carroll, and as a new faculty member he began working out with coach John Gagliardi. The explanation for Hunthausen's success as a coach depends on whom you talk to: Hunthausen credits Gagliardi for handing on winning game plans, but Father Joseph Sullivan, who played football and basketball under Hunthausen, calls his former coach "a great strategist who knew how to play to the strengths of his team." In four years of coaching football, basketball, baseball, track, and golf, Hunthausen's teams won eight conference championships, and the winning coach was inducted into the National Association of Intercollegiate Athletics Hall of Fame. (He also installed the sprinkler system and turf for the new football field himself.)

By 1957, Hunthausen was president of Carroll College and thought he had found his ultimate niche. He was comfortable, attached, and not much troubled. But five years later he was appointed bishop of Helena. It was an unlikely event, since his predecessor also had been from Montana, and native-son bishops are rare. "Becoming a bishop was the remotest thing from my mind," Hunthausen says. "I wanted to run away because I was sure I didn't have what it takes. Finally I said if God wants this, it'll have to be his doing. He'll have to make me big enough for the job."

It has been said more than once that God changed the job to fit Raymond Hunthausen. Personally unassertive and little interested in politics or administration, Hunthausen probably would not have fit into the ranks of traditional American prelates. These were the "brick-and-mortar" bishops, the autocratic administrators who built the physical structure of an immigrant church. While amassing money to open parishes, schools, orphanages, and hospitals in the prewelfare era, they also built up the church's political power and civic prestige, and controlled that power with iron hands. In many cases, the traditional bishop's interest lay more in the strength of the institution than in the souls it was meant to serve.

Just two months after Hunthausen's appointment in 1962, however, Pope John XXIII convened the Second Vatican Council, an event that was to transform the church, its bishops, and their relation to its people more radically than any since the Reformation. Concerned about Roman Catholicism's declining credibility, the pope called for a sweeping reexamination of the church's doctrines, liturgy, and relation to the world. The question he posed to the assembled magisterium was: are we being faithful to the Gospel?

Mark Allison
Matthews

The tall and commanding minister of the First Presbyterian Church in Seattle, Mark Allison Matthews dominated much of the city's morals and politics from 1902 to 1940. He built up a large church and expanded his influence by pioneering use of the radio. The scope of Matthews's sway reminds one of the blue-nosed traditions of Seattle. That tradition waged many a war with the open-city mores of a seaport town.

From "Mission in the Wilderness," by David M. Buerge, Seattle Weekly, December 25, 1985. Copyright © 1985 David M. Buerge. Reprinted by permission.

Few congregations were as ambitious as Seattle's First Presbyterian Church under the leadership of the Reverend Mark Allison Matthews. From 1902 to 1940 he was undoubtedly the most influential church figure in town. Matthews was raised in the South. His commanding preaching style and sympathy for farmers and workers made him a leader in Populist and Progressive reforms and the Social Gospel. Accepting the pastorate offered him in 1902 by First Presbyterian, he made his goal the religious development of Seattle as a righteous community that would be an important staging area from which missionaries could embark for Asia to complete the Christian conquest of the world and usher in its transformation.

Under his dynamic leadership, First Presbyterian's congregation soon numbered in excess of 6,000, eventually becoming the largest Presbyterian church in the world. It plunged into community work, operating a day nursery, the city's first successful kindergarten, and an unemployment bureau. It . . . offered English classes for Japanese immigrants. It supported development of a juvenile court and established the city's first anti-tuberculosis center, the ancestor of Firlands Sanitorium.

Matthews called for the development of city parks, art galleries, and libraries, and the development of a medical school at the University of Washington. He campaigned for the concepts of initiative, referendum, and recall, worked for the institutions of the direct primary and supported labor-management negotiations and consumer protection. But if Matthews dazzled reformers with his progressive zeal, he was in no sense a liberal on moral issues, and he used his great influence in an attempt to make Seattle conform to his moral vision of a "holy city."

A fanatical prohibitionist, Matthews once described the saloon as "the most fiendish, corrupt and hell-soaked institution that ever crawled out of the slime of the eternal pit." Prohibition was a major component of Progressive reform and the one in which the churches, as the "praying wing" of the movement, exercised the most influence. The prohibition movement that gathered steam as the century turned was very much a reaction against the type of society America had become: urban, cosmopolitan, technical, and dynamic. Prohibitionists longed nostalgically for the supposed virtues and stasis of an earlier, rural time, and if they could not restore the pastoral, they could at least strike down some of the more egregious modern blights.

The cast of characters in the new century was much as it had been in the old: property-owning middle class families against transient workers and business-men. After women lost the vote in '87, the temperance movement lost much of its political clout, and gambling, horse racing and prostitution took its place on the moral agenda. Matthews led the fight: he sent numerous church agents into the red-light district to ferret out evidence of official graft, and he was a vociferous opponent of mayoral candidate Hiram Gill.

In one of the pendulum swings of the perennial battle between the reformers and the business community, Hiram Gill had run for mayor on the issue of "wide-open town" and won, promising his supporters that he would protect saloons and gambling halls and permit prostitution in the skid road district. "Hell!," he once said to a friend, "this is a seaport town, ain't it?" As long as the abuses were not too flagrant, the city seemed willing to tolerate in public what it might abhor privately. And there were the familiar economic reasons: the economy was slow and vice was an important source of municipal revenue.

But in 1910, the forces of reform were resurrected when the vote was returned to women, and then, serendipitously, Gill blundered. He had promised to keep prostitution within the skid road area, but then it was made public that he had given some of his friends the contract to build what was described as the "world's largest brothel" south of it in Georgetown.

Matthews and others pressed for a recall vote, and, marshaling the women's vote, Gill was "diselected" in 1911. The brothel was converted into a rooming house. After that, Matthews's influence in the city was immense. According to his biographer, Dr. Dale Soder, many believed that George Dilling, the man who succeeded Gill in office, took his orders from Matthews, and that the subsequent election of George Cotterill, the reform candidate who had written the 1910 suffrage amendment, was due largely to Matthews's support.

Once under way, the reform movement gained momentum. Pitting themselves against the business community, the

Mark Allison Matthews

Evangelical churches led by Matthews worked for the passage of Initiative 3, which called for an end to the manufacture and sale of liquor by January 1, 1916. The initiative won statewide, and even though it lost in Seattle, 39 percent of the city's voters approved it. In 1917, the state Legislature banned the importation of liquor, and in 1919, with no opposition, it ratified the 18th Amendment to the Federal Constitution. Prohibition had won.

Prohibition was *the* great Protestant crusade of the 20th century, "the last grand concert of the old moral order." As such, its ultimate failure marked the end of Protestant ascendancy in American life. As it became obvious that prohibition could not or would not be enforced, the optimism of those who hoped it could bring about the restoration of virtue and the agrarian dream turned to despair. In the Protestant churches, this was compounded by a growing rift between the supporters of the Social Gospel and those who revolted at what they perceived as its excesses: the substitution of sociology for theology, the secularization of the spiritual. These sought to return to what they identified as the fundamentals of Christianity.

In its search for the answers, the council concluded for the first time that the church was subject to history, time, and change, that its fundamental truths might be expressed differently in different cultures, and that each individual "has the duty, and therefore the right, to seek the truth in matters religious, in order that he may with prudence form for himself right and true judgments of Conscience." Before Vatican II, most doctrines and details of the Mass had been frozen with adamantine finality, their administration the sole province of the clergy. But in redefining the church as "the whole people of God," whose faith was a matter of personal experience as well as submission to ecclesiastical authority, the council empowered the laity to help define Catholic morals and to share in the governance and ritual life of the church.

Above all, explains Hunthausen, "Vatican II called us back to the primacy of love in our lives. We had become overly reliant on the power of law and discipline, and had put aside the very principle that undergirds the church's existence. The council and the Gospels tell each one of us to be *responsible,* to discern as we can in the spirit of love just what God is asking us to do."

Many Catholics found such ideas devastating to the doctrinal clarity and absolutism that had been the basis of traditional Catholicism. Many still do. But the young Bishop Hunthausen, for whom the awesome council was in effect a training ground, welcomed each acknowledgment of the individual conscience and each step toward collegiality, pluralism, and social involvement. He was already so firmly convinced that "the spirit of God moves among all people" that it was natural for him to open the governance of his diocese to parish priests and lay people. "He made the church a democracy," says Robert Beaulieu, a priest who served under the new bishop of Helena. "He expected us to be mature in applying Gospel principles to our jobs, and it gave the whole diocese a new sense of energy and life." Even before Vatican II, Hunthausen believed that racial, class, and sexual inequities conditioned the individual moral response, so he naturally addressed the church's energies to improving social justice. By temperament, his interest already lay in the church as a community, not a corporation. In other words, it required no change in principles and no redirection of focus for Hunthausen to become the new "pastoral" bishop envisioned by the Second Vatican Council. From the earliest days of his appointment, in fact, he has been called "the quintessential Vatican II bishop."

Without that reputation, Hunthausen might not have come to Seattle. By the early seventies, many priests and nuns here were chafing under the old-style authoritarianism of Archbishop Thomas Connolly, who many credit with having built the church of Western Washington, but who could not let go of the power he acquired in the process. Encouraged by Vatican II to believe a change was possible, the clergy submitted a profile of their ideal archbishop to the Most Reverend Jean Jadot, then Rome's apostolic delegate to the United States. They asked for a man of deep spirituality, a man sensitive to social concerns, com-

He has stopped short of calling for the ordination of women as priests, but he insists that the issue cannot be sidestepped.

477

mitted to decentralized, democratic management, and able to enliven the church community with a fresh spirit of love.

It was a prescription for Hunthausen, but his appointment in 1975, like every important turning point in his life, was not on his personal agenda. "I never wanted to leave Montana," the archbishop admits. "I'm not a big-city product, and I found coming here an extraordinary change in my life. I told God I just didn't see it, that if he wanted it, he'd have to provide."

Despite his initial reluctance, Hunthausen soon put his personal stamp on nearly every part of church life. "There is no archdiocese in America where the spirit of Vatican II is taken more seriously," says the Reverend William J. Sullivan SJ, president of Seattle University. Guided by a wisdom of the heart that routinely overrules caution, Hunthausen has reached out to divorced Catholics, those who have had abortions, women, homosexuals, refugees, and minority communities. In the fall of 1983, for example, he allowed a group of Catholic homosexuals called Dignity to celebrate mass at St. James Cathedral, knowing it was "a no-win choice." The archbishop realized his decision could be interpreted as condoning homosexual activity, which the church forbids. "Yet they are Catholics," he says simply. "How could I deny them a church?" A few weeks later he announced that he would support any parish in the archdiocese whose people decided to extend public sanctuary to Latin American refugees, even though that would involve an act of civil disobedience.

"I am challenged increasingly by the nonviolent truth of the cross, by the call of the God of Love to lose our lives for peace."

Hunthausen has endorsed the Equal Rights Amendment, and in 1980 wrote what is thought to be the first pastoral letter by an American archbishop identifying concrete steps the church was to take to "value the gifts of women equally with those of men in its decision-making and the carrying out of its mission." He has stopped short of calling for the ordination of women as priests, but he insists that the issue cannot be sidestepped. Despite Pope John Paul II's warning to American bishops to "withdraw all support" from groups that advocate ordination for women, he regards his brother bishops' decision to issue a pastoral letter on women's rights as "a joyous moment in our history."

If the archbishop's pastoral ministry has won strong loyalty, however, it also has made him vulnerable to critics at home and to suspicion in Rome. In ministering to "the people," he has offended the conservative Catholic elite, many of whom miss the pomp, majesty, and stability of the old church. "He behaves with excessive humility," complains a former member of Archbishop Connolly's kitchen cabinet. "He'll carry your coffee; if you don't watch him, he'll turn into a waiter. He never has understood that kings wore elegant clothes for a reason, that he should look and live like a bishop to give the Roman Church visibility in the secular world." Others fault Hunthausen for not cultivating civic and political power outside the church. His predecessor, they recall, wielded considerable clout in Olympia and in Seattle.

478

Archbishop Raymond
Hunthausen: Are we being faithful
to the Gospel?

It was probably inevitable that Hunthausen's collegial style of management, which worked well enough in the sixty-five parishes of Helena, has drawn fire in the more complex 130-parish archdiocese of Seattle. Since he arrived, the chancery has burgeoned into a bureaucracy with a host of services, and as it has grown the archbishop has delegated what even chancery insiders consider excessive authority to his staff. If parish priests, nuns, and lay workers felt they were too tightly controlled under Connolly, many now complain that no one is in charge, that in consulting everyone about everything, the archbishop has dropped the reins. Ironically, they say, Hunthausen has become a prisoner of his own bureaucracy: the net effect of delegating so much is not true collegiality, but oligarchical rule by a staff that follows only its own liberal agenda.

Most of these complaints reflect the frustration any unwieldy bureaucracy causes its inhabitants, but not much more. "The archdiocese isn't a smoothly sailing ship," remarks

479

Sam Sperry, a lay veteran of several boards, "but it's no Seafirst." In fact, the books are comfortably in the black. And despite the internal chaos, the National Pastoral Planning Conference, an association of about sixty archdioceses around the United States, looks to Seattle as a model of effective long-range planning.

To reach his admittedly radical stand against nuclear arms, Hunthausen has followed his familiar pattern. First came the call to conscience, then the pressure of events, other people, and God. In this case the catalyst was a meeting in 1976 with former Catholic theologian Jim Douglass, who was bound for Washington DC to lead a peace vigil against the navy's plans to base the Trident submarine at Bangor. Unable to ignore the example of a man he felt was following a conscience informed by the Gospels, Hunthausen alerted his priests to Douglass's activities, joined a protest march at Douglass's Ground Zero Center outside the future base, and offered mass at the county jail when Douglass was arrested.

In the spring of 1981, Hunthausen attended a bishops' conference where he heard another prelate say he would withhold part of his taxes as a way to alert people to the escalating arms race. Hunthausen already had agreed to speak to a local Lutheran conference in June, and in that speech he declared that "the teaching of Jesus tells us to render to a nuclear-armed Caesar what that Caesar deserves—tax resistance." At that point he had not decided to disobey the tax laws himself, and he had misgivings about having spoken out so strongly. But when he concluded several months later that withholding half of his own taxes was a personal moral obligation, his doubts disappeared. He never read the tax laws to see what penalties might lie ahead, and admits that the federal taxes on his ten thousand dollar annual income "wouldn't buy a bolt or screw on a single weapon." He is convinced, though, that "the Spirit has been working" to bring him to this point. (Nearly eighteen months after Hunthausen first acted, the IRS sent a computer printout telling him he is in arrears.)

By the fall of 1981, the archbishop had grown bolder, partly because his tax stand had brought in more than eight hundred invitations to speak. He told a peace rally sponsored by the Nuclear Weapons Freeze Campaign that if the Soviets would not agree to a nuclear weapons freeze, the United States should disarm unilaterally. With that, the truly radical element of Hunthausen's thinking emerged: "I am challenged increasingly by the nonviolent truth of the cross, by the call of the God of Love to lose our lives for peace," he said then. "What further steps that will mean in my life, I hope to leave to God's will, as that will is revealed in response to prayer. Whatever it is, I am certain it will be harder than anything I have in mind today. I think one consequence of praying our way into nonviolence is that God takes us more seriously than we wish. A prayerful nonviolence is dangerous to our lives."

It is rare indeed for a modern leader of any stripe to acknowledge that the course he endorses could lead to totalitarian rule or death. Yet Hunthausen has not backed away from either as a possible result of unilateral disarmament. "If the Soviets do not respond in kind as we disarm," he told a Target Seattle audience in 1982, "I am willing to grant that in the end, the worst thing short of nuclear war might occur." The bedrock of his willingness is that Christ died rather than allow his disciples to kill others in his defense. "Human life is sacred," Hunthausen says. "The ultimate evil is that as a nation we are willing to destroy life to protect our lifestyle. There can be no justification whatever for the killing of millions of people. You can't look at the life of the Lord and come to any other conclusion."

This "Gospel logic," as he calls it, brought Hunthausen first to conclude that St. Augustine's theory of the "just war" has been rendered obsolete by modern weapons. Traditionally invoked by Catholic thinkers to justify wars of self-defense, the just-war theory includes the principles of proportionality—the amount of damage done must be proportionate to the end sought—and discrimination—noncombatants must be spared. Clearly, Hunthausen says, neither of these conditions could be fulfilled in a nuclear war. He then rejected the United States policy of deterrence, since "the intention alone to wage nuclear war is an inconceivable sin," and he called for complete renunciation. "From the rejection of any intention whatever to use nuclear weapons, it follows that unilateral disarmament is an unavoidable moral imperative. If we cannot morally use them, nor intend to use them, how can we justify having them?"

While Hunthausen's critics consider this a suicidal form of pacifism, the archbishop sees it as the only true form of self-protection, for he believes that trusting our safety to an arsenal of deadly weapons is the greatest form of danger. He describes unilateral disarmament as a step-by-step process which, by planting the first seeds of trust in a people who do not want to die any more than we do, will lead the Soviets to follow suit. "Unilateral initiatives are not a substitute for disarmament treaties," he insists. "They are a way to make such treaties possible." In Hunthausen's view, such initiatives would "create an alternative power of love in us and in others, and, indeed, a new kind of world."

Few others have followed Hunthausen this far, and more than one ideological opponent has seized the ammunition the archbishop himself has supplied by sometimes getting his facts wrong. He has called the Trident missile a first-strike weapon, though many experts contend the term is to be applied only to faster, more accurate weapons capable of destroying enemy silos or command centers. His labeling the Trident base "the Auschwitz of Puget Sound" may have alienated more people than it convinced in a region heavily dependent on the defense industry. In addition, says one close observer, "he lost lots of potential support when he took the path of civil disobedience." "He doesn't understand the power of the symbols he creates," adds another. "If he were more careful about his facts and more astute about people's political sensibilities, he'd make his point much more strongly."

He was given to understand this was just a friendly visit—although everyone else knew it was an inquisition.

John Leffler

Men of the cloth have not played an especially prominent part in this state, but one who did was the dean of Seattle's St. Mark's Episcopal Cathedral, John Compton Leffler. At a time of racial tension and generation gaps, Leffler's quiet, humorous, tolerant espousal of Christian compassion won him a legion of admirers and helped Seattle through a time that cost many other cities a heavy toll of violence and hostility.

From "The Long, Happy Life of John Compton Leffler," by David Brewster, Seattle Weekly, *December 9, 1981.*

John Leffler came to be dean of Seattle's St. Mark's in 1951, when the cathedral was a troubled church barely out of bankruptcy. St. Mark's needed a liberal to contrast with the Anglo-Catholic local bishop, Stephen Bayne, a popular preacher to revive the congregation, and a skilled diplomat to soothe the anger of the other Anglican clergy, who resented the cathedral's ruinously expensive ambitions. When Leffler arrived in 1951, he found "a dirty, grimy, dismal church" with blackout paint still on some windows from the degrading days when it had been closed, put up for sale, and used briefly as an Army training center for an anti-aircraft contingent.

Indeed, St. Mark's had become an awkward symbol for Seattle's normally faltering stab at religion. Conceived in grandiose scale as a victory cathedral to celebrate the end of World War I (complete with a 250-foot-high tower), it achieved only a truncated portion of its intended size, fell into debt, and was foreclosed in 1941. No one would buy it, so "The Holy Box" struggled back to life in 1944, retired the mortgage (thanks to a civic crusade by Henry Ketcham, Emil Sick, and Dave Beck—the latter regularly grumbles that he gets precious little credit from the city's first families for saving their church), beat back more architectural fantasies, and ended up as a touching half-ruin of raw concrete walls and massive wooden beams in the roof. Stunted, drab, and vast, it stood as an empty shell awaiting some new spirit to fill the vacuum.

The Dean plunged in, and in the process of succeeding he became an antidote to the town's previous great religious leader, the stern Presbyterian moralist Mark Matthews. Leffler's approach was to downplay the monarchical overtones of a cathedral and instead to treat St. Mark's as a whopping parish church in which all the tumultuous, colorful, flamboyant, and questing spirit of the Capitol Hill population could find a home. In this, St. Mark's echoed the national experience of the Episcopal Church, which discovered in the 1960s that a church with a history of political moderation and antiquated parish routines was being outclassed by secular politics and the introspective fashions of a caring (and sometimes self-indulgent) new philosophy. The church, worried about decline and the poor quality of applicants to seminary, threw itself into support of radical political movements, guitar liturgies, and "repentant activism." When St. John's Cathedral in New York hosted a vast antiwar ceremony organized by anti-Trotskyite Marxists in 1971, it threatened to become, in the sarcastic phrase of Paul Seabury, "a recreation hall for the counterculture." Where the Christian content was in all this was open to considerable question.

Dean Leffler never went so far as his more famous counterparts, in part because he had to placate the first families who were still an essential part of the cathedral. He hired the remarkably talented Peter Hallock to direct the choir and ultimately help secure the cathedral's magnificent Flentrop baroque-style organ. He latched onto the notion of Sunday night compline services, with monastic chants and plainsong, and watched the service become "jammed with hippies who liked Bach, Rock, and Gregorian." He convinced a devoted parishioner, Dorothy Bullitt, president of KING, to televise Christmas Eve services, and followed this up with weekly fireside chats "From the Dean's Desk."

If the ceremonies were still religious, the political activities were also local and not so global and trendy. Leffler blasted the McCarthyites and the Birchers, once even taking out a full-page ad in *The Seattle Times* to excoriate local Republicans who tried to link ungodliness with the Democratic party: "Truth is Slain in the Streets!" proclaimed the headline for the ad. "A group of Republican friends gave me a terrible evening over that ad," recalls Leffler, "but I think you can now safely conclude that the Episcopal Church, on the West Coast at least, is no longer 'the Republican Party at prayer.'"

But what was it? St. Mark's was certainly riding the whirlwinds of change, with a Dean who kept saying that everything would be okay and that all this dynamic change was far better than "the sweet reasonableness of Jesus." In a typical Leffler sermon, he would justify the new ideas, chide them for their excesses at the same time scoffing at Episcopal stuffiness

John Leffler

and fear of emotions, and then sneak the Bible and church doctrine into the back door at the end of the talk. "God gave me a flexible mind," Leffler muses today, and he exemplified that trait by favoring the ordination of women, the modernized prayer book, abortion, war resistance, and some aspects of the counterculture. He invited a hippie priest up from San Francisco to conduct a light show with rock music, and then capped the show by giving a sermon himself on drugs in a command performance coupled with a rock band. (The show was dubbed The Old Man and Uncle Henry, the latter being the name of the band.) The cathedral took a lead in draft counseling. "The church was certainly on the antiwar side of the Vietnam question," recalls one Capitol Hill activist, "though the young priests didn't quite wear black pajamas."

Leffler had succeeded in lifting the church from its ashes and making it into a conscience of the town. The peak came in 1969 at a massive service for the slain black leader Ed Pratt, member of St. Mark's and dear friend of the Dean. Despite an enormous snowfall, the cathedral was jammed to the rafters. When the throng sang "Mine eyes have seen the glory" and "tears shone on every face," the cathedral became for a moment the true heart of the city.

But Hunthausen has resolutely refused to deliver his message in any but moral terms. "I'm not going to argue megatonnage," he insists, "when the fundamental issue is the destructive nature of *any* nuclear weapon, and the unspeakable, life-denying sin of using them." The archbishop's sole appeal, even on this highly complex question, is stunningly simple: "What I am doing is challenging people to look at the choices and to make a decision," he explains. "Life has only two fundamental issues: love and hate, life and death, God and Satan. We always struggle to choose one or the other, and that is our greatest glory. We don't want to accept the fact of a God who expects us to make decisions, yet that responsibility is our greatest privilege, and people can't relieve themselves of trying to cope. I say to people, you must decide. I don't say how to do it."

Hunthausen's reluctance to tell people "how to do it" which he translates as treating them like adults led directly to a second controversy, in which he became the most famous symbol, not of resistance to secular evil, but of his church's determination to repress American dissent. In the fall of 1985, Rome forced him to transfer much of his authority to a Vatican-appointed auxiliary, Bishop Donald Wuerl. The scandal caused by that unprecedented Roman crackdown rocked the Catholic church across the United States. Headlines, mass meetings, collection-basket boycotts, even wild talk of a priests' strike have been the result. The church has sustained considerable long-term hurt.

How had Dutch Hunthausen, neither wily politician nor suave theologian, gotten in such hot water with the Holy See? The story extended back a full decade.

Only three years after Raymond Hunthausen was consecrated archbishop of Seattle in 1975, the Holy See began questioning his conduct of his episcopal office as a result of "the high volume of complaints that were sent to Rome by priests, religious, and faithful in the archdiocese." Hunthausen corrected some improper pastoral practices and erroneous teaching, but the complaints continued. Mostly, it is generally agreed, they were inspired by a small, right-wing group calling itself "Roman Catholic Laity for Truth." Members of such groups around the country, liberals gripe, enjoy remarkable ability to reach the inner circles of the Vatican, even to John Paul himself. Hunthausen thought he was dealing with Rome's worries as they came up, but his replies, according to the Vatican, offered further evidence that something was seriously amiss in Seattle. In 1983, the Holy See sent Archbishop James A. Hickey of Washington, one of the more conservative members of the episcopate, to investigate Hunthausen.

Here the accounts begin to diverge. Apostolic delegate Pio Laghi claims that Hunthausen was thoroughly briefed and consulted as to what was going on. Hunthausen argues that his treatment was "not just," insofar as he was given to understand this was just a friendly visit—although everyone else knew it was an inquisition—was never allowed to confront his accusers, and never saw Hickey's final report. Laghi says that the chief evidence of error in the archdiocese came, not from hostile testimony, but from Hunthausen's own testimony and documents, as well as his determination to discount Vatican concerns.

In September 1983, auxiliary Bishop Nicholas Walsh retired. Normally, Hunthausen would have been allowed to nominate a new assistant, and it is widely known that he would have named Father Michael Ryan, his effective second-in-command. He was not allowed to do so. What happened during the next two years is unclear, in part because Hunthausen, overworked and enduring considerable stress, suffered a heart attack in 1984.

Certainly by the fall of 1985, the Vatican had concluded that Hunthausen was, in Laghi's icy phrase, "lacking the firmness necessary to govern the archdiocese." Laghi's public statements have cited six different areas where the alleged softness was manifest. Most deal with issues of sexuality, a realm in which American practice and church teaching bear no noticeable resemblance to one another.

The portrait that emerges is one of Uncle Raymond, who might tell people what the church says they should do, but would not follow them around issuing orders and cracking a whip. One self-described "middle of the roader" among diocesan priests puts it this way: "He kind of looked the other way at things that were going on. He would never have cracked down with a lot of fuss. Basically, he's not the kind of person who cracks down."

Bishop Wuerl turned out to be the very model of a rising young priest, following the career path Raymond Hunthausen did not take.

Catholics here tend to be happy with that attitude, both because they think the rules are wrong and because they prefer to be treated like adults. To many Americans—particularly the nonreligious—Hunthausen's loving approach is what Christianity is supposed to be all about. To Rome, which counts protection of the church's authority high among the duties of an archbishop, Hunthausen's spirit looks like weakness or passive subversion of the rules. If you really want to be everybody's favorite uncle, ought you to take on the father's or the teacher's role?

Rome's answer was to leave Hunthausen clothed in the dignity of the archbishop, but hand the actual power to someone else. In the fall of 1985, Rome and Seattle negotiated an agreement under which the Holy See would name a new auxiliary bishop for Seattle and Hunthausen would hand his new assistant final authority over the areas in which he had been found lacking. Rome promptly appointed the exceedingly orthodox Donald Wuerl to the auxiliary post. Hunthausen could maintain the fiction that he had an auxiliary like any other. The move was unprecedented. Until two recent cases, including Hunthausen's, the Holy See had given substantial powers to auxiliaries only when the nominal archbishop was mishandling funds, insane, or otherwise incompetent. But it was also a less extreme measure than the Vatican at one point contemplated, whereby Wuerl would have been named a coadjutor, or equal to the archbishop, with a right to automatic succession.

Late in 1985, the plan went into effect. A letter from Archbisop Laghi—widely misinterpreted as vindicating Hunthausen—concluded the Hickey visitation. Wuerl was formally appointed, consecrated in Rome (no one was taking any chances with a service in Seattle), and the affair disappeared for a while from the broader public eye. To deal with the concerns outlined in the Laghi letter—and a more complete version issued by Cardinal Joseph Ratzinger, the head of the Congregation for the Doctrine of the Faith—Hunthausen appointed a committee consisting of Bishop Wuerl, Chancellor Ryan, and Father Michael McDermott, the archdiocesan director of administration.

Soon there were problems. Bishop Wuerl turned out to be the very model of a rising young priest, following the career path Raymond Hunthausen did not take. Forty-five years old at the time of his consecration, he had spent much of the last twenty years in Rome, under the patronage of Cardinal John Wright of his native Pittsburgh. He has written close to a shelfful of books and innumerable articles—solidly orthodox work, full of appeals to authority, but not displaying any particular human insight. He spent much of his career in secretarial posts. Most recently, he was the real power behind a Vatican-ordered study of United States seminaries. Clearly, this is a man being groomed for higher things. When not picking his way through the local minefield, he is warm, eager to reach out and establish relations with people he knows. Equally plainly though, he was completely lacking the kind of pastoral experience that would equip someone to deal with the decidedly tense situation in Seattle. It probably did not help that his guide would turn out to be Father Ryan, a former classmate in Rome, and Hunthausen's preferred auxiliary.

In any case, Wuerl was quickly labeled the "Vatican watchdog," the "spy," and the "KGB." Wuerl himself has spoken of how "very painful" those months were, pointing out to the diocesan newspaper, "I had had no experience as a bishop. It was a whole new part of the world to come to know. All new people to come to know. All of the support system that was part of my life was removed. And then to find I would be somewhat living under a cloud because I am associated with the visitation. Sometimes I get the real feeling when I read some of the articles in the press and see some of the quotations, I'm not seen as me. I'm seen as somehow the incarnation of the visitation."

By April 1986, the eruption came. Both archbishop and pro-nuncio have subsequently claimed that the other side must have misunderstood and that they do not see how the misunderstanding was possible. Hunthausen has also said that, though he was informed as to the Vatican's "power-sharing" plan, he simply refused to believe the Holy See meant it. He said, "I stated my concern and my strong feelings, my opposition really, to that whole concept so strongly that I really could not bring myself to believe, it didn't even cross my mind that that was what was intended."

It turned out that Hunthausen did not surrender any of his powers. In April, the archbishop and auxiliary were in a meeting to determine the archdiocese position on King County's decision to include homosexuals under equal-employment protections. Wuerl supported repeal of the ordinance, in line with what was to become the church's position on gay rights; Hunthausen supported its retention, the traditional position of the church here. Argument ensued over who was really in charge, followed by both sides appealing to

Laghi and, ultimately, to Rome. When the final, no-wiggle-room decision came in July to assign the faculties to Wuerl, Hunthausen says he nearly resigned, "preferring the course of resignation to what would amount to pretending to be what, in fact, I was not." Then he edged back from the precipice, making "a very reluctant decision to remain...for the ultimate good of the church in the archdiocese of Seattle."

He also called a press conference, September 4, to explain the new arrangement. All hell now broke loose, with priestly meetings and vigils and headlines around the country. Some thirteen thousand of the region's three hundred thousand Catholics signed petitions calling for Hunthausen's restoration. Wuerl and Hunthausen announced they would go to Rome to seek such a restoration. (The archdiocese later "clarified" the statement to say that they had not actually meant they would travel to Rome: Rome must have said no.) Somehow, the public was given to understand that this entire auxiliary business was only temporary. The next stop was the bishops' meeting scheduled for the second week in November, where Hunthausen was planning to speak.

In an effort to calm the gathering storm, Laghi attempted to get the National Conference of Catholic Bishops to endorse his version of the events in Seattle, specifically a chronology that repeatedly emphasized the participation of the American episcopacy in the decision to discipline Hunthausen. The bishops declined, partly because a "solid minority" backed Seattle's archbishop, and partly because they wanted to give a fellow bishop room to maneuver. The conference leadership, under considerable Vatican pressure, agreed only to distribute Laghi's chronology. Hunthausen reserved his reply for the bishops' meeting. So rather than quelling the controversy, Laghi's actions heightened the expectations for the bishops' convention in Washington DC in 1986. Raymond Hunthausen was back on the front page of *The New York Times*.

But there is a problem with casting Hunthausen as the patron saint of dissent. "The archbishop is not a dissenter," insists diocesan theologian Michael Raschko. "He's not." Hunthausen has carefully told his fellow bishops," I am not a dissenter from the church's teaching." His colleagues add that the portrayal of the archbishop as a theological renegade has hurt him more than anything else in this whole controversy. When the members of the archdiocesan Respect Life Committee resigned en masse, they blamed chancery staff for its lack of commitment and, to a lesser extent, Hunthausen for failing to follow through. They did not fault the archbishop's *beliefs*.

Why hasn't Hunthausen followed through on those doctrines? We are back to the "lacking the firmness" issue again. Archdiocesan officials say Hunthausen believes people are adults who deserve to be taught, yes, but also are entitled to respect. This outlook corresponds with a pragmatic pastoral belief that battering the erring faithful does not work. The trouble is that Hunthausen's tendency to tolerate dissension can all too easily be viewed—by both sides—as approval of the dissension, as well as love of the dissenter. But it took

At the heart of the Hunthausen affair is a struggle for the future of the Roman Catholic church in America.

months of behind-the-scenes maneuvering. The November, 1986 bishops' meeting ended inconclusively, with a public relations victory for Hunthausen that almost eclipsed his failure to gain his fellow bishops' intervention on his behalf. The real denouement emerged over the first six months of 1987.

The church ultimately chose to vindicate Hunthausen, but not his preference for the pastoral, as opposed to a more authoritarian, archibishopric. The denouement came over the first six months of 1987. Rumors swirled that the Vatican intended to restore Hunthausen's powers while also forcing him into retirement, which set off widespread protests. Bishop Wuerl was hamstrung in his attempts to exercise his special faculties, proving Hunthausen's claim that the shared-power arrangement was "unworkable." When a trio of fellow American prelates weighed in with a report in June of 1987, that intervention was something of a victory for Hunthausen's view of a collegial church, even though the document came down in favor of the authority of the pope. The report also damned Seattle's archbishop for "generating, or a least accepting, a climate of permissiveness in which some feel free to design their own policies and practices."

The harsh reality turned out to be that the negotiations were really over timetables, and who might choose the archbishop's successor. In June of 1987, Hunthausen's powers were restored. Wuerle was removed, eventually to be consecrated the bishop of his home diocese of Pittsburgh. Hunthausen also acquired a coadjutor archbishop (and automatic successor) in the form of Montana's Bishop Thomas Murphy. The genial Murphy was neither the slap in the face represented by Wuerl, nor Hunthausen's own choice.

Whether Hunthausen retires soon or years from now, at the heart of the Hunthausen affair is a struggle for the future of the Roman Catholic church in America. That church has much to offer the universal church as well. Brought up on democratic ideals and ecumenicism, the American theologians were well equipped to develop the integration of the Gospel and the modern world that was demanded by Vatican II. The resulting theological renaissance, in areas as diverse as Biblical scholarship and sexual ethics, has been impressive.

Just as important, America still cares about the Catholic church. Unlike much of Catholicism in Western Europe, where the church was too closely associated with wealth and authority, the American church never lost touch with the working class, identifying itself with such movements as the development of trade unions. Even when it was intellectually moribund, the American church took care of its souls. As a result, American Mass attendance rates, and other evidence of devotion, are traditionally among the highest in the world. The church here may be messy; but it is alive. In much of Europe, it is not.

American Catholicism is also in trouble. Although the proportion of Americans who are Catholic has remained fairly steady over the last twenty-five years—a reflection of burgeoning populations of Latin American and Asian immigrants—the numbers of baptisms, conversions, nuns, and seminarians have all plunged dramatically. Of particular concern is the aging of the priesthood, caused in large part by the wholesale departure—for marriage and family, mostly—of much of the younger generation. David Jaeger, the director of seminarians who was picketing at the bishops' conference, is one of just three local members of his seminary class who has remained a cleric. The *median* age of priests has climbed to fifty-three; the total number of priests has dropped 10 percent in the last two decades. An entire generation of Catholic children is growing up, knowing priests as nothing but old men. Are such arguably tangential doctrines as celibacy among priests worth that kind of price?

The Vatican crackdown is demolishing the vague hope that, somehow, the American church would be allowed to develop along a slightly divergent, Americanized path, accepting contraception in practice and using the laity in the liturgy to compensate for the shortage of priests, while awaiting the day when the church changes its position on the vexed sexual issues.

Certainly Hunthausen is not everyone's cup of religious tea. Moreover, disaffection with him extends beyond those right-wingers who see him as a Machiavellian politician. Some conservatives simply want an archbishop who enforces the rules far better than Hunthausen does. Some moderates believe Hunthausen should stop proclaiming simplistically about nuclear war and spend his time running the diocese.

That is not going to happen. Since the apparent end of the controversy with Rome, Hunthausen has more than ever taken on the role of witness for justice and peace, whether speaking at national conferences of disarmament advocates, or in front of the Legislature in Olympia.

For most local Catholics, Hunthausen is beloved as a simple, possibly saintly man. Even at the height of the battle with Rome, fewer than 20 percent of the faithful opposed him, about the same number would have lain down in front of an oncoming train on his behalf, and the remainder were somewhere in the middle. John Hough, a banker and father of four and no one's definition of a raging radical, expresses his admiration this way: "By the strength of his commitment to peace and the poor he has demonstrated his commitment to all the people, not just the comfortable ones." He adds, "I don't stand in front of the trains at Bangor. I don't not pay some of my taxes. But I admire and support his conviction and his expression of it. It is open and straightforward and it's the strongest expression he can make to his community."

In the end, it is as such a witness for personal Christian commitment that Dutch Hunthausen will be remembered in the larger community of Washington, and even, perhaps, in the great body of the faithful in his church. ◢■

TEAM NORDSTROM

THE NORDSTROM CLAN (1901–)

FRED MOODY

The Nordstrom family is the Mount Rainier of the Northwest's civic and cultural landscape. As the mountain symbolizes the beauty and splendor of the Northwest, so the Nordstrom name has come to epitomize a certain Northwestness of character, a set of drives and values that we regard as being unique to our corner of the country. In addition, the Nordstroms—although conspicuously absent when it comes to supporting the arts—exert a Rainier-like influence over civic life, whether through retailing, downtown development, charities, sponsorship of events like the annual Beat-the-Bridge Run, or ownership of a well-loved professional football franchise.

The family remains shrouded in nearly impenetrable mists of self-imposed secrecy. In spite of their obvious ambition, the Nordstroms often seem to have ascended to the heights of wealth, prominence, and achievement almost against their will. They eschew interviews, refuse to be photographed, and assiduously avoid attention directed at them rather than at their commercial enterprises. Whether from *Seattle Weekly* or *The New York Times,* would-be interviewers are told the same thing: that family publicity is detrimental to the esprit of the company as a whole. Along with the many values (probity, prudence, propriety, stolidity, sternness, stoicism, old-fashioned Scandinavian-Episcopalian values, family closeness, dedication, etc.) that we have come to regard as characteristic of the Nordstroms, their storied shyness is one more example of a trait, often seen in others as something comic or suspicious in nature, that in their case comes across as simply admirable.

Our reflexive admiration for all things Nordstrom comes so naturally and is so deep-rooted that the mere association of the name with any enterprise now tends to confer an immediate sense of legitimacy and stability to it. The name reassures and comforts in the same mysterious, unconscious way that the mention of Ivar Haglund's name invariably brings a fond smile to the native face. (Haglund and the Nordstroms, in fact, have always epitomized for me the two sides of the quintessentially Northwest character: the folksy, unpretentious, laid-back, avuncular nonconformist on the one hand, and the quiet, upright, hardworking, decidedly unfrivolous paternal figure on the other.)

In the beginning, there was but one Nordstrom, John W., and one store, at Fourth and Pike in downtown Seattle.

Some knowledgeable sources have characterized the renegotiation in the early 1980s of the Kingdome leases of the Mariners and the Seahawks in a way that dramatically highlights the stature and power of the Nordstroms in the community. They note that the Nordstroms artfully waited for the Mariners to introduce the theme of renegotiation to county politicians. Then the Mariners, being the first to approach the county and being represented by a blustery, unpopular *California* owner, took the brunt of the public's and the politicians' outrage over rewriting a contract that had already been signed. Once the Mariners had forced a better deal out of the county, the Seahawks stepped forward and quietly renegotiated their lease. The Nordstroms are held in such high esteem that neither county nor public raised so much as a whimper in protest, and the Seahawks—already one of the National Football League's hottest properties—ended up with a new lease that made them even more salable. "They used the Mariners," said one longtime observer of the Seahawks, "to get their own house in order for the sale of the team."

Engendered during a 1969 golf game between Lloyd Nordstrom and Vince Lombardi, the Seahawk enterprise has been a classic Nordstrom operation from Day One, and one can see the family touch at work throughout the franchise. Particularly when it comes to secrecy, team transactions—whether player trades or the 1988 sale of the franchise to California multimillionaire Kenneth Behring—typically included a provision forbidding all parties from discussing terms of the transactions in questions with the media.

Most Nordstromesque was the low-key, controlled behavior of the Seahawk ownership, right up to the family's 1988 sale of the team. In a league known as much for the high profiles of its owners as for the exploits of its players, the Nordstrom approach to sports ownership was a definite anomaly. Like the architects of the Dallas Cowboy franchise, the Nordstroms opted to exert their control solely through the budget, delegating football decisions to experts. While many owners consistently meddle in football matters ranging from draft choices to play selection, the Nordstroms, win or lose, always stayed resolutely in the background.

At the same time, they were just as resolute in their "hands-on" approach to running the business side of the team. Knowledgeable observers characterized the Seahawks as one of the best-run franchises in all of professional sports. By budgeting intelligently in the team's early years, by securing a radio contract that rivals those of teams in bigger media markets like Los Angeles and New York, and by carefully managing the team's money, the Nordstroms made the Seahawks immensely profitable. The team is reputed to have made money in every year save for the strike-shortened 1982 and 1987 seasons and is in the NFL's top 25 percent in terms of revenue produced. The Nordstroms' initial investment of $8 million—the cost to them in 1975 for 51 percent of the team—paid off handsomely 13 years later, when they bought the remaining 49 percent of their franchise for $35 million and sold the entire package for $80 million.

From left: James F. Nordstrom,
Robert E. Bender, John N.
Nordstrom, Bruce A. Nordstrom,
John A. Mcmillan

493

Curt Warner

The acquisition of Penn State star running back Curt Warner by the Seattle Seahawks in 1983 signaled a dramatic change in direction for the Seattle franchise. Warner was the first super star signed by the Seahawks, and his arrival meant that the Nordstrom family would no longer be content merely to be a respectable member of the NFL. They put their franchise on a course to become one of the league's premier teams.

From "The Seahawk Nobody Knows," by Fred Moody, Seattle Weekly, December 2, 1987. Copyright © 1987 Fred Moody. Reprinted by permission.

Part of football's appeal to [Seahawk running back] Curt Warner lies in its extreme danger. "There are big people flying at you," he says, "and they're quick. And they have a nasty attitude at the same time. It's exhilarating and it's exciting and it's fun. It may not seem like fun at the time, but it is. You're aware of everything around you and you're just wide awake because you know there's someone over there on the other end who's going to take his best shot at you."

After his 1984 knee injury, Warner realized that all the joys and glories of the game could be taken away forever, in an instant. "I appreciated the game more when I got back. But more importantly, I appreciated my God-given talents and abilities, and I realized that at any given time, on any given play, it can be over for me."

It is important to Warner that he not forget the source of his abilities. He regards the improbable path in his life from rural near-poverty to the heights of glory as proof that he is guided from above. A devout Christian—his great-grandfather was an itinerant minister—Warner sees his career as a form of ministry. "I know that I've been blessed. I have to be thankful. You break it all down and you look at it and say, 'It's not just that I've been struck by a magic wand—it's by design.' And having a Christian background, I do believe that. Every time I walk out on that field, I'm definitely assured of it—that this is not just by luck, my friend. This was given to me. For a purpose, I guess. It's part of a design that can't be seen."...

Alive as he is to the danger around him, and tuned in as he is to his team, Warner finds himself in a private world, inaccessible to others, during a game. "With all that stuff going on, you're sort of in your own little world at the same time. It's like you're getting away from it all for a while. You're in your own world within yourself." It is in many ways a private emotional maelstrom. "There are plateaus in a game, and momentum shifts. You probably go through more emotions during a football game than you go through for three or four months of living. You go through a lot, I'll tell you. You're not only physically drained but you're emotionally drained, too."...

Always there lurks the alluring possibility of making a great play. "There will be a few glimpses when you're watching film," Warner says, "a few moments where you can sit back and say, 'That was a nice play.' It's not like every time or even every game. It's like beating your head against the wall, sometimes—you're banging against the wall and then in that one moment—BOOM!—there's a great play. I think that's what it's all about."

For all of the game's seductions, Warner occasionally feels tremendous shivers of wonder and fear. It is as if in order to stay out on the field he has to deny the reality of what is happening around him. "It's a violent game," he says. "I mean, I'm sitting on the sidelines and I'm going, '*Why* are we out here? *Why* are we doing this?' I'm asking myself that in the middle of a timeout sometimes. 'What are we doing out here? Are we crazy?' Then the timeout's over and it's back in the huddle and you forget. Time to get it on again. But I find myself laughing sometimes. Why are we out here? Well, because we're dumb."

Bad as the pain from playing can be—and in Warner's case it is particularly bad—football is more painful to watch than to play. "To see it is to see the reality of it. But to be in it, you can't think about it, it's not a presence of mind. There are some things that you're able to block out. The mind, for some reason, will not accept it. Because of the fear. I don't think any of us would be any good if we really realized what we were doing. If we sat down and

Mike Urban

Curt Warner

thought about it and really, really took a look at it—I don't think any of us would be out there doing it. But the mind has an ability to kind of make it a little bit softer than it really is."

Seahawk co-owner Herman Sarkowsky, a developer, is widely credited for the team's success on the ledger. Having built the Portland Trailblazers—arguably one of the two or three best-run pro basketball teams in the country—Sarkowsky helped make the Seahawks at least as successful as Portland, if not more so. His prominent role in the team's formative years—although a minority owner, he was the operation's managing general partner—reflects the time-honored Nordstrom management method of delegating as much authority as possible to people they consider more expert than themselves.

A more telling reflection of the Nordstrom management method came in 1982, when the family took firmer control of the team, fashioning it even more strongly along traditional Nordstrom lines. A player strike—along with then-head coach Jack Patera's hard-line stance against player expressions of union solidarity, the most notable was his cutting from the team roster of player-union representative Sam McCullum—left the Seahawk image at an all-time low. The Nordstroms were presented with two options: either sell out to their minority partners (they came close to doing so for somewhere around $20 million), or use their muscle to implement dramatic change. Deciding against leaving the team on a sour note, the family opted for the latter and acted with characteristic decisiveness. They fired Patera and general manager John Thompson, replaced Sarkowsky with Elmer Nordstrom, and installed Mike McCormack as general manager. The moves opened the door for the hiring of head coach Chuck Knox, who in turn ushered in the Seahawks' best years—not only on the field, but in the hearts of fans as well.

Knox is himself temperamentally and tactically so much like the Nordstroms that he could almost be mistaken for a member of the family. Under him, the Seahawks have become remarkably similar to the Nordstrom retail operation. There are now two things that set the Seahawks distinctly apart from almost all other NFL franchises: the team's positive image in the mind of the public and the unflagging loyalty of its players. The Nordstroms' success at building the Seahawk image was the envy of the NFL, and observers pointed to the remarkable number of Seahawks who have made their permanent homes in the Northwest as a sign not only of the devotion of the players to the franchise but also as a significant factor in the team's image-making. During the football season and off, Seahawk players are said to be far more available for charitable and promotional events than players from other teams.

Sportswriters and players alike credit Chuck Knox—known throughout the league as a "player's coach"—for inspiring such unusual dedication in the team's athletes, but it is clear that the Nordstrom touch is at work as well. Everything the owners have done, from building a new state-of-the-art headquarters to making their head coach the second-highest-paid in the NFL to retiring a Seahawk jersey in honor of their fans, has shown the Nordstroms' characteristic concern for class and quality. Such shrewd moves have contributed to the image of Seattle as a great franchise—one that players are proud to be playing for and fans are proud to cheer.

Not so surprisingly to those who have endured mind-numbing interviews with football coaches and athletes on the subject of motivation, you learn much more about the magic of the Nordstroms' Seahawk enterprise by looking at their retail operation than by listening to their football people. In many ways, their chain of stores is run like a sports franchise. They play to win.

Nordstrom, Inc.—which at the turn of the century was a single Seattle shoe store—has rung up world-class numbers in just about every statistical category used to measure the performance of the retailers. Nordstrom has become the country's, if not the world's, largest independent fashion specialty retailer. *The New York Times,* citing marketing and retailing analysts, calls it "one of the best-managed retailers in the country." Lately, Nordstrom seems to be growing larger by the minute. Net sales increased from $107 million in 1976 to a whopping $1,301,857,000 in 1985, when sales grew 34 percent over 1984's $958,678,000. Net earnings in 1985 were just over $50 million, a 23 percent increase over the previous year's $41 million. In 1986—to cite a statistic with a certain sporting attention to detail—Nordstrom was selling $293 worth of merchandise for every square foot of retail space it owns.

In the beginning, there was but one Nordstrom, John W., and one store, at Fourth and Pike in downtown Seattle. Then John W. begat Everett, Elmer, and Lloyd: the three sons who bought the business from him in 1920 and built it into the biggest shoe retailer in the country. Elmer—now the sole surviving son of John—begat John and Jim, Everett begat Bruce, and this third generation of Nordstroms—together with Jack McMillan, who married Lloyd's daughter Loyal—took over the family business and engineered its expansion across the country. The Nordstrom family owns 57 percent of the company stock, with John and Bruce co-chairmen of the board of directors, Jim director and president, Jack McMillan director and executive vice president, and a fourth generation of Nordstroms working its way up from the sales floor.

There is no end to the list of reasons for the company's continuing success. Experts cite such disparate factors as the Nordstrom policy of meeting competitors' prices, a decentralized management policy that allows department managers—rather than a central personnel department—to hire their own salespeople, a "hire from within" policy that requires all managers to be recruited from the store's sales force, a purchasing system that is directed from below—with each department helping stock its own shelves—rather than from above, and Nordstrom's inventory per square foot, which is nearly double that in other department stores.

The store has humble roots, which also helps. It took off after the shoe store purchased

a fashion store, Best's Apparel, in 1963, and carried over into the fashion trade the high-service, commission-based sales system of the lowly shoe business. Unlike department stores, with their large lines of space-consuming durable goods and their union-hallowed, noncommission compensation structures, Nordstrom could concentrate on moving densely packed soft goods tailored to the downtown trade, and it could create a sell-or-go spirit in the work force.

The Nordstrom buyers are skilled merchandisers, but the store is not really the trendsetter most think it is. It likes to build a glittering environment, packed with merchandise displayed in a crisp manner (a Nordstrom trick is to put lots of items at right angles to each other, thus combining clarity with energy). Things look expensive, so when the price tag is inspected, a sense of bargain is achieved. Nordstrom has pioneered the quick granting of credit, on very easy terms. Other stores discount nearly all the time, but sales events at Nordstrom are infrequent and genuine. The sales staff is very young, mostly drawn from outgoing people unjaded from any previous store work. Consequently, walking into a Nordstrom store is quite different from the laid-back, condescending feel of many competitors' operations. You feel welcome, you feel ready to buy, you get hooked early in life.

"They were always asking you things like, 'What is your goal in the company?' 'How much do you want to sell today?' "

Then there is the example of the family. Not a new store opens without Nordstroms themselves being there, unpacking shoe boxes and working the floor. One year when Nordstrom experienced a downturn, family members (all of whom started off by working in sales) returned to the floor for stints of selling and pitching in to meet goals.

Probably the single most oft-cited factor is Nordstrom's ability to motivate its employees, particularly when it comes to the company's vaunted attention to customer service. Nordstrom salespeople are cajoled and goaded into superlative sales and service performance in much the same way athletes are, and they take an athlete's pride in the overall performance of the Nordstrom "team."

A Nordstrom salesperson is powered by meetings, skits, goals, awards, folklore, commissions, and profit-sharing—all fueled with motivational speeches, seminars, and positive-thinking literature from the Pacific Institute, a performance- and motivation-enhancing enterprise based in Seattle. New employees are given a handbook, view an inspirational videotape (*The Nordstrom Story*, which details the enterprise's history, beginning with John W. Nordstrom's migration from Sweden through Alaska to Seattle, where he opened his first shoe store in 1901 with money made from the sale of his Klondike gold claim), and are initiated into the Nordstrom system.

The system is an inspired mix of hardheaded, sound business practices with a folksy, cornball psychology of the workplace. An old-fashioned brand of employee loyalty to the store is forged from a combination of rigid discipline with praise, rewards, and a semiformal, family feel to the store organization. "We're like a family, all the stores," says a saleswoman in the downtown Nordstrom. "I really can't describe it, it just happens. It's

498

like the Nordstroms are my uncles or something."

On the hardheaded business side, salespeople are paid either a base salary or a commission on their sales—whichever is greater—and those who do not regularly surpass their base salary with sales commissions ("make their draw," or "make their book," in employee parlance) are fired, often very abruptly.

Salespeople also can be fired for failing to meet Nordstrom's rigid standards for proper on-the-job appearance and behavior. "You are expected," says a former Nordstrom employee whom I'll call Emily, "to dress a certain way, and have a certain demeanor. They want you to be accountable for everything you say, do, or think." Having worked in both a California branch and the downtown Seattle Nordstrom, Emily remembers standards for appearance and behavior as being far harder to meet than standards for sales performance. "I always made my draw," she says. "But you always felt like thumbscrews were being applied. We weren't allowed, for instance, to tuck pencils behind our ears. We weren't allowed to point—it isn't polite—even when giving directions. We were always expected to look 'fashion forward.' And when you get hired, they encourage you to go down to the makeup counter and get yourself made over. There's a definite Nordstrom look—you can spot Nordstrom workers on the downtown streets."

Like all Nordstrom employees, Emily was required to keep a "personal trade book," in which she recorded the names, addresses, and tastes of her customers. Salespeople are required to send customers thank-you notes and letters telling them of upcoming sales or new products. Nordstrom regards this program as one of the store's primary personal touches—an example of the kind of service and attention that sets Nordstrom apart. "I worked for one manager," Emily remembers, "who wanted five thank-you notes from each of us on his desk every Friday."

For lapses in service and sales performance, employees can be "written up," according to Emily, and "if you get written up three times, you're fired." (*The Nordstrom Employee Handbook* takes an even harder line, listing seven performance shortcomings— "poor customer service," "failure to meet expected performance levels," and so on— which can result in "dismissal after one established warning.") The demands, judging from company figures, are hard to meet. Salesperson turnover at Nordstrom is estimated to be between 50 percent and 70 percent per year—most of which is due to seasonal layoffs— with turnover among permanent salespersons ranging from 15 percent to 20 percent. The company estimates that 7 percent to 10 percent of its employees are fired.

Even given adjustment for seasonal work, 60 percent is a high turnover rate for a retailer's work force. Yet Nordstrom—which is said to receive two hundred applications for work per day—does not consider turnover a significant problem.

Nordstrom employees work in a highly charged atmosphere of relentless purpose, dedication, reward, and praise. Salespeople work toward such an array of personal, depart-

Both Knox and the Nordstroms present their demands in a relentlessly, almost maniacally positive way.

Nordstrom today

mental, and store goals that one goal or another is in their minds almost constantly. Every salesperson has a personal yearly sales goal, and salespeople who are "on target" are publicly praised—often in the form of a letter or announcement from one of the Nordstroms—at frequent intervals throughout the year. Each sales department has a daily goal of trying to surpass sales on the previous year's corresponding day by a certain set amount, and each salesperson is trying to meet a personal daily sales goal. During sales, employees try to surpass the previous year's sales—again, by a certain set amount. Each department manager is expected to meet a monthly sales goal, which determines, to an extent, the size of his department's daily goal. If one day is low, for instance, the next day's goal may be pegged higher to get the two days' total sales back on track to meet the month's goal.

Goals are kept in the forefront of employees' minds through frequent reminders. Shifts often begin with a reminder of what the day's particular goals are, salespeople are often asked during a workday what their day's goals are, and a previous day's successes are always praised. "The goals aren't easy," says a salesperson I'll call Vera, "but we just have to push a little harder. It's something to work for."

The importance to Vera of Nordstrom's motivational milieu is underscored by her description, in the vocabulary of the athlete, of her store manager's psychological skills. "Our store manager," she says, "is a good positive force. He'll get on the public-address system and say, 'Good morning, everyone, we had good day yesterday, we hope to have another today.' Then he'll tell a story about someone—maybe a girl who sold one thousand dollars in cosmetics to one person the day before, or something. He's a good store manager—he gets everybody pumped up." In the case of employees singled out for praise, the managerial positive force is enhanced throughout the day, Vera says, by employees. "Like sometime during the day I'll go by cosmetics and say something like, 'Congratulations! That was a nice sale yesterday.'"

Employees who make their yearly personal sales goals are admitted to Nordstrom's "Pacesetter's Club." Pacesetters are given a certificate, a new business card with "Pacesetter" emblazoned on it, a 33 percent discount on Nordstrom merchandise for a year (the standard employee discount is 20 percent), and a lavish evening out on the town.

More important, from the motivational standpoint, is a certain air of theatricality accompanying the whole topic of goals at Nordstrom. This ongoing goal drama is remarkable enough to figure prominently in a 1979 Harvard Business School study of Nordstrom prepared by Harvard Associate Fellow Manu Parpia. In dry, academic prose that nonetheless betrays a certain breathless fascination with what appears to be a distinctly exotic way of doing business ("The Nordstroms did not even have an organization chart"), Parpia describes the Nordstrom enterprise in the manner of an anthropologist who has stumbled

The birth of an empire

onto some hitherto unknown tribe. He is particularly taken with the structure of a Nordstrom motivational meeting for managers and buyers:

> Goal setting was achieved through means of peer pressure. Every year a meeting attended by all the regional buyers and the store managers was held at each region's headquarters. The regional manager or, in the case of Washington state, the Nordstroms, would call on each individual manager (or buyer, as the case may be) in turn to present his or her sales target for the year. As the figures were called out, the regional manager wrote the amounts against the individual's name on a large chart. Next to the figure in turn was a space on which the regional manager had written his target for each manager. That target figure was kept covered during the initial part of the meeting in which the managers gave their target figures for the year. Then, amidst great excitement and suspense, the regional

manager tore off the slip of paper which covered his target for each individual manager. If the sales target of the manager was under that of the regional manager, the assembly would boo the unfortunate manager. However, if the manager's target was above that of the regional manager, then the group of persons would break out into cheers. One manager described the scene as being similar to that of a classroom before an exam, or perhaps during an exam, with all the store managers and buyers doing feverish calculations as they heard what their peers were setting as targets and were tempted to revise their own targets.

This air of competition among managers filters down to the sales force as well, according to Emily. Salespeople have ready access, she says, to sales figures from all departments and stores in the Nordstrom chain, and frequently check on one another's sales to see where they themselves are placing in the hierarchy of performance.

Employee meetings, at which salespeople are singled out for praise and at which instructive or motivational skits are performed, are held frequently. "We get a lot of recognition at those meetings," says Vera, "for the good things we've done." Skits vary from the instructional—in which actors will portray both the right and wrong way to handle certain customer-service situations—to what Emily calls the "rah-rah" genre. A regular attendee at Sunday morning meetings in the California Nordstrom, Emily remembers one skit in particular. "They got everyone in the men's clothing department to dress up in weird, ill-fitting suits and cowboy hats to do this parody of Cal Worthington ads. They sang, 'If you want customer service, go see Al!' That kind of thing."

Emily, a remarkably enthusiastic and energetic woman—in short, a classic Nordstrom personality—nonetheless soured on the Nordstrom motivational method after one year. Still she seems more bemused—admiring, even—than bitter about her experience. "Everything is goal-oriented there," she says. "They were always asking you things like, 'What is your goal in the company?' 'How much do you want to sell today?' 'How much merchandise do you want to move in the pay period?' During sales, they would ask, 'What is your personal goal?' 'How much do you want your department to sell?' It was this controlled, rabid lather. It was amazing how they could make you incredibly mercenary without making you feel sleazy."

The Nordstrom service ethic is a genre unto itself. Everyone has a Nordstrom service tale. There is the one about the clerk who took a customer's new shirts upstairs and ironed them herself, so he could wear them for an important, immediate meeting. There is the one about the saleswoman whose customer needed a dress from another store before the normal interstore delivery could arrive. The clerk drove out to the other store, then delivered the dress to the customer's home. There is the one about the clerk who paid a customer's fine when her car was towed away for being parked by a fire hydrant.

Circulation of these tales is strongly encouraged by Nordstrom, both through what

Emily calls "lunchroom lore" and through institutionalization of the "heroics" system. Employees who see another employee perform some customer service "above and beyond the call of duty" write up a "heroic" detailing the incident, and the document is circulated in a weekly collection of heroics. Clerks who are habitually heroic can be elected to the VIP club—an honor that is accorded weekly—or they can be named "Employee-of-the-Month" (a designation more popularly known as "All-Star"), and their pictures are mounted in the Customer Service Room.

The attainment of All-Star status affords Nordstrom yet another opportunity for instructive, motivational hoopla. "When I became an All-Star," Vera says with obvious pride, "my manager wrote a letter to the Nordstroms, saying, 'Vera was a Pacesetter last year, she's on target this year, and is our department's leading salesperson.' " Circulation of the letter serves a double function: it rewards the honoree, and it serves as a reminder to others of what is expected of them.

The net effect of the relatively high-pressure Nordstrom approach depends upon the perspective of the salesperson in question. For some, it creates a positive, productive frame of mind. Others find themselves fraught with anxiety over individual productivity and relations with customers. For Emily—whose penchant for decidedly un-Nordstromesque irreverence comes out when she refers to the store's Town Square department as "Squaretown" and "the polyester palace"—the pressure to perform was exhausting, and the never-ending, uncomplaining deferral to the demands of the customers was demeaning.

Say what you will about the Nordstrom method, it works. It is also remarkably similar to Chuck Knox's Seahawk method. Both are uncompromising. In both cases, employers demand, and get, superlative performances out of their employees. Both Knox and the Nordstroms present their demands in a relentlessly, almost maniacally positive way, working hard to create a working environment in which almost everything that happens is beneficial. Both are adept at convincing their charges that they can improve themselves, their fates, their abilities, their performance, their workplace, and their lives through the power of positive thinking. Both are generous with praise and reward, without robbing them of their value. Both cleverly manage to mix a feeling of solidarity and purpose, of teamwork, with intrateam competition. Just as the Seahawk player who has lost his starting position to a teammate will praise his conqueror, so Nordstrom employees compete with one another, measure their performances against their fellow workers, and yet still retain a definite sense of shared purpose. And whether on the football field or in the department store, the Nordstrom worker is an overachiever, who comes away from the demands of the job feeling fulfilled in a way that few of us ever are by work.

Vera, who has worked at Nordstrom's downtown store for three years, is a case in point. A Pacesetter, she sells nearly three hundred thousand dollars worth of merchandise for Nordstrom each year. In her comments about herself and her company I hear the echoes of hundreds of Seahawk interviews I have conducted during the Chuck Knox era.

The Nordstroms, in spite of their enthusiasm for the franchise, are incapable of putting it ahead of a business that would strike most of us as hopelessly drab by comparison.

"We really do feel," she says, "that we're the best Nordstrom store. It's a feeling that, 'We want to be better than the best.' We don't compete with the other Nordstroms, but at the same time we have to be the best. And I do think that our store is better than all the others. Others may have more merchandise and stuff, but we have the best service."

She is as loyal to the Nordstroms as Seahawk players are to Chuck Knox, and it is clear that she takes personal pride in the Nordstrom expansion—particularly when she uses the first-person-plural pronoun whenever she talks about the corporation. "We're breaking into all these new markets," she says at one point, "and we're very excited about it. And it's kind of neat to be working at the *main store*. People come up from California, they say, 'Oh, this is the main store!' It's really neat."

Vera prides herself on her ability to go the extra mile. Her personal trade book has five hundred names and addresses in it, and she sends out two letters a day to customers. More telling, though, is her pride in letters that have been written to Nordstrom—or by Nordstrom management—about her. "I have lots of letters written about me," she says, "and I keep all of them." Her file contains copies of letters written to John Nordstrom about her, copies of his replies to customers, and copies of letters written to the Nordstroms by her supervisors. "Dear Mr. Nordstrom," begins one typical customer letter, "Whenever I come into your store, Vera immediately goes into high gear." The letter, which is quite long, goes on to pile accolade upon accolade, in a nearly endless paean of praise that strikes me—whose mail is littered with terms like "woman-basher" and "idiot"—as unattainable by mortals. It is a powerful motivating force for Vera—so much so that she rates it far ahead of her salary (a combination of commissions and bonuses that amounts to well over twenty thousand dollars per year) in her list of reasons for liking her job.

That susceptibility to praise, which is also characteristic of successful athletes, sets the successful Nordstrom employee apart. It is part and parcel of the feeling, as articulated by Vera, that Nordstrom workers are a breed apart, and that they are part of an enterprise that is special. Nordstrom salespeople seem possessed by a sense of privilege and adventure, as if there is something about their jobs that distinguishes them from identical jobs in other organizations.

Most mystifying, to my mind, is the intense personal loyalty the Nordstroms, like Chuck Knox, are able to inspire in their workers. Having sat through countless Knox sessions filled with clichés and platitudes about positive thinking, dedication, and hard work—topics that generally leave me cold—I have nonetheless come away every time filled with an inexplicable affection for him. And his football players, whatever their role on the team, are fanatically loyal. The Nordstroms seem to elicit the same kind of response from their employees.

As with Knox, there seems to be some indefinable quality about the Nordstroms that makes them seem particularly personable. At times I think it may come from a touching awkwardness or discomfort with their status that is demonstrated by some of their halfhearted aspirations to informality. Take the way they choose to be addressed by their employees: They are known as Mr. Elmer, Mr. Jim, Mr. Bruce, Mr. John, as if they can't quite pull off the friendliness-and-approachability act that Ivar (who was never Mr. Haglund) made into an art form.

If there is any one reason for the singular dedication of Nordstrom employees—whether they wear shoulder pads or snazzy suits—it is probably some combination of the Nordstroms' Knoxian charisma and single-minded dedication to the family's name and business. And while tales of heroic Nordstrom dedication are nearly as abundant in company folklore as tales of employee heroics, none of them illustrates the family's dedication to its stores more dramatically than its decision, made in 1986, to sell the Seahawks. Having competed very successfully against their peers in the NFL, having realized—given the sport's rapidly changing economics—as much profit as they ever will, and finding themselves increasingly absorbed by their stores' unprecedented expansion, the Nordstroms, in spite of their enthusiasm for the franchise, are incapable of putting it ahead of a business that would strike most of us as hopelessly drab by comparison. Their ability to divest themselves of the Seahawks for the sake of improving their retail business is a remarkable, classic example of the kind of attitude toward Nordstrom that they expect of their employees. It is an apotheosis of shopkeeping.

It is also the beginning of the end for what could have been one of the proudest franchises in the NFL. "They're great owners," sports impresario Bob Walsh once said. "They've been able to take what they've done with their stores—which have become one of the most successful business ventures probably in the world—and move it over to sports. With most owners, that just doesn't happen. I mean, there are a million examples of owners that couldn't do that. The franchise is extremely successful, and you never know what's going to happen when it changes hands."

In mid-1988, in a prelude to outright sale of the franchise, the Nordstrom family abruptly bought out their minority partners, assuming full control of the Seahawks. With the minority owners' right of first refusal thus done away with (they had had six months to match any offer the Nordstroms accepted), the team's sale appeared imminent.

Given what sets the Nordstroms apart from their fellow NFL owners, the 1988 sale of the Seahawks bodes ill for the future of the franchise. Probably the most distinguishing feature of Nordstrom sports ownership—aside from superb, prudent fiscal management—has been the family's heroic abstinence from using its franchise as an alter ego. By not tinkering with it in the manner of a Robert Irsay, George Steinbrenner, Lamar Hunt, Georgia Frontiere, or George Argyros, they have allowed their players, coaches, and front-office people to be driven by the same kind of pride and personal investment that ignites Nordstrom salespeople like Vera. The characterization among sports people of the Nordstroms as a rare breed of owner is so widespread and so strongly stated that it is impossible to imagine a second owner with their skills coming along hard on their heels.

The kind of drive to overachieve that turned the Seahawks from pre-1982 also-rans into Knox-era contenders reminds me, oddly, of the consistent excellence of maverick owner Al Davis's Los Angeles Raider franchise. Davis, described by one source as "one of the toughest and smartest men in the world," runs one of the NFL's most financially successful franchises, enjoys probably the fiercest player loyalty in the league, and wins almost constantly. His personal style is polar-opposite to that of the Nordstroms (a difference that adds a certain richness to the storied rivalry between the Seahawks and Raiders), but Davis shares with them an ability to motivate players with something besides money, an ability to win, and a knack for turning a handsome profit.

Where he differs from them is in his passion for football. His passion is matched only by the Nordstroms' zeal for retailing. For Davis, football is everything. For the Nordstroms, it has always been secondary to the family enterprise.

There was considerable sentiment in the Nordstrom family for keeping the Seahawks, but in the end the rapid expansion of their retail business into California and the eastern seaboard consumed too much of the family's time and energy. Some of the Nordstroms simply found the football season's demand for time—particularly on weekends—more than they could bear. For six months out of the year, hard weeks spent in the stores culminated in weekends spent traveling with and working on the football operation. Finally, the family decided to do the prudent thing—the Nordstrom thing to do—by selling the franchise so they could devote their undistracted energy to retailing. Sources close both to the family and to football are unanimous in their characterizations of the Nordstroms as obsessively dedicated to their stores, to the point that *nothing*—however glamorous—can distract them. ◥

FURTHER READING

General

America's Spectacular Northwest. Washington, D.C.: National Geographic Society, 1982.

Bancroft, Hubert Howe. *History of Washington, Idaho, and Montana*. San Francisco: History Company, 1890.

Bingham, Edwin R., and Glen A. Love, eds. *Northwest Perspectives: Essays on the Culture of the Pacific Northwest*. Seattle: University of Washington Press, 1979.

Clark, Norman H. *Washington: A Bicentennial History*. New York: W.W. Norton, 1976.

Dodds, Gordon B. *The American Northwest: A History of Oregon and Washington*. Arlington Heights: Forum Press, 1986.

Gates, Charles Marvin, ed. *Readings in Pacific Northwest History*. Seattle: University Book Store, 1941.

Johansen, Dorothy O., and Charles M. Gates. *Empire of the Columbia: A History of the Pacific Northwest*. 2d ed. New York: Harper & Row, 1967.

Lavender, David. *Land of Giants: The Drive to the Pacific Northwest, 1750–1950*. Garden City, N.Y.: Doubleday, 1958.

Meinig, D.W. *The Great Columbia Plain: A Historical Geography, 1805–1910*. Seattle: University of Washington Press, 1968.

Pomeroy, Earl. *The Pacific Slope: A History of California, Oregon, Washington, Idaho, Utah, and Nevada*. New York: Alfred A. Knopf, 1965.

Preston, Ralph N. *Early Washington Atlas*. Portland: Binford & Mort, 1974.

Robbins, William G., Robert J. Frank, and Richard E. Ross, eds. *Regionalism and the Pacific Northwest*. Corvallis: Oregon State University Press, 1983.

Vaughan, Thomas, ed. *The Western Shore: Oregon Country Essays Honoring the American Revolution*. Portland: American Revolution Bicentennial Commission of Oregon and Oregon Historical Society, n.d.

Creators

Anderson, Bern. *Surveyor of the Sea: The Life and Voyages of Captain George Vancouver.* Seattle: University of Washington Press, 1960.

Bakeless, John. *Lewis and Clark: Partners in Discovery.* New York: William Morrow, 1947.

Barkan, Frances B. *The Wilkes Expedition: Puget Sound and the Oregon Country.* Olympia: Washington State Capital Museum, 1987.

Barnett, Homer Garner. *Indian Shakers: A Messianic Cult of the Pacific Northwest.* Carbondale and Edwardsville: Southern Illinois University Press, 1975.

Beckham, Stephen Dow. *Requiem for a People: The Rogue Indians and the Frontiersmen.* Norman: University of Oklahoma Press, 1971.

Bowen, William A. *The Willamette Valley: Migration and Settlement on the Oregon Frontier.* Seattle: University of Washington Press, 1978.

Burns, Robert Ignatius, S.J. *The Jesuits and the Indian Wars of the Northwest.* New Haven: Yale University Press, 1966.

Cole, Douglas. *Captured Heritage: The Scramble for Northwest Coast Artifacts.* Seattle: University of Washington Press, 1985.

Collins, June McCormick. *Valley of the Spirits: The Upper Skagit Indians of Western Washington.* Seattle and London: University of Washington Press, 1974.

Cook, Warren L. *Flood Tide of Empire: Spain and the Pacific Northwest, 1543–1819.* New Haven: Yale University Press, 1973.

Deloria, Vine, Jr. *Indians of the Pacific Northwest.* Garden City, N.Y.: Doubleday, 1977.

Drury, Clifford M. *Marcus and Narcissa Whitman and the Opening of Old Oregon.* 2 vols. Glendale, Calif.: Arthur H. Clark, 1973.

Faragher, John Mack. *Women and Men on the Overland Trail.* New Haven: Yale University Press, 1979.

Graebner, Norman A. *Empire on the Pacific: A Study in American Continental Expansion.* New York: Ronald Press, 1955.

Hendrickson, James E. *Joe Lane of Oregon: Machine Politics and the Sectional Crisis, 1849–1861.* New Haven: Yale University Press, 1967.

Jeffrey, Julie Roy. *Frontier Women: The Trans-Mississippi West, 1840–1880.* New York: Hill and Wang, 1979.

Johannsen, Robert W. *Frontier Politics on the Eve of the Civil War.* Seattle: University of Washington Press, 1955.

Josephy, Alvin M., Jr. *The Nez Perce Indians and the Opening of the Northwest.* New Haven: Yale University Press, 1971.

Merk, Frederick. *Manifest Destiny and Mission in American History: A Reinterpretation.* New York: Alfred A. Knopf, 1963.

Morgan, Murray. *Puget's Sound: A Narrative of Early Tacoma and the Southern Sound.* Seattle: University of Washington Press, 1979.

Murray, Keith A. *The Modocs and Their War.* Norman: University of Oklahoma Press, 1959.

Ramsey, Jarold, ed. *Coyote Was Going There: Indian Literature of the Oregon Country.* Seattle: University of Washington Press, 1977.

Relander, Click. *Drummers and Dreamers; The Story of Smohalla the Prophet and His Nephew Puck Hyah Toot.* Seattle: Pacific Northwest National Parks & Forests Association, 1986.

Richards, Kent D. *Isaac I. Stevens: Young Man in a Hurry.* Provo, Utah: Brigham Young University Press, 1979.

Ronda, James P. *Lewis and Clark among the Indians.* Lincoln: University of Nebraska Press, 1984.

Ruby, Robert H. and John Brown. *Half Sun on the Columbia: A Biography of Chief Moses.* Norman: University of Oklahoma Press, 1965.

Scheuerman, Richard. *The Volga Germans: Pioneers of the Northwest.* Moscow: University Press of Idaho, 1980.

Stern, Theodore. *The Klamath Tribe: A People and Their Reservation.* Seattle: University of Washington Press, 1966.

Tharp, Louise. *Company of Adventurers: The Story of Hudson's Bay Company.* Boston: Little Brown and Company, 1946.

Thompson, Erwin N. *Shallow Grave at Waiilatpu: The Sagers' West.* Portland: Oregon Historical Society, 1973.

White, Richard. *Land Use, Environment, and Social Change: The Shaping of Island County, Washington.* Seattle: University of Washington Press, 1980.

Wynecook, David. *The Children of the Sun: A History of the Spokane Indians.* Washington: Wellpinit, 1969.

Visionaries

Abbott, Carl. *The Great Extravaganza: Portland and the Lewis and Clark Exposition.* Portland: Oregon Historical Society, 1981.

Allen, Howard W. *Poindexter of Washington: A Study in Progressive Politics.* Carbondale: Southern Illinois University Press, 1981.

Athearn, Robert G. *Union Pacific Country.* Chicago: Rand McNally, 1971.

Clark, Norman H. *The Dry Years: Prohibition and Social Change in Washington*. Seattle: University of Washington Press, 1965.

Coman, Edwin, and Helen Gibbs. *Time, Tide and Timber*. Palo Alto: Stanford University Press, 1949.

Cox, Thomas R. *Mills and Markets: A History of the Pacific Coast Lumber Industry to 1900*. Seattle: University of Washington Press, 1974.

Dembo, Jonathan. *Unions and Politics in Washington State, 1885–1935*. New York: Garland, 1983.

Fahey, John. *The Inland Empire: Unfolding Years, 1879–1929*. New York and London: University of Washington Press, 1986.

Gates, Charles M. *The First Century at the University of Washington*. Seattle: University of Washington Press, 1961.

Hedges, James B. *Henry Villard and the Railways of the Northwest*. New Haven: Yale University Press, 1930.

Hidy, Ralph W., Frank Ernest Hill, and Allan Nevins. *Timber and Men: The Weyerhaeuser Story*. New York: Macmillan, 1963.

Hyman, Harold M. *Soldiers and Spruce: Origins of the Loyal Legion of Loggers and Lumbermen*. Los Angeles: University of California Press, 1963.

LeWarne, Charles Pierce. *Utopias on Puget Sound, 1885–1915*. Seattle: University of Washington Press, 1975.

McGregor, Alexander Campbell. *Counting Sheep: From Open Range to Agribusiness on the Columbia Plateau*. Seattle: University of Washington Press, 1982.

Mills, Randall V. *Railroads Down the Valleys: Some Short Lines of the Oregon Country*. Palo Alto, Calif.: Pacific Books, 1950.

Moynihan, Ruth Barnes. *Rebel for Rights: Abigail Scott Duniway*. New Haven: Yale University Press, 1983.

——. *Stern-Wheelers Up Columbia: A Century of Steamboating in the Oregon Country*. Palo Alto, Calif.: Pacific Books, 1947.

Morgan, Murray. *Skid Road: An Informal Portrait of Seattle*. 1951. Rev ed., Seattle: University of Washington Press, 1982.

Mumford, Esther Hall. *Seattle's Black Victorians: 1852–1901*. Seattle: Ananse Press, 1980.

Nesbit, Robert C. *"He Built Seattle": A Biography of Judge Thomas Burke*. Seattle: University of Washington Press, 1961.

O'Connor, Harvey. *Revolution in Seattle*. New York: Monthly Review Press, 1964.

Oliphant, J. Orin. *On the Cattle Ranges of the Oregon Country*. Seattle: University of Washington Press, 1968.

Paul, Rodman Wilson. *Mining Frontiers of the Far West, 1848–1880.* 1963. Reprint, Albuquerque: University of New Mexico Press, 1974.

Roe, JoAnn. *Frank Matsura, Frontier Photographer.* Seattle: Madrona Publishers, 1981.

Sale, Roger. *Seattle, Past to Present.* Seattle: University of Washington Press, 1976.

Schwantes, Carlos A. *Radical Heritage: Labor, Socialism, and Reform in Washington and British Columbia, 1885–1917.* Seattle: University of Washington Press, 1979.

——. *Coxey's Army: An American Odyssey.* Lincoln: University of Nebraska Press, 1985.

Sone, Monica. *Nisei Daughter.* Seattle and London: University of Washington Press, 1979.

Throckmorton, Arthur L. *Oregon Argonauts: Merchant Adventurers on the Western Frontier.* Portland: Oregon Historical Society, 1961.

Trimble, William J. *The Mining Advances into the Inland Empire.* Madison: University of Wisconsin, 1914.

Tyler, Robert L. *Rebels of the Woods: The I.W.W. in the Pacific Northwest.* Eugene: University of Oregon Books, 1967.

Weinstein, Robert A. *Grays Harbor, 1885–1913.* New York: Viking, 1978.

Woodhouse, Philip R. *Monte Cristo.* Seattle: The Mountaineers, 1979.

Contemporaries

Brown, Bruce. *Mountain in the Clouds: A Search for the Wild Salmon.* New York: Simon & Schuster, 1982.

Chasan, Daniel Jack. *The Water Link: A History of Puget Sound as a Resource.* Seattle: University of Washington Press, 1981.

Cumming, William. *Sketchbook: A Memoir of the 1930s and the Northwest School.* Seattle and London: University of Washington Press, 1984.

Downs, Vaughn L. *The Mightiest of Them All: Memories of Grand Coulee Dam.* Fairfield, Washington: Ye Galleon Press, 1986.

Ficken, Robert E. *Lumber and Politics: The Career of Mark E. Reed.* Seattle: University of Washington Press, 1979.

Friedheim, Robert L. *The Seattle General Strike.* Seattle: University of Washington Press, 1964.

Lowitt, Richard. *The New Deal and the West.* Bloomington: Indiana University Press, 1984.

McKinley, Charles. *Uncle Sam in the Pacific Northwest: Federal Management of Natural Resources in the Columbia River Valley.* Berkeley: University of California Press, 1952.

Nash, Gerald D. *The American West Transformed: The Impact of the Second World War.* Bloomington: Indiana University Press, 1985.

Neuberger, Richard. *Our Promised Land.* New York: Macmillan, 1938.

Peirce, Neal R. *The Pacific States of America: People, Politics, and Power in the Five Pacific Basin States.* New York: Norton, 1972.

Sanders, Jane. *Cold War on the Campus: Academic Freedom at the University of Washington, 1946–64.* Seattle: University of Washington Press, 1979.

Seufert, Francis. *Wheels of Fortune.* Portland: Oregon Historical Society, 1980.

Sundborg, George. *Hail Columbia: The Thirty-Year Struggle for Grand Coulee Dam.* New York: Macmillan, 1954.

Extracted from Experiences in a Promised Land. *G. Thomas Edwards and Carlos A. Schwantes, eds. Seattle and London: University of Washington Press, 1986.*

ACKNOWLEDGMENTS

Bagley, Clarence B., ed. "Journal of Occurrences at Nisqually House," *Washington Historical Quarterly*, Vol. VI, No. 3, July 1915.

Bell, Daniel. "Labor's New Men," *Fortune*, June 1953.

Boren, Rebecca. "Young Booth Gardner," *Seattle Weekly*, July 18, 1984.

Brewster, David. "Behind the Times," *Seattle Magazine*, November 1969.

——. "The Long, Happy Life of John Compton Leffler," *Seattle Weekly*, December 9, 1981.

Buerge, David M. "Mission in the Wilderness," *Seattle Weekly*, December 25, 1985.

Budlong, Julia N. "What Happened in Seattle," *The Nation*, August 29, 1928.

Cornish, Nellie C. *Miss Aunt Nellie: The Autobiography of Nellie C. Cornish*. Seattle: University of Washington Press.

Cumming, William. *Sketchbook: A Memoir of the 1930s and the Northwest School*. Seattle: University of Washington Press, 1984.

DeVoto, Bernard, ed. *The Journals of Lewis and Clark*. New York: Houghton Mifflin Company, 1981.

Douglas, Patrick. "The Family of Two Revolutions," *Seattle Magazine*, January 1969.

Douglas, William O. *Go East, Young Man; The Early Years*. New York: Random House Inc., 1984.

Evans, Walter. "The Mercer Girls," *Seattle Post-Intelligencer*, September 7, 1975.

Fargo, Lucile F. *Spokane Story*. New York: Columbia University Press, 1950.

Henderson, David. *Jimi Hendrix: Voodoo Child of the Aquarian Age*. New York: Doubleday, 1978.

Holbrook, Stewart H. "Jim Hill Built An Empire," *The American Mercury*, Vol. LXV, No. 283, July 1947.

——. *The Far Corner*. Sausalito, CA: Comstock Editions, 1986.

Houston, Darrell Bob. "Kerouac in the Cascades," *Seattle Weekly*, October 18, 1978.

Howay, Frederic W., ed. *Voyages of the "Columbia" to the Northwest Coast (1787-1790 and 1790-1793)*. Boston: The Massachusetts Historical Society, 1941.

Johnson, Jalmar. *Builders of the Northwest*. New York: Dodd, Mead & Company, 1963.

Kirk, Ruth. "Richard Daugherty" *The Seattle Times*, March 23, 1980.

The Literary Digest, "His Majesty the Jazz King Who Enjoys the Last Laugh," December 24, 1932.

Meeker, Ezra. *Pioneer Reminiscences of Puget Sound*. Seattle: Lowman, Hanford, 1905.

Moody, Fred. "The Seahawk Nobody Knows," *Seattle Weekly*, December 2, 1987.

Prochnau, William W. and Richard Larsen. *A Certain Democrat: Senator Henry M. Jackson*. New York: Prentice-Hall, 1972.

Rexroth, Kenneth. "The Visionary Painting of Morris Graves," *Perspectives U.S.A.*, Winter 1955.

Rochester, Junius. "The Many Crusades of Wing Luke," *Seattle Weekly*, January 28, 1987.

Roe, JoAnn. *Frank Matsura, Frontier Photographer*. Seattle: Madrona Publishers, 1981.

Romeo, Margaret. "A Hammer in Her Hand," *Seattle Post-Intelligencer*, February 24, 1980.

Ross, Nancy Wilson. *Westward The Women*. San Francisco, CA: North Point Press, 1985

Ruby, Robert H. and John A. Brown. *Half-Sun on the Columbia: A Biography of Chief Moses*. Norman: University of Oklahoma, 1965.

Sale, Roger. *Seattle: Past to Present*. Seattle: University of Washington Press, 1976.

Satterfield, Archie. "He Sold the Klondike," *The Seattle Times*, January 2, 1972.

Smith, Wendy. "Ivan Doig," *Publishers Weekly*, September 18, 1987.

Sperlin, O.B., ed. "Our Official Horticulturalist," *Washington Historical Quarterly*, Vol. XXI, No. 4, October 1930; Vol. XXII, No. 1, January 1931.

Stimson, William. "Happy-go-lucky Spokane Beginnings of an American Legend," *Spokane Magazine*, Vol. 1, No. 9, December 1977.

——. *Going to State*. Walla Walla, WA: Washington State University Press, 1989.

Strong, Anna Louise. *I Change Worlds: The Remaking of an American*. Seattle: The Seal Press, 1979.

Tateishi, John, ed. *And Justice for All: An Oral History of the Japanese American Detention Camps*. New York: Random House Inc. 1984

Taylor, Ella. "Funny Girl: Lynda Barry Draws on Her Own Experience," *The Boston Globe Magazine*, December 13, 1987.

Tobey, Mark. *The World of a Market*. Seattle: University of Washington Press, 1964.

Wagner, Henry R., *Spanish Explorations in the Strait of Juan de Fuca*. Santa Ana, CA: Fine Arts Press, 1933.

Watson, Emmett. "Tex Johnston," *The Seattle Times*, August 3, 1986.

Whitman, Narcissa. *Letters of Narcissa Whitman*. Fairfield, WA: Ye Galleon Press, 1986.

INDEX

* Page number in italic indicates an illustration.